LEGAL ISSUES IN ANESTHESIA PRACTICE

LEGAL ISSUES IN ANESTHESIA PRACTICE

William H. L. Dornette, M.D., J.D.
    Law Medicine Specialist
    Kensington, Maryland

 F. A. DAVIS COMPANY • Philadelphia

Printed in the United States of America

Last digit indicates print number: 10 9 8 7 6 5 4 3 2 1

As new scientific information becomes available through basic and clinical research, recommended treatments and drug therapies undergo changes. The author(s) and publisher have done everything possible to make this book accurate, up to date, and in accord with accepted standards at the time of publication. The authors, editors, and publisher are not responsible for errors or omissions or for consequences from application of the book, and make no warranty, expressed or implied, in regard to the contents of the book. Any practice described in this book should be applied by the reader in accordance with professional standards of care used in regard to the unique circumstances that may apply in each situation. The reader is advised always to check product information (package inserts) for changes and new information regarding dose and contraindications before administering any drug. Caution is especially urged when using new or infrequently ordered drugs.

This book is intended to provide guidance in reference to legal issues that may arise in anesthesia practice. It is not the intent of the book's authors, editors, or publisher to render professional legal or medical advice. Readers seeking such advice should obtain the services of a competent professional. This admonition is especially pertinent as it applies to legal advice, given: (1) the diversity of statutory and common law among the 51 U.S. jurisdictions, and (2) the everchanging nature of those laws in response to technological advances in associated problems.

Library of Congress Cataloging-in-Publication Data

Dornette, William H. L. (William Henry Lueders), 1922–
  Legal issues in anesthesia practice / William H.L. Dornette.
    p.   cm.
  Includes bibliographical references and index.
  ISBN 0-8036-2721-1 (alk. paper) .
  1. Anesthesiology—Law and legislation—United States.
2. Anesthesiologists—Legal status, laws, etc.—United States.
I. Title.
  [DNLM: 1. Anesthesia—legislation—United States.   WO 33 AA1 D71]
KF2910.A5D67   1991
344.73'0412—dc20
[347.304412]
DNLM/DLC
for Library of Congress   91-19934
                                                                                 CIP

To
Betty Jane
whose patience, while the editor spent evenings and week-
ends during the first years of our marriage working on this
book, is gratefully acknowledged and appreciated.

PREFACE

For quite a few years, anesthesiologists have enjoyed the unenviable reputation of being rated by professional liability insurance underwriters as having one of the riskiest of medical practices. The premium rates for independently practicing certified registered nurse anesthetists (CRNAs) and for those employing anesthesia professionals have risen in an almost parallel fashion. The reasons for these high ratings stem from certain factors *inherent* in the practice of this specialty. Eight of these are related to the untoward side effects of certain commonly used agents or techniques:

1. The dosage of agent(s) required to produce general anesthesia usually is more than 50% of the lethal dose.

2. General anesthetic agents deprive patients of their protective reflexes, setting the stage for airway obstruction, aspiration of foreign materials (e.g., vomitus), and related complications.

3. Airway management problems are not uncommon; for example, the anatomic configuration of the upper respiratory tract of many patients interferes with direct laryngoscopy, precludes ready insertion of an endotracheal catheter, and thus sets the stage for acute respiratory obstruction and hypoxia. What often follows was aptly described by John Scott Haldane (1860–1936), British physiologist, a number of years ago: "Anoxia not only stops the machine, it wrecks the machinery."

4. Some general anesthetics, and all muscle relaxants, depress or obliterate spontaneous respiratory activity. The compensatory airway or ventilatory support in turn may be inadequate, leading to chronic or acute respiratory depression.

5. Some components of balanced general anesthesia adversely affect sympathetic nervous system activity, vasomotor tone, and myocardial function, especially in patients who are receiving antihypertensive drugs, setting the state for hypotension, myocardial depression, and possible circulatory arrest.

6. Some forms of regional anesthesia, notably epidural techniques, may cause cardiovascular collapse from a toxic reaction to the local agent or inadvertent "total spinal" anesthetic.

7. Attempts to produce spinal anesthesia may result in a high or total spinal, or produce spinal nerve or spinal cord injury, with attendant sensory and motor loss that may be permanent.

8. Modern techniques of invasive monitoring are mandated under certain circumstances. The injury-producing potential of these techniques is small, but real and finite, and the complications that may ensue can be lethal.

Two additional factors, while not directly related to the anesthetic or to monitoring, and not productive of complications per se, are inherent in the delivery of anesthesia care. These contribute to the possibility that, given an untoward outcome, anesthesia personnel will be named party defendants, thus increasing their *exposure* to litigation and, in turn, elevating their liability insurance premiums. These factors are:

9. The practice of this specialty conventionally involves very-short-term patient contact; when the administrator of the anesthetic is other than the professional who made preop-

erative rounds, this contact is limited even more—sometimes to the very short interval that the patient is in the operating room awaiting induction of anesthesia. Thus the "anesthetist" (be he or she a physician, CRNA, or other) in the mind of the patient becomes a poorly defined and vaguely remembered entity, whose major impact seems limited to the large invoice for professional services. Disgruntled patients contemplating litigation are much more likely to sue such an individual than one with whom they have had more extended contact.

10. Lawyers representing patients in malpractice actions today are aware of the modern team concept of health care delivery. In incidents involving a team, these lawyers are prone to name *all of its members*. For example, in an action stemming from an allegedly improperly performed open-heart procedure, it is customary practice to name as individual party defendants, initially at least, all persons in the operating room, including anesthesia personnel. Even though the "fault" may later be found to lie with one other than anesthesia personnel (e.g., a member of the operating team, pump technicians, or OR nurse), the carrier insuring those "at the head of the table" will be required at least to initiate a defense. If these legal fees are significant, the cost must be passed along to the insured, ultimately to be reflected in higher premiums (i.e., a higher rating) for those anesthesia personnel involved in open-heart procedures.

Given the potentialities for disaster noted above (factors 1 through 8), plus those other factors (9 and 10) that tend to encourage the filing of lawsuits, it is not surprising that a fairly large body of common law has developed from problems in the practice of this specialty. One of the purposes of this book is to afford health care professionals—in medicine, nursing, dentistry, and related fields—a comprehension of this case law. But understanding case law is not the only purpose, nor are health care providers the sole intended readership, of this book. Beyond this case (common) law are a host of other laws and legal processes that impinge on healing arts practice. These, along with much more on medical jurisprudence (impact of laws on health care delivery), are covered in this book. The primary intent of the editor and authors is to explain law and medical jurisprudence to health care providers. Nonetheless, attorneys representing clients involved in anesthesia-related problems may well find both the medical background and legal issues germane to their practice, either for their own edification or for that of their clients.

This book is divided into six parts, and contains several appendices. Part 1 and the Glossary of Legal Terminology serve to introduce the health care provider to those aspects of the law pertinent to medical jurisprudence. Part 2 reviews certain steps that are essential in minimizing one's exposure to liability. Part 3 covers particular techniques and procedures that may produce special problems, while Part 4 considers a number of ancillary activities with which not all anesthesia practitioners become involved. Part 5 is an introduction to the litigation process and to a very important part of that process—giving testimony under oath. Finally, Part 6 details some of the business aspects of anesthesia practice, including two subjects that are germane to practice today: (1) the relationships between anesthesiologists and nurse anesthetists and (2) indemnification for acts of professional negligence via insurance or similar means of protection.

In general, the chapters in this book need not be read in any particular sequence, the only caveat being that the first six chapters are offered as a background for health care providers with little knowledge of laws and legal processes. The authors' and editor's approach throughout this book is to stress minimizing or avoiding liability by *emphasizing medical and medical-legal pitfalls*, and how to avoid them. It *is not* our intent to dwell upon loopholes, including case law in which health care providers avoided liability through legal technicalities. It *is* our intent to offer suggestions that will help promote the delivery of high-quality anesthesia care and, if it later becomes necessary, to be able to defend that care by readily proving its quality.

William H. L. Dornette

ACKNOWLEDGMENTS

It is incumbent on anyone setting out to edit a book to first determine its purpose, its potential readership, and in some detail its subject matter. Next, in the case of a publication directed to a professional audience, one needs to select as authors professionals knowledgeable in their fields who will produce manuscripts that fulfill the just-stated goals and meet editorial deadlines. It is also helpful if those manuscripts require minimal editing. Fortunately, I was able to obtain the services of 14 such professionals—5 lawyers, 4 physician-lawyers, 3 physicians, 1 nurse anesthetist, and 1 oral surgeon—who met those requirements. These authors attacked the initial production of their manuscripts enthusiastically and, inasmuch as this book has been in preparation for over 5 years, also helped update the material as statutory and common law evolved during that interval. Without them, it would not have been possible to produce a book of this timeliness and quality. I owe them a special debt of gratitude.

One of the responsibilities of the editor is clarification or verification of references. The research librarians of the National Library of Medicine and the Library of Congress simplified this task immeasurably, one of the real benefits of residing in the Washington, D.C., area. Current data on HIV infections and related problems also were readily available, thanks to personnel operating the Public Health Service's AIDS Hotline, and to publications of the Center for Infectious Diseases at the Centers for Disease Control.

Every author needs an editor, *as does every editor!* The different perspective placed on portions of our manuscripts by several Davis' editors who scrutinized them is refreshing. I am especially beholden to Linda Weinerman, Bernice Wissler, and Elizabeth Egan, whose labors in this area were outstanding. And, because it took so long for me to finish this project, I wish to acknowledge with appreciation the forbearance of concerned persons at F. A. Davis, including former Senior Editor Sylvia Fields and Robert H. Craven, Sr., Chairman.

A final note. The editor would have been hard-pressed to function without his personal computers and associated hardware and software, all of which greatly simplified and speeded up manuscript and graphics production. The very first manuscripts were prepared on a Lisa computer. The Lisa's dot matrix–printed hard copy subsequently was scanned into a Macintosh II, using a Hewlett Packard ScanJet Plus scanner. These data then were converted to Microsoft Word v.4.0 documents with the Caere Corporation's OmniPage optical character recognition software. The majority of the manuscripts and the tables, appendices, Glossary, and Figure 11-1 were prepared directly on MS Word. The graphics were created with Claris' MacDraw II, Computer Associates' Cricket Graph, or Innovative Data Design's MacDraft. They then were printed on an Apple LaserWriter NT printer.

CONTRIBUTORS

Steven E. Brown, M.D.
Assistant Medical Director
Woodburn Surgical Center
Staff Anesthesiologist, The Fairfax Hospital
Fairfax, Virginia
Former Medical Director, Ambulatory Surgery Center
Walter Reed Army Medical Center
Washington, D.C.

Donald E. Demkee, D.D.S.
Oral and Maxillofacial Surgeon
Wooster, Ohio
District Team leader for Office Evaluations, General
   Anesthesia
Ohio State Dental Board
Clinical Instructor in Oral and Maxillofacial Surgery
Department of Surgery, Division of Oral and
   Maxillofacial Surgery and Dentistry
University of Cincinnati Medical Center
Cincinnati, Ohio

William H. L. Dornette, M.D., J.D.
Law Medicine Specialist
Kensington, Maryland
Adjunct Professor of Anesthesiology
University of Maryland School of Medicine
Baltimore, Maryland
Member of the Ohio bar

W. Stuart Dornette, J.D.
Partner and member of the Litigation Department
Taft, Stettinius & Hollister
Cincinnati, Ohio
Member of the Ohio, Virginia, District of Columbia, and
   Federal bars

H. Thomas Foley, M.D., J.D.
Medical Officer
Health Professions Support Agency
U.S. Army Medical Department
Walter Reed Army Medical Center
Washington, D.C.

Brad Lee Hilaman, M.D., J.D.
Obstetrician and Gynecologist
Walnut Creek, California
Member of the Pennsylvania bar

Thomas C. Hill, J.D.

Partner and member of the Litigation Department
Taft, Stettinius & Hollister
Cincinnati, Ohio
Member of the Ohio and Federal bars

Susan A. Jenny, J.D.

International Development Attorney
The Marriott Corporation
Bethesda, Maryland
Former Associate, Taft, Stettinius & Hollister
Cincinnati, Ohio
Member of the Ohio bar

Ronald A. MacKenzie, D.O.

Assistant Professor of Anesthesiology, Mayo Medical
    School
Consultant and Vice Chairman, Department of
    Anesthesiology
Mayo Clinic
Rochester, Minnesota

Clement Markarian, C.R.N.A., M.A.

Program Director, School of Nurse Anesthesiology
    (Proposed)
Carraway Methodist Medical Center
Birmingham, Alabama
Former Director, Anesthesia Nursing Program
Walter Reed Army Medical Center
Washington, D.C.

William B. Markovits, J.D.

Partner, Markovits & Greiwe
Cincinnati, Ohio
Member of the Ohio, District of Columbia, and Federal
    bars

Bence A. Sell, M.D.

Staff Anesthesiologist
Tallahassee Memorial Regional Medical Center
Tallahassee, Florida
Former Medical Director, Post Anesthesia Recovery
    Service
Walter Reed Army Medical Center
Washington, D.C.

Melvin S. Shotten, J.D.

Partner and member of the Corporate Law Department
Taft, Stettinius & Hollister
Cincinnati, Ohio
Member of the Ohio and Federal bars

Michael M. Wilson, M.D., J.D.

Practicing attorney
of counsel, Edward C. Bou, P.C.
Rockville, Maryland
Member of the New York and District of Columbia bars

CONTENTS

Clement J. Markarian, C.R.N.A., M.A.

William H. L. Dornette, M.D., J.D.

William H. L. Dornette, M.D., J.D.

William H. L. Dornette, M.D., J.D.
Bence A. Sell, M.D.

William H. L. Dornette, M.D., J.D.

Steven E. Brown, M.D.

PART 4.   **Ancillary Activities** **245**

CHAPTER **19.**   The Training Program............................. **247**

William H. L. Dornette, M.D., J.D.
Clement J. Markarian, C.R.N.A., M.A.

CHAPTER **20.**   Practice in the Federal Sector................. **263**

William H. L. Dornette, M.D., J.D.

CHAPTER **21.** Anxiety and Pain Control in Dentistry..................... 270

Donald E. Demkee, D.D.S.

CHAPTER **22.** Products Liability 282

William H. L. Dornette, M.D., J.D.

PART 5. **Courts, Litigation,
and Expert Testimony**................................ 295

CHAPTER **23.** The Process of Litigation 297

W. Stuart Dornette, J.D.

William B. Markovits, J.D.

Ronald A. MacKenzie, D.O.

Introduction to
the Law

EDITOR'S NOTE

We live in a complex society. Various laws, regulations, and legal processes govern our practices, our daily lives, and our relationships with fellow citizens, patients, and governments, both federal and state. Long before the anesthesiologist or nurse anesthetist administers the first anesthetic, he or she will have complied with many of these laws. Part 1 first reviews the sources of these laws, discusses how they govern our legal relationships with our patients and other health care providers, and sets forth the basis for the health care provider–patient relationship. Subsequent material covers legal actions for professional negligence—that is, malpractice—and other civil wrongs called nonnegligent or intentional torts. The last chapter of this section discusses vicarious liability, which relates to liability to third parties for the wrongful act of an employee or partner.

Part 1 is intended to introduce the health care provider to the law. It is recommended reading for those who have little knowledge of the law but who are interested in reviewing the legal implications of the practice of anesthesia as they are discussed in Parts 2 through 6.

W. H. L. D.

1

William H. L. Dornette, M.D., J.D.

Overview of Our Legal System

Relationships of Medicine and Law

Sources of Laws

    Constitutions

    Statutes

    Administrative Regulations

      The Common Law

Interrelationship of Laws

Substantive Versus Procedural Law

Immunity—Charitable, Governmental, and Statutory

RELATIONSHIPS OF MEDICINE AND LAW

Medicine and law are interrelated in two areas. The area that developed initially was *forensic medicine*, that is, medicine introduced into the *forum* or court of law for the settlement of a controversy. (See Glossary of Legal Terminology.) Forensic medicine assumed a role of importance in litigation during the latter part of the 19th century as information from a variety of scientific disciplines and discoveries—for example, blood typing, pathology, toxicology, and the like—was introduced into legal proceedings to help resolve them. Today, these scientific disciplines, plus those of neurosurgery, obstetrics, gynecology, orthope-

dics, psychiatry, and many other specialties, play a significant role in modern litigation—civil and criminal issues as well as worker's compensation. The physician in turn has become essential as an expert witness in introducing scientific evidence to help resolve these matters.

Another field of interaction between medicine and law, called *medical jurisprudence*, concerns the impact of the law and legal processes upon the practice of medicine and the other health sciences. With the rise in professional liability litigation, increasing numbers of physicians, nurses, dentists, and other health care providers have been faced with this aspect of the impingement of the laws upon their professional practices. This book is princi-

3

pally concerned with the overall impact of laws, legal processes, and regulations on the practice of anesthesia. That is, it is concerned with *anesthesia jurisprudence.*

SOURCES OF LAWS

A good starting point for understanding how the various laws impact on one's practice is to review their sources and interrelationships. Laws come from federal and local constitutions, legislatures (statutes), administrative agencies (administrative regulations), and appellate courts (judge-made or common law). While the origin of each differs, all are interrelated, as discussed below.

Constitutions

Constitutions establish the framework of the government entity, be it federal or state. The U.S. Constitution created a tripartite form of government—a *legislative branch* (Article I), an *executive branch* (Article II), and a *judicial branch* (Article III). The legislative branch adopts the laws, the executive branch administers them, and the judiciary interprets them. The Constitution specifically reserves certain powers for the individual states and still others for the people. Each state has adopted a state constitution, which in turn establishes the three-part government in that individual state.

For the most part, the U.S. Constitution is the overriding legal force that governs—that is, places constraints on—all state constitutions and all statutes, administrative regulations, and common law decisions, both federal and state. Through the Constitution and its amendments, the powers of the federal government are delineated, as are those rights and powers retained by the states and those retained by the individual citizens of this republic. The rights of the citizens are set forth for the most part in the Bill of Rights (the first 10 amendments to the Constitution), but these rights are also incorporated in some of the subsequent amendments. These rights may not be altered by either statute or common law.

Article I, § VIII of the Constitution gives the U.S. Congress the power "to . . . provide

for the . . . general welfare. . . ." This clause has allowed the enactment of Medicare and Medicaid laws and the creation of such agencies as the Food and Drug Administration (FDA) and the Environmental Protection Agency (EPA). The power of the Congress to enact patent and copyright laws also flows from the Constitution, that is, "The Congress shall have the power . . . to promote the progress of science and useful arts, by securing for limited times to authors and inventors the exclusive rights to their writings and discoveries."

The "due process" clause of the Constitution has come to the fore strongly in recent years in the health care field. Growing numbers of physicians are challenging denial by state licensing boards and hospital staff committees of the privilege of practicing medicine. Due process of law refers to both *substantive* and *procedural* due process. The application of due process in credentialing and decredentialing procedures is discussed in Chapter 27 and, as it applies to a training program, in Chapter 19.

Another constitutional provision, the "equal protection" clause, has been invoked recently as the constitutional basis for invalidating certain statutes involving health care delivery. For example, a number of state legislatures have enacted statutes limiting the amount of recovery for pain and suffering in medical malpractice actions. These statutes result from efforts to achieve so-called tort reform, thereby attempting to mitigate the liability of professionals and reduce the cost of professional liability insurance (see Chapter 29). In several instances, patients injured by professional negligence have alleged the denial of equal protection under the law, inasmuch as someone similarly injured but as a result of, for example, a defective product or a transportation accident rather than negligence would have the ability to sue, demand, and collect even greater general damages. Some of these challenges have been successful, and the statutes have been overturned.[1]

Statutes

Physicians, nurses, dentists, and many other health care professionals are licensed under one of the healing arts licensing statutes of the jurisdiction in which they practice. All states have such statutes. One of the powers retained by the states at the time of the adoption of the U.S. Constitution was the power to protect the health and well-being of the citizens of that state. That is the constitutional basis for each of these licensing statutes. To be constitutionally valid, these statutes must afford equal protection to all those governed by them, be they citizens of that or any other state. In its interpretation and enforcement, the statute must also afford *due process*. One of the interpretations of due process is that there must be a reasonable connection (called a *nexus* in legal terminology) between the activity being regulated and the purpose of the statute. Finally, the legislature must have the power to enact the statute. A state legislature could, for example, pass a statute forbidding the use of a certain anesthetic agent within that state if a reasonable nexus could be established between the use of that agent and dangers to patients who are citizens of that state. The same legislature would not, however, have the power to enact a statute prohibiting an out-of-state manufacturer from shipping the same agent across the state for use in another state. Such a statute would fly in the face of the commerce clause of the Constitution, which states in part, "[n]o state shall enact any statute interfering with commerce between the several states."

National Conference of Commissioners on Uniform State Laws

State statutes are passed by individual legislatures, each of which is made up of individuals with diverse interests. These statutes frequently vary widely among states. There are certain types of transactions, notably commercial sales, banking, and the like, that involve parties residing in more than one state. It became apparent early during the development of commerce in this country that it would be desirable to have laws governing such transactions that were uniform among the states. The task of developing such a uniform code fell to the National Conference of Commissioners on Uniform State Laws. Each state nominates

one or more representatives to sit on the commission. The commissioners meet more or less regularly, and uniform statutes are adopted by consensus action. Each individual state legislature then may (but is not required to) incorporate the uniform statute as part of its own laws. Thus, adoption can only be on a state-by-state basis. The Uniform Commercial Code (see Chapters 17 and 22, and the discussion of warranties contained therein) has been adopted by all U.S. jurisdictions. Of interest to the medical profession are a number of other uniform acts, not all of which have been adopted by all jurisdictions.

Administrative Regulations

State healing arts licensing boards are administrative agencies. These agencies are created by each state legislature and derive their power from the executive branch. Their purpose is to adopt and enforce specific regulations pertaining to (in the case of health care) the respective healing arts professions in that state. Because it is not practical for the legislature to adopt by statute all of the necessarily detailed provisions governing the practice of each healing art, the responsibility for adoption of these regulations is delegated to these administrative agencies, the boards themselves. Even though these regulations have not been created by the statutory drafting process and signed into law by the governor, they nevertheless have the force of law upon those licensed practitioners working within that jurisdiction. The FDA, EPA, and Public Health Service are examples of health-related administrative agencies at the national level.

The Common Law

Long before the colonists sailed from England to establish what was to become the United States, they were governed by a body of laws known as the common law of England. The term *governed* as used in the previous sentence does not refer to regulation of individual conduct by the Crown, but rather to the relationships between one English citizen and another. The common law, then and now, consists of a body of judicial decisions handed down to finally resolve disputes between one individual and another, or between one individual and an entity of the government.* The publication (in the *reporter systems*, regional and federal) and recognition (by courts in the same and other jurisdictions) of common law decisions promote orderly and uniform relationships between individual citizens. When the colonists came to this country, they brought with them the common law of England to help establish law and order on this continent. The United States (except for Louisiana), along with all of the countries of the British Commonwealth, has adopted this common law.

In its early days, the common law was relatively simplistic, reflecting the lack of complexity of the times during which it arose. As the Industrial Revolution swept Europe first and then this country, industrial accidents led to litigation, which in turn led to judicial decisions. These expanded the common law and increased its complexity. Today, injuries from products, transportation vehicles, and health care delivery have contributed generously to a growing body of common law.

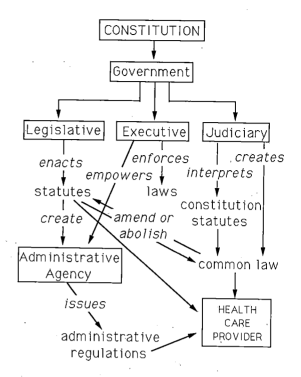

Figure 1–1 Sources of laws, their interrelationship, and potential impact on the health care practitioner.

INTERRELATIONSHIP OF LAWS

Common law, statutory law, administrative law and regulations, and constitutional law are all interrelated. This interrelationship is depicted in Figure 1-1. All judicial decisions (common law) must be subservient to the constitutions (both federal and state) and generally to pertinent statutes within that jurisdiction. Although a judicial (common law) decision might interpret a constitutional provision, it may not overrule it. For example, the right of privacy, while not specifically spelled out in the Constitution, was held by a Supreme Court justice as springing from that document.[2] Initially, this constitutional "right" was interpreted as limiting the federal government's power to interfere with or invade one's personal privacy. A number of years later in *Roe v. Wade*,[3] the Supreme Court included within this right a woman's right to have an abortion under certain circumstances. In issuing this decision, the high court overturned a number of state statutes outlawing abortion[†] (at least during the first trimester).

A judicial or common law decision may also interpret a statute. For example, for some time, the statute of limitation of actions for professional negligence in Ohio had been 1 year. A patient who had been operated upon in a Cleveland hospital did not discover that a sponge had been left in his abdomen until 11 years after the operation. He sued the hospital. The hospital defended the lawsuit on the ground that the 1-year limitation had long since expired. In a landmark decision, the Supreme Court of Ohio held that the statute did not commence to run in the case of a foreign body until the patient knew, or through the use of a reasonable amount of diligence should have known, that the foreign body was present.[4] This is an example of common law interpretation of a statute. In 1975, the Ohio legislature modified this common law decision by placing an absolute limit on the length of time suits may be filed in foreign body cases.[5] Such an action is, of course, within the prerogative of a legislature. At the same time, that legislature modified the statute of limitation of actions for professional negligence pertaining to minors. It abolished the provision of the Ohio Civil Code that tolled the running of the 1-year limitation of actions until the minor reached the age of 18 years. In 1986, the Ohio Supreme Court overturned this statute on the grounds that it failed to afford due process and equal protection to minors who might not be in a position to initiate litigation until they became of legal age.[6]

There are, of course, examples of the reverse action, that is, common law decisions being overturned by statutory action. For example, next of kin have always had a common law right that the body of a loved one shall be buried without any trauma, including an autopsy or removal of organs.[7] The Uniform Anatomic Gifts Act[8] abolishes by statute this common law right.

SUBSTANTIVE VERSUS PROCEDURAL LAW

Laws are both substantive and procedural. The duties of health care providers to their patients, which will be discussed in Chapter 2, have been created by common law decisions; they are substantive in nature. If a patient elects to sue a physician for alleged professional negligence, the duties to which the physician will be held (see Chapter 3) have been defined by this substantive law. On the other hand, the rules by which the case will be tried are set forth under the procedural laws of that jurisdiction. Chapter 23 contains a discussion of the application of some of these procedural laws to the litigation process.

IMMUNITY—CHARITABLE, GOVERNMENTAL, AND STATUTORY

Health care providers think of immunity as the processes by which the body fights infections or prevents their development in the first place. At law, the term *immunity* means freedom not from micro-organisms but from liability. Immunity may be of common law or statutory origin. Many of the colonists who came to this country were endeavoring to escape the tyranny of the British king. It is perhaps ironic that in bringing the common law with them, they imported the doctrine of sovereign immunity. This doctrine holds that the sovereign (translated into American jurisprudence, the government) can do no wrong. Therefore, it would be purposeless to sue any governmental entity unless the entity waives immunity (generally by statute) and allows such litigation to take place. Federal governmental immunity, and its partial waiver by statute, is further reviewed in Chapter 20 as it relates to the Federal Tort Claims Act.

Charitable immunity was created by common law decisions to prevent charitable organizations from being inundated with lawsuits and deprived of monies intended for charitable purposes. Even as late as the beginning of this century, practically all hospitals were considered to be charitable institutions in one form or another; few were operated for commercial gain. Times have changed. While some hospital support still comes from charitable sources, much is derived from governmental entities, health care insurance, and patients themselves. In consequence, there are few truly charitable hospitals in this country today, and the courts no longer feel any need to afford these hospitals the protective umbrella of the charitable immunity doctrine.[9]

Statutory immunity is just what the name implies—immunity created by legislative action. Child abuse reporting statutes, which have been enacted in most U.S. jurisdictions, all contain immunity provisions. These statutes provide that any person who reports suspected child abuse to authorities will be immune from civil or criminal liability provided that the report was made in good faith (i.e., the reporter had reasonable grounds to believe that the abuse had taken place).[10]

CONCLUSION

Laws and legal processes will always be with us. They establish the framework of our governments and, just as importantly, define our relationships with those governments and our fellow humans. It is inevitable that we live within the constraints imposed by these laws and far better that we do so in harmony. However, achieving a harmonious relationship is but one of a number of advantages stemming from even a brief study of the law. A comprehension of the sources of these laws, and how they are interrelated, contributes immeasurably toward our understanding of the laws themselves. Such understanding in turn constitutes an important initial step toward the acquisition of a better grasp of anesthetic jurisprudence.

REFERENCES

1. *See, e.g.*, Andrews, T: Infant tolling statutes in medical malpractice cases, J Leg Med 5:469, 1984; Strahler v. St. Luke's Hosp., 706 S.W.2d 7 (Sup. Ct. Mo. *en banc*, 1986).
2. Olmstead v. United States, 277 U.S. 438, 487, 72 L. ed. 944, 956 (1928).
3. Roe v. Wade, 410 U.S. 113, *reh'g denied*, 410 U.S. 959 (1973).
4. Melnyk v. Cleveland Clinic, 32 Ohio2d 198, 290 N.E.2d 916 (Sup. Ct., 1972).
5. *See* Dornette, WHL: Ohio strives to resolve malpractice problem. J Leg Med 4(no 1, Jan):D30, 1976.
6. Mominee v. Scherbarth, 28 Ohio St.3d 270 (Sup. Ct., 1986).
7. Wasmuth, CE and Stewart, BH: Medical and legal aspects of human organ transplantation. Cleve-Mar L Rev 14:442, 1965.
8. *See* Dornette, WHL (ed): Legal Aspects of Anesthesia. FA Davis, Philadelphia, 1972, Appendix 8, pp 570 *et seq.*
9. *See, generally*, Smith, JW: Hospital Liability. Law Journal Seminars Press, New York, 1988, §§ 2.01 *et seq.*
10. See, *generally*, Meriwether, MH: Child abuse reporting laws: Time for a change. Fam L Q 20:141, 1986.

2

William H. L. Dornette, M.D., J.D.

The Health Care Provider–Patient Relationship

THE LEGAL BASIS OF HEALTH CARE DELIVERY

The legal relationship between health care providers and their patients revolves about one or more *service contracts* (in contrast to *sales contracts*) for the delivery of that care. One definition of a contract is *an agreement, based upon sufficient consideration, to do, or refrain from doing, a certain lawful thing.*[1] An agreement involves the mutual assent of the parties. The patient *consents* to the proposed diagnostic-therapeutic regimen and the pay for the service, and the health care provider agrees to deliver that care for a certain sum (the obliga-

tions of each party to a contract of this type are detailed later in this chapter). In the health care field, contracts may be based upon *implied, express, constructive,* or *statutory* consent. Also, they may be ordinary service contracts, or those for service by a specific individual. Each type deserves elaboration.

Types of Consent and Associated Contracts

Implied Consent

This type of consent abounds in health care delivery. Implied consent results from

9

action (or inaction) rather than from verbal or written (express) communication. If the health care provider asks, "May I take your blood pressure?" and the patient remains silent but proffers his or her bare arm, the latter is implicitly (by a specific action) consenting to this noninvasive procedure. The query "May I draw some blood to send to the laboratory?" might elicit an identical response by the patient, this time to an invasive procedure. Thus, in both instances the patient would have granted legally binding consent, even though it was not express. When a patient voluntarily seeks the services of a health care provider, the former *by implication* submits to an examination by the latter and agrees to pay for that service.

Express Consent

When an individual health care provider agrees to care for a specific patient, an *express contract* is entered into. Generally, this contract is a verbal one, although patients who join a health maintenance organization or similar plan are required to execute a written contract. In general, while contracts may be implied from the facts, express contracts are mandatory prior to the commencement of diagnostic or therapeutic endeavors of any significance.

Written Versus Verbal Consent

If the patient and health care provider mutually assent and execute a verbal contract for health care delivery, it is just as binding as a written contract. In point of fact, most outpatient care is rendered under verbal contracts. The details of verbal contracts may be harder to prove at a later date, however, and the statute of limitation of actions is shorter under a verbal contract than a written one. For the former reason, especially, it is customary to obtain written consent for major procedures, the most notable example being operative intervention and the administration of attendant anesthetics (see also Chapter 9).

Constructive Consent

Consent may be *constructive* (construed by the law from the facts of the situation) in nature. This type of consent results in the formation of a constructive contract, as epitomized by the case of an unconscious accident victim who is brought to the hospital unaccompanied by friends or relatives. An examination of the patient reveals that emergency operative intervention is needed to save his or her life. Must hospital personnel waste precious minutes endeavoring to locate any next of kin? The courts recognize that health care providers do have a duty to act promptly in emergencies. Therefore, courts have held health care providers to a constructive duty to proceed in the absence of consent. There are two provisos: first, that the procedure must be necessary to save life, preserve limb, prevent disfiguration, or allay suffering; and, second, that *reasonable* efforts to locate next of kin should be made if the necessary time is available. The same type contract, that is, one based upon constructive consent, would be created in the case of the unemancipated minor who faces a similar emergency procedure and whose parent or guardian cannot be located.

Statutory Consent

Most states have enacted statutes permitting health care providers to treat minors without parental consent in certain situations, notably for management of sexually transmitted diseases and unwanted pregnancy. Anesthesia personnel might be involved in a therapeutic abortion to be performed under such consent. (The refusal to administer anesthesia for abortions because of personal or religious convictions is another issue.) The pertinent statute would cover consent for all associated services.

Sales Versus Service Contracts

As noted above, health care is delivered under service contracts and for the most part is not considered to be a sale of goods. This distinction is important. Warranties of fitness and merchantability (see Chapters 17 and 22) may apply to contracts for sales. In the 1960s, courts in this country began construing the transfusion of blood products to constitute sales of goods, a trend that was subsequently reversed by statutory action (Chapter 17) in most U.S. jurisdictions.

Service Versus Personal Service Contracts

The contract for personal services is unique, as compared with the usual service contract. An example of the difference is the patient who goes to a specific health care provider versus one who joins a health maintenance organization or similar health plan. In the former case, when the health care provider agrees to examine and treat that patient, a contract for personal services is entered into. This contract is unique in that the patient expects that particular health care provider, and only that one, will carry out whatever diagnostic and therapeutic steps become necessary. The health care provider cannot unilaterally substitute another health care provider in delivering the needed services. Should he or she do so, there could be liability to the patient for *breach of contract*. (Breach of contract, which is actionable under contract rather than tort law, is discussed later in this chapter.) Furthermore, if the treatment continues over an extended period of time, the health care provider may not unilaterally transfer the care of the patient to another health care provider without the patient's consent, except under certain limited circumstances, which are discussed later in this chapter.

On the other hand, the patient-subscriber of the health maintenance organization or similar health plan would expect, and be entitled to receive, services by any appropriate health care provider employed by the plan, but not personal services by a specific provider. Duties owed by each party to the health plan contract would be set out by both common law (as described below) and the provisions of the contract. The fundamental principles of the health care provider–patient relationship would remain the same, however.

Individual Versus Group Practice

It is probable that most anesthesiologists engage in some type of group practice. Night and weekend coverage is achieved on a rotational basis, and, with the possible exception of purely elective cases, the professional who makes rounds may not be the one who administers the anesthetic. Patients who are to be anesthetized by a member of a group must be apprised of the rotational nature of the coverage generally afforded by members who have such affiliations. This apprisal should take place at the time of the first contact between a member of the group and the patient. Patients who are fully apprised of procedures for coverage are unlikely to object to substitutions, even last-minute ones. From a legal standpoint, each member of such a group is on the same footing as every other member (assuming, of course, that all possess the same anesthesia privileges within the institution).

Anesthesia professionals who are engaged in solo practice must anticipate their need for substitutes and apprise their patients in advance of the service for which a substitute will be supplied. Given the well-recognized right of all patients to self-determination, those who object to care by a particular professional must, except possibly in emergencies, be afforded care by a substitute who is satisfactory to those patients.

The Nature of the Health Care Provider–Patient Relationship

A very important aspect of this relationship is that is it fiduciary in nature. The term *fiduciary* means something of highest trust. In the course of making a diagnosis, the health care provider is expected to probe deeply into the patient's past history, both medical and, at times, nonmedical. Information gained from the patient by the health care provider generally tends to be of a very highly personal nature. This need for full disclosure by the patient, plus the possession by the health care provider of this highly personal information, creates what the law calls a *fiduciary relationship*. The health care provider may not divulge outside the health care setting personal information gained from or about that patient within that setting. If he or she does so, breach of confidence, an intentional tort (see Chapter 5), could occur.

Other well-known fiduciary relationships exist in modern society. The priest-penitent, lawyer-client, spouse-spouse, and trustee-beneficiary relationships are of the same nature. In each situation, information obtained by one of the parties from the other during the course of the relationship may not be disclosed outside of that relationship. This admonition leads to a consideration of the concept of the privileged communication.

Privileged Communications

The term *privilege* has several connotations. It is *a freedom on the part of one person to do, or refrain from doing, a certain act*, "[t]hat which releases one from the performance of a duty or obligation, or exempts one from a liability which he would otherwise be required to perform."[2] Members of the U.S. Congress frequently make comments from the floor of the House or Senate that are considered privileged. These are privileged in the sense that that particular representative or senator is free to do so without exposing himself or herself to any liability for potentially defamatory remarks made. *Privilege* also has another connotation. When a patient makes a disclosure of personal information to a health care provider within the health care delivery setting, the patient holds a privilege that the provider will not disclose this information outside that particular setting. Such communications are called privileged communications.

The concept of the privileged communication was not recognized by the common law. A health care provider who was called into court would have to testify as to the details of such communications. Times have changed, however. At the present time, a number of states[3] have enacted legislation that establishes a statutory health care provider–patient privilege and defines the degree of confidentiality with which the courts must view such communications.

It is important to note that it is *the patient*, not the health care provider, who holds the privilege. A patient may, however, waive the privilege. Such a waiver automatically occurs when a patient files a lawsuit against a health care provider, thereby making the condition of his or her health a public issue (documents filed to initiate litigation become public documents) (see Chapter 23). Once a patient waives the privilege, a treating health care provider can be compelled to testify about the disclosures made to him or her.

Disclosure of Privileged Communications

If, as a result of a court order, a health care provider is required to make a disclosure under oath, that disclosure is considered privileged (i.e., he or she is privileged to make it without threat of liability). In this respect, the first use of the term is applied. The health care provider could not be held liable for defamation, breach of confidence, or invasion of privacy (see Chapter 5).

DUTIES OF HEALTH CARE PROVIDERS

As in any contract, the personal service contract places certain duties on each party. The health care provider owes his or her patient five duties: (1) to practice at the professed level of care, (2) to make full disclosure, (3) to protect confidences, (4) to offer continuing treatment, and (5) to seek consultation when indicated. Each of these duties is discussed below, with examples drawn from the anesthesiologist-patient and nurse anesthetist–patient relationship.

1 *The duty to practice at the professed level of care.* The health care provider who holds himself or herself out to be a practitioner in a particular field, or an expert in the treatment of certain problems, is expected to deliver that degree of expertise in patient care. The board-certified anesthesiologist and certified registered nurse anesthetist are expected to practice at those respective levels of care. The level expected of trainees would be considerably less. Trainees pose other, special problems, including those related to adequate supervision and informed consent. These problems are reviewed in Chapter 19.

2 *The duty to make full disclosure.* Health care providers are under a duty to disclose fully to the patient any significant risks created by the proposed diagnostic or therapeutic

procedure. This duty, like most of the others, is of common law origin. It was first articulated by a California Court of Appeals in 1957 in the famous case of *Salgo v. Trustees of Leland Stanford Hospital*.[4] The court held that one of the health care provider's duties, when obtaining a patient's consent for a procedure that posed a risk, was the duty to *inform* the patient of the risks created by that procedure, as well as its benefits, the risks and benefits of alternative procedures (if any), and the risks of not having any procedure at all. Since that case, courts in almost every U.S. jurisdiction have incorporated this legal concept within their common law (see Chapter 9, and especially Appendix 9-2).

Since the Salgo case, the courts have expanded the informed consent doctrine to include the duty to inform the patient of the progress of the treatment, or lack of it (a duty not really applicable to anesthesia care), and the duty of obtaining informed refusal.[5]

3 *The duty to protect confidences.* Every health care provider who learns of personal information about a patient must keep that information within the health care setting. Disclosure of such information to outsiders would expose the health care provider to the possibility of an action for breach of confidence or invasion of privacy (intentional torts —see Chapter 5). Protecting confidences, and preventing a breach thereof, are of distinct concern to health care providers who learn that a patient has acquired immunodeficiency syndrome (AIDS) or is infected with the virus that causes it (see Chapter 18).

4 *The duty to offer continuing treatment.* The courts have held that once a health care provider–patient relationship is entered into, it may not be terminated unilaterally by the health care provider. This same admonition also applies to other health care providers. Failure to offer continuing treatment could result in allegations of, and potential liability for, abandonment. The health care provider would not be liable for abandonment under the following circumstances:

a The patient unilaterally terminated the contract for health care, or it was terminated by mutual agreement.

b The health care provider became incapacitated through illness, or died.

c The health care provider obtained a mutually agreeable substitute.

d The illness for which the treatment was commenced was cured, or the course of treatment otherwise completed.

e The health care provider formally notified the patient, by restricted delivery certified mail with a return receipt requested, that the contract was being terminated unilaterally, and the patient was given ample (customarily 20 to 30 days) notice to obtain a substitute health care provider.

Most of these exceptions do not apply to anesthesia personnel. The principal problem that could develop from anesthesia care, and one that might lead to allegations of abandonment, is substitution of the caregiver. For example, an anesthesiologist expressly agrees to personally administer a patient's anesthetic. After the patient is anesthetized, the anesthesiologist turns the care over to another practitioner. Even though the delegatee might be fully competent, it would constitute abandonment for the anesthesiologist to substitute another health care provider without the patient's express knowledge and consent. The patient might also allege breach of contract, and possibly fraud. Inasmuch as the patient had not given the substitute consent to administer the anesthetic, allegations of battery (Chapter 4) against the substitute also might be raised.

5 *The duty to seek consultation when indicated.* The final duty of the

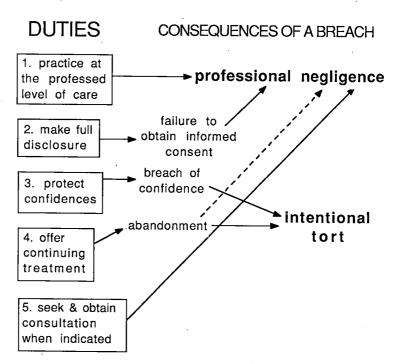

Figure 2–1 Each health care provider in general owes each patient five duties, shown on the left side of this figure. A breach of any of these duties— by commission or omission—as shown on the right, may result in liability either for professional negligence (malpractice) or a nonnegligent, intentional tort. Because professional liability insurance does not offer coverage for intentional torts, some members of the plaintiff's bar may allege negligence following an act of abandonment (broken arrow), to be assured that a source of assets will be available to satisfy any judgment.

health care provider involves two steps: first, the health care provider must recognize his or her limitations. Second, when the problem at hand exceeds those limitations, the provider has a duty, created by common law, to obtain consultation. The significance of and need for this duty are especially important when reviewing those legal issues that emanate from training programs (Chapter 19).

If the health care provider departs from the first, second, or fifth duties, an act of professional negligence or malpractice (rather than breach of contract—see below) is said to have occurred (Fig. 2-1). Malpractice is the subject of the next chapter. Breach of the third or fourth duty could result in allegations of intentional tort (Chapter 5).

DUTIES OF PATIENTS

Under the contract for health care delivery, patients also have legally recognized duties. There are three of them: (1) making full disclosure themselves, (2) cooperating in the therapeutic regimen, and (3) paying for services rendered. The courts do recognize the importance of these duties and might consider a breach of one or more of them to constitute sufficient contributory negligence (see Chapter 3) on the part of the patient to offset a departure from the duty of care by the health care provider. For example, it is important that the patient make full disclosure. During the preanesthetic visit (Chapter 8), anesthesia personnel must become aware of those aspects of the patient's history that have a direct bearing on the selection and management of the anesthetic. Failure of the patient to divulge this information could result in the use of an agent or technique that should have been contraindicated (i.e., patient fails to tell about prior adverse reaction to halothane, and that agent is administered). If consequent harm befalls the patient, the anesthesiologist or nurse anesthetist would have as a valid defense the contributory negligence of the nondisclosure by the patient. Cooperating in the therapeutic regimen (e.g., "Take nothing by mouth after midnight") likewise is vital (see also Chapter 15).

BREACH OF CONTRACT VERSUS NEGLIGENCE

As noted at the beginning of this chapter, the legal basis of each health care provider–patient relationship is a contract. Each party to that contract owes the other certain duties. Yet, as noted above and discussed at greater length in the next chapter, if a health care provider deviates from this contract by the breach of one or more of these duties, it has generally been considered malpractice or professional negligence, rather than breach of contract, and thus is treated as a tort (Chapter 1). The courts have created this dichotomy, at least in part, on the basis of three distinctions:

1 *The nature of the services.* In general, courts have treated professional activities differently from ordinary ones, so that negligence committed within a professional's practice usually is considered to be malpractice, even though that act might stem from the breach of one of the duties set forth above.

2 *The absence of any intent to do wrong.* The courts have long recognized that professionals who err in their practice generally do not intend to make a mistake or cause harm to the client-patient.

3 *The absence of assertions that a given result will be forthcoming.* Health care providers customarily do not guarantee a specific result; thus they give their patients scant ground for a breach of contract action. Should one do so, and proof of that guarantee be established, he or she could be held liable for failure to perform as promised.

It is also significant that health care providers customarily are indemnified (for the most part, at least) by professional liability insurance that *covers negligence but not breach of contract.* Hence lawyers, preferring some assurance that there will be a readily available source of funds (i.e., the carrier), tend to frame their causes of action in terms of negligence rather than contract law.

CONCLUSION

Health care is delivered under one or more service contracts, some of which may be for the services of a specific health care provider, thus *mandating* those services. Most of these contracts are express, verbal ones, which are just as binding as written contracts. Each contract creates duties for both health care providers and patients. *All parties* to those contracts, including patients,* should understand the "terms" (i.e., rights and duties of all parties) and the necessity of adhering to them. By following these recommendations, both health care providers and patients will have taken a major step toward maintaining the best possible interrelationships, and much misunderstanding and the potential for litigation will be forestalled.

REFERENCES

1. 17 *American Jurisprudence 2d Contracts* § 1.
2. State v. Grosnickle, 206 N.W. 895, 896 (Sup. Ct. Wisc. 1926).
3. 8 *Wigmore Evidence* § 3280 and n. 5 (rev. ed. 1961).
4. Salgo v. Trustees of Leland Stanford Hosp., 154 Cal. App.2d 560, 317 P.2d 170 (1957).
5. Truman v. Thomas, 105 Cal. Rptr. 308, 611 P.2d 902 (Sup. Ct., Calif. 1980). This holding should come as no surprise to those familiar with the evolution of the informed consent doctrine in U.S. common law; since the initial informed consent decision (Salgo, *supra*), courts have required the disclosure of both *risks* and *benefits*; the appellate court in *Truman* was merely articulating the doctrine from the opposite perspective, that is, emphasizing the importance of advising the patient of the *risks of refusing* the recommended procedure, which would count among the *benefits of acquiescing* to that same procedure.

---

*While health care providers are not under a legally recognized duty to instruct their patients on the finer points of contract law, it is only common sense and makes for good public relations that patients somehow are made to appreciate that full disclosure and complete cooperation on their part are absolutely vital.

3

William H. L. Dornette, M.D., J.D.

Professional Negligence

Ladies and gentlemen of the jury, this case involves the alleged medical malpractice of the physician who is the defendant in this action. His former patient accuses him of improper treatment, with the result that she has been injured. Malpractice is a form of negligence. Negligent conduct may be defined as having an obligation to behave in a certain way toward another person, and then failing to behave in that way. If the failure to act properly results in an injury to that other person or to his or her property, then the actor is considered to have been negligent. The injured person is then entitled to receive compensation to make him or her whole. This compensation is called damages and takes the form of a monetary award or payment.

Malpractice is negligence committed within a professional activity. This case involves a physician. If the physician, in treating his

patient, did something he should not have done, or did not do something that he should have done, and that act of commission or omission caused an injury or monetary damage to the patient, then that physician has committed malpractice. In every case, the defendant—here, the physician—comes to court presumed to be not liable. The plaintiff, the injured patient in this case, must introduce evidence to prove that the defendant physician did in fact commit negligence. The plaintiff must prove her case by a preponderance of the evidence. She must prove each element of her case by a preponderance of evidence. By a preponderance, I mean that the weight of the plaintiff's evidence must just exceed that of the defendant; that is, it must be greater than 50%. If you find that the plaintiff has established her proof of each element and has done so with proof that is at least 1% greater than that presented by the defendant, then the plaintiff has sustained the burden of coming forward with the evidence, and you must find for the plaintiff. On the other hand, if you find that the plaintiff's evidence in each and every element is not greater than that of the defendant, then you must find for the defendant.

In this manner, a judge might begin his or her charge to the jury in a typical case involving the alleged malpractice of a physician. Medical malpractice is negligence committed by a professional within the health care delivery setting. Negligence is but one type of tort or civil wrong (for a discussion of some of the nonnegligent torts, see Chapter 5).

ANALYSIS OF NEGLIGENCE

The word *tort* is derived from the Latin *tortus*, meaning "twisted." "The metaphor is apparent: a tort is conduct which is twisted, or crooked, not straight."[1] At law, a tort is a civil wrong that one person commits against another, either by an act of omission or commission. The law recognizes such an act to be a wrong, and the courts will award compensation to the injured party through the litigation process. There are a number of different types of torts; they fall into two categories—negligent and intentional. An intentional tort (see Chapter 5) results from an act that on its face appears to have produced its intended result. Negligence, on the other hand, represents an act that was not intended to produce the (wrong) result that followed. This chapter will begin with an analysis of the five elements of proof that comprise a professional negligence action involving a health care provider: (1) the duty of care owed the patient, (2) breach of that duty, (3) nature of the injury, (4) proximate causation (between the breach and the injury), and (5) extent of the monetary damages.

The Duty Owing

The health care provider–patient relationship is analyzed in the previous chapter. At law, this relationship is embodied in a contract for services. For example, once a member of the health care team agrees to administer an anesthetic, a contract has been entered into. Obviously, no contract exists until the health care provider has agreed to care for that patient. Until then, there would be no duty of care and no possibility of the health care provider being found liable for negligence.

As noted in the prior chapter, each party to that contract (as with any contract) owes the other party certain duties; the other party possesses correlative rights that these duties will be carried out. The first duty of the health care provider is to care for the patient at that level of skill, training, and experience, including any specialization, at which he or she professes to possess. Thus, one who holds himself or herself out to be a certified registered nurse anesthetist or a board-certified anesthesiologist would be expected to deliver care at that respective level. In introducing evidence in a professional negligence action to prove the plaintiff-patient's case (see Chapter 23), the lawyer must prove exactly what the health care provider's duty was at the time of the care in question. This level of care is what is known as the *standard of care*, that level at which physicians of similar training and experience practicing in the same community would perform under the same or similar circumstances. As noted in the next chapter, the standard of care has undergone much change since this country was founded. While one may say that the community standard still exists, the "community" now has been broadened to encompass the entire United States.*

Breach of the Duty

Having established the level of the standard of care to which the defendant should have practiced, plaintiff's counsel then must introduce evidence to prove that the defendant departed from that standard and

*There are important exceptions to this broad statement. Common law decisions (see Chapter 1) and legislative action have established the informed consent doctrine, which differs among the several states (see Chapter 9). Statutes drafted to attempt to attenuate the medical malpractice "problem" are the work of individual state legislatures; the contents of these statutes vary markedly and thus may affect the standard of care quite differently across this country.

hence breached the duty of care. That is, proof must be introduced showing the manner in which the defendant committed the act of commission or omission that in turn allegedly led to the patient's injury.

At this juncture, mention should be made that the courts have held that an *error in judgment* does *not* constitute a departure from the duty of care. Giving an intravenous anesthetic agent to a known alcoholic, with an accompanying cross-tolerance and need for the administration of large amounts of the thiobarbiturate, might constitute an error in judgment. Administering spinal anesthesia to a patient with a history of back trauma might be another example. Still another can be drawn from the changing standard of care. As discussed in the next chapter, the standard of care does change as newer agents and techniques that are more efficacious or possess fewer side effects than the older ones are introduced into practice. At some time, the standard will shift to use of the newer modality. This change does not occur everywhere overnight. Rather, it tends to be progressive and takes place in medical centers and other large institutions first. Thus, it may take some time before the standard has changed completely across the United States. The courts would probably hold that as long as a "substantial minority" of practitioners still employ the older technique or agent, it is not a departure from the standard of care to continue to use the older modality.

Nature of the Injury

The nature of the patient's injury, even though obvious, also must be proved. In most cases, there will be scant objection to admission of medical records and other evidence detailing that injury. An expert may be required to give an opinion about future loss of function and permanent disability. Such proof is needed to help establish duration and extent of future loss of earning capacity, both essential in computing monetary damages.

Proximate Causation

The next step in the introduction of the plaintiff's evidence involves proving that the defendant's breach of the duty—departure from the standard of care—caused the patient's injury to the exclusion of other factors. This element is essential in the chain of proof. Lawyers use the term *proximate cause*, which means that the physician's breach more likely than other factors caused the injury—that there was a greater than 50% chance that it did. Proximate cause does not mean absolute cause. On the other hand, if there are two or more probable causes and the physician was responsible for only one of them, the courts have held that it would be speculative to determine which of them was the operative one. In such an instance, the judge must, on proper defense motion, take the case from the jurors and grant a directed verdict for the defendant.

Customarily, proof of the standard of care, breach of the standard, and proximate causation require expert testimony in a case of professional negligence. Jurists reason that in the usual cases involving a professional, the duty of care, the manner in which it was breached, and how the breach caused the resultant injury are by their very nature so complex that the only ready explanation can come from someone who is skilled in that professional field.*

Extent of the Monetary Damages

Once the plaintiff's lawyer has established proof of the first four elements of the negligence action—duty of care, breach of the duty, nature of the injury, and proximate causation—the next step is to introduce evidence as to the dollar value that should be applied to the injury, in an effort to make the patient "whole." Damages are of three types—special, general, and punitive. *Special damages* are based upon the actual economic losses—past, present, and future—suffered by the plaintiff. These include medical and hospitalization costs, loss of income, and cost of any special training to compensate for residual disabil-

*Expert testimony may not be required in cases in which the plaintiff elects to establish the proof through the creation of an *inference* of negligence, by invoking the doctrine of *res ipsa loquitur*; this doctrine is discussed later in this chapter.

ities. Customarily, an economist is retained by the plaintiff as an expert witness to testify as to damages that are projected into the future in cases of permanent disability or death. In wrongful death cases, the surviving spouse usually demands and, if he or she is the winning party, obtains compensation for the projected future earnings of the decedent. In cases where the plaintiff is married or the parent of small children, derivative action(s) will be filed on behalf of these next of kin. These actions are described later in this chapter.

In addition to special damages, *general damages* are customarily awarded. These compensate the injured person for the pain and suffering. They are calculated as a multiple of (e.g., two to three times) the special damages.

General and special damages are intended to compensate the injured person for monetary losses and for pain and suffering. They are not intended to punish the defendant. In cases of intentional torts, however, the plaintiff may seek *punitive* damages. These damages may be quite large, depending upon whether the tort was particularly egregious. Intentional torts are discussed in Chapter 5.

EXAMPLES OF NEGLIGENT ACTS

The basis for an action in negligence is a failure of the defendant to carry out one (or more) of the duties of care (enumerated in Chapter 2) owed the plaintiff. Although these duties emanate from a contract, a breach of any of them generally will expose the health care provider to allegations of *negligence* rather than *breach of contract*.[2] (The background for this apparent dichotomy is explained at the end of Chapter 2.) Ready examples of breach of some of these duties may be found in health care delivery. The duty to make full disclosure is the basis of the informed consent doctrine, discussed in Chapter 9. Failure to obtain informed consent when counseling the patient for a procedure that poses a risk is considered negligence. Once treatment is started, the health care provider has a duty to keep the patient apprised of the therapeutic progress. Attempting to conceal a complication from a patient could amount to a breach of the duty to disclose. It could also constitute fraudulent concealment, a nonnegligent or intentional tort (Chapter 5).

Failure to maintain confidences traditionally is an intentional tort, although the patient's lawyer might file an action for negligence, inasmuch as professional liability insurance policies cover negligent acts but not intentional ones. Some might argue that failure to provide continuing treatment is abandonment, also an intentional tort, although when it is alleged, it is usually included within the scope of negligence actions. Turning the anesthetic administration over to someone significantly less skilled, with a consequent complication that probably would not have occurred in more skilled hands, would be an example of this tort in the field of anesthesia. Another example would be leaving a patient who is not fully recovered from the effects of the anesthetic in the recovery room when the anesthetist or anesthesiologist knows that the recovery room is inadequately staffed. Potential legal problems associated with postanesthesia follow-up care are discussed in Chapter 13.

The fifth duty, seeking consultation when indicated, evolved through common law decisions as medical knowledge expanded to the point that no single practitioner can be expected to know all there is to know about medicine. Jurists, jurors, and appellate courts recognize that this overabundance of knowledge mandates that much care is specialized, and it must therefore fall within the province of a specialist. Decisions in these cases hold that the physician must recognize the limits of his or her expertise and know when to call for help. Failure to refer in a timely fashion is considered a departure from the duty of care. Failure to seek consultation in a pedagogical setting is discussed in Chapter 19. Other examples of negligent acts occurring in anesthesia practice are discussed in Chapters 4, 6, 8, 11, 12, 14 through 18, 21, and 22).

DOCTRINE OF RES IPSA LOQUITUR

As noted above, proof in a negligence action involves the introduction of evidence pertaining to each of the five elements of that action. The plaintiff is always shouldered with this burden, the defendant always coming to court *presumed* to be not liable. This manner of proof follows one of the rules of evidence (see Chapter 23). There is another rule that can be used in an effort to create an *inference* (or even *presumption*) of negligence if actual proof of the negligent act is lacking. That rule is embodied in the doctrine of *res ipsa loquitur*,[3] which requires five elements: (1) the instrumentality causing the injury must have been under the *exclusive control* of the defendant or defendants, (2) the patient-plaintiff must *not* have been *contributively negligent* and (3) not in a position to have observed the negligent act, (4) the nature of the injury must have been such that it *could not have occurred in the absence of someone departing from the duty of care*, and (5) it must be *common knowledge* among laypersons (as those who sit on juries) that the injury could not have occurred in the absence of negligence. In effect, the plaintiff's lawyer, in addressing the judge or jury (in a foreign body case), would state:

> The defendant anesthesiologist and surgeon in this case were in exclusive control of everything, including my client, while she was anesthetized for the operation. My client was at all times unconscious under the effects of the anesthetic and could neither have observed nor contributed to her own injury. Surgical clamps are not left in wounds without one of the surgeons or other member of the operating team having made a mistake. Furthermore, even laypersons recognize that fact.

At the appropriate time following introduction of all of the evidence (see Chapter 23), the plaintiff's lawyer requests that the judge give the jurors a *res ipsa loquitur* instruction. The following might be such an instruction in a case involving a patient who was burned by a fire in the operating room drapes:

> If you believe by your own knowledge that the defendant members of the operating room team must have made a mistake in allowing a fire to develop in the sterile drapes, which fire burned the plaintiff, then you may infer that the defendants breached their duty

to the plaintiff, and you may bring in a verdict for the plaintiff.

Except in a few jurisdictions, introduction of evidence via the *res ipsa loquitur* doctrine creates only an *inference* of negligence. The jurors *may infer* that there was a departure from the duty of care that allowed the hemostat to remain in the abdomen, or they may not. The defense would still have the opportunity to introduce evidence to the effect that it was not a departure from the duty of care to leave a clamp in the wound. In this example, liability would seem straightforward.

Considerably more weight is given to this doctrine in a minority of jurisdictions.[4] Courts in California, Colorado, Indiana, Louisiana, Mississippi, Montana, and North Carolina have held that either a *presumption* of negligence is created or the burden of coming forward with the evidence is actually shifted to the defendant. In either event, the defendant would have to introduce evidence rebutting this presumption or risk having the court direct a verdict for the plaintiff.

Two cases in which this doctrine was applied to establish an inference of negligence sufficient to sustain the plaintiff's burden of proof stand out. In *Sawyer v. Jewish Chronic Disease Hospital*,[5] a New York anesthesiologist administered open ether to a malnourished infant with an upper respiratory infection. The defendant was found liable for the death of the infant. In the other case, a circulating nurse placed the ground electrode of a unipolar high-frequency electrosurgical device on a patient's buttock, as was customary practice. Because the electrode was not in complete contact, the patient suffered an electrical burn at its site. The plaintiff's lawyer invoked the *res* doctrine against the anesthesiologist, and the inference of negligence was so strong that the anesthesiologist was found liable for failure to adequately supervise placement of this electrode.[6]

There are numerous applications of the *res* doctrine in which jurors have found for the defendant health care provider. Some of the best examples of unsuccessful, and also successful, use of this doctrine involve positioning patients and subsequent peripheral nerve injuries. This case law is discussed in Chapter 11.

ACTIONS FOR INJURY TO FAMILY MEMBERS

If the plaintiff is married, is a parent, or has other close relatives, actions may be filed by, or on behalf of, these next of kin for loss of the care, comfort, companionship, and society of the injured spouse, parent, sibling, or the like. These common law–based actions initially were available only to husbands whose wives were injured. In 1950 the Court of Appeals for the District of Columbia held that a wife may sue for loss of her husband's care, comfort, and society.[7] Actions for injuries to family members automatically fail if there is a defense verdict on the primary action and may have a good chance of success if there is a plaintiff's verdict. Parents who observe a negligent act that injured one of their children may sue the tort-feasor for the negligent infliction of emotional harm (see Chapter 5). A father who watches a traumatic delivery of his child could allege such a tort.

DEFENSES TO MALPRACTICE ACTIONS

There are a number of possible defenses to actions for *ordinary* negligence (in addition to the rather obvious one of proving that the defendant's conduct met the standard of care). These include *contributory negligence, assumption of the risk,* and *consent.* In a case of *professional* negligence, however, the only possible defense might be the contributory negligence of the plaintiff, and then under relatively few factual situations. One example would be a patient scheduled for "same-day surgery" (see Chapter 15) who is told to "take nothing by mouth after midnight." The patient disregards that admonition, eats a full breakfast, and, before the start of the case, makes no mention of having eaten. During induction of anesthesia, the patient vomits, aspirates, develops asphyxia and circulatory arrest, and suffers permanent brain damage. In any subsequent legal action, anesthesia personnel would offer as a defense the contributory negligence of the patient in having eaten. At common law, contributory negligence forms an absolute bar to recovery.

Many state legislatures, recognizing that the universal application of this doctrine barred recovery in cases in which the negligence of the defendant was particularly strong while that of the plaintiff relatively mild, adopted *comparative negligence* legislation (an example of changing the common law by statute.) By 1989, all state legislatures except those in Alabama, the District of Columbia, Maryland, North Carolina, Tennessee, and Virginia had adopted the comparative negligence doctrine.[8] It operates by weighing the relative magnitude of the negligence of the plaintiff against that of the defendant. Thus, if the negligence of the plaintiff contributed 20% to the injury and that of the defendant 80%, the reward would be reduced by 20%. In the just cited food-in-the-stomach example, the plaintiff might allege that anesthesia personnel departed from the duty of care themselves on the morning of the procedure by failing to inquire whether the patient had followed the nothing-by-mouth advice.

In a fairly recent case[9] involving a Jehovah's Witness and refusal to accept a blood transfusion, both the comparative negligence and assumption of the risk doctrines were invoked.

The Witness-patient, Mrs. Doreen Shorter, was a candidate for a dilatation and curettage to remove a dead fetus. She refused to allow the administration of any blood product under any circumstances. Her husband joined with this admonition, and both executed what the court later found to be a valid release. The general practitioner who was to perform the D & C warned both Shorters of the possible risk of a perforated uterus and excessive bleeding. During the performance of the D & C, the uterus was perforated. Unfortunately, the general physician did not become aware of the perforation until Mrs. Shorter commenced bleeding profusely while in the recovery room. She was taken back to the operating room, where a team of surgeons attempted to repair the perforation. It became necessary to perform a hysterectomy and massive blood loss ensued. The surgeons were unable to stop the flow of blood sufficiently to save Mrs. Shorter's life.

Subsequently, her husband filed a lawsuit against the general physician. The jury found for the Shorters but reduced the damages by 75% on the grounds that the Shorters had assumed the risk by refusing to accept blood, and that in doing so they were contributively negligent. The case was appealed, and the Supreme Court of Washington affirmed the decision of the trial court. The Court held that while the refusal to permit a blood transfusion did not release the general physician from his negligence in perforating the uterus, there was sufficient evidence presented to the jury to find that the refusal to receive the blood was done voluntarily and with full knowledge of the risk. Therefore, the court reasoned, the refusal was valid. The court stated that a refusal to permit blood transfusion which released physicians from responsibility for unfavorable reactions because of that refusal was not against public policy. The husband, the court stated, did not assume the risk of the general physician's negligence, but did assume the risk of death as a consequence of refusal to allow the blood to be administered.

This case resulted in a landmark decision. It is good law and should also *place health care providers on firm notice of the risk that they face any time they endeavor to conditionally* (i.e., "We will not give you any blood even if it might be lifesaving") *care for anyone who refuses a blood product*, the use of which might later have been lifesaving.

Although assumption of the risk is a possible defense in medical malpractice actions, it would be likely to succeed only under very limited factual situations.[10] A hypothetical case might involve a patient with inoperable carcinoma who was offered a new chemotherapeutic agent that had considerable therapeutic promise, yet possessed a high incidence of serious side effects. Without this experimental drug, the patient would be expected to die within 6 months. The patient elects to receive the experimental agent. Just as its therapeutic benefits are becoming manifest, the patient develops severe myocardial toxicity and dies of acute myocardial failure. Although the oncologist has obtained the patient's informed consent, the estate sues on general negligence theories. One of the defenses could be assumption of the risk.

ROLE OF THE MEDICAL RECORD

One cannot stress strongly enough the importance of thorough, accurate, and legible documentation (see Chapter 10) of the care rendered each patient. Patients commonly equate the bad result with a departure from the duty of care. The untoward result that is not accompanied with an adequate explanation, especially when it is coupled with a breakdown in communication between patient and health care provider, is very likely to send the patient off to seek legal counsel; litigation may well be in the offing. If the defendant physician is lucky, the plaintiff will retain a competent trial lawyer who will want to review the medical records, possibly even before he or she agrees to take the case. If those records accurately reflect the reasons for the untoward result, the lawyer may refuse to accept the individual as a client and might even endeavor to convince the client that the case has no merit.

Cases that do come to trial inevitably involve extensive use of medical records. Customarily, these records carry significant evidential weight. If the defendant health care provider can demonstrate that the care was adequate, through the modality of neat, legible, carefully executed, and generously informative medical records, there is a good chance that a defense verdict will be forthcoming.

CONCLUSION

Litigation involving professional negligence or malpractice receives wide publicity in the professional, as well as the lay, press. It is also reflected in professional liability insurance rates that once again (see Chapter 29) appear to be on the rise, in part at least because of the frequency and amount of judgments rendered against health care professionals. Health care professionals naturally are quite anxious to reduce their exposure to the threat of malpractice. Specifically germane to this end is Chapter 7. It covers some of the risk management steps that health care providers, and especially anesthesia personnel, can take to minimize the danger of injuries to one's patients and, even in the presence of an untoward result, minimize the risk of litigation and liability.

These steps are worth pursuing. Health care providers and patients both are human, and hence not perfect. The potential for hidden illnesses, adverse pharmacologic interactions, or both, lurks for unwary members of the anesthesia team in a significant number of patients. Some of these risks can be identified during careful preanesthetic evaluation (Chapter 8). Positioning the patient, monitoring the vital signs, administering general or regional anesthesia, and following the patient postoperatively (Chapters 12 through 15) bring additional risks to the fore. Accompanying these risks are opportunities for adverse outcomes, and hence sources of potential litigation. Personnel who are alert to these will take appropriate steps to ameliorate these hazards before they materialize into accidents and injuries. In doing so, they will have taken the first major step in preventing complications, adverse outcomes, and potential litigation.

REFERENCES

1. Keeton, WP (ed): Prosser and Keeton on Torts, ed 5, West, St Paul, 1984, p 2.
2. *Ibid*, pp 186–187.
3. *Ibid*, pp 242 *et seq*.
4. *Ibid*, pp 258–259.
5. 234 N.Y.S.2d 372 (1962).
6. Wiles v. Myerly, 210 N.W.2d 619 (Iowa, 1973).
7. Hitaffer v. Argonne Co., 87 U.S. App., D.C. 57, 183 F.2d 811, *cert. denied*, 340 U.S. 852, 71 S. Ct. 80, 95 L. Ed. 624 (1950).
8. Tingley, J: Comparative Negligence Manual, Appendix II. Callaghan, Chicago, 1989.
9. Shorter v. Drury, 103 Wash. 2d 645, 695 P.2d 116 (Sup. Ct., 1985).
10. *See, generally*, discussion of assumption of the risk, in Keeton, *supra* 1, pp 480 *et seq*.

4

William H. L. Dornette, M.D., J.D.

The Standard
of Care

Traditionally, as indicated in Chapter 3, the standard of care has been the level of care that physicians of similar training and experience practicing in the same community would provide under the same or similar circumstances. As noted in the discussion of negligence in Chapter 3, the standard of care is one element of proof necessary for establishing negligence. That is, the health care provider will be found liable only if there was a departure from this standard and that departure caused an injury to the patient. This level of care, to which the health care provider has a duty to adhere, becomes important from both a practical and legal posture—from a practical posture because it is the best and safest method of delivering that care, and from a legal posture because failing to adhere to it could well lead to liability. It thus becomes important to review how the standard is established and the factors involved in changing it. This chapter covers the historical development of the standard of care in medical practice, delineates the role of courts as well as of the advances in medicine in setting and changing the standard, and proffers suggestions for meeting the standard of care in today's changing anesthesia practice.

HISTORICAL PERSPECTIVE

To fully appreciate the standard of care in the practice of anesthesia today, it is helpful to understand how medical practice standards in the United States have evolved. At the beginning of the 19th century, there were several thriving medical centers on the eastern seaboard. Across the Allegheny Mountains on the banks of the Ohio River, a medical school was founded in Cincinnati in 1819. That school, which eventually became a part of the University of Cincinnati, was geographically isolated from the health care facilities in Boston, Philadelphia, and New York. Communications were slow, and movement of physicians from one area to another sporadic. There were no national organizations of physicians, much less specialists. Medical books were scarce, and journals (except for the *Boston Medical and Surgical Journal,* now the *New England Journal of Medicine)* essentially nonexistent. Anesthesia had not yet come into being. It is understandable that physicians of that era were held to what was called the locality standard—the level of care administered by practitioners who worked within that particular *community.*

Times have changed. National associations of physicians and specialists have been founded. Journals as well as books are published with nationwide circulation. Specialty boards have evolved since the period immediately preceding World War II. Examinations given by these specialty boards are the same across the country. Considering the ready means of communications that have developed, the national scope of publications, the board examinations and organizations, and the universality of the sciences of medicine, nursing, and other health care, it is apparent that the standard of care has, of necessity, expanded to become nationwide. One may say that the community standard still exists, but

now that "community" encompasses the entire United States.

THE STANDARD OF ANESTHESIA CARE TODAY

As one might surmise, the evolution of standards of anesthesia practice has paralleled that of health care in general. As noted below, specialty organizations, training programs, and publications have played principal roles, with governmental agencies and individual institutions also contributing. Today, in the United States and Canada there are at least five organizations that were founded by anesthesia professionals for the promotion, among other things, of safe anesthesia practice. Among them are the American Association of Nurse Anesthetists (AANA), the American Board of Anesthesiology (ABA), the American Society of Anesthesiologists (ASA), the Canadian Anaesthetists Society, and the International Anesthesia Research Society. Each of them, through the publication of journals, presentation of annual meetings, workshops, refresher courses and the like, and (in the case of the AANA and ABA) offering certifying examinations, clearly achieves its intended goal of elevating the level of anesthesia care in this country. In doing so, each helps establish the standard of care. Residency programs and schools of nurse anesthesia, functioning under the guidelines of the respective accreditation organization or council, also promote sound anesthesia practice and further the establishment of the standard of care. Books, journals, recommendations of governmental agencies, and even possibly the courts (as discussed below) contribute to this standard.

Variations in the Standard

While it is true that the community standard encompasses the entire United States, there still may be some differences. These primarily relate to the level of care in the large hospital versus the small one. As is well recognized, U.S. health care delivery is carried out in primary, secondary, and tertiary care institutions. This tripartite arrangement is necessitated by subspecialization and the often complex and expensive equipment needed to carry out many of the most modern procedures. Thus, while the overall standard in the United States is the same nationwide, there are major differences between small and large (especially tertiary care) hospitals in carrying out some highly specialized medical and surgical services, and in the equipment needed to accomplish those services. A notable example of specialized equipment (i.e., the mass spectrometer) has become a part of modern monitoring practice in some large institutions (see Chapter 12).

CHANGING THE STANDARD OF CARE

Anyone who has been in the practice of anesthesia for more than a few years realizes that the standard of care may change very quickly and dramatically. The availability of a new drug or new item of equipment may suddenly take the health care community by storm. Attributes such as enhanced safety, fewer side effects, better muscle relaxation, more complete total effect, or more profound analgesia frequently will produce a dramatic shift from one agent to another. The same is true of innovative equipment. New monitoring equipment is a case in point. The introduction of new drugs and equipment frequently elevates the standard of care. It also poses interesting problems for those who deliver that care. When should the new drug or item of equipment be added to one's practice? When should one drop an old item of equipment or pharmaceutical? In this respect, two quotations come to mind. When one reads glowing reports about new pharmaceuticals, Balfour's rather dour comment deserves repetition:

Considering the enthusiasm that moves the world, it is unfortunate that so few enthusiasts can be entrusted to speak the truth.

The second quotation is by Oliver Wendell Holmes:

Be not the first by whom the new is tried, nor yet the last to lay the old aside.

The standard of care of anesthesia practice is not static, nor does it progress evenly across the country. One way to approach the question "When does the standard of care change?" is to consider a hypothetical case. Assume that antibiotic A is the only one available to treat a certain infection. It has recognized side effects, one of which is permanent deafness. The patient has developed a renal infection for which antibiotic A is the drug of choice. Failure to use antibiotic A would probably result in loss of the kidney; the infection might even prove fatal. During the process of discussing this therapy with the patient, the side effects are specifically mentioned. The patient's informed consent is obtained, and the therapy is started. The patient is cured of the infection but becomes permanently deaf. Clearly, under that set of facts, the patient would have no cause of action against the treating physician.

Let us now change the facts slightly. Some time before the patient's illness, Miracle Laboratories is licensed by the Food and Drug Administration (FDA) to market a new drug, antibiotic B. This agent has fewer and less serious side effects and is just as efficacious as antibiotic A in managing that type of renal infection. At what point should the practitioner become aware of this new drug and prescribe it instead of antibiotic A? At some time the standard of care will change because of the increased safety of antibiotic B over antibiotic A. Perhaps the standard will not change until the drug has been used sufficiently in the postclinical trial period for the medical profession to be fully convinced of its safety and efficacy. The process of changeover may be gradual or abrupt. The courts have held that as long as a *respectable minority* of the medical profession still uses the older drug, the standard of care has not yet changed. Admittedly such an argument may seem of little solace to the practitioner who has failed to jump on the antibiotic B bandwagon and is now being sued because of the side effects mentioned. The lawyer for the deaf patient-plaintiff will probably be able to find a bright young practitioner who will testify that he started using B just as soon as it was marketed and has never experienced any problems with it. The defendant

THE STANDARD OF CARE **27**

would endeavor to introduce evidence to the effect that at the time of the patient's treatment, a respectable minority (or more) of the profession still employed antibiotic A. I use this example to reiterate the importance of each practitioner's keeping up with the standard of care. Fortunately, there are relatively few, if any, anesthetic agents that are capable of producing side effects as serious as those described in this hypothetical case.

Practicing at a Higher Level of Care

To meet the expectations of the courts (e.g., in offering a defense in an action for negligence), the practitioner must practice at the level of care of similar practitioners working under the same or similar circumstances. The reader who works in a large university hospital may have available elaborate equipment for the administration of anesthesia and monitoring patient's vital signs. Many of these new monitoring devices do achieve a degree of assessment of vital function far more detailed and precise than the devices commonly in use in the average hospital in the United States. Will this institution or practitioner be held to a standard of care above that of the average in the community or nation? The answer to this question clearly is yes. One may establish a higher level of care, but if one does so, one will be held to that higher level of care.[1] This fact is presented not to discourage hospitals and individual providers from practicing at a higher level of care, but merely to point out the legal position they create for themselves when they do so.

Changing the Standard of Care by Common Law

One would naturally expect that the standard of care, reflected by common law decisions, would be advanced only by enhancements in the professional or other activity involved. Such is not always the case. It is possible for a court to change the standard of care based upon the evidence presented to it.

The lead case in this area involved the *T. J. Hooper* and the *Montrose*, two oceangoing tugs that left Norfolk, Virginia, for New York City in the early 1920s, each with three barges of coal. At that time the Navy broadcast twice-daily reports from a radio station in Arlington, Virginia, of weather conditions in the vicinity, and made forecasts for the ensuing 12 to 24 hours. It was not then the standard practice for seagoing tugs to be equipped with receiving sets; a few tugboat pilots did own their own personal radios. The sets were not overly expensive, a fact taken into consideration during the subsequent litigation. The pilots of four tugs heading north along the coast and preceding the *Hooper* and *Montrose* did have radio receiving sets. Sometime prior to approaching the Delaware River breakwater, they picked up a report from Arlington radio indicating the possibility of a storm. All four tugs with their barges heaved to behind the breakwater. The masters of the *Montrose* and *Hooper* arrived at the breakwater sometime later. Not having receiving sets, they were unaware of the impending storm and continued northward. The tugs encountered the storm off the coast of Atlantic City. Each lost one barge from its tow. In affirming the District Court opinion against the operators of the tugs, the Court of Appeals[2] held that an entire calling—business, industry, or profession—may lag behind in keeping up with the standard of care. The tugboat owners-operators were found liable for the unseaworthiness of their vessels; that is, they did not supply themselves with a receiving set, which they could have done at relatively low cost, and which, according to the admissions of the masters of the tugs, would have alerted them to the prudent step of following the other tows behind the Delaware River breakwater.

Closer to home (from a factual standpoint) is an Ohio case that involved the standard of care in counting sponges. At the time of the missing sponge, all Cleveland surgeons apparently relied on their circulating and scrub nurses for the correctness of the count. Following a mistaken count and retained sponge, Mrs. Ault developed an abdominal abscess and subsequently sued Dr. Hall. His defense was understandably based upon what was customary practice. The Supreme Court of Ohio disagreed, stating (in part):

Methods employed in any trade, business or profession, no matter how long continued, cannot avail to establish as safe in law that which is dangerous in fact.[3]

It is clear that a court may elevate the standard of care for any activity if a higher (safer) standard is readily available, the higher standard is not unduly burdensome or prohibitively expensive, and following that higher standard would have prevented the accident and injury.

VOLUNTARY STANDARDS-MAKING ORGANIZATIONS

A voluntary standards-making organization is an organization, association, or similar group, membership in which is voluntary, that drafts codes, standards, manuals, recommended guidelines, or practices for the enhancement of safety, or for other purposes, within an activity or endeavor that is affected by those standards. The primary purpose of these organizations is developing and promoting the standards. Examples of voluntary standards-making organizations affecting the practice of anesthesia include the American National Standards Institute, the Association for the Advancement of Medical Instrumentation, the Compressed Gas Association, the Joint Commission on Accreditation of Healthcare Organizations (JCAHO, formerly the JCAH), and the National Fire Protection Association (NFPA). The AANA, the ABA, and the ASA do not draft standards as a primary activity. Yet, some of the publications of these organizations create, and serve to elevate, the standard of care of anesthesia practice in this country (see, e.g., the publications of the ASA and AANA in reference to various aspects of anesthesia practice that are contained in Appendixes 4-1, 4-2, 8-1, 12-1, 12-2, 13-1, and 15-1, and Table 10-1).

Legal Status of Voluntary Standards

Whether voluntary standards will be recognized in a court of law as establishing or influencing the standard of care of a given activity will depend upon whether the standard is adopted by statute, or the individual or institution involved in the activity is a member of or accredited by the voluntary standards-making organization. When introducing evidence to prove negligence (Chapter 3), the duty of care owing becomes the cornerstone of the case. A voluntary standard can be introduced into evidence in such an action; it would have a different procedural effect under each of the following circumstances.

Statutory Incorporation of the Standard

If a state had adopted a statute that specifies a standard, it is incumbent upon those practicing within that state to adhere to that standard.

For example, the Tennessee legislature adopted what was formerly NFPA 56A—Standard for the Safe Use of Inhalation Anesthetics, as well as the National Electrical Code (NEC). Assume, further, that a patient is electrocuted in an operating room in a hospital within that jurisdiction. The cause of the accidental electrocution is traced to faulty wiring. An investigation of the wiring reveals that it did not follow the recommendations of either the NEC or NFPA 56A. The estate of the patient sues the hospital. The lawyer for the estate introduces copies of the NEC and NFPA 56A into evidence. The argument is made that these publications were incorporated by reference in a statute and, therefore, failure of the institution to comply with them was a violation of a statute. The lawyer would then argue that the injured party was a member of that class of persons that the statute was adopted to protect, and that the harm suffered was of the type that the statute was enacted to prevent.

A majority of courts in this country hold that the nonexcused violation of a statute is *conclusive evidence of negligence* (i.e., a departure from the duty of care proximately causing the patient's injury).[4] The jury would be so instructed. The defenses of contributory negligence of, or assumption of the risk by, the plaintiff still would be available to the defendant. It is, of course, hard to envision how an unconscious patient could be contributively negligent under such circumstances. Further, no patient would knowingly enter an operating room and assume the risk of improper wiring that might result in accidental electrocution.

Some (a minority) of the courts would hold that violation of the statute resulted in strict liability.[5] In such a situation, the judge would direct a verdict for the plaintiff. Any defenses, such as contributory negligence or assumption of the risk, would not be available to the defendant hospital under those circumstances.

Membership in the Voluntary Organization

If an institution is a member of (or accredited by) a voluntary organization that has adopted a standard, the institution is expected to adhere to that standard. The effect of such membership is epitomized by the holding in the case of *Darling v. Charleston Community Memorial Hospital.*[6]

Clarence Darling was injured in a football game one Saturday afternoon and was taken to Charleston Community Memorial Hospital. The physician covering the emergency room was a family practitioner who had not done any orthopedic procedures in 2 years and had not set a femoral fracture in 4 years. The physician performed a closed reduction and applied a hip-to-toe cast. Clarence recovered from anesthesia complaining of pain. The nurses administered meperidine as per postoperative orders. His complaints of pain continued, and Clarence's toes were noted by nursing personnel to first become pale, then blue. The family physician was notified. He bivalved the cast, but in spite of that treatment, the circulation in Clarence's leg continued to deteriorate. The nurses did not notify their superiors of this problem, and the family physician did nothing else to prevent the subsequent gangrene.

Eventually Clarence was transferred to Barnes Hospital in St. Louis, where his leg was amputated. He lost his college basketball scholarship. Clarence, through his parents, sued the hospital and the physician. The physician settled for the limits of his policy. The case against the hospital went to trial, during which the standards of the (then) JCAH were introduced into evidence. The case eventually reached the Supreme Court of Illinois, which affirmed the trial court's decision for Clarence.

Germane to this particular discussion was the holding that the standards of the JCAH may be introduced as evidence of customary practice of an accredited hospital. Charleston Community Memorial Hospital was so accredited.

The Darlings' lawyer alleged violation of a number of standards. To quote from the complaint[6] (see Glossary of Legal Terminology definitions):

That the defendant hospital failed to conform and to observe one or more of the following standards customarily required of and adhered to by accredited [emphasis the editor's] hospitals in the area involved at that time:

(1) *Failed to provide a licensed, graduate, professional nursing service available to all parties at all times, and particularly to the plaintiff here;*
(2) *Failed to provide qualified personnel adequate to supervise and conduct the supervision of medical patients and, in particular, the plaintiff here;*
(3) *Failed to make adequate provision for hematology and serology examinations as pertains to this plaintiff, and to conduct such other blood tests and examinations as would have disclosed the progressive deterioration of the circulation in this plaintiff's right leg;*
(4) *Failed to maintain a modern and adequate medical library relating to modern orthopedic methods and casting techniques;*
(5) *Permitted the defendant physician to be appointed as a member of the active staff when he was not qualified professionally to perform orthopedic surgery, which, as a member of such staff, he was permitted to do;*
(6) *Failed, through its medical staff, to review the treatment rendered to the plaintiff and violated its duty to make certain that the attending physician in this case did not fail in the matter of calling consultants as needed, there being doubt as to the best therapeutic measures to be utilized, and it being apparent under the circumstances of this case that a qualified orthopedist should have been called into consultation;*
(7) *Failed to have reports of a tissue committee on orthopedic cases previously handled by the said physician, in order to determine his qualification to do surgery of that type and character, and failed to have monthly meetings to review surgical procedures following in*

this and in other cases;

(8) *Failed to have a sufficient number of licensed, graduate, professional nurses for the bedside care of all patients at all times, and thus failed to have such nurses available for bedside care of the plaintiff at all times capable of recognizing the progressive gangrenous condition of the plaintiff's right leg, and of bringing the same to the attention of the hospital administration and to the medical staff so that adequate consultation could have been secured and such conditions rectified.*

This case stands as a landmark decision in other respects. It has not been overturned. In a case such as this one in which voluntary standards are admissible as evidence of customary practice, it would not be necessary for the plaintiff to introduce expert testimony to authenticate those standards.

The Nonmember Institution

Even if an institution is not a member of such a voluntary organization, it could be held that standards adopted by such an organization would apply even to a nonmember institution. Assume that a similar accident occurs in a hospital that is not accredited by the (now) JCAHO. What role would a JCAHO standard play in the trial of the case? In such an instance, the plaintiff would have to obtain an expert who would testify that even though the hospital was not so accredited, the standard of care in the United States, even in nonaccredited hospitals, was set or at least strongly influenced by JCAHO standards. The extent to which such an argument would prevail would, in large measure, depend upon the persuasiveness of the plaintiff's expert witness, as well as the expertise of the lawyers trying the case.

Effect of Reducing a Voluntary Standard

Even if a voluntary standards-making organization lowered the safety requirements of one of its standards, an argument could successfully be made that the standard of care is not automatically lowered. The JCAHO recently removed the requirement for isolated power from nonflammable anesthetizing locations. This requirement, a holdover from the days when flammable anesthetics were the agents of choice for general anesthesia, offers an extra layer of safety against electrocution in the often wet environment of the operating room. Personnel, standing on a floor wet from spills of biological fluids or irrigating solutions, are in practicality themselves grounded. They would not be electrocuted, however, if they accidentally (because of an electrical fault in an item of line-powered equipment) contacted either one of the live conductors, as long as that equipment was supplied by isolated power. Such would not be the case in the operating room supplied by conventional (one side grounded, the other side hot to ground) power.

Assume that a patient or member of the staff suffers an electrically induced injury as a result of the use of a defective item of electrical equipment in an operating room equipped with a conventional, grounded electrical supply circuit. The injured person would be unable to allege violation of a statute or requirement of the JCAHO, since such a requirement no longer exists. That person would have to obtain an electrical engineer or other expert to testify that a higher quality of electrical service (i.e., through an isolated circuit) would, had it been present, have prevented the injury. Considering the precedent set by the *T. J. Hooper* case, it would seem inconceivable that the court would accept the argument that the standard of care now required a lesser degree of protection. It would further seem that the injured patient or staff member would have little difficulty in obtaining the services of such an expert.

THE STANDARD OF CARE IN THE COURTROOM

In the final analysis, real concerns about the standard of care relate to its application in actual litigation—how it would be determined in the courtroom for the resolution of an actual case. The lawyer for the patient-plaintiff would endeavor to establish the standard at as high a level as possible. In doing so, the task of proving to the trier of fact that the defendant practiced below that level of care would be simplified. A plaintiff's lawyer might even endeavor to show the level of practice at the time of the trial. (It is, of course, a well-accepted evidential tenet that the level of care is the one in effect *at the time* of the incident complained of; further, remedial measures taken afterward to prevent future such incidents may not be used in evidence to show the preferable level of that care.) Conversely, the defense lawyer will introduce evidence of the usual and customary level of care contemporaneous with the event(s) that generated the litigation. Both lawyers will utilize expert witnesses (see Chapter 24) to offer opinions on the standard of care. Bolstered by their respective qualifications, these witnesses will employ their own expertise and may reinforce their opinions through the use of articles from well-known journals, chapters from learned treatises, current researches, and any other authoritative information that they may find and bring to bear as part of their testimony.

The Role of Books, Articles, and Other Learned Treatises

Publications have always been useful in the courtroom—by expert witnesses to bolster their own opinion on direct examination and by lawyers during cross-examination in attempts to discredit an opponent's expert witness. In either event, some expert witness must testify that the publication is authoritative if it is to be afforded evidential weight. The amount of weight will vary, depending on the scope (local, statewide, or national) and nature (directed to that particular specialty or more general in nature) of the publication, as well as the prestige of the author and his or her institution. For example, in 1986 an article[7] appeared in *The Journal of the American Medical Association* (JAMA) describing the monitoring methodology in use at the teaching hospitals affiliated with the Harvard Medical School. The authors pointed out that the use of those techniques would be efficacious in reducing morbidity and mortality. In litigation involving the standard of monitoring care, what weight would (or should) this article be given in establishing that standard? JAMA is prestigious but is not published

specifically for anesthesia personnel. Harvard Medical School is also prestigious, but perhaps no more or less so than a number of medical centers in this country. One would expect the article to carry significant weight in Boston, and perhaps throughout New England, but progressively less the greater the distance of the site of the trial from the Boston area.

The Standard of Care and Ultimate Liability

Does proof that the standard of care was met ensure a defense verdict? Failure to meet the standard resulted in payments to over 80% of patients, according to a closed claims study reported by Cheney and coworkers.[8] Yet these same authors found that "if the anesthesiologist provides appropriate care there is still a greater than 40 percent chance that payment will be made." This seeming dichotomy might be explained by the relative experience of the trial lawyers and degree of expertise of witnesses for each side. There are a number of almost intangible factors that are taken into consideration in deciding to effectuate settlement.

In the final analysis, the standard of care in any given case will be that which the trier of fact (in personal injury cases, generally the jurors) becomes convinced it is—no more and no less—based upon the persuasion of the expert witnesses. The greater the expertise of a given witness, and of the lawyer on whose behalf the expert is testifying, the greater will be the degree of this persuasion.

CONCLUSION

Considering the many modern advances in pharmaceutical therapy and medical equipment, it is apparent that the standard of care has changed and will do so in the future. All health care providers are expected to be aware when it does change and to adjust their practices as appropriate. Whether any new item of equipment or pharmaceutical will replace an older one, and hence change the standard of care, will depend upon whether the item, technique, or pharmaceutical carries out its intended task more efficiently, with a greater degree of safety, or both, as compared to older agents or methods. Time-worn but still efficacious agents and techniques will continue to be used only if they can be used as safely and effectively as the newer ones.

Finally, personnel should remain alert to any changes in *any* standards that create a more hazardous situation or increase the likelihood of an untoward result. The standard of care, as the courts ultimately must determine it, will not automatically be reduced by a dilution or lowering of any such standards.

REFERENCES

1. Keeton, WP (ed): Prosser and Keeton on Torts, ed 5. West, St Paul, 1984, p 185.
2. *T. J. Hooper*, 60 F.2d 737 (C.A. 2 1932).
3. Ault v. Hall, 119 O.S. 442, 164 N.E. 518 (Sup. Ct. 1928)
4. Keeton, *supra* ref. 1, p 230.
5. *Ibid.*, p 231.
6. Darling v. Charleston Community Memorial Hosp., 50 Ill. App.2d 253, 200 N.E.2d 149 (App. Ct. 4th Dist. 1964); *aff'd* 33 Ill.2d 326, 211 N.E.2d 253 (Sup. Ct. 1965).
7. Eichhorn, JH, et al: Standards for patient monitoring during anesthesia at Harvard Medical School. JAMA 256:1017, 1986.
8. Cheney, FW, et al: Standard of care and anesthesia liability. JAMA 261:1599, 1989.

APPENDIX

4-1

ASA GUIDELINES FOR PATIENT CARE IN ANESTHESIOLOGY*

(AMENDED BY THE HOUSE OF DELEGATES ON OCTOBER 16, 1985)

I Definition of Anesthesiology:

Anesthesiology is a discipline within the practice of medicine specializing in:

A The medical management of patients who are rendered unconscious and/or insensible to pain and emotional stress during surgical, obstetrical and certain other medical procedures (involves preoperative, intraoperative and postoperative evaluation and treatment of these patients);

B The protection of life functions and vital organs (e.g., brain, heart, lungs, kidneys, liver) under the stress of anesthetic, surgical and other medical procedures;

C The management of problems in pain relief;

D The management of cardiopulmonary resuscitation;

E The management of problems in pulmonary care;

F The management of critically ill patients in special care units.

II Anesthesiologist's Responsibilities:

---

*Reprinted with the permission of the ASA.

Anesthesiologists are physicians who, after college, have graduated from an accredited medical school and have successfully completed an approved residency in anesthesiology. Anesthesiologists' responsibilities to patients should include:

A Preanesthetic evaluation and treatment;

B Medical management of patients and their anesthetic procedures;

C Postanesthetic evaluation and treatment;

D On-site medical direction of any non-physician who assists in the technical aspects of anesthesia care to the patient.

III Guidelines for Anesthesia Care:

  A The same quality of anesthetic care should be available for all patients:

    1 Twenty-four hours a day, seven days a week;

    2 Emergency as well as elective patients;

    3 Obstetrical, medical, and surgical patients.

  B Preanesthetic Evaluation and Preparation means that the responsible anesthesiologist:

    1 Reviews the chart.

    2 Interviews the patient to:

      a Discuss medical history including anesthetic experiences and drug therapy.

      b Perform any examinations that would provide information that might assist in decisions regarding risk and management.

    3 Orders necessary tests and medications essential to the conduct of anesthesia.

    4 Obtains consultations as necessary.

    5 Records impressions on the patient's chart.

  C Perianesthetic Care means:

    1 Re-evaluation of patient immediately prior to induction.

    2 Preparation and check of equipment, drugs, fluids, and gas supplies.

    3 Appropriate monitoring of the patient.

    4 Selection and administration of anesthetic agents to render the patient insensible to pain during the procedure.

    5 Support of life functions under the stress of anesthetic, surgical, and obstetrical manipulations.

    6 Recording the events of the procedure.

  D Postanesthetic Care means:

    1 The individual responsible for administering anesthesia remains with the patient as long as necessary.

    2 Availability of adequate nursing personnel and equipment necessary for safe postanesthetic care.

    3 Informing personnel caring for patients in the immediate postanesthetic period of any specific problems presented by each patient.

4 Assurance that the patient is discharged in accordance with policies established by the Department of Anesthesiology.

5 The period of postanesthetic surveillance is determined by the status of the patient and the judgement of the anesthesiologist. (Ordinarily, when a patient remains in the hospital postoperatively for 48 hours or longer, one or more notes should appear in addition to the discharge note from the postanesthesia care unit.)

IV Additional Areas of Expertise:

A Resuscitation Procedures.

B Pulmonary Care.

C Critical (Intensive) Care.

D Diagnosis and Management of Pain.

E Trauma and Emergency Care.

V Quality Assurance:

The anesthesiologist should participate in a planned program for evaluation of quality and appropriateness of patient care and resolving identified problems.

APPENDIX

4-2

AANA STANDARDS FOR NURSE ANESTHESIA PRACTICE*

A characteristic of any profession is its responsibility to the public for promulgating standards by which the quality of practice rendered by its members can be assessed. Standards, based upon sound philosophy, theory, science and principles, serve to upgrade clinical practice.

As the representative of the profession, the Board of Directors of the American Association of Nurse Anesthetists adopt and promulgate standards of practice with input from the members of the Association. The primary responsibility for implementing these standards rests with the practitioners, Certified Registered Nurse Anesthetists (CRNAs). As an organization composed of health care providers, the American Association of Nurse Anesthetists recognizes that the principles of anesthesia practice should be clearly described as professional standards which guide the practitioner in maintaining and improving the delivery of quality anesthesia care.

PURPOSE OF STANDARDS

These standards are intended to assist the CRNA practitioner in providing consistent, safe anesthesia care. The standards are descriptive, providing a basis for evaluation of the practice and reflecting the rights of those receiving anesthesia care. The AANA recognizes it may not be possible for the CRNA to comply with each of these standards in certain extraordinary or emergency situations. It is expected that the CRNA should assess each patient situation and utilize professional judgment in selecting a course of action, and that in each case, the CRNA can demonstrate that the decisions made were in the best interest of the patient. In addition, while the standards are intended to encourage high quality patient care, they cannot insure specific patient outcomes.

Their intent is to:

1 assist the profession in evaluating the quality of care provided by its practitioners.
2 provide a common base for practitioners to use to coordinate care and unify their efforts in the development of a quality practice.
3 assist the public in understanding what to expect from the practitioner.
4 support and preserve the basic rights of the patient.

STANDARD I

A thorough and complete preanesthetic assessment shall be performed.

Interpretation

The responsibility of a CRNA begins before the actual administration of the anesthesia. Except under unusual or emergency situations, the CRNA has an obligation to determine that relevant tests have been completed and thorough assessment of the patient has been made.

STANDARD II

Informed consent for the planned anesthetic intervention shall be obtained from the patient or legal guardian.

Interpretation

The CRNA shall obtain or verify that an informed consent has been obtained by another qualified provider. Anesthetic options and risks should be discussed with the patient and/or legal guardian in language the patient and/or legal guardian can understand. The patient's medical record should reflect that informed consent was obtained.

STANDARD III

A patient-specific plan for anesthesia care shall be formulated.

Interpretation

The plan of care is developed by the CRNA in coordination with appropriate health care providers in a systematic manner based upon assessment, analysis, anticipated procedure, patient preference and current anesthesia principles. It must be coordinated with appropriate health care providers.

STANDARD IV

The anesthesia care plan shall be skillfully implemented and the plan of care adjusted as needed to adapt to the patient's response to the anesthetic. Vigilance shall be maintained for untoward identifiable reactions and corrective actions initiated as required.

Interpretation

The CRNA shall induce and maintain anesthesia at required levels. The CRNA shall continuously assess the patient's response to the anesthetic and/or surgical intervention and intervene as required to maintain the patient in a homeostatic, physiologic condition.

STANDARD V

The patient's physiologic condition shall be monitored consistent with both the type of anesthesia care and specific patient needs.

Interpretation

Monitoring modalities shall be instituted in accordance with AANA Patient Monitoring Standards [See Appendix 12-2, Editor.]

STANDARD VI

There shall be prompt, complete and accurate documentation of pertinent information on the patient's record.

Interpretation

Documentation should be criteria-based, reflecting the standards of anesthesia practice. Documentation should include all anesthetic interventions and patient responses.

Accurate recording facilitates comprehensive patient care, provides information for retrospective review and research data and establishes a medical-legal record. The CRNA is responsible for assuring that the care provided by the CRNA is properly documented.

STANDARD VII

The responsibility for the care of the patient shall be transferred to other qualified providers in a manner which assures continuity of care and patient safety.

Interpretation

The CRNA shall assess the patient's status and determine when it is safe to transfer responsibility for care to other qualified personnel. The CRNA shall accurately report the patient's condition and all essential information to the personnel assuming responsibility for the care of the patient.

STANDARD VIII

Appropriate safety precautions shall be taken to minimize the risks of fire, explosion, electrical shock and equipment malfunction.

Interpretation

Safety precautions and controls, as established within the institution, shall be strictly adhered to, so as to minimize the hazards of electricity, fire and explosion in areas where anesthesia care is provided. The anesthetic machine shall be inspected by the CRNA according to guidelines before use. The CRNA shall check the readiness, availability, cleanliness and working condition of all equipment to be utilized in the administration of the anesthesia care. Documentation shall be made on the patient's medical record that the anesthesia machine and equipment were checked. Policies for routine safety and maintenance checks of anesthesia equipment and monitors shall be developed and adhered to by the appropriate individuals and departments within the institution.

STANDARD IX

Appropriate safety precautions shall be taken to minimize the risk of infection for the patient, CRNA and other staff.

Interpretation

Written policies on infection control shall be developed and followed in order to minimize the risks of infectious disease.

STANDARD X

Anesthesia care shall be assessed to assure its quality.

Interpretation

The CRNA shall participate in the ongoing review and evaluation of the quality and appropriateness of anesthesia care that he or she provides. Evaluation shall be performed based upon appropriate outcome criteria and reviewed on an ongoing basis.

STANDARD XI

The CRNA shall participate in a continual process of self-evaluation and strive for excellence in anesthesia practice.

Interpretation

Self-evaluation is accomplished in several ways, including quality assurance, peer review, annual performance appraisal, review of clinical privileges and ongoing assessment of clinical practice. The CRNA shall incorporate into practice new techniques and knowledge which have been acquired through formal, self-directed study.

STANDARD XII

The CRNA shall respect and maintain the basic rights of patients, demonstrating concern for personal dignity and human relationships.

Interpretation

The CRNA shall support and preserve the basic rights of patients to privacy, independence of expression, decision and action.

5

William H. L. Dornette, M.D., J.D.

Nonnegligent, Intentional Torts

TORTS IN THE HEALTH CARE INDUSTRY

As noted in Chapter 3, a tort is a civil wrong, other than a breach of contract, for which one party may be liable to another. Negligence is one type of tort. An act of negligence committed within the practice of a profession is called *malpractice*. Acts of negligence are considered *unintentional*. There are, however, a number of so-called *intentional* or nonnegligent torts that have evolved under the common law. Some, but not all, originated in English common law. These torts include abandonment, assault, battery, breach of confidence, defamation,

false imprisonment, fraud, intentional infliction of emotional harm, and invasion of privacy. Each of them has occurred or could occur in a health care setting. Anesthesia personnel could commit any one of these torts, except possibly false imprisonment. The common law also recognizes two additional intentional torts, namely abuse of process and malicious prosecution. These are mentioned at the end of this chapter in the discussion of actions in response to frivolous claims.

Although these torts are well-recognized common law causes of action, there are not many reported cases involving intentional torts committed during health care delivery. Why is this? Lawyers representing patients who might have such a cause of action generally prefer to allege breach of a duty of care, that is, professional negligence or malpractice, rather than an intentional tort. The reason is straightforward. As noted in Chapters 2 and 29, the large majority of U.S. physicians carry professional liability (malpractice) insurance, which covers only acts of negligence. If the defendant physician is found liable for professional negligence, the insurance carrier has a contractual duty to pay the judgment. These policies, however, customarily are not written to cover judgments for intentional torts. Nor do they cover breach of contract.[1] (In a similar vein, the Federal Tort Claims Act[2] covers acts of negligence by agents of the federal government but, with one possible exception, not intentional torts; this act is discussed in Chapter 20.) In the following paragraphs, these torts are considered in alphabetical order rather than in any order of significance.

Abandonment

The most clear-cut example of abandonment is the unilateral termination of the delivery of health care by the provider. This tort must be distinguished from the designation of a substitute who is just as qualified as the original provider, an act the courts have held not to be actionable in and of itself provided that the substitute is carefully selected.[3] In a case of agreeing to administer an anesthetic in advance of the date of the operation, it is obviously far better public relations to anticipate one's needs and inform the patient beforehand of the possibility of, say, being away at a meeting and not being able to provide the service. Actionable abandonment could occur if a practitioner, after inducing anesthesia, turns the care over to one less skilled, and a complication arises because of the inability of the substitute anesthesiologist or anesthetist to handle the problem. Delivering a patient to the recovery room who is still under the effects of the anesthetic agent or muscle relaxant and failing to ensure that recovery room personnel are available and capable of managing the patient's problems could constitute abandonment.

Another example is agreeing to administer anesthesia but, after the patient had been given preliminary medication and is in the operating room awaiting induction of anesthesia, failing to administer it. Courts have also interpreted abandonment as failing to give proper advice on follow-up care,[4] failing to instruct the patient to return for a follow-up visit,[5] and failing to advise the patient to have additional treatments when the physician had reason to believe that the patient was not cured.[6]

Battles v. Alderhold[7] involved an anesthesiologist who, while administering a transfusion to an 80-year-old patient undergoing an aortofemoral bypass graft, was requested to correct respiratory problems in a patient in the recovery room. The anesthesiologist remained with his first patient in the operating room and was later sued for his failure to assist in the recovery room.

The appellate court held that there was no breach of duty for failing to go to the recovery room. Had he done so to the detriment of care of the bypass patient, there probably would have been a viable action against him for abandonment.

While some courts have treated abandonment as an intentional tort, others have considered it to be negligent conduct, that is, a breach of the duty to offer continuing treatment. Lawyers who plan to file one of these actions may be placed on the horns of a dilemma. If they allege negligent conduct, the health care provider's liability insurance carrier would be expected to defend the case and pay any judgment. If the act of abandonment were particularly egregious, the lawyer might allege that an intentional tort had occurred, thereby opening the doors to the possibility of punitive damages, which can be quite large (see below). The insurance carrier in turn probably would defend "with reservation of rights" (see "Consequences of Intentional Torts," later in this chapter). Thus, although the lawyer might obtain a large judgment, the insurance carrier would be under no obligation to pay and the health care provider might be unable to satisfy the judgment from personal assets. The latter probably would be forced to declare bankruptcy, grossly limiting the amount of the recovery available to the lawyer's client.

Assault

Assault is defined as placing one in fear of a battery from someone having the capability of carrying out that act. As noted in the next paragraph, a battery is the intentional touching of the body of another without the other's consent. For example, assume that a patient refuses to have a spinal anesthetic. For valid medical reasons, the anesthesiologist may sincerely believe that a spinal anesthetic is the method of choice for that particular patient at that time. If the anesthesiologist proceeds to have the patient positioned and approaches the patient with the lumbar puncture needle ready to administer the spinal anesthetic, an assault will have occurred.

Battery

The right of persons in general to be free from any intentional touching of their bodies is a fundamental concept of the common law. Such touching, which can include even *medically indicated* health care, constitutes a battery. Consent is a defense to an action for battery. The need for consent is well articulated in an early New York decision by Benjamin Cardozo, a renowned jurist who was later appointed a justice of the Supreme Court of the United States:

> Every human being of adult years and sound mind has a right to determine what shall be done with his body; and a surgeon who performs an operation without his patient's consent commits ... [a battery] for which he is liable in damages.[8]

It is clear that treating without any consent at all constitutes a battery. A battery may also occur as a result of operating on the wrong part of the body; extending an operation beyond the scope set forth in the operative consent form, in prior discussions with the patient, or both; performing a procedure that is not medically indicated; and conducting the procedure under circumstances other than those under which the original consent was granted.

Battery is perhaps the intentional tort that is most commonly alleged in the course of the delivery of health care in this country. The primary reason relates to the undisputed fact that the average health care provider knows more about health care delivery than does the average patient. Additionally, especially in the not-too-distant past, many physicians adopted a paternalistic attitude toward their patients. These two factors fostered a widely prevalent "Doctor knows best" attitude, which resulted in physicians performing nonconsensual procedures on the assumption that they were acting in their patients' best interests. It has only been in recent years, most notably with the adoption of a *patients' bill of rights*, that the right of self-determination of each patient has been widely recognized. (Whether and under what circumstances a patient may voluntarily forego a lifesaving procedure is beyond the scope of this chapter; for a brief consideration of this fascinating topic, see Chapter 17.)

In the example of the spinal anesthetic noted above, if the anesthesiologist proceeded to administer that anesthetic without the patient's consent, he would have committed both assault and battery. On the other hand, assume that the anesthesiologist informed the patient that he would not give the spinal anesthetic but proceeded to administer intravenous anesthesia. After rendering the patient unconscious, he then administered the spinal anesthetic. This action would constitute a battery without an assault. The anesthesiologist, because of his assertions that he would not give the spinal anesthetic, would also have committed *fraud*, discussed below.

Breach of Confidence

One of the duties of health care providers, discussed in Chapter 2, is to protect confidences. It is well recognized that one of the patient's duties—to make full disclosure—is vital to the history-taking process, to ensure that an accurate diagnosis is made. Thus, health care providers must, of necessity, obtain a great deal of confidential information from each patient. If this information is disseminated outside the immediate health care circle (i.e., beyond those communications between health care providers required to ensure the delivery of careful and complete health care, to those with a "need to know"), a breach of confidence will have occurred. The unnecessary dissemination of information about a patient's human immunodeficiency virus antibody (HIV-ab) seroreactivity (see Chapter 18) is an example of a clear-cut breach of confidence.

Anesthesia personnel obtain much confidential information from their patients during the preanesthesia interview. This author was unable to locate any common law decisions relating to breach of confidence in the anesthesia setting. A 1985 Oregon case[9] involving an obstetrician, however, is worthy of discussion, as it is illustrative of how the courts handle cases involving this tort.

On reaching the age of 21, an adopted child was able to learn the name of the obstetrician who delivered her. She requested the aid of the obstetrician in locating the name of her natural mother. Using as his excuse the daughter's faked concern that the mother had ingested diethylstilbestrol during the pregnancy, the obstetrician obtained the mother's name from hospital records and so informed the adopted child. The latter confronted her natural mother, who became quite upset and subsequently sued the obstetrician. The Supreme Court of Oregon found the obstetrician liable for breach of confidence.

Defamation

Defamation is the dissemination of false information about an individual. If this dissemination is in writing, it is called *libel*; if verbal, *slander*. Truth of the statement is an absolute defense to the action for defamation. As noted in Chapter 18, spreading news that an HIV-infected, HIV-ab–positive person has full-blown AIDS could constitute defamation.

False Imprisonment

False imprisonment is the unlawful detention or other restriction of the free movement of an individual against his or her will. It is unlikely that an allegation of false imprisonment could stem from the delivery of anesthesia care. Emergency

room personnel or psychiatrists who admit patients against their will could be accused of false imprisonment. In one actual case, a hospital administrator ordered nursing personnel not to release a patient's clothing until she paid her bill. The patient successfully sued the hospital and the administrator for false imprisonment.

Fraud

Fraud involves the intentional concealing of information, or knowingly giving false information, with the intent to deceive another person to the latter's detriment. One court defined fraud as

A false representation of a matter of fact, whether by words or by conduct, by false or misleading allegations, or by concealment of that which should have been disclosed, which deceives or is intended to deceive another so that he shall act upon it to his legal injury.[10]

So-called ghost surgery of days gone by constituted a classic example of fraud. A surgeon agreed to operate upon a patient. General anesthesia was administered. The surgeon did not operate, however, but substituted the services of a colleague, all without the patient's knowledge and consent. Such an act constitutes fraud on the part of the original surgeon. It is also a battery as far as the operating surgeon is concerned, inasmuch as the patient did not give his or her consent for the procedure. In anesthesia practice, the anesthesiologist who agrees to administer anesthesia to a patient but who then turns the anesthesia care over to someone less skilled, without the knowledge and consent of the patient, would be committing a fraudulent act.

Intentional Infliction of Emotional Harm

It is difficult to envision an intentional tort of this type resulting from the delivery of anesthesia care. An example in modern-day medicine could arise from a terminally ill patient who requests that cardiopulmonary resuscitation (CPR) not be administered. If a health care provider proceeded to perform CPR over the patient's express desires not to be coded, the patient, and possibly the next of kin, in all likelihood would have a valid cause of action for intentional infliction of emotional harm.

Invasion of Privacy

This tort is similar to breach of confidence except that the information divulged is of a private, but not necessarily confidential, nature. Courts in some but not all jurisdictions have recognized this tort as part of their common law, although it was not part of the common law at the time the latter was imported from England during the 17th and 18th centuries. Invasion of privacy is dissemination of personal information about a patient without the patient's consent. The best example of this tort is the nonconsensual publication of photographs of the patient.[11-14] Among these cases are a number involving biological photography. They point up the absolute necessity of obtaining patients' permission, preferably in writing, before photographs are taken.

CONSEQUENCES OF INTENTIONAL TORTS

The courts have always treated intentional torts differently from the tort of negligence. The courts consider these torts to be avoidable, and as such there is an inference that the actor *intended* that the act occur, hence the name "intentional tort." Expert testimony is not required as it is in an action for professional negligence. Damages can be quite large (seven-figure awards are not uncommon) because punitive damages (see Chapter 3) customarily are demanded, and awarded. What should be of special concern to health care providers is that a professional liability insurance policy does not indemnify a health care provider found liable for one of these torts. It is not likely that the carrier would even offer to supply legal counsel for the defense of the case, unless the complaint (see Chapter 23) was couched in terms of malpractice as well as the intentional tort. In that event, the carrier probably would "defend with reservation of rights," as discussed above.

ALLEGING A MALPRACTICE LAWSUIT WAS FRIVOLOUS

Before considering this subject, it is important to define certain terms. Health care providers often learn about cases in which physicians, against whom seemingly groundless medical malpractice actions have been filed, have in turn filed what they call "counterclaims" against the plaintiff and his or her legal counsel. Used in this context, the term *counterclaim* is a misnomer. Counterclaims are not uncommon in certain types of litigation, notably those involving contracts. The defendant in a breach of contract action might, for example, allege that the plaintiff breached one of the duties under the contract and for that reason owes the defendant money. In the case of a seemingly frivolous malpractice lawsuit, the response would not be a counterclaim (which, incidentally, must be filed before the original lawsuit is tried) but an action for one or several negligent or intentional torts, described below.

The judicial system has always been troubled by the concept of such counteractions, for a number of reasons. First, the fundamental premise of U.S. jurisprudence is that every plaintiff should be able to have his or her "day in court." Second, there is always the possibility that frivolous counteractions will be filed to attempt to detract from the main issue, namely the liability of the original defendant. Finally, there has not been any clear-cut common law cause of action that could be used to retaliate for the frivolous lawsuit. Even though the allegations of the plaintiff about the health care rendered by the defendant are untrue, if they are limited to the complaint, pleadings (formal papers that initiate and document the progress of the case; see Chapter 23), and testimony, they become "privileged" communications, and there would be no cause of action for defamation.

Lawyers for aggrieved physicians have filed lawsuits alleging abuse of process, negligence on the part of the original plaintiff's lawyer for failing to investigate the facts, malicious prosecution, and even intentional infliction of emotional harm.[15] Such suits cannot be filed unless and until the original action is finally resolved, and in favor of the defendant *with prejudice* (the original plaintiff is forever barred from any further action on the original lawsuit). To my knowledge, only one such suit has been successful when pursued through the appellate process.

The Supreme Court of Kentucky affirmed a trial court verdict for an orthopedic surgeon and his partner.[16] The patient had fallen from an examining table in a hospital. The patient's lawyer sued not only the hospital but also the two orthopedic surgeons who examined and treated the patient after the fall. The lawyer finally did drop his case against the orthopedic surgeons literally "on the steps of the courthouse" just before the trial was to commence.

Although the amount of the damages awarded was not large, the decision did have a very salutary effect on members of the plaintiff's bar in the immediate area (northern Kentucky, southwestern Ohio), at least. These lawyers began making very serious efforts to investigate allegations, and obtain opinions from medical experts, before filing medical malpractice actions. Help may be on the way, at least in the federal district courts, and in those jurisdictions[17] that have adopted versions of the Federal Rules of Civil Procedure containing the current text of rule 11 for governing the trial of civil cases in the respective state courts. Federal rule number 11 now provides that if the losing party promotes a cause of action, or a defense, that has no merit, that party shall pay the court costs and fees of the opposing counsel. Implementation of this new rule should reduce significantly the furtherance in these courts of malpractice (and other) cases (or defenses in those cases) that have no merit.

CONCLUSION

The courts consider intentional torts not only *avoidable* but also sufficiently egregious to allow recovery of large amounts of punitive damages. Therefore, it is apparent that health care providers must prevent their occurrence. To this end, the following admonitions should be helpful:

1 Once you have undertaken, or agreed to undertake, the care of a patient, be certain to fulfill that obligation or obtain a mutually satisfactory substitute.
2 Be certain that the recovery room is adequately staffed and able to manage the postanesthesia recovery of your patient (Chapter 13); if not, you may have to sit with that patient until all protective reflexes have returned.
3 Obtain each patient's consent, as appropriate, for the care you are about to render (consent is also covered in Chapter 9; see also Chapter 17 for managing situations in which consent is refused).
4 Never give even an impression of initiating any care against a patient's express refusal.
5 Maintain confidences; if there is no "need to know," then do not divulge personal information about any of your patients.
6 Select and use words carefully, both verbally and when charting; be certain that what you say or write about a patient is the literal truth.
7 Be forthright and completely honest when dealing with all of your patients. Avoid evasion; do not conceal the role that substitutes or trainees (see Chapter 19) will play in any patient's care, especially if the patient inquires.
8 When assigned to the CPR team, maintain awareness of the possibility of "No Code" or "DNR" orders being in effect; abide by any such orders.
9 Respect each patient's right of privacy; if you need to take biological photographs for any reason, obtain the patient's written consent beforehand if there is any possibility of the patient's being identified from the photographs.

Intentional torts are creatures of the common law. They are considered by the courts to be *serious offenses against persons*, as well as acts that are *totally avoidable*—hence the willingness of these courts to award large amounts of punitive damages. Furthermore, the conventional professional liability insurance policy does not provide indemnification for liability stemming from the commission of any intentional tort. It should be apparent to the reader that every effort must be made to avoid acting in any way that might lead to allegations of an intentional tort. Understanding the contents of this chapter, and implementing the admonitions set forth, should contribute significantly toward the accomplishment of that end.

REFERENCES

1. Safian v. Aetna Life Ins. Co., 260 A.D. 765 (1st. Dept. N.Y. 1940).
2. 28 U.S.C. §§ 1346(b), 2671 *et seq.* (1948).
3. *See,* e.g., Jacknwicz v. Knobloch, 265 N.W. 799 (Sup. Ct. Mich. 1936); Stohlman v. Davis, 220 N.W. 247 (Sup. Ct. Neb. 1928); Young v. Jordaan, 145 S.E. 41 (Sup. Ct. W.Va. 1928).
4. Orendino v. Clark, 402 P.2d 527 (Ore. 1965).
5. Doan v. Griffith, 402 S.W.2d 855 (Ky. 1966).
6. McGulpin v. Bessmer, 43 N.W.2d 121 (Sup. Ct. Iowa 1950).
7. Battles v. Alderhold, 430 So.2d 307 (La. App. 3 1983).
8. Schoendorff v. Soc. of N.Y. Hosp., 105 N.E. 92 (N.Y. 1914); as a "classic" example of battery, see Pizalotto v. Wilson, 437 So.2d 859 (Sup. Ct. La. 1983) in which the court specifically delineated the difference between battery and malpractice.
9. Hamphers v. 1st Interstate Bank of Oregon, 298 Ore. 706, 696 P.2d 527 (1985).
10. Brainerd Dispatch Newspaper Co. v. Crow Wing Co., 196 Minn. 194, 264 N.W. 779, 780 (Sup. Ct. 1936) (in its opinion, the high Oregon court specified that liability was not predicated on invasion of privacy).
11. Feeney v. Young, 191 A.D. 501, 181 N.Y.S. 481 (1st Dept. 1920).
12. Griffin v. Med. Soc. State of N.Y., 11 N.Y.S. 109 (Spec. Term N.Y. Co. 1939).
13. Clayman v. Bernstein, 38 D&C 534 (Phila. Co. Pa. 1940).
14. Estate of Barthiaume v. Pratt, 365 A.2d 792 (Sup. Ct. Me. 1976).
15. *See, generally,* Witlin, LT: Countersuits by medical malpractice defendants against attorneys. J Leg Med 9:421, 1988.
16. Raine v. Drasin, 621 S.W.2d 895 (Sup. Ct. Ky. 1981).
17. As of 1986 (the last year a survey was made), legislative bodies or supreme courts in Alabama, Alaska, Arizona, Colorado, the District of Columbia, Hawaii, Indiana, Kentucky, Maine, Massachusetts, Minnesota, Montana, New Mexico, North Dakota, Ohio, Rhode Island, South Dakota, Tennessee, Utah, Vermont, Washington, West Virginia, and Wyoming had adopted what the authors of this survey termed "replicas" of the Federal Rules of Civil Procedure (FRCP) to govern civil cases in their respective state courts; additionally, legislators in Arkansas, Delaware, Idaho, Mississippi, Nevada, and South Carolina adopted versions of the FRCP that contained rule 11; legislators in the 21 other jurisdictions had adopted other variations of the FRCP that might or might not contain a version of rule 11; see Oakley, JB and Coon, AF: The federal rules in state courts: A survey of state court systems or civil procedure. Wash L Rev 61:1367, 1986.

6

William H. L. Dornette, M.D., J.D.

Vicarious Liability

There are numerous situations in just about every activity—daily living, business, commerce, industry, and especially the delivery of services, notably health care—wherein one person may be liable to a third party for the acts of another person. This type of liability is termed *vicarious liability*; it is based upon the business relationship between employers and those who consume or for whose benefit the employer's goods or services are delivered. It is an accepted economic concept that employees work for the economic gain of their employer. The courts have reasoned that any economic losses occasioned by the negligent act of an employee therefore should be imputed to the employer.[1]

AGENCY LAW AND ASSOCIATED RELATIONSHIPS

The rules governing vicarious liability are bound up in the *law of agency*. The word *agency* is derived from the Latin *agentia*; it denotes the person or actor who accomplishes something. A large body of case law has developed from disputes arising from agency relationships. A party who was injured by the act of another sues not only the prime tortfeasor (the person who committed the negligent act) but also his or her employer. Agency law recognizes several distinct relationships between the actor and the person or persons for whose benefit the act is performed. In each of these relationships, liability for the negligence of the actor to a third party (in medical practice cases, the patient) differs somewhat. There are three basic relationships in agency: *master-servant*, *principal-agent*, and *independent contractor*. Each of these relationships may be encountered in the practice of anesthesia.

Master-Servant

The relationship between an employer and employee is a typical master-servant relationship. Under it, the master has the power to direct the acts of the employee or servant. Whether the master actually exercises that power is immaterial; as long as he or she possesses the power, he or she is considered the master. All activities of the servant that are carried out within the scope of the servant's employment may be imputed to the master, including any acts that are negligent (with one exception, discussed below). Thus, the anesthesiologist who hires a nurse anesthetist is creating an employer-employee or master-servant relationship. If the nurse anesthetist commits a negligent act and a patient is injured thereby, the anesthesiologist as the employer could be held liable under the doctrine of *respondeat superior*. This doctrine literally means "let the master respond." The surgeon who employs a nurse anesthetist has the same master-servant relationship with the anesthetist. An institution employing house staff would be liable for the negligent acts of such individuals (see Chapter 19), as well as those of nurses and other employees.

The employer is not without remedy, however. He or she can (and should!) be careful in selecting and training employees and assigning responsibilities to them. Liability insurance can be purchased to cover the acts of those employees. If a hospital is contemplating becoming self-insured, liability for acts of all employees, including members of the house staff, must be taken into consideration. Finally, if an employer is held liable for an employee's negligence, he or she can sue the negligent employee to attempt to recover the loss. On at least two occasions, such an action has been taken by hospitals against professional members of the staff whose alleged negligence injured a patient.[2,3] Of course, the injured person may still sue the prime tortfeasor (i.e., the one who committed the act causing the injury).[4]

The Borrowed-Servant Doctrine

As with most legal principles, there are exceptions to the *respondeat superior* rule. One exception is embodied in what is known as the borrowed-servant doctrine. At times, an employee may have to work under the immediate supervision of someone other than his or her own employer. A classic medical example is that of the surgeon who "borrows" certain hospital employees, for example, the circulating nurse, scrub nurse, nurse anesthetist, and possibly a member of the house staff, to assist during an operation. Under ordinary circumstances, as their employer the hospital would be responsible for their acts. During the course of an operation, however, the rules change, since the courts have recognized the impracticality of having more than one individual in charge. These employees are considered temporary servants of the surgeon, borrowed from the hospital. In general, any negligence of such employees during the course of the operation is imputed to the surgeon.[5] The nurse anesthetist is usually, although not always, included under the borrowed-servant rule; the anesthesiologist, however, customarily is not included (see discussion of independent contractors below).

Although courts generally hold that an individual can serve only one master at a time, it is possible under certain circumstances (as, for example, joint treatment efforts, discussed below) that a court might hold both the true master and the borrower jointly liable. In reviewing the facts in a given case, the court would instruct the jurors to consider whether the borrowed servant was still performing acts for his or her employer, whether the employer or the borrower had the power to control the acts of the servant, and for whose benefit the acts were being carried out.

Principal-Agent

An agent is one who works on behalf of the principal but is not under the direct control of the latter. The agent has the power to change a legal relationship of the principal and bind him or her to a course of action.[6] For example, a professional liability insurance agent executes a contract on behalf of a carrier. The carrier is then bound to the terms of the policy. Physicians frequently enter into either partnerships or corporations. The partnership or corporation is considered to be a principal in one of these principal-agent relationships. Each individual partner or incorporator has the power to act as an agent for the principal, namely the partnership or corporation. In any of these relationships, the principal will be liable for any acts of negligence of the agent acting within the scope of his or her authority.

Independent Contractor

Independent contractors are in business for themselves. Even though they may work for someone, they do not do so as a servant or an employee: "He acts not as a servant because he is not under the control of the employer, and because he is engaged not in the employer's enterprise but one of his own."[7] The anesthesiologist generally is considered to be an independent contractor in reference to the surgeon. The anesthesiologist, like the surgeon, makes his or her own contract with the patient. Each of these independent contractors owes the patient the duty of care according to the standards of that individual's own specialty. This duty is parallel to and separate from the duty owed by each other independent contractor. As a general rule, independent contractors are liable for their own torts, but not for the torts of another independent contractor. In fact, in health care delivery, liability is not imputed to another independent contractor except under certain, rather limited circumstances:

1 One independent contractor observes the negligent act of another independent contractor but fails to call it to the latter's attention.
2 Two or more independent contractors are working closely together, in what the courts call a joint treatment effort (discussed below).
3 Or one independent contractor is

negligent in selecting a second independent contractor; as an example, a surgeon requests the professional services of an anesthesiologist whom he or she knows to be incompetent, but does so because the anesthesiologist is available at the time the surgeon wants to operate; if it can be shown that the anesthesiologist was known to be incompetent, the surgeon, too, could be found liable if the patient was injured by a negligent act of the anesthesiologist.

A burning issue in anesthesia care today (discussed at greater length in Chapter 25) is whether nurse anesthetists are, or should be considered, independent contractors. In those jurisdictions in which nurse anesthetists are allowed to function independently, invoice patients separately, make their own preoperative and postoperative visits, and write their own orders, it would seem that such individuals would be considered independent contractors and thus have the same legal status as the anesthesiologist. This concept, however, flies in the face of the traditional relationship between the nurse anesthetist and the surgeon as relating to medical practice regulations. It is generally accepted that the administration of anesthetic agents involves diagnosis and therapy. As such, it constitutes the practice of medicine.* Because only a physician is licensed to practice medicine, the "medical" practice of the anesthetist would be imputed to the surgeon. The latter then would be considered to be engaged in the practice of medicine insofar as the administration of anesthetics by the nurse anesthetist was concerned. This concept, plus the captain-of-the-ship and borrowed-servant doctrines, has traditionally made the surgeon liable for the negligence of the nurse anesthetist.[8]

Some recent case law, however, has imputed the negligence of the nurse anesthetist to the hospital (under the master-servant doctrine) on the grounds that certain of the acts were committed at a

*A number of jurisdictions have resolved this potential dilemma by administrative regulation or statute.

time in which the surgeon had no control over the anesthetist.[9] It would be interesting to see whether courts recognize the independent contractual status of the nurse anesthetist in those states in which he or she has been granted practice (i.e., for writing orders, billing, and the like) autonomy. It is obvious, under those circumstances at least, that independently functioning nurse anesthetists must purchase ample professional liability insurance to cover their own acts.

Exceptions

As with all principles derived from the common law, there may be exceptions. This is especially true in agency law, wherein all questions of vicarious liability must be decided on the facts in each individual case. Sometimes these facts differ significantly from those that form the basis of a previous, precedent-setting decision. One of the advantages of the common law approach to resolving disputes is that each dispute is decided on its own merits—based upon the specific factual situation from which it developed. For example, in at least one case a surgeon was held liable for the acts of an anesthesiologist.[10] In a case involving partial loss of a patient's hand following the accidental intra-arterial injection of thiopental, the surgeon testified that he had the power to control the selection and administration of the anesthetic, even when it was being administered by an anesthesiologist. Although he had not exercised that power in the case in question, he was held jointly liable with the anesthesiologist for the negligence of the latter. This holding, however, is contrary to usual common law decisions in this area.[11]

Joint Treatment Efforts

Considering the complexities of modern health care, especially that rendered on an inpatient basis, it should be apparent that few health care providers act alone. The concept of the team approach to the delivery of health care is probably best epitomized by activities in the operating room.[12] Anesthesia, surgical, and operating room nursing personnel have a joint responsibility (and potential exposure to joint liabili-

ty) for properly (or improperly) identifying the patient, moving the patient to the operating table, and positioning the patient for the proposed operative procedure (see also Chapter 11). Mistakes and consequent injuries that occur during these procedures *could result** in joint liability among members of these three groups of individuals, even though the anesthesiologist and surgeon were independent contractors and not employees of the hospital.

Agency by Estoppel

One possible exception to the independent contractor concept is embodied in an application of the *agency-by-estoppel* doctrine. Under certain circumstances, a court might rule that because the relationship between the employer and independent contractor *overtly appeared* to be one of master-servant or principal-agent, the employer can be estopped (prevented) from denying both an agency relationship and the associated vicarious liability. This doctrine is applied not infrequently to hospital-physician contracts, notably in the furnishing of emergency room services by independently practicing physicians under contract with the institution.[13]

In *Seneris v. Haas*,[14] a group of anesthesiologists had an exclusive contract to cover all anesthesia services in the hospital. Under the terms of that contract, members of the group were designated as independent contractors. One member of that group subsequently was found liable for professional negligence. The plaintiff had also named the hospital as a party defendant, a position that the hospital challenged based upon the terms of the contract. The contract called for the anesthesia group to offer its anesthesia services solely to patients hospitalized at that institution. The hospital, in turn, agreed not to utilize the services of other anesthesiologists for this purpose.

The court held that the mutual exclusivity of the terms of the contract created an agency-by-estoppel relationship. That is, the

---

*Again, it is important to stress that there are no hard rules defining joint liability; in such cases, the court (presiding judge) will examine the facts closely, apply the laws of agency, and instruct the jury to determine which party or parties are liable, based upon those facts and laws.

hospital was estopped from denying that an agency relationship existed and therefore was compelled to participate in the payment of the damages.

OTHER EXAMPLES OF AGENCY LAW IN ANESTHESIA PRACTICE

Anesthesia Assistants

Using an anesthesia assistant poses two potential areas of concern—the legality of the practice under the healing arts licensing statutes of the particular jurisdiction[15] and the potential exposure to vicarious liability. It should be obvious that one's practice must not be inconsonant with admonitions set forth in the licensing statute. Failure to abide by such a statute or administrative regulation very likely would subject the employer of the anesthesia assistant to sanctions for the violation. Additionally, in a subsequent malpractice action the court might hold the defendant-employer liable as a matter of law.[16] Or, as happened in a case involving a patient injured by an injection given by a licensed practical nurse (LPN) in a physician's office,[17] such an action might raise an inference of negligence. The statute in that particular jurisdiction forbade LPNs from giving hypodermic injections, because such a practice required skills possessed only by registered nurses. Inasmuch as LPNs did not possess that knowledge, a jury could infer that the injection was performed negligently.

Quite apart from the legality of utilizing an anesthesia assistant for direct patient care are issues of vicarious liability. Inasmuch as the anesthesiologist–anesthesia assistant relationship would most likely be akin to a master-servant one, the rules applicable to any employee would govern potential liability.

House Staff

Generally, interns and residents are employed by the hospital, and their liability is imputed to their employer (see Chapter 19). On the other hand, what if a patient were injured while a privately practicing anesthesiologist was directly supervising a member of the house staff? A court would probably hold the anesthesiologist vicariously liable under the borrowed-servant rule.[17] Alternatively, that same court might find direct liability of the supervisor, either because of negligence for inadequate supervision or because the anesthesiologist was a party to a joint treatment effort. It is, of course, possible that a plaintiff's lawyer will allege all three as viable causes of action.

Staff Privileges

In general, privately practicing physicians who hold staff privileges are considered independent contractors, and the hospital would not be held liable for their negligence.[18] Certain factual situations may create agency relationships, however.[19,20]

The General Partnership

A partnership creates a principal-agent relationship between the entity and each individual partner. Utilizing a partnership for the delivery of anesthesia care is both advantageous and disadvantageous. The advantages—relative simplicity in creation and sharing the caseload, preoperative and postoperative rounds, call, vacation and meeting times, and the like—may be obvious. Such a close practice relationship may, however, set the stage for serious personality conflicts. As one author succinctly states:

> The success of a partnership will depend upon the professional and personal compatibility of its members. . . . Prospective members should know each other and be exposed to each other's idiosyncrasies for a long time before considering partnership.[21]

One distinct disadvantage is the *unlimited personal liability* of each partner. Thus, if a judgment rendered against an individual partner exceeds that partner's share of the partnership and the personal assets of that partner, the available assets of the entire partnership, and then the personal assets of each of the other partners, would be used to satisfy it. Wording of agreements becomes very important, and each party should be represented by *competent* legal counsel (see, especially, Chapter 26). For example, an incompetently drafted employment contract could result in one physician employee being forced to furnish indemnification for the negligence of another employee.[22]

Limited Partnership

This type of partnership consists of at least one general partner and a number of limited partners. The liability of the limited partners covers only their share in the assets of the partnership. The agency relationship—one of principal-agent—is the same as in the general partnership, however. The general partner would have *unlimited personal liability*.

The Professional Corporation

Under a conventional principal-agent relationship, each incorporator acts as an agent of the corporation.

Although a successful plaintiff in a malpractice action could reach the assets of the corporation, the personal assets of the individual incorporators (with the exception of the one who committed the negligent act) would be protected. One of the principal advantages of the corporation is the limited (to their share in the assets of the corporation) liability of the incorporators. On the other hand, if such a corporation had insufficient assets to even begin to satisfy a judgment, a court might hold that the corporation was a sham, and allow a successful plaintiff to "pierce the corporate veil," so to speak, and reach the personal assets of the incorporators. (Given the availability of professional liability insurance to protect assets, however, the real advantage of a professional corporation would seem to lie in the ability of the incorporators to fund attractive retirement plans. There are other advantages in establishing a professional corporation, all of which are beyond the scope of this book.) Consultation with competent legal counsel (Chapter 26) before entering into any type of partnership or corporation is an obvious necessity.

CONCLUSION

In the final analysis, it is important for each health care professional to recognize his or her own individual responsibility to each patient, the responsibility owed to other members of the health care team, and the responsibility for the acts of employees, both actual and borrowed. When one is engaged in joint treatment efforts, joint exposure to liability is always a real possibility. Thus, while identifying mistakes and calling them to the attention of others might not be popular, it will not only promote patient safety but also minimize one's own possible exposure to liability. Joint treatment efforts by anesthesiologists and surgeons often bring up the time-honored question "Who is the most important person in the operating room?" The answer clearly is neither the anesthesiologist nor the surgeon; it is the *patient*. Personnel who are able to put aside petty differences and, working together as a team, place the welfare of the patient ahead of other factors, will be practicing their profession as an art as well as a science. Maintaining such an attitude can only promote the delivery of patient care of the highest quality. It will also constitute an important risk management step toward reducing the exposure of all members of the operating room team to litigation and possible liability.

REFERENCES

1. Mecham, FR: Outlines of the Law of Agency, ed 4. Callaghan, Chicago, 1952, pp 237 *et seq.*
2. Hall, GD: Professional liability insurance for intern and resident (citing Emanuel Lutheran Hosp. v. Bockhaven). JAMA 193:55, 1965.
3. McFadden v. Turner, 195 N.J.Super. 360, 388 A.2d 244 (1976).
4. 12 ALR 3d 1017.
5. *Ibid.*
6. Mecham, *supra* ref. 1 at 8.
7. *Id.* at 288.
8. *See, e.g.,* McConnell v. Williams, 361 Pa. 355, 65 A.2d 243 (Sup. Ct. 1949).
9. Cavero v. Franklin Gen. Benevolent Soc., 36 Cal.2d 301, 223 P.2d 471 (1950); Kemalyan v. Henderson, 45 Wash.2d 963, 277 P.2d 372 (1954).

10. Rockwell v. Kaplan, 404 Pa. 572, 178 A.2d 54 (Sup. Ct. 1961).
11. Andrepont v. Ochsner, 84 So.2d 63 (La. 1955) (explosion of cyclopropane); Crits v. Sylvester, 3 D.L.R. 181 (High Ct. Ont. 1955); 3 D.L.R.2d 502 (Ct. App. Ont. 1956); 5 D.L.R.2d 601 (Sup. Ct. Canada 1956) (explosion of ether-oxygen mixture); Dohr v. Smith, 104 So.2d 29 (Fla. 1958) (fracture and aspiration of tooth); Huber v. Protestant Deaconess Hosp. Ass'n, 127 Ind. App. 565, 133 N.E.2d 864 (App. Ct. 1856) (paralysis following spinal anesthesia); Paton v. Parker, 15 Australian L. J. 285 (1942) (patient burned when spilled ether ignited); Thompson v. Lillehei, 164 F.Supp. 716 (D.C. Minn. 1958) (air embolism during open heart operation); Wiley v. Wharton, 41 N.E.2d 255 (Ohio 1941) (broken spinal needle); Woodson v. Huey, 261 P.2d 199 (Okla. 1953) (injury following spinal anesthetic that patient had refused).
12. Wasmuth, CE and Wasmuth, CE, Jr: Law and the Surgical Team, Chapter 1. Williams & Wilkins, Baltimore 1969, pp 1–44.
13. Griffin v. Matthews, 522 N.E.2d 1100 (Ohio App. 1987); Pamperin v. Trinity Memorial Hosp., 423 N.W.2d 848 (Wis. 1988).
14. Seneris v. Haas, 291 P.2d 915 (Sup. Ct. Calif. 1955).
15. Central Anesthesia Associates v. Worthy, 254 Ga. 728, 333 S.E.2d 829 (Sup. Ct. 1985).
16. Id. at 833.
17. Barber v. Reinking, 68 Wash.2d 139, 411 P.2d 861 (Sup. Ct. 1966).
18. For cases holding instructors or members of the house staff liable under the borrowed-servant rule, see Graddy v. New York Medical College, 243 N.Y.S.2d 940 (1963); Rockwell v. Stone, 404 Pa. 561, 173 A.2d 48 (Sup. Ct. 1961); Frazier v. Hurd, 149 N.W.2d 226 (Mich. 1967); McConnell v. Williams, 361 Pa. 355, 56 A.2d 243 (1949); Terhune v. Hague Maternity Hosp., 164 A.2d 75 (N.J. 1960).
19. Byrd v. Marion Gen. Hosp., 162 S.E. 738 (N.C. 1932); Fiorentino v. Wegner, 227 N.E.2d 296 (N.Y. 1967); Lundahl v. Rockford Memorial Hosp., 235 N.E.2d 671 (Ill. 1968); Moon V. Mercy Hosp., 373 P.2d 884 (Colo. 1961).
20. Brown v. Moore, 247 F.2d 711 (C.A. 3d 1957); Carrol v. Richardson, 100 S.E.2d 193 (Va. 1959).
21. Hirsh, BD: Business Management of Medical Practice. CV Mosby, St. Louis, 1964.
22. McGray v. Cobb, 152 N.W. 262 (Sup. Ct. Minn. 1915).

Minimizing
Exposure to Liability

EDITOR'S NOTE

There are certain activities or procedures that have become a part of the delivery of health care in this country. Some of these are related to all health care, including obtaining the patient's consent and informed consent, keeping good medical records, and developing and implementing a risk management program for injury prevention and liability control. Other steps lie mainly within the province of anesthesia care, for example, preanesthesia evaluation, moving and positioning, monitoring, and postanesthesia follow-up. Implementation of some of these steps (i.e., obtaining informed consent) is mandated by common law, others by the standard of care (preanesthesia evaluation, postanesthesia follow-up), still others (e.g., record keeping, monitoring) by voluntary standards promulgated by such associations as the American Society of Anesthesiologists or the Joint Commission on Accreditation of Health Care Organizations. Whatever their origin, these activities are intended to facilitate the delivery of health care, and anesthesia services, of a high quality. In maintaining care at such a level, these steps will also help ameliorate the exposure to liability of health care providers in general and anesthesia personnel in particular.

H. Thomas Foley, a board-certified internist with a law degree, is currently a civilian member of the staff of the U.S. Army Claims Service, Fort Meade, Maryland. His special interests include consent and informed consent, the right to refuse treatment, the right to die with dignity, and terminating life support. As an oncologist, he has utilized numerous chemotherapeutic agents that may produce serious side effects. Dr. Foley addresses the issues of battery, consent, informed consent, and informed refusal from the standpoint of an internist who has had many years of experience with diagnostic and therapeutic procedures that pose a definite risk to the patient.

Clement J. Markarian is a certified registered nurse anesthetist who currently is developing a new graduate program in nurse anesthesiology for Carraway Methodist Medical Center, Birmingham, Alabama, and will be director of the proposed program. While his several contributions to this book were being prepared, he was Director of the Anesthesiology Program for ANC Officers at Walter Reed Army Medical Center, in Washington, D.C., and Anesthesia Nursing Consultant to the Department of Legal Medicine at the Armed Forces Institute of Pathology. He has contributed chapters on record keeping, risk management, and, in Part 4, training programs.

Bence A. Sell obtained his medical degree from Emory University College of Medicine and currently is a staff anesthesiologist at Tallahassee Regional Medical Center in Tallahassee, Florida. At the time he co-authored Chapter 13, Dr. Sell was serving on active duty in the Army Medical Department and was Medical Director of the Post Anesthesia Recovery Service, Walter Reed Army Medical Center.

W. H. L. D.

7

William H. L. Dornette, M.D., J.D.
Clement J. Markarian, C.R.N.A., M.A.

Risk Management

Although risk management (RM) is a relatively new concept to the health care field, it has been used extensively in the past in business, industry, and the construction trades. For years, casualty insurance companies have developed various approaches to RM for use by those insured by them in an effort to reduce accidents, injuries, and other losses. By taking these steps, the carriers are able to minimize claims, stabilize premium rates, remain competitive, and earn a profit. Formal RM programs did not enter the health care field until the medical malpractice crisis of the 1970s. Among the state legislatures, Florida's was the first to mandate RM in hospital health care delivery. This provision was incorporated in an omnibus medical malpractice statute that was adopted to attempt to resolve the difficulty in, or high cost of, obtaining professional liability insurance during that era. Since then, numerous hospitals, recognizing the value of becoming self-insured (and thus not having to pay premiums based on the loss experiences of other institutions), have adopted various forms of RM programs. Each of the uniformed services has a formal RM program embodied in its respective regulations pertaining to health care delivery.[1] Personnel who have become involved in health care delivery–related RM activities report the experience to be interesting, challenging, and rewarding.

Early evidence of the forthcoming liability insurance crisis started to surface in the late 1960s, as insurance premiums began a slow and, as it turned out, progressive rise that has continued almost unabated to the present time. In 1970 one of us published an article[2] giving the reasons then believed to be the cause of this increase. They included a number of interacting factors (Fig. 7-1), which produced an almost synergistic increase in the number of lawsuits, dollar amount of losses, and cost of liability insurance. By the following year, the stage was set for the next series of events: the rapidly escalating cost of this insurance and its unavailability at any cost for some specialists in some parts of this country. (Chapter 29, which covers professional liability insurance, updates the issues of losses and coverage.)

In order to underwrite insurance in any jurisdiction, the prospective carrier must demonstrate to the insurance commissioner financial stability in the form of sufficient reserves. Sufficiency constitutes an ample ratio of dollar value of reserves to dollar value of total coverage in effect. If the reserves fall, the amount of insurance in effect must be reduced. These reserves are

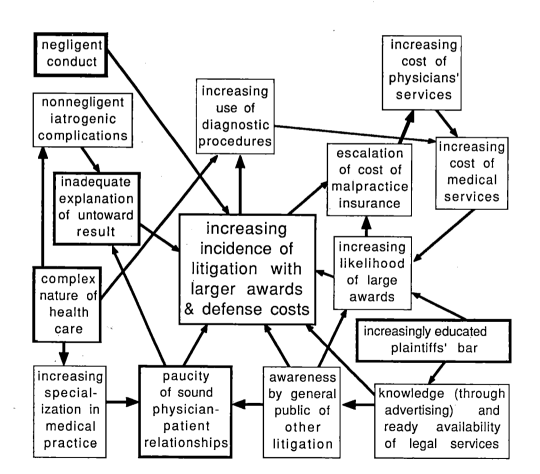

Figure 7–1 Diagram of the genesis of the ongoing medical professional liability problem. Interrelated etiologic factors act synergistically to fan the flames of litigation and larger awards. The most significant factors are highlighted in boldface.

initially obtained from premiums paid by insured entities, such as hospitals and health care providers. By investment of these reserves, the carrier is able to increase their value, thus providing a cushion for any catastrophic losses. The cost of premiums is carefully calculated from past loss experience (hence the high premiums of anesthesia personnel—see Preface). Traditionally, these methods have proved adequate for the casualty insurance industry.

But what will happen if losses suddenly escalate because of costs of defending and paying out a much larger number of more costly judgments or settlements? What happens if a major investment turns sour? Or if the stock market, in which the carrier has invested heavily, takes a sudden and dramatic plunge? All three of these events took place in the early 1970s in an industry already beset with rising costs from increasing claims and payouts at the end of the 1960s. Reserves fell, causing some of the larger carriers to subsidize professional liability reserves with those from other lines. Some carriers stopped underwriting in areas of excessive losses (notably California) or for high-risk specialists. Others discontinued underwriting medical malpractice insurance altogether. The net result—excessive premiums or no coverage at all—has been addressed, and for the most part resolved, by physicians' associations, state legislators, and insurance commissions.

The details of many of the methods used by those entities are beyond the scope of this book (Chapter 29 does cover some of these approaches). One of them, however—reducing losses by developing and implementing RM plans—is the subject of this chapter. After reviewing the mechanics of RM and its application in anesthesia practice, we will attempt to cover those lessons that may be drawn for the 1990s and beyond.

HANDLING RISKS

Risks are inherent to everyday living. Purchasing insurance, sending one's children to driving school, keeping sidewalks free of ice in winter—all consist of one or more methods of handling risks. In fact, there are five methods: assumption, trans-ferral, sharing, avoidance, and attenuation (Fig. 7-2).

Methodology

Assumption

Risk assumption means just that. The individual, institution, or other entity assumes all of the risks of the endeavor. The totally self-insured hospital does just that. So does the United States government in the operation of those Army, Navy, Air Force, Public Health Service, and Veterans Administration facilities that make up the federal health care delivery system.

Transferral

Risk transferral means shifting the entire risk onto another entity, for example, purchasing a zero-deductible insurance policy for one's automobile or home. The insurance carrier agrees to indemnify (pay for damages) the insured for all losses sustained during the term of the policy. This is total indemnification, and because the carrier is required to pay all losses, the premiums can be very expensive.

Sharing

Risk sharing is best epitomized by the insurance policy with a deductible clause. The insured assumes the responsibility for the first $100 to $200 of the loss. The carrier then pays the balance. In reality, risk sharing is a combination of assumption and transferral. The premiums of insurance policies with a deductible clause are much lower than those of policies with no deductible clause.

Avoidance

Risk avoidance simply means avoiding the risk by not carrying out the activity. The automobile driver who allows his or her insurance to lapse may elect to avoid the risks of a catastrophic loss by storing the automobile and using a bicycle or public transportation. A hospital with a little-used but potentially high-risk service (e.g., obstetrics, emergency service) located in proximity to another hospital with a similar, very active service, may elect to close the high-risk, little-used service and send all patients requiring that particular type of care to the other hospital. That is risk avoidance.

Attenuation

Risk attenuation involves taking those steps that will reduce the risk while still engaging in the activity. *Risk attenuation is what risk management is all about.*

INSTITUTIONAL RISK MANAGEMENT

There are two parts to risk management —injury prevention and liability control (see Fig. 7-2). Injury prevention primarily involves looking ahead, identifying sources of losses, determining how those losses may be prevented, and taking the necessary steps to prevent them from occurring. Liability control, on the other hand, looks back and endeavors to manage, in one way or another, problems generated by accidents and injuries that have already occurred and to minimize any liability stemming from those incidents. An RM program must *aggressively* pursue both aspects on a continuing basis.

Injury Prevention

Injury prevention commences before the incident, accident, or injury has occurred. It involves four steps.

1 A *data base* is created. It is com-

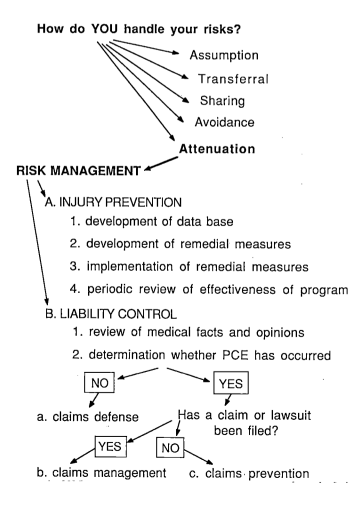

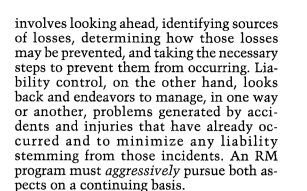

Figure 7–2 Of the five methods for handling risks, attenuation is the most important—from a standpoint of efficiency, economy, practicality, and plain common sense. Risk attenuation is commonly referred to as "risk management" and comprises injury prevention and liability control. Each of these procedures involves several steps.

posed of information derived from a variety of sources (Fig. 7-3). To be effective, this data base must identify all pertinent causes of incidents, accidents, and injuries.

2 Once the data base is established, *remedial measures are developed.* These are directed to the specific risks identified as the data base is constructed.

3 *The remedial measures that have been developed are implemented.* Implementation obviously may take a variety of forms because of the varied nature of the risks that have been identified. It may range from simple changes in procedures to major structural alterations in the building.

4 Finally, *periodic reviews of the effectiveness* of the program are performed. This step is crucial and cannot be overemphasized. Some of the remedial measures recommended may not be acted upon by the administration of the institution. Others that have been implemented may prove ineffective in eliminating or controlling the risk. Hence, it is absolutely essential that this fourth step be carried out through regular meetings of the RM committee (see below). These meetings serve not only to update the data base and further the development of remedial measures, but also to assess the effectiveness of past recommendations.

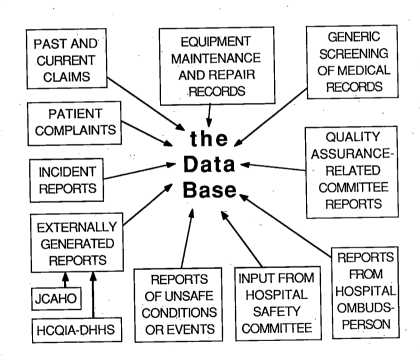

Figure 7–3 Development of a data base, the first step in injury prevention, involves identifying all risk-associated activities within the institution or department. Shown here are the sources of such information in private-sector institutions. A departmental data base for an anesthesia department would also receive reports from recovery room personnel and would include data pertaining only to anesthesia equipment and anesthesia records. Information sources in federal institutions are similar, the principal differences being in nomenclature ("patient representative" rather than "ombudsperson," "reports of unusual occurrence" rather than "incident reports"). Uniformed-services hospitals may receive investigative reports from the Inspector General as well as reports from the JCAHO and DHHS. (JCAHO = Joint Commission on Accreditation of Healthcare Organizations; HCQIA = Health Care Quality Improvement Act; DHHS = Department of Health and Human Services.)

The Risk Management Committee

Each hospital should have an RM committee, the suggested composition of which is depicted in Figure 7-4. The committee should be chaired by a senior physician to help promote ready communication with, and compliance of its recommendations by, the other members of the medical staff. The risk manager, a member of the committee, reports *directly* to the chief executive officer of the institution. Many risk managers are lawyers. Knowledge by one committee member of pertinent substantive (informed consent doctrine, what constitutes negligence, and the like) and procedural (e.g., how to protect sensitive documents) laws is imperative if RM committee meetings and other activities are to be conducted intelligently and in an unfettered manner. If the risk manager is not a lawyer, the house counsel for the institution, or a member of the firm representing the institution, should be a member of the RM committee, and *attend all of its meetings*. The presence of a member of the bar helps ensure that the minutes of the meetings will be protected and not be subject to discovery (discussed later). Additionally, those committee members who are non-lawyers will be able to acquire some knowledge of pertinent substantive and procedural law.

The Role of Incident Reports

As noted in Figure 7-3, incident reports are one source of information for the data base, and thus may contribute significantly to injury prevention. They are important documents:

> Hospital incident or accident reports play a significant role in the facility's risk management program. These reports memorialize important factual data and enable isolation of potential areas of recurring liability. It also facilitates accident investigation necessary to structure an adequate defense of the hospital should litigation later arise.[3]

In their latter role, these reports furnish valuable information to those involved in identifying accidents that could lead to successful litigation against the institution (called potentially compensable events or PCEs, discussed later) and carrying out claims management or defense functions, as covered in the following paragraph. To be effective, these reports should be accurate, objective, frank, and complete. Properly drafted in this manner, such a report on its face might well constitute an admission of liability. Thus, it should be prepared carefully and have limited distribution to protect it from disclosure by opposing counsel in any adversary proceeding (see later discussion).

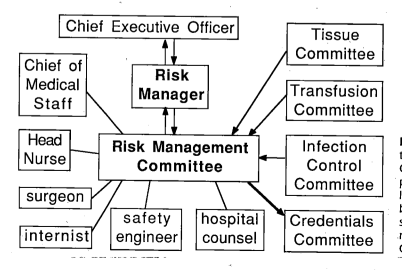

Figure 7–4 Typical composition of a Risk Management Committee and sources of input to it. In cases of gross negligence or egregious conduct by a member of the medical staff, information may be transmitted to the Credentials Committee.

Liability Control

Liability control involves those steps that are taken after an accident, incident, or injury has occurred. Depending upon the status of the incident, and whether a claim or lawsuit already has been filed, one approaches liability control from one of three perspectives: claims management, claims defense, or claims prevention.

Claims Management

Claims management is put into motion after a claim or lawsuit has already been filed. The risk manager or legal counsel for the institution obtains the medical records, any radiographs, and all other related materials pertaining to the care of the claimant. It is important that this data-gathering process be complete. Next, the personnel who cared for the patient are interviewed. Having completely assembled the medical record and procured statements from treating personnel, the risk manager then obtains an objective assessment of the case from an independent medical expert. The purpose of this step is to determine whether there was a departure from the standard of care and, if so, whether that departure caused the problem about which the patient is complaining. That is, was there any negligence? If, after such independent, objective review, it is determined that a departure from the duty of care owed the patient did occur, and that the departure caused the patient's injury, efforts are made to manage the claim by compromise or settlement.

Carriers underwriting professional liability insurance in the United States today will rarely endeavor to defend in court a case involving an injury proximately caused by a health care provider's departure from the duty of care, a situation in which there was obvious negligence. Uniformly, these cases are settled, unless the claimant is demanding damages far in excess of what the case is worth.

Claims Defense

Defense of claims starts out in a manner similar to the procedure involved in claims management. The medical record is assembled, together with any radiographs or other materials, and statements are taken from treating personnel as appropriate. The file is then sent to an independent expert for review. If the expert determines that there was no departure from the duty of care, that there was no injury (i.e., the "injury" complained of was an extension of the disease process), or that there was no relationship between a possible departure from the duty of care and the untoward result, a decision is made to deny the claim and, if litigation ensues, offer a strong defense.

When discussing claims denial versus claims defense, it is important to stress the difference between medical malpractice and *iatrogenic complications*. Any sequel of health care is an iatrogenic complication (derived from the Greek *iatros*, meaning "medical," and *genesis*, "caused by"). All complications of medical malpractice are iatrogenic in nature, but *the reverse is not true. Good medical records*, substantiating the reason for the less-then-perfect result, *generally form a very sound defense* in such a situation. Thus, the importance of records that are legible, complete, generously informative, and medically logical (see Chapter 10) cannot be overemphasized.

Claims Prevention

Through a variety of methods (some of which are described below), RM committees and others in the health care setting frequently become aware of a PCE long before the patient even thinks about obtaining legal counsel or filing a claim or lawsuit. As noted above, a PCE is an adverse outcome that might have been caused by a departure from the duty of care. One key to a successful RM program is the ability to identify these PCEs early during the patient's care (in the case of the hospitalized patient, before discharge). Armed with the information that the untoward result may have been compensable, the risk manager and other health care delivery personnel are in an ideal position to take steps toward reducing the likelihood of a claim or lawsuit being filed. Steps involving identification of PCEs (Fig. 7-5) include occurrence screening of medical records, review of incident reports and patient complaints, establishment and promotion of the posi-

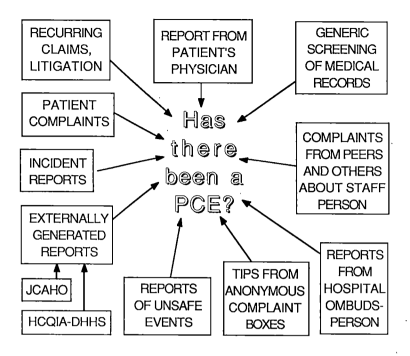

Figure 7–5 Members of the Credentials Committee must remain forever alert to the occurrence of potentially compensable events (PCEs) to be able to fully implement the claims prevention aspect of liability control. This figure illustrates some of the sources of information needed to further this end.

tion of hospital ombudsperson, and review of complaints of one health care provider about another.

Inasmuch as the last area may be an important source of information about potentially serious problems (e.g., the impaired health care provider), some hospitals have found it extremely helpful to establish an anonymous-complaint system. Boxes are placed at strategic locations throughout the institution; personnel are encouraged to submit anonymous complaints, comments, and other data in reference to conditions or situations that might result in injuries to patients or personnel. The risk manager or a member of the RM committee then reviews these comments and complaints, evaluates them, and considers making recommendations to the entire committee about possible remedial measures.

Thus, a review of the information obtained from anonymous complaints serves not only for liability control but also for injury prevention. Institutions that have utilized this system feel that it works admirably and promotes a much freer flow of information than if the individual has to identify himself or herself at the time the complaint is made. Quite obviously, at least some of the data gathered thereby (notably complaints lodged against individuals) is of a confidential nature, and must remain so, at least until acted upon by the appropriate authority (e.g., personnel director, credentials committee).

Handling a Potentially Compensable Event

Is the Event Truly a PCE?

In all cases, especially those involving an injury of considerable magnitude, it is desirable to verify that the event in truth is a compensable one, as compared to one that is only questionably so. Review of the facts by an independent, out-of-house expert, and procurement of an objective opinion, would seem to be an ideal (and perhaps the only) solution. Members of the institution's staff should not be placed in the position of having to criticize a colleague's work, even before a closed session of the RM committee, when the damages are large. An obvious exception would be when the care was so egregious that a decredentialing process is in the offing.

It must also be remembered that not all

care resulting in adverse outcomes can be neatly categorized as being negligent or not negligent. Nor is it possible to precisely state in every instance that proximate causation exists. In the 7 years' experience of one of us (W.H.L.D.) reviewing cases of alleged malpractice emanating from federal health care facilities, there were quite a few claims and potential claims that did not present clear-cut evidence of departures from the duty of care, the existence of proximate causation, or either. It is situations such as these that make case review both challenging and rewarding.

Informing the Patient or Next of Kin

That an adverse outcome has occurred does not necessarily mean that the event is potentially compensable. Considering the complex nature of therapy and the equally complex makeup of the human being, some adverse outcomes will occur that, though unfortunate, are not related to a departure from the duty of care. Hence, before any adverse outcome is discussed with a patient in terms of its being a PCE, every effort must be made, as noted above, to objectively ascertain that there was a departure from the duty of care and that the departure did, in fact, cause the adverse outcome.

Once it is determined that a PCE has occurred, the patient, next of kin, or both should be apprised. How this step is accomplished will influence whether the patient will subsequently file a claim or lawsuit. Comments such as "We really messed up things here, didn't we?" or "This is the worst case of malpractice I have ever seen!" have no place in a health care provider's contacts with any patient. The health care provider obviously must express genuine concern. The statement "There is nothing either one of us could have done to prevent this complication" is inappropriate when the event has been identified as being potentially compensable. It is our opinion that when a PCE is identified, the best statement to make is, "We are sorry. What happened *probably* should not have happened. We will do our best to correct the problem," or words to that effect. The patient or next of kin then

should be given an explanation in lay terminology of the situation in reference to how the adverse outcome occurred. Following this interview, it is desirable to refer the patient to the risk manager of the institution. The risk manager should be apprised before the patient's visit of the nature of the problem and the reasons why the event is considered potentially or actually compensable. Whether the legal counsel for the institution should become involved at this point, or at some later time, is a decision that should be made jointly by the risk manager and legal counsel.

Correction of the Medical Problem Created by the PCE

Appropriate medical-surgical care to correct the complication caused by the PCE should be undertaken in a timely fashion, an admonition that emphasizes the importance of early identification of PCEs. It is disconcerting to note the number of PCEs that have not had timely detection by the health care team.

Achieving at Least Partial Compensation

Once a PCE has occurred, concerted efforts should be made to attempt to make the patient "whole." These might include forgiving some portion or all of the patient's hospital bill. This is one of the reasons why it is essential that the risk manager report directly to the executive staff or chief executive officer of the institution (see Fig. 7-4).

Maintaining an Open Line of Communication

If the liability control program is to succeed, it is imperative that open communication be maintained with the patient and next of kin. Every effort must be made to continue, or to rebuild and restore, rapport. Openness and honesty lead to trust. If total trust can be maintained, the likelihood of a patient filing a claim or lawsuit will be minimized. If health care providers adopt a stonewall approach, litigation is inevitable.

When the Event Is <u>Not</u> Potentially Compensable

As noted above, it is absolutely vital that each untoward outcome be evaluated objectively to determine whether a PCE has occurred. If one has not occurred, it is important to so apprise the patient (or next of kin, or both, as appropriate) at the earliest possible opportunity. This meeting should be conducted in an unhurried and relaxing atmosphere. The patient, and next of kin as appropriate, should be given a thorough explanation in lay terminology of the disease entity, treatment administered, and reason(s) for the untoward outcome. This discussion should allay all fears, remove doubts, and dispel any guilt feelings that anyone may have. As following a PCE, all questions by the patient and next of kin should be answered in a straightforward manner. It is also essential that trust, rapport, and open communication be maintained, as detailed earlier, before and subsequent to the patient's discharge from the institution. Careful, complete, and thorough documentation obviously is essential in support of the determination that an untoward outcome is noncompensable.

The Role of Personnel in an Institution's RM Program

Personnel who are not formally involved in the institution's program (e.g., as members of the RM committee) still play an important role in it. They should report unsafe conditions, unsafe practices, and the "near miss." Personnel should also serve willingly on quality assurance and RM-related committees (see, e.g., Fig. 7-4). Following the occurrence of a PCE, personnel should cooperate fully in the investigation. Finally, personnel should *never* discuss such events or outcomes with anyone other than their immediate supervisor, the hospital risk manager, the executive officer of the hospital, or the lawyer representing the hospital.

The Relationship Between RM and Quality Assurance

Some are of the opinion that quality assurance and RM mean the same thing. In actuality, each involves a slightly different form of activity, although there is some overlap between the two. This relationship is shown in Figure 7-6. RM and quality assurance each encompass separate spheres of activity, part of each of which is common to the other. Quality assurance involves optimal utilization of resources; optimal utilization includes injury prevention. RM also involves injury prevention and, additionally, liability control.

A DEPARTMENTAL RM PROGRAM

The RM program of the anesthesia department is much like the one of the institution itself (see Figs. 7-2 and 7-3). It involves both injury prevention and liability control. Occurrence screening of anesthesia records forms one vital source of information for this data base. Table 7-1 gives examples of events that might trigger an anesthesia case review, as well as fur-

QUALITY ASSURANCE   RISK MANAGEMENT

optimal utilization of resources   injury prevention   liability control

Figure 7–6 One may consider quality assurance and risk management as two overlapping circles, with injury prevention being common to both activities.

nish information for the data base.

Once the data base is developed and remedial measures determined, efforts obviously must be made to implement those measures in a timely manner. Obviously, these measures will vary widely, and if they are costly, it may be necessary to assign priorities to them. Whatever the recommendations, one cannot stress strongly enough the importance of periodically determining whether these measures are being implemented and, just as important, whether the implementation appears to be effective in mitigating the associated hazard(s). All of these responsibilities fall on the shoulders of the risk manager or the entire RM committee.

Liability control at the departmental level involves four steps:

1 There must be timely identification of PCEs.
2 Data from these events must be fed into the departmental data base (and possibly that of the institution as well).
3 The institutional risk manager must be made aware of any serious problem so that those relationships with the patient, next of kin, or both that are recommended above may be established and implemented, or maintained, as appropriate.
4 Those individual practitioners directly (or indirectly, as witnesses) involved in the adverse outcome must cooperate in the investigation and adhere to those admonitions covered above.

AN INDIVIDUAL RM PROGRAM

Each trainee should develop his or her own individual RM program early during the training period. This program would be directed principally toward injury prevention, since liability control (once a PCE has occurred) involves more than just the individual resident or student nurse anesthetist. The first step is obviously to

TABLE 7-1. Events That Might Trigger an Audit of the Anesthesia Record

Absence of notation of preoperative laboratory data (except in *true* emergencies).
Absence of preanesthesia counseling note (except in emergencies).
Anesthesia machine or monitoring systems malfunction, misuse, or failure resulting in patient injury.
Aspiration from emesis or "silent regurgitation."
Blood product replacement.
Circulatory or cardiac arrest.
Critical incidents resulting in patient injury.
Emesis during induction, maintenance, or recovery from anesthesia.
Episode of malignant hyperthermia.
Failed regional anesthesia (unplanned supplementation with general anesthesia).
Failure of anesthesia personnel to brief postanesthesia care unit (PACU) personnel on condition of patient at time of admission.
Failure to regain consciousness in the PACU.
Greater than 5-minute interval between recorded blood pressure determinations.
Hoarseness or other difficulty in speaking longer than 24 hours postoperatively.
Hypoxic insult.
Inability to perform endotracheal intubation.
Incidence of air embolism.
Injury to teeth or gums.
Intermittent or continued motor and/or sensory loss following regional anesthetic techniques.
Intraoperative patient memory recall.*†
Myocardial dysfunctions.
Neurological insult of any dimension.
Occurrence of life-threatening arrhythmia.
PAR score of 5 or less 60 minutes after admission to the PACU.
Pharmacological interactions or reactions causing physiological problems.
Prolonged induction of anesthesia, unexplained.
Prolonged (greater than 5 minutes) hypertension or hypotension.
Pulse rate greater than 110 beats per minute or less than 60 beats per minute.
Recurarization or renarcotization in PACU.
SaO_2 desaturation below 90%.
Stay in PACU longer than norm, unplanned.
Unstable patient condition upon admission to the PACU.
Unusual narcotic expenditure.*
Use of vasopressors or inotropic drugs.
Ventilatory inadequacy or unplanned respiratory support postoperatively.

---

*Areas of concern that might indicate addictive or abusive drug behavior among anesthesia care providers.
†This complication could occur if the anesthesia provider had substituted a less effective agent, using the charted anesthetic for himself or herself.

develop a data base. The sources for this data base are depicted in Figure 7-7. As the data are assembled, they may be stored in a loose-leaf notebook or similar instrument. As the data base increases in size, it may be desirable to develop a system of file folders.* From these data, the individual trainee will be able to determine remedial measures. These may take the form of a safety manual that encompasses procedures for performing various techniques, drug interactions, special problems created by disease entities, and the like.

As noted above, the third step in injury prevention is implementation. The individual practitioner incorporates within his or her practice the information developed by the first two steps. Finally, there should be periodic reassessment of this implementation. In the case of the trainee, the assistance of a senior fellow trainee or junior member of the staff might be elicited. Trainees should also remember the admo-

---

*Personnel with access to a personal computer may want to build a computerized data base. One excellent way for doing so is embodied in HyperCard running on an Apple Macintosh computer with ample memory. Data base management software obviously is also available in the MS/DOS environment.

nition attributed to Michael DeBakey: "No matter how well you do today, you can do better tomorrow!" What follows should be the delivery of anesthesia care at increasingly higher levels of quality.

LEGAL RISKS

Are there any legal risks associated with RM? Interestingly, there are several. One area that does not create a risk is the adoption of remedial measures to prevent a similar accident in the future. Such an activity might appear to constitute an admission that a hazardous situation previously existed. Fortunately, the courts have long held that evidence of any such remedial measures may not be introduced to prove the negligence of the defendant.[4] This common law doctrine is now codified in the Federal Rules of Evidence.[5]

Minutes of RM Committee Meetings

Lawyers who frequently represent injured patients in medical malpractice actions commonly endeavor to obtain copies of the

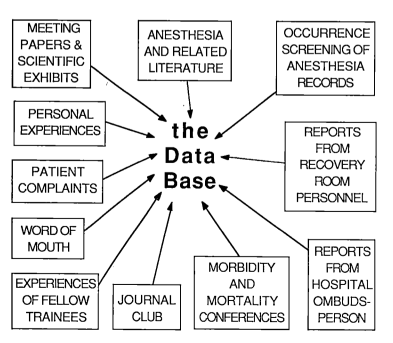

Figure 7-7 Sources of information for an individual practitioner's data base.

minutes of the RM committee meeting at which the client's case was discussed. The modern tendency in both state and federal courts is to forestall the element of surprise by promoting rather free access to pertinent documents in possession of the opposing party via appropriate motions for discovery (the process of obtaining copies of documents pertinent to the litigation in the possession of one's opponent in the litigation— see Chapter 23). The general rule, however, is that these minutes are not subject to discovery,[6] for a very valid reason. In order for RM deliberations to be successful, they must be open and frank, and anything that would impede the free flow of information (notably threat of discovery of the minutes) would be counterproductive. Congress has enacted legislation affording statutory protection for RM minutes and related documents generated in uniformed-services health care facilities.[6] To prevent discovery, the lawyer representing the institution might invoke the attorney-client privilege*[7] or the argument raised in Bredice.[8] Documents prepared for, and statements made to, one's lawyer or insurance carrier *solely* in preparation for litigation are not subject to discovery.

Legal Status of Incident Reports

As discussed above under injury prevention, incident reports become important sources of information for the injury prevention data base. They also contribute to the data that become useful in building a defense. One authority on health law[9] suggests that each institution should:

1 Treat incident reports as confidential documents, clearly marked as such.
2 Strictly limit the number of copies made and the distribution of the reports in the institution.
3 Not place a copy of the report in the patient's medical record or in the

inner file.
4 Limit the content of the report to the facts, not conclusions or assignment of blame.
5 Address the report to the hospital's attorney or claims manager by name.
6 Train hospital personnel to complete incident reports with the same care used in completing a medical record.

Taking these steps will help ensure accuracy and objectivity in each report's preparation. It will also limit exposure of the institution, and individual professionals mentioned in it, should the report somehow fall into the hands of opposing counsel.

The Risks of Not Having a Program

There is no question but that an effectively managed RM program will accomplish its objectives in terms of enhanced quality of care, a reduction in exposure to liability, and a lowering of professional liability insurance premiums. There are, however, a number of other, not so obvious advantages.

A favorite question asked of a defendant by the patient-plaintiff's lawyer in a medical malpractice action is: "*Doctor, how much sleep did you get the night before my client's injury?*" Members of the plaintiffs' bar have a whole series of such potentially embarrassing queries, directed to creating at least an inference of the defendant's incompetence.

Another series relates to RM. The following could be directed to a defendant anesthesiologist: "*Doctor, you do recognize the importance of risk management in your practice, don't you?*" (There can be only one answer; if the witness professes ignorance about the subject, the lawyer conducting the cross-examination is certain to subsequently introduce evidence about the importance of RM in injury prevention, and that RM is an essential component of health care delivery today, thereby inferentially discrediting the defendant's care of the plaintiff.)

The next question might be: "*Doctor, you do* (or *your department does*) *have an active risk management program, isn't*

---

*Communications between lawyer and client are considered to be "privileged"; the client holds the privilege that the lawyer will not disclose them to others without the client's permission. The physician-patient privilege is discussed in Chapter 2.

that so? Just answer 'yes' or 'no'!" (A "no" answer places the witness in the same position as does a "no" answer to the previous question; a "yes" might lead to a request for details about that program.) Asking the anesthesiologist to "*... describe your program*" would be a dangerous question for a cross-examiner to ask, however. If there were a good RM program in effect, and the anesthesiologist were deeply involved in it, he or she would be able to describe the program clearly and concisely, thereby making valuable points for the defense *while still on cross-examination*! By the careful use of leading questions (questions that suggest the answer—see Chapter 23), on the other hand, the cross-examiner could determine if there was no really strong program, or that the witness is only vaguely familiar with it. In that event, the witness's answers

will reflect ignorance, casting doubt on his or her previous "yes" answer, and thereby bring discredit on the entire testimony.

The moral to this not-so-hypothetical colloquy is straightforward. It should serve to give emphasis to the one real legal risk of a RM program—not having one! Every anesthesia service should have some type of formal program, and all members of that service should be active participants in it.

CONCLUSION

RM has become a permanent fixture in the health care field. Some form of RM and quality assurance is required of accredited institutions by the Joint Commission on Accreditation of Healthcare Organizations.[10] Every health care provider, in anes-

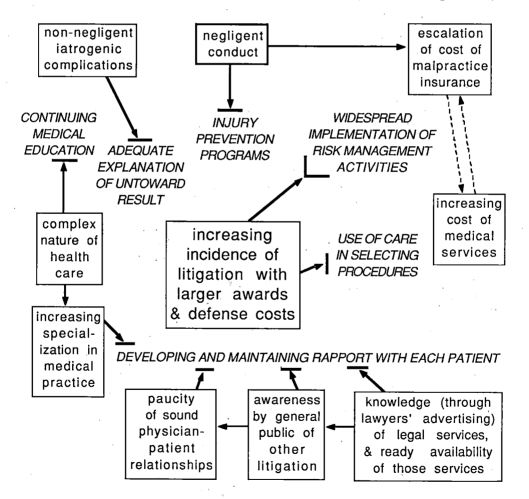

Figure 7–8 Risk management activities (italicized) can block the factors shown in Figure 7-1 from causing increasing litigation and larger awards and can mitigate the effects of litigation on the costs of insurance and medical services, promoting fiscal soundness in the health care delivery process.

thesia and in other specialties, should recognize the importance of RM. It is incumbent upon every departmental director to ensure that some type of RM activity is embodied within the operation of his or her department. These programs should be fully implemented on an ongoing basis. All personnel working in the department must be made aware of these programs and of their individual roles in them. Further, one cannot stress strongly enough the desirability for each individual anesthetist and anesthesiologist, both at the training level and in posttraining practice, of maintaining one's own personal RM program. These activities do pay off in terms of decreased risks to patients, reduction in morbidity and mortality, and the personal satisfaction that accrues from the delivery of anesthesia care of high quality.

This book has been in preparation for 4 years. During that interval, professional liability insurance premiums once again have been on the rise, at least for some specialists in some segments of this country (Chapter 29). Does this mean that RM as a concept has failed? That it has not enjoyed widespread adoption? Or, that where adopted, it has not been implemented as it should have been? There are no ready answers to these questions. Suggestions that some morbidity and mortality may be inevitable in the practice of medicine, and therefore all patients should be insured with what one of us (W.H.L.D.) calls *medical injury insurance*,[11] may deserve further study. Still, it does appear that there can be further reductions in anesthesia-related morbidity and mortality. Perhaps anesthesia personnel should look even more carefully at those facets of care that are productive of incidents, complications, and adverse outcomes.[12] In many instances those outcomes turn out to be not only potentially compensable but also preventable.[13] A review of the facts in other such cases—ones that have gone on to claims and litigation—leads us to believe that substandard care does occur, and that this care often is responsible for the sometimes large awards or settlements, as well as major defense costs. Figure 7-8, modified from Figure 7-1, both sets forth the problem and proffers a solution.

Simply stated, the root cause of all malpractice actions is the complication associated with health care delivery. Quite a few such complications, however, can occur in the absence of professional negligence, that is, fault on the part of a health care provider. Additionally, some untoward results represent an inevitable progression of an already existing disease process. It is important that health care professionals make absolutely certain that patients and next of kin fully understand these differences. Such understanding, it is to be hoped, will reduce the likelihood of the filing of unfounded claims. Beyond that, the basis for comprehending, and resolving, the malpractice problem is identifying fault and endeavoring to correct those practices that lead to fault during health care delivery. Fault identification and elimination are what injury prevention—a key element of risk management—is all about.

REFERENCES

1. AR 40-47 (1987); NAVMEDCOMINST 6320.24 (1987); AFR 168-13 (1987, 1990).
2. Dornette, WHL: Professional liability insurance. Anesthesiology 33:535, 1970.
3. Smith, JW: Hospital Liability. Law Journal Seminars Press, New York, 1988, § 14.07 [1].
4. Chadbourn, JH: Wigmore on Evidence, Vol 2. Little, Brown & Co, Boston, 1979, § 283.
5. Federal Rules of Evidence, Rule 407.
6. Bredice v. Doctor's Hosp., 50 F.R.D. 249; adhered to 51 F.R.D. 187; *aff'd*. 479 F.2d 920 (C.A.D.C., 1973).
7. 10 U.S.C. § 1102 (1987).
8. Smith, *supra* note 4, §§ 14.07 [2], [3].
9. Lasky, PC (ed): Hospital Law Manual. Aspen Systems, Rockville, MD, 1983, p. 76.
10. *See, e.g.*, Standard on Quality Assurance. Accreditation Manual for Hospitals, 1991. The Joint Commission on Accreditation of Healthcare Organizations, Chicago, 1990, p. 219.
11. Dornette, WHL: Medical injury insurance. J Leg Med 1:28, 1973; Dornette, WHL: Medical injury insurance: Proposed model legislation. J Leg Med 3: 24, 1975.
12. Caplan, RA, et al: Unexpected cardiac arrest during spinal anesthesia: A closed claims analysis of predisposing factors. Anesthesiology 68:5, 1988; Cohen, MM and Duncan, PR: Canadian four-center study targets patient outcomes. Anesthesia Patient Safety Foundation News Letter 3:36, 1988.
13. See Eichhorn, JH, et al: Standards for patient monitoring during anesthesia at Harvard Medical School. JAMA 256:1017, 1986. "Of the cases involving major morbidity or death, *most were believed to be preventable*" [emphasis supplied].

8

Clement J. Markarian, C.R.N.A., M.A.

Preanesthesia Evaluation

This chapter is designed to highlight key factors in the preanesthesia evaluation. The implementation of these factors will enhance patient care by minimizing the possibility of missing essential information without which the correct anesthetic might not be selected and administered. This chapter also reviews pertinent common law generated by cases involving failure to properly evaluate patients preoperatively. This chapter does not offer a detailed explanation of how to evaluate a patient preoperatively, conduct a physical examination, or determine which tests are necessary, nor does it discuss the manner in which "preoping" is most efficiently achieved and documented, as these topics are thoroughly covered in other publications.

RATIONALE AND GOALS

Preoperative and preanesthetic evaluation and preparation are one and the same process. This evaluation-preparation process in reality initiates anesthetic management. Each patient's preoperative evaluation-preparation preferably is accomplished by the individual who is scheduled to administer the anesthetic. Early participation by the anesthesia provider is of utmost importance to that person's integral involvement in the patient's care. Ideally, the assessment process is initiated far enough in advance of the operative procedure so that the evaluation may be conducted in a leisurely fashion and free from anxiety. This initial meeting with the patient allows the provider to accomplish several goals:

1 Secure pertinent information about the patient's medical and social history.
2 Conduct a physical examination.
3 Allow the development of rapport with the patient.
4 Provide an opportunity for the patient to express any concerns about the forthcoming procedures, learn something about pertinent aspects of anesthesia, and have any questions answered (steps that are essential if one is to reduce to the extent possible any anxiety that may be present).
5 Allow a direct interaction to formalize what in reality becomes a contractual agreement between both parties—anesthesia provider and patient.
6 Afford the opportunity for obtaining informed consent.

The successful management of all candidates for anesthesia, with or without disease, is based on a thorough preoperative evaluation that covers the past and present history, relevant laboratory data, and physical condition of the patient. Depending upon institutional routines, it may not always be possible to accomplish these three steps in the sequence mentioned. Generally, a battery of predetermined laboratory tests will have been performed prior to the preoperative visit. One can usually find in the chart a report of the admitting physician's history and physical examination (H & P) as well as the laboratory test results even before making initial contact with the patient. Unfortunately, at times one may find absolutely no documentation whatsoever in the medical chart. If the information is available, a chart review can provide a wealth of data and assist in tailoring the interview according to the individual physical and mental needs of the patient. Nonetheless, the H&P of the anesthesia provider must be independent of that of the surgeons and other health care providers. Despite redundancy, each specialist will focus on his or her area of concern, thus blending the multidisciplinary modalities into the overall care of the patient. Often, entities missed by one provider will be picked up and evaluated by another.

THE PROCESS OF EVALUATION

Ultimately, the history, physical examination, and laboratory results should collectively yield enough in-depth information to allow the inquiring provider to ascertain whether there is functional impairment of any system—impairment that will affect or be affected by anesthesia, the operation, or both.

The Patient's History

The process of taking the history must be careful and methodical—absolutely nothing of importance should be overlooked. The attitude that "a little anesthesia" requires only a cursory evaluation may set the stage for serious complications and massive litigation. Thus, all preoperative workups need to be as complete as possible. A sensible guide to what constitutes "complete" is based upon the patient's physical status (PS). A complete workup for a healthy PS I patient would not be as detailed as that required for someone with a multisystem illness. There are a number of aphorisms that one must remember, one of which is: *If you do not ask, the patient will probably not volunteer the information.* Even when questioned, some patients do not disclose all the facts necessary to provide the best discussion-making circumstances possible. Rephrasing one's questions may help to reduce such hazards. It is important to *record what the patient denies as well as admits,* that is, negative as well as positive findings. (Documentation is covered in greater detail in Chapter 10; denial of HIV infectivity by HIV antibody [HIV-ab]–positive persons is discussed in Chapter 18.)

Depending on the information elicited during history taking, it may be necessary to procure the patient's prior medical records. For example, if a patient with a prior diagnosis of squamous cell carcinoma of the genitourinary-tract cannot remember the name of the drug employed for chemotherapy, then follow-up is definitely indicated. To dismiss the past pharmaceutical history without verifying that this agent was not a bleomycin-type compound, or one that will not cause some other type of serious pharmacological interaction, is unsound. If one is unable to retrieve the necessary information or if the situation calls for immediate action, then to prevent pulmonary complications and toxicity, one should avoid an anesthesia technique requiring an F_{IO_2} greater than 0.25.[1] Follow-up, when indicated, is the absolute rule.

Physical Examination

The physical examination should validate disclosures made during history taking. Once again, the extent of the examination depends on the patient's physical status; minimum standards for examination should be developed and followed meticulously. Certain criteria must be incorporated because they pertain both to the conduct of the anesthesia and any anticipated (especially invasive) monitoring. As an example germane to invasive monitoring, every patient should have an Allen's test to assess the patency of the arches between the ulnar and radial arteries in the hand. Even if the contemplated anesthetic involves a local or regional technique, during which patient cooperation is still possible intraoperatively, the test should be completed preoperatively and results documented. An anesthetic that commences as a local or regional can easily progress to a general that is fraught with complications and requires radial arterial puncture for blood gas sampling or pressure determination. Without a prior negative Allen's test, digital circulatory impairment is always a distinct possibility. Despite methodology allowing performance of the Allen's test in unconscious patients, it is a rare occasion that one is able to obtain a Doppler ultrasonic monitor while an emergency is in progress. Only when routine use of pulse

oximetry becomes the standard of care employed by every anesthetist and anesthesiologist will this technique provide a readily available method of Allen's testing.

Laboratory Data

As noted above, patients often undergo a series of predetermined laboratory tests as part of routine preoperative screening. Depending on standard operating procedures, these tests may include hemoglobin level, hematocrit, blood chemistries, liver function tests, coagulation studies, and urinalysis. An electrocardiogram and chest film are included for those over 40 years of age.[2] Pulmonary function studies may be indicated in elderly patients; the incidence of respiratory disease increases significantly in these patients.[3] Standard operating procedures should be meticulously followed for all patients. They set the standard of care, and failure to adhere to such a routine could create an inference of liability should there be any subsequent adverse outcome. Given identical surgical procedures for inpatients and outpatients, the preanesthesia workup should be the same unless more strict criteria are established for the latter group.

Usefulness of Screening Tests

Currently, there seems to be much controversy whether many of the above-noted laboratory studies are being used truly for "screening" purposes, that is, to uncover unsuspected conditions or disease entities. Thanks to the today's medical legal climate, frightened practitioners have seemed to order "everything in the book" just to cover all possible legal exposure; many of these tests are inappropriate for the intended use, i.e., preoperative evaluation. Recently, the clinical usefulness of many of them has been questioned, and emphasis is being placed on evaluating the cost-effectiveness of tests in detection of abnormalities. The federal program of prospective payment relating to diagnosis-related groups has effectively reduced the amount of unnecessary testing on inpatients, especially that conducted as part of a "teaching process." A varied number of authors have consistently demonstrated that multiphasic routine laboratory testing of patients who have a negative history and physical findings has no significant value, wastes finite resources, and does not alter the perioperative anesthetic course.[4-9] Therefore, it probably makes better sense to first obtain a detailed history and examine the patient. Positive findings will then dictate which laboratory tests are required. Ultimately, the clinician's judgment will serve as the guide; there are no national "routines" that have established a norm.

Other Laboratory Testing

Not all laboratory tests are used for screening purposes. Sound medical practice does dictate that certain tests are necessary for management of disease entities. For example, because of the frequency of arrhythmias during anesthesia in patients with potassium or sodium electrolyte imbalance, levels of these ions should be checked in patients where such imbalances are expected, for example, hyperkalemic patients in uremia, hyponatremic or hypokalemic patients, or those on hyperaldosterone therapy. There are other disease entities that when present mandate certain diagnostic evaluation, but this evaluation should be carried out long enough prior to the operation to allow for corrective therapeutic intervention. For example, patients with chronic obstructive pulmonary disease (COPD) consistently have a higher incidence of postoperative respiratory complications, particularly following upper abdominal and thoracic procedures, compared with patients with normal respiratory tracts. COPD patients will benefit from pulmonary function testing and attempts to optimize their respiratory function.[10] There is one additional legitimate reason for preoperative testing—to have a baseline for comparison with values obtained in the intraoperative or postoperative period. Such baseline data will give subsequent values far greater diagnostic significance.

Timing of Testing

Routine admissions, workups, and laboratory testing generally are completed the day before the date of elective operations. Most likely, anesthesia personnel will see patients at the end of the workday; late interviews lend themselves to late evaluations. If an abnormal test result is discovered at that time, the question arises whether the abnormality will or might affect the patient's care or desired outcome. In fact, if your care is not altered by test results that are either positive or negative (except to determine baseline data), then perhaps that test should not have been ordered in the first place. On the other hand, if the anesthetic plan will be altered by the results, then the test should be considered necessary. If abnormal results are noted and repeat studies ordered, the latter may not be reported by the time the procedure is scheduled to commence. Should an operation be postponed or canceled because the laboratory cannot handle routine testing during the late evening or night prior to the operation? If minimum standards for evaluation cannot be met and adequate treatment depends on access to the results of repeat testing, the procedure should be delayed.

Abnormal findings that have clinical significance should be followed up, and repeat studies obtained, since adverse outcomes and exposure to litigation may otherwise follow. Repeat testing to rule out false positives or clinically correlated values should be performed, and awareness of these findings properly documented. The key here lies in documentation. Merely repeating the test or ordering additional ones because of abnormal results offers insufficient safeguards against errors and possible lawsuits. It certainly does not improve patient care. Studies by Parkeson[11] and by others have shown that 50% to 95% of abnormal laboratory results are never recorded preoperatively on medical charts. Existence and knowledge of these reports is always questionable when documentation is absent. Finally, one should also be concerned about the needless anxiety generated in patients when test results are falsely positive.

Consultations

In this age of specialization, appropriate consultations should be requested if, in the opinion of the anesthetist or anesthesiologist, there is any possibility that the patient would benefit from such expertise. Consultations should not "clear" any patient for anesthesia, since it is the anesthesia care provider who is the expert in the physiological processes, anesthetic agents, and their interactions.

At least two questions should be addressed by a consultant: First, what is the nature and extent of the disease process; and, second, is the patient in the best possible physiological and psychological condition for the operation? Occasionally, in answering the second question, it may be necessary to defer an elective operation until the patient is optimally prepared, and thus reduce any chance of morbidity or even mortality. The luxury of deferment may not be feasible if the operation is urgent or emergent; in that event the risk-benefit ratio of deferral must be weighted carefully. This situation generates a third and final question for the consultant: namely, whether any particular problems that might be encountered by going ahead with the operation while any organ system is not in optimum condition can be effectively treated. Herein lies the importance of the preoperative evaluation process. It plays a dominant role in the intraoperative and postoperative outcomes and takes the knowledge and judgment of anesthesia personnel to correctly handle all of these difficult challenges.

The consultant should impart information in the form of recommendations that can be integrated into the patient's total care. Caution is advised—once a consultation is requested, it is prudent to wait until it is completed. Also, it is wise to acknowledge awareness of the consultant's recommendations by written entry in the patient's chart. Not all suggestions need be followed; however, a note explaining why any recommendation of this "expert" is not adhered to should be placed in the record. It could prove vital in defending one's position if something should go amiss. For example, restricting fluid intake in a patient who is bordering a state of pulmonary edema may be very appropriate in most instances. If this same patient is about to incur a sympathetic block from a regional anesthetic, fluid restriction may not be sound therapy; an explanation justifying fluid preloading with careful monitoring would be an intelligent approach to such a display of opposition. Careful documenta-

tion is the only means by which the events can be completely and accurately reviewed years after the incident. Since the written consultation becomes a permanent part of the medical chart, the decision process to approve or reject the expert's recommendations should also be detailed on the record.

The Surgeon's Operative Requirements

No preoperative assessment is complete without knowledge of the surgeon's requirements. Open communication with the primary surgeon is essential. One needs to know the patient's position(s) throughout the procedure; any specialized techniques needed to produce controlled hypotension, neuromuscular blockade, airway management, and fluid and blood replacement regimens; and any unique needs or idiosyncratic wishes of the members of the operating team.

PREPARATION AND THE ANESTHETIC PLAN

Once all the surgeon's specific needs are coupled with the data from the H & P, laboratory studies, and the wishes of the patient, an optimal anesthetic plan can be developed. The anesthetist carefully prepares this plan (and possibly alternate plans) to manage any emergency that could arise intraoperatively. Paramount to the preoperative evaluation is identifying what the patient will need and addressing all anticipated (and possibly even some unanticipated) requirements. When planning the anesthetic management, one should include alternatives. At times the just cited steps may fail. One may need to shift plans quickly and on short notice because life-threatening crises may ensue. Thorough and hence optimal preparation can and does reduce the overall risk to the patient. It also helps avoid litigation, inasmuch as pitfalls and complications are anticipated and avoided.

Education of the Patient

Preparation of the patient includes psychological preparation. First-time candidates for operative intervention and anesthesia do not know what to expect during their forthcoming surgical experience. Certain explanations are of paramount importance during preanesthesia and preoperative counseling, counseling that must take place during the anesthetic interview. Beginning with the events of the evening before the operation, the patient should be verbally taken through each phase, to become comfortable with the events that will take place:

- Dispensing of sleeping medications
- Remaining "NPO" after a prescribed time
- The routines of morning care (emptying bladder, brushing teeth, removing jewelry, and the like)
- Injection of preliminary medication, with its attendant grogginess
- Expected time of trip to the operating room
- Start of intravenous lines, application of monitoring leads, and route of administration of anesthesia
- Anticipated duration of the surgical procedure
- The sequence of events following emergence and transfer to the postanesthesia recovery unit

The communication of these vital pieces of information is necessary to adequately prepare the patient. The patient should also be told about the presence of expected catheters, the magnitude of postoperative discomfort, the treatment methods for handling that discomfort, and any other therapies required to prevent postoperative complications. Personnel must take time to answer all of the patient's questions in such a manner that the patient will truly comprehend what will happen. Not only should all this information be covered, but the reasons for and importance of these expectations or requests should be reinforced during these discussions. If, for example, patients understand why they need to breathe deeply and cough vigorously while in the recovery unit, their complete cooperation may in fact prevent serious postoperative complications.

In summary, the anesthesia interview not only provides a forum for gathering and putting to use information that will ulti-mately ensure proper anesthetic management, but also serves as an informational interchange that will help allay anxiety, foster confidence, and establish the basis for a sound health care provider–patient relationship. Expectations of both parties can be determined. The patient's wishes must precede all others except, of course, if acceding to those wishes would lead to substandard anesthesia care.

Similar educational exchanges also apply to the members of the patient's family, who may have corresponding fears and anxieties, especially if the patient is at the extremes of age. Parents want children protected. Every family member wants the elderly protected. In fact, in today's climate, everyone wants all patients to be protected, and the legal system (rightly or wrongly) ensures that the public is indeed entitled to that protection.

Counseling

Counseling the patient, and obtaining his or her informed consent (see Chapter 9), is one of the most important goals of the preoperative visit. The patient's consent to the anesthetic must be preceded by some explanation of the anesthetic risks, potential complications, and benefits. While there is agreement that proper counseling and disclosure eliminate exposure to liability for lack of informed consent, there is disagreement as to the amount of detail that constitutes proper disclosure. Suffice it to say that a proper disclosure will depend upon the patient and the individual circumstances surrounding each case. The duty of disclosure dictates it be made up of facts, and opinions as to risks and benefits based upon those facts. If there is any doubt, one probably should lean toward overdisclosure, rather than withholding information.

Special Problem Areas

Recently, the human immunodeficiency virus (HIV) that causes the acquired immune deficiency syndrome (AIDS) has created a flurry in the medical community (see also Chapter 18). Since the law follows the *stare decisus* principle, the legal ramifications of this dreaded disease are yet to be

fully realized. Patients are concerned about
being infected, especially from administration of blood or blood products. Health care
providers are concerned about exposure to
HIV by contact with infected patients. Because of the serious nature of this disease
(ultimately fatal with no cure in sight at the
present time), I firmly believe that all surgical patients should be screened for antibodies to the virus (see Chapter 18).
Patients should also be counseled about
possible HIV exposure when blood transfusions will or might be needed in conjunction with the surgical procedure. The use of
autologous donations for the replacement
of blood should be considered when blood
product therapy is anticipated and the operation is elective (see Chapter 17).

Identity of Anesthesia Personnel

When anesthesia is practiced under a
"team" concept, one must be certain that
the patient becomes aware of the identity
of the individual(s) who will be administering the anesthetic. (Informed consent problems in a pedagogical setting are discussed
in Chapter 19.) If the interviewer will not
be the one providing direct and primary
anesthetic care to the patient, it is necessary to disclose that fact. Patients have the
right to reject entering into a contract with
a health care provider when they have not
had the opportunity to interview and evaluate for themselves.

Language Barriers

Communication problems arise in every
aspect of human endeavor; they must be
held to a minimum to avoid legal problems.
If a language barrier exists, then an interpreter must be utilized for every portion of
the H & P, patient education, and especially during the counseling session when
informed consent is obtained. The name of
the interpreter should be recorded and that
person should cosign the written consent
form along with the patient. Clear communication and comprehension are essential
in preventing misunderstanding and allied
problems.

Adequately Informing the Patient

Although consent and informed consent
are discussed in Chapter 9, one element of

informed consent deserves emphasis here.
This concept *assumes* that consent is obtained from an *informed, uncoerced, re-
laxed, unmedicated* patient who has *intact
mental faculties* and is of *legal age*. Under
these (and preferably only under these) circumstances, the patient makes a decision
to proceed with the anesthetic and any
monitoring in light of full knowledge of the
risks, complications, and the alternatives,
if any, all of which should have been presented by the interviewer. This decision-
making process does require time; if the
patient is not afforded an ample opportunity to contemplate the options, it is questionable whether a truly informed consent
has been obtained. Obviously, counseling
sessions held as far in advance of the pending operation as possible satisfy the time
element best. Excluding emergency procedures, "informed" consent obtained while
the patient is on the operating table clearly
does not provide the patient with the opportunity to meaningfully analyze risks
and benefits and select appropriate
alternatives.

Preliminary Medication

The anesthesia interview and enlighten-
ment of the patient that takes place during
this meeting may do more to allay the patient's anxiety than any pharmaceuticals
employed for that purpose. Pharmacologic
adjuncts may be deemed necessary and
they will often provide a smooth anesthetic
induction, perioperative course, and
postanesthetic recovery. Modern anesthesia practice has witnessed a changeover
from the traditional sedative, narcotic, an-
ticholinergic, and barbiturate agents to
more concern for the therapeutic drug regimens that the patient's pathophysiology
mandates. Continuation of antihypertensive agents, beta-blockers, steroids, antibi-
otics, and similar regimens now dominates
the pharmaceutical preparation. Dosage ad-
justments may be required but there are
few exceptions (MAO inhibitors and anti-
coagulants) to the practice of continuing
existing therapy. Potential adverse interactions of current drug therapy and anesthetics are of primary concern to anesthesia
personnel. Prior therapy with some of these
agents will often dictate the selection of

agents and techniques as well as monitoring methods needed to ensure patient safety. Nonparticulate antacids, antiemetics, H_2-receptor antagonists, and newer sedatives are frequently used for preliminary medication, while narcotics, anticholinergics, and barbiturates generally are administered intravenously immediately prior to or in conjunction with the anesthetic induction.

Just as preliminary medication regimens have changed because of philosophy and availability of newer drugs, so have the routes of drug administration. More medications are currently administered orally; just a decade ago, this practice was considered heresy. Additionally, today's patients are often allowed to play an active role in drug selection, and even whether they prefer to be medicated (i.e., depressed) at all.

LEGAL ISSUES

As noted in Chapter 2, all health care providers owe certain duties to their patients—practice at the professed level of competence, maintain confidences, make full disclosure, seek consultation when indicated, and offer continuing treatment. How these duties are specifically interwoven with preanesthesia evaluation and preparation is depicted in Figure 8-1. They become the standard of care for personnel engaged in these essential steps. This standard requires that each patient receive a properly conducted evaluation—history, physical examination, and laboratory testing—to determine what anesthetic may or may not be indicated. Then, preoperative preparation commences, a process that in reality is the beginning of the anesthetic. A published source of this standard is the guidelines (Appendix 8-1) of the American Society of Anesthesiologists (ASA). These guidelines have become the standard of care (see Chapter 4) for members of the ASA. More stringent guidelines, if established by departments or individuals, must, of course, be followed carefully.

Of corollary but special importance is

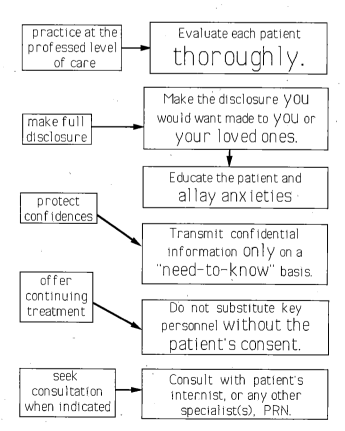

Figure 8–1 The five duties of the health care provider as they apply to preoperative evaluation of the candidate for anesthesia administration and operative intervention.

preserving the confidentiality of information obtained during the process of history taking (Chapter 5). Likewise, making a full disclosure in obtaining the patient's consent (Chapter 9) and obtaining consultations as required (Chapter 2) all play important roles. Anesthesia personnel also have responsibility for preparing an anesthesia plan—to include monitoring as required (Chapter 12)—and administering the anesthetic (Chapter 14). All of these steps must be consonant with the data acquired during the thorough review and analysis of the complete H & P conducted previously, and of the laboratory findings. Finally, the patient is owed a duty of continued care once the health care provider accepts the contract for anesthesia services. This continuum of care extends well into the postanesthesia period (Chapter 13).

Just as anesthesia personnel have certain legally recognized duties, so does each patient (see also Chapter 2). In the context of preoperative evaluation and preparation, these include *making a full disclosure of pertinent aspects of the past medical history, cooperating in the therapy* (e.g., taking nothing by mouth after midnight, stopping smoking several weeks in advance of the date of the operation, or the like), and *paying for services rendered.*

All of the aforestated duties are created and become enforceable once the agreement to render anesthesia services has been entered into. Litigation, if it arises, generally stems from a breach of one or more of the health care provider's duties, coupled with a therapeutic result that is less than desirable. If the patient's lawyer can prove to the trier of fact that there was a breach of a duty, and the untoward result was caused by that breach, a prima facie case of negligence (Chapter 3) will have been established.

Pertinent Common Law Decisions

It should come as no small surprise that there are a number of reported cases [12-18] involving instances in which anesthesia personnel have failed to become aware of pertinent medical problems in their patients or, if they were so aware, failed to appreciate the significance of the positive

findings or otherwise ignored them. The Jackson case[15] is a particularly egregious example of disregard of the significance of a preoperative illness.

On the day before the tonsillectomy, Mrs. Jackson apprised the surgeon who was to perform it that her daughter had a cold and runny nose. The surgeon said that "he would have to operate the next day because he was leaving town, and it did not matter that she had a cold." Judith never regained consciousness following the diethyl ether anesthetic, developed hyperpyrexia and convulsions later that day, and died early the following morning. The appellate court reversed the jury verdict for the surgeon, and ordered a new trial.

The consequential untoward results in the other cases also led to litigation and, ultimately, verdicts for the patient-plaintiffs. This body of common law clearly sets forth the principle that anesthesia personnel are under a legally recognized duty to thoroughly familiarize themselves with each patient's past medical history, current pharmacologic therapy, any associated problems, and the significance of those findings. The courts are willing and ready to impose liability for failing to be aware of and to apply this information to the enhancement of anesthesia administration.

Conversely, courts will not impute liability to anesthesia personnel in situations wherein there is no duty to inquire about a particular aspect of a patient's problem. The plaintiff in a fairly recent California case alleged that the anesthesiologist who visited the patient preoperatively for a procedure that was subsequently canceled should be liable for failure to examine radiographs of the patient's cervical spine and detect a fracture of the odontoid process that might or might not have been present at the time of the rounds. The appellate court held that there was no duty to do so.[19]

CONCLUSION

The ideal evaluation conducted prior to and in anticipation of any form of anesthesia consists of a blending of the art of interpersonal relationships and the science of medicine and nursing. The best protection against legal action is the conservative and safe approach to a state-of-the-art practice, coupled with complete documentation. Reducing perioperative morbidity is directly proportional to the adequacy of the process of evaluation and preparation detailed in this chapter. *Primum non nocere!*

REFERENCES

1. Allen, SC, et al: Bleomycin therapy and anaesthesia. Anaesthesia 36:60, 1981.
2. Tornebrandt, K and Fletcher, R: Pre-operative chest x-rays in elderly patients. Anaesthesia 37:901, 1983.
3. Wahba, WN: Influence of aging lung function. Clinical significance of changes from age twenty. Anesth Analg 62:764, 1983.
4. Sandler, G: Costs of unnecessary tests. Br Med J 2:21, 1979.
5. Durbridge, TC, et al: Evaluation of benefits of screening tests done immediately on admission to hospital. Clin Chem 22:968, 1986.
6. Rabkin, SW and Horne, JM: Preoperative electrocardiography: Effect of new abnormalities on clinical decisions. Can Med Assoc J 128:146, 1983.
7. Delahunt, B and Turnbull, PRG: How cost effective are routine preoperative investigations? N Zealand Med J 92:431, 1981.
8. Wood, RA and Hoekelman, RA: Value of the chest x-ray as a screening test for elective surgery in children. Pediatrics 67:477, 1981.
9. Krieg, AF, Gambino, R, and Galen, RS: Why are clinical laboratory tests performed? When are they valid? JAMA 233:76, 1985.
10. Gracey, DR, et al: Preoperative pulmonary preparation of patients with chronic obstructive pulmonary disease. Chest 76:123, 1979.
11. Parkeson, GR, Jr: Determination, recognition, and follow-up of abnormal laboratory values. J Fam Prac 7:341, 1978.
12. Butler v. Layton, 266 Mass. 117, 164 N.E. 920 (Sup. Ct. Mass. 1929) (liability for complications resulting from administration of general anesthesia [diethyl ether] to a child with a "severe cold").
13. Cook v. Lichtblau, 176 So.2d 523 (C.A. 2 Fla. 1965) (failure to become aware of full stomach, with regurgitation during recovery from anesthesia and aspiration, acute asphyxia, circulatory arrest, and severe residual CNS damage).
14. Graddy v. New York Medical College, 243 N.Y.S.2d 940 (App. Div. 1963) (lack of appreciation by resident of significance of patient's respiratory infection, with circulatory arrest followed by 4 days of coma and minor but long-term neurological deficits).
15. Jackson v. Mountain Sanitarium, 234 N.C. 222, 67 S.E.2d 57: *reh'g denied* 235 N.C. 756, 69 S.E.2d 29 (1961).
16. Moore v. Bell, 187 Tenn. 366, 215 S.W.2d 787 (1948) (failure to perform complete preoperative workup prior to general anesthesia in physician's office, with patient's consequent failure to regain consciousness and death a short time later).
17. Quintal v. Laurel Grove Hosp., 41 Cal. Rptr. 577, 397 P.2d 161 (Sup. Ct. 1964) (apprehensive, uncooperative 6-year-old develops circulatory arrest during general anesthesia for correction of strabismus; inability of ophthalmologist to open chest for direct cardiac massage [in 1960] leads to delay in resuscitation and consequent severe CNS damage).
18. Sanzari v. Rosenfeld, 34 N.J. 128, 167 A.2d 625 (Sup. Ct. 1961) (failure of dentist to take history and become aware of patient's hypertension, followed by use of epinephrine and subsequent, ultimately fatal cerebrovascular accident in dental chair).
19. Mann v. Cracchiolo, 38 Cal.3d 18, 210 Cal.Rptr. 762, 694 P.2d 1134 (1985).

ASA STANDARD FOR PREANESTHESIA CARE*

This standard applies to all patients who receive anesthesia or monitored anesthesia care. Under unusual circumstances (e.g., extreme emergencies) this standard may be modified. When this is the case, the circumstances shall be documented in the patient's record.

STANDARD I

An anesthesiologist shall be responsible for determining the medical status of the patient, developing a plan of anesthesia care, and acquainting the patient or the responsible adult with the proposed plan.

The development of an appropriate plan of anesthesia care is based upon:

1 Reviewing the medical record.
2 Interviewing and examining the patient to:
  a Discuss the medical history, previous anesthetic experiences and drug therapy.
  b Assess those aspects of the physical condition that might affect decisions regarding perioperative risk and management.
3 Obtaining and/or reviewing tests and consultations necessary to the conduct of anesthesia.
4 Determining the appropriate prescription of preoperative medications as necessary to the conduct of anesthesia.

The responsible anesthesiologist shall verify that the above has been properly performed and documented in the patient's record.

---

*This Standard was approved by House of Delegates of the American Society of Anesthesiologists on October 14, 1987. Reprinted with permission of the ASA.

9

H. Thomas Foley, M.D., J.D.
William H. L. Dornette, M.D., J.D.

Consent and Informed Consent

The common law has recognized the right of individuals to be free from the intentional touching of their bodies by another. The law characterizes such touching as a battery (Chapter 5). Treating a patient in any manner without any consent at all (except in an emergency) constitutes a battery. It is quite obvious that the administration of anesthesia, an intentional act, involves the "touching" of the body of the patient. To verify that patients have consented to the administration of the necessary anesthetics, operative consent forms customarily include a provision for consenting to anesthesia as well as to the operation itself.

While courts have long recognized the need for consent, except possibly in emergencies, the formal doctrine of informed consent is of only fairly recent origin. The following discussion concerns principally this legal doctrine, which, like much current medical jurisprudence, is of common law origin.

THE LEGAL AND SOCIETAL BASIS OF INFORMED CONSENT

On the basis of a single factual situation, a patient-plaintiff's attorneys may, and often do, assert more than one theory of recovery.

1 They may allege that the patient did not give permission for the procedure and that, therefore, the physician committed a battery for which both compensatory and punitive damages should be awarded.
2 They may allege that although the patient consented to the procedure, the patient's consent was invalid because the physician negligently failed to disclose sufficient information upon which the patient could make an informed consent (see Glossary of Legal Terminology); and that, as a result of lack of informed consent, the patient underwent a procedure to which he or she would not have consented had he or she been adequately informed. Lack of informed consent is an independent basis for recovery even if the procedure itself is nonnegligently performed.
3 They may allege that although the procedure was performed with an informed consent, the procedure itself was negligently executed in one or more ways.

Each theory of recovery—no consent, lack of informed consent, and negligent performance—is sufficient, if proved by a preponderance of the evidence, to hold the physician liable for damages. The issue of informed consent is reviewed in this chapter. After reviewing it, the reader should conclude that all that is required by this doctrine is that the physician practice good medicine.

Right of Privacy

The societal basis for the doctrine of informed consent is that every human being of adult years and sound mind has a right to determine what shall be done with his or her own body. This right of self-determination is included in the general common law right to privacy, the right to be let alone. It is a right that, when government is involved, is protected by the Fourth and Fourteenth Amendments to the U.S. Constitution. Both the common law and constitutional right to privacy are expressions of the value our society places on the sanctity and dignity of the individual. It is a right that should not be violated without justification.

Fiduciary Relationship

A second basis for this doctrine is found in the fiduciary nature of the doctor-patient relationship. In general, a fiduciary relationship exists when one of two parties to a transaction must trust and rely upon the other. Under such circumstances the party with superior knowledge regarding the transaction is under a legal duty to disclose all material information about the transaction to the other party. If the superiorly positioned party fails to disclose all material information he or she has or should have, and if the other party is adversely affected as a result of that failure, the party in the superior position will be held liable for injury sustained by the dependent party. Because the physician-patient relationship is obviously fiduciary in nature, the duty to disclose continues as long as the relationship exists. It is critical at the time decisions must be made, especially when invasive diagnostic or therapeutic procedures are being proposed.

CAPACITY TO CONSENT

Before obtaining the patient's consent for the proposed course of action, the physician must be assured that the patient has the capacity to consent, capacity being the legal power to grant or withhold consent. Except for the exceptions discussed below, a competent patient has virtually an absolute right to consent to, or refuse, a proposed procedure or treatment. Refusal is merely an indication, usually verbal, that consent is being withheld.

When treating minor children, or adults who have been legally adjudged incompetent, a physician must obtain consent from a parent or the incompetent person's legal guardian. The right of the parent or legal guardian to consent or refuse (especially refuse), however, is not coextensive with the right accorded to the competent adult. For example, the highest court of Massachusetts has held that if an incompetent individual refuses antipsychotic drugs, the legal guardian must have judicial approval before authorizing forcible administration of such medication.*

While the legal guardian is the only person who may consent to procedures upon and treatment of an incompetent adult, one of his or her relatives—commonly the spouse or an adult child—customarily is asked to grant permission if the physician believes that patient to be incompetent, even though the individual has not been so adjudged by a court. Legally, however, consent given by a relative who is not the legal guardian of an incompetent is a nullity. All adults are presumed to be competent until adjudged otherwise, and no other person, related or not, may assume rights that belong exclusively to another. Just as a wife may not sell or convey her husband's automobile without authority, she may not consent to invasion of his person unless properly authorized. Because most, if not all, hospital bylaws require that consent be obtained from a relative when the physician believes the patient to be incompetent, such consents must be obtained. While they have no legal validity, they do have the practical effect of showing

*The reader should be alerted that in these matters the law of one state is not necessarily the law in another. The examples used in this chapter serve merely to illustrate how some courts dispose of these issues. When faced with one of these issues, the reader would be well advised to seek the assistance of someone familiar with the case law of his or her own jurisdiction. Because the issue is most frequently faced in hospitals, the hospital administrator or hospital counsel would be the logical person with whom to consult.

that the physician has discussed the proposed procedure or treatment with someone who presumably knows the patient and has his or her best interests at heart.

CONSENT VERSUS INFORMED CONSENT

Historically, the physician obtained the patient's consent in order to avoid an accusation of the intentional tort of battery, the impermissible touching of one person by another. In one respect, informed consent is much like the concept of agreement in contract law; it is a meeting of the minds with both parties talking about the same subject matter. Similar to agreement in contract law, consent may be *implied* or *express*. An example of implied consent would be a patient's rolling up his sleeve and extending his arm when the physician asks for a blood sample. Express consent, which may be verbal or written, obviously is necessary as a prerequisite to major diagnostic and all therapeutic procedures.

To the extent required by hospital bylaws, written consents must be obtained. In addition, when the issue of lack of informed consent arises, written consent forms, like written contracts, serve as evidence that the physician and patient discussed the subject matter noted on the form. Lawyers describe consent forms as "good" evidence, because they are tangible and contemporaneous, that is, executed when the consent was obtained, at a time when the issue of consent was not in litigation.

Defective Consent

Like written contracts, written consent forms may be attacked on the basis that the terms were nonspecific or that the patient did not understand the meaning of the technical terms used. An example of the former is the general consent form wherein the patient agrees to all treatments and procedures; an example of the latter might be a patient with a second-grade education who consents to a pancreatoduodenectomy. The problem of lack of patient understanding is best avoided by using forms that allow for the insertion of a description of the procedure in common rather than technical terms. Another serious problem revolves about a patient being asked to acknowledge the granting of an informed consent before being informed of any risks. On point is the following case[1] that involved a number of key issues, the most important of which (from the standpoint of this chapter) was the dismissal by the trial judge of the plaintiffs' claim that patient Brown's informed consent was not obtained:

On the afternoon of February 24, 1980, Mr. Brown entered Harrison Memorial Hospital in Bremerton (Washington) for exploratory surgery to be performed the following day. When Mr. Brown checked into the hospital, he signed several admission forms, including one that indicated *he was aware of the risks associated with anesthesia* (emphasis supplied) and consented to anesthesia. After completing the forms, which took about 15 to 20 minutes, Mr. Brown was sent by the admissions' secretary to consult with Dr. Dahl, one of the defendants, for a preanesthetic evaluation. While waiting to meet with Dr. Dahl, Mr. Brown completed a preanesthetic evaluation "checklist." Mr. and Mrs. Brown testified that during the ensuing consultation, Dr. Dahl told them that he recommended a general anesthetic procedure (sodium Pentothal) for the surgery and *would personally perform the proposed procedure* (emphasis supplied). They also testified that although Dr. Dahl asked them whether they had any questions about the proposed anesthetic procedure, he did not disclose any of the risks associated with the proposed procedure, nor any of the available alternative anesthetic procedures.

Mr. Brown was taken to the operating room the following morning where he was met by codefendant Susan Korte, a nurse anesthetist. She testified that she explained to Mr. Brown that she was going to perform the general anesthetic procedure and that Mr. Brown voiced no complaints about her performing the procedure or to the absence of Dr. Dahl.

After completing standard preanesthetic preparations and selection of the anesthetic agents, Nurse Korte began to administer general anesthesia to Mr. Brown. As the anesthetic began to take effect, Mr. Brown's airway became partially blocked and he experienced difficulties in breathing. Nurse Korte attempted corrective measures that proved unsuccessful. She then called for help. The elapsed time between Nurse Korte's first discovery of Mr. Brown's breathing problems

to when she first called for help was a hotly contested issue at trial. Within moments after Nurse Korte's call for help, several doctors arrived at the scene, including Dr. Dahl.

After several attempts, doctors were successful in establishing an airway for Mr. Brown. Shortly thereafter, however, Mr. Brown sustained a cardiac arrest. Mr. Brown suffered significant mental and physical impairments.[1]

In its opinion, the appellate court noted that "because they signed a consent to anesthesia, plaintiffs have the burden of rebutting the presumption of having given their informed consent." The court of appeals decided that the plaintiff had successfully rebutted the presumption. The court

. . . held that (1) evidence that patient's injuries resulted from risks associated with general anesthesia, that physician failed to inform patient of the risks of general anesthesia and available alternatives, and that patient only signed consent form after being told that he would not receive treatment without signing was sufficient to present the issue of informed consent to the jury; (2) proof of failure to provide informed consent does not require expert testimony showing that risks of alternatives were less than treatment actually administered.[1]

It should be added, perhaps parenthetically, that failure to obtain Mr. Brown's informed consent was not the only departure from the duty of care owed him in conjunction with the administration of his anesthetic. As noted in Chapter 2, health care is delivered under personal services contracts. Duties under these contracts for the most part are not delegable. Agreeing to perform such a duty, and then delegating that duty to one less skilled without the patient's express knowledge and consent, constitutes a breach of one's fiduciary duty to one's patient. It could also be construed to be a fraudulent act (Chapter 5) as well as a negligent one (Chapter 3).

In modern times, the physician has been held liable not only for battery (for failing to obtain the patient's consent) but also for negligence in failing to disclose sufficient information so that the patient could make a knowledgeable decision or, in other words, give informed consent. If the patient-plaintiff should prevail on the negligence theory of recovery, he or she is entitled only to compensatory damages, the measure of damages for unintentional torts, which is the legal category in which professional negligence (malpractice) belongs. That result—compensatory damages only—should be compared with the case wherein the physician fails to obtain any consent. In that case the physician could be found liable for battery, and the patient could be awarded punitive damages in addition to compensatory damages.

EXTENT OF DISCLOSURE REQUIRED

Having established that the physician has a duty to make disclosures to the patient, it becomes necessary to define the scope of that duty—which disclosures must the physician make to avoid liability for failure to make adequate disclosure. Fortunately, *what the law requires and what constitutes good medical practice are identical.* In general, both require that the physician disclose to the patient:

- The diagnosis
- The proposed course of action and the probability of success
- The risk of doing nothing
- The substantial inherent risks or dangers of the proposed course of action
- The existence, and risks and benefits, of alternative courses of action (if any), either collectively or in particular

As applied to the practice of anesthesia, certain of those required disclosures are of greater relevance to the anesthesiologist than they would be to other specialists. In the preanesthesia interview, it would be wise for anesthesia personnel to review with the patient his or her understanding of the diagnosis and the surgical procedure for which anesthesia is required. Obviously, the probability for success of general anesthesia is so great as to require no discussion; however, when either local or spinal anesthesia is proposed, it would be wise to advise the patient of the possibility that general anesthesia might be required if the proposed method proves ineffective. If more than one type of anesthesia could be

used for the procedure, it would be wise for anesthesia personnel to inform the patient of the alternatives and the reason why the proposed method is preferable. For example, if either regional or general anesthesia could be used for the procedure, and if the anesthesiologist or nurse anesthetist was of the opinion that general anesthesia was preferable, anesthesia personnel should disclose that either type of anesthesia could be used, but that the recommendation in this case is that general anesthesia is preferable.

Finally, the anesthesiologist or nurse anesthetist should inform the patient as to the substantial inherent risks posed by this recommendation. It has been suggested that the disclosure of risks includes informing patients of the risks associated with the alternatives that are not recommended. At this point, patients have the choice of giving their now informed consent or refusing. Patients who consent should be requested to acknowledge that consent by signing a consent form. If the patient expresses a desire for a type of anesthesia not recommended (for example, spinal anesthesia), the anesthesiologist has the choice of withdrawing from the case or agreeing to administer anesthesia according to the patient's desire.

The discussion thus far outlines what must be disclosed, not the manner in which it is to be disclosed. Disclosure can and should be accomplished in such a way that the patient is not unduly alarmed and the anesthesiologist is not perceived as callous or indifferent. For example, in informing the patient that one of the risks of general anesthesia is death, the anesthesiologist should simultaneously inform the patient not only that the risk is extremely small, but also that the patient would be monitored very carefully so that the proper measures can be instituted if signs of impending cardiac arrest appear.

Standards for Disclosure

Although the physician must disclose to the patient the substantial risks or dangers inherent in or collateral to the proposed course of action, this does not mean that the physician must disclose all known risks or dangers. Nor must the patient be given a complete medical education during the preanesthesia interview. Since it is only substantial risks that must be disclosed, the problem is to define which risks are "substantial." Unfortunately, there is no bright line separating substantial from non-substantial, significant from insigificant, or material from immaterial. There are guidelines, however, for determining which risks to disclose.

These guidelines vary depending upon which jurisdiction's law governs. In most jurisdictions, this standard has been set by common law (Appendix 9-1), although it is statutorily defined or mandated in 23 jurisdictions (Appendix 9-2). One jurisdiction uses the subjective standard; some use the professional standard; others use the reasonable-patient or objective standard.

Subjective Standard

The subjective standard focuses on the possible risks considered significant by the patient when he or she is deciding whether to follow the recommended course of action.[2] If the physician does not warn the patient of a particular risk and that complication subsequently develops, this standard asks whether the patient, had he or she been informed of that risk, would have agreed to the procedure. An obvious difficulty with the subjective standard is that the patient who has *already* experienced the complication would tend to testify (in retrospect) that he or she *would have considered* its risk significant.

Professional Standard

In those states using the professional standard, the patient-plaintiff, in order to prevail on the informed consent issue, must produce expert testimony as to what other physicians disclose in similar circumstances.[3,4] A criticism of this standard is that it gives too much authority to the medical profession in deciding the appropriate degree of disclosure.[5]

Reasonable-Patient Standard

States using the reasonable-patient or objective standard do not require an expert with regard to the informed consent issue. All that the patient-plaintiff is required to show is that the physician failed to disclose information that a reasonable patient (prudent person in a similar position) would want to know and would consider significant. A District of Columbia appellate court described the reasonable-patient standard:

> The test for mandatory disclosure of information on treatment of the patient's condition is whether a reasonable person in what the physician knows or should know to be the patient's position would consider the information material to his decision. The information is material if the reasonable person in what the physician knows or should know to be the patient's position would be likely to attach significance to the risks in deciding to accept or forego the proposed treatment.[6]

Choice of Standard

The reasonable-patient standard is considered by most experts to be the better one and to be the direction in which the law is moving, as shown by the fact that a growing number of states are changing to it from the professional one. Because the reasonable-patient standard is more comprehensive than the professional standard, it would be wise for physicians to adopt it in their practices even if their state uses the professional standard. Regardless of which standard a physician's state uses, he or she would balance the frequency with which a particular complication occurs against the severity of the injury in determining which complications to disclose. If the injury stemming from the complication is severe, then the possibility of that complication should be disclosed even if its occurrence rate is very low. For example, a 1% paraparesis rate associated with laminectomy has been held to be material information that should have been disclosed preoperatively by the surgeon.

Proof in an Action Alleging Lack of Informed Consent

In order for a patient-plaintiff to prevail in a malpractice suit based on lack of informed consent, he or she must prove that disclosure to a prudent person in the patient's position would have resulted in a decision against the proposed course of action. This is the objective standard used in a deciding informed consent cases. A patient-plaintiff's assertion that he or she would not have submitted to the proposed procedure if he or she had known about a particular complication (the subjective standard) is insufficient proof to sustain an allegation of lack of informed consent.

EXCEPTIONS TO THE REQUIREMENT FOR INFORMED CONSENT

There are three major exceptions to the requirement that the physician must obtain the patient's informed consent prior to treatment.

1 The physician should not pursue the matter if the patient expresses the desire not to be informed.
2 Informed consent is presumed to have been granted in an emergency situation, defined as a problem posing imminent danger to life or limb in an apparently incompetent patient, for example, unconscious patients, patients with delirium tremens, or senile, guardianless patients with gangrenous limbs.
3 The therapeutic exception—the physician's belief that disclosure is contraindicated for medical reasons (e.g., avoiding unduly alarming a candidate for an urgently needed procedure). This exception is carefully circumscribed so that the exception does not devour the rule.

INFORMED CONSENT IN ANESTHESIA PRACTICE

That the administration of anesthetics poses a number of significant risks is well known. For example, anesthesia care today frequently requires the ancillary use of some form of invasive monitoring. Although the techniques for insertion of arterial and central venous lines are straightforward, use of these techniques is not without risk. It may be incumbent on personnel who plan to employ these modalities to warn the patient of the associated risks and benefits. Anesthesia personnel frequently participate in the decision to initiate a transfusion (see

Chapter 17). In many situations, the possible need for a transfusion is known preoperatively. These personnel (along with the surgeon) may have a duty to inform the patient during the preanesthesia counseling session that there is a chance of contracting non-A, non-B hepatitis, cytomegalovirus, or HIV. Finally, there are a number of other risks relating to specific agents or techniques, and differing from patient to patient, from operation to operation, and even from surgeon to surgeon.

Anesthesia personnel, after listening to a discussion of the informed consent doctrine, frequently raise very cogent questions in several areas. These pertain to the extent of disclosure desired, its documentation and true value, and whether the professional who will administer the anesthetic must be the one who obtains the informed consent.

Risks to Be Discussed

We believe that all possible complications do not necessarily need to be mentioned to every patient when obtaining that patient's informed consent. Anesthesia personnel should follow the suggestions set forth in the preceding pages. *In purely elective cases, a very complete disclosure should be made.* On the other hand, in an emergency, one probably need say relatively little, simply because the risks of any procedure are intimately entwined with its benefits. The benefit of an emergency operation, which may be lifesaving, clearly outweighs many of the risks of anesthesia, including those of invasive monitoring and blood product therapy.

There is one more suggestion concerning the extent of disclosure. We do not believe that the counseling session should be cluttered with a discussion of complications that *would not be expected to occur in the absence of negligence.* The courts have long held that one who is in a superior position (e.g., a health care provider) cannot employ a contract or a consent form to insulate oneself from liability—for example, by warning of injuries that can develop only if one is negligent.[7] The practical application of this statement is that one need mention very few complications of the anesthetic administration itself. One of these complications that does deserve mention pertains to instrumentation about the mouth. For example, patients with one or more porcelain jacket crowns on their incisor teeth need to be appraised of possible damage to those prostheses, and to the underlying tooth or teeth as well.[8]

Invasive monitoring poses a special informed consent problem. Arterial cannulas, Swan-Ganz catheters, and even central venous pressure catheters all are associated with significant risks. For example, a number of anesthetic and equipment-related accidents and injuries have occurred in uniformed-services hospitals. In one case there was a loss of a patient's thumb following a competently inserted arterial cannula; in another patient, a perforation of the innominate artery occurred following Swan-Ganz catheter placement; and in a third, the tip of a CVP line perforated the wall of the right ventricle. We believe that disclosure of these risks is mandatory in the elective case (see Chapter 12), although very likely not necessarily in the emergency.

Documentation

We have not usually listed in the preanesthesia counseling note all potential risks discussed during the counseling session. So-called laundry lists have been recommended by some "authorities." The problem with such a list is that if you fail to note the complication that actually occurs, you have made things difficult for yourself, and may even have "sold the farm," so to speak.

Patients' Recall of the Preanesthesia Visit

Studies of patients' recall have demonstrated that a significantly large percentage of patients, especially candidates for major operative procedures, remember very little of what they are told during the preanesthesia visit when they are informed of the risks and their consent for the anesthetic and monitoring is obtained. The responsible anesthesiologist or nurse anesthetist should make every effort to verify that the patient (or next of kin or both, as appropriate) understands what is discussed *at the*

time of the preanesthesia visit. Having someone from the nursing unit present as a witness may be a sound idea under certain circumstances. Some anesthesiologists have even proposed that the counseling session be tape recorded. Other anesthesiologists do not feel that one needs to go to this extreme, although there certainly is no harm in doing so.

Who Must Obtain the Informed Consent?

We believe that a health care provider other than the one who is to administer the anesthetic may obtain the patient's informed consent *provided that* the disclosure is essentially the same as the one that would have been made by the actual anesthetist or anesthesiologist. On point is an opinion of a New York State appellate court decision involving a case in which a registered nurse customarily obtained patients' informed consent for the physician with whom she worked regularly.[9]

Other Informed Consent Issues

Who determines which risk(s) to disclose is, for the most part, set forth by the common law of each jurisdiction, as noted above. The standard of disclosure is not uniform across the United States (see Appendix 9-1). A number of state legislatures have invaded the province of their judiciary in creating the common law by enacting statutes that either mandate informed consent or specify the standard for disclosure. These statutes are tabulated in Appendix 9-2; some of their pertinent provisions are also incorporated in Appendix 9-1. The majority of these statutes (12) specify the professional standard, three specify the objective one, and seven are silent. One author[10] is of the opinion that a statute mandating application of the professional standard was enacted in New York at the behest of organized medical interests to attempt to mitigate health care professionals' exposure to liability; that is, it is another of the steps taken to afford tort reform (see Chapter 29).

Special informed consent issues arise for patients who are hospitalized in teaching institutions. These issues are discussed in Chapter 19. Caring for HIV-infected patients, or having staff persons who are carriers of HIV, creates unique informed consent questions, as reviewed in Chapter 18. What to tell patients about the risks of blood products, and under what circumstances, is covered in Chapter 17.

CONCLUSION

In summary, the informed consent doctrine really places no additional burden on the health care provider beyond what has always been required as part of the delivery of complete, competent care. The concepts of the right of privacy and the fiduciary relationship with one's patients—upon which the informed consent doctrine is based—antedated the initial informed consent decision[11] by a number of years. By fulfilling the legal requirements of this doctrine, the anesthesia care provider will have taken a major step both in the preanesthetic preparation of, and the promotion of sound rapport with, the patient.

REFERENCES

1. Brown v. Dahl, 705 P.2d 781 (Wash. App. 1985).
2. Canterbury v. Spence, 464 F.2d 772 (D.C. Cir. 1972) ("Optimally for the patient, exposure of a risk would be mandatory whenever the patient would deem it significant to his decision, either singly or in combination with other risks. Such a requirement, however, would summon the physician to second-guess the patient, whose ideas on materiality could hardly be known to the physician."), *cert. denied*, 409 U.S. 1064 (1972).
3. *Id.* at 783 ("The majority of courts dealing with the problem have made the duty depend on whether it was the custom of physicians practicing in the community to make the particular disclosure to the patient [footnote omitted]").
4. *See, e.g.*, Bly v. Rhoads, 216 Va. 645, 222 S.E.2d 783 (1976) (Court required expert testimony to establish the scope of disclosure that a reasonable medical practitioner would provide under similar circumstances).
5. Canterbury v. Spence, *supra* ref. 3 at 784 ("Respect for the patient's right of self-determination on particular therapy demands a standard set by law for physicians rather than one which physicians may or may not impose upon themselves." [footnotes omitted]); Myers, MJ: Comment: Informed consent in medical malpractice. Calif L Rev 55:1396, 1967.
6. Crain v. Allison, 443 A.2d 558, 562 (D.C. App. 1982).
7. Keeton, WP (ed): Prosser and Keeton on Torts, ed 5. West, St. Paul, 1984, pp 482 *et seq.*
8. Dornette, WHL: Care of the teeth during endoscopy and anesthesia. Chapter 14 in Dornette, WHL (ed): Legal Aspects of Anesthesia. FA Davis, Philadelphia, 1972, p 213.
9. Hoffson v. Orentreich, 144 Misc.2d 411, 543 N.Y.S.2d 242 (Sup. Ct., N.Y. Co., Trial Term, Part 43, 1989).
10. Annas, GJ: Avoiding malpractice suits through informed consent. Leg Med Ann 29:228, 1977.
11. Salgo v. Trustees of Leland Stanford Hospital, 154 Cal.App.2d 560, 317 P.2d 170 (Sup. Ct. 1957).

COMMON LAW STANDARDS FOR INFORMED CONSENT DISCLOSURE BY JURISDICTION

Jurisdiction	Citation	Year	Standard
Alabama	Fain v. Smith, 479 So.2d 1150.	1985	Objective
Alaska	Informed consent mandated by Alaska Stat. § 09.556(a).	1983	Not specified
Arizona	Gaston v. Hunter, 112 Arriz. 33, 588 P.2d 326.	1978	Professional
Arkansas	Pegram v. Sisco, 406 F. Supp. 776 (W.D. Ark.), *aff'd*, 547 F. 2d 1172 (8th Cir. 1976), applying state law.*	1976	Professional
California	Cobbs v. Grant, 8 Cal.3d 229, 104 Cal.Rptr. 505, 502 P.2d 1.	1972	Objective
Colorado	Bloskas v. Munay, 618 P.2d 719 (App.)	1980	Professional
Connecticut	Logan v. Greenwich Hosp. Ass'n., 191 Conn. 282, 465 A.2d 294.	1983	Objective
Delaware	Coleman v. Garrison, 327 A.2d 757 (Super. Ct. 1974), *aff'd*, 349 A.2d 8.	1975	Professional
District of Columbia	Canterbury v. Spence, 464 F.2d 772 (D.C.Cir.); *cert. denied* 409 U.S. 1064.	1972	Objective
Florida	Meretsky v. Ellenby, 370 So.2d 1222 (Fla. App.).	1979	Professional
Georgia	Physician's duty limited to disclosure in general terms of nature of proposed procedure. Ga. Stat. Ann. § 31-9-6(d).	1975	Doctrine not viable in Georgia
Hawaii	Informed consent mandated by Hawaii Rev. L. § 671-3 (6) R 16-85-25.	1982	Statutory†
Idaho	Riedinger v. Colburn, 361 F. Supp. 1073 (D.), applying state law.*	1973	Professional
Illinois	Carrnan v. Dypold, 63 Ill. App.3d 419, 379 N.E.2d 1365.	1978	Professional
Indiana	Revord v. Russell, 401 N.E.2d 763, 766 (C.C.A.4th).	1980	Professional
Iowa	Perin v. Hayne, 210 N.W.2d 609.	1973	Professional
Kansas	Funke v. Fieldman, 212 Kan. 524, 512 P.2d 539.	1973	Professional
Kentucky	Holton v. Pfingst, 534 S.W.2d 786.	1975	Professional
Louisiana	Percle v. St. Paul Fire and Marine Ins. Co., 349 So.2d 1289 (La. App.); *cert. denied*, 350 So.2d 1218	1977	Objective
Maine	Downer v. Vielleux, 322 A.2d 82.	1974	Professional
Maryland	Sard v. Hardy, 281 Md. 432, 379 A.2d 1014.	1977	Objective
Massachusetts	Harnish v. Children's Hospital Medical Center, 387 Mass. 152, 439 N.E.2d 240.	1982	Objective
Michigan	Roberts v. Young, 369 Mich. 133, 119 N.W.2d 627.	1963	Professional
Minnesota	Cornfeld v. Tongen, 262 N.W.2d 684.	1977	Mixed‡
Mississippi	Lathan v. Hayes, 495 So.2d 453.	1986	Objective
Missouri	Roberson v. Menorah Medical Center, 588 S.W.2d 134 (App.).	1979	Objective
Montana	Negaard v. Estate of Feda, 152 Mont. 47, 446 P.2d 436.	1968	Professional
Nebraska	Informed consent mandated by Neb. Rev. Stat. § 44-2816.	1978	Professional¶
Nevada	Informed consent mandated by Nev. Rev. Stat. § 41A.110.	1981	Not specified

Jurisdiction	Citation	Year	Standard
New Hampshire	Informed consent mandated by N.H. Rev. Stat. Ann. §§ 507-C:1 (III), 507-C:2 (II).	1983	Professional
New Jersey	Largey v. Rothman, 110 N.J. 204, 540 A.2d 504.	1988	Objective
New Mexico	Henning v. Parsons, 95 N.M. 454, 623 P.2d 574.	1982	Mixed‡
New York	Ogden v. Bhatti, 92 A.D.2d 658, 460 N.Y.S.2d 166.	1983	Professional
North Carolina	Dixon v. Peters, 306 S.E.2d 477 (App.) (affirming constitutionality of N.C. Gen. Stat. § 90-21.13).	1981	Objective
North Dakota	Wasem v. Laskowski, 274 N.W.2d 219.	1979	Objective
Ohio	Congrove v. Holmes, 37 Ohio Misc. 95, 308 N.E.2d 765.	1973	Objective
Oklahoma	Scott v. Bradford, 606 P.2d 554.	1979	Objective
Oregon	Arena v. Gingrich, 733 P.2d 75 (App.).	1987	Subjective
Pennsylvania	Cooper v. Roberts, 220 Pa.Super. 260, 286 A.2d 647.	1971	Objective
Rhode Island	Wilkinson v. Versey, 110 R.L 606, 295 A.2d 676.	1972	Objective
South Carolina	Hook v. Rothstein, 316 S.E.2d 690 (App.).	1984	Professional
South Dakota	Wheeldon v. Madison, 374 N.W.2d 367.	1985	Objective
Tennessee	German v. Nichopoulos, 577 S.W.2d 197 (App.).	1978	Professional
Texas	Wilson v. Scott, 412 S.W.2d 299.	1967	Professional
Utah	Informed consent mandated by Utah Code Ann. § 1909.	1977	Not specified
Vermont	Small v. Gifford Memorial Hosp., 133 Vt. 552, 349 A.2d 703.	1975	Objective
Virginia	Bly v. Rhoades, 217 Va. 645, 222 S.E.2d 783.	1976	Professional
Washington	Miller v. Kennedy, 11 Wash. App. 272, 522 P.2d 852	1974	Objective
West Virginia	Cross v. Trapp, 294 S.E.2d 446.	1982	Objective
Wisconsin	Scaria v. St. Paul Fire and Marine Ins. Co., 68 Wis.2d 1, 227 N.W.2d 647.	1975	Objective
Wyoming	Stundon v. Stadnik, 649 P.2d 16.	1970	Professional

*State courts in neither Arkansas nor Idaho have addressed the informed consent issue; the federal jurists in these cases are assuming that the appellate courts would so hold.

†Statute sets forth substantive nature of disclosure.

‡Combination of objective and professional standards.

¶Statute mandates use of professional standard.

STATES MANDATING INFORMED CONSENT BY STATUTE

Jurisdiction	Date	Standard
Alaska Stat. § 09.55.556	1983	Not specified
Delaware Code Ann. tit. 18 § 6852 (Supp.)	1982	Professional
Florida Stat. Ann. § 768.46 (West Supp.)	1983	Professional
Hawaii Rev. Stat. § 671-3 (1976 & Supp.)	1982	Not specified
Idaho Code §§ 39.4301-.4306	1977	Professional
Iowa Code Ann. § 147.137 (West Supp.)	1983–1984	Not specified
Kentucky Rev. Stat. § 304.40-320	1981	Professional
Louisiana Rev. Stat. Ann. § 40:1299.40 (West)	1977	Not specified
Maine Rev. Stat. Ann. tit. 24, § 2905 (Supp.)	1983–1984	Professional
Nebraska Rev. Stat. § 44-2816	1978	Professional
Nevada Rev. Stat. § 41A.I10	1981	Not specified
New Hampshire Rev Stat. Ann. §§ 507-C 1 (III), 507-C:2 (II)	1983	Professional
New York Pub. Health Law § 2805-d (McKinney)	1977	Professional
North Carolina Gen. Stat. § 90-21.13	1981	Professional
Ohio Rev. Code Ann. § 2317.54 (Page)	1981	Not specified
Oregon Rev. Stat. § 677.097	1981	Professional*
Pennsylvania Stat. Ann. tit. 40, § 1301.103 (Purdon Supp.)	1983–1984	Objective
Rhode Island Gen. Laws § 9-19-32 (Supp.)	1983	Not specified
Tennessee Code Ann. § 29-26-118	1980	Professional
Texas Rev. Cit. Stat. Ann. art. 4590i, §§ 6.01-.07 (Vernon Supp.)	1982–1983	Objective†
Utah Code Ann. § 78-14-5	1977	Not specified
Vermont Stat. Ann. tit. 12, § 1909 (Supp.)	1983	Professional
Washington, Rev. Code Ann. §§ 7.70.050, 7.70.060 (Supp.)	1983–1984	Objective

*This statutory provision mandating a professional standard for disclosure was overturned by Arena v. Gingrich, 84 Or.App. 25, 733 P.2d 75 (C.App. 1987), which mandates a subjective disclosure.

†Statute requires creation of a Texas medical disclosure panel to determine both which risks must be disclosed and the substantive nature of that disclosure.

10

Clement J. Markarian, C.R.N.A., M.A.

The Anesthesia Record

HISTORICAL BACKGROUND

Although the first anesthetic was introduced to the medical profession in 1846 at the Massachusetts General Hospital (MGH), details of anesthetic administrations were not documented until nearly half a century later. The earliest known anesthesia records were first prepared in 1894, some 50 years after the discovery of surgical anesthesia.[1] Two medical students, Cushing and Codman, frequently were delegated to administer anesthesia at MGH; they worked out a system of intermittently recording the pulse and respirations.[2] These first records were known as "ether charts." In 1902 Cushing incorporated the intermittent graphic recording of blood pressure following his familiarization with Riva-Rocci's instrument for assessing this newly measured physiologic parameter.[2] Thus, with the addition of this

datum, the anesthetic record was established, and it became the basis of the record
we know today.

PURPOSES OF
DOCUMENTATION

Since the early ether charts, anesthesia
personnel have been faced with increasing
responsibilities for record keeping. Indeed,
the importance of documenting all aspects
of medical care has long been recognized.
The Standard for Medical Record Services
(MR 1.2) of the Joint Commission on Accreditation of Healthcare Organizations
(JCAHO) lists the purposes of the medical
record as follows:

*MR.1.2.1 To serve as a basis for planning pa-
tient care and for continuity in the evaluation of the patient's condition and treatment;*
 *MR.1.2.2 To furnish documentary evi-
dence of the course of the patient's medical
evaluation, treatment, and change in condition during the hospital stay, during an ambulatory care or emergency visit to the hospital, or while being followed in a
hospital-administered home care program;*
 *MR.1.2.3 To document communication
between the practitioner responsible for the
patient and any other health care professional who contributes to the patient's care;*
 *MR.1.2.4 To assist in protecting the legal
interest of the patient, the hospital, and the
practitioner responsible for the patient; and*
 *MR.1.2.5 To provide data for use in con-
tinuing education and in research.[3]*

If good records are essential to the development of any science, then the discipline
of anesthesia has progressed more rapidly
from an art to a science than perhaps any
other specialty in medicine or nursing.
From Cushing's first charts that recorded
the three basic vital signs—blood pressure,
pulse, and respiration—the modern anesthetic record has become a thorough, legible (it is hoped!), complex, sequential, informational account of the patient's
anesthetic encounter. Every physiological
parameter that is to be monitored should be
not only more or less continuously measured, but also recorded. Properly prepared
following careful monitoring, the modern
record will reflect all pertinent findings,
documented at sufficiently frequent inter-

vals to allow concurrent, or later, assessment of the patient's condition at any giv-
en moment during the surgical procedure
and anesthetic administration.

Proof of Care

As previously stated, an anesthetic
record should be prepared in such a manner
that anyone at a later time can reconstruct
exactly what occurred during the administration of the anesthetic. Therefore, the
record must be neat, legible, accurate,
clear, precise, complete, and somewhat
concise. The last element may be impossible if all of the former elements are entirely satisfied. Nonetheless, if any element is
omitted or performed in a haphazard manner, then the events that took place become
tainted, and any later attempt at recon-
struction of those events becomes quite difficult or impossible.

Additionally, the record should be prepared contemporaneously with the event(s)
it purports to document. This admonition,
which may be difficult to accomplish during some inductions and most emergencies, is discussed further below.

The old adage "If it isn't in the record, it
wasn't done" has a firm jurisprudential basis. Lack of a notation creates a strong inference that there was an act of omission,
an inference that is very difficult to overcome in a court of law (discussed later). On
the other hand, it is inconceivable that an
absolutely complete anesthetic record has
ever been written. There are countless observations—of skin characteristics and va-
sodilation, to name a couple—that are never recorded on even the most diligent
professional's chart. How often are vital
signs checked at intervals shorter than the
traditional 5 minutes and never charted?
One easily runs out of space attempting to
insert entries on and then between these 5-
minute vertical grid lines.

Additionally, unexplained entries can
render charts incomplete. A misinterpreta-
tion can occur when a dose of lidocaine is
administered and the chart does not explain that the drug was utilized as an intravenous laryngeal-tracheal anesthetic and
not as an antiarrhythmic. Spacial limitations account not only for incompleteness
but also for illegibility and inaccuracies.

When several events occur almost simultaneously and must be charted in confined spaces, the record may become illegible. Inaccuracies then develop during any later attempt to determine the exact sequence of events. Other discrepancies may occur during periods of maximum activity when charting must of necessity be delayed and recorded later. Data committed to memory until they can be documented are always subject to error. Personnel should endeavor to develop a methodology for preparing short but legible notations, from which data can later be transferred to the anesthesia record.

To fulfill one of its purposes, an anesthetic record must offer proof of adequate anesthesia care. Anesthesia personnel therefore must be able to submit documentary evidence that each has continuously taken care of the patient to his or her best knowledge and ability. The common law has held that anesthesia personnel must conduct their professional practices in accordance with accepted medical and nursing standards (Chapters 2 and 3). Traditionally, these standards are equated with those in the same community. These standards now are national in scope (as, for example, those of the JCAHO cited earlier) and apply to all aspects of care, including documentation. Each anesthetist and anesthesiologist is expected to bring to his or her practice a reasonable degree of skill, knowledge, and experience, and to exercise reasonable care. The best way to verify that these ingredients are present is by meticulous documentation. It is not negligent per se to engage in poor record keeping (unless, of course, the faulty record proximately leads to an untoward outcome). Yet, trial courts have taken a dim view of records that are messy, inaccurate, illegible, unclear, imprecise, incomplete, or have been altered in any manner.

Individual Forms

Before addressing the anesthetic record itself, it should be clearly understood that the particular design of any record is not as important as having all the information available in an interpretable format. It is possible that every institution in this country has its own record; often these incorporate the particular whims of its designer or user. One can review the relevant literature on form design and incorporate the industry's standards to improve most forms currently in use. Some recommendations include:

- Use of separate forms, obviating the need to place information on the back of forms, thereby being able to view the complete record at any one time without flipping pages
- Use of similar graphs in anesthetic and recovery room records to facilitate easy comparison
- Avoidance of sections that utilize specific printed names of drugs or techniques, thus wasting space if those particular items or methods are not employed
- Adherence to a minimal amount of repetition from form to form

Of utmost importance is that the well-designed record should be clearly understood at a glance and prepared in such a manner that upon reading it, another professional or a layperson (e.g., a judge or juror) can reconstruct the fundamental facts and the course of the anesthetic as it really was administered.

COMPONENTS OF THE ANESTHESIA RECORD

When the words *anesthesia record* are used, what comes to most persons' minds is the *anesthesia graphic chart*, that portion of the record used to document what happens to the patient in the operating room. In actuality, the anesthesia record consists of four components—preanesthesia note, intraoperative record, recovery room record, and postanesthesia note. (I prefer the terms *preanesthesia* and *postanesthesia note* to *preoperative* and *postoperate note*, reserving the latter for entries by the surgeon.) Standard practice suggests that anesthesia records include a minimum of three written documentations. These are delineated in the published guidelines for maintaining anesthesia records by the JCAHO under Surgical and Anesthesia Services, SA.1.5,[4] and by the American Society of Anesthesiologists (Table 10-1).

TABLE 10-1. Documentation of Anesthesia Care*

I   Preanesthesia Evaluation[†]
  A Patient interview to review:
    1 Medical history
    2 Anesthesia history
    3 Medication history
  B Appropriate physical examination.
  C Review of objective diagnostic data (e.g., laboratory, ECG, x-ray)
  D Assignment of ASA physical status
  E Formulation and discussion of an anesthesia plan with the patient and/or responsible adult
II Perianesthesia (time-based record of events)
  A Immediate review prior to initiation of anesthetic procedures:
    1 Patient re-evaluation
    2 Check of equipment, drugs and gas supply
  B Monitoring of the patient[‡] (e.g., recording of vital signs)
  C Amounts of all drugs and agents used, and times given
  D The type and amounts of all intravenous fluids used including blood and blood products, and times given
  E The technique(s) used
  F Unusual events during the anesthesia period
  G The status of the patient at the conclusion of anesthesia
III Postanesthesia
  A Patient evaluation on admission and discharge from the postanesthesia care unit
  B A time-based record of vital signs and level of consciousness
  C All drugs administered and their dosages
  D Type and amounts of intravenous fluids administered including blood and blood products
  E Any unusual events including postanesthesia or postprocedural complications
  F Postanesthesia visits

---

*Approved by House of Delegates of the American Society of Anesthesiologists on October 12, 1988; reprinted with permission of the ASA.
[†]See ASA Standard for Preanesthesia Care (Table 8-1).
[‡]See Standards for Basic Intraoperative Monitoring (Table 12-1).

Preanesthesia Note

Initially, the preanesthesia evaluation is conducted during a preoperative interview and the appropriate documentation is recorded in the patient's medical record. The preoperative interview furnishes anesthesia personnel with a wealth of information, all of which should be recorded. Nearly all the preoperative data are available elsewhere in the patient's chart; anesthesia personnel often will transfer this information onto the preanesthesia portion of the anesthesia record form. While the patient's preoperative status is evaluated by both the surgical and anesthesia staffs, the anesthesia interview serves to focus on information that has specific implications in the conduct of the anesthetic.

Following the preanesthetic interview and evaluation, or preferably during the interview, the information and physical findings should be entered on an overprint form, on a section of the anesthetic record specifically designed for preoperative documentation, or written in longhand in the doctor's progress notes under the title "anesthetic preop note." The following information should be included:

- Usual patient identification data of name, age, hospital register number, race, sex, height, weight
- Date and time of interview; diagnosis and proposed procedure with its time or urgency (emergency or elective)
- American Society of Anesthesiologists (ASA) physical status (PS) classification
- Whether the patient was interviewed, the chart reviewed, or both
- Pertinent facts relating to the patient's history with emphasis on previous anesthetics and any problems encountered
- Family history regarding the same
- Personal habits of smoking, drink-

ing, and drug history, both pre-scribed and others
- Allergies if any
- A brief statement of physical examination findings with reference to all systems or organs directly related to the administration of anesthesia
- Vital signs, including temperature
- All laboratory results
- The proposed anesthetic technique and any alternatives, if applicable
- The counseling note and the patient's consent to the proposed plan (i.e., documentation that informed consent to anesthesia has been obtained)
- Any questions that the patient may have that have been satisfactorily answered
- The signature of the interviewing anesthetist or anesthesiologist

Some practitioners may include the proposed preliminary medication in their note; however, this information usually can be found in the physician's order sheet, where sleeping medications, nothing-by-mouth (NPO) status, and any additional lab, x-ray, or consultations also will be ordered.

Occasionally a patient will refuse the primary anesthetic agent or technique recommended by anesthesia personnel. *First,* when this happens, I recommend that the refused agent or technique be listed in the preanesthesia counseling note, as well as the alternative anesthetic that will be administered. This listing precludes one particularly vexing problem. Whether the patient refuses or accepts your first choice might seem immaterial until you are forced to explain from the witness stand why the plaintiff's expert witness just testified that the best choice was the one you never documented as having offered the patient. Thus, one's proposed technique could list two or even more alternatives with a remark that the initial proposal(s) was (were) refused by the patient. *Second,* it may not be desirable to list specific drugs or agents. By doing so, the anesthetist is locked into administering, for example, a halothane endotracheal anesthetic rather than a general endotracheal anesthetic. There may be a good reason to change agents intraoperatively, as in the case of substituting another volatile liquid for halothane if the sur-

geon suddenly decides to use excessive amounts of a local anesthesia with epinephrine.

Finally, it would behoove anesthesia personnel to have patients sign or initial the counseling statement wherein the proposed technique and the range of risks and complications have been explained in writing. This simple measure may preclude filing of a claim or lawsuit, and satisfy the irate family member who contends that their relative would never have consented to anything that could result in an intraoperative cardiac arrest and death. This precaution is in addition to the standard anesthesia and operative consent form commonly employed in most medical treatment facilities and routinely signed by patients, thus documenting the fact that they consented to these procedures and precluding actions for battery.

Preoperative notes need not be single entries; they often require follow-up notations, especially if return visits are required. An example of such a revisit could be necessitated by having to counsel parents or a legal guardian who may not have been present at the time of the initial visit to an unemancipated minor. Under these circumstances, the second entry should note that the parents or guardian were counseled and understand and accept the risks and complications of the anesthetic for the minor.

Similarly, laboratory or radiographic data that were not available the evening before should be incorporated in a separate note added the morning of the operation prior to induction of anesthesia. This note would include data from any additional or repeat tests ordered prior to the operation. Such an entry will then complete the preoperative assessment (which would otherwise be incomplete), thus precluding any later allegation that the anesthetist or anesthesiologist was unaware of these data should an untoward event or complication occur that could be directly related to the missing information.

Intraoperative Anesthesia Record

The classic anesthesia record incorporates patient identification information as well as quantitative patient data. Identification information usually includes the addressograph plate elements, date of procedure, names of surgeons, signature(s) of anesthesia personnel, and the operation performed. Other pertinent information that must be immediately available during the anesthetic is often transferred from the preoperative evaluation sheet. Height, weight, age, as well as the important laboratory data of hemoglobin, hematocrit, potassium, blood glucose, and similar results are transferred along with the ASA PS, allergies, and preliminary medication with time and route administered. It is also a reasonable idea to chart the effects of the preliminary medication for future reference. A simple four-star evaluation system does nicely—four stars indicate excellent sedation and tranquility; three, good; two, fair; and one, poor or undesirable. Additionally, estimated blood volumes, tidal volumes, and calculations for minute ventilation and hourly fluid maintenance rates should be recorded and readily available.

With the recent introduction of sophisticated electronic equipment and gas anesthesia apparatus, anesthesia personnel must necessarily make an entry on the anesthesia record that these various devices have been checked and are functioning properly. A detailed note is not necessary if a routine is established and followed for each equipment check. For example, the manufacturer of the Modulus One machine recommends some 39 procedures to verify that this gas anesthesia apparatus is safe for patient use. In this case, a single entry of "Modulus machine no. _____ checked" would be sufficient, in lieu of documenting each of the 39 items covered in the procedure. As long as the routine remains the same, and the anesthetist can verify that each machine check is done in the same manner (i.e., high- and low-pressure checks, purging of all vaporizers, checking each fail-safe valve, checks of the oxygen analyzer, high and low tension, and so on), then documenting the extensive and timely machine check can be simplified as previously described. (Fortunately for practitioners, the newer Modulus Two has simplified these check devices, conserving time and eliminating many of the above-mentioned steps.)

The major portion of the record is occupied by two graphs and a series of smaller boxes, each designated for a specific entry or purpose. Generally the top graph gives the dynamic picture of the anesthetic technique and management, and the second graph shows the patient's responses. The vertical lines represent 5- and 15-minute time intervals. The horizontal lines in the upper section are used to delineate and record the anesthetic agents and adjunctive drugs. Each agent or drug is correctly identified by percent concentration if applicable and appropriate units of measurement and dosage. Given the available pharmaceutical armamentarium, it would be extremely difficult to record all agents in a uniform manner. Gases must be charted in liters per minute (L/min); most adjunctive drugs in milligrams (mg) and occasionally in milliliters (ml) if the milligram figures occupy more space than the time interval blocks allow. Obviously certain potent drugs may require dosages registered in micrograms. Ultimately, timeliness and accuracy take precedence over uniformity in units for recording drug dosages.

When specifically calibrated vaporizers are used for volatile liquids, the percent concentrations of the agents generally are charted. If a universal vaporizer (e.g., Kopper Kettle or Vernitrol) is employed, however, it is far better to chart the parameters known or given rather than a calculated percent concentration. Thus, instead of charting calculations that could also be computed incorrectly, it is far safer to chart given facts as vaporizer temperature, milliliters of flow over the liquid in the vaporizer, and total gas flow, and allow the inquisitive individual to do his or her own calculations. Of course, it is important to know that flowing 110 ml/min over halothane at 20°C (a vapor pressure of 243 mm Hg) and a total diluent gas flow of 5 L will yield 1% of halothane. In a court of law, however, where one cannot absolutely guarantee that 1% halothane was being delivered under the same set of circumstances, it would be hazardous to have charted anything but facts. From a practical standpoint, the patient received "quantity sufficient" rather than a calculated percent.

The second graph is provided for recording vital signs, the values for which are on a vertical axis, numbered 0 to 240 and marked with universally understood symbols (Appendix 10-1). Respirations are further charted as being spontaneous, assisted, or controlled and, if the last, whether manually or mechanically achieved. If a mechanical ventilator is employed, one also needs to indicate the type of ventilator, tidal volume setting (preferably verified by a mechanical device, e.g., Wright respirometer), and the pressures generated so that changes in lung compliance and muscle relaxation can be noted. Ultimately, it is not important what symbols and abbreviations are used in charting; of utmost importance is the use of a reference section on the anesthetic record to explain the meaning of the symbols and acronyms.

Space is usually provided to indicate if the induction is satisfactory or unsatisfactory. If an induction sequence was recorded as unsatisfactory, an explanation should follow, indicating why. Singultus, laryngeal spasm, prolonged excitement, bronchospasm, and emesis or regurgitation certainly qualify as a few of the unsatisfactory events that complicate inductions. Space is also provided to show the surgical position of the patient and, if there are intraoperative posture changes, these are recorded against the time graph. Positions can either be written longhand or diagrammed with self-explanatory stick symbols.

The section on airway management requires documentation of:

- Type of airway
- The size of a laryngoscope blade
- Endotracheal catheter size and whether oral or nasal and cuffed or uncuffed
- Method of intubation, direct vision or blind
- Number of intubation attempts
- Utilization of stylet or Magill forceps
- Anesthetic ointment or lubricant
- Amount of air injected into cuff
- Use of pharyngeal pack
- Whether insertion of the device(s) was accompanied by trauma or damage to the tissues, lips, teeth, tongue, or any other surface exposed to endoscopy and intubation

One often sees a remark in this section reading "atraumatic intubation times one under direct vision" indicating an ideal in-

tubation. Only upon suctioning, prior to extubation, does the anesthetist find sufficient amounts of bloody sputum to indicate that "atraumatic" was not the case at all. Under such circumstances, it may be more prudent to make an entry indicating the intubation was accomplished "times one, under direct vision and without apparent difficulty" rather than documenting something that one assumes rather than definitely knows to be factual.

Special horizontal columns, again plotted against time, should be available for charting temperature, central venous pressure, continuous electrocardiography, oxygen saturation, precordial or esophageal heart and breath sounds, peripheral nerve stimulation monitoring, estimated intraoperative blood loss, Foley and nasogastric catheter outputs, pulmonary wedge pressures, and any other physiological parameter or output monitored.

All infusions including blood transfusions are graphically recorded, again being plotted against the time axis. Information about cannula, needle, or catheter used for venipuncture or cutdown—denoting the type, size, its location, and type of infusion administered—is also documented.

The volumes infused should be noted periodically so one can determine exactly, at any given time, the total replacement of all fluids, whole blood, and blood fraction(s). When a type-specific blood product is employed, the identification numbers, blood type, verification procedures, reactions, and expiration dates of all products must be recorded on the anesthetic record. Similarly, all measured or estimated (as accurately as possible) blood and fluid losses, including sequestered and third spacing, are noted on the record.

The final two predesigned spaces on the typical anesthetic record are for recording the method or technique and the anesthetic level, the former summarizing all of the anesthetic technique(s)—including general, regional, and local—and all agents including total dosages. If a regional technique is employed (e.g., subarachnoid block), the anesthetist would routinely chart:

- The position of the patient while administering the block
- Type of prep, including agent uti-

lized and number of applications

- Vertebral interspace level and anatomical approach (midline versus lateral) of the lumbar puncture
- Concentration and agent used for dermal anesthesia
- Gauge of introducer (if one is employed) and that of the lumbar puncture needle
- Number of insertions or attempts
- Presence or lack of paresthesias (with location when elicited)
- Character of cerebrospinal fluid and its flow
- Quadrant changes
- Aspiration or flow of cerebrospinal fluid both prior to and following injection
- Concentration of spinal anesthetic agent injected with total volumes and dosages of solutions and vasoconstrictors (if added to the mixture)
- The manufacturer's name, lot number, and expiration date of any disposable tray used

If any drugs are substituted or added to the tray, then their manufacturer nomenclature, lot numbers, and expiration dates also should be recorded. The level of sensory and motor block can be charted in the space provided for that purpose and levels should be assessed as soon as feasible following administration of the block. Sensory level determination is especially important at the onset of the block, at the time of drug fixation, at the end of the operative procedure, and once in the recovery room.

There remains a host of details that have no specific section allotted for their entry and could never be recorded graphically. Therefore, a "Remarks" column serves to accommodate all the additional observations, treatments, difficulties, reactions, and complications that accompany the anesthetic experience. When numbered, these remarks can be entered along the corresponding time slot for proper sequencing of events. Typical remarks could read:

1 Ohio 30/70 machine no. 001843 checked.
2 Patient identified and 16-ga Jelco (2-in cath) inserted in right basilic vein with Bacitracin ointment and dressing.

3 Transfer to operating room table and monitors applied.
4 Preoxygenation by mask.
5 Induction.
6 Endoscopy and LTA with 4% lidocaine, 160 mg total.
7 Intubation.
8 Bilateral and equal breath sounds (B = BS).
9 Esoph steth, oral temp probe and small Berman airway inserted.
10 Lacrilube ointment OU and taped.
11 Turned over to surgeons (TOTS).
12 Surgical shave and prep.
13 Ventilator on: VT = 1000 cc, rate = 8 PM, 20 cm of H_2O pressure, B = BS.
14 Tourniquet up on left arm to 300 mm Hg at 0805 hrs.
15 Arterial stick X1 right radial artery with 25-ga needle, spec—lab for ABG.
16 Surgeon notified of 1-hr tourniquet time.

and so on.

The same detailed notes apply for the remainder of the procedure through emergence, extubation, and transfer to the recovery suite. Obviously, the list is dependent on the event and whether it is considered important enough to be noted by the anesthetist. It is desirable to record not only anesthesia comments but also surgical aspects of the procedure that are related to changes in the patient's condition. Examples of the latter include

- Clamping times of major vessels
- Surgical manipulations causing bradycardia or hypotension, and remedial measures
- Placement of surgical packs with possible compression of blood vessels or diaphragmatic excursions
- Removal of specimens
- Results of sponge count
- Drains inserted, layers closed
  and any other pertinent information.

Starting and ending times of both anesthesia and operation are sometimes recorded in the remarks section as well as marked on the zero line utilizing their respective symbols. The significance of distinguishing between these routine times and a TOTS time is that there is documented evidence of why the "downtime" occurs. Past practice has often operated on the premise that "all things being equal, anesthesia is to blame." If the start of anesthesia of 0730 hours and the TOTS time is recorded at 0740 hours, the reasonable utilization of 10 minutes required to induce, intubate, and stabilize the patient before releasing him or her to the surgeon is documented. If the operative procedure is commenced at 0900 hours, it is obvious that the surgical prep, positioning, and the like are responsible for the additional delay. Without a TOTS indication or remark explaining a delay, it would appear that 90 minutes elapsed between the start of anesthesia and the start of the operation, with the anesthesia service most likely to take the brunt of the blame.

In summary, the intraoperative record, consisting of both graphic entries and written notations, should accurately and dynamically reflect a patient's status during the operative and anesthetic course.

Recovery Room Records

The actual records kept in the recovery room are not the direct responsibility of anesthesia personnel.* Upon arrival from the operating room, however, anesthesia personnel are responsible for a transfer report and note. This transfer note is often referred to as a "postop" note and its time frame is correctly reflected by the term "postop." It is the first note written immediately after the operation and is prepared in conjunction with the anesthesia person's verbal report to the professional member of the recovery staff responsible for the patient. It is important to note that one is *transferring the responsibility* for care of the patient *from one professional to another.*

In order to ascertain the professional strata, one must look at the structure of the recovery room staff. If a physician is part of that staff and physically present in the unit, then the hierarchy begins with the physician. Many institutions have an anesthesi-

*A member of the anesthesia staff generally has responsibility for overall supervision of the operation of the recovery room; hence, he or she is indirectly responsible for ensuring that recovery room record keeping meets current standards; see Chapter 13.

ologist in charge of the recovery room, who will usually discharge those patients who have recovered from their anesthetic. He or she is not continually present, however, and therefore the claim will normally begin with a registered nurse.

The anesthetist's *verbal* report informs the recovery room personnel of the following information about the patient:

- Name, age, ASA classification, weight
- Any significant preop physical conditions
- History of allergies and drug therapy, both prior to admission and since hospitalized
- Preliminary medication and its effects
- Operative procedure(s) carried out
- Anesthetic technique with agents utilized, including the time of the last dose of any narcotic
- Reversal of any drugs
- Findings
- Sizes and locations of catheters, tubes, and drains, both visible and under dressing
- Total fluids: input to include crystalloid and colloid
- Output of all drains and catheters
- Transfusions and the last intraoperative hematocrit
- Reactions
- Vital sign trends
- Closing pressures or values for oxygen saturation, central venous pressure, temperature, pulmonary wedge, and similar monitoring parameters
- Any observations or areas of caution that the anesthetist or anesthesiologist wants to reinforce (see also Chapter 13)

Inasmuch as all the just-cited information is already included on the well-prepared anesthetic record, there is no need to reiterate it on the transfer note. The recovery room *transfer note* should contain:

- The date and time
- Location of transfer
- Physical and mental condition of the patient, including types of responsiveness, reflexes, and level of consciousness
- Vital signs as established by recovery room personnel

- Position, patency, and condition of all infusion and monitoring lines
- Any therapy initiated since leaving the operating room with all pertinent data
- Any complaints of the patient
- The person taking the report, who will be identified by title and name
- Any item of concern that was reinforced in the verbal report
- The anesthetist's or anesthesiologist's signature

Postoperative Visit and Note

The postoperative visit provides for continuity of patient care and furnishes data regarding the acceptability of the anesthetic to the consumer. The opportunity to explain untoward responses to drugs or that the patient presented with a difficult intubation or other problem is of vital importance. Such information can contribute to a more informed patient and may prevent serious anesthetic problems in the future. This invaluable data should be retrievable from medical records for future procedures in which the patient requires an anesthetic. Unfortunately, this is a theoretical statement rather than a truism, since in reality, past medical records are seldom available for review.

A minimum of one postoperative note, excluding the recovery room transfer note, was required under the old Joint Commission on Accreditation of Hospitals (JCAH) standards if no anesthetic complication was found during the first postoperative visit. This requirement mandated that the note make *specific* reference to the presence *or absence* of anesthetic complications.[5] If a complication was noted, subsequent visits were made and the condition followed until it was resolved or the patient was discharged. The new JCAHO standards have been revised to reflect current changes in the delivery of anesthesia care. The wording of the new standards has taken on a very generalized translation rather than the specific interpretation under the older ones. The new standards call for notes in the medical record to explain "any unusual events or postoperative complications and the management of those events."[6] It

would appear that adhering to the older, more stringent standard could enhance patient care by providing follow-up through resolution and/or discharge. Of course, the facts surrounding any visit are documented in the progress notes.

Documenting Complications

What comprises an anesthetic complication may vary according to institutional policy and personal bias. A typical example of the latter would have the chief of surgery maintaining that any surgical patient who has a postoperative temperature elevation has an anesthetic complication. Most true anesthetic complications are obvious, however, and generally not dictated by such policies or individuals.

The postoperative note addresses:

- The numbered postoperative day
- Location of the visit
- The operative procedure performed, which may be different from what was originally scheduled
- The anesthetic technique, which might also differ
- Any sequelae arising from intraanesthetic complications, for example, an infection from a submucosal dissection during nasal intubation
- Memory recall
- Lacerations, and other soft tissue injury
- Sore throat or dental injury
- Specific patient complaints

The note gives particular emphasis to systems prone to develop complications secondary to anesthesia, for example, respiratory, cardiovascular, central nervous, and hepatorenal. The signature of the person conducting the postoperative interview, date, and time will complete the postoperative note.

Occasionally, a patient may be discharged before a postoperative visit can be conducted; a note still should appear in the medical record. Under these circumstances, the note should reflect that the patient's chart and progress notes were reviewed without the patient being interviewed and no apparent anesthesia complications were found or noted by the discharging physician.

Finally, the postoperative note will help identify cases that should be present at the anesthesia morbidity and mortality conference or other staff meeting. (No mention should be made in the record that the case has been so identified, however.)

CHANGES IN RECORD-KEEPING METHODOLOGY

Anesthesia practice has in recent years become so complex that it is increasingly difficult for one individual to attend to all aspects of ideal patient care. Sophisticated electronic equipment has become routine in anesthesia care, and this equipment requires setup preparation, calibration, and continual monitoring throughout an anesthetic procedure. Meticulous charting—to the degree previously discussed—has also become a full-time task. An excellent record is of little value if the anesthetic was poor; quite obviously, care of the patient should never be sacrificed for the sake of the paperwork. Still, if we operate on the premise that records serve in identifying deficiencies in one's practice, the dilemma is quite obvious.

Perhaps it is time to place the anesthetic record in its proper perspective and resolve this dilemma. Should the anesthetic record portray the continuous moment-to-moment physiologic response to anesthesia? This traditional concept has become distorted and certainly has been capitalized upon by one's adversaries in the courtroom. It is entirely plausible that Cushing and Codman meant their ether charts to represent a mere summary of the monitoring of the physiologic responses to surgery and anesthesia rather than a documented beat-by-beat log. The magnitude of effort required to prepare a "legally acceptable" modern-day anesthetic record cannot help but distract from attentiveness to the patient. Conversely, the law expects certain things from professionals engaged in anesthesia practice. That expectation is to care for the patient in a manner that meets the recognized and accepted standard of care within the anesthesia specialty. Anesthesia personnel cannot administer anesthesia, continually monitor the patient, and document that process in its entirety. At best,

an acceptable medium is exercised and this balance is where anesthesia practice has been carried out for a number of years. The anesthetist administers the anesthetic, cares for the patient, and prepares a chart that reflects a periodic assessment of the parameters monitored.

LEGAL ASPECTS OF THE RECORD

Much has been written on the legal aspects of medical record keeping.[7-10] The influence of charting upon liability (or lack of it) stems from the rationale that maintaining complete and accurate records contributes to quality patient care and reduces the likelihood of some types of patient injury. If a complication does occur despite good care, and the latter is documented well in the records, the likelihood is strong that no liability will be forthcoming. Good documentation and good care go hand in hand, often with complete mitigation of liability. Good documentation not only provides strong evidence of good care, but allows health care providers to accurately refresh their memories several years later when litigation ripens and review of prior care becomes essential. If a case does come to trial, a *sine qua non* for anesthesia personnel is to be able to accurately reconstruct the events, by completely reviewing those events as documented in the record.

Introduction of Records Into Evidence

It is estimated that as many as 85% of all civil cases litigated involve medical evidence of one type or another. The medical record generally becomes a vital piece of evidence in such cases. Traditionally, records could not be introduced under the hearsay rule. Unless the individual who prepared the record was in court to give direct testimony and be cross-examined about what was written, the material contained in the record constituted hearsay. Hearsay is evidence that does not come from the personal knowledge of the witness, but is only a repetition of what he or she has heard others say. The problem with hearsay evidence is not the veracity of the witness who is attempting to give it, but that the individual who made the original statement is not in court to be cross-examined on it.

There are, however, several common law, statutory, and judicial exceptions to this rule. Of foremost importance is the Uniform Business Records as Evidence Act.[9] Records that are kept as part of the regular course of business, and prepared at or near the time the event they intend to portray took place, will be admitted providing the custodian of the record (e.g., the medical records librarian) testifies as to the mode of preparation, and that it meets the aforestated criteria. Each person who made an entry into the record need not be present subsequently to testify to bolster that record's admission.

There are several other methods for introducing medical records. The Shopbook Rule originated in England,[11] the shopbook being an original record kept by a shopkeeper indicating services performed and accounts due for the work. Documents that qualify as official public records constitute another method for introducing certain medical records. Finally, statutes in a number of states allow direct and specific admissibility of certain hospitals' medical records. Photocopies and microfilms of original records, and computer printouts, also can be admitted under the aforestated criteria. Finally, if the parties to the litigation stipulate (agree) that the records may be admitted, the hearsay rule and its exceptions become irrelevant.

Privileged Information and Confidentiality

Communications between a patient and health care provider are considered privileged. The patient holds the privilege that the health care provider will not divulge the information outside of the health care setting (see also Chapter 2). Once a patient places his or her medical condition at issue by filing a lawsuit alleging that he or she was harmed through the negligent care of a health care provider, however, the medical records are no longer privileged insofar as they have evidential value in the litigation. Disclosure of this information beyond the extent necessary in furtherance of the litigation would still constitute a violation of the physician-patient privilege.

Spoliation

The term *spoliation* refers to any alteration, destruction, or loss of a record pertinent to the litigation at hand. The question may arise whether an individual who alters a medical record does so in a conscious attempt to avoid responsibility for his or her actions. Does such an act constitute a fraudulent attempt to suppress evidence? Should the burden of proof be shifted to the custodian of the record who lost or altered it, to come forward and show why he or she should not be held in contempt of court? Or should the spoliation instruction by the judge to the jury suffice? In effect, this instruction allows the trier of fact to *infer* that the missing or altered record would have supported the cause of the party who did not have custody of the record. Perhaps one solution to problems of this type would be having the court take custody of the documents by a writ of attachment once a suit is filed. Such a writ would limit the opportunities for spoliation, if not eliminate it altogether.

Changing Entries in the Medical Record

While it is legally impermissible to delete entries from an "official" document (and the medical record is considered one), one may change an incorrect notation by lining it out, inserting the correct data, and initialing the change. *The original entry must remain legible.* The change should be initialed by the individual making the alteration. It is also possible to make a later addition to the record to document events that took place earlier. The later entry should be dated and timed to indicate exactly when it was placed on the chart. It should indicate the reason(s) why it was entered later, rather than in a timely fashion. It is considered fraud to predate an entry on the record to attempt to make it appear that it was written at an earlier time.

COMPUTERIZED RECORDS

The medical and nursing professions have kept abreast of technological advances in monitoring equipment, therapeutic modalities, newer pharmaceuticals, and research techniques. Unfortunately, however, in perhaps the majority of institutions, medical records and the associated paper load continue to be handled in much the same fashion as during the early days of anesthesia. As noted in the following paragraphs, computer-assisted anesthesia record keeping is a reality at the present time. Would failure to computerize anesthesia record keeping constitute a departure from the duty of care to one's patients?[12] Have a substantial number of practitioners changed their practice to incorporate computerized record keeping? Liability may be imposed for failing to adopt this new methodology, even though the majority of providers still adhere to older techniques, and customary practice does not yet mandate the use of computers.[12]

Changes in surgical practice have followed advances in medicine, pharmacology, and other scientific disciplines. These advances have been exemplified by the more intensive care of more seriously ill patients, who in consequence undergo more extensive operations. Furthermore, as the complexity of the modern anesthetic increases, there is less time to chart all of the monitoring variables as frequently and as accurately as required. Given the pitfalls of preparing ideal anesthetic records and the inability to produce them, the answer may lie with a semiautomated anesthesia record system. Certainly the technology and computer hardware components necessary to produce an automated system are available. It appears to this author that such an approach poses the most viable alternative and solution to the dilemma.

An automated anesthesia data system can provide not only relief for the anesthetist attempting to produce the ideal chart but also the means for instantaneous retrieval of patient data from any area within the hospital equipped with the system. Laboratory test results and ward progress notes could easily be brought into the operating room at the touch of a key. Likewise, intraoperative data can be transferred to the postoperative area once the operation is completed. The increased accuracy, timeliness, and uniformity in style and legibility thus would truly enhance record keeping. Intraoperatively, the rapid availability of calculated patient data (e.g., vital sign trends, cardiac outputs) would markedly enhance patient care. Automatic notification of drug allergies, overdosages, and incompatibilities, as well as calculations for drug doses, can be easily incorporated into the system. For patient safety, instantaneous notification of preset out-of-limit conditions to detect hypotension, tachycardia, hyperthermia, hypoxia, and so forth, can be programmed. Finally, automated systems can provide easy access to archived data and provide greater ease in patient billing.

Several investigators[13,14] have evaluated semiautomated record systems and compared these systems to traditional handwritten anesthesia records. Shaffer and colleagues[13] showed a number of limitations caused by hurried handwritten manual forms. Easy misalignment of carbon and copies while charting, crowding due to limitations in space, overlooked or incomplete entries, illegible copies, and losses were some of the inadequacies reported. Additional problems in the storage and retrieval of data were also shown by these authors. Apple and associates[14] found that the most common omission for both keypad and handwritten records was blood pressure. Keypad omission errors tended to be related to data that were neither obtained nor entered into the system. Handwritten errors resulted from inaccurate pressure entries or incorrect time entries. Since keypad records are made in real time versus handwritten records, which are made after the fact, it would seem that temporal inaccuracies would essentially be eliminated by a computerized system.

Computerization does not in itself guarantee error-free records. Studies by Burton and colleagues have verified that the recording of vital signs is the poorest reflection of actual events during anesthetic administration.[15] Many of the failings of a computerized system are related to the use of noninvasive techniques. Naturally, noninvasive monitoring devices are more desirable since they make the procedure as risk-free as possible. However, noninvasive techniques may be less accurate, and are significantly more prone to artifacts created by motions of the patient and third parties, improper placement of transducers, and transmission of extraneous noise to Doppler-type sensors.

A simple noninvasive system is schematically diagrammed in Figure 10-1. It could employ an Arteriosonde to measure systolic and diastolic blood pressure every 2 minutes by the Doppler method, a commercial oxygen analyzer to measure the oxygen tension in the inspiratory limb of the inhalation anesthesia apparatus breathing circuit, and a Hewlett-Packard ear oximeter to continuously assess photometrically the ear pinna blood oxygen saturation or pulse oximetry to assess SaO_2. It could also monitor routine temperature and EKG, as well as respiratory activity derived from an analog technique sensing a waveform of the EKG or thoracic cage movement.

Computerized records reflect a greater degree of reliability, accuracy, and timeli-

ness than handwritten ones.[15,16] More importantly, there is a greater frequency of data collected and recorded while freeing the clinician to pay full attention to the patient and administration of the anesthetic. With increased frequency of entries, and without missing any vital signs, subtle changes can be more readily plotted and recognized and serve as early warnings of pending significant physiologic changes. These machine-made records reduce preparation time and document a course of events far more accurately and convincingly than recourse to memory, so necessary in the preparation of handwritten charts. Immediacy of charting leads to credibility of record keeping. Finally, automated systems print factual data without omissions, thereby decreasing the chance of preparing

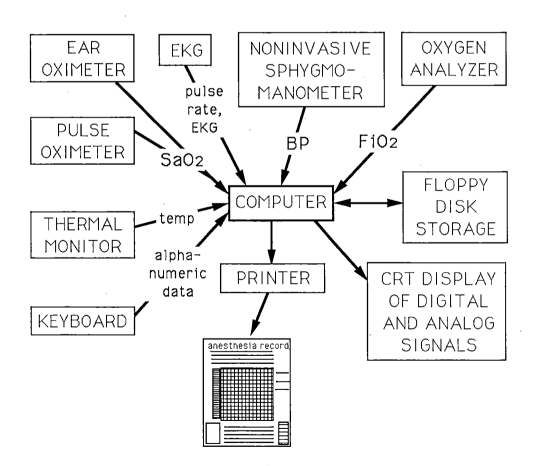

Figure 10-1 Block diagram of a computerized system for monitoring vital signs and other parameters during anesthesia. The printout does not resemble a conventional anesthesia graphic chart, however.

a fictitious record by attempting to fill in missing information.

Physicians and nurses occasionally are reluctant to document any unfavorable patient event directly attributable to their care. Most people like a smooth record, as it implies a better management of the case. Given identical undesirable patient outcomes, however, the record that shows difficulties or complications denotes better patient care than the "straightline" uneventful anesthetic record. The latter situation leads to questions of withholding facts, since most untoward events generally do not occur precipitously. An artificial sense of clinical stability may be not only inappropriate but often can be detected by another experienced and proficient clinician. Worse still, such a record could easily indicate inattentiveness or even lack of concern for the patient's well-being. Therefore, computerization adds yet another safeguard for quality assurance in anesthesia care.

Suggested Hardware

One of the simplest computerized anesthetic record systems has been reported by Prentice and Kenny.[17] The system they described was based on an Apple II microcomputer linked to a Datascope noninvasive arterial pressure monitor. Permanent records were produced on an inexpensive printer and data were stored on floppy disks. Most entries were made with a light pen from selections off a menu. When necessary to enter data not on the light pen menu, the information was typed via the keyboard. These authors readily expanded the system to measure ventilatory variables such as end-tidal carbon dioxide concentrations, gas flows, and other parameters not usually monitored during routine anesthesia cases. Other systems have been proposed, developed, and are now on line.[18-21]

There may be some resistance to moving with modern technology. Arguments based on the inability to type, thereby wasting time, and the capital expenditures associated with equipment purchases have been heard often. Keyboard entries do create a time delay factor for the nontypist. Voice recognition computers that allow quantitative inputs by speech alone have also been evaluated.[22,23] Once fully computerized records are recognized and established as effective for use in the anesthetic area, the objections of anesthesia personnel based on time and lack of ease should be eliminated.

Advantages and Disadvantages

There remains only the task of integrating the various components into an ideal system that can produce the ideal anesthetic record. Theoretically, the system will be noninvasive to minimize the patient risks and complications, will be responsive to the clinician's needs, and will decrease the time involved in record keeping. Ultimately, the completed hard copy will exit the printer at the end of the case, and the anesthetist will only have to affix a signature to make the record a legal document.

Adoption of these highly sophisticated devices may not pose an unmixed blessing, however. Personnel responsible for the selection of a given device, including hardware and software, must be certain that it will function at the expected level, and be relatively troublefree. Liability could flow to the institution, and the individual provider, if a system's failure caused injury to a patient.[24]

Computerized records pose yet another potential legal problem. How can the confidentiality of computerized records be assured? Electronically stored data are always subject to unauthorized access, as well as tampering. How does one ensure that a record has not been altered? And, in the same vein, how would one then authenticate a record? Workable solutions have been introduced using voiceprints. Codes and other methodologies have also been proposed.[25] Reality indicates that not all potential legal problems have been identified, much less solved!

CONCLUSION

Developments in record keeping have lagged behind other advances in medicine and nursing, and record keeping in anesthesia has drifted even further behind documentation in other critical care areas. This shortcoming may be related to the minute-to-minute changing variables involved in monitoring and ministering to the anesthetized patient. It may also relate to the lack of recording equipment sophisticated enough to handle adequately the prolific outputs of multiple monitoring devices. With the advent of monitoring equipment tracking similar physiologic responses in seriously ill patients in intensive care units, automated record-keeping systems have been developed for accurately and contemporaneously recording these many signals. These systems are on line in many locations, and they have progressed in capability and reliability. Several studies and authors[13-17] have proved that the stylus of a printer is not only mightier than the pen, but also more accurate and contemporaneous.

Clear and complete anesthesia records are the hallmark of the anesthesia professional. Those records become a vital part of each patient's operating room experience. All anesthesia personnel must now use the best method for documenting the details of that experience so that the professional's sole role is patient care. The anesthetist administers the anesthetic, the computerized system documents beat-to-beat responses throughout the anesthetic course, and the patient is the subject of undivided attention of anesthesia personnel.

Clearly, the standard of care in anesthesia record keeping has not yet shifted to the use of computerized detection and recording of patients' vital signs even though the necessary equipment is now commercially available. However, until that equipment is adopted on a widespread scale, and the standard of care shifts accordingly, anesthesia personnel will continue to employ the conventional graphic chart and pen. These modalities have survived the test of time. To the end that they will, for the immediate future at least, continue to furnish medical safeguards (for our patients) and legal safeguards (for ourselves), the following admonitions are in order.

- Before you start any case, synchronize your watch with the OR wall clock; it may be difficult to explain later why the circulating nurse (according to his or her notes) called a code before you had started the anesthetic!

- Endeavor to keep your running entries in the anesthesia graphic chart current, especially during the induction and recovery phases of the anesthetic when events may occur in rapid sequence.
- Abbreviations are to be encouraged and may help keep documentation current with events.
- Use standard abbreviations; if you must be innovative, it may be desirable to append some type of glossary to the patient's anesthesia record.
- Do not put anything in the medical record that has nothing to do with patient care.
- Do not place copies of incident reports, or references to them, in the patient's record.
- Do not make references to morbidity and mortality conferences anywhere in the record.
- Do not put anything in the record that you would not want your worst enemy to read.

The handwritten record that is accurate, complete, legible, and generously informative still will furnish eloquent evidence, both out of court and in, of the anesthesia care it purports to document.

REFERENCES

1. Beecher, HK: The First Anesthesia Records. Surg Gynecol Obstet 71:689, 1940.
2. Cushing, H: On routine determinations of arterial tension in operating room and clinic. Boston Med Surg J 149:250, 1903.
3. Accreditation Manual for Hospitals, 1991. Joint Commission on Accreditation of Healthcare Organizations, Chicago, 1990, p 87.
4. *id*, pp 272–273.
5. Program in Hospital Accreditation Standards Manual, 1982. Joint Commission on Accreditation of Hospitals, Chicago, AS 22.
6. Accreditation Manual for Hospitals, 1991. Joint Commission of Accreditation of Healthcare Organizations, Chicago, 1990, SA.1.5.5.1.5, p 273.
7. Dornette, WHL: Medical records. In Dornette, WHL (ed): Legal Aspects of Anesthesia. FA Davis, Philadelphia, 1972, p 189.
8. Dornette, WHL: Medical records in a malpractice case. In Wasmuth, CE (ed): Legal

Problems in the Practice of Anesthesiology. Little, Brown, & Co, Boston, 1973, p 165.

9. Wasmuth, CE: Law for the Physician. Lea & Febiger, Philadelphia, 1966, p 439.

10. Smith, JW: Patient medical records. In Hospital Liability. Law Journal-Seminars Press, New York, 1988, §§14.01 *et seq.*

11. Dornette, WHL: *supra* note 7, p 166.

12. Watson, BL: Liability for Failure to Acquire or Use Computers in Medicine. Proceedings, 5th Annual Symposium on Computer Applications in Medical Care. Institute of Electrical and Electronic Engineers, New York, 1981, p 879; Gibbs, RF: The present and future medicolegal importance of record keeping in anesthesia and intensive care; the case for automation. J Clin Monit 5:251, 1989.

13. Shaffer, MJ, et al: Manual record-keeping and statistical records for the operating room. Med Instrum 12:192, 1978.

14. Apple, HP, et al: Design and evaluation of a semiautomatic anesthesia record system. Med Instrum 16:69, 1982.

15. Burton, LW: Pinnacles and Pitfalls of Network-Based Patient Monitoring. Proceedings of the Association for the Advancement of Medical Instrumentation, 17th Annual Meeting, Arlington, VA, 1982, p 21.

16. Baetz, WR, et al: The anesthesia keyboard system. In Gravenstein, JS, et al. (eds): Monitoring Surgical Patients in the Operating Room. Charles C Thomas, Springfield, IL, 1979.

17. Prentice, JW and Kenny, GNC: Microcomputer-based anesthetic record system. Br J Anaesth 56:1433, 1984.

18. Karliczek, GF, et al: Carola, a computer system for automatic documentation in anesthesia. Intl J Clin Monit Comput 4:211, 1987.

19. Block, FE: Automatic anesthesia record keeping. J Clin Monit 4:284, 1989.

20. Gravenstein, JS: The uses of the anesthesia record. J Clin Monit 5:256, 1989.

21. Ream, AK: Automating the recording and improving the presentation of the anesthesia record. J Clin Monit 5:270, 1989.

22. Reddy, RA: Speech recognition by machine: A review. Proc IEEE 64:501, 1976.

23. Dixon, NR and Silverman, HF: A general language-operated decision implementation system. IEEE Trans: Acoust Speech Sig Proc 24:137 (No. 2, April) 1976.

24. Norris, JA and Szabo, DS: Removing some impediments to development of America's third and fourth generation health care delivery systems: Legal aspects of computer medicine. Am J Law Med 7:5, 1982; see also Gibbs, RF: *supra* note 12.

25. Miller, R, et al: Ethical and legal issues related to the use of computer programs in clinical medicine. Ann Intern Med 102:529, 1985.

10-1

ABBREVIATIONS THAT MAY APPEAR ON THE ANESTHESIA GRAPHIC CHART

ABG	arterial blood gas
An Blk	ankle block
AR	assisted respirations
art/L	arterial line
ASA I-V	American Society of Anesthesiologists classification of physical status of patients—I (healthy) to V (moribund); VI (decreased, organ donor); E suffix = emergency
AW	airway
Ax Blk	axillary block
B = BS	bilateral and equal breath sounds
Bains	non-rebreathing system (inhalation anesthesia technique)
Br Blk	Bier block
BS	breath sounds
BSA	body surface area
cc(s)	cubic centimeter(s)
CCA	closed circle absorption (inhalation anesthesia technique)
CD	continuous IV drip
cm (s)	centimeter(s)
CPRAM	controlled partial rebreathing anesthesia method
CR	controlled respirations
CVP	central venous pressure
C°	centigrade degree(s)
D_5N/S	5% dextrose in normal saline
D_5RL	5% dextrose in Ringer's lactate solution
D_5W	5% dextrose in water
drip	IV drip
DTC	D-tubocurarine
EBL	estimated blood loss
EBV	estimated blood volume
EMV	estimated minute ventilation
ET	endotracheal
ETC	endotracheal catheter
FIO_2	inspired oxygen concentration
Fr	French (catheter size— refers to circumference in cm)
F°	Fahrenheit degree(s)
ga	gauge
gtt(s)	drop(s)
H_2O	chemical formula for water—dihydrogen oxide
Hct	hematocrit

ABBREVIATIONS THAT MAY
APPEAR ON THE ANESTHESIA
GRAPHIC CHART—Continued

Hg	mercury
Hgb	hemoglobin
Ht	height
I	intermittent
IC	indwelling catheter
ICP	intracranial pressure
⇑ICP	increased intracranial pressure
IJ	internal jugular vein
IRR	irregular rate and rhythm
IV	intravenous line, or intravenously
IVP	intravenous push (given rapidly)
IVPB	intravenous piggyback (feeding second IV solution through first IV set)
K	potassium
kg	kilogram
L	lumbar (region of body)
lb(s)	pound(s)
LpM, L/M	liter(s) per minute
mg	milligram(s)
ml	milliliter(s)
mm	millimeter(s)
MS	morphine sulfate
MV	minute ventilation
N	nasal
N/S	normal saline
N_2O	nitrous oxide
Na Pent	sodium Pentothal (generic name: thiopental)
NP	nasopharyngeal
NRB	non-rebreathing system
NSR	normal sinus rhythm (EKG monitoring)
NTG	nitroglycerine
O	oral
O_2	oxygen
OD	right eye
OS	left eye
OU	both eyes
p	pressure
PA	pulmonary artery
PAC(s)	premature auricular contraction(s)
PAP	pulmonary artery pressure
PCB	pancuronium bromide (generic name for Pavulon)
PNS	peripheral nerve stimulator
PRBC	packed red blood cells
PVC(s)	premature ventricular contraction(s)

ABBREVIATIONS THAT MAY APPEAR ON THE ANESTHESIA GRAPHIC CHART—Continued

PVR	peripheral vascular resistance
PWP	pulmonary wedge pressure
RL	Ringer's lactate
RR	[heart] rate regular
RR	recovery room
RRR	[heart] rate and rhythm regular
S	sigh
S/G	Swan/Ganz catheter (for monitoring pulmonary artery pressure)
SAB	subarachnoid block (also spinal anesthetic block)
SaO_2	arterial oxygen saturation
SC	semiclosed (technique of inhalation anesthesia)
SC	subclavian [vessel]
SCCA	semiclosed circle absorption (technique of inhalation anesthesia)
SLB	superior laryngeal nerve block
SO	semiopen (technique of inhalation anesthesia)
SR	sinus rhythm
SR	spontaneous respirations
sux	succinylcholine
SV	spontaneous ventilation
T	thoracic (region of body)
T	tourniquet
T_4	train of four (neuromuscular blockade monitor response)
T⇑	tourniquet (pressure) up
T⇓	tourniquet (pressure) down
TPN	thiopental (generic name for sodium Pentothal)
TTB	transtracheal block
TTT	total tourniquet time
µg	microgram(s)
ung	ointment
VS	vital signs
WB	whole blood
Wt	weight
XX	start and end of anesthesia administration
◉ ◉	start and end of operation
•	pulse rate (on graphic chart)
○	respiratory rate
v	systolic blood pressure, indirect
	diastolic blood pressure, indirect
⊥	systolic blood pressure, direct
T	diastolic blood pressure, direct

11

William H. L. Dornette, M.D., J.D.

Identifying, Moving, and Positioning the Patient

Identifying, moving, and positioning the candidate for operative intervention are obvious prerequisites to the administration of anesthesia and performance of operative procedures. One would not expect these activities to produce accidents, injuries, or litigation. Unfortunately, accidents, injuries, and litigation have developed from these activities in the past, and undoubtedly will continue to do so in the future.

Anesthesia, surgical, and operating room personnel are human; mistakes in patient identification, movement, and positioning do occur. This chapter points up some of the possible hazards associated with preparing the patient for the administration of the anesthetic, delineates methodology for preventing such problems, and discusses some of the case law that has stemmed from injuries of this type.

113

IDENTIFYING THE PATIENT

Obviously it is imperative that each patient be delivered to the operating room scheduled for that patient and that the intended procedure be performed on the correct body part. Unfortunately, for a variety of reasons detailed below, patients may be brought to an operating room scheduled for another patient, or positioned improperly, so that the wrong structure is operated upon. Generally, these mix-ups result from breakdowns in communication that in turn stem from one or sometimes several gross errors.

Problem Areas

Patients who are young, very old, or who have language problems are potential candidates for incorrect identification. If patients cannot tell you their names and the site of the intended operation, extra precautions must be taken. I investigated one case that probably stemmed from a language barrier.

The patient, a Mexican-American, spoke English poorly. At least four different health care providers made mistakes preoperatively that culminated in the performance of a meniscectomy on his left instead of right knee. The operative request form, which was not signed, specified the left knee. Operating room personnel, in processing this form to prepare the operative schedule for the following day, should not have accepted an unsigned form. The operating room nurse and the nurse anesthetist both visited the patient on the nursing unit the evening before the procedure; neither discussed the site of the pending operation with the patient. When the patient was brought to the operating room the following morning, the same nurse anesthetist and operating room nurse again did not discuss with him the site of the operation. When the senior orthopedic surgeon and first assistant (who was to perform the procedure) came into the operating room, neither of them checked the radiographs, and thus neither noticed that they were about to operate on the incorrect knee. They proceeded with the operation and did not discover the mistake until immediately afterward.

In another case, also unreported, the anesthesiologist administered general anesthesia to a candidate for a nephrectomy and positioned the patient with the incorrect side up. When the surgeon came into the operating room, he did not notice the improper positioning, and proceeded to remove the less-diseased kidney. The mistake was not discovered until sometime during the postoperative period. The patient was able to receive a very generous settlement for this gross incompetence.

The case of *Huggins v. Graves* occurred a number of years ago in Chattanooga, Tennessee. Mr. Huggins was scheduled for a hemorrhoidectomy. Somehow his chart was switched with that of another patient who was a candidate for hernia repair and orchidectomy for an undescended testicle. Mr. Huggins was taken into the wrong operating room. The anesthesiologist did not check the identity of his patient, and proceeded to induce anesthesia. Mr. Huggins was subjected to hernia repair and removal of a normally located testicle. He sued the hospital and surgeon, but did not name the anesthesiology group, a member of which had given him the anesthetic. The surgeon filed a third-party complaint* against the group of anesthesiologists, bringing them into the litigation and compelling them to contribute their share to the $100,000 judgment.[1]

Several pediatric cases have come to my attention. Fortunately, none of them resulted in performance of the wrong operation. In one case, a candidate for an operation was in the bathroom and another patient was sitting on his bed. The orderly took the other child to the operating room, where the mistake was immediately detected by operating room personnel. In another case, the wrong patient was taken to the operating room simply because the orderly did not check the wristband. Fortunately, the child was old enough to tell operating room personnel that she was not supposed to be operated upon.

Obviously, mistakes in identifying patients cannot be condoned, and operating on the wrong patient is indefensible. The introduction of permanently affixed wristbands has helped considerably in preventing errors of this type. Unfortunately, some personnel still do not routinely read the

---

*An action that in effect will add the third party to the original lawsuit as an additional defendant.

wristband and compare the information contained therein to the chart and the patient's responses to direct questions about identity. It is my opinion that identifying candidates for operative procedures should involve at least three persons, each acting independently. Identification should be carried out by:

1 The surgeon, who should know the patient well from preoperative evaluation
2 The member of the anesthesia team, who presumably made preoperative rounds some time prior to the operation
3 A member of the operating room nursing staff

The process of identification should involve comparing the patient's name as the patient states it with the wristband, the patient's medical record, and the operative schedule. The site of the operation should be identified by a similar procedure. Safety involves redundancy. Special attention must be given to operations on paired organs, especially excision of a paired organ. When patients are unable to respond positively to the query "Tell me your name," extra steps should be taken. Patients who are elderly, unconscious, and in the pediatric age range all deserve these extra steps. Operating on the wrong patient or the wrong side of the body is simply an inexcusable act. It constitutes an intentional tort (a battery; see Chapter 5) for which punitive damages should be forthcoming.

MOVING THE PATIENT

Members of the operating team are well aware of the absolute necessity of having available a sufficient number of persons with strong backs to transfer patients from the stretcher onto the operating table. In spite of these efforts, patients have slipped from the hands of these personnel.[2] My attention was called to an accident that occurred while a patient was being slid along the operating table to position him for a thoracotomy. The anesthesia resident had induced general anesthesia and had inserted the endotracheal catheter. Before he had a chance to secure it, and apparently without any warning, the surgeons slid the patient cephalad along the operating table. The anesthesia resident was left at the head of the table holding the Y connector and endotracheal catheter. Efforts to reinsert the catheter quickly were to no avail, and the patient suffered circulatory arrest and severe brain damage. While accidents of this type are rare, they point up the absolute necessity, once general anesthesia has been induced, of the anesthesiologist or nurse anesthetist being in control and directing the actions of all personnel who are to move the patient. Accidents such as these become totally indefensible.

POSITIONING THE PATIENT

Positioning patients for operative procedures involves the cooperative effort of surgical, anesthesia, and operating room nursing personnel. The operating surgeon should have reasonably optimal access to the site of the operation, access that affords reasonably comfortable working conditions. Concurrently, the function of vital structures and systems—respiratory function (movements of the thoracic cage and diaphragm), cardiovascular function (venous return to the heart), and peripheral nerve function—must not be compromised. These admonitions deserve special emphasis.

Preventing Respiratory and Cardiovascular Compromise

Whether the patient is to be breathing spontaneously or having respirations assisted or controlled, the movement of the thoracic cage and abdominal wall (indirectly, the diaphragm) must not be compromised. Figure 11-1 shows the effects of various positions on respiratory and cardiovascular activity. In general, the more extreme the position, the greater the potential degree of compromise. While the average patient of physical status I or II can sustain some degree of externally induced interference with these vital functions, patients who are more seriously ill cannot. Anesthesia personnel should be thoroughly familiar with the mechanisms for pro-

POSITION

FUNCTION	SUPINE	PRONE	PRONE-JACKKNIFE	TRENDEL-ENBURG	SITTING	REVERSE TRENDEL-ENBURG	LATERAL, TABLE BROKEN
venous return	▲	▼	▼	▲	▼	▼	▼
heart rate	▼	▲	▲	▼	▲	▲	▲
stroke volume	▲	▼	▼	▼	▼	▼	▼
cardiac output	▲	▼	▼	▼	▼	▼	▼
resp. rate	▼	▲	▲	▲	▲	▲	▲
tidal volume	▲	▼	▼	▼	▼	▼	▼
vital capacity	▼	▼	▼	▼	▼	▲	▼

Figure 11-1 The effects of various positions on cardiorespiratory functions. The importance of avoiding extreme positions, thereby significantly interfering with vital functions, should be obvious.

duction of respiratory and cardiovascular compromise as detailed in this figure.

Preventing Peripheral Nerve Injuries

Whereas the problems discussed in the previous section generally are self-limited, injury to a peripheral nerve may produce long-term or permanent impairment. Inasmuch as these injuries are preventable, it is essential that personnel be acutely aware of their pathogenesis, pathology, and sites of involvement.

Pathogenesis

There are a number of factors that contribute to a peripheral nerve injury. First, and perhaps of greatest concern, is the nerve that passes over a joint. When a patient is rendered unconscious, and especially following use of muscle relaxants, joints may be subjected to positioning that would be extremely uncomfortable or impossible during the conscious state. As a result, nerves that pass across these joints may be stretched sufficiently to produce a peripheral nerve injury. A second mechanism of injury relates to the nerve that lies in direct contact with a bony structure. Such a nerve is much more prone to develop ischemia from external pressure, by counterpressure from the underlying bone, than one completely surrounded by soft tissue. A third factor is the tendency of some persons to experience positional peripheral nerve ischemia more readily than others. The importance of asking patients whether they frequently wake up at night with numbness in the sensory distribution of one of their peripheral nerves is discussed below. A fourth factor relates to the patient whose nutritional status is inadequate (e.g., vitamin B deficiency) or who may have peripheral neuritis. Such patients are especially prone to neurapraxia or axonotmesis (discussed below) and require extra attention during the positioning process.

Pathophysiology

Peripheral nerve injuries are of three types—neurapraxia, axonotmesis, and neurotmesis. These pathophysiologic changes are best understood by referring to Figure 11-2, which depicts a typical neuron. Impulses pass from the dendrites through the cell body to the axons. Each axon is in immediate contact with and surrounded by the myelin, which in turn is surrounded by sheath cells of Schwann. Both structures help protect the axon. At regular intervals along the course of the nerve, the sheath cells of Schwann terminate at what is known as the nodes of Ranvier. These relationships are also depicted in this figure (for purposes of illustration, there is considerable foreshortening of the length of the axons and each individual sheath cell).

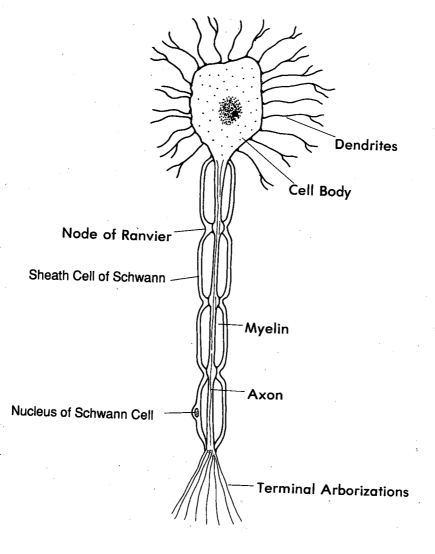

Figure 11–2 Diagram of a "typical" neuron, depicting various components involved in axonotmesis and subsequent regeneration. See text. Figure taken from Dornette WLD: Compression neuropathies; medical aspects and legal implications. Chapter 9 in Hindman BJ: Neurological and Psychological Complications of Surgery and Anesthesia. International Anesthesiology Clinics, Vol. 24, No. 4 (Winter) 1986, p. 203, and used with permission.

Neurapraxia

Peripheral nerves receive their nutrition and oxygen from small blood vessels that enter the peripheral nerve trunk via the vasa nervorum. Although these nerves are much less susceptible to ischemic or hypoxic injury than those of the central nervous system, not-too-prolonged periods of external pressure can produce what is known as neurapraxia. Nerve transmission comes to a halt. The conscious individual experiences numbness and a tingling sensation in the portion of the extremity supplied by a sensory nerve. If a motor nerve is involved, the muscles are transiently paralyzed. This phenomenon frequently occurs during natural sleep. The subject is stimulated sufficiently by the numbness and tingling to awaken enough to turn over. This repositioning allows the circulation to return. Within seconds these peripheral nerve trunks will have been adequately resupplied with oxygen, and the numbness, tingling, and muscle weakness will disappear.

Neurapraxia is a transient phenomenon, provided that the individual retains the ability to awaken sufficiently for repositioning. Inasmuch as some patients are more prone to developing neurapraxia than others, it is my opinion that during preoperative rounds all patients should be queried whether they frequently awaken during the night with numbness of an extremity. If they answer "yes," extra care should be taken in positioning them to protect peripheral nerves, as noted below.

Axonotmesis

This is the second type of peripheral nerve injury. Its pathogenesis is fundamentally the same as that of neurapraxia. If the external pressure is not removed in a timely fashion, the axon experiences enough ischemia to lose viability at the point of the pressure. The axon then undergoes neurolysis in a peripheral direction from the point of the injury to the terminal arborizations, and proximally to the next node of Ranvier. Because there has not been any disruption of the sheath cells of Schwann, they remain intact. Following such an injury, the axon commences regeneration peripherally through the intact tunnel of myelin and sheath cells of Schwann; the sensory endings or motor fibers ultimately are reinner-

vated. Regeneration, which commences immediately after the ischemia is relieved, progresses at a rate of approximately 1 mm/day. Thus, if, for example, the ulnar nerve of the average individual is compressed as it passes through the olecranon groove, it would take about 400 days (approximate distance, 40 centimeters) for regeneration to take place.

Neurotmesis

The third and most serious type of peripheral nerve injury is neurotmesis. Both the axon and the sheath cells of Schwann are disrupted. Such an injury can occur from stretching the peripheral nerve as it passes through or around a joint. A marked degree of external pressure might also cause such an injury, either directly or, if residual scar tissue is laid down, following the injury. This last type of injury is evidenced by the progressive development of signs and symptoms of nerve palsy over a several-month interval after the initial insult. Examples of injuries of this type are detailed below. Because of the disruption of the sheath cells of Schwann, peripheral regeneration rarely is complete. The importance of safeguarding patients from injury of this type is quite obvious.

Sites of Neurological Injury

Injury of a transient or permanent nature may occur to a number of the cranial nerves, the brachial plexus, and various peripheral branches of the spinal nerves.*

The Cranial Nerves

Optic Nerve

The retina and portions of the optic nerve are supplied by the central artery of the retina. This artery, a branch of the ophthalmic artery, enters the optic nerve just proximal to the optic foramen and passes to the eyeball in that nerve. If through improper po-

---

*For illustration of the mechanism for the various nerve injuries, see Dornette, WHL: Compression neuropathies: Medical aspects and legal implications. In Hindman, BJ (ed): Neurological and Psychological Complications of Surgery and Anesthesia, Little, Brown & Co, Boston, 1986, p 201.

sitioning of the head, pressure is applied to the eyeball continuously for 4 minutes or longer, retinal blindness will result. A seemingly insigificant amount of pressure usually is sufficient to overcome the pressure within the retinal artery, stopping flow through this artery and causing acute retinal ischemia. The rod and cone cells respond to oxygen deprivation in the same manner as do the giant Betz cells of the central nervous system.

Trigeminal Nerve

The skin of the face in the vicinity of the eyes and nose is innervated via the supraorbital, infraorbital, supratrochlear, and infratrochlear nerves, which are branches of the trigeminal nerve. Excessive pressure from an anesthesia mask placed in the vicinity of these nerves can produce neurapraxia or even axonotmesis. The patient will experience a small area of numbness in the vicinity of the eyes or nose. While the duration of any subsequent paresthesia would be quite short, care still must be taken in positioning the anesthesia mask in order to avoid applying excessive pressure to any of these nerves.

Facial Nerve

This nerve innervates the muscles of the face. It may be injured if pressure is applied at the point the nerve passes around the lower edge of the ramus of the mandible. Facial nerve palsy results in a face drop. Care must be taken when using the anesthesia mask and inhaler retainer (head strap) to avoid contact between a strap and the lower edge of the ramus of the mandible.

Brachial Plexus

The brachial plexus is formed by the anterior primary rami of the fourth through the seventh cervical spinal nerves and the first thoracic nerve. It also receives branches from the third cervical and second thoracic nerve. It descends through the posterior triangle of the neck, passes over the dome of the thoracic cage and behind the clavicle, and enters the axilla adjacent to the medial head of the humerus. It may be injured by pressure applied externally. Axonotmesis or even neurotmesis could occur. The second mechanism for injury relates to the mobility of the shoulder girdle during general anesthesia and muscle relaxation. If the patient is placed in a Trendelenburg's position and restrained either by a shoulder brace applied over the acromioclavicular joint, by wrist bracelets, or both, the patient may slide cephalad on the operating table, depressing the shoulder girdle, and stretching the upper roots of the plexus, possibly causing neurapraxia.

A third injury-producing mechanism relates to the structures adjacent to the plexus as it passes behind and beneath the clavicle and around the head of the humerus. When the patient's arm is abducted, the head of the humerus rotates inward. At the same time the plexus, affixed between the spinal nerve roots and the upper arm, tends to be stretched around the head of the humerus.

Radial Nerve

The radial nerve, one of the peripheral nerves supplied by the brachial plexus, passes into the arm and courses around the midportion of the shaft of the humerus. At that point it is in direct proximity to the bone and close to the surface of the skin. If an orthopedic tourniquet is inflated to too great a pressure, axonotmesis may occur. The nerve also may be injured by pressure from a Mayo stand, ether screen, or improper padding of the dependent arm when the patient is in the lateral decubitus position. The patient will develop wrist drop and loss of sensation of the skin over the dorsum of the radial two-thirds side of the hand.

Ulnar Nerve

The ulnar nerve is perhaps the most commonly injured peripheral nerve. It is vulnerable because of its direct opposition to the bony prominences of the distal humerus and proximal ulnar as it passes around the elbow.

Median Nerve

This nerve commonly is not subject to positional injuries. It may, however, be directly traumatized during inept attempts at venipuncture in the antecubital fossa. The lateral antebrachial cutaneous nerve may be injured in a similar fashion.

Peroneal Nerve

Although injuries of the peroneal nerve are not as common as those of the ulnar nerve, the mechanism for the production of injuries of both nerves is very similar. The peroneal nerve crosses the knee joint lateral to and behind the proximal head of the fibula. Externally applied pressure at this point, because the nerve is in direct opposition to bone, can result in a peripheral peroneal nerve palsy, with foot drop and numbness of the lateral aspect of the leg and dorsum of the foot.

Other Nerves in the Lower Extremity

The lateral femoral cutaneous nerve, tibial nerve, sural nerve, and superficial peroneal nerve also may be injured by a variety of mechanisms. Table 11-1 depicts these and other sites of peripheral nerve injury, etiology, and resultant neurological deficits.

THE LEGAL ISSUES

It should come as no surprise that peripheral nerve injuries and consequent litigation have enriched the common law. In the usual negligence action (Chapter 3), the patient-plaintiff must introduce proof, by a preponderance of the evidence, of each element of this action—notably breach of the duty of care and proximate causation. In the large majority of cases of peripheral nerve injuries, the plaintiff is unconscious from the effects of general anesthesia and has no way of identifying the act or acts of negligence that did or might have produced the peripheral nerve injury. Thus, peripheral nerve injuries become proof problems for plaintiff's lawyers, who frequently must resort to the doctrine of res ipsa loquitur.

Doctrine of <u>Res Ipsa Loquitur</u>

As noted in Chapter 3 on proof of negligence, there are certain circumstances in which an *inference of negligence* may be created. If the instrumentality causing the injury is under the direct control of the defendant or defendants, if the plaintiff was in

no way contributorily negligent, and if it is well known, even among laypersons who sit on the bench and in the jury box, that such an injury could not occur in the absence of the negligence of someone, then an inference of negligence may be created. The trier of fact may accept that inference and find for the plaintiff. The defendant would, of course, have the opportunity to rebut any such circumstantial evidence. From a practical standpoint, utilization of the res doctrine as a modality of proof is very risky. On the other hand, it may be the only approach that the plaintiff can employ under the circumstances. Much of the peripheral nerve injury case law involves use of the res doctrine. Judges and juries have gone both ways in deciding these cases.

The Case Law

One the earliest cases involving peripheral nerve injuries and the utilization of the res ipsa loquitur doctrine occurred in 1939.

Joseph Ybarra was hospitalized at Stanford University Hospital for acute appendicitis. At the time he was placed on the operating table prior to induction of general anesthesia, he remembered that there was something pressing painfully against his right shoulder and neck. He lost consciousness shortly thereafter. When he awakened postoperatively he noted severe pain and weakness in his right shoulder and arm. The muscles subsequently became paralytic and atrophied (neurotmesis). Since he had no way of knowing which member of the operating room team had positioned him improperly, Ybarra sued the surgeons, anesthesiologists, operating room nurses, and hospital. His lawyer was unable to introduce any evidence of negligence, and invoked the res ipsa loquitur doctrine to prove his case. One of the essential elements of the res doctrine, however, is that the defendant must have been in exclusive control of the instrumentality that allegedly caused the injury. Inasmuch as no single member of the operating team could have been considered in exclusive control, the defense based its request for a nonsuit on this particular element. When the trial court granted the defense motion, Ybarra appealed. In December 1944,[3] the Supreme Court of California held that the res ipsa loquitur doctrine could be applicable to more than one defendant, reversed the holding of the trial court, and ordered a new trial.

TABLE 11-1. Mechanisms of Peripheral Nerve Injury in the Unconscious Patient*

Nerve or Trunk	Site of Injury	Mechanism(s) of Injury	Impairment
Infraorbital n. Infratrochlear n. Supraorbital n. Supratrochlear n.	Face adjacent to orbit or nose	Excessive pressure from inhalation anesthesia mask too tightly applied	Limited area of sensory loss of skin innervated by affected nerve
Facial n.	At point(s) at which fibers of nerve pass under lower edge of mandible	Too tightly applied inhaler retainer (head-strap) used to hold inhalation anesthesia mask in place	Sensory anesthesia and motor paralysis of structures innervated by roots affected; patient may develop face drop
Brachial plexus	Trunks or cords	Shoulder brace placed too close to the supraclavicular area	Sensory loss and motor paralysis of varying extent, severity, and permanence, depending on location of injury and degree of disruption of nerve trunks
	Upper roots, trunks, or cords	Sliding of anesthetized patient, restrained only by wrists for procedure in Trendelenburg's position, toward head of table, depressing shoulders and stretching upper components of plexus	Sensory loss in skin of radial two-thirds of palm, and ends of dorsum of index and middle fingers; inability to flex or separate thumb and two radial fingers; inability to oppose thumb and little finger
	Junction of cords with peripheral nerves, in axilla adjacent to head of humerus	Abduction of arm to 90° or more from the trunk, allowing the head of the humerus to descend into the axilla; brachial plexus stretched around the head of the humerus, causing both stretch and compression injury	Wrist drop; sensory anesthesia of the skin over the dorsum of radial two-thirds of hand
Median n.	In antecubital fossa	Puncture of nerve during attempts at venipuncture of one of antecubital veins, or extravasation of neurotoxic medications intended for intravenous injection	Sensory anesthesia of little finger, ulnar half of ring finger, ulnar third of hand; claw hand (contracture of muscles of little and ring fingers)
Radial n.	At middle of arm at point where nerve spirals around lateral aspect of humerus	(1) Injections of medications into substance of nerve; (2) too tightly applied orthopedic tourniquet; (3) external pressure from Mayo stand, ether screen or improper padding of the dependent arm with the patient in the lateral decubitus position	Foot drop; anesthesia of skin over leg and foot
Ulnar n.	As nerve passes through the ulnar groove	(1) External pressure (very little may be required) from poorly padded arm board with forearm fixed in prone position; (2) contact with operating table rail with forearm supinated; (3) hands above head with patient in the prone position on the operating table	Causalgias or sensory loss over skin of anterior thigh
Sciatic n.	Adjacent to sciatic foramen	Injection of neurotoxic substance into nerve during intramuscular injection	Foot drop; anesthesia of skin of foot and leg

121

TABLE 11-1. Mechanisms of Peripheral Nerve Injury in the Unconscious Patient (Continued)

Nerve	Site	Mechanism	Result
Lateral femoral cutaneous n.	Anterior thigh just inferior to inguinal ligament	Direct pressure with patient in prone position on inadequately padded operating room table with table broken at level of hips and thighs flexed on trunk	Causalgias or sensory loss over skin of anterior thigh
Common peroneal n.	Lateral aspect of head of femur	(1) Inadequate padding of dependent knee with patient in lateral decubitus position; (2) inadequate padding of knee and/or use of stirrups on lateral aspect of knee, with patient in lithotomy position	Sensory loss over lateral aspect of leg below knee and dorsum of foot; foot drop
Superficial peroneal n.	Lateral aspect of calf	Same as for common peroneal nerve	Same as for common peroneal nerve
Deep peroneal n.	Posterior aspect of lower leg, just below knee	Pressure on posterior aspect of leg from improper placement of patient's knee over break in table	Foot drop; inability to invert foot, sensory loss over great and second toe
Posterior tibial n.	Posterior aspect of lower leg, just below knee	Same as for deep peroneal nerve	Sensory loss over plantar surface of foot and atrophy of small muscles of foot
Sural n.	Posterolateral aspect of ankle	Patients who are inadvertently anesthetized with their legs crossed may suffer injury to the superficial peroneal nerve of the dependent leg and the sural nerve of the appendent leg, because of pressure from the opposite leg.	Sensory loss in skin of lateral aspect of heel and foot
Superficial peroneal n., terminal branches	Dorsum of foot		Sensory loss in skin over dorsum of foot

*From Dornette, WHL: Legal Aspects of Anesthesia. FA Davis, Philadelphia, 1972, p 358; used with permission.

Since that time a number of other cases involving peripheral nerve injuries in the unconscious candidate for operative intervention have been tried and taken to appeal. They are summarized in Table 11-2. Most of these cases[3-14] involved application (not always a successful one) of the *res* doctrine, although negligence was alleged in a few.[15-17] These cases do reiterate the strict application by the courts of evidential rules in establishing liability; that is, an injury in the absence of proof of negligence leads to a defense verdict. But that fact obviously must not deter members of the operating team from employing *extra diligence* in preventing these neurological injuries.

CONCLUSION

Injuries and accidents of the type described in this chapter are for the most part preventable. Properly identifying patients and the side and site of the proposed opera-

TABLE 11-2. Peripheral Nerve Injury Cases Involving Res Ipsa Loquitur

Citation	Injury	Doctrine Applicable?	Verdict
Calvin v. Jewish Hosp. of St. Louis[4]	Radial n. palsy	Yes	Plaintiff's trial verdict reversed on other grounds
Congelton v. Baton Rouge Genl. Hosp.[5]	Left ulnar n. palsy	Yes	Congelton
Duff v. Yelin[15]	Right ulnar n. palsy	No	Defense
Holloway v. Sou. Baptist Hosp.[7]	Left ulnar neuropathy and causalgia	Yes	Holloway—action of lower court reversed
Hoover v. Gaston Memorial Hosp.[8]	Left ulnar n. palsy	No	Defense—elements of doctrine not met
Horner v. Northern Pacific Ben. Assoc. Hosp.[6]	Severe traction injury bracheal plexus	Yes	Horner
Hoven v. Rice Memorial Hosp.[9]	Bilateral ulnar n. palsy	Yes	Hoven—directed defense verdict improper
Marrero v. Goldsmith[16]	Left antebrachial cutaneous n. (blood donor injured by phlebotomist)	No	Defense—plaintiff's trial verdict reversed
Mozzer v. Bush[10]	Left ulnar n. palsy	No	Defense
Parks v. Perry[11]	Right ulnar n. palsy	Yes	Parks—reversing lower court decision for defendants
Schmidt v. St. Joseph's Hosp.[13]	Left ulnar n. palsy	No	Defense—plaintiff failed to make *prima facie* case
Talbot v. Dr. W. H. Groves Latter-Day Saints Hosp.[14]	Nerves of right arm and back	No	Defense
Wiik v. Rathmore[17]	Left ulnar n. palsy	No	Defense
Ybarra v. Spangard[3]	Nerves of right shoulder and arm	Yes	Ybarra—defense trial verdict reversed

*Superior numbers refer to reference list.

tion, moving patients carefully, and positioning them with full knowledge of the anatomic structures and associated physiologic functions will help ensure both safety for one's patients and the delivery of anesthesia care of high quality.

REFERENCES

1. Huggins v. Graves, 210 Fed Supp 98 (E.D. Tenn. 1962).
2. For a general discussion of falls in the hospital, *see* 9 ALR 4th (1987); *see also* 31 ALR 3d 1114 (1970) § 7.
3. Ybarra v. Spangard, 25 Cal.2d 486, 154 P. 2d 687 (1945), Annot. 162 A.L.R. 1258 (1946).
4. Calvin v. Jewish Hosp. of St. Louis, 746 S.W.2d 602 (Mo.App. 1988).
5. Congelton v. Baton Rouge Genl. Hosp., 444 So.2d 174 (La. App. 1 Cir. 1983).
6. Horner v. Northern Pacific Ben. Assoc. Hosp., 62. Wash. 2d 351, 382 P. 2d 518 (1963).
7. Holloway v. Sou. Baptist Hosp., 367 So.2d 871 (La.App. 4 Cir. 1978).
8. Hoover v. Gaston Memorial Hosp., 11 N.C.App. 119, 180 S.E.2d 479 (1971).
9. Hoven v. Rice Memorial Hosp., 386 N.W.2d 752 (Minn. App. 1986).
10. Mozzer v. Bush, 527 A.2d 727 (Conn. App. 1987).
11. Parks v. Perry, 68 N.C.App. 202, 314 S.E.2d 287 (1984).
12. Rhodes v. DeHann, 184 Kan. 473, 337 P.2d 1043 (1959).
13. Schmidt v. St. Joseph's Hosp., 736 P.2d 135 (N.M. App. 1987).
14. Talbot v. Dr. W. H. Groves Latter-Day Saints Hosp., 21 Utah 2d 73, 440 P. 2d 872 (1968).
15. Duff v. Yelin, 721 S.W.2d 365 (Tex. App. 1986).
16. Marrero v. Goldsmith, 448 So.2d 543 (Fla. App. 3, 1984).
17. Wiik v. Rathore, 487 N.E.2d 235 (Mass. App. Ct., Middlesex, 1986).

12

William H. L. Dornette, M.D., J.D.

Monitoring the Anesthetized Patient

In just a few short years, dramatic changes have occurred in the equipment and techniques utilized for monitoring the anesthetized patient. Devices now are available for assessing many more physiologic parameters than ever before. Some items of equipment (e.g., the Dinemapp blood pressure manometer) are automatic, eliminating the need for manual operation. Many invasive monitoring practices have been implemented to replace or complement noninvasive techniques. All of these changes have altered dramatically the standard of monitoring care in this country. These advances are not necessarily unmixed blessings, however, even though much additional information about the patient is determined through their use. This chapter reviews the changes in the standard of monitoring care, assesses the current impact of monitoring on the quality of that care, and reviews the potential exposure of anesthesia personnel to liability for using, or failing to use, some of these modern monitoring devices.

THE STANDARD OF MONITORING CARE

Each health care provider owes each patient the duty to practice at the professed level of care (see Chapter 2), as a board-certified or board-eligible anesthesiologist, a certified registered nurse anesthetist, or a trainee aspiring to either vocation. That level of care includes the selection and use of appropriate agents, techniques, and equipment to deliver anesthesia safely to each patient. Failing to meet that level or standard of care, with resultant injury to the patient or other adverse outcome, might lead to allegations of negligent conduct (Chapter 3). In such an action, the injured party must prove that the defendant departed from the duty of care (to practice at the level of the standard of care) and that that departure was the cause of the adverse outcome. The standard of care (Chapter 4) thus becomes an important element, not only in the negligence action but also in the delivery of safe anesthesia. Obviously, certain monitoring techniques do enable anesthesia personnel to maintain better awareness of the patient's condition, and thus forestall serious complications and morbidity or even mortality. How is the standard of care of monitoring the anesthetized patient developed, and what is its level at the present time?

The Evolving Standard

It was not too many years ago that monitoring the anesthetized patient consisted of applying a blood pressure cuff and stethoscope to one of the patient's arms and then, with a finger on the patient's temporal artery, manually determining the blood pressure and counting the pulse and respiratory rates at regular intervals. Over the years, additional monitoring equipment and techniques have been introduced into practice, first as research tools and later as part of the accepted armamentarium of the complete anesthetist or anesthesiologist. The introduction of a precordial or esophageal stethoscope connected to a molded earpiece, the use of electrocardiographic monitors later equipped with rate alarms, and the introduction of the Clark oxygen electrode are but a few of the advances of the not too distant past.

Perfection of devices to regularly reinflate the blood pressure cuff and sensors to detect the pressure at which the Korotkoff sounds disappear and reappear (as embodied in the Dinemapp monitor) has resulted in a major noninvasive monitoring breakthrough. No longer do anesthesia personnel need to interrupt other activities by manually reinflating the blood pressure cuff at regular intervals and carefully auscultating to the Korotkoff sounds while observing the manometer. While manual recording is still a necessity, the use of computers to assimilate and print out this information is not only possible but has been implemented in some institutions (see Chapter 10).

The most recent, and very innovative, addition to monitoring practices has been the introduction of mass spectrometry[1] for assessing respired gas concentrations. The PO_2, PCO_2, PN_2, and partial pressure of inhaled anesthetic agents now can be readily monitored in both inspired and expired gases. The use of one of these devices furnishes more data than the concentration of the anesthetic agent and whether there is enough oxygen in the breathing circuit. One can also detect the physiologic changes associated with endobronchial intubation, a collapsed lung, accidental disconnection of the endotracheal catheter from the Y piece, and other malfunctions. Mass spectrometry has become standard practice in some larger institutions. It has not been accepted as part of the standard of care in all hospitals across this country, however, at least not at the time of this writing.

The just-described techniques are noninvasive. Modern monitoring practice also mandates the application of certain invasive techniques under certain circumstances. Central venous and arterial lines for continuous pressure monitoring and Swan-Ganz catheterization of the pulmonary vein have become standard practice during many complex operative procedures, or for monitoring seriously ill patients.

Steps in Changing the Standard

The widespread availability and generalized use of many of these devices have changed monitoring practice dramatically in this country. By acquiring and applying this equipment, anesthesia personnel have elevated the U.S. standard of monitoring care. These changes have evolved slowly but progressively because of a variety of factors. First, there was an expressed need for the device by anesthesia personnel. Equipment manufacturers were apprised of or otherwise recognized this need. These manufacturers, using technological developments* in the field of instrument engineering and design, developed at first prototype models and then later production devices. As a final step, anesthesia personnel and hospitals, for varied reasons, but perhaps foremost out of a desire to enhance patient care and prevent accidents, injuries, and litigation, acquired these newer devices and put them into use. At some point, after a sufficient number of practitioners and hospitals commenced use of a given device, the standard of monitoring care shifted (see Chapter 4). From that point onward, it would be considered a departure from the duty of care to fail to incorporate that device in one's armamentarium.

The advantages that accrue from the use of many of these new devices are obvious. More physiological parameters are monitored. Automation frees anesthesia personnel from the routine operation of certain equipment, allowing them to carry out other tasks while at the same time the vital signs are detected regularly and at more frequent intervals. All of these factors afford greater safety for anesthetized patients.

ADVERSE OUTCOMES RELATED TO MONITORING

Unfortunately, thexse advances are not necessarily all positive ones. Perhaps of foremost importance is the fact that some

*Much modern instrumentation equipment and practices are spinoffs of developments by the National Aeronautics and Space Administration for monitoring the astronauts.

of this equipment (notably the mass spectrometer) is extremely expensive, thus limiting its use, at least at present, to larger institutions. Considerable time may be involved in checking out the equipment and applying it to each patient; that time might not be available in the true emergency situation, during which the equipment would probably serve its most useful function. The equipment is also highly complex, and there is an associated greater potential for maintenance problems. Even if the equipment is in good working order, a number of other potential pitfalls await anesthesia personnel. These include inherent risks (notably involving invasive devices), failure to obtain informed consent when indicated, failure to utilize a device when the standard of care so requires, and misplaced reliance on an item of equipment.

Finally, once anesthesia personnel come to rely on one of these complex devices, its unavailability because of malfunction or routine servicing may result in a serious lowering of the standard of care. This would be especially true if personnel became so accustomed to use of the device that to be required to switch to a more simplistic one would seriously interfere with their ability to deliver a safe anesthetic. One's potential exposure to liability when using, or not using, today's complex and sophisticated equipment is a fascinating subject, and one that is considered throughout this chapter. But first, it is desirable to review some of the injuries that may stem from monitoring practice.

Direct Versus Indirect Injuries

Monitoring equipment may cause direct injuries to a patient. This same equipment, or the lack of it, also may indirectly injure a patient. An example of a direct injury would be a perforation of a vessel or viscus by a monitoring probe, or electrical shock caused by faulty circuits or lack of proper grounding. An indirect injury might stem from misplaced reliance upon a device, or the display of incorrect readings that resulted in the wrong therapeutic decision. An indirect injury also might occur during unavailability if the availability and use of the instrument would have prevented an adverse outcome. The following paragraphs detail some of the legal pitfalls stemming from both direct and indirect injuries caused by modern monitoring practice.

Inherent Risks of Some Monitoring Techniques

There are a number of procedures, both diagnostic and therapeutic, associated with a small but finite and known risk of injury. Some of these procedures involve relatively simple techniques, for example, catheterizing a major blood vessel. The insertion of a catheter into the right side of the heart for central venous pressure monitoring can result in perforation of a vessel or wall of the heart in roughly 4 instances out of each 1000 insertions.[2] In reviewing monitoring equipment–related accidents in uniformed-services hospitals, I have encountered several cases of serious complications—loss of a thumb following the placement of radial artery cannula in the presence of a negative Allen's test; perforation of a major vein in the neck with consequent hemothorax; and passage of a central venous catheter through the wall of the right ventricle with subsequent hemopericardium, cardiac tamponade, and circulatory arrest. The fact that these inherent risks exist raises the issue of informed consent, and whether and under what circumstances there is a duty to inform the patient of them.

Informed Consent Issues

The informed consent doctrine, which is discussed at length in Chapter 9, revolves about a disclosure to the patient of the *risk-benefit ratio*. Many invasive monitoring procedures are performed in emergency or semiemergency situations. The risks posed by the patient's medical or surgical problems and impending operative procedure generally far outweigh *those risks* created by the presence of the monitoring lead(s). At the same time, the information gained (the *benefit*) from the monitor may be indispensable for the safe management of the case. Thus, the individual making preanesthesia rounds may need to discuss very little, if anything, about the risks of proposed

monitoring. Such might also be true in the case of a badly needed semielective procedure (e.g., coronary artery bypass grafting to correct severe left-sided stenosis) in an extremely apprehensive patient.

There can be little argument that in many situations the advantages of the monitoring clearly outweigh its risks. But what if the medical indications are not clear-cut, or the operative procedure itself is purely elective (e.g., total hip replacement wherein potential major blood loss may mandate invasive vascular monitoring)? What if, in a teaching situation (Chapter 19), invasive monitoring is performed for largely elective (pedagogical) reasons? In such an instance, it would be especially important to obtain the patient's informed consent.

Failing to Keep Up With the Standard of Care

The standard of care (Chapter 4) is defined as care rendered by reasonably prudent practitioners under the same or similar circumstances, and *is essentially the same nationwide*. When considering the application of complex equipment, however, there *may be differences among communities, and even in the same community*. Large—especially tertiary-care—hospitals, wherein more-complex operative procedures are routinely carried out, would be expected to have more-complex equipment to monitor patients during those procedures. Such hospitals, in turn, would be held to a higher standard of care than the average, smaller institution. The smaller hospital could, however, hold itself out at a much higher level of care by purchasing and using this equipment and offering those services. Failure to keep up with the standard of care and have the equipment available when needed would be considered one of the elements in an action for negligence if the standard of care required the availability of equipment and its unavailability resulted in an adverse outcome to the patient.

Failure to Employ a Given Device When Indicated

One equipment-related injury deserves special emphasis, namely, indirect harm resulting from omission to use a given device in a particular situation. The decision to employ, or not to employ, any monitoring technique is principally a medical one that nevertheless has strong legal overtones. This decision often is complex; the factors that may possibly enter into the decision-making process are depicted in Figure 12-1. If the standard of care requires such an application, then failure to employ it would probably constitute a departure from the duty of care. If any consequent untoward event would not have occurred had the device been used, it would seem that the injured patient could establish a clear-cut cause action for negligence.

Legal Consequences

As noted earlier in this chapter, the standard of monitoring care is changing. If anesthesia personnel do not keep abreast of these advances, a court might step in and, by judicial decision, elevate that standard. One court, in a case involving reliance by a surgeon on the accuracy of a circulating nurse's sponge count, articulated its willingness to accept a higher than purely community standard in the following language:

> *Methods employed in any trade, business or profession, however long continued, cannot avail to establish as safe in law that which is dangerous in fact.*[3]

A hospital will be liable for failure to keep its equipment standards up to date. Unavailability of a given device, once the standard of care has shifted to its use, would not excuse the health care provider who proceeded with patient care knowing that the device was essential to that patient's well-being. If such equipment is not available, there may be an affirmative duty to inform the patient before the start of the anesthetic. If the procedure is carried out, rather than transferring the patient to another treatment facility wherein appropriate equipment would have been available, both physician and hospital may be liable if an untoward result ensues.[4]

Equipment Failures

Even simple items of equipment can fail. The more complicated they are, however,

the greater the likelihood of something going wrong. Generally, most health care–related equipment manufacturers recommend that the more sophisticated devices receive regular preventive maintenance. The importance of this maintenance and who should perform it are discussed below.

Failure of an item of equipment would be expected to result in its not being available, which may create a worse situation than if it had never been purchased at all. Unfortunately, once personnel come to rely upon some of this new, innovative equipment, its unavailability can seriously interfere with the delivery of the quality of care afforded by the use of the equipment, and the patient could suffer a consequential indirect injury. Another type of indirect injury might be caused by spurious signals on which anesthesia personnel relied. I was a party to such a situation a number of years ago. It involved a simple aneroid manometer. This case is worth reiterating, as it shows how potentially serious problems can result from rather simple equipment failures.

For reasons that I do not remember, I took the patient's blood pressure before I brought the patient to the operating room. Once in the operating room, I connected the blood pressure cuff to an aneroid manometer that was stored in a drawer in the gas anesthesia apparatus. Unfortunately, I did not take the patient's blood pressure again until after I had administered the spinal anesthetic. The patient's pressure had been running at 125/80 before the anesthetic was administered. Afterwards, I noted that it was 80/40. I gave the patient some intravenous phenylephrine, but the pressure did not return to preanesthesia levels. The surgeon, who was scrubbed and ready to make the incision, was consulted. Because two doses of phenylephrine did not restore the patient's blood pressure, we mutually decided to cancel the procedure. I took the patient to the recovery room and rechecked his blood pressure using the mercury manometer affixed to the wall behind the head of the bed. His pressure was normal. I later checked the aneroid manometer and found that it was registering 46 mm Hg less than it should have. Fortunately, the only sequel involved was an unnecessary anesthetic. The patient was taken to the operating room 2 days later and a "normotensive" spinal anesthetic was administered for his hernia repair. There were no adverse legal consequences; in today's litigious climate, there could well have been.

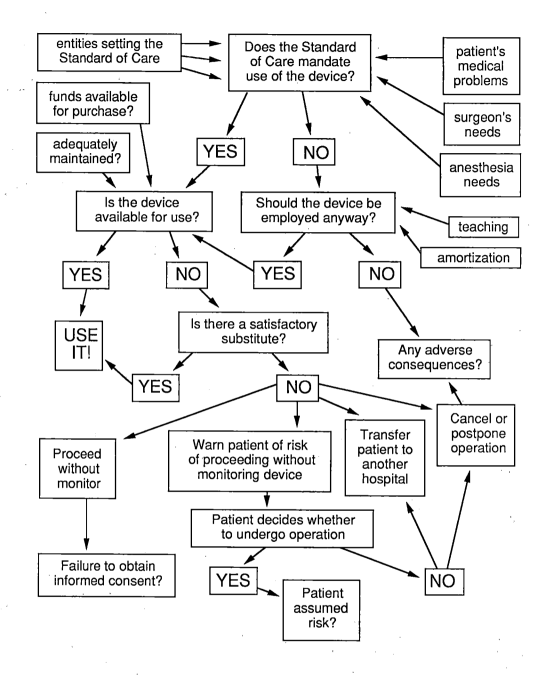

Figure 12–1 The interrelationship of the potentially numerous factors involved in the decision to employ a given (generally complex) monitoring device. The decision-making process commences at the top left with a consideration of the standard of care, the sources of which are enumerated in the text. Assuming the device is essential to that patient's care and is not available, the process terminates at the bottom right with three rather hard choices, one of which might lead to an indirect injury. Fortunately, one would not expect to encounter the need for this decision tree with any regularity.

An aneroid manometer is a relatively simple device. Most monitoring equipment is much more complex, and hence much more prone to malfunction.[5] Equipment may be defective at the time it is put to use. It may also become defective after normal use, after misuse, or after being used an excessively long period of time without maintenance or replacement. If the equipment is defective at the time of purchase, the manufacturer will be liable. There is a growing body of products liability case law (see Chapter 22) that holds the supplier liable as well.[6-8] The fact that either the manufacturer, supplier, or both become liable does not necessarily exonerate the user, however. If the defect in the equipment is obvious, the person who employs it would be expected, in the application of reasonable care, to discover the defect.[9] Failure to do so would constitute negligence on the part of that person. In some situations, the user would be liable for latent defects if a check of the equipment before use was customary practice, that is, if there was a duty to be watchful for latent but foreseeable defects.[10]

Equipment may be in good working order when first installed and put to use, but may develop a malfunction after a period of time. If this period is relatively short, one would expect liability similar to that discussed in the preceding paragraph to apply. If the failure of the device followed long use, however, the manufacturer and supplier probably would not be liable. "Long use before failure is evidence of absence of any initial defect."[11] The best-made equipment can be expected to wear out in time. Plaintiffs' lawyers in such cases may use ingenious methods to prove excessive use. In a case involving a broken needle, the plaintiff was able to obtain through discovery

procedures (see Chapter 23) the defendant's purchase orders for needles. By introducing copies of those orders into evidence, the plaintiff's lawyer was able to prove that the needles had been reused for an excessively long period of time, and the defendant was therefore negligent in not replacing them with new ones more often.[12] Generally, if an instrument breaks down because of abuse, liability would fall squarely on the shoulders of the user.

Maintenance and Repair

Users of equipment have a duty to maintain it in safe operating condition,[13-14] including inspection for "such deterioration which is bound to follow ordinary use."[15] While one court held that the user would not be liable for injuries caused by a latent defect in an instrument that was in daily use,[16] it seems apparent that the majority of courts will weigh the length of time that the instrument or device has been in service, and the maintenance given to it, if any. Figure 12-2 diagrams the potential liability of the manufacturer, supplier, user, or all three in the various situations just described.

Importance of Preventive Maintenance Contracts

All equipment should be subjected to periodic preventive maintenance. Such maintenance is mandatory for complex devices. Unless the hospital can be assured of competent in-house personnel to service this equipment, it is far wiser to subject it to maintenance by a qualified outside company, especially one that is affiliated with the manufacturer. Many manufacturers of gas anesthesia apparatus and monitoring equipment offer preventive maintenance

Figure 12–2 The potential liability of user, manufacturer, or both, for direct (see text) injuries caused by defective equipment. In this figure, as well as in Figures 12-3 and 12-4, injuries to personnel as well as to patients are possible. (Adapted from Dornette, WHL: Legal Aspects. In Dornette, WHL (ed): Monitoring in Anesthesia. FA Davis, Philadelphia, 1973, pp 125–136.)

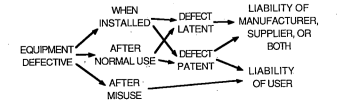

POTENTIAL LIABILITY FOR DEFECTIVE EQUIPMENT

contracts. Serious consideration should be given to the purchase of one of these contracts. In doing so, the ultimate liability, if any, will be at least shared with, and possibly completely shouldered by, the out-of-house service concern.

Faulty Repairs

Figure 12-3 diagrams the potential liability for injuries caused by faultily repaired equipment. Because of the complexity of most of this equipment, it is desirable to utilize a skilled repair person. Having a preventive maintenance contract with the manufacturer, supplier, or a reputable repair service company (see the previous paragraph) may be preferable. The user of the equipment (e.g., the hospital) obviously would be liable if a patient injury resulted from a repair performed in a faulty manner by one of its own employees. Furthermore, the user would be liable if the defect was patent or the user was negligent in selecting a repair service, even though the latter functioned as an independent contractor (see Chapter 6). The user is, however, justified in relying upon repair personnel who are carefully selected. In general, negligence of such an independent contractor would not be imputed to the owner-user of the equipment.

Equipment manufacturers today are under a duty to furnish recommendations for servicing and repair in the absence of offering a sound service program of their own. If these recommendations prove inaccurate, and a patient is injured because of improperly performed repairs, the manufacturer would be liable. The repair person might be liable also if the instructions were patently incorrect.

Other Equipment-Related Injuries

The equipment may be in perfect working order, and yet an equipment-related injury still may follow its use. Considering the sophisticated nature of some of the devices available today, and the lack of an engineering or other electronic background among physicians and hospital purchasing agents, it is to be expected that the user shopping for new equipment will rely upon the expertise of the manufacturer or supplier. "The greater the complexity of the product, the greater is the reliance placed upon the seller's skill and judgment by the consumer."[17] In general, a purchaser and user who relies upon the judgment of the manufacturer is protected by the implied warranty of fitness for a particular purpose that accompanies goods sold in this country. This warranty is created by the Uniform Commercial Code that has been adopted by all state legislatures in this country.

> *Where the seller at the time of contracting has reason to know any particular purpose [emphasis the author's] for which the goods are required and the buyer is relying on the seller's skill or judgement to select or furnish suitable goods, there is unless excluded or modified . . . implied warranty that the good shall be fit for such purpose.*[18]

If it was obvious that the goods were unfit for

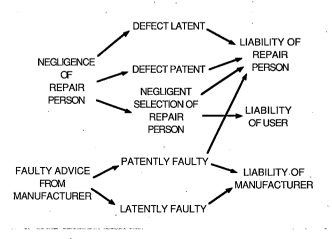

Figure 12-3 The potential liability of repair person, user, or manufacturer for direct injuries caused by faulty repairs. (Adapted from Dornette, WHL: Legal Aspects. In Dornette, WHL (ed): Monitoring in Anesthesia. FA Davis, Philadelphia, 1973, pp 125-136.)

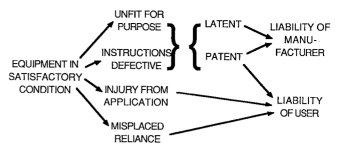

Figure 12–4 The potential liability for other injuries, both direct and indirect. Indirect injuries related to misplaced reliance or unfitness for purpose were further covered in Figure 12-1. (Adapted from Dornette, WHL: Legal Aspects. In Dornette, WHL (ed): Monitoring in Anesthesia. FA Davis, Philadelphia, 1973, pp 125–136.)

a particular purpose, the user most likely would be found liable as well as the seller.

The manufacturer of complex equipment is under a legal obligation to furnish an operation manual or other instructions detailing the application of the device. Liability for a defect in the manual or instructions would be imputed to the manufacturer (Fig. 12-4). For example, an absence of adequate warning on an otherwise safe instrument would create manufacturer's liability.[19] It should be obvious, however, that the user would be under a legally recognized duty to read, and heed, these warnings and instructions. They in effect become a legal document similar to the package literature that by FDA regulation accompanies pharmaceuticals sold in this country. Failure to read the instructions might or might not relieve the manufacturer of liability for any deficiencies in them.[20] Reading and understanding the instructions should help the user to apply them as indicated and avoid other problems (see also Fig. 12-4) such as injury from application of the leads or misplaced reliance on the capabilities of the instrument.

HOSPITAL VERSUS PHYSICIAN LIABILITY

Under most circumstances, complex equipment is purchased by the hospital. Frequently the purchase is recommended by those health care providers who will use that equipment. Interesting questions of potential liability arise when equipment owned and maintained by the hospital, but under the direct use of a private physician who is not a hospital employee, causes injury to a patient. Whether the physician, the hospital, or both would be liable would depend upon the various factors discussed in the previous paragraphs. At times, individual physicians, nurse anesthetists, or partnerships of physicians will purchase smaller items of equipment. Monitoring devices frequently fall into this category. What about physician-owned equipment and injuries to a patient? Would the hospital be liable? Resolving these questions becomes important inasmuch as approximately 70% of all medical malpractice cases stem from in-hospital care, and since (at least in the not-too-distant past) an estimated "almost half"[21] to "a majority"[22] of malpractice cases or claims involve equipment.

Liability of a physician or nurse anesthetist for equipment-related injuries would be predicated upon the common law of medical malpractice. The health care provider would be liable only if he or she "failed to use reasonable skill, care, or diligence."[23] Using an instrument improperly, failing to notice a patent defect, or not performing any monitoring at all when it was indicated would be considered a lack of reasonable skill, care, or diligence. Before putting equipment to use, personnel should inspect it for patent defects and test it for possible latent defects. Taking these steps would reduce the possibility of injury, mitigate liability, and help bolster the defense should litigation ensue following an adverse outcome.[24]

The hospital is expected to keep up with the developments of monitoring practice[25] (as well as other practices) and supply equipment "reasonably fit for the uses and purposes intended under the circumstances."[26] This duty extends to keeping the equipment in good operating order and replacing old, worn-out equipment as indicated.[12] On the other hand, if custom, the standard of care, or the nature of the equipment dictated that it be inspected for defects before being put to use by physicians, nurse anesthetists, or others, and there was a failure to conduct such an inspection, the liability would shift to the individual health care provider, although the hospital still might be liable.[27]

If the health care provider owns the equipment, a different type of problem could arise. Hospitals should have safety regulations pertaining to personnel equipment brought into the hospital by the members of its staff. The National Fire Protection Association* (NFPA) makes certain recommendations for the use of equipment in anesthetizing locations in Code 99. This publication provides[28]:

(a) *No electrical equipment except that judged by the engineering department of _____ Hospital as being in compliance with NFPA 99-1987, Section 12-4.1, "Anesthetizing Locations," shall be used in any anesthetizing location.*

(b) *When a physician wishes to use his or her personal electrical equipment, it shall first be inspected by the Engineering Department and, if judged to comply with NFPA 99-1987, Section 12-4.1, "Anesthetizing Locations," it will be so labeled.*

(c) *Photographic lighting equipment shall be of the totally enclosed type or so constructed as to prevent the escape of sparks or hot metal particles.*

It is possible that these or similar regulations have not been adopted by all hospitals. These rules do point up what is customary practice in some hospitals, however. Thus, they would have evidential value in any litigation stemming from an injury caused by a physician's personal equipment. A court might hold, as it did in *Darling*[25] (involving injuries of another type), that published standards are admissible as evidence of customary practice, and that one of the duties of the hospital is to enforce regulations governing the activities of members of its staff.

---

*For a discussion of the role of the NFPA and other voluntary standards-making organizations in setting the standard of care, see Chapter 4.

A LOOK INTO THE FUTURE

In 1985 the American Society of Anesthesiologists (ASA) commenced the development of, and on October 21, 1986 adopted and subsequently published, the ASA Standards for Basic Intra-operative Monitoring.[29] These standards are reproduced in Appendix 12-1. The AANA has developed and published similar standards (Appendix 12-2). Although neither the ASA nor the AANA are voluntary standards-making organizations per se, they do publish standards and thus contribute to the uniformity and elevation of the level of anesthesia care in this country. Will those standards automatically elevate the standard of monitoring care? They most certainly will, for both anesthesiologists and nurse anesthetists. Furthermore, they can be expected to have significant evidential value in any future litigation involving monitoring practice in this country, especially if one of the parties to the action is a member of the ASA or certified by the AANA. (See Chapter 4 for a discussion of how the courts treat published standards that are introduced as evidence to establish the "standard of care" in a negligence action.)

Another interesting development in standards making appeared in a 1986 article published in the *Journal of the American Medical Association*.[30] The article detailed the standards for anesthesia monitoring practices adopted for the nine teaching hospitals that are affiliated with Harvard Medical School. These standards (Appendix 12-3) were developed to prevent what was postulated to be inadequate-monitoring–related morbidity and, possibly, mortality. Will this article have an effect on the standard of care similar to that of the ASA's publication? Unquestionably, it probably already has, at least in Boston. Whether that effect has or will spread beyond New England is not an easy question to answer. There are, of course, many similarities between the ASA and Harvard standards. Good practices are good practices, whether developed by a national organization or a large medical center. Furthermore, there usually is more than one method for achieving a given result.

Of importance in assessing any practice, whether in the operating room or courtroom, is the final outcome. Did (or does) that practice enhance the quality of care? Would the care have been any better had the alternative practice (often espoused by the plaintiff's expert witness) been employed? What is the opinion of the defendant's expert? As noted throughout this book, the standard of care—as accepted to resolve any action for malpractice—is almost always established by expert testimony.

At the beginning of this chapter, I commented on the use of the mass spectroscope to detect the partial pressures of various respired gases and determine from these data certain malfunctions before an adverse outcome ensues. I then stated that mass spectrometry "has not been accepted as part of the standard of care in all hospitals across this country . . . at least not at the time of this writing." Mass spectrometry is not specifically included in the monitoring standards of either the ASA or the Harvard Medical School (although spectrometry certainly will help fulfill these standards as they apply to ventilatory monitoring). Will the standard of monitoring care across the United States eventually change to incorporate mass spectrometry? If so, in all hospitals and all patient care situations? Only in larger, tertiary-care institutions (in many of which the standard has already changed)? Or will the standard come to rest somewhere in between? The last situation is most likely, given the cost of mass spectrometry, and the impracticality of its use in small hospitals.

Clearly, advances in the art and science of monitoring do enhance patient care.[31] One example may be taken from the comments of law-medicine expert David Rubsamen, who follows the professional liability scene in California. Addressing the standard of care in monitoring practices, and changes that have taken place in the recent past, he wrote:

> It is particularly interesting to note the effect of new [monitoring] technology on the risk of liability for the anesthesiologist. It was commonly felt in 1974 that California anesthesiologists might soon be uninsurable . . . because there were so many . . . verdicts and . . . settlements against anesthesiologists. But with increased sophistication of anesthesia machines and adherence to constant pulse monitoring, the incidence of anesthesia disasters over the past 10 years has steadily declined. . . . One of the major California carriers now rates anesthesiologists at about the same classification as general surgeons.[32]

RECENT CASE

Washington v. Washington Hospital Center[33] is a fascinating case involving the standard of monitoring care, how it is developed, the role of voluntary standards in that process, and whether the monitoring standard as of November 1987 incorporated end-tidal carbon dioxide monitors. According to the case report, Mrs. Washington was admitted to the defendant hospital for an elective laparotomy. She was taken to the operating room on the morning of November 7, 1987, general anesthesia was administered, an endotracheal catheter inserted, and its positioning checked and reportedly found proper. Unfortunately, Mrs. Washington was noted to be deeply cyanotic shortly thereafter. Circulatory arrest subsequently ensued. Mrs. Washington never recovered consciousness and currently is "essentially awake but unaware" of her surroundings.[34] Her next of kin retained legal counsel and a lawsuit was filed on her behalf and that of her estranged husband and others. The nurse anesthetist, anesthesiologist, and hospital were among the several defendants.

It was the plaintiffs' contention that the hypoxic episode was caused by inadvertent and undiagnosed esophageal intubation, that the use of an end-tidal carbon dioxide monitor would have afforded a timely diagnosis of this mistake, that the standard of care at that time required use of such a device, and that failure to employ one breached the standard. As part of the plaintiffs' proof, the monitoring standards of the American Society of Anesthesiologists (first version adopted October 1, 1985) and the Harvard monitoring standards (see Appendices 12-1 and 12-3) were introduced into evidence. These publications were referred as practices to be "encouraged" or "recommended," and the standards as "emerging" or "developing."[35] It was the defense posture that this terminology did not mandate such practices. In response, the appellate jurists commented:

> A standard of due care . . . necessarily embodies what a reasonably prudent [emphasis the court's] hospital would do [citation omitted], and hence care and foresight exceeding the minimum required by law or mandatory professional regulation may be necessary to meet that standard. It certainly cannot

*be said that the 1986 recommendation
of a professional association (which
had no power to issue or enforce
mandatory requirements), or an article
speaking of an "emerging" standard in
1986, have no bearing on an expert
opinion as to what the standard of
patient monitoring equipment was fully one year later. . . .*[36]

During trial, the defendant anesthesiologist
and anesthetist reached effective settlements,
and the case proceeded against the hospital.
The jury returned a verdict against the hospital for $4.586 million on behalf of Mrs. Wash-
ington and $68,000 on behalf of her estranged
husband for loss of consortium.[37]

Among other things, this case points up the
willingness of courts to accept voluntary
standards and allow their use in bolstering the
opinions of expert witnesses in medical malpractice cases.

CONCLUSION

A great many modern medical advances
have been made possible only by the availability of monitoring equipment that often
is highly complex. The application of this
equipment has elevated the level of medical care and has changed the standard of
care. It might be considered a departure
from this standard to fail to have this
equipment available, to fail to use it if it is
available, or to fail to understand and interpret its output. Because it is complex,
modern equipment is subject to malfunction. It requires skilled maintenance and
repair services. Both direct and indirect injuries can follow the use of this equipment.
For all of these reasons, I offer the following suggestions for minimizing the injury-
producing potential of using (or not using)
this equipment and, hence, mitigating exposure to liability.

1 Keep up with the standard of care.
   Have equipment available, *and use
   it,* as the standard mandates.
2 If needed equipment is not available, and proceeding without it
   would increase the risk to the patient, consider postponing the procedure or transferring the patient

to an institution wherein the
equipment is available.
3 Purchase equipment only from reputable manufacturers. The warranties that accompany the device
   then will have real force.
4 Remember that it is the responsibility of the manufacturer to supply operating manuals and instructions. It is the responsibility of the
   user to read and understand those
   instructions.
5 Be certain that all personnel who
   operate the equipment are thoroughly trained in its proper use.
6 Keep the equipment in good repair;
   if it is complex, it should be ser-
   viced only by qualified personnel.
7 It is highly desirable to purchase
   a preventive maintenance contract with the manufacturer, supplier, or reputable repair service
   company.
8 Any safety precautions embodied
   in such documents as NFPA 99
   should be understood, read, and
   followed.
9 One must remember that, properly
   selected and adequately functioning equipment notwithstanding,
   the *most essential* element in
   sound monitoring practice is *the
   presence of a responsible anesthesiologist or anesthetist in the operating room with the patient at all
   times.*
10 Everyone should also remember
   that while one cannot prevent lawsuits from being filed, one can, by
   following these suggestions, mitigate exposure to liability and bolster one's defenses significantly
   should an untoward accident and
   patient injury occur.

REFERENCES

1. Lichtiger, M: Respiratory monitoring to detect and avoid anesthetic disasters; mass
   spectrometry. Semin Anesth 3:206, 1986.
2. Jay, AWL and Kehler, CH: Heart perforation
   by central venous catheters (editorial). *Can
   J Anaesth* 34:333, 1987.

3. Ault v. Hall, 119 Ohio State 422, 164 N.E. 518, 60 A.L.R. 128 (Sup. Ct. 1929).

4. Carrasco v. Bankoff, 33 Cal. Rpt. 673 (Ct. App. 2d Dist., Div. 1, 1963).

5. Grace, CH and Kahoe, SM: Injuries from electronic power sources. Cleveland State Law Rev 19:23, 1970.

6. McKisson v. Sales Affiliates, Inc., 416 S.E. 2d 787 (Sup. Ct. Tex. 1967).

7. Read v. Safeway Stores, 70 Cal. Rptr. 454 (Ct. App. 1st Dist., Div. 3, 1968).

8. State Stove Mfg. Co. v. Hodges, 189 So. 2d 113 Sup. Ct. Miss. 1966).

9. Vlases v. Montgomery Ward & Co., 377 F.2d 846 (3d Cir. 1967).

10. Swartz, EM: Products liability: Manufacturer's responsibility for defective or negligently designed medical and surgical instruments. DePaul Law Rev 18:348, 1969.

11. Melanson Co. v. Hupp Corp., 282 F. Supp. 859 (D.N.J. 1966).

12. Ribando v. American Cyanamid Co., 37 Misc., 2d 603, 235 N.Y.S. 2d 110 (Sup. Ct., Spec. Term, N.Y. Co., 1962).

13. American Policyholders Insurance Co. v. Michota, 156 O.S. 578, 103 N.E. 2d 817 (Sup. Ct. Ohio 1952).

14. Nelson v. Swedish Hosp., 241 Minn. 511, 64 N.W. 2d 38 (Sup. Ct. 1954).

15. Goar v. Village of Stephen, 157 Minn. 228, 196 N.W. 171 (Sup. Ct. 1923).

16. Johnston v. Black Co., 33 Cal. App. 363, 91 P. 2d 921 (Dist. Ct. App. 1st Dist., Div. 2, 1939.

17. Kopet v. Klein, 275 Minn. 525, 148 N.W. 2d 385 (Supr. Ct. 1967).

18. UNIFORM COMMERCIAL CODE § 2-315. The exact citation to this section of the code will vary from state to state.

19. Lillehald v. E. I. DuPont de Nemours Co., 268 F. Supp. 791 (S.D.N.Y. 1966).

20. Douglas v. Bussabarger, 438 P. 2d 829 (Sup. Ct. Wash. 1968).

21. Kirchner, AA. Do we carry adequate malpractice coverage? JAMA 178:402, 1961.

22. The equipment factor in medical professional liability, Fort Wayne, Medical Protective, p 1.

23. *Annot.* Malpractice: attending physicians' liability for injury caused by equipment furnished by hospital. 35 A.L.R. 3d (1968).

24. Tennant v. Barton, 164 Wash. 279, 2 P. 2d 735 (1931).

25. Darling v. Charleston Community Memorial Hosp., 50 Ill. App. 2d 253, 200 N.E. 2d 149 (App. Ct., 4th Dist., 1964); *aff'd.* 33 Ill. 2d 326, 211 N.E. 2d 253 (Sup. Ct. 1965).

26. South Highlands Infirmary v. Camp. 279 Ala. I, 180 So. 2d 904, 14 A.L.R. 3d 1245 (1965).

27. *Annot.* Hospital's liability to patient for injury sustained from defective equipment furnished by hospital for use in diagnosis or treatment of patients. 14 A.L.R. 3d 1954.

28. National Fire Protection Association: NFPA 99—Health Care Facilities, Appendix C. National Fire Protection Association, Boston, 1987, pp 99–164, 165.

29. Eichhorn, JH: Are there standards for intraoperative monitoring? Act Anesth 5:1, 1988.

30. Eichhorn, JH, et al: Standards for patient monitoring during anesthesia at Harvard Medical School. *JAMA* 256:1017, 1986; for the preoperative and intraoperative monitoring standard of the JCAHO, see Surgical and Anesthesia Services Standard **SA.1.5** in Accreditation Manual for Hospitals. Joint Commission on Accreditation of Healthcare Organizations, Chicago, 1990, p 272.

31. Eichhorn, *supra* note 29, at 20.

32. Rubsamen, DS: The standard of care and where it comes from. Semin Anesth 5:237, 1986.

33. Washington v. Washington Hospital Center, 579 A.2d 177 (D.C. App. 1990).

34. Id. at 180.

35. Id. at 182.

36. Ibid.

37. Id. at 180.

APPENDIX

12-1

ASA STANDARDS FOR BASIC INTRA-OPERATIVE MONITORING†

These standards apply to all anesthesia care although, in emergency circumstances, appropriate life support measures take precedence. These standards may be exceeded at any time based on the judgement of the responsible anesthesiologist. They are intended to encourage high quality patient care, but observing them cannot guarantee any specific patient outcome. They are subject to revision from time to time, as warranted by the evolution of technology and practice. This set of standards addresses only the issue of basic intraoperative monitoring, which is one component of anesthesia care. In certain rare or unusual circumstances, 1) some of these methods of monitoring may be clinically impractical, and 2) appropriate use of the described monitoring methods may fail to detect untoward clinical developments. Brief interruptions of continual‡ monitoring may be unavoidable. *Under extenuating circumstances, the responsible anesthesiologist may waive the requirements marked with an asterisk (*); it is recommended that when this is done, it should be so stated (including the reasons) in a note in the patient's medical record.* These standards are not intended for application to the care of the obstetrical patient in labor or the conduct of pain management.

STANDARD I

Qualified anesthesia personnel shall be present in the room throughout the conduct of all general anesthetics, regional anesthetics and monitored anesthesia care.

Objective

Because of the rapid changes in patient status during anesthesia, qualified anesthesia personnel shall be continuously present to monitor the patient and provide anesthesia care. In the event there is a direct known hazard, e.g., radiation, to the anesthesia personnel which might require intermittent remote observation of the patient, some provision for monitoring the patient must be made. In the event that an emergency requires the temporary absence of the person primarily responsible for the anesthetic, the best judgement of the anesthesiologist will be exercised in comparing the emergency with the anesthetized patient's condition and in the selection of the person left responsible for the anesthetic during the temporary absence.

STANDARD II

During all anesthetics, the patient's oxygenation, ventilation, circulation and temperature shall be continually evaluated.

---

†Approved by House of Delegates of the American Society of Anesthesiologists on October 21, 1986; last amended October 23, 1990; to become effective January 1, 1991. Reprinted with permission of the ASA.

‡Note that "continual" is defined as "repeated regularly and frequently in steady rapid succession" whereas "continuous" means "prolonged without any interruption at any time."

OXYGENATION

Objective

To ensure adequate oxygen concentration in the inspired gas and the blood during all anesthetics.

Methods

1 Inspired gas: During every administration of general anesthesia using an anesthesia machine, the concentration of oxygen in the patient breathing system shall be measured by an oxygen analyzer with a low oxygen concentration limit alarm in use.
2 Blood oxygenation: During all anesthetics, a quantitative method of assessing oxygenation such as pulse oximetry shall be employed.* Adequate illumination and exposure of the patient is necessary to assess color.*

VENTILATION

Objective

To ensure adequate ventilation of the patient during all anesthetics.

Methods

1 Every patient receiving general anesthesia shall have the adequacy of ventilation continually evaluated. While qualitative clinical signs such as chest excursion, observation of the reservoir breathing bag and auscultation of breath sounds may be adequate, quantitative monitoring of the CO_2 content and/or volume of expired gas is encouraged.
2 When an endotracheal tube is inserted, its correct positioning in the trachea must be verified by clinical assessment and by identification of carbon dioxide in the expired gas.* End-tidal CO_2 analysis, in use from the time of endotracheal tube placement, is encouraged.
3 When ventilation is controlled by a mechanical ventilator, there shall be in continuous use a device that is capable of detecting disconnection of components of the breathing system. The device must give an audible signal when its alarm threshold is exceeded.
4 During regional anesthesia and monitored anesthesia care, the adequacy of ventilation shall be evaluated, at least, by continual observation of qualitative clinical signs.

CIRCULATION

Objective

To ensure the adequacy of the patient's circulatory function during all anesthetics.

Methods

1 Every patient receiving anesthesia shall have the electrocardiogram continuously displayed from the beginning of anesthesia until preparing to leave the anesthetizing location.*

2 Every patient receiving anesthesia shall have arterial blood pressure and heart rate determined and evaluated at least every five minutes.*

3 Every patient receiving general anesthesia shall have, in addition to the above, circulatory function continually evaluated by at least one of the following: palpation of a pulse, auscultation of heart sounds, monitoring of a tracing of intra-arterial pressure, ultrasound peripheral pulse monitoring, or pulse plethysmography or oximetry.

BODY TEMPERATURE

Objective

To aid in the maintenance of appropriate body temperature during all anesthetics.

Methods

There shall be readily available a means to continuously measure the patient's temperature. When changes in body temperature are intended, anticipated or suspected, the temperature shall be measured.

APPENDIX

12-2

AANA PATIENT MONITORING STANDARDS*

(AN ELABORATION OF STANDARD V OF STANDARDS FOR NURSE ANESTHESIA PRACTICE) [SEE APPENDIX 4-2.—ED.]

Basic to safe anesthesia care is the application of qualitative and quantitative monitoring which enables the anesthetist to administer anesthesia and evaluate its effect in a manner that optimizes desired responses while minimizing the risks of anesthesia. Fundamental to this endeavor is the use of multiple monitoring modalities which play vital roles in assisting anesthetists to provide conscientious care to patients receiving anesthesia.

These patient monitoring standards are intended to assist the CRNA practitioner in providing consistent, safe anesthesia care.

These standards apply to patients undergoing general, regional or monitored anesthesia care for diagnostic or therapeutic procedures in designated anesthetizing locations. In extenuating circumstances, the CRNA must use clinical judgment in prioritizing and implementing these standards. All of these standards do not normally apply to epidural analgesia for labor or pain management therapy. The standards may be exceeded in any or all respects at any time at the discretion of the anesthetist, as required by individual patient needs.

While the standards are intended to encourage high quality patient care, they cannot insure specific patient outcomes. It is recognized that appropriately used monitoring modalities may fail to detect untoward clinical developments. Further, it is recognized by the AANA that under some circumstances certain monitoring standards may not be applicable. While this is a fact of practice, the omission of one or more monitoring standards should be documented and the reason stated on the patient's anesthesia record. Interruptions in monitoring may be unavoidable. Occasionally, the anesthetist must work at some distance from the patient because of an environmental hazard such as, but not limited to, radiation. Under such circumstances, provisions for monitoring the patient must be made and documented on the patient's anesthesia record.

Adequate facilities must exist to enable remote patient monitoring.

The standards are subject to review and revision from time to time, as indicated by technology and practice.

ANESTHESIA PROVIDERS

Continuous clinical observation and anesthetist vigilance are the bases of safe anesthesia care. The anesthetist, or nurse anesthesia student, shall be in constant attendance of the patient until the responsibility for care has been accepted by another qualified health care provider.

PATIENT MONITORS

Ventilation

Purpose

To assess adequate ventilation of the patient.

STANDARD

Ventilatory adequacy shall be assessed by continuous auscultation of breath sounds. Correct placement of an endotracheal tube must be verified by auscultation, chest excursion and end tidal CO_2 monitoring when available. Other quantitative ventilatory devices may be used in conjunction with auscultation, such as spirometry and ventilatory pressure monitors.

Breathing system disconnect monitor: When the patient is ventilated by an automatic mechanical ventilator, the integrity of the breathing system must be monitored by a device that is capable of detecting the disconnection of any component of the breathing system. Such a device shall be equipped with an audible alarm which is activated when its limits are exceeded.

Oxygenation

Purpose

To assess adequate oxygenation of the patient.

STANDARD

Adequacy of patient oxygenation shall be monitored continuously with pulse oximetry. In addition to pulse oximetry, oxygenation shall also be monitored by observations of skin color, the color of the blood in the surgical field and arterial blood gas analysis when indicated.

During general anesthesia, the oxygen concentration delivered by the anesthesia machine shall be monitored continuously with an oxygen analyzer with a low oxygen concentration limit alarm. An oxygen supply failure alarm system shall be operational to warn of low oxygen pressure to the anesthesia machine.

Circulation

Purpose

To assess adequacy of the cardiovascular system.

> **STANDARD**
>
> Blood pressure and heart rate shall be determined and recorded at least every 5 minutes.
> The patient's electrocardiogram shall be monitored continuously during the course of the anesthetic.
> Circulation also shall be assessed by at least one of the following measures: digital palpation of pulse, auscultation of heart sounds, continuous intra-arterial pressure monitoring, electronic pulse monitoring or pulse oximetry.

Body Temperature

Purpose

To assess changes in body temperature.

> **STANDARD**
>
> Body temperature shall be intermittently or continuously monitored and recorded on all patients receiving general anesthesia; the means to monitor temperature shall be immediately available for use on all patients receiving local or regional anesthesia and used when indicated.

Neuromuscular Function

Purpose

To assess neuromuscular function.

> **STANDARD**
>
> The means to evaluate the patient's neuromuscular function by the use of a nerve stimulator shall be available immediately when neuromuscular blocking agents have been used.

ANESTHESIA EQUIPMENT

A complete equipment safety check shall be performed daily and an abbreviated check of all equipment shall be performed before each anesthetic is administered.

All anesthesia machines and monitoring equipment shall conform to the appropriate national and state standards. An ongoing preventive maintenance program shall be established and enforced.

APPENDIX

12-3

HARVARD STANDARDS

(ADAPTED IN REVISED FORM JULY 3, 1985)*

These standards apply for any administration of anesthesia involving Department of Anesthesia personnel and are specifically referable to preplanned anesthetics administered in designated anesthetizing locations (specific exclusion: administration of epidural analgesia for labor or pain management). In emergency circumstances in any location, immediate life-support measures of whatever appropriate nature come first with attention turning to the measures described in these standards as soon as possible and practical. These standards encourage high-quality patient care but observing them cannot guarantee any specific patient outcome. These standards are subject to revision from time to time, as warranted by the evolution of technology and practice.

Anesthesiologist's or Nurse Anesthetist's Presence in Operating Room

For all anesthetics initiated by or involving a member of the Department of Anesthesia, an attending or resident anesthesiologist or nurse anesthetist shall be present in the room throughout the conduct of all general anesthetics, regional anesthetics, and monitored intravenous anesthetics. An exception is made when there is a direct known hazard, e.g., radiation, to the anesthesiologist or nurse anesthetist, in which case some provision for monitoring the patient must be made.

Blood Pressure and Heart Rate

Every patient receiving general anesthesia, regional anesthesia, or managed intravenous anesthesia shall have arterial blood pressure and heart rate measured at least every 5 minutes where not clinically impractical. Under extenuating circumstances, the attending anesthesiologist may waive this requirement after so stating (including the reasons) in a note in the patient's chart.

ECG

Every patient shall have the ECG continuously displayed from the induction or institution of anesthesia until preparing to leave the anesthetizing location, where not clinically impractical. Under extenuating circumstances, the attending anesthesiologist may waive this requirement after so stating (including the reasons) in a note in the patient's chart.

Continuous Monitoring

During every administration of general anesthesia, the anesthetist shall employ methods of continuously monitoring the patient's ventilation and circulation. The methods shall include, for ventilation and circulation each, at least one of the following or the equivalent.

For ventilation—Palpation or observation of the reservoir breathing bag, auscultation

---

*Reproduced with permission from the Risk Management Committee, Department of Anesthesia, Harvard Medical School.[30]

of breath sounds, monitoring of respiratory gases such as end-tidal CO_2, or monitoring expiratory gas flow. Monitoring end-tidal CO_2 is an emerging standard and is strongly preferred.

For circulation—Palpation of a pulse, auscultation of heart sounds, monitoring of a tracing of intra-arterial pressure, pulse plethysmography, or ultrasound peripheral pulse monitoring.

It is recognized that brief interruptions of the continuous monitoring may be unavoidable.

Equivalence is to be defined by the chief of the individual hospital department after submission to and review by the department heads, Department of Anesthesia, Harvard Medical School.

Breathing System Disconnect Monitoring

When ventilation is controlled by an automatic mechanical ventilator, there shall be in continuous use a device that is capable of detecting disconnection of any component of the breathing system. The device must give an audible signal when its alarm threshold is exceeded. (It is recognized that there are certain rare or unusual circumstances in which such a device may fail to detect a disconnection.)

Oxygen Analyzer

During every administration of general anesthesia using an anesthesia machine, the concentration of oxygen in the patient breathing system will be measured by a functioning oxygen analyzer with a low concentration limit alarm in use. This device must conform to the ANSI Z.79.10 Standard. Under extenuating circumstances, the attending anesthesiologist may waive this requirement after so stating (including the reasons) in a note in the patient's chart.

Ability to Measure Temperature

During every administration of general anesthesia, there shall be readily available a means to measure the patient's temperature.

Rationale—A means of temperature measurement must be available as a potential aid in the diagnosis and treatment of suspected or actual intraoperative hypothermia and malignant hyperthemia. The measurement/monitoring of temperature during every general anesthetic is not specifically mandated because of the potential risks of such monitoring and because of the likelihood of other physical signs giving earlier indication of the development of malignant hyperthemia.

13

William H. L. Dornette, M.D., J.D.

Bence A. Sell, M.D.

Postanesthesia Care

The recovery room, or postanesthesia care unit (PACU) as it currently is called, became an integral and essential part of health care delivery during the period immediately following the Second World War. Its purpose is obvious—to afford each patient recovering from the acute effects of the anesthetic and operation adequate monitoring and respiratory and vascular support until the patient's condition has stabilized and the recovery process is fairly complete. Since the advent of the PACU, operative procedures and concomitant anesthetic administrations have become much more complex. The patient population has expanded to include greater numbers of those at the extremes of age and of poorer physical status than ever before. In response to these demands, the care rendered in the PACU has progressed accordingly, thanks to advances in design, equipment, and staffing. This chapter reviews the standard of care in the operation of the modern PACU (Appendixes 13-1 and 13-2), and points out some of the potential causes of accidents and litigation that have developed, or might occur in the future, because of inadequacies in the care of patients in the postanesthesia period.

EQUIPPING AND STAFFING

Physical Plant

Much has been written about the design, construction, and operation of the PACU.[1-3] A number of features of the physical plant should be obvious. Ideally it is located on the same floor as and immediately adjacent to the operating suite. The number of patient bed positions must be sufficient to accommodate the expected surgical load. The nurses' station should be centrally located and afford personnel at the desk an unobstructed view of all patients if possible.

Fixed Equipment

Each bed position should be equipped with at least one oxygen outlet, possibly one compressed air outlet (filtered air), one vacuum inlet, and an adequate number of electrical outlets that are automatically switched to the hospital's standby electrical power system[4] in event of a power outage. General and task illumination also should be adequate (e.g., 40 to 50 foot-candles) for general observation of the patient and the performance of specific procedures as starting an intravenous line, performing lumbar or intra-arterial puncture, or initiating other invasive monitoring.

Movable Equipment

Equipment available for monitoring, ventilatory support, parenteral therapy, resuscitation, and other purposes should be comparable with that available in the operating room. It may be desirable for each bed position to be equipped with an electrocardiographic monitor. While each bed position need not be equipped with an automatic ventilator, enough should be available to cover whatever needs may arise. Airway support equipment (laryngoscopes, endotracheal catheters, oral and nasal airways) as well as a sufficient number of Ambu bags or their equivalent must be immediately available. While a defibrillator and pacemaker need not be physically located within the PACU, these devices should be available on short notice. For example, the smaller hospital may have one set of these devices that is kept in the operating suite and available for PACU use. Finally, all fluids and pharmaceuticals that might be needed for support, resuscitation, or other purposes, must be close at hand.

Staffing Patterns

A sufficient number of adequately trained personnel must be available to afford ample coverage for the customary patient load. Practicality dictates that the number of these personnel may fluctuate with the volume of the surgical load on any particular day. In 1986 the American Society of Post Anesthesia Nurses published their Standards of Nursing Practice,[5] which cover both preanesthesia and postanesthesia nursing care for hospitals and ambulatory care facilities. These standards, which were endorsed by the House of Delegates of the American Society of Anesthesiologists in 1986, suggest various patient-to-staff ratios for the PACU.[6] These ratios vary from 3:1 to 1:1, depending on the severity of the patients' medical problems and complexity of the operative procedures. These recommendations may not yet have established the standard of care across this country. Nonetheless, in litigation involving allegations of inadequate staffing, they would provide a patient-plaintiff's lawyer fertile grounds for arguing that they should constitute the standard of care.

In many hospitals it is customary practice to assign the responsibility for overall supervision of the PACU to an anesthesiologist or to the anesthesia service, to be covered by a member of that service on a rotational basis. That person must ensure that the number and qualifications of personnel are adequate to cover the expected patient load, both quantitatively and qualitatively. That person is also responsible for the development of policies and procedures for admitting, monitoring, and discharging patients, as described below.

POLICIES AND PROCEDURES

It is highly desirable that a procedural manual be developed detailing all aspects of PACU operation. Such a manual serves as an excellent starting point for the training of new personnel. Its availability at the nurses' station as a day-to-day reference also helps ensure that the standard of care of the unit will be maintained at a high level.

Admissions

It is generally desirable to admit all patients who have received any anesthetic, except possibly those receiving a local anesthetic of limited scope. Quite obviously, some patients "recover" almost completely while still in the operating room and have little need for additional close observation. By adopting a blanket rule covering all patients, no one requiring even the slightest amount of care will inadvertently be sent directly to the nursing unit.

Admissions Briefing

It is customary for the individual responsible for the administration of the anesthetic to accompany the patient to the PACU and brief personnel about the patient's condition. Table 13-1 lists the various facts and events about which personnel should be briefed. While the briefing is in progress, PACU personnel will be connecting the appropriate monitoring leads and other lines (e.g., nasal oxygen, chest suction, and the like), and will determine and record the patient's vital signs in the pres-

ence of the anesthesiologist or nurse anesthetist who was responsible for the anesthetic. That professional should be aware of these vital signs, and thus be assured that the patient's condition is stable, before he or she leaves the PACU.

Supervision and Record Keeping

The Joint Commission on Accreditation of Healthcare Organizations (JCAHO, formerly the JCAH) standards[7] mandate the evaluation of patients' status and documentation of these observations (Table 13-2). The PACU policy manual should delineate the monitoring procedures to be carried out on each patient, including the intensity of supervision, frequency of determination of vital signs, and need for performance of any other procedures. The procedural manual should detail the methodology for documenting vital signs and other observations.

It is very helpful to keep a running "score" of the patient's recovery from anesthesia. A postanesthesia recovery (PAR) scoring system, similar to the Apgar system, has been developed. The scoring scheme in current use at Walter Reed Army Medical Center is detailed in Table 13-3. While this system was developed for keeping track of the recovery progress of individual patients, it is also helpful when assessing the overall effectiveness of the PACU. The system is invaluable when reviewing the quality of care rendered by an individual anesthesiologist or anesthetist. For example, it may be found that patients who were anesthetized by a specific person are remaining in the PACU for longer-than-average periods of time, and their PAR

TABLE 13–1. Recovery Room Admissions Briefing

- Pertinent medical history
- Diagnosis
- Previous operations (if significant)
- Operation just completed
- Anesthetic agent(s) and technique(s)
- Blood loss; how determined
- Blood, fluid therapy
- Any other medications
- Vital signs during procedure
- Complications while in operating room
- Current state of recovery
- Status of protective reflexes
- Complications for which to be watchful
- Pertinent surgical orders or comments
- Any other recommendations

TABLE 13–2. JCAHO PAR Monitoring Standard

SA [Surgical and Anesthesia Services].1.5.5 The postoperative status of the patient is evaluated on admission to and discharge from the postanesthesia recovery area.*
  SA.1.5.5.1 Documentation includes a record of
    SA.1.5.5.1.1 vital signs and level of consciousness;
    SA.1.5.5.1.2 intravenous fluids administered, including blood and blood products;
    SA.1.5.5.1.3 all drugs administered;
    SA.1.5.5.1.4 postanesthesia visits; and
    SA.1.5.5.1.5 any unusual events or postoperative complications and the management of those events.

*The asterisked item is a key factor in the accreditation decision process.

Source: Accreditation Manual for Hospitals. Joint Commission on Accreditation of Healthcare Organizations, Chicago, 1990. Reprinted with permission.

scores generally are much lower than those of patients anesthetized by other members of the department. This type of information can be extremely helpful for counseling a trainee or taking adverse personnel action against a member of the staff (see Chapters 19 and 27).

Discharge Policies

The procedural manual also must cover discharge policies and criteria, especially delineating the length of time patients should be at a specific level of recovery before it is permissible to discharge them. Obviously, patients who are candidates for in-and-out procedures (see Chapter 15) will have to remain in the PACU longer than inpatients, unless provisions are made for them to be moved to a separate area in which they will become fully ambulatory. It is highly desirable that a responsible physician—generally an anesthesiologist—sign each patient out of the PACU. The JCAHO standards[7] also specify patient discharge policies (Table 13-4).

TABLE 13–3. Postanesthesia Recovery Scoring*

Activity	2	Able to move 4 extremities voluntarily or on command
	1	Able to move 2 extremities voluntarily or on command
	0	Not able to move any extremities voluntarily or on command
Respiration	2	Able to breathe deeply and cough freely
	1	Dyspnea on limited breathing
	0	Apnea
Circulation	2	BP ± <20% of preanesthetic value
	1	BP ± 20% to 50% of preanesthetic value
	0	BP ± >50% of preanesthetic value
Consciousness	2	Fully awake
	1	Arousable on calling
	0	Not responding

*Utilized in the Recovery Room, Walter Reed Army Medical Center.

Notes:
1. Each patient is scored on admission and again after intervals of 30 and 60 minutes.
2. The scores for each system are totaled; 8 is a perfect score; 0 is the poorest rating.

TABLE 13–4. JCAHO PAR Discharge Policy

SA.1.5.6 A licensed independent practitioner who has appropriate clinical privileges and who is familiar with the patient is responsible for the decision to discharge a patient from a postanesthesia recovery area or, when the surgical or anesthesia services are provided on an ambulatory basis, from the hospital.*

  SA.1.5.6.1 When the responsible licensed independent practitioner is not personally present to make the decision to discharge or does not sign the discharge order,

    SA.1.5.6.1.1 the name of the licensed independent practitioner responsible for the discharge is recorded in the patient's medical record; and*

    SA.1.5.6.1.2 relevant discharge criteria are rigorously applied to determine the readiness of the patient for discharge.

      SA.1.5.6.1.2.1 The discharge criteria are approved by the medical staff.

*The asterisked items are key factors in the accreditation decision process.
Source: Accreditation Manual for Hospitals. Joint Commission on Accreditation of Healthcare Organizations, Chicago, 1990. Reprinted with permission.

LEGAL ISSUES AND CASE LAW

Although there are relatively few cases appearing in American common law relating to litigation stemming from incidents in the PACU,[8-16] the legal issues are fairly well defined. They pertain to the duties of health care providers, negligence, intentional torts, and vicarious liability.

Potential Legal Issues

The duties of health care providers, discussed in Chapter 2, include practicing at the professed level of care and offering continuing treatment. The concept of PACU care is based upon the delegation of certain duties of anesthesia personnel—namely, monitoring the patient during the final phases of the recovery process—to those in the PACU. This delegation raises a very fundamental issue—whether and, if so, when this duty may be delegated. It is a fundamental common law principle that a person who places another in a position of peril owes the duty of rescue.[17] The patient who has been rendered unconscious and deprived of his or her protective reflexes is, in truth, in a position of peril. While patients may well have recovered consciousness by the time they enter the PACU, they may not be in full possession of all of their reflexes. The purpose of the PACU is to en-

sure that these reflexes will have returned completely before the patient is sent to the nursing unit. It is, of course, the primary duty of the responsible anesthetist or anesthesiologist to ensure that the patient has recovered these reflexes. On the other hand, given a very busy service, the anesthesiologist or nurse anesthetist cannot in effect "special duty" all patients until their reflexes have fully returned. This truism raises an important query: At what point may the anesthesiologist or nurse anesthetist delegate to PACU personnel the responsibility for continuing care of these patients while they are still under some of the effects of the agents administered by anesthesia personnel? This query deserves comment. If there is a legally recognized duty to continue administering to a patient, a court might find that the duty was not delegable, setting the stage for an action for alleged abandonment. Abandonment may be considered negligence (Chapter 3) or an intentional tort (Chapter 5). There is, however, case law to substantiate the opinion that under certain circumstances anesthesia personnel may delegate the duty of supervision of the patient during final phases of recovery to others. In *Prack v. United States Fidelity and Guaranty Co.,*[12] the court held:

> It is a matter of common knowledge that doctors successively give their attention to one patient after another, and in those instances where there is no probability of the occurrence of an emergency *it would be* entirely

unreasonable *to expect a doctor to deny his attention to a patient in need simply upon the basis that another patient* might possibly develop *a condition which required emergency attention [emphasis the authors'].*

This delegation may occur without exposure to liability for abandonment provided that the PACU personnel are appropriately skilled and trained and are thoroughly briefed in the patient's condition and any anticipated problems (see Table 13-1). Furthermore, at the time of the patient's admission the staffing pattern must be sufficient to cover the patient in question.

The second possible exposure to liability relates to the duties of the anesthesiologist (as is common practice) who is responsible for the overall operation of the PACU. It is his or her responsibility to make certain that the procedural manual covers problems that may be anticipated, and that the recommendations made to the hospital for equipping and staffing are in fact adequate. It would then become the responsibility of the hospital to ensure that these recommendations were followed. Failure on the part of the hospital to do so would shift the liability for any related patient injury to the hospital rather than the responsible anesthesiologist. Conversely, if the latter did not draft safe operational policies, or request adequate equipment or staffing, liability for injuries related to such inadequacies would tend to fall on the anesthesiologist's shoulders.

Other Case Law

Some of the case law relating to PACU litigation is disturbing. *Thomas v. Seaside Memorial Hospital*[13] involved a young child who was given diethyl ether for removal of a "birth mark" from her shoulder. To quote from the opinion:

She was in the operating room for approximately one hour and was returned to her crib, at which time she was sleeping; she was placed on her abdomen with a small pillow under her and her head and face slightly lower than her abdomen; she was lying on her right cheek, with her face showing toward her mother; Mrs. Thomas remained at the side of her child for 15 or 20 minutes during which time the baby continued to sleep, but was throwing her arms around; . . . there were two

other visitors in the room; Mrs. Mitchell, the nurse in charge, came into the room and ordered Mrs. Thomas and the other mothers to leave while the nurses bathed the other children; Mrs. Thomas protested against being compelled to leave her unconscious baby but was told by the nurse that the hospital rules required that she go out of the room while the other children were bathed; when Mrs. Thomas and the other mothers left the room the baby was lying on her abdomen with her pillow under her and her face on the right side; she was breathing and had stopped throwing her arms around.

When Mrs. Thomas returned to the room about 30 minutes later she found her baby pale and cold. An examination revealed that the child had developed respiratory and circulatory arrest. The surgeon later testified that the baby had died from atelectasis, and that "there are symptoms that a skilled doctor or nurse could discover right after the onset of atelectasis." The court found for the plaintiff on the grounds that the supervision of Mrs. Thomas' baby by the nurses had been inadequate.

A number of other cases—*Hicks,*[9] *Jackson,*[10] *Nave,*[11] and *Prack*[12]—also involve inadequate supervision of patients recovering from general anesthesia. *Jackson* involved a child who had been given general anesthesia during which she presumably suffered a hypoxic episode, as she failed to regain consciousness after termination of the anesthetic. The surgeon did not visit her in the immediate postoperative period. "The mother asked him why he did not come and attend to Judith. He said he was so busy he just did not have the time to attend to her." Judith developed hyperpyrexia and convulsions, and died about 19 hours postoperatively.

In *South Highlands Infirmary v. Galloway,*[16] a 78-year-old patient had a transurethral resection performed under spinal anesthesia. He was also given several doses of Pantopon during the procedure to achieve a somewhat balanced effect and allay apprehension. Postoperatively, although the spinal anesthetic had worn off, he was still groggy. During an interval when he was not adequately supervised, he attempted to climb from the bed, fell, and broke his hip. The hospital was found liable for inadequate supervision. In the case of *Ranelli v. Society of New York Hospital*[15] a patient rolled out of bed in the PACU and injured her nose. The court found the hospital liable for inadequate supervision.

CONCLUSION

Unquestionably, the PACU has become an essential part of modern operative intervention. Given the large and continuously growing number of patient admissions to recovery rooms in the United States, it is somewhat remarkable that there is a relative paucity of case law stemming from this aspect of patient care. Perhaps this dearth of cases relates to the careful, meticulous operation of recovery rooms in hospitals today. Perhaps it relates to the understandable tendency of defendants to settle lawsuits in which the plaintiffs' cases are meritorious. In 1920, long before the advent of the PACU, Benjamin Cardozo, then an appellate court judge who later became a Justice of the Supreme Court, writing on changes and growth of the law, stated:

Existing rules and principles can give us our present location, our bearings, our latitude and longitude. The inn that shelters for the night is not the journey's end. The law, like the traveler, must be ready for the morrow. It must have the principle of growth.[18]

Plato, writing many centuries earlier, stated:

Human beings do not ever make laws; it is the accidents and catastrophes of all kinds happening in every conceivable way, that make laws for us.[19]

To the end that readers of this book contribute to the enhancement of patient care in the PACU, the following admonitions are offered:

1 "Awaken" the patient to the extent possible at the termination of the anesthetic.
2 If untoward problems ensue, or if the recovery room is short-staffed, it may be preferable to keep the patient in the operating room until the problems are resolved, or until the patient is in *full possession* of all protective reflexes.
3 Adhere meticulously to guidelines

for briefing recovery room nurses (Table 13-1).
4 Personally supervise the application of any respiratory therapy appliances.
5 As an anesthesiologist, play an active and continuing role in PACU design, staffing, administration, personnel training, and policy development and implementation.

With well-thought-out admission and discharge policies, state-of-the-art equipment, adequate staffing, and comprehensive supervision based upon awareness by personnel of the particular problems that might be encountered in each patient, "accidents and catastrophes" will not happen. And those involved in postanesthesia recovery care will not become parties to the further "growth" of the common law.

REFERENCES

1. Dornette, WHL: Hospital Planning for the Anesthesiologist. Charles C Thomas, Springfield, IL, 1959, p 33.
2. Sadove, MD and Cross, JH: The PACU. WB Saunders, Philadelphia, 1956.
3. Willock, MM and Willock, GM: Design of the recovery room. In Israel, JS and DeKornfeld, TJ (eds.): Recovery Room Care. Charles C Thomas, Springfield, IL, 1982, p 8.
4. Klein, BR (ed): Health Care Facilities Handbook, ed 2. National Fire Protection Association, Boston, 1987, §§ 3-2.4 et seq.
5. Standards of Nursing Practice. American Society of Post Anesthesia Nurses, Richmond, VA, 1986.
6. Id, p 18.
7. Joint Commission on Accreditation of Healthcare Organizations: Accreditation Manual for Hospitals. JCAHO, Chicago, 1990.
8. Grimes-Graeme v. North Short Hosp., Civil Case No. 6204160, Sup. Ct., Nassau County, N.Y., 1964 (facts not available as case not reported in National Reporter).
9. Hicks v. Harlan Hosp., 231 Ky. 60, 21 S.W.2d 125 (App. 1929) (surgeon instructed recovery room head nurse about patient's postoperative airway management; head nurse delegated duty to another nurse, who in turn delegated it to a third; the last failed to follow instructions, and respiratory arrest followed by circulatory arrest ensued;

jury verdict for defendants affirmed on appeal, plaintiff having been unable to introduce evidence of negligence).

10. Jackson v. Mountain Sanitarium, 234 N.C. 222, 67 S.E.,2d 57; *reh'g denied* 235 N.C. 758, 69 S.E.2d 29 (1951) (apparent failure to regain consciousness after the anesthetic, and failure of surgeon to follow patient postoperatively ["The mother asked him why he did not come and attend to Judith. He said he was so busy he just did not have the time to attend to her"]; patient developed hyperpyrexia, convulsions, and died about 19 hours postoperatively; trial court granted defendant hospital's motion for summary judgment and jury returned verdict for physician; on appeal judgment for hospital sustained, but new trial ordered as to physician because prejudicial jury instructions prevented jury from rendering a fair verdict).

11. Nave v. Ryan, 266 F.Supp. 405 (D.Conn. 1967) (inattention postoperatively with circulatory arrest, brain damage, and death 15 days later; deceased's mother sued the surgeon and anesthesiologist; she later amended her complaint to include the anesthesiologist who made preoperative rounds; judge granted latter's motion to dismiss case against him on grounds that the filing was beyond the time set by the statute of limitation of actions).

12. Prack v. United States Fidelity and Guaranty Co., 187 So. 2d 170 (La. 1966) (patient returned to nursing unit, recovery room having closed earlier; special duty nurse unable to maintain airway; as noted in body of text, anesthesiologist was found not liable).

13. Thomas v. Seaside Memorial Hosp., 80 Cal. App. 2d 841, 183 P. 2d 288 (1947).

14. Miners Memorial Hosp. Assn. v. Miller, 341 S.W. 2d 244 (Ky. 1960) (hospital not liable for patient's fall after apparent recovery from anesthesia).

15. Ranelli v. Soc. of New York Hosp., 269 App. Div. 906, 56 N.Y.S. 2d 481; *aff'd. without op.* 295 N.Y. 850, 67 N.E. 2d 257 (1945) (hospital liable for failure to install sideboards postoperatively).

16. South Highland's Infirmary v. Galloway, 233 Ala. 276, 171 So. 250 (1936) (fall from bed in immediate postoperative period; new trial granted after jury verdict for hospital, on grounds of probable negligence of nurse, a hospital employee).

17. Keeton, WP (ed.): Prosser and Keeton on the Law of Torts. West, St. Paul, 1984, p 274.

18. Cardozo, BN: Growth of the Law. Yale University Press, New Haven, CT, 1924, p 20.

19. Plato, Laws IV, 709.

13-1

ASA STANDARDS FOR POSTANESTHESIA CARE*

These Standards apply to postanesthesia care in all locations. These Standards may be exceeded based on the judgment of the responsible anesthesiologist. They are intended to encourage high quality patient care, but cannot guarantee any specific patient outcome. They are subject to revision from time to time as warranted by the evolution of technology and practice.

STANDARD I

All patients who have received general anesthesia, regional anesthesia, or monitored anesthesia care shall receive appropriate postanesthesia management.

---

1 A Postanesthesia Care Unit (PACU) or an area which provides equivalent postanesthesia care shall be available to receive patients after surgery and anesthesia. All patients who receive anesthesia shall be admitted to the PACU **except** by specific order of the anesthesiologist responsible for the patient's care.
2 The medical aspects of care in the PACU shall be governed by policies and procedures which have been reviewed and approved by the Department of Anesthesiology.
3 The design, equipment and staffing of the PACU shall meet requirements of the facility's accrediting and licensing bodies.
4 The nursing standards of practice shall be consistent with those approved in 1986 by the American Society of Post Anesthesia Nurses (ASPAN).

STANDARD II

A patient transported to the PACU shall be accompanied by a member of the anesthesia care team who is knowledgeable about the patient's condition. The patient shall be continually evaluated and treated during transport with monitoring and support appropriate to the patient's condition.

STANDARD III

Upon arrival in the PACU, the patient shall be re-evaluated and a verbal report provided to the responsible PACU nurse by the member of the anesthesia care team who accompanies the patient.

---

*Approved by House of Delegates of the American Society of Anesthesiologists on October 12, 1988. Reprinted with permission of the ASA.

1 The patient's status on arrival in the PACU shall be documented.
2 Information concerning the preoperative condition and the surgical/anesthetic course shall be transmitted to the PACU nurse.
3 The member of the Anesthesia Care Team shall remain in the PACU until the PACU nurse accepts responsibility for the nursing care of the patient.

STANDARD IV

The patient's condition shall be evaluated continually in the PACU.

---

1 The patient shall be observed and monitored by methods appropriate to the patient's medical condition. Particular attention should be given to monitoring oxygenation, ventilation and circulation. While qualitative clinical signs may be adequate, quantitative methods are encouraged.
2 An accurate written report of the PACU period shall be maintained. Use of an appropriate PACU scoring system is encouraged for each patient on admission, at appropriate intervals prior to discharge, and at the time of discharge.
3 General medical supervision and coordination of patient care in the PACU should be the responsibility of an anesthesiologist.
4 There shall be a policy to assure the availability in the facility of a physician capable of managing complications and providing cardiopulmonary resuscitation for patients in the PACU.

STANDARD V

A physician is responsible for the discharge of the patient from the postanesthesia care unit.

---

1 When discharge criteria are used, they must be approved by the Department of Anesthesiology and the medical staff. They may vary depending upon whether the patient is discharged to a hospital room, to the ICU, to a short stay unit, or home.
2 In the absence of the physician responsible for the discharge, the PACU nurse shall determine that the patient meets the discharge criteria. The name of the physician accepting responsibility for discharge shall be noted on the record.

APPENDIX

13-2

ASPAN STANDARDS OF NURSING PRACTICE

The American Society of Post Anesthesia Nurses (ASPAN) was founded in 1980 to develop and disseminate information relative to enhancing the preanesthesia and postanesthesia care of patients, and to form an association of licensed nursing personnel working in preanesthesia holding areas and recovery rooms. To further these and other ends, the society developed, and in 1984 published, standards relative to postanesthesia care. Their standards, which were revised in 1986, now incorporate preanesthesia and postanesthesia care and cover ambulatory care facilities. The standards were endorsed by the House of Delegates of the American Society of Anesthesiologists on October 21, 1986. Persons interested in purchasing a copy of them should write:

> American Society of Post Anesthesia Nurses
> P.O. Box 11083
> Richmond, Virginia   23230

3

Special Problem Areas

EDITOR'S NOTE

The delivery of anesthesia care often requires that the anesthesiologist or anesthetist function in situations in which special risks lurk—to patient, personnel, or both. Some of these hazards are inherent to the patient, practice, agent, or technique. Others may materialize only under certain circumstances. Failure to fully appreciate those risks may lead to accidents, morbidity, or even mortality, and consequent litigation. Part 3 covers five such problem areas—specific agents and techniques, anesthesia in the ambulatory care setting, anesthesia for the pregnant patient, the use of blood products, and the legal implications posed by the presence of the human immunosuppressive virus (HIV) in today's health care setting.

A number of specific anesthetic agents and techniques have, in the past at least, been productive of morbidity, mortality, litigation, and enrichment of the common law. Fires, explosions, hepatic injury, spinal cord damage, and the like, caused by the application of these agents or methodologies, are considered in Chapter 14.

Chapter 15 reviews some of the problems associated with the administration of anesthetics to outpatients. Potential sources of difficulty include lack of absolute control over the patient's preanesthetic oral intake and over the patient's management subsequent to discharge from the facility. The lack of common law in this field bespeaks the care with which this technique has been applied during the several decades since it was introduced.

Chapter 16 is concerned with the potential vicissitudes of delivering anesthetic care to the pregnant woman—both for delivery-related and non–delivery-related surgical problems. In addition to avoiding substances and situations that may cause fetal malformation or, during the latter stages of pregnancy, fetal injury or premature labor, anesthesia personnel must be alert to those factors directly affecting the mother, and especially the mother who is at high risk. Certain agent-technique combinations may be productive of serious complications; litigation following those complications is reviewed. Finally, the controversial subject of *fathers in the delivery room* is considered, along with the recently developed common law concept of *negligent infliction of emotional harm*.

Blood products are perhaps the second most commonly employed therapeutic agents (after anesthetics themselves) in the armanentarium of anesthesia personnel. The fascinating common law background of blood product therapy is reviewed in Chapter 17. Additionally, suggestions are offered for mitigating exposure to liability during the use of these products. Given the remote, albeit finite, possibility of HIV transmission through a blood product, and the not-so-remote possibility of hepatitis transmission, the dual issues of informed consent and liability for nonindicated therapy become both real and significant.

The presence of the HIV in today's health care scene may generate three possible allegations of wrongdoing: (1) you discriminated against me because I am infected, (2) you negligently infected me, (3) you placed me at risk of becoming infected. Occupational exposure is real, especially to those practicing in metropolitan areas (Fig. 18-1) in which large numbers of infected persons live. Chapter 18 considers the legal implications created by this virus as they concern health care providers in general and anesthesia personnel in particular.

Steven E. Brown is an anesthesiologist with extensive experience in the management of outpatient anesthesia. Prior to leaving active military service, and during the preparation of the manuscript for Chapter 15, he was medical director of the Ambulatory Surgery Center, Walter Reed Army Medical Center in Washington, D.C. Currently he is a staff anesthesiologist at the Fairfax Hospital in Fairfax, Virginia, and assistant medical director of its ambulatory care facility, the Woodburn Surgical Center.

Brad Lee Hilaman, author of Chapter 16, received his medical degree from Thomas Jefferson University in Philadelphia and his law degree from Georgetown University Law School. He is a member of the Pennsylvania bar. Currently, he practices obstetrics and gynecology in Walnut Creek, California, and holds staff privileges at John Muir Medical Center and Mount Diablo Medical Center. Dr. Hilaman also serves as a consultant to the U.S. Army Claims Service and several malpractice insurance carriers in the San Francisco area in reference to claims involving obstetrics and gynecology.

Michael M. Wilson received both his law and medical degrees from Georgetown University. Currently, he is a practicing attorney representing primarily plaintiffs in personal injury actions. He is a member of the New York and District of Columbia bars. Chapter 17, which he authored, was first drafted in partial fulfillment of the requirements of an elective course taken during his senior year in medical school.

W. H. L. D.

14

William H. L. Dornette, M.D., J.D.

Some Problems Related to Specific Agents and Techniques

General Anesthesia
    Ventilation and Airway Problems
    Fires, Thermal Injuries, and
    Explosions
    Hepatic Injuries
    Mechanical Injuries From Use of
    Equipment

    Intravenous Anesthetics
    Balanced Techniques
Regional Anesthesia
    Spinal Anesthesia
    Epidural Anesthesia
    Documentation

Anesthesiologists and independently practicing certified registered nurse anesthetists are considered by professional liability insurance underwriters to be engaged in some of the riskiest health care delivery in this country; their premium rates are correspondingly high. The reasons for their high exposure stem from certain factors inherent to anesthesia practice. These factors are enumerated in the preface, reviewed in Chapter 7 (on risk management), and alluded to throughout this book.[1] Still other factors related to health care delivery in general create an atmosphere in which the patient with a less-than-optimal outcome tends to seek legal counsel (see the preface and Chapter 7). Given the inherent hazards of our specialty, plus those other factors that encourage patients to consult lawyers and file lawsuits, it is not surprising that a fairly large body of common law has developed from problems generated by the practice of anesthesia.

One of the purposes of this book is to afford health care professionals in medicine, nursing, dentistry, and related fields, and the lawyers who represent them, a comprehension of not only this case law but also

TABLE 14–1. Anesthesia Mismanagement Incidents That Are Both Common and Preventable

Respiratory Mismanagement	Other Mismanagement
Breathing circuit disconnection	Ampule swap
Breathing circuit leak	Syringe swap
Breathing circuit misconnection	Drug overdose (technical)
Loss of oxygen or nitrous oxide supply	IV line disconnection
Inadvertent change in gas flow	Inadequate fluid replacement
Esophageal or endobronchial intubation	Wrong blood transfused
Inadvertent extubation	
Premature extubation	
Wrong choice of airway management technique	
Laryngoscope malfunction	
Hypoventilation (operator error)	
Ventilator malfunction	

Source: Modified from Table 1 in Newbower, RS, Cooper, JB, and Long, CD: Failure analysis—the human element. In Gravenstein, JS, et al (eds): Essential Non-invasive Monitoring in the Operating Room. Grune & Stratton, New York, 1980, p 268.

its genesis. Armed with this knowledge, it is the hope of this and the other authors that the complications forming the basis for these law suits will be reduced to the extent possible.

This chapter covers complications related to specific agents—inhalation, intravenous, regional—and techniques—general, endotracheal, intravenous, spinal, epidural, and regional (Table 14-1). Complications caused by identifying and moving patients are reviewed in Chapter 11, and complications caused by monitoring techniques in Chapter 12. Interestingly, two of the best inhalation anesthetic agents, cyclopropane and diethyl ether, possess wide margins of safety and a high degree of patient acceptance. Unfortunately, their flammability has forced their departure from American hospitals. These valuable agents have been replaced by nonflammable inhalation agents and balanced techniques that are far less safe, as detailed in the case reports that follow.

GENERAL ANESTHESIA

General anesthesia poses risks relating to absence of awareness, loss of protective reflexes, and use of specific agents and techniques. Peripheral nerve and other injuries caused by improper positioning, which generally occur only during general anesthesia because patients are unconscious

and unable to perceive pain, are discussed in Chapter 11.

Ventilation and Airway Problems

It is very likely that the majority of complications stemming from general anesthesia revolve about failure to maintain adequate ventilation, because of respiratory obstruction, depressed ventilation, or both.[2] One such case involved an anesthesia assistant:[3]

A physical status II patient was undergoing general anesthesia for laparoscopy. There was evidence of inadequate monitoring of the patient's respirations by the assistant with a resultant 10- to 15-minute bout of hypoxia before the anesthesiologist was notified. Apparently the endotracheal catheter was occluded or dislodged, and the patient was later diagnosed as having "delayed hypoxic encephalopathy." A jury verdict for the hospital and assistant was reversed on appeal as being contrary to the weight of the evidence.

The case of *Theophelis v. Lansing General Hospital* also involved failure to maintain adequate ventilation:

Glen Schneider, a 7-year-old boy admitted for tonsillectomy and bilateral tympanoplasty, developed circulatory arrest during the procedure. Cardiac and respiratory activity were restored only "after extensive resuscitative efforts," but he never regained consciousness. He arrested again on the first postoperative day, required continuous respirator support, and on the sixth postoperative day a diagnosis of brain death was made and he was taken off the respirator. "The pathologist diagnosed anesthetic death."

Glen's parents sued the hospital, the CRNA who had administered the anesthetic, the anesthesiologist who had supervisory responsibility over the CRNA, the surgeon, and the pediatrician who had cared for Glen postoperatively. Prior to trial, the anesthesiologist's insurer settled for $172,739, the CRNA's for $85,000, and the plaintiffs proceeded to trial against the remaining defendants. Allegations against the hospital included failure to have regulations mandating use of a precordial stethoscope and the presence of an anesthesiologist throughout the case. The jury found for the surgeon and pediatrician, but against the hospital in the amount of $1 million, to be reduced by the payments made on behalf of the anesthesiologist and surgeon. The hospital appealed and the holding of the trial court initially was upheld.[4] On a second appeal, however, the court overturned the verdict against the hospital, on the grounds that the plaintiffs had not established proof of any negligence of the hospital in promulgating operating room safety regulations.[5]

Although the hospital ultimately prevailed, this case underscores the importance of having pertinent regulations for safe anesthesia practices and other safety standards in place, and then adhering to them (standards of practice are covered in Chapters 3 [application], 4 [derivation], and 12 [applied to monitoring]).

Brown v. Dahl[6] also involved acute respiratory obstruction, circulatory arrest, and severe central nervous system damage. The Browns' lawyer alleged negligence and lack of informed consent, and endeavored (unsuccessfully) to invoke the doctrine of *res ipsa loquitur* (see Chapters 3 and 11). The trial judge dismissed the informed consent complaint and the jury subsequently rendered a defense verdict. The Browns appealed. The appellate court reversed and remanded the case for a new trial on various grounds, including the error in refusing to allow a *res* instruction and in dismissing the informed consent claim (this claim is discussed in Chapter 9).

A significant (in that it is both *preventable* and *rapidly lethal*) cause of respiratory obstruction is unrecognized intubation of the esophagus. Most anesthesia personnel would agree that it is not a departure from the duty of care to accidentally intubate the esophagus rather than the trachea. Although all would agree that it is a clear-cut departure to fail to recognize such an incorrect placement, some anesthesia personnel apparently do just that. The case of *Ward v. Epting*[7] is on point. Mrs. Ward, aged 22 years and apparently in good health, had undergone a sagittal split osteotomy under general anesthesia administered through a nasotracheal catheter. The following direct quotation from the South West 2d series of the *National Reporter* (with lay explanation of medical terminology omitted) details what happened after the completion of the operation around 11 o'clock.[7]

> *Dr. Epting awoke Mrs. Ward and removed the [endotracheal catheter]. She testified Mrs. Ward was breathing on her own and was alert enough to respond to directions. Mrs. Ward was taken to the recovery room at 11:05. At 11:06 she began experiencing respiratory problems and turned blue. . . . Dr. Epting testified Mrs. Ward was having a laryngospasm. . . . Mrs. Ward did not respond when Dr. Epting attempted to give her oxygen with a face mask and ambu [sic] bag. Dr. Epting estimated she pumped approximately a gallon of air into Mrs. Ward's stomach through the esophagus, since the oxygen could not pass through an apparent obstruction in her trachea.*
>
> *Dr. Epting then entubated [sic] Mrs. Ward with an endotracheal tube. She testified Mrs. Ward responded to this attempt and very shortly began to breathe on her own; however, she soon became cyanotic again. Dr. Epting repositioned the tube and ordered drugs to dilate the bronchi of the lungs. These attempts helped briefly, according to Dr. Epting. Mrs. Ward, however, continued to have difficulty. At approximately 11:30 Dr. Epting used a [fiberoptic] bronchoscope to check [the location and patency of the endotracheal catheter]. Dr. Epting and a respiratory therapist both testified they saw the rings and the carina of the trachea. . . .*
>
> *Mrs. Ward's condition continued to deteriorate. A "mayday" was declared in the recovery room. CPR was administered to her at approximately 11:40. At 11:40 Dr. Epting cut the wires holding Mrs. Ward's jaw shut and*

viewed the tube's position with a laryngo-scope. A blood gas study taken at that time showed profound inadequacy of oxygen. At that point, Mrs. Ward's pupils were fixed and dilated, indicating severe brain damage. At approximately 12 noon, a portable chest x-ray was taken. Resuscitation attempts were continued until 12:45, at which point Mrs. Ward was declared dead.

Both the 12 o'clock x-ray film and later autopsy showed that the endotracheal catheter was in the esophagus. The autopsy also showed erosion of the mucosa of the upper esophagus at the area of its contact with the end of the endotracheal catheter. Mr. Ward's medical expert testified that the catheter had been removed prematurely at the end of the case, and that the efforts to reestablish the airway were below the level of the standard of care. A jury verdict for Mr. Ward against Dr. Epting in the amount of $400,000 was sustained on appeal. In doing so, the appellate court took note of the fact that Dr. Epting failed to take cognizance of the radiographic finding of the esophageal intubation during the entire interval of the CPR following preparation of the x-ray film.

Another cause of inadequate ventilation is the undiscovered accidental disconnection of the endotracheal catheter at its point of connection to the Y piece of the breathing circuit. If the patient's head is covered with drapes, this complication may be unrecognized for a sufficiently long interval to produce severe hypoxic injury of the central nervous system. That there are only a few such cases reported in the American common law [8-10] speaks perhaps more of an informed defense bar effectuating settlement than a dearth of such incidents.

Clearly, airway management problems do play a significant role in anesthesia-related morbidity and mortality. Newbower and associates[11] listed 19 common incidents that may occur during the administration of anesthesia, and *which are preventable.* Of these, 12 relate directly to respiratory management (see Table 14-1).

Regurgitation and Aspiration

One must consider every candidate for emergency operative intervention to be in possession of a full stomach. Any time such a person is given a general anesthetic, there is a real possibility of regurgitation and aspiration. Acute respiratory obstruction, hypoxemia, circulatory arrest, and permanent central nervous system damage are real possibilities.[12-13] The plaintiff in one of these cases[13] reportedly was the wife of an internist. The case was settled for $383,000 (a large amount in those days). This case is believed to have formed the factual basis for the motion picture *The Verdict*.

Aspiration of acidic gastric contents can also cause acute chemical pneumonitis and fulminating pulmonary edema, a phenomenon first described by Mendelson.[14] Unless quickly and appropriately treated, including use of steroids and high oxygen tension with positive end-expiratory pressure (PEEP), Mendelson's syndrome generally proves fatal. A fairly recent case, *Keys v. Mercy Hosp. of New Orleans*,[15] is on point. Following administration of thiopental and succinlycholine to Mrs. Keys, a candidate for emergency cesarean section, CRNA West attempted to insert an endotracheal catheter. She was unsuccessful. Mrs. Keys regurgitated gastric contents and aspirated. Although Mrs. Keys recovered consciousness, she developed "bronchopneumonia" and subsequently died. A jury verdict of $350,000 was sustained on appeal.

Overdose of Inhalation Anesthesia

Anesthesia personnel rarely encountered problems with overdosage of the older inhalation anesthetic agents cyclopropane and diethyl ether. With the advent of the newer, much more potent, rapidly acting agents as halothane and isoflurane, overdosage became a much more serious hazard. Fortunately, thanks to equipment engineers and manufacturers, vaporizers accurately calibrated for delivery of specific agents in precise concentrations have been introduced into the market, removing much of the calculations and guesswork that took place in the not-too-distant past. The advent of these newer devices clearly elevated the standard of anesthesia care, in both this country and abroad.

All general anesthetics (except diethyl ether, an inhalation agent used only sparingly today because of its flammability) produce some degree of respiratory depression. When intravenous muscle relaxants are added to a regimen of balanced anesthesia, the extent of this depression may be profound. While a review of the common law reveals only one case in which respiratory depression was believed to play the principal role in the hypoxemia-induced central nervous system injury,[16] undoubtedly there are many others. Five not-too-recent cases of respiratory inadequacy leading to litigation resulted from tonsillectomies.[12,17-20] One wonders in how many of these an endotracheal catheter was employed (if any!) and, if one had been employed, whether these adverse outcomes would have developed. It is clear that modern anesthesia practice mandates the use of an endotracheal catheter whenever general anesthesia is to be employed for a tonsillectomy and adenoidectomy.

Fires, Thermal Injuries, and Explosions

Fires and explosions in hospital operating rooms, once an all-too-frequent occurrence,[21,22] largely disappeared from the American health care delivery scene long before the abandonment of flammable agents, thanks to efforts of the National Fire Protection Association in drafting safety standards for hospital operating rooms and promoting their enforcement.[23,24] Another factor may be the reporting of cases in the medical literature.[25,26] Only a few cases appear in the common law,[27-30] suggesting that health care providers involved in a fire or explosion will settle rather than attempt to defend any ensuing litigation.

Flammable agents produce safe anesthesia as long as appropriate precautions are taken. In spite of this fact, and the exceptional properties of such flammable agents as diethyl ether and cyclopropane, anesthesia personnel in very recent years have abandoned the use of flammable agents because of potential exposure to liability. To compound the problem for practitioners who would like to continue to employ these agents, some carriers who insure hospitals reportedly have refused to write policies covering incidents involving the use of flammable agents.

Even though a hospital may have abandoned the use of all flammable inhalation anesthetic agents, the risk of fire still exists. Fires from the inadvertent ignition of still-liquid alcohol-containing skin preparation fluids, with resultant patient injuries, have occurred in a number of hospitals. In their haste to commence operating, surgeons all too often fail to allow the alcohol to evaporate before commencing use of the high-frequency electrocautery. If enough residual alcohol remains, it will ignite and cause second- and even third-degree burns. Admonitions for the safe use of flammable germicidal preparation solutions are contained in NFPA publication Code 99.[31]

Another source of ignition is the laser beam. Otolaryngologists are employing this source of energy to fulgurate and excise neoplasms in the upper respiratory tract and larynx. The patient first must be given general endotracheal anesthesia, necessitating the presence of an endotracheal catheter within the oropharynx. These catheters generally are manufactured of materials that will burn if ignited. The presence of an oxygen-enriched atmosphere within the lumen of the catheter compounds the problem. Anesthesia personnel must take positive steps to assure that their catheter is appropriately protected.

Hepatic Injuries

Halothane is a polyhalogenated volatile liquid agent of the methane series. It is well known that halothane may produce liver damage under certain circumstances.[32-55] A number of lawsuits were filed in the 1960s in consequence to severe and sometimes fatal hepatotoxicity, although few if any of these cases reached the appellate level.[56] Because this agent is nonflammable, possesses a rapid onset of action, and affords rapid recovery, it still is employed widely, along with the newer nonflammable agents enflurane and isoflurane. Certain individuals may be more susceptible than others to hepatic injury, and anesthesia personnel must be aware of the importance of careful and complete history taking during preanesthesia evaluation (see Chapter 8). Suggestions for the safe administration of this agent, discussed in detail elsewhere,[57] include being certain that: the agent is medically indicated; the patient has no underlying liver disease; the agent is not employed repeatedly, especially in the older patient; and it is not employed if there is any evidence of a sensitization reaction following its prior use.

Mechanical Injuries From Use of Equipment

Insertion of endotracheal catheters, airways, parenteral therapy lines, and monitoring leads (both invasive and noninvasive) can produce mechanical injuries of various types. Generally these complications are not as severe as those described in the preceding paragraphs. Injuries from the application of monitoring devices are covered in some detail in Chapter 12.

Inept attempts in performing laryngoscopy may injure the teeth or gums[58] with ensuing litigation.[59-62] Although the number of these common law cases is small, alleged dental injuries make up 265 of 1067, almost one fourth, of the claims involving anesthesia care reported by a large carrier specializing in professional liability insurance.[63] Injuries to the nasopharynx, larynx, trachea, and adjacent structures may also occur.[64-78] A recently reported case involving residual scarring of the tracheal mucosa in the immediate subglottic region is worthy of mention.[79]

Marion Cangelosi, a 68-year-old, diabetic, postmyocardial-infarction patient with a pacemaker and congestive heart failure, was taken to the operating room on December 2 for a cholecystectomy under general endotracheal anesthesia. He withstood these procedures well and, on return to the nursing unit with the endotracheal catheter in situ, was placed on a respirator for medical reasons not later questioned. Catheter cuff pressure was monitored regularly by a member of the respiratory therapy service of the hospital. Respiratory therapy was discontinued and the endotracheal catheter removed on the morning of December 5, the third postoperative day. No problems were noted on extubation. Laryngeal edema, requiring Mr. Cangelosi's readmission to the intensive care unit, developed the following day. It responded to therapy, and by the sixth postoperative day he was

asymptomatic. On January 4, Mr. Cangelosi was seen for hoarseness and shortness of breath, a problem that was later attributed to rapidly forming scar tissue in the mucosa of the tracheal lumen immediately beneath the larynx. Initially, a tracheotomy was required. He subsequently was subjected to multiple laser treatments to remove the scar tissue and maintain the patency of his airway.

Mr. Cangelosi retained legal counsel and sued the hospital and various treating physicians; some of the defendants were dropped from the case before or during trial. His lawyer was unsuccessful in obtaining either evidence of negligence or a res ipsa loquitur instruction, and the jury found for all remaining defendants. On appeal, the intermediate appellate court affirmed, noting that the circumstances surrounding the injury were not consonant with a res ipsa loquitur instruction.

This case has important lessons for anesthesia personnel who work in the operating room, intensive care facility, or both. The facility by which endotracheal catheters are placed, their size, and other details of laryngoscopy and intubation should be documented carefully. So should the medical indications for prolonged use of a catheter, and the steps taken to prevent injury to the vocal cords, tracheal lumen, and adjacent structures if the catheter is allowed to remain in situ beyond the duration of the anesthetic administration. There is no doubt but that such documentation contributed immeasurably to the defense verdict in the Cangelosi case.

Intravenous Anesthetics

Thiopental and thiamylal are the salts of a strong base (sodium) and a weak acid (barbituric); hence, a solution of either agent is strongly alkaline. The inadvertent introduction of one of these agents into an artery can have disastrous consequences. Such an occurrence constitutes one of the true emergencies in anesthesia practice, and appropriate steps must be taken in a timely fashion to prevent loss of tissue or even the hand and part of the forearm.[80] Litigation resulting from extravenous administration of intravenous agents has produced some interesting case law,[81-84] perhaps the most noteworthy of which is *Rockwell v. Stone*[83] involving an intra-arterial injection of thiopental. Anesthesia personnel failed to recognize the significance of the complication and initiate appropriate therapy until several hours after the injection. In consequence, Rockwell lost his left arm 3 days later, but won the ensuing lawsuit.

Balanced Techniques

Balanced anesthesia, a concept developed in the early 1950s, involves the use of a number of intravenously administered agents, each of which alone will produce only one of the desired effects of total general anesthesia, namely, analgesia, amnesia, muscle relaxation, or loss of consciousness, but when given together will achieve a balanced effect. Balanced techniques have both advantages and serious drawbacks. It is theoretically possible to achieve a total anesthetic effect with much lower dosage than if one attempts to produce the entire anesthetic effect with one agent. Unfortunately, some agents employed for balanced anesthesia have potentially serious side effects. Fentanyl, a potent, ultrashort-acting analgesic, may be associated with a delayed respiratory depressant action, the onset of which may occur some time after the patient apparently has recovered spontaneous respirations following the initial administration of this agent. Recovery from certain muscle relaxants may also be prolonged. The case of *Pearson v. St. Paul*[84] illustrates the dangers of delayed return to full respiratory activity following use of a balanced technique.

Judith Pearson was admitted to United Hospitals Orthopedic Center for arthroscopy of her left knee. Balanced anesthesia was administered by CRNA St. Paul. At the termination of the procedure, St. Paul, accompanied by two residents, brought Ms. Pearson to the recovery room and "all three left almost immediately thereafter." Disputed evidence was offered relative to the extent of Ms. Pearson's recovery from the effects of the anesthetic at the time of her admission, the CRNA maintaining that there was a greater recovery than did the recovery room nurse. "Some 10 or 15 minutes later" the recovery room nurse was alerted by Ms. Pearson's shallow breathing and was unable to arouse her. Help was summoned from the anesthesia service; the ad-

ministration of Narcan, prostigmine, and atropine did not restore either consciousness or spontaneous respiratory activity. Ms. Pearson developed circulatory arrest followed by "severe brain damage," remained in a coma for 5 days, and died.

Ms. Pearson's mother sued the hospital, the CRNA, the recovery room nurse, and others, alleging negligence in the administration of the anesthetic and in managing Ms. Pearson's postoperative care. At the end of the plaintiff's proof, the trial judge granted the defense motion for involuntary dismissal and Mrs. Pearson filed an appeal.

The appellate court overruled the trial judge and remanded the case for a new trial. In doing so the appellate court found that the plaintiff's expert witness had established a *prima facie* case (one that patently has a cause of action) of negligence that should have gone to the jury. Mrs. Pearson's medical expert testified that excess narcotic was administered as part of the balanced anesthetic, that an oral airway should have been inserted at the time Ms. Pearson was transferred to the recovery room, that the CRNA should have alerted the recovery room nurse about the excess narcotic, and that the extent of Ms. Pearson's central nervous system injury could not have developed "in the absence of negligence of the medical personnel in charge of the recovery room...." This last portion of the opinion supported an application of the *res ipsa loquitur* rule of evidence (see Chapters 3 and 11).

Another agent commonly used for sedation and balanced anesthesia, droperidol, will produce α-adrenergic blockade, and may be associated with severe hypotension if given for preliminary medication in a patient who develops ganglionic blockade (an expected side effect) following a subsequent spinal anesthetic. Patients who are dehydrated may also develop hypotension following use of droperidol.

Failure to Render a Patient Unconscious

Among the drawbacks of balanced anesthesia is failure to achieve complete loss of consciousness in a patient who, because of the effects of muscle relaxants, is unable to communicate with anesthesia personnel. The common law has few such cases. In *Turner v. Malone*[85] the patient complained that he had felt insertion of the "rib spreader" in preparation for a thoracotomy for carcinoma of the lung. The appellate court in that case held that the defendant anesthesiologist was not liable.

REGIONAL ANESTHESIA

Just about every form of regional anesthesia may cause side effects, which are many and varied.[86] Only those complications that are serious and produce either a permanent neurological deficit or an acute, life-threatening problem will be discussed. These complications are of four types: spinal cord injuries, nerve root injuries, total spinal anesthesia, and generalized toxic reactions to the local anesthetic agent.

Spinal Anesthesia

A number of years ago a New York neurologist collected a series of cases of patients who developed permanent sequelae from spinal anesthesia.[87-90] The common law contains a number of case reports detailing instances of permanent injuries following use of this technique.[91-107] Anesthesia personnel today recognize that the advantages of a well-administered spinal anesthetic far outweigh its potential risks. This statement is buttressed by the work of several authors who have evaluated this technique carefully and prospectively.[108-111]

Permanent spinal anesthesia–related deficits are caused either by spinal cord or nerve root injury. The former may stem from the introduction of a contaminant into the subarachnoid space with the development of adhesive arachnoiditis, scarring, and pressure transection of the spinal cord.[112-113] The cord also may be injured by the tip of the lumbar puncture needle if the latter is introduced inadvertently at too high a level.[96,100,114-115] Another possible cause of spinal cord or conus medularis injury is a low-lying conus.[96,116]

Nerve root injury results from failure to introduce the lumbar puncture needle in the midline. As the needle is advanced, the spinal nerve is impinged by the tip of the needle against the body or pedicle of the vertebra. The patient experiences excruciating pain radiating to the side, and later develops numbness, paralysis, and other signs and symptoms of nerve root injury.[99]

One other complication deserves mention. In *Clark v. Gibbons*[117] the injury was an indirect result of the spinal anesthetic, but proximately connected nonetheless. The patient was undergoing an orthopedic procedure on his ankle; the operation took longer than anticipated. The spinal anesthetic wore off, forcing the surgeon to terminate the procedure before he had completed it. (The case report is unclear as to why supplemental general anesthesia could not have been used.) Postoperative complications ensued, and the patient's ankle joint developed a permanent malfunction. His lawsuit against the anesthesiologist was successful.

In many instances, so-called complications of spinal anesthesia are not really caused by this technique. Greene, in his excellent treatise on complications of spinal anesthesia,[111] lists four disease entities or complications that might develop concurrently with, but not be causally connected to, the spinal anesthetic:

1 Pre-existing neurologic disorders that progress without being affected by the spinal anesthetic, as for example, a neoplasm metastasizing to the spine.
2 Pre-existing neurologic disorders, the signs and symptoms of which may appear to be accelerated by the anesthetic, e.g., a spinal cord meningioma.
3 Neurologic deficits caused by other factors as surgical retractors or positioning.
4 Idiopathic neurologic deficits that mimic complications of spinal anesthesia, but may follow general anesthesia or no anesthesia at all.

Whenever spinal anesthesia is contemplated, it is extremely important for the person making preanesthesia rounds to query the patient about any possible pre-existing neurologic deficits. Allegations that a deficit was anesthesia-related would be negated by its identification prior to the anesthetic. When one of the neurologic conditions noted above pre-exists, it might be desirable to consider another technique as the method of choice, to avoid any possible future allegations of there being a causal connection.

"Total" Spinal Anesthesia

As noted below, a total spinal anesthetic is a recognized complication of epidural anesthesia. It may also occur at the time spinal anesthesia is induced. Patients who are given a spinal anesthetic must not be permitted to attempt to move their bodies. In making a move, the patient involuntarily tightens the muscles of the abdominal wall. There is a concomitant increase in intra-abdominal pressure, which is transmitted to the epidural veins, causing them to engorge and press against the dura. This pressure in turn forces the spinal fluid cephalad, and along with it the local anesthetic agent. It is not difficult to manage this complication—supporting the blood pressure, ventilating the patient's lungs, and sedating the patient to mitigate the uncomfortable feeling of total paralysis. The problem should resolve without sequellae. Failure to take all of these steps may result in successful litigation against anesthesia personnel.[118]

Epidural Anesthesia

Epidural anesthesia enjoys many of the advantages of spinal anesthesia. By utilizing a catheter for the introduction of fractional doses of the local anesthetic agent, one may control almost precisely the duration of effect, preventing the possibility of complications as those noted in the Clark[117] case. Unfortunately, epidural anesthesia is not an unmixed blessing.[119] The proximity of the epidural needle or catheter to the subarachnoid space invites accidental puncture of the dura with introduction of the local anesthetic into the subarachnoid space. The relatively large volume (as compared with that required for intentional spinal anesthesia) will result in the onset of total spinal anesthesia.[120] The size of this volume may contribute to the development of a systemic toxic reaction, with convulsions, respiratory, and, possibly, circulatory arrest.[121,122] Epidural anesthesia has become very popular on obstetrical services for patient and obstetrician alike and is used widely. The legal consequences of some of the complications of the use of this technique in obstetrics are discussed in Chapter 16.

Documentation

The need for complete documentation is discussed in Chapter 10. Of special importance when performing regional anesthesia is recording all details of the technique, any complications, and how those complications were managed. For example, the following note might appear in the remarks column of the anesthesia graphic chart to document the technique employed for a spinal anesthetic:

LP 23 ga L3-4 1st pass, clear tap, no pares [lumbar puncture with 23 gauge needle on first attempt with clear tap and no paresthesias] [followed by list of agents and dosages, and sensory level ultimately achieved]

If a paresthesia does occur and the lumbar puncture needle is withdrawn and redirected away from the side of the paresthesia, these facts are recorded.

CONCLUSION

This chapter reviews some of the complications that may be associated with the administration of anesthetic agents. Could any or many of them have been prevented? Need anesthesia always be a two-edged sword? Anesthesia rarely is an end in and of itself. Customarily, it is employed to facilitate the performance of other (e.g., operative) procedures. Given the secondary role of anesthesia in the care of the candidate for operative intervention, it seems apparent that morbidity and mortality accompanying or following the administration of anesthetics should be minimal or absent altogether, and that with appropriate efforts the complications described in this chapter might be eliminated.

Such may not always be the case, however, for a variety of reasons, including the condition of the patient and other factors over which anesthesia personnel have little or no control. Yet morbidity and mortality can be minimized, and possibly eliminated altogether, by using due care throughout the entire patient care process, from initial interview to final postoperative visit. Those parts of that process pertinent to this chapter are especially important, because of the severe nature of the complications that may ensue from improper ventilatory maintenance, or mismanagement of one or another of the multitude of other possible adverse outcomes described in this chapter. By maintaining awareness of these potential problems, one should be able to eliminate those factors that are essential to the genesis of the complication, to the end that accidents will be prevented and overall patient care significantly enhanced.

REFERENCES

1. *See also* Smith, JW: Hospital Liability. Law Journal-Seminars Press. New York, 1988, § 10.03 Anesthesia.
2. Mills, DH and Engel, HL: Malpractice prophylaxis: an analysis of ventilatory problems in anesthesia. In Dornette, WHL (ed): Legal Aspects of Anesthesia. FA Davis, Philadelphia, 1972, p 455.
3. Sanders v. Mt. Sinai Hosp., 487 N.E.2d 588 (Ohio App. 1986).
4. Theophelis v. Lansing General Hosp., 366 N.W.2d 249 (Mich. App. 1985).
5. Theophelis v. Lansing General Hosp., 384 N.W.2d 823 (Mich. App. 1986).
6. Brown v. Dahl, 705 P.2d 781 (Wash. App. 1985).
7. Ward v. Epting, 351 S.E.2d 867 (S.C. App. 1986).
8. Schneider v. Albert Einstein Medical Center, 257 Pa. Super. Ct. 348, 390 A.2d 1271 (1978).
9. Kemalyan v. Henderson, 45 Wash. 2d 693, 277 P. 2d 372 (1954).
10. Whitfield v. Whittaker Memorial Hospital, 210 Va. 176, 169 S.E. 2d 563 (Sup. Ct. App. Va. 1969).
11. Newbower, RS, Cooper, JB, and Long, CD: Failure analysis—the human element. In Gravenstein, JS, et al (eds): Essential Non-invasive Monitoring in the Operating Room. Grune and Stratton, New York, 1980, p 268.
12. Cavero v. Franklin General Benevolent Society, 223 P.2d 471 (Cal. 1950); Cook v. Lightblau, 176 So. 2d 523 (Fla. 1965).
13. Katz v. Easton, reported by Torey, JH: Lessons from a malpractice verdict. Med Econ, October 1967, p 75.
14. Mendelson, CL: Aspiration of stomach contents into the lungs during obstetric anesthesia. Am J Obstet Gynecol 52:191, 1946.
15. Keys v. Mercy Hosp., 485 So.2d 514 (La. App. 4 Cir. 1986).
16. Edelman v. Zeigler, 44 Cal rptr. 114 (Dist. Ct. App., 1st Dist., Cal. 1965).
17. Butler v. Layton, 164 N.E. 920 (Sup. Ct. Mass. 1929).
18. Jackson v. Mountain Sanitarium, 234 N.C. 222, 67 S.E. 2d 57; *reh'g denied* 235 N.C. 758, 69 S.E. 2d 29 (1951).
19. Linhares v. Hall, 257 N.E. 2d 429 (Sup. Ct. Mass. 1970).
20. Stites v. Searle and Gebauer, Docket No. A254510, Court of Common Pleas, Hamilton County, Ohio.
21. Woodbridge, PD: Incidence of anesthetic explosions. JAMA 113:2308, 1939.
22. Greene, BA: Hazard of fire and explosion in anesthesia; report of a clinical investigation of 230 cases. Anesthesiology 2:144, 1941.
23. Dornette, WHL and Yuelling, DP: Safety in hospitals and nursing homes. Fire J 64:23, 1970.
24. Dornette, WHL: Anesthesiologists, hospitals and the NFPA. Anesth Analg 51:271, 1972.
25. Nicholson, MJ: Case history: Anesthetic explosion. Anesth Analg 46:410, 1967.
26. Nicholson, MJ and Crehan, JP: Fire and explosion hazards in the operating room. Anesth Analg 46:412, 1967.
27. Philipp v. Shaw, 280 App. Div. 999, 116 N.Y.S. 2d 889 (Sup. Ct. App. Div., 2d Dept. 1952).
28. Andrepont v. Ochsner, 84 So. 2d 63 (Ct. App. La. 1955).
29. Dierman v. Providence Hosp., 188 P.2d 12 (Sup. Ct. Cal. 1947).
30. McKinney v. Tromly, 386 S.W. 2d 564 (Tex. Civ. App. 1954).
31. NFPA Code 99, § 3-2.7.8. National Fire Protection Association, Boston, 1990.
32. Aach, R. Halothane and liver failure. JAMA 211:2145, 1970.
33. Armstrong, CA and Wade, WG: Fatal jaundice after halothane. Lancet 2:393, 1965.
34. Barton, JDM: Jaundice and halothane. Lancet 1:1097, 1959.
35. Brody, GL and Sweet, RB: Halothane as a cause of hepatic necrosis. Anesthesiology 24:29, 1963.
36. Buncker, JP and Blumenfeld, CM: Liver necrosis after halothane anesthesia. N Engl J Med 268:531, 1963.
37. Burnap, TK and Vandam, LD: Anesthetic, circulatory and respiratory effects of Fluothane. Anesthesiology 19:307, 1958.
38. Chadwick, DA and Jennings, RC: Massive hepatic necrosis associated with halothane anesthesia. Lancet 1:793, 1964.
39. Chamberlain G: Liver damage after halothane anaesthesia. Br Med J 5344:1524, 1963.
40. Griner, PE: Hepatitis after repeated exposure to halothane. Ann Intern Med 65:753, 1966.
41. Heidenberg, WJ, et al: Halothane hepati-

tis—an American disease. Lancet 1:1135, 1963.

42. Herber, R and Specht, NW: Liver necrosis following anesthesia. Arch Intern Med 115:266, 1965.

43. Klatskin, G and Kimberg, DV: Recurrent hepatitis attributable to halothane sensitization in an anesthetist. N Engl J Med 280:515, 1969.

44. Lecky, JH and Cohen, PJ: Hepatic dysfunction without jaundice following administration of halothane. Anesthesiology 33:371, 1970.

45. Lindenbaum, J and Leifer, E: Hepatic necrosis associated with halothane anesthesia. N Engl J Med 268:525, 1963.

46. Lomanto, C and Howland, WS: Problems in diagnosing halothane hepatitis. JAMA 214:1257, 1970.

47. McReynolds, EC, Thorogood, A, and Morris, LE: Clinical comparison of halothane (Fluothane) and chloroform. Arch Surg 86:633, 1963.

48. Morganstern, L, et al: Postoperative jaundice associated with halothane anesthesia. Surg Gynecol Obstet 121:728, 1965.

49. Nowill, WK: Death due to acute hepatic necrosis, secondary to administration of halothane anesthesia. Anesth Analg 49:355, 1970.

50. Peters, RL, et al: Hepatic necrosis associated with halothane anesthesia. Am J Med 47:748, 1969.

51. Subcommittee on National Halothane Study of Committee on Anesthesia, National Academy of Sciences—National Research Council: Summary of national halothane study: Possible association between halothane anesthesia and postoperative hepatic necrosis. JAMA 197:775, 1966.

52. Tornetta, BJ and Tomaki, HT: Halothane jaundice and hepatotoxicity. JAMA 185:658, 1963.

53. Trey, C, et al: Fulminant hepatic failure. N Engl J Med 279: 793, 1968.

54. Trey, C, Lipworth, L, and Davidson, CS: The clinical syndrome of halothane hepatitis. Anesth Analg 48:1033, 1969.

55. Winkler, K, Sejersen, P, and Rask, H: Halothane. Lancet 2:902, 1965.

56. The anesthesiologist in a 1987 appellate decision in a case involving "massive hepatic necrosis" developing 9 days after a halothane anesthetic was found not liable; see Grando v. Madsen, 720 S.W.2d 866 (Tex. App. 1987).

57. Dornette, WHL: Some problems in anesthesia. In Dornette, WHL (ed): Legal Aspects of Anesthesia. FA Davis, Philadelphia, 1972, p 295.

58. See, generally, Dornette, WHL and Hughes, BH: Care of the teeth during anesthesia. Anesth Analg 38:206, 1959; Dornette, WHL: Care of the teeth during endoscopy and anesthesia. In Dornette, WHL (ed): Legal Aspects of Anesthesia. FA Davis, Philadelphia, 1972, p 213.

59. Hastings v. Hughes, 438 S.W. 2d 349 (Ct. App. Tenn., 1968).

60. Morwin v. Albany Hosp., 185 N.Y.S. 2d 85 (1959).

61. Meyer v. St. Paul-Mercury Indemnity Co., 61 So. 2d 901 (La. 1952).

62. Dohr v. Smith, 104 So. 2d 29 (Sup. Ct. Fla. 1958).

63. St. Paul Fire and Marine Insurance Company, Physician and Surgeon Professional Liability Countrywide Summary Report by Allegation (1978).

64. Bamforth, BJ: Complications during endotracheal anesthesia. Anesth Analg 42:727, 1963.

65. Baron, SH and Kohlmoos, HW: Laryngeal sequelae of endotracheal anesthesia. Ann Otol 60:767, 1951.

66. Deming, MV and Oech, SR: Steroid and antihistamine therapy for postintubation subglottic edema in infants and children. Anesthesiology 22:933, 1961.

67. Gillespie, NA: Endotracheal Anesthesia, ed 2. University of Wisconsin Press, Madison, 1948, p 151 et seq.

68. Hartsell, CJ and Stephen, CR: Incidence of sore throat following endotracheal intubation. Can Anaesth Soc J 11:307, 1964.

69. Jackson, C: Contact ulcer granuloma and other laryngeal complications of endotracheal anesthesia. Anesthesiology 14:425, 1953.

70. Powell, JB and Keown, KK: Endobronchial aspiration of a tooth. An unusual anesthetic complication. Anesth Analg 44:355, 1965.

71. Scott, M and Brechner, VL: Retrobulbar hemorrhage from nasotracheal intubation. Anesthesiology 20:717, 1958.

72. Smith, RH, Pool, LL, and Volpitto, PO: Subcutaneous emphysema as a complication of endotracheal intubation. Anesthesiology 20:714, 1959.

73. Snow, JC, Harano, M, and Balogh, K: Postintubation granuloma of the larynx. Anesth Analg 45:425, 1966.

74. Warner, WA: Laryngeal band: Possible relation to prolonged nasotracheal intubation. Anesthesiology 28:466, 1967.

75. Wasmuth, CE: Legal pitfalls in the practice of anesthesiology. Part 2. Complications of endotracheal anesthesia. Anesth Analg 39:128, 1960.

76. Wylie, WD: Hazards of intubation. Anaes-

thesia 5:143, 1950.

77. Young, N and Stewart, S: Laryngeal lesions following endotracheal anesthesia: A report of 12 adult cases. Br J Anaesth 25:32, 1953.

78. Bell v. Umstatd, 402 S.W. 2d 306 (Tex. Civ. App. 1966).

79. Cangelosi v. Our Lady of the Lake Regional Medical Center, 542 So.2d 90 (La. App. 1 Cir. 1989).

80. Dornette, WHL: Some problems in anesthesia. In Dornette, WHL (ed): Legal Aspects of Anesthesia. FA Davis, Philadelphia, 1972, p 304.

81. Hornbeck v. Homeopathic Hosp. Assn., 197 A. 2d 461 (Del. 1964).

82. Miller v. Raaen, 276 Minn. 109, 139 N.W. 2d 877 (1966).

83. Rockwell v. Stone, 404 Pa. 561, 574, 173 A.2d 48, 54 (Supr. Ct. 1961); *see also* Wolfsmith v. Marsh, 337 P.2d 70 (Cal. 1959), wherein the anesthesiologist, finding no veins in his obese patient's arm, endeavored to administer thiopental into a varicose vein in her leg; extravasation of the solution, tissue necrosis, slough of skin, scarring, and a plaintiff's verdict ensued.

84. Pearson v. St. Paul, 220 N.J.Super., 531 A.2d 744 (N.J.Super.A.D. 1987).

85. Turner v. Malone, 176 Ga. App. 132, 335 S.E.2d 404 (1985).

86. Dornette, ref. 80, pp 310–313.

87. Kennedy, F, Somberg, HM, and Goldberg, BR: Arachnoiditis and paralysis following spinal anesthesia. JAMA 129:664, 1945.

88. Kennedy, F, Effron, AS, and Perry, C: Grave spinal cord paralysis caused by spinal anesthesia. Surg Gynecol Obstet 91:365, 1950.

89. Ayers v. Parry, 192 F. 2d 181 (3d Cir. 1951).

90. Beausoleil v. Providential Sisters of Charity, 53 D.L.R. 2d 65 (Quebec Ct., Queen's Bench, Appeal Side, 1964).

91. Brune v. Belnikoff, 235 N.E. 2d 793 (Sup. Ct. Mass. 1968).

92. Chambers v. Nottenbaum, 96 So. 2d 716 (Dist. Ct. App., 3d Cir., Fla. 1957).

93. Costley v. United States, 131 F. 2d 723 (5th Cir. 1950).

94. Douglas v. Bussabarger, 438 P. 2d 829 (Wash. Sup. Ct. 1968).

95. Erban v. Kay, 174 N.E. 2d 667 (Mass. 1961).

96. Funke v. Fieldman, 212 Kan. 524, 512 P.2d 539 (Sup. Ct., 1973).

97. Gravis v. Physicians and Surgeons Hospital of Alice, 415 S.W. 2d 647 (Ct. Civil App. Texas 1967); *rev'd* and *rem.* 427 S.W. 2d 310 (Sup. Ct. Texas 1968).

98. Hall v. United States, 136 F. Supp. 187 (D.C., W.D., La. 1955).

99. Herbert v. Travelers Indemnity Co., 221 So. 2d 619 (Ct. App., 4th Cir., La. 1970).

100. Huber v. Protestant Deaconess Hosp. Assn., 133 N.W. 2d 864 (Ind. 1956).

101. Mayor v. Dowsett, 240 Ore. 196, 400 P. 2d 234 (1965).

102. Porter v. Puryear, 258 S.W. 2d 182 (Tex. Ct. Civ. App. 1953).

103. Ramsland v. Shaw, 166 N.W. 2d 894 (Mass. 1960).

104. Seneris v. Haas, 291 P. 2d 915 (Sup. Ct. Cal. 1955).

105. Walker v. Distler, 296 P. 2d 452 (Sup. Ct. Idaho 1963).

106. Wiley v. Wharton, 69 O. App. 345, 41 N.E. 2d 255 (Ct. App. Summit Co. 1941).

107. Woodson v. Huey, 261 P. 2d 199 Sup. Ct. Okla. 1953).

108. Dripps, RD and Vandam, LD: Long-term follow-up of patients who received 10,098 spinal anesthetics. JAMA 156:1486, 1954.

109. Vandam, LD and Dripps, RD: Long-term follow-up of 10,098 spinal anesthetics; incidence and analysis of minor sensory neurological defects. Surgery 38:463, 1955.

110. Vandam, LD and Dripps, RD: Long-term follow-up of patients who received 10,098 spinal anesthetics; neurological disease incident to traumatic lumbar puncture during spinal anesthesia. JAMA 172:1483, 1960.

111. Greene, NM: Neurological sequelae of spinal anesthesia. Anesthesiology 22:682, 1961.

112. Wolley and Roe v. Ministry of Health, reported by Cope, RW: The Wolley and Roe case. Anaesthesia 9:249, 1954.

113. Denson, JS, et al: Effects of detergents intrathecally. Anesthesiology 18:143, 1957.

114. Baras v. Aetna Casualty and Surety Co., 263 So.2d 375 (La. App. 1972).

115. Puryer v. Porter, 153 Tex. 92, 264 S.W. 2d 689 (1954).

116. Reimann, AF and Anson, BJ: Vertebral level of termination of the spinal cord with report of a case of sacral cord. Anat Rec 88:127, 1944.

117. Clark v. Gibbons, 58 Cal. Rptr. 125, 426, P. 2d 525 (Sup. Ct. 1967).

118. Ayers v. U.S., 750 F.2d 449 (3d.Cir. 1984).

119. *See, generally,* Vandam, LD: Complications of spinal and epidural anesthesia. In Orkin, FK and Cooperman, LH (eds): Complications in Anesthesiology. JB Lippincott, Philadelphia, 1983. p 75.

120. *Id*, p 103.

121. *Ibid.*

122. Douglas v. Lombardino, 236 Kan. 471, 693 P.2d 1138 (1985).

15

Steven E. Brown, M.D.

The Ambulatory Care Setting

The administration of anesthesia to non-hospitalized patients, a technique known as "outpatient anesthesia," "one-day surgery," "in-and-out surgery," and "anesthesia for the ambulatory patient," is now employed almost universally across this country.[1] Statistics indicate that anywhere from 60% to 88% of hospitals in the United States provide some sort of ambulatory surgical care. It is estimated that 20% of all surgical procedures in the United States are currently performed on an outpatient basis, with the capacity to increase this number to the 40% range.[2] The concept of adminis-tering short-acting general or regional anesthetic agents for selected operative procedures has been practiced since the turn of the century. Early efforts at establishing outpatient surgery as an accepted practice included Ralph Waters' Down-Town Anesthesia Clinic in Sioux City, Iowa, in 1916.[3] The practice of outpatient surgery continued informally until the 1960s but remained relatively unpopular.

The concept of administering short-acting general or regional anesthetic agents for selected operative procedures on the outpatient was formally reintroduced by Wallace

171

Reed, an anesthesiologist in Phoenix, Arizona, in the 1960s. It was Reed's intent to offer safe anesthesia for suitable candidates for selected operative procedures without the necessity of hospitalizing them for even a short period of time.[4] Reed felt that this practice would significantly lower the cost of care and, as a possible added advantage, eliminate the psychic trauma frequently associated with hospitalization, especially in the young.

Outpatient surgery is a concept whose time has arrived. With major concerns about the rising cost of health care, the economic benefits of surgery performed on an outpatient basis with potential savings of 50% to 75% was self-evident.[2] The economic benefits include less time lost from work for patients or their family members, and a more efficient use of existing hospital beds with decreased requirements for new beds and the associated medical infrastructure that is required to maintain them in nursing, administrative, and ancillary personnel. The elimination of the psychological trauma of hospital admission the night prior to the operation has also been of benefit in easing the stress for both adults and children. The success of Wallace Reed's Surgicenter, a freestanding unit, led to the development of other, similar facilities, as well as hospital-based outpatient surgery, which is much more common today.

This chapter reviews the requirements for the freestanding facility—housing, equipment, staffing patterns, and operating procedures—that have been developed over the years and have become the standard of care (see Chapter 4) for ambulatory anesthesia facilities and practices. It does not take into consideration any state laws or local ordinances governing the design, licensing, or operation of ambulatory care facilities in a particular jurisdiction. Such regulations are far beyond the scope of this chapter.

FACILITY DESIGN AND EQUIPMENT

In most but not all instances, the hospital-based facility uses existing operating and recovery rooms. This chapter reviews the physical plant and equipment used by freestanding facilities.

Physical Plant

It should be obvious that the rooms housing the facility, equipment, and the like must be comparable with those found in the hospital. The operating, recovery, instrument, cleanup, storage, office, and waiting rooms all should be of adequate size to accommodate the respective function. The recovery room should be adjacent to the operating room, and the recovery room nurses' station should afford ready view of all recovery bed locations.

Installed Equipment

General and task illumination in both the operating room and recovery room should be of sufficient intensity to meet at least minimal lighting requirements. Central piping of oxygen to the operating room and each bed position in the recovery room is essential. Depending upon the number of cases of general anesthesia to be administered, it may be desirable to install a central piping system for nitrous oxide. A central suction system, with outlets available in the operating room and at each bed location in the recovery room, is also essential. The anesthesia machines should be equipped with a central system for scavenging waste anesthetic gases. NFPA 99, Standard for Health Care Facilities,[5] requires the availability of an alternate source of electrical power[6] for the freestanding ambulatory care facility if inhalation anesthetics are employed for general anesthesia.[7] Battery-operated sources of illumination, of sufficient intensity and designed for automatic activation in the event of a power failure, are permitted "if inhalation anesthetics are not administered in any concentration."[8] Adequate electrical power must also be available for suction devices in the event of a power outage.[9]

Movable Equipment

The operating table must be of modern design, capable of placing the patient in Trendelenburg's position quickly, and achieving other positions as required by the surgeons. The anesthesia machine should also be of modern design and equipped to deliver the required inhalation agents. The monitoring equipment should be comparable to that found in the modern operating room. The criteria for the application of these monitors should be the same as those in the inpatient facility. Obviously, because of the nature of the procedures performed in the ambulatory care facility and its patient population, invasive monitoring is not appropriate. The minimum acceptable standards for monitoring these patients should, however, include those monitors suggested in the recent Harvard recommendations,[10] as well as the continual presence of an anesthesiologist or nurse anesthetist whenever these monitoring modalities are employed. Provisions should be made for upgrading these monitoring capabilities as the standards of practice for minimal acceptable monitoring change.

It is realistic to predict that some additional monitoring modalities (e.g., an end-tidal carbon dioxide analyzer and pulse oximeter) will be included as a part of the minimal standards for monitoring, to decrease the risk of untoward occurrences during outpatient anesthesia. Such niceties as mass spectrometry are not required at this time, but might be in the future. Pharmaceuticals and devices for resuscitation are of course mandatory, including those for cardiac monitoring and defibrillation and airway management. The agents for the administration of anesthesia and resuscitation, similar to those found in the modern inpatient operating room, must also be readily available.

STAFFING PATTERNS

The operating room must be supplied with a sufficient number of operating room nurses, technicians, or both, to carry out the tasks required and assist the surgeon as appropriate. The anesthetic may be administered by a certified registered nurse anesthetist (CRNA) or an anesthesiologist. If the operating surgeon is not a physician (e.g., a dentist), some jurisdictions mandate that an anesthesiologist be present in the operating room while the anesthetic is being administered (see Chapter 25). Except in the case of a hospital-based ambulatory care facility, it may not be desirable

to have trainees administer anesthesia, even though they are under the direct supervision of an anesthesiologist or CRNA.

The recovery room, likewise, must be staffed with a sufficient number of personnel, appropriately trained in postanesthesia recovery, to cover the maximum number of patients that might be in the room at any one time. It is desirable to have an anesthesiologist available for supervising care in the recovery room from the time the first patient enters the room until the last patient is discharged. This practice will avoid any allegations of abandonment (see Chapters 5 and 13).

OPERATING POLICIES

Before the facility accepts its first patient, its medical director (generally an anesthesiologist) must develop and adopt a procedural manual that covers all operating policies. This manual, which must at least meet the standard of care of other such facilities in this country, contains criteria for patient selection, preparation, and consent; operative procedures to be performed within the facility; policies on preoperative medications, anesthetic agents, and techniques; monitoring modalities to be utilized; discharge criteria; and staffing patterns. Of particular importance to the freestanding facility is the establishment of an affiliation with an inpatient facility for those patients who fail to meet minimum discharge criteria or need hospitalization because of an unforeseen complication. These policies should adhere to the recommendations put forth by the Joint Commission on Accreditation of Healthcare Organizations[11] or by the ASA (see Appendix 15-1).

Patient Selection

In the early days of ambulatory surgical care, it was customary practice to select only patients of ASA physical status (PS) I or II as candidates for care on an outpatient basis. With the experience generated by caring for these healthy patients, and a national agenda of controlling health care costs, most ambulatory care centers are now finding themselves challenged to provide safe anesthetic care for patients of ASA PS III.[12] These patients should have a stable medical condition and should have undergone appropriate evaluation and therapy to medically optimize their condition prior to their appearance at the ambulatory care center. The extremes of age have not been a factor in denying care in the ambulatory surgical setting; however, it has been the policy in some facilities to admit infants less than 3 months of age for observation postoperatively because of the immaturity of their respiratory organs.[12]

Each patient must be a candidate for a selected operation appropriate to an ambulatory surgical center. In the past, duration of the operation had been a consideration in determining the appropriateness of a procedure performed in the outpatient facility. Experience has now led to the performance of procedures that can take up to 4 to 5 hours. As long as adequate time is allotted to the recovery process, problems related to recovery and discharge have been negligible. Other criteria for procedure suitability on an outpatient basis include those not involving major incisional entry into a body cavity, no expectation of significant blood loss or fluid shifts, and no requirement for parenterally administered pain medications postoperatively.[12] Candidates for emergency procedures obviously are not usually acceptable, as one of the key elements of safe ambulatory anesthesia, particularly now that ASA PS III patients are undergoing outpatient anesthesia, is a thorough preanesthetic evaluation and preparation, steps that must be initiated and completed before the day of the procedure. The formal protocol detailing the patient selection process must be adhered to assiduously.

Preliminary Workup

Each candidate for anesthesia must be worked up in a manner similar to that employed for hospitalized patients. It must be apparent to surgeons, anesthesiologist, and the public that the standard of care in an outpatient facility is the same as, if not higher than, that of the inpatient facility, because of the additional requirement of discharge of the patient to a nonmedically monitored environment.

The patient is required to visit his or her personal physician some time prior to the day of the procedure. The physician obtains a medical history and performs a physical examination. The patient is also sent to a clinical laboratory for a urinalysis, a complete blood count, possibly automated chemistry, and, if the patient is a female of childbearing age, a pregnancy test (see Chapter 16). Further lab work may be indicated by the patient's individual medical history or by the nature of the medications that the individual is taking. An EKG for patients over 40 years of age and a chest x-ray film for those over 60 are also required.

The results of the physician's screening together with the laboratory data assist in determining the patient's physical status and hence whether the anticipated procedure may be performed on an outpatient basis. The results of this evaluation should be documented completely in the records that the patient hand-carries to the facility at the time of the preanesthetic interview.

It must be stressed that these recommendations are minimal standards that may have to be elevated on a case-by-case basis, where indicated. The results of all of these tests must be available and documented prior to the procedure, at the very latest by the time of the patient's arrival at the outpatient facility. Both the physical examination and laboratory testing should be carried out sufficiently early enough before the day of the procedure so that additional testing may be obtained as required.

Consent for Anesthesia and Operation

A consent form similar to that employed for inpatients should be utilized. It is desirable that the patient meet with the surgeon in his or her office some time before the operation to discuss the procedure, its risks, and its benefits. The surgeon must be certain that all of the patient's questions have been answered and that both consent and informed consent (see Chapter 9) for the operative procedure are obtained. Inasmuch as these procedures are purely elective, fully informing the patient of all significant risks is imperative! It is a foregone conclusion that being subjected to an anesthetic and operation in the ambulatory care setting must in no way pose any greater risk than having the same procedures as an inpatient. The standards of care for the outpatient facility should be at least as stringent as those in effect in the inpatient setting.[13-15] There are those who might argue that the ambulatory surgical setting should set a higher standard than the inpatient facility because of the intention of subsequently discharging patients on the day of the operation.

The patient should also visit the ambulatory care facility sometime prior to the day of the operation and discuss the proposed anesthetic with the anesthesiologist. The anesthesiologist will take into consideration the elicited history and available laboratory data in the formulation of the anesthetic plan. The proposed anesthetic with all its implications should be discussed, all questions answered, and the patient's consent and informed consent obtained at this time. By the inherent nature of the ambulatory surgical center's structure, the anesthesiologist performing the preanesthetic interview and counseling may or may not be the one who will administer the anesthetic. The usual problems in the physician-patient relationship inherent to the practice of anesthesia are exacerbated in the ambulatory setting. Because of this discontinuity in preoperative counseling and subsequent performance of the delivery of the anesthetic, all discussions with the patient should be carefully documented and become part of the patient's ambulatory care record.

Preparation of the Patient

As with any operative procedure, preparation of the patient may have to be started a number of weeks prior to the administration of the anesthetic. For example, heavy smokers should stop smoking completely for at least 2 weeks before the operation. Those who have badly diseased teeth may need to visit their dentist and have their mouths thoroughly cleaned up. Patients on various medication regimens might need preoperative manipulation of their drug schedule (e.g., discontinuation of aspirin). Obviously, patients with problems such as these may not be satisfactory candidates for ambulatory care anesthesia even after such preparation.

Each facility should have a written list of preoperative instructions for the patient (e.g., "take absolutely nothing by mouth after midnight," what you should wear, whom you should bring and where you should report on the day of the procedure, and what you should do if you develop a cold). This list should be given to the patient (or responsible next of kin in the case of a minor) during the visit to the facility prior to the day of procedure. The instructions currently in use at the Walter Reed Army Medical Center ambulatory care facility are contained in Table 15-1. Compliance has been found to be optimal when verbal directions related to the preoperative considerations are combined with written instructions. The prospective patient acknowledges the receipt of this list of instructions in writing on a copy of the instruction sheet, which is included as a part of the medical record.

On the morning of the procedure, the patient should be specifically queried whether the admonitions have been followed, and the patient's responses documented on the record. While failure to follow these admonitions might be considered comparative (barring a portion of any recovery) or contributory (barring any recovery) negligence should, for example, the patient ingest food, vomit, and aspirate, preventing such an occurrence obviously is the preferable approach. If upon questioning the patient it is discovered that the preoperative instructions were not followed, a medical decision must be made whether to delay the procedure or cancel and reschedule it for another day. That is, a patient ingesting fluids prior to arriving at the ambulatory facility may have the procedure delayed depending on the nature and quantity of the fluid ingested, as opposed to a cancellation because of ingestion of a solid meal.

Under the contract for health care (see Chapter 3), patients as well as physicians have legally recognized duties. Duties of the patient pertinent to this discussion include making full disclosure and cooperating in the therapeutic regimen. Patients must divulge all pertinent aspects of their medical history that have or might have any bearing on their physical status and suitability as candidates for these procedures. They must also truthfully comment

TABLE 15–1. Medical Record—Supplemental Medical Data

WRAMC* Pre-Surgical Instruction Sheet

Your safety depends on you following these instructions:

1 Do not eat or drink anything (including water) after midnight of the evening before your planned procedure.
2 Following your surgical procedure you will not be permitted to drive, take a taxi, or a bus home. You must be escorted to the hospital by a responsible adult, who will be required to remain in the Ambulatory Surgical Center during the entire time of your surgical procedure and recovery period.
3 Anticipate a stay of approximately two (2) hours following your surgical procedure. You will be discharged only when an anesthesiologist and your surgeon feel your recovery is satisfactory.
4 Leave all valuables, including money, credit cards, and jewelry at home. You will need your military ID card.
5 You must remove all make-up and nail polish before coming to the hospital.
6 Please remember that it is not safe to care for a child that has had surgery and drive a car at the same time; therefore, if your child is to have surgery on our unit you will be required to bring a second adult to care for your child on the way home.
7 Wear old, loose fitting clothing to the hospital on the day of your surgery.
8 If there is any change in your condition prior to surgery, please contact your surgeon and the Ambulatory Surgical Center. Such things as a cold, flu, fever, sore throat, or diarrhea may require that the procedure be postponed to a later date.

    Point of Contact: Ambulatory Surgical Center 0700-1600
                      Phone: (202) 576-3953/54; AUTOVON 291-3953/54
                      Surgeon: _____
                      Phone: (202) _____

9 Special instructions:

10 I understand that if the above instructions are not followed as written and explained my surgery may be cancelled and rescheduled.

---

*Walter Reed Army Medical Center, located in the District of Columbia.
Source: Reprinted with the permission of the WRAMC.

on their compliance with preoperative instructions that might have an impact on their anesthetic care.

The patient should be instructed to wear loose-fitting clothing that can be readily removed prior to the anesthetic but, more importantly, easily put back on with assistance afterward. Finally, the patient must be instructed that he or she can leave the facility only if accompanied by a responsible adult and transported home either by a private vehicle or taxicab. To prevent the situation of a patient postoperatively insisting on leaving alone, it is our policy that the adult who will be responsible for accompanying the patient home also accompany the patient to the ambulatory surgical facility in the morning. The presence of this accompanying adult on arrival at the ambulatory surgical facility helps to assure his or her availability at the time of patient dis-

charge. It is preferable, though not required, for procedures performed on small children that two adults transport the child home postoperatively (i.e., one to drive and the other to tend to the needs of the child). Even in the presence of another responsible adult, it is undesirable to use public transportation.

Preliminary Medication and Anesthetic

On the morning of the procedure the patient is allowed to undress and put on a hospital gown or other appropriate attire. Clothing, glasses, and so forth, are secured in a locker (patients are instructed to leave valuables at home). The patient is next brought to a preanesthetic holding area where an intravenous line is started. Preliminary medication may be administered (though rarely is) if deemed appropriate, provided that it will have minimal impact on postoperative recovery and not delay the ultimate patient discharge.[16]

The patient is next brought to the operating room where monitors are applied (e.g., EKG, blood pressure cuff, and the like) and the anesthetic is administered. Each anesthetic, be it a general or a regional with one of the shorter-acting agents, should be tailored to provide adequate intraoperative coverage while at the same time possessing minimal recovery requirements. Whether regional anesthesia will be used depends in large measure upon the patient's ASA physical status, the operative procedure, and the policies of the facility.

Spinal anesthesia with a short-acting agent may be indicated under certain circumstances as long as allowances are made for adequate recovery of both sensory and motor function, and duration of recumbency to diminish post-subarachnoid block headaches. Unfortunately, if the operative procedure exceeds the duration of the effect of the spinal anesthetic and supplemental general anesthesia is required, one is faced with the disadvantages of both and the advantages of neither.

Continuous (fractional) epidural anesthesia may be preferable to subarachnoid anesthesia in the outpatient facility because it allows precise control of the duration of the anesthetic by fractional injection through the catheter, as well as a diminished risk of postlumbar-puncture headaches.[17]

Caudal anesthesia, particularly as an adjunct to general anesthesia, is also useful in the ambulatory facility among pediatric patients. It offers a diminution of general anesthetic requirements and may result in a pain-free experience for the child in the recovery room and a speedy discharge.[18]

Intravenous regional local anesthetic administration (Bier block), conduction block of the brachial plexus by the axillary approach, and peripheral nerve block are also acceptable methods of providing regional anesthesia for the surgical outpatient. Because patients remain in the ambulatory care facility only for a finite period of time, and the performance of a regional anesthetic may consume much of that time, special arrangements may have to be made to allow this technique to be utilized efficiently. Thus the administration of general anesthesia in the ambulatory setting is probably more common.

Discharge Policy

The freestanding ambulatory care facility must have formal discharge criteria to ensure that all patients have recovered adequately from anesthesia at the time of their discharge. A physician, preferably an anesthesiologist, should verify that each patient meets these criteria at the time the patient is "signed out." These criteria should include an assessment of the patient's vital signs, ensuring their stability. The patient should have any nausea and emesis controlled pharmacologically and should be able to tolerate fluids by mouth. Additionally, patients' sensorium should be intact, and they should be able to ambulate with assistance.

After these criteria have been met, the patient and the most responsible accompanying adult are both counseled verbally as to limitations on activity and other postoperative expectations. Most importantly, inasmuch as the patient is being discharged to an environment without trained medical observers, the patient and the accompanying adult must be warned about those postoperative complications to watch for that might necessitate their return to a medical facility. They are given information detailing who to call about postoperative problems and where to go if medical intervention becomes necessary. This information is provided to the patient and the accompanying adult both verbally and in writing (Table 15-2). The patient is then transported by wheelchair to the car or taxi and taken home by the accompanying adult.[13,14]

Inherent in the nature of outpatient anesthesia is the nonavailability of the patient on the ward for postanesthetic interview on the day after the procedure. The postanesthetic interview ordinarily is performed by telephone the next day by a member of the anesthesia care team or a nurse assigned to the recovery room. Any problems unearthed are brought to the attention of the anesthesia care team responsible for the case, and appropriate remedial measures taken. In our institution this process has

TABLE 15–2. Postoperative and Postanesthetic Instructions*

1 Although you will be responsive soon after your anesthetic, small amounts of the anesthetic remain in the body for 24 hours. Return home and rest for this period.
2 Nausea, vomiting, dizziness, or drowsiness may be present the first 12 to 24 hours. If this should occur, lie down if being transported home. If at home, return to bed.
3 When you return home, follow your doctor's orders regarding medications, diet, and rest. Unless instructed differently, resume clear liquids for 6 hours after surgery, then light meals until morning.
4 Tasks that require physical or mental alertness should not be attempted for 24 hours. DO NOT: drive a car, sign any legal documents, or engage in any legal transactions during this time.
5 It is advisable to have someone home with you the rest of the day.
6 It is not safe to care for a child who has had surgery and drive a car at the same time. Please bring another adult along to care for him.
7 Any postoperative problems related to your surgery, that is, bleeding, fever, inability to void within 8 to 12 hours should be reported to:

    Name:

    Phone:

    Or:

    Special Instructions:

    Signature:

    Date:

*Utilized on the Ambulatory Care Service, Walter Reed Army Medical Center.

brought to light postoperative complications that necessitated medical intervention but had been ignored by the patient (e.g., a patient with excessive bleeding after an outpatient dilation and curettage). An important requirement for safety in the outpatient setting is not only the proper management of patients in the recovery room but also adequate follow-up after they leave the facility.

COMPLICATIONS AND CASE LAW

During the preparation of this chapter, I researched the WestLaw* data base in

---

*A computerized data base containing text of essentially all common law (appellate court) decisions in United States federal and state courts over the last several decades. One may access this data base via a modem connected to a personal computer equipped with communications software and search for cases containing key words or phrases such as "anesthesia" and "outpatient" and the like.

search of cases involving anesthesia administered to ambulatory patients. This data base, which covers the time before the advent of the widespread administration of anesthesia to ambulatory patients, did not contain any reported cases specifically involving this technique, at least none that I was able to discover with this search. (Had there been any such cases, one would have expected them to relate to complications during recovery from anesthesia. There is, for example, an abundance of cases pertaining to inpatients recovering from the effects of anesthesia—see Chapter 13.)

In all likelihood, this dearth of case law relates to several factors. As noted above, the formalized concept of 1-day surgery did not begin until the 1960s, and did not take full hold in this country until the 1970s. Possibly because the concept is so new, there is essentially no case law involving complications developing from these procedures. This paucity of reported cases may also stem from two other factors. First, ambulatory care anesthesia was initiated by experienced anesthesiologists who recognized the potential problems inherent to this technique and adopted adequate safeguards to prevent complications. These safeguards included:

- Careful patient selection and work-up
- Restricting candidates for anesthesia to those of ASA PS I and II status and (most recently) stable, well medically controlled patients of PS III status
- The use of short-acting agents
- Meticulous monitoring, during both maintenance of and recovery from anesthesia
- A discharge policy ensuring that each patient will reach home safely that same day but still allowing for re-entry into the medical care system if the need later arises

Another factor may relate to the realization by professionals, and those who insure them, that cases in which the plaintiff's side has merit should be settled rather than tried. Additionally, a physician or hospital who loses a case in court generally, except under exceptional circumstances, will not appeal that decision. Hence, the common law (see Chapter 1) is essentially silent pertaining to litigation concerning ambulatory care anesthesia.

That is not to say, however, that incidents cannot and do not occur. The complication rates for surgical procedures and for anesthetic complications (i.e., bronchospasm, malignant hyperpyrexia, and the like) are not magically diminished by performing the procedure on an outpatient basis. The performance of anesthesia on patients coming from and returning directly to their home on the same day does allow for other potential problems. Consider the following incident that occurred at a large tertiary-care hospital in the private sector.[19]

The hospital had an international reputation, and the majority of the patients came from other communities. Ambulatory care anesthesia was standard practice, with no restrictions being placed on where the patient resided. Late one afternoon, an adult male had fully recovered from the effects of the anesthetic. As was customary practice in that hospital, the patient had been informed that he must be accompanied home by a responsible adult. Af-

ter the patient was ready for discharge from the recovery room, he told personnel that he had rented a car that was parked in the hospital garage, and he desired to leave, drive the car to the airport, and return home. He was told by personnel that he could not do so, whereupon the patient informed them that he wanted to go to the car to get some clothing. One of the nurses walked to the garage with him. The patient opened the car door, suddenly jumped in, started the engine and sped away, leaving the dismayed nurse to explain to other personnel what had happened. Fortunately, the patient was able to drive, turn in the car at the airport, board the aircraft, and make it home safely.

It is interesting to speculate what would have happened if the patient had been involved in an accident on the way to the airport and injured himself or others. Would the hospital have been liable? Or would the contributory negligence of the patient have been sufficient to offset any allegations on his part, or those of third parties injured in any such accident, and thus have relieved the hospital of liability? It would seem under those circumstances that the hospital had acted reasonably, and that the contributory negligence of the patient would have completely offset any potential exposure of the hospital to liability under those circumstances.

CONCLUSION

The administration of anesthesia in the ambulatory care setting is here to stay. It has proven itself to be a safe, effective, and cost-efficient method of providing anesthesia care for selected patient populations and procedures. Unquestionably, with continued adherence to appropriate safeguards, it will remain a safe substitute for inpatient anesthesia for a goodly number of operative procedures in appropriately selected patients.

REFERENCES

1. O'Donovan, TR and O'Donovan, PG: The future is now. In Wetchler, BV (ed): Anesthesia for Ambulatory Surgery. JB Lippincott, Philadelphia, 1985, p 1.
2. White, PW: Anesthesia for ambulatory surgery. Anesthesia Review Course Manu-

al, International Anesthesia Research Society Annual Meeting, Reno, NV, 1984, p 185.

3. Waters, RM: The down-town anesthesia clinic. Am J Surg Anesth (Suppl) 33:71, 1919.
4. Ford, JL and Reed, WA: The surgicenter—an innovation in the delivery and cost of medical care. Ariz Med 26:801, 1969.
5. NFPA 99, Standard for Health Care Facilities. National Fire Protection Association, Boston, 1987.
6. *Id.*, §§ 8-3.1 *et seq.*
7. *Id.*, §§ 8-5.1 *et seq.*
8. *Id.*, § 8-5.1(a)
9. *Id.*, § 8-4.4.2(b)
10. Eichhorn, JH, et al: Standards for patient monitoring during anesthesia at Harvard Medical School. JAMA 256:1017, 1986.
11. 1991 Accreditation Manual for Hospitals. Joint Commission on Accreditation of Healthcare Organizations, Chicago, 1990, pp 57–67.
12. Roizen, M, et al: The relative roles of history and physical examination, and laboratory testing in preoperative evaluation for outpatient surgery; the "Starling curve" of preoperative laboratory testing. Anesth Clin North Am 5:15, 1987.
13. Epstein, BS: Outpatient anesthesia. Refresher Course, American Society of Anesthesiologists Annual Meeting, Atlanta, 1983, pp 125–126.
14. Griffith, JL and McLaughlin, SH: Legal implications. In Wetchler, BV (ed): Anesthesia for Ambulatory Surgery. JB Lippincott, Philadelphia, 1985, p 33.
15. Montedonico, J and Tazzara, PM: Legal considerations of outpatient anesthesia. Anesth Clin North Am 5:227, 1987.
16. Clark, AJM and Hurtig, JB: Premedication with meperidine and atropine does not prolong recovery to street fitness after outpatient surgery. Can Anaesth Soc J 28:390, 1981.
17. Mulroy, M and Bridenbaugh, LD: Regional anesthetic techniques for outpatient surgery. In Woo, SW (ed): Ambulatory Anesthesia Care. Little, Brown & Co, Boston, 1982, p 71.
18. *Id.* at 77.
19. Dornette, WHL: Personal communication, 1988.

ASA GUIDELINES FOR AMBULATORY SURGICAL FACILITIES*

The ASA endorses and supports the concept of Ambulatory Surgery and Anesthesia and encourages the anesthesiologist to play a role of leadership in both the hospital and free-standing setting.

  I An ambulatory surgical facility may be hospital affiliated or freestanding. The facility is established, equipped and operated primarily for the purpose of performing outpatient surgical procedures.
 II ASA Standards, Guidelines and Policies should be adhered to in all areas except where they are not applicable to outpatient care.
III A licensed physician, preferably an anesthesiologist, must be in attendance in the facility at all times during patient treatment, recovery, and until medically discharged.
 IV The facility must be established, equipped, constructed, and operated in accordance with applicable local, state and federal laws.
  V Staff shall be adequate to meet patient and facility needs, and consist of:
    A Professional Staff
       1 Physicians and other practitioners who are duly licensed and qualified.
       2 Nurses who are duly licensed and qualified.
    B Administration Staff
    C Housekeeping and Maintenance Staff
 VI Physicians providing medical care in the facility should be organized into a Medical Staff which assumes responsibility for credentials review, delineation of privileges, quality assurance and peer review.
VII Personnel and equipment shall be on hand to manage emergencies. The facility must have an established policy and procedure concerning unanticipated patient transfer to an acute care hospital.
VIII Minimal patient care shall include:
    A Pre-operative instructions and preparation.
    B An appropriate history and physical exam by a physician prior to anesthesia and surgery.
    C Pre-operative studies as medically indicated.
    D Anesthesia shall be administered by anesthesiologists, other qualified physicians or medically directed non-physician anesthetists.
    E Discharge of the patient is a physician responsibility.
    F Patients who receive other than unsupplemented local anesthesia must be discharged to the company of a responsible adult.
    G Written post-operative and follow-up care instructions.
    H Accurate, confidential and current medical records.

---

*Amended by House of Delegates of the American Society of Anesthesiologists on October 12, 1988. Reprinted with the permission of the ASA.

16

Brad Lee Hilaman, M.D., J.D.

Anesthesia During Pregnancy, Labor, and Delivery

The administration of anesthesia during pregnancy carries with it all the medical and legal risks of anesthesia administration to nonpregnant patients, as described elsewhere in this book. The presence of a fetus, however, creates additional medical risks, as well as medical-legal ones, including the potential for independent legal action brought by or on behalf of an injured newborn infant. It seems reasonable, then, for anesthesia providers to be acutely conscious of the specific risks attendant to the administration of anesthesia to the pregnant patient. It is the goal of this chapter to familiarize the reader with these risks and some of the methodology for mitigating them.

SCOPE OF THE PROBLEM

When anesthesia personnel undertake to care for a pregnant patient, they are not only caring for a mature adult but also a developing fetus. In that situation, personnel will be held not only to the standard of care customarily provided by the theoretical "reasonable anesthetist," but possibly also to the standards of practice developed and mandated by the American College of Obstetrics and Gynecology (ACOG) as they pertain to anesthesia services, as well as to any applicable common law standards of care established following adjudication of obstetrical malpractice cases. ACOG is a voluntary standards-making organization (see Chapter 3) concerned with quality care standards in this specialty. The ACOG requirement of being able to start a cesarean section within 30 minutes of the decision to do so serves as a pertinent example.[1] In addition, anesthesia personnel may find themselves inadvertently embroiled in the management of various conditions unique to obstetrics—that is, disseminated intravascular coagulation following stillbirth or the management of insulin infusion in a class D diabetic—which may ultimately lead to the birth of a damaged fetus and result in the potential for a multimillion dollar damage award.

Both the type and frequency of administration of obstetrical anesthesia have changed over the last 10 years, partly because of the trend toward "prepared" or "natural" childbirth. The medical-legal issues associated with anesthesia administration during pregnancy have multiplied, reflecting the underlying problem unique to the administration of obstetric analgesia and anesthesia—it is the mother who wishes relief from the pain, but both mother *and*

fetus must be protected from inadvertent harm caused by agents given to produce that relief. Creative plaintiffs' attorneys have continued to develop new and novel causes of action under which the person administering the anesthetic may be held liable. Many of these claims are based upon changes in the standard of practice resulting from the development of new technology. This chapter reviews some of these changes, claims, and outcome of subsequent litigation.

DETERMINATION OF PREGNANCY

Although the teratogenicity of anesthetic agents has not been established, the underlying 4% fetal malformation rate and 20% miscarriage rate makes the possibility of a claim, based upon the temporal association between a fetal loss or malformation and the anesthetic administration, likely in today's litigious society. It is, therefore, important that *all females in the childbearing age be considered pregnant* unless it is determined that they are not. Traditionally, pregnancy was diagnosed by establishing the last menstrual period while taking the patient's medical history, and confirming one's suspicion with a urinary pregnancy test. Despite reasonable precautions, the lack of sensitivity and specificity of this test in the past resulted in some very early pregnancies not being diagnosed until days or weeks after an anesthetic administration. With the advent of the serum beta-HCG analysis, even early pregnancy can virtually be ruled in or out. Women who are on the obstetrical or gynecologic service almost always have had their pregnancy status determined prior to any operation. For other surgical services, the thought of possible pregnancy may not be entertained. *It should be part of the preanesthesia workup to ascertain that pregnancy is not reasonably likely.* Abstinence or reliable use of a contraceptive and a normal last menstrual period indicate with a reasonable degree of assurance that pregnancy is unlikely. In the absence of this historical information, the clinician should consider obtaining a beta-HCG level to exclude an undiagnosed pregnancy. As noted above, administering general anesthesia to a patient not known to be pregnant may be courting litigation. Although such a claim might not be successful, it seems prudent to take steps to rule out pregnancy and thereby avoid any possibility of a claim being filed. When pregnancy is diagnosed and the operation is indicated but is not emergent, it is prudent to wait until 14 to 16 weeks of gestational age to avoid the embryologic phase of development and time of highest spontaneous fetal loss, namely the first trimester.

In an emergency necessitating operative intervention and the administration of an anesthetic to a woman with an undiagnosed pregnancy, general principles of common law would preclude liability for any untoward outcome related thereto. It should be apparent under those circumstances that the standard of care required anesthetic and surgical intervention.

SURGICAL DISEASES DURING PREGNANCY REQUIRING ANESTHESIA

Appendectomy, correction or removal of twisted adnexa or adnexal mass, and placement of a cervical cerclage for incompetent cervix are examples of emergent or indicated surgical procedures during pregnancy that will require anesthesia administration. Those conditions just cited commonly occur during the embryogenesis of the first trimester. Because each of these complications is associated with a high potential for fetal loss through premature labor, the risk of malpractice claims against the obstetrician and anesthesia personnel is increased.

Commonly, the surgical literature reports the removal of normal appendices in 20% of cases of "appendicitis." Because of the increased incidence of fetal loss attending delayed diagnosis of appendicitis during pregnancy, it is likely that 30% of appendices removed during pregnancy will be normal.[2] Anesthesia personnel should not be hesitant to anesthetize pregnant women with signs and symptoms of an inflamed appendix. The site of the operative intervention (in the lower abdomen) lends itself to regional techniques. Additionally, regional agents carry the added advantage of less systemic absorption. General anesthesia is not absolutely contraindicated, however. The practitioner's legal duty is to choose an agent not known to adversely affect uterine blood flow, and one that has no known teratogenic properties.[3] Maternal hypotension also must be avoided.

In this scenario, the physician's most important duty is to provide adequate informed consent. Inasmuch as the choice of anesthetic technique is limited to general versus regional block, the risks and benefits of each type should be carefully reviewed with each patient. Some of these risks are covered in general terms elsewhere in this book. They are discussed in this chapter within the context of obtaining informed consent from the pregnant woman.

INTRAPARTUM CARE

The advent of the concept of "natural" childbirth techniques (Lamaze) has altered drastically the way patients desire to experience childbirth and the way they desire the professional staff to manage delivery. Many patients seek to avoid all narcotic agents; the use of "twilight sleep" has all but vanished from the practice of obstetrical anesthesia. Other patients desire a more traditional "pain-free" labor and delivery process, and the use of caudal or epidural anesthesia is found to be desirable. It is not uncommon for the obstetrician to request that anesthesia personnel insert a catheter for fractional epidural anesthesia to aid in the management of a patient who has become uncontrollable secondary to the pain of labor. Additionally, conditions such as cerebral aneurysm necessitate epidural anesthesia as part of the management of the labor and delivery process to decrease the intracranial pressure associated with "pushing" during the second stage of labor.

Current standards of practice dictate the availability of separate personnel to treat anesthetic and obstetric complications should they occur simultaneously. In this respect, it is to be hoped that the days of one medical person attending to both the anesthetic and obstetrical needs of the patient have passed. *Responsibility* for the administration of the initial and repeat doses of anesthetic agents, as well as monitoring the patient's vital signs, continues to remain with members of anesthesia service, despite the delegation of these tasks to other personnel. Any mishaps that occur while the patient is under the care of alternate personnel—who have other concomitant duties or lack of proper anesthesia qualifications—may be perceived as an *abandonment* (see also Chapter 5) by those anesthesia persons who are properly qualified, as well as negligent conduct on the part of the substitute.

Hypotension during the administration of a spinal or epidural anesthetic is of major concern. Patients who have been in labor for hours and kept on nothing by mouth are likely to be volume-depleted unless they are fluid-loaded prior to the beginning of the regional anesthetic block. Hypotension rarely is a catastrophic problem for the adult, but may well cause a significant fetal bradycardia.

Importance of Fetal Monitoring

The anesthetist can be made aware of adverse fetal response only if there is *adequate* fetal surveillance. Although this monitoring can be accomplished by intermittent auscultation, it seems more reasonable to use electronic fetal monitoring (EFM), which provides the easiest and probably most sensitive way to monitor fetal heart rate. It is my belief that anesthesia personnel *have a duty to determine that there is no fetal distress* before initiating a spinal or epidural anesthetic, and before administering any repeat doses of regional agent for this technique. If an infant in the intrauterine environment is already compromised by decreased uterine blood flow, or hypoxia caused by placental insufficiency or cord compression, regional block–induced maternal hypotension will probably cause additional compromise by decreasing the uterine blood flow. This added insult may result in additional brain damage or death of the infant. When the EFM is already in place, the preanesthetic record should reflect an evaluation of fetal status as determined by the monitor. A comment in the medical record concerning the presence of a normal heart rate, good variability, and lack of periodic decelerations, or the assurance from the obstetrician that the tracing is interpreted as normal, should be

sufficient to insulate anesthesia personnel from liability arising over controversies surrounding the pre-existing fetal condition at the time the anesthetic was induced.

Informed Consent and Regional Anesthesia

Obtaining informed consent under these circumstances involves the same steps as in the nonpregnant individual (see Chapter 9); that is, risks, benefits, and alternatives must be disclosed. In the pregnant woman, one must also include in the discussion any material risks to the fetus. These include the possibility of fetal distress induced by hypotension. The latter in turn may require emergent abdominal delivery if conservative intrauterine resuscitative measures fail. The possession of this information by the patient is considered *legally* necessary, because the patient, in theory, at least, has the alternative of utilizing Lamaze techniques for pain control, solely or in addition to an intravenous, intramuscular, or subcutaneous analgesic agent. It is the availability of all of these choices, together with the serious nature of some of these risks, that makes the need for obtaining informed consent so imperative. Anesthesia personnel must also be mindful of the concept of *informed refusal*, inasmuch as obstetrical or anesthesia personnel may receive an unusual request by the patient for an anesthetic agent or technique that is a poor choice, or actually contraindicated.

The Concept of Informed Refusal

In 1980, the California Supreme Court formally recognized this concept in *Truman v. Thomas*,[4] a case involving refusal of a patient to have a recommended Pap test. The court faulted the physician for failing to impress upon his patient the importance of the test by failing to emphasize the risks of not having it performed (in this case, carcinoma of the cervix that turned out to be inoperable by the time it was discovered). Would the availability of this doctrine excuse obstetrical or anesthesia personnel who acquiesced to using a medically contraindicated technique that the patient insisted upon having? That is, would the patient's truly informed refusal to receive the recommended agent or technique, coupled with informed consent to receive that which was less desirable, insulate anesthesia and obstetrical personnel from liability if the foreseeable risk materialized? I think not! It is a well-accepted common law principle that it is a departure from the duty of care to employ that which is medically contraindicated. It is a like departure to allow another to compromise one's professional judgment. Decisions as to the choice of agent and technique should have been made far enough in advance of delivery so that any conflicts between the patient's choice and ability of anesthesia personnel to adhere to that choice would have been resolved under nonemergent circumstances. Anesthesia personnel must not be asked to compromise their judgment at the last minute, when the infant's life, and possibly that of the mother as well, may revolve about split-second decision making.

What if the type of anesthetic demanded by the mother-to-be would create a substantial risk for the infant? Fortunately, such factual situations are rare. Again, I do not believe that any health care provider should compromise his or her professional judgment. This is the type of case in which a court, following appropriate motions by the hospital's legal counsel, could intervene, on the grounds that the mother-to-be's behavior constituted a risk to the life or well-being of her soon-to-be-born offspring.

General Anesthesia

The availability and administration of general anesthesia to the pregnant woman, as with the use of regional techniques, places anesthesia personnel in a position of being responsible for additional duties and at risk of potential exposure to additional liability. The ACOG requires being able to institute cesarean delivery within 30 minutes from the decision by the obstetrician to do so.[1] Another example is the requirement for fetal monitoring in the anesthesia preoperative holding area.

The physiology of the pregnant woman is altered in many ways. These alterations affect the techniques for administering general anesthesia to the pregnant woman. Delayed gastric emptying during pregnancy is a recognized risk that exposes every pregnant woman to the danger of aspiration of gastric contents during induction of general anesthesia. It has become the standard of practice to use rapid-sequence induction techniques to decrease this risk. Failure to use these techniques, without overriding justification, would likely be found substandard care in every instance if aspiration occurred and litigation ensued. Likewise, failure to accomplish endotracheal intubation without adequate justification would be met with expert testimony certifying it to be substandard medical care based upon the risk of aspiration.

The ACOG does not require that the labor and delivery unit have full-time anesthesia personnel available. It does require that the hospital must possess the *minimum* capability of beginning cesarean section within 30 minutes of the decision that abdominal delivery is indicated.[1] In addition, the ACOG has established as a minimum standard that "a person qualified to administer anesthesia should be readily available to administer appropriate anesthetic and maintain support of vital functions in any emergency."[5] This ACOG "standard" of practice, may well be less than what a court adopts as the legal standard of care.[6] That is to say, the court, in establishing what it perceives the standard of care should be, may require less than 30 minutes' interval between decision to initiate and the initiation of cesarean delivery. A tertiary-care hospital almost certainly will be held to a standard of initiating abdominal delivery within 10 to 15 minutes or less. In any litigation involving alleged delay in initiating the induction of anesthesia, the standard will be established and will be based upon the plaintiff's expert's testimony as presented to the court and accepted by the trier of fact. In addition, the ACOG standard suggests "in larger facilities caring for high risk patients, 24-hour, in-house anesthesia coverage is strongly recommended."[5]

These criteria have established a duty upon the obstetrician to alert the anesthesia and operating room personnel to the possibility of the need for emergent cesarean section and to request their presence in the hospital on a standby basis when "in-house" coverage is not required. If the anesthetist fails to agree to this request and then an emergency follows resulting in fetal injury from delayed delivery, it is likely that most courts will find the anesthetists' action negligent based upon the ACOG standards.

The ACOG also requires that a woman who has been placed on EFM while in labor continue to be monitored in the anesthesia holding area as well as the operating room until the abdominal skin preparation has begun (if external devices are used) or delivery (if internal devices are used).[5] Continued EFM is apparently required even in the situation where there has been a previously normal fetal heart tracing and the indication for cesarean delivery is "failure to progress in labor."

It is obviously both medically and legally necessary that once the inhalation of oxygen has been initiated during labor, it must be continued during transport and in the operating room holding area.

Informed Consent for General Anesthesia

In addition to the requirements for proper informed consent (discussed in Chapter 9) associated with the administration of general anesthesia in the nonpregnant state, there is need for provision of additional information by way of informed consent to the pregnant patient. It is reasonably accepted that it is preferable to maintain patients undergoing cesarean delivery under general anesthesia at a light level using thiopental, nitrous oxide, and a paralyzing agent until the fetal umbilical cord is clamped. Only at that time is complete anesthesia, using an intravenous or inhalation technique, commonly achieved. This anesthesia sequence is intended to avoid exposing the infant to narcotics or inhalational agents that could potentially affect the child's respiration, reflex activity, and tone for an extended postbirth period. Valium administered intrapartum has been found to be responsible for extended neonatal depression and decreases in the Apgar scores. Without adequate justification (for example, control of seizures), the use of Valium should be avoided before the clamping of the umbilical cord. This will avoid an allegation of negligently caused neonatal de-

pression, whereas the actual cause was preexisting injury.

Plaintiffs' attorneys are now filing claims based on physical pain and mental anguish for failed or inadequate anesthesia during cesarean delivery. These claims appear to be based upon the patient's recall of the initial stages of the cesarean section prior to the clamping of the cord and the administration of more effective analgesic agents. In reality, this is an issue of complete patient informed consent. Certainly, it is medically justifiable to conduct the initial part of the cesarean section without total anesthesia coverage, based upon the small percentage of patients who will have recall of the procedure postoperatively. This practice further serves to protect the infant from the possible detrimental effects of the analgesic agents. *The pregnant woman should therefore be advised that a small number of patients may remember some of the initial operating room procedures*, but that this is a result of an *intentional* action on the part of the anesthetist designed to protect the infant while balancing the risks and benefits to both mother and her unborn infant. It is to be hoped that when the patient and her family are advised of the rationale underlying her initial discomfort, a lawsuit will not be filed. If one is filed, the insurance carrier or defense attorney should reasonably be able to dispose of the case favorably for the physician as long as proper informed consent covering this issue has been obtained *and* documented in the record.

Positioning of the Patient

As in any other situation, positioning of the patient, although probably a joint responsibility between the anesthetist and the obstetrician, remains the primary duty of the operating room personnel under the direction of the anesthetist (see also Chapter 11). Placement of a "roll" under the mother's right side, or the use of other lateral displacement devices, is a standard of practice designed to displace the uterus laterally off of the inferior vena cava. Avoiding supine hypotension and the associated fetal distress that may result is imperative in avoiding claims for aggravation of fetal injury or brain damage.

Special Conditions of Pregnancy Affecting Anesthetic Management

The anesthetist must not only be totally familiar with the usual anesthetic complications and their prevention and management, but also with those obstetric complications that affect the administration of anesthesia. Recognizing these problem areas will help prevent compounding the injury to an already compromised mother, fetus, or both.

Postdate Pregnancy

A "postdate" pregnancy is considered medically, and therefore legally, a high-risk situation. There is an increased risk of fetal distress because of decreased efficiency of the placenta in CO_2 and O_2 exchange, caused in turn by aging and associated fibrosis. This places all health care personnel caring for the mother and infant at a higher duty of surveillance for hypoxia and fetal distress, based upon the underlying risk of placental insufficiency. The risk of meconium aspiration is also increased when the pregnancy extends beyond 42 weeks' gestation. Electronic fetal monitoring and careful attention to maternal oxygenation are mandatory when there is any question of fetal hypoxia and postdate pregnancy.

Intrauterine Fetal Demise With Associated Intravascular Coagulation

Disseminated intravascular coagulation (DIC) is a recognized complication of intrauterine fetal demise (IUFD). The potential for the bleeding diasthesis must be recognized by the anesthetist when called to attend to either a vaginal or abdominal delivery of a stillborn infant. Because of the anxiety associated with delivery of a stillborn, "heavy" analgesia or anesthesia is commonly requested by the obstetrician. It is incumbent upon the anesthetist to recognize his or her duty to ensure that the laboratory values for the clotting factors as well as the platelet count are normal. The anesthetist must be aware of the association of DIC and IUFD, and recognize the complications, such as DIC, associated with administration of anesthesia to persons with a preexisting bleeding diasthesis.

Pre-eclampsia and Eclampsia

Care of the pre-eclamptic or eclamptic patient obviously involves the medical management of her hypertension and seizures if present. Controversy surrounding the use of regional anesthetic blocks continues, with the argument centering around the appropriateness or inappropriateness of utilizing regional techniques in the presence of an intravascularly volume-depleted patient with pre-eclampsia or eclampsia.[7] It is an accepted legal principle that there are different schools of thought as to the "best" mode of management of many disease processes. The anesthesia practitioner needs to recognize the pre-eclamptic patient's state of intravascular volume depletion despite the outward appearance of cellular edema. Hydration must be managed so as to avoid hypotension secondary to the sympathetic blockade associated with or resulting from administration of regional anesthesia. That is to say, the selection of a regional block for a pre-eclamptic or eclamptic patient, although not accepted fully across the country, is not a negligent decision; rather, it is a question of medical judgment.

Infant Resuscitation

Occasionally, the situation arises wherein an infant requires cardiopulmonary resuscitation in the operating or delivery room while the anesthesiologist or anesthetist is present and attending to the needs of the mother. It is my opinion that *the primary duty of the anesthesia person is to the mother.* For the anesthetist to be able to leave the mother and attend to an infant without risking allegations of abandonment requires that (1) the mother's condition be stable, and (2) some trained individual be able to attend to monitoring of her vital signs and observing her during the anesthetist's temporary "absence" for infant resuscitation. The overall responsibility for infant resuscitation should be charged to the pediatric team, unless the anesthetist can reasonably and safely turn the duties of maternal monitoring over to another trained individual. Thus, while assistance from anesthesia personnel is always welcomed, and may be urgently needed in some cases of infant resuscitation, it must be remembered that the primary legal duty of the anesthetist is to the mother.

NEW TECHNIQUES AND LIABILITY ISSUES

Vaginal Birth After Cesarean Section

Traditionally, once a woman delivered by cesarean section, she was forever precluded from vaginal delivery, because of the risk of rupture of the uterus at the site of the scar, and subsequent probable loss of the infant and possibly the mother. Currently, under certain circumstances, vaginal births after cesarean section (VBAC) may be preferable to repeat sections (see below). Anesthesia personnel need be concerned about the implementation of this new technique, as it necessitates early availability of personnel.

Although the maternal mortality associated with a cesarean section is only 1 death per 10,000 operative deliveries, it does constitute a 10-fold increase over vaginal deliveries, the rate of which is 1 in 100,000. The morbidity accompanying cesarean section is even more striking. ACOG is now advocating VBAC as the delivery method of choice for all women who satisfy the following criteria:

1 *Early during the prenatal course the woman and her physician should discuss fully the option of a trial of labor. The patient should be made aware of the benefits and potential risks.*
2 *Absolute cephalopelvic disproportion, although rare, remains a contraindication to labor.*
3 *A previous classical uterine incision remains a contraindication to labor.*
4 *There should be only one fetus, and the estimated fetal weight should be less than 4000 grams.*
5 *There should be continuous electronic fetal heart rate and uterine activity monitoring throughout labor, as well as staff and facilities required to respond to acute obstetrical emergencies.*[8]

It is reported that 58% of patients with

low transverse uterine scars who attempt to deliver vaginally have successful vaginal births.[9] The risks of VBAC include rupture of the uterus, possible intra-abdominal hemorrhage, fetal loss by placental abruption, or combinations thereof. To mitigate these risks, the ACOG institutional requirements for VBAC include:

1 Continuous uterine activity monitoring
2 Continuous fetal heart rate monitoring
3 Ability to initiate emergency cesarean section within 30 minutes

While current ACOG guidelines do not require in-house anesthesia coverage for hospitals performing VBAC, they do mandate that anesthesia be initiated within 30 minutes. This is the same criterion published by ACOG for routine vaginal delivery.[1] Thus, any institution meeting ACOG's criteria for vaginal deliveries should be able to perform VBAC. It is my opinion, however, that a creditable argument could be made by a plaintiff to the effect that obstetrics and anesthesia personnel should have been forewarned about the parturient's pre-existing risk of uterine rupture and, therefore, they should have been able to initiate the cesarean section *in less than 30 minutes.* A search of the national reporter system* failed to uncover any appellate cases dealing with this issue. It does seem appropriate, however, that where anesthesia personnel are on call for obstetrical anesthesia and a VBAC attempt is in progress, all efforts should be made to be available and ready to initiate induction of anesthesia within a "reasonable time" of 30 minutes or (preferably) less.

Refusal to Administer Anesthesia

Some health care providers refuse, on religious or related grounds, to participate in operations to terminate pregnancy or prevent it in the future (i.e., sterilization). A

*Computerized data base covering all state and federal appellate court decisions going back a number of years; it is possible to perform a topical search for specific phrases such as "vaginal birth (or delivery) after cesarean section."

general discussion of a professional's right to refuse to care for a patient is contained in Chapter 18. In those instances of health care providers being disciplined or fired for refusing to participate in an abortion or tubal ligation, the courts customarily have favored the provider.[10] Some legislatures have enacted statutes specifically delineating individuals' rights to refuse to participate in such cases.[11]

COMPLICATIONS THAT HAVE LED TO LITIGATION

It should come as no surprise that the common law is replete with obstetrical anesthesia-related case law. What follows are a few typical examples of complications that ended in litigation, appeals taken from trial court judgments, and a consequent enrichment of the common law.

Failure to Provide Adequate Anesthesia

In *Rosa v. Kulkarni*,[12] Marcel Rosa alleged that she suffered "unnecessary pain and injury, as well as psychotrauma" for "failure to make appropriate arrangements for the administration of anesthesia during delivery, [and] for not promptly providing her with anesthesia. . . ." The dispute centered around "whether [the] anesthesiologist delayed 45 minutes or only 30 seconds in arriving at [the] delivery room." The case was remanded to the medical malpractice panel for a hearing after the court determined the case merited a hearing and not just summary dismissal. In my experience reviewing claims against the U.S. government, this case serves as a typical example of the manner in which plaintiffs' attorneys frame their allegations for what most commonly is a delay in the arrival of the anesthetist in the operating room or delivery suite, or the complaint of recall of the initial portions of the cesarean delivery by the patient.

Bupivacaine Cases

In "Dear Dr." letters mailed on August 22, 1983, the Food and Drug Administra-

tion (FDA) and the manufacturers of Marcaine and Sensorcaine warned physicians not to use these agents in 0.75% concentration for obstetrical anesthesia. In pregnancy, the epidural veins may be enlarged, increasing the risk of inadvertent intravascular injection during attempted epidural injection. Bupivacaine's increased cardiotoxicity is thought to be related to its high lipid solubility.[13] Obstetrical patients who receive the 0.75% concentration of Bupivacaine have an eight times greater chance of having a seizure followed by a cardiac arrest than those who have been administered the 0.5% concentration.[14] Reported deaths have occurred with the 0.5% concentration, raising the issue of whether its risks exceed the benefits of its use. In this case, there appears both an informed consent issue (was the anesthetic really necessary?) and a question of possible negligence.

In *Barreto v. Justin*,[15] Marcaine was administered as a caudal anesthetic during labor. Inadvertent intravascular injection resulted in a fatal respiratory and cardiac arrest. This suit was settled for $1.1 million, based upon an allegation that the caudal anesthetic was unnecessary and that a drug less dangerous than Marcaine should have been used.

In *Love v. D.C.*,[16] a woman undergoing a cesarean section died after the Marcaine block reached too high a level. Summary judgment affixing liability against the hospital was issued by the court.

Marcaine was again the agent implicated in the malpractice action of *Henry v. St. John's Hospital*.[17] In this case, two doses of Marcaine were administered in the form of a paracervical block by the obstetrical staff. Fetal bradycardia occurred, which lasted until the infant's birth. At 24 months the child had evidence of a severe cerebral-palsy–type injury. The court held that the doses were too close together and that the second dose was excessive. An additional fact in this case was that the resident physician altered the nursing notes* in an attempt to reflect a decreased amount of Marcaine being administered in the second dose. The court found that, "based upon a reasonable degree of medical certain-

---

*A certain way of ensuring that the trier of fact brings in a large verdict for the plaintiff; see the discussion of spoliation in Chapter 10. [Ed.]

ty, it is likely that the perinatal asphyxia was related to the bradycardia . . . and absent a predisposition for cerebral palsy," the bradycardia was found to be the cause of the injury. The court awarded the successful plaintiff $10,000,000.

In *Wentling v. Medical Anesthesia Services, P.A.,*[18] a verdict of $786,166 was sustained for mismanagement of labor in November of 1979. Marcaine in a 0.75% concentration was administered as a spinal anesthetic after a prior epidural had been placed using 0.25% Marcaine. After injection by the nurse anesthetist, the patient sustained immediate seizure, cardiac arrest, and loss of consciousness. The infant was born by cesarean delivery without problems, but the mother died 4 days later from complications of the cardiac arrest. Liability was admitted by the defendant, with the trial centering on a controversy as to the reasonableness of the damages.

Informed Consent Obtained During Labor

Patterson v. VanWiel[19] involved two important allegations against the anesthesiologist: informed consent and proper location of necessary resuscitation equipment.

The obstetrician requested an epidural or caudal anesthetic be initiated for pain management during induction of labor and episiotomy. The anesthesiologist entered Mrs. Patterson's room and identified himself. He advised her that he had been told that she desired an epidural anesthetic. The patient agreed that she wanted the epidural anesthetic "now." The anesthesiologist told her of the technique which was to be used and that there was "some kind of risk involved," but that the risk of serious complications was 1 in 1000. Mrs. Patterson was asked if she had any questions, which she did not. "'She was in much discomfort at that time; she was anxious to receive an anesthetic. She understood the nature of his questions and there was no impairment to her ability to consent to the anesthetic."[20]

Following the anesthetic administration, Mrs. Patterson suffered a respiratory arrest, which was followed by a cardiac arrest lasting less than 1 minute. The resuscitation was successful and the baby was born without complications. The suit alleged the failure to obtain informed consent to the epidural anesthesia and the failure to have the necessary resuscitation equipment available.

The court noted that consent to medical treatment may be oral or written. Under the facts of this case, despite the presence of the pain associated with labor, the patient's consent was adequate to protect the anesthesiologist from liability. This was so even in the situation where Mrs. Patterson claimed she had no memory of the presence of the anesthesiologist nor of the "shot in her back." She could not recall the anesthesiologist telling her anything about anesthetics. Testimony that this conversation had taken place was accepted as factual, because of the complete medical record and the adequate explanation as to why Mrs. Patterson could not remember the consent conversation that was given to the trier of fact.

Although the evidence indicated that the resuscitation equipment was not in the patient's room at the time that it was needed, it was in the obstetrical suite. This location of the equipment was accepted by the court as consistent with the standard of practice. The court therefore held in favor of the anesthesiologist and the hospital on all issues.

Liability for Fathers in the Delivery Room

In *Justice v. Atchison,*[21] the father-plaintiff, who was in the delivery room prior to the attempted delivery, alleged that the defendant obstetrician improperly attempted to deliver his wife's baby. A prolapsed umbilical cord resulted in fetal death. The action was filed for negligent infliction of emotional harm, the father claiming that he felt (presumably by placing his hand on his wife's abdomen) fetal movement initially but not subsequently, and that his observation of the cessation of fetal life caused "shock and distress." The cause of action and the claim were denied, because the court found that the death of the fetus was hidden from the husband's *contemporaneous perception.* The court also based its verdict precluding recovery on the fact that the husband was in the delivery room *voluntarily.*

In California, at least, the distinction between parents' (husbands') voluntary or involuntary presence at the scene of the injury, as distinguished in *Justice,*[21] has been disapproved. The subsequent *Austin* case involved a husband who also was voluntarily present in the delivery room, and whose wife and unborn child died during delivery. The *Austin* court held that the father had stated a cause of action that was triable for negligent infliction of emotional distress. The claim for emotional distress resulting from the death of his unborn child was based upon the theory that while in the delivery room, he had been able to "feel life in the unborn child" and had observed cessation of life in the fetus, causing shock and distress. The court reasoned that the husband's triable cause of action arose because he had a "sensory and contemporaneous observance of the accident."[22]

The reader must remember that to have a successful claim for negligent infliction of emotional distress in these cases, there must be a negligent act that results in harm which the father observes. It is the *observed act coupled with the observed harm* that triggers the cause of action and potential liability, not just the act itself. Furthermore, the father need not know at the time of the act that it was tortious (i.e., a departure from the duty of care).[23] Fortunately, by their very nature the number of these cases should be limited.

CONCLUSION

The cases cited in this chapter constitute a mere sampling of the types of claims that appear in the various state and federal court reporter systems and directly or indirectly involve providers of obstetrical anesthesia. The complications that generated these lawsuits are preventable for the most part, given the availability of a competent member of the anesthesia service. It should be the goal of all anesthesiologists and nurse anesthetists to apply both the general principles of safe delivery of anesthesia service (delineated throughout this book) and those principles that are specific for the obstetrical patient (set forth in this chapter). Of specific import are identifying areas of risk in one's practice—as, for example, anticipating the obstetrician's needs and taking whatever steps are necessary to ameliorate those risks—such as being able to commence induction of anesthesia less than 30 minutes after a decision is made to go ahead; and carefully, completely, and legibly documenting one's care in the patient's medical record.

REFERENCES

1. American College of Obstetricians and Gynecologists. Standards for Obstetric-Gynecologic Services, 6th ed. ACOG, Washington, DC, 1985, p 29.
2. Black, WP: Acute appendicitis during pregnancy. Br Med J 1:1938, 1960.
3. *See, generally,* Smith, BE: Teratogenicity. In Orkin, FK and Cooperman, LH (eds): Complications in Anesthesiology. JB Lippincott, Philadelphia, 1983, p 523.
4. Truman v. Thomas, 27 Cal.3d 285, 165 Cal. Rptr. 308, 611 P.2d 902 (Sup. Ct. 1980).
5. *Supra* note 1, p 36.
6. Helling v. Carey, 84 Wash. 2d 514, 519 P.2d 981.
7. Pritchard, JA, Cunningham, FG, and Pritchard, SA: The Parkland Memorial Hospital protocol for treatment of eclampsia: Evaluation of 245 cases. Am J Obstet Gynecol 148:951, 1984.
8. American College of Obstetrics and Gynecology, ACOG Committee Statement: Guidelines for Vaginal Delivery After a Previous Cesarean Section. ACOG, Washington, DC, 1982; revised 1984.
9. Gibbs, CE: Planned vaginal delivery following cesarean section. Clin Obstet Gynecol 23(2):507, 1980; Merer, PR and Porreco, RP: Trial of labor following cesarean section: A two year experience. Am J Obstet Gynecol 144(6):617, 1982; Merril, BS and Gibbs, CE: Planned vaginal delivery following cesarean section. Obstet Gynecol 52(1):50, 1978; Pregnancy management after prior cesarean section: An invitational symposium. J Reprod Med 29(1), 1984.
10. *See, e.g.,* Swanson v. St. John's Hosp., 597 P.2d 702 (Mont. 1979).
11. Mich. Comp. Laws Ann. §§ 333.20181–.20184 (1980).
12. Rosa v. Kulkarni, 452 N.Y.S. 2d 441, 80 A.D. 2d 529 (1982).
13. Albright, GA: Cardiac arrest following regional anesthesia with Etidocaine or Bupivacaine (editorial). J Anesth 51:285, 1979.
14. Report of Anesthetic and Life Support Drugs Advisory Committee Meeting, Rockville, MD, October 4, 1983, pp 1–57.
15. Barreto v. Justin, Cal., Santa Barbara Co. Sup. Ct., No. SM 15783 (1987).
16. Love v. D.C., D.C. Sup. Ct. C.A., No. 14739–79, 1983.

17. Henry v. St. John's Hospital, No. 4-86-0604, Appel. Ct. of Ill., 4th Dist. (1987).
18. Wentling v. Medical Anesthesia Services, 701 P.2d 939, 237 Kan. 503 (1985).
19. Patterson v. VanWeil, 570 P.2d 931, 933 (C.A. New Mex. 1977).
20. *Id.*, p 934.
21. Justice v. Atchison, 19 Cal. 3d 564, 139 Cal. Rptr. 97, 565 P.2d 122 (1977).
22. Austin v. Regents of Univ. of Calif., 152 Cal. Rptr. 420, 89 Cal. App.3d 354 (1979).
23. Ochoa v. Superior Ct. (Santa Clara County) (Cal.) 216 Cal. Rptr. 661, 39 Cal.3d 159, 703 P.2d 1, 54 U.S.L.W. 2107 (1985).

17

Michael M. Wilson, M.D., J.D.

The Use of Blood Products

The transfusion of whole blood and blood products plays a significant role in operative as well as critical care anesthesiology. Many, if not most, modern advances in surgery would not have been possible without the availability of sometimes large volumes of blood products. Organ transplantation and coronary artery bypass grafting are two examples of operations that often require multiple transfusions. Approximately 12 million units of whole blood and packed red cells were transfused in 1988.[1] All of these transfusions pose a significant risk. Transfusion-related morbidity and mortality have led to a substantial body of law—comprising decisions, statutes, and regulations—that provides rules both for safe practices and for determining liability for complications under various circumstances. This chapter presents a survey of these rules so that anesthesia personnel can achieve a better understanding of the application of legal principles to disputes that may arise.

Initially, the chapter will review the legal bases of liability for complications arising from transfusions. Each patient's informed consent for transfusion generally should be obtained whenever possible, and considerations for obtaining this consent under various circumstances will be discussed, along with the four primary theories of liability for transfusion complications—battery, negligence, strict liability in tort, and breach of implied warranty for sale of goods. These theories will be considered as they apply to specific complications.

A successful transfusion requires the procurement of whole blood; the processing, storage, typing, and cross-matching of blood; the preparation of components; the decision to transfuse; and the performance of the transfusion. Complications related to each of these steps can and do occur, and they are associated with potential liability. A significant source of this liability relates to the fact that transfusions may transmit disease. Concern about hepatitis still exists, although cytomegalovirus and the human immunodeficiency virus (HIV, which causes acquired immunodeficiency syndrome, or AIDS) currently pose potentially significant, additional threats. The potential liability of the donor, blood bank, hospital, and physician for transfusion-associated hepatitis and HIV infection will be discussed.

LEGAL ISSUES AND ASSOCIATED LIABILITY

Consent to Transfusion

The physician who orders any blood product should obtain the prior consent of the patient for the transfusion if at all possible. The consent may be a part of the written consent to the administration of anesthesia or operation, although the risks of transfusion should be discussed apart from those of anesthesia. The transfusion of any blood product to a patient without consent may constitute a battery,[2] a legal theory of liability discussed below (see also Chapter 5). A physician who is found to have committed a battery ordinarily would be liable

for all damages caused by the transfusion, even though he or she did not commit any negligence (i.e., the transfusion was medically indicated). Therefore, obtaining a valid consent protects the physician as well as the patient.

While the surgeon often obtains the patient's consent to any needed transfusions while obtaining consent to the operative procedure, it is wise for the anesthesiologist also to obtain the patient's consent to transfuse as part of the anesthesia consent. Because they are monitoring the patient's vital signs closely and are perhaps the first members of the operating room team to become aware of falling blood volume (increasing heart rate, decreasing systolic pressure, narrowing of the pulse pressure, and the like), anesthesia personnel frequently participate in the decision to initiate the transfusion.

Informed Consent

A consent is ordinarily valid only if the patient is "informed" of the nature of the procedure and its attendant risks (see Chapter 9). As discussed below, if transfusion risks are not adequately explained, the consent will not be informed, and thus may be defective. Anesthesia personnel can be certain that the risks are adequately understood only by adequately explaining those risks. Furthermore, consent is limited to the specific procedure described to the patient, and any errors in such a description could invalidate the consent. Since a valid informed consent offers considerable legal protection for nonnegligent complications, anesthesia personnel should obtain this consent to transfusion directly (as noted above), if not impracticable under the circumstances. The legal standard for assessing the adequacy of the information provided varies from jurisdiction to jurisdiction. There are three standards—subjective, reasonable patient (objective), and professional—as defined and discussed in Chapter 9.

Only a few litigated cases have considered the adequacy of the discussion of risks of transfusions; these cases have been primarily concerned with whether the physician must warn of a risk of hepatitis. In *Fischer v. Wilmington General Hospital*, a woman contracted hepatitis after receiving

500 mg per dl of whole blood during a dilation and curettage. She argued that the hospital and physician had a duty to warn her of the risk of hepatitis. The hospital produced several affidavits to the effect that the customary practice of physicians in the community was not to inform patients of the risk of hepatitis, because the risk of infection, estimated at 0.45% to 1.0% was slight in relation to the risk of shock from blood loss. These affidavits were not contradicted by the patient-plaintiff. The court refused to allow the plaintiff to proceed to trial, placing particular emphasis on the standard of practice for disclosure in the community. It is also possible that the court was influenced by one affidavit that compared the "very great danger of fatality from blood loss" with the "temporary disability and discomfort associated with hepatitis."[3]

In *Parr v. Palmyra Park Hospital, Inc.,*[4] the patient also was not informed of the risk of hepatitis, which he later contracted. He argued that the consent was not "informed" because of the failure to warn of hepatitis. The court held that the consent was valid and refused to allow the case to proceed to trial.[5] The court applied the Georgia statute covering consent to medical treatment, which provided:

> A consent to medical and surgical treatment which discloses in general terms the treatment or course of treatment in connection with which it is given and which is duly evidenced in writing and signed by the patient or other person or persons authorized to consent . . . shall be conclusively presumed to be a valid consent in the absence of fraudulent misrepresentations of material facts in obtaining the same.[6]

The court followed previous cases that construed this statute to require only that the physician describe the procedure "in general terms" without describing the attendant risks. The court held that the consent was valid under the statute since the plaintiff produced no evidence of fraudulent misrepresentation. This holding represents straightforward application of the state statute and applicable precedent, but the resulting rule is unfair to patients as a policy matter. Patients are effectively denied the right to obtain information concerning the risks of medical treatment prior to pro-

viding consent to receive the proposed treatment.[7]

Finally, in *Sawyer v. Methodist Hospital*[8] the U.S. Court of Appeals for the Sixth Circuit also found no duty to warn of hepatitis. The court emphasized that over a 5- to 6-year period, approximately 60,000 units of blood were transfused at the defendant Methodist Hospital, with only eight cases of hepatitis, an incidence of 0.013%. Perhaps the court may have reached a different result had the incidence been significantly greater.

Refusal of Patient to Consent

Occasionally, a patient may refuse to consent to an entire course of treatment, or to one or more specific procedures within a proposed course of treatment. Objection to receiving a blood product is rather common, because of fear of contracting a disease or on religious grounds. The general rule is that the patient has authority over his or her body,[9] which includes the right to refuse treatment, even that which may be potentially lifesaving. In general, courts will refuse to order nonconsensual treatment. As one jurist stated:

> The makers of our Constitution . . . sought to protect Americans in their beliefs, their thoughts, their emotions and their sensations. They conferred, as against the Government, the right to be let alone—the most comprehensive of rights and the right valued most by civilized man.[10]

An especially difficult problem is posed by the patient who consents to an operation but refuses blood transfusions, a common occurrence among Jehovah's Witnesses.[11] What should the surgeon and anesthesia personnel do in such a situation? The physician could obtain a documented consent to the operation subject to the condition that blood products not be transfused (informed refusal), and then participate in the operation. Whether the physician will choose to follow this option will depend upon the risk-benefit analysis of the importance to the patient of undergoing the operation without benefit of possible transfusions.[12] This approach carries with it another risk of liability, being unable to compensate for massive blood loss that was caused by a negligent act. (A case of this nature is discussed later.) Another option is for the concerned surgeon or anesthesiologist to withdraw* from the case, with a referral, if possible, to other physicians who would discuss with the patient the possible performance of the procedure subject to the refusal to accept a transfusion. This option generally is not available in an emergency.

In emergency situations, the physician may be placed in an untenable position—between performing the procedure subject to the limitation or abandoning the patient. In such a dilemma, the hospital may decide to seek a court order authorizing the refused transfusion or other procedure. Whether the court will authorize such an order depends on the law of the particular jurisdiction, as well as the facts of the particular case.[13] How the courts would handle this issue varies, and revolves about whether the patient is a child or adult, and if the latter, whether pregnant, a parent, or neither. Representative cases of this nature will be discussed.

Adults

The principal case on the refusal of an adult Jehovah's Witness to consent to a blood transfusion for nonelective care is *Application of President & Directors of Georgetown College, Inc.*[14]

The patient, Mrs. Jones, was a 25-year-old mother of a 7-month-old child. Mrs. Jones was brought to the emergency room with a ruptured ulcer, having already lost two thirds of her total blood volume. The treating physicians advised that she would die without receiving a transfusion, but would have a 50% chance of survival with transfusions. The patient and her husband were both practicing Jehovah's Witnesses, and both refused to consent to the transfusion.

Counsel for the hospital appealed to the district court for an order authorizing transfusions, and the requested order was refused. Counsel then proceeded to the chambers of U.S. Court of Appeals Judge J. Skelly Wright, and requested immediate review of the district court's refusal to enter the order. Judge Wright spoke to the treating physicians by telephone, went to the hospital, and inter-

---

viewed the patient and her husband. He was informed by both husband and wife that neither would feel responsible for the transfusion if ordered by the court. He also decided that the patient was incompetent to provide or withhold consent because of being "in extremis."

Judge Wright entered the requested order authorizing the transfusions for four reasons. First, and most important, he desired to preserve the life of the mother ("I was determined to act on the side of life"). Second, he wanted to serve the best interests of innocent third parties, in this case, the 7-month-old child who could have been without a mother. Third, he sought to prevent suicide.[15] And fourth, he wanted to maintain and support the ethical and legal responsibility of the hospital and medical profession to preserve life.

Mrs. Jones recovered and subsequently petitioned for a rehearing by all justices of the Court of Appeals to determine whether the order should have been granted. The request for rehearing was denied by a majority vote of the entire court. Judge Miller dissented, however, with Judges Bastian and Burger concurring, on the ground that Judge Wright did not have the authority to enter the order as a single appellate judge, without serving on a duly constituted panel. Judge Burger also dissented, with Judges Bastian and Miller concurring, arguing that the hospital had no legally enforceable right sufficient to overcome the patient's "right to be left alone."

The cases subsequent to *Georgetown College* pertaining to adults have been divided. Several cases have followed the *Georgetown* holding and ordered that the blood be given. *United States v. George*[16] also involved a patient with a bleeding ulcer, and the court reached the same result, although the patient had "greater rational capacity." A New York judge ordered a transfusion in 1965 for a female Jehovah's Witness in an emotional opinion concluding with "I could not let her die."[17] A subsequent New Jersey opinion ordered a transfusion for a 22-year-old single Jehovah's Witness, holding that the state had a compelling interest in preserving life.[18]

Transfusions were not, however, ordered in several other cases. In *In Re Osborne*,[19] the refusal of a 34-year-old father of two to be transfused was observed, with the facts of a competent patient, well-established religious beliefs, and adequate provisions for the maintenance of the children deemed sufficient to refuse to order the transfusion.

In *In Re Brooks*[20] a transfusion order was reversed in a patient with adult children, even though the patient was deemed incompetent by virtue of blood loss.[21] And in a lower New York court, the refusal of a competent adult patient to receive a transfusion was respected, with little importance attached to the state interest in preserving life.[22]

How will these precedents be applied to the facts of a particular case? The result will differ from jurisdiction to jurisdiction, depending on the importance attached to the state's interest in preserving the life of the patient. Other factors that will be considered by the courts are the existence and status of dependent third parties, particularly children; the degree of lucidity of the patient at the time the transfusion is refused; and the duration and significance of the patient's religious beliefs. Considerable uncertainty in result will exist in those jurisdictions that lack case law on this issue.[23]

Children

Traditionally, a minor could not consent to medical treatment, and the consent of the parents or guardian was required except in an emergency or similar other exigency.[24] Exceptions to the common law for "mature minors" and "emancipated minors" were judicially carved out in some jurisdictions. Now, the majority of states have statutes that set forth criteria for "emancipation" or define an "age of consent." For example, Colorado combines emancipation and age criteria in the following statute:

> [A] minor eighteen years of age or older, or a minor fifteen years of age or older who is living separate and apart from his parent, parents, or legal guardian, with or without the consent of his parent, parents, or guardian, and is managing his own financial affairs, regardless of the source of his income, or any minor who has contracted a lawful marriage may give consent to the furnishing of hospital, medical, dental, and surgical care of himself.[25]

In situations wherein the child may not validly consent to a lifesaving transfusion or other procedure and the parents refuse consent due to religious or other reasons, the courts will intervene to protect the child and order the transfusion.[26] Where the transfusion is necessary for an operation indicated to further the health of the child but not necessary to preserve the child's life, the courts will attempt to balance the state's interest in health, the parents' interest in freedom of religion, and the child's interest in self-determination.[27]

Pregnant Women

The leading case in which a pregnant woman refused to consent to a transfusion considered necessary to save both her life and the life of the unborn fetus is *Raleigh Fitkin-Paul Morgan Mem. Hospital v. Anderson*.[28] The Supreme Court of New Jersey ordered the transfusion primarily to protect the interest of the unborn child, but noted that the interest of mother and child were inseparable, and that the state had sufficient interest in preserving the life of the mother to order the transfusion on that ground alone. After *Roe v. Wade*,[29] it is probable that a court could not order a transfusion solely to protect the fetus until the point of viability, but could order the transfusion if necessary to protect the life of the mother.

LIABILITY FOR COMPLICATIONS

Liability of the physician to the patient is premised on the violation of a legally recognized right of the patient. Four bases of liability are most closely related to transfusions of blood and blood products—battery, negligence, tort liability without fault, and breach of implied product warranty. Each of these potential bases of liability, or "causes of action," will be discussed.

Battery

A battery is an intentional touching of a person to which there is no consent[30] (see also Chapter 5). Generally, this touching is harmful or offensive, although in the case of health care the physician need not intend it to be. The key element is the *intent to cause the touching* of the patient, and not any intent to do harm. The consent to touching must be an "informed consent," as discussed above. A physician who is considered to have committed a battery upon the patient will ordinarily be liable for all of the harmful consequences of the touching, whether the consequences were intended or even foreseeable.

As an example, assume that through oversight neither the surgeon nor anesthesiologist obtains a patient's consent for a transfusion. Despite proper cross-matching and administration, the patient suffers a rare allergic reaction to the transfused blood and dies. Under these facts, the anesthesiologist who started the blood is likely to be considered to have committed a battery in transfusing blood because he or she intentionally caused a "touching" of the patient without the patient's consent. The requisite intent of battery would be satisfied, although the anesthesiologist intended only to properly transfuse blood, since he or she intended to cause the act to which no valid consent existed. The anesthesiologist need not intend to cause any harm to the patient. If a battery were deemed to occur, the anesthesiologist would be liable without regard to the fact that there was no negligence. Furthermore, even though the complication was not foreseeable, as in a case of the rare allergic reaction just hypothesized, the anesthesiologist still would be liable.

The primary significance of liability of the anesthesiologist for battery is that he or she must obtain consent to any administration of anesthesia or other procedure, or else risk liability for all consequences of the procedure without regard to fault. If an injury occurs, counsel for the plaintiff will carefully consider if consent was obtained, the consent was "informed," and the anesthesiologist exceeded the scope of the consent (in that event, negligence need not be proven).

Negligence

Negligence is the legal term that encompasses what is commonly termed *medical malpractice* (see Chapter 3). Negligence is the failure to adhere to the applicable standard of care. It comprises five elements: (1) duty, (2) breach of the duty, (3) nature of the injury, (4) causation, and (5) damages.[31] Each of these elements will be explained in the context of transfusions.

The Duty and Its Breach

A person, blood bank, hospital, and physician each has a duty to exercise reasonable care to patients or others with whom some relationship exists that gives rise to that duty. The precise standard of reasonable care will vary according to the factual situation and may be established by custom, expert testimony, or statutes and regulations (see Chapter 4). Once the existence of a duty and the standard of care are established, breach of duty is shown by demonstrating that the defendant did not meet the standard of care during the period of time under consideration.

The Injury

The nature of the injury is simply the complication that developed, the harm that ensued, and any sequalae thereof.

Causation

Causation has two elements: (1) causation in fact and (2) proximate causation. Causation in fact refers to whether the breach of duty did in fact cause the injury complained of. For example, if a homosexual patient developed AIDS following a transfusion, was HIV transmitted by the transfusion or by the sexual practices of the patient?[32] Proximate causation refers to the doctrine of "foreseeability," whereby some damages are so far beyond the scope of the risk that liability should be cut off as a matter of law. Assume, for example, that an anesthesiologist provided two units of blood at a time when only one unit was necessary, and that the second unit was infected with HIV, which was transmitted to the patient. Assume further that the chance of becoming infected was 1 in 1,000,000.* One could argue that the occurrence of HIV was sufficiently unlikely and unrelated to the risk of administering one unnecessary unit of blood that the anesthesiologist should not be liable for the subsequent disease.[33]

Damages

The fifth element is damages, attaching a

---

*In actuality, this risk is between 1 in 40,000 and 1 in 1,000,000; see discussion below on HIV transmission through blood products.

monetary figure to the harm to the patient proximately caused by the physician's breach of the standard of care.

Res Ipsa Loquitur

A doctrine closely related to negligence liability is that of *res ipsa loquitur*, which translated from Latin literally means "the thing speaks for itself." The importance of this doctrine (discussed in Chapters 3 and 11) is that the plaintiff may have his or her case submitted to the jury despite the absence of specific evidence of negligence.[34]

Responsibility for Negligence

Donor

The donor has a duty to behave as a reasonable person under the circumstances. For example, donors would generally have a duty to refrain from donating blood if they knew that they were carrying an infectious disease,[35] and to respond truthfully to questions posed in interviews and on written questionnaires.[36] Given the fact that members of high-risk groups have given blood contaminated with HIV,[37] litigation against such individuals is not without the realm of possibility.

Blood Bank

A blood bank[38] has a duty to the donor to avoid injuring him or her, by the use of disposable equipment (to prevent infection) and health screening (to verify that the donor will not be harmed by losing a unit of whole blood). The bank also has a duty to the ultimate recipient of the blood or blood product to exercise reasonable care in carrying on the functions of a blood bank,[39] which include donor selection; blood collection; donor blood testing; labeling, storage, and transport; compatibility testing; and issue of blood for transfusion.[40] A well-developed body of knowledge has been established for procedures for the accomplishment of these functions.[41] Each blood bank is responsible for developing and observing a procedures manual, which could be used to establish the standard of care at that particular blood bank.

The standard of care for blood banks differs according to the case law of each jurisdiction. Some courts adopt the general standard of the "reasonably prudent" blood bank.[42] At least one court has held that compliance with all federal regulations, all accreditation standards of the American Association of Blood Banks, and the blood bank's own internal regulations is conclusive evidence that the applicable standard of care has been met.[43]

Hospital

The hospital has a duty of care to the patient, arising out of the hospital-patient relationship.[44] As with physicians, the hospital does not guarantee the health of the patient or efficacy of the treatments, but instead has a duty of exercising reasonable care. With respect to blood transfusions, the hospital must exercise reasonable care in the selection of supplies, in the storage of blood, and in issuing and enforcing safety procedures. The hospital must also exercise reasonable care in the selection and maintenance of equipment and in the selection, training, and retention of blood bank or transfusion service employees and staff physicians. Failure to do so might hold the institution to *prime liability*. A hospital may also be *vicariously liable* for the negligence of its employees.[45] This liability is created by the doctrine of *respondent superior*, which is discussed in Chapter 5. Under this doctrine, the hospital is held responsible for the actions of its employees acting within the scope of their employment without a showing of specific fault by the hospital.

Physician

The duty of anesthesia personnel arises from the existence of the health care provider–patient relationship (Chapter 2). Once this relationship is created, those personnel must demonstrate the "knowledge, skill, and care" ordinarily possessed by anesthesiologists in good standing.[46] In the absence of the physician-patient relationship, this duty would not exist. For example, if an anesthesiologist or anesthetist was merely observing an operation and anesthetic administration, he or she ordinarily would not be liable even for gross errors by the anesthesiologist or nurse anesthetist actually administering the anesthetic.[47] Breach of duty in the context of anesthesia is the failure to conform to the requisite standard of care of other anesthesia practitioners. Breach of duty is generally established by expert testimony from other similar specialists in good standing (see also Chapters 3 and 23).

The One-Unit Transfusion. One potential negligence issue that is certain to be litigated more widely is whether a transfusion was medically indicated. If one takes into consideration the risks, including exposure to the viruses causing hepatitis and AIDS, along with the potential benefits,[48] the one-unit transfusion may be suspect. Some physicians believe that if only one unit is required, then the transfusion is not likely to be necessary.[49] The "scientific" basis for this hypothesis is that each working day more than 10,000 Americans lose (as blood donors) "one unit" of whole blood without any consequent morbidity or mortality. Therefore, a patient would not be harmed by a 500-ml deficit caused by operative blood loss. This argument fails to consider the fact that the patient in possible need of a blood product, under the effects of an anesthetic and operative intervention, is a far cry from the average healthy donor.

Under some circumstances, it may be appropriate to transfuse a single unit of blood, re-evaluate the patient's status, and perhaps then decide that no further blood is necessary. (It is important to remember that administering the second unit *doubles* the risk of contracting an infection.) If the transfusion is not medically indicated, the physician ordering it may be liable for any subsequent infections—including possibly hepatitis or AIDS—caused by that transfusion. Patients are deemed to refuse nonindicated therapy, which *in the eyes of the law becomes nonconsensual*, to which all legal consequences of a battery (see discussion above and Chapter 5) attach.

The principal importance to anesthesia personnel of the doctrine of negligence in the administration of blood and blood products is that, absent other liability theories being applicable, he or she is *not an insurer* against any complications that may result. Liability only follows fault—the breach of the duty of care—and any damages proximately flowing from that breach. This concept should always be kept in mind, inasmuch as some complications will inevitably result from the administration of whole blood or blood products to large numbers of people.

Tort Liability Without Fault

Strict liability in tort is the imposition of liability without regard to fault for bodily injury resulting from the use of a defective product.[50] (For a consideration of products liability, see Chapter 22.) The imposition of liability without regard to fault for a defective product is arguably justified for two reasons—it provides an incentive to manufacturers to market safe products,[51] and it spreads the risk of loss, thereby minimizing the impact on injured individuals.[52] Strict liability in tort is based on Section 402A of the *Second Restatement of the Law of Torts*,[53] *Special Liability of Seller of Product for Physical Harm to User or Consumer.* This section provides that:

> (1) *One who sells any product in a defective condition unreasonably dangerous to the user or consumer or to his property is subject to liability for physical harm thereby caused to the ultimate user or consumer, or to his property, if (a) the seller is engaged in the business of selling such a product, and (b) it is expected to reach the user or consumer in the condition in which it is sold.*
> (2) *The rule stated in subsection (1) applies although (a) the seller has exercised all possible care in the preparation and sale of his product, and (b) the user or consumer has not bought the product from or entered into any contractual relation with the seller. An exception to strict liability is provided for a product that is unavoidably unsafe, has unquestioned utility, and is accompanied by an adequate warning.*[53]

These exceptions, which are provided in Comments j and k to Section 402A, are of critical importance to those concerned with the administration of blood products and the many pharmaceuticals that are essential to modern health care delivery but unavoidably unsafe.

Comment j. Directions or Warning

In order to prevent the product from being unreasonably dangerous, the seller may be required to give directions or warning, on the container, as to its use.

Comment k. Unavoidably Unsafe Products

There are some products which, in the present state of human knowledge, are quite incapable of being made safe for their intended and ordinary use. These are especially common in the field of drugs. . . . Such a product, properly prepared, and accompanied by proper directions and warning, is not defective, nor is it unreasonably dangerous. . . . The seller of such products, again with the qualification that they are properly prepared and marketed, and proper warning is given, where the situation calls for it, is not to be held to strict liability for unfortunate consequences attending their use merely because he has undertaken to supply the public with an apparently useful and desirable product, attended with a known but apparently reasonable risk.[53]

Section 402A represents the law in most states, but some exceptions and variations to this doctrine do exist in particular jurisdictions. Section 402A applies to "any product." Therefore, if blood is a "product," then strict liability will ordinarily apply to transfusions of blood components, although Comment k would also be applicable. If blood is considered to be a "service," then strict liability would not apply, and negligence would need to be proven to establish liability.

The first case concerning this issue, *Perlmutter v. Beth David Hospital*,[54] held that supplying blood was a service, although by a 4 to 3 vote. Until 1967 all subsequent cases followed *Perlmutter* in holding blood transfusions to be a service.[55] In 1967 to 1968, however, appellate courts in Florida held that the furnishing of blood by a blood bank was a sale of goods.[56] Courts in other states, notably Illinois,[57] New Jersey,[58] and New York[59] followed Florida in holding that a transfusion constituted a sale of the whole blood or blood product. These cases caused considerable consternation among medical, hospital, and blood-banking interests. Intense lobbying efforts, directed to legislators across the country, led to the enactment of "medical service" statutes in most jurisdictions. These provide protection against strict liability by declaring the use of blood products to be a service, to which no warranties will apply.[60] At the present time 48 jurisdictions[61] have enacted various forms of protective legislation to

provide a negligence standard, rather than strict liability, for transfusions of blood and blood products. Appendix 17-1, contains a list of statutory citations together with provisions of some of these statutes.

One form of state statute merely declares a transfusion of blood and blood products to be a service.[62] Another form of state statute expressly restricts strict liability in tort and implied product warranties.[63] Still another form of state statute only limits strict liability in tort and implied product warranties in cases involving the transmission of hepatitis.[64] Whether the courts (by common law interpretation of these statutes) would extend a state statute pertaining only to hepatitis to AIDS transmission remains open to question. A federal district judge sitting in Baltimore refused to do so in a case[65] involving HIV transmission before the Maryland legislature amended its medical service statute to incorporate any viral transmission.[66] The court ruled that Maryland statutes and common law in effect at the time the plaintiff contracted HIV did not bar an action for strict liability based on alleged defects in the factor concentrate, but that there could be no action for strict liability based on duty to warn.

At the time of this writing, three jurisdictions—New Jersey, Vermont, and the District of Columbia—have not enacted any protective legislation. By case law, New Jersey provides protection to hospitals and blood banks,[67] and the District of Columbia to hospitals[68] from strict liability for transfusions. No cases could be found concerning the status of blood transfusion in Vermont. The prohibition of strict tort liability and implied product warranties for transfusions of blood products has been criticized by one legal commentator on the ground that innocent victims of disease transmission will be left uncompensated where fault cannot be established. He argues that the risk of loss would be better born by a state insurance fund.[60] A review of state statutes did not disclose any state that has adopted such a proposal.

Breach of Implied Warranty

The fourth potential basis of liability is breach of implied warranty. Implied warranties frequently arise out of sales contracts between merchants and buyers. Thus, strict tort liability and implied warranty in contract are distinct and independent bases of liability.[69] While this distinction is valid in theory, in practice the elements of breach of implied warranty are so nearly identical to those of strict tort liability that some consider it redundant to have two theories. The distinction is significant, however, where one or more procedural aspects differ, as the duration of the statute of limitation of actions, or in jurisdictions where the doctrine of strict tort liability is not recognized.

If a transfusion of blood is considered the sale of a product, then the Uniform Commercial Code provides for two possible implied warranties: an *implied warranty of merchantability*[70] and an *implied warranty of fitness for intended use*.[71] An implied warranty of fitness for intended use would normally be expected to accompany a transfusion that is considered a "sale" because the patient normally relies on the physician, hospital, and blood bank to exercise "skill or judgment" to "select or furnish" suitable blood. Once an implied warranty is considered to exist, the patient may recover for damages arising from breach of the warranty without establishing the existence of fault on the part of the seller.

The important aspect of implied warranty liability for the purposes of this chapter is that if a transfusion of whole blood or blood product is considered to be a "service," then the Uniform Commercial Code and its associated implied warranties would not apply.[72] Since most states have enacted statutes providing that transfusions of blood and blood products are to be considered as a "service," implied warranty liability is no longer generally applicable to such transfusions. For the purposes of this chapter, the theory of breach of implied warranty can either be considered to be inapplicable because of a state statute or case law, or essentially similar to strict tort liability, depending upon the context. Therefore, the theory of breach of implied warranty will no longer be discussed independently of strict liability in tort, and the two will be referred to together as liability without fault.

Constitutionality and Applicability of "Medical Service" Statutes

The constitutionality of Tennessee's statute was attacked by a Mrs. McDaniel who contacted hepatitis in a Memphis Hospital. The Court of Appeals for the Sixth Circuit held that the statute did not deprive her of equal protection.[73] A hemophiliac who became infected with HIV sued Hyland Laboratories, manufacturer of the Factor VIII concentrate used to correct his bleeding problem. He contended that California's statute did not apply to companies that prepared such blood derivatives as factor concentrate. The Supreme Court of California held that the statute covered products from commercial as well as noncommercial sources.[74] Litigation in other jurisdictions generally has supported the constitutionality and applicability of these statutes,[75] although some courts have refused to apply them retroactively.[65,76]

APPLICATION OF LIABILITY THEORIES TO SPECIFIC MEDICAL SERVICES

The performance of a transfusion can be divided into at least four steps: obtaining the blood from the donor; processing, storing, typing, and cross-matching it; deciding that the transfusion is indicated; and performing the transfusion. Complications and errors in judgment or negligence can occur at each of these steps. Selected cases will be reviewed to discuss the application of the legal theories of liability to the assessment of liability for complications.

Obtaining Blood and Blood Products

The donation of blood is the first step in the transfusion process. The blood bank owes a duty of care to the donor of blood as well as to the recipient, and donors have sued for alleged breaches of this duty. A blood bank has a duty to the recipient to exercise reasonable care in screening donors for disease, particularly hepatitis and HIV infection. Alleged breaches of this duty are considered below in the discussion of each disease.

Processing, Storage, Typing, and Cross-Matching

The processing, storing, typing, and cross-matching of blood has been associated with errors and complications giving rise to a substantial number of cases.[77] There are two legal issues that frequently arise. The first issue is whether those who prescribe and administer the blood product (in this instance the surgeon, the anesthesiologist or anesthetist, or combinations thereof) will be held liable for the negligence of laboratory technicians.

In *Mazer v. Lipschutz*[78] the patient was transfused with incompatible blood after mislabeling with an incorrect room number. The jury found that the surgeon and the anesthesiologist were not negligent in administering the mislabeled blood. The U.S. Court of Appeals, however, held that the trial court erred in failing to instruct the jury that the surgeon may be liable for negligence of the head technician under the "captain of the ship" doctrine.[79] The anesthesiologist was held not to have responsibility for negligence of the head technician under the that same doctrine, inasmuch as Pennsylvania law was construed as barring the existence of two "captains of the ship" in the same operating room.

In *Davis v. Wilson*[80] a patient also was transfused with incompatible blood after improper labeling by the laboratory technician. Neither the surgeon nor the anesthesiologist was held liable because of the absence of supervisory responsibilities over the negligent laboratory technician.

The second issue concerns the liability of the hospital for the negligence of laboratory technicians in typing, cross-matching, and labeling blood under the doctrine of *respondeat superior* previously discussed. In the typical situation where the laboratory technician is hired and paid directly by the hospital as an employee, the hospital would be liable for the technician's negligence in typing, cross-matching, and labeling blood.[81]

The Decision to Transfuse

One of the most important steps in the transfusion process is the decision of the surgeon, anesthesiologist, or nurse anesthetist to order the transfusion. Liability may attach when unnecessary or contraindicated transfusions are ordered, or where a necessary transfusion is not ordered. Arguments for and against the "one-unit" transfusion are presented above. Three cases will serve to illustrate typical factual situations in this category.

In *Necolayff v. Genesee Hospital*,[82] a hospitalized patient was mistakenly administered blood ordered for another patient. The transfusion was administered by a team made up of a nurse and fourth-year medical student. The hospital was held liable, although the court did not clearly specify whether liability was predicated on negligence or the doctrine of *respondeat superior*.

In *James v. Holder*,[83] an anesthesiologist employed by the city of New York allegedly failed to provide an adequate amount of blood to a patient who bled excessively internally following a cesarean section. She went into shock and died on the operating table during the subsequent attempt to stop the bleeding. The First Appellate Division of the Supreme Court held that the city may be liable for the negligence of its employee under the *respondeat superior* doctrine.

Conversely, another case involved the transfusion of an alleged excessive amount of blood.

In *Powell v. Fidelity and Casualty Company*,[84] a woman in her 35th week of pregnancy was provided two units of blood; she subsequently died from pulmonary edema. Expert testimony was presented to the effect that women in the latter stages of pregnancy usually have an increased blood volume, and that transfusions should be provided to such women only after extensive testing, which was not performed. The attending physician entered into a compromise settlement with the decedent's estate.

Performing the Transfusion

The fourth step is the performance of the

transfusion, and again errors and complications can occur. Two cases are on point.

In *Sherman v. Hartman*,[85] the needle came out of the vein being transfused, and approximately 200 cc of blood extravasated into the soft tissues of the patient's forearm, causing considerable pain and swelling. The nurse failed to check the position of the needle, although she noticed that the transfusion was running slowly. The appellate court reversed the trial court's refusal to submit claims against the hospital to a jury, holding that evidence of negligence existed and that the doctrine of *res ipsa loquitur* was applicable.

In *Sommers v. Sisters of Charity of Providence in Oregon*[86] the plaintiff developed a staphylococcic infection at the site of the infusion, allegedly because of the use of a nonsterile needle. The evidence established that the hospital did use sterile disposable needles. Furthermore, the trial court refused to apply the doctrine of *res ipsa loquitur*, finding that staphylococcus infections may occur at intravenous sites in the absence of negligence. The trial court entered judgment for the defendant hospital; it was affirmed on appeal.

APPLICATION OF LIABILITY THEORIES TO DISEASE TRANSMISSION

Hepatitis

Medical Background

Three primary forms of viral hepatitis are recognized—A; B; and non-A, non-B. Approximately 55,000 cases of all types of viral hepatitis were reported in the United States in 1983, about 25 per 100,000 population. Hepatitis A constituted approximately 40%, B 41%, and non-A, non-B 14%.[87] Most experts believe that only a small percentage of hepatitis cases are actually reported. Based upon Bove's subsequent analysis[87] of a number of studies, the risk of posttransfusion hepatitis of all forms is now *estimated* to range between 4% and 18% of all patients transfused, depending on the geographic location of the study.

Hepatitis A, also called "infectious hepatitis," is primarily transmitted by the fecal-oral route. It is rarely transmitted by transfusions, for two reasons. First, there is

no hepatitis A carrier state, and the viremic stage lasts only approximately 1 week. Thus, a relatively small window of donor infectivity exists. Second, even during the viremia, there is a low concentration of A virus in the blood. Hepatitis B, also called "serum hepatitis," accounts for 5% to 10% of transfusion-transmitted hepatitis.[88] Hepatitis B is primarily transmitted percutaneously, as by infected needles, or parenterally, as by contact with blood and other tissue fluids.[87] All blood is now screened for the hepatitis B surface antigen, which, along with the decreased use of paid professional donors, has resulted in a concomitant decline of transfusion-transmitted hepatitis B.

In 1985 non-A, non-B hepatitis reportedly accounted for "well over 90%" of all posttransfusion hepatitis cases.[87] It is chiefly transmitted parenterally. No specific serological marker exists to detect the existence of non-A, non-B infectivity, possibly because of a very low level of circulating antigen. The donor's alanine aminotransferase (ALT) level, however, is a sensitive but nonspecific marker for non-A, non-B infectivity.[89] One study reported that the test is cost-effective and could prevent as many as 30% of transfusion-associated non-A, non-B hepatitis cases.[90] Serum glutamic pyruvic transaminase (SGPT) is also a nonspecific marker for non-A, non-B hepatitis. Use of such nonspecific markers is called *surrogate testing*. Recently, blood-banking organizations in the United States have included testing for ALT and SGPT as a part of routine screening of donated blood.

Bases of Liability

There are three grounds for liability associated with transfusion transmission of a disease—battery, liability without fault, and negligence.

Battery

The first basis of liability for transfusion-associated hepatitis is battery. A failure to obtain any consent would ordinarily constitute a battery, for which the physician, and possibly the hospital, would be liable without fault.[91] Inasmuch as patients are presumed to refuse treatment that is not medically indicated, any such therapy would be considered to be nonconsensual—and hence a battery—for which liability and damages for all sequelae would flow.

Liability Without Fault

The second basis of liability for transfusion-associated hepatitis is strict liability in tort or implied warranty in contract, where these doctrines have not been limited by state statutes or case precedent. Nearly all states, however, provide protection to the blood bank, hospital, and physician from liability without fault. Where such protection is not provided, the hospital and blood bank each could be liable for transfusion-associated hepatitis without fault.

Negligence

The third basis of liability is negligence. Four potential defendants exist: the donor, the blood bank, the hospital, and the physician. The potential liability in negligence of each party will be discussed.

Donor. The plaintiff could attempt to establish that the donor of blood was negligent in, for example, failing to report a history of hepatitis or IV drug abuse. One problem in seeking recovery against the donor is the difficulty in identifying the specific unit of blood in multiunit transfusions, in identifying and locating the donor, and in collecting a judgment even if liability were established. A patient who contracted hepatitis from a transfusion did sue an alleged donor in one reported case.[92] The case was dismissed because the plaintiff failed to allege that the donor knew or had reason to know that she was infected with hepatitis prior to donating blood, and because the plaintiff would be barred for procedural reasons from examining the alleged donor even if the complaint were properly amended.

Blood Bank. To establish negligence on the part of the blood bank, it must be shown that the blood bank's actions fell below the applicable standard of care. For example, a blood bank would ordinarily be required to exercise reasonable care in the selection and screening of prospective donors. In one case, testimony that the blood bank had failed to ask any questions concerning hepatitis was ruled sufficient to create an issue of negligence.[93] A more recent San Francisco case, *Borchelt v. Irwin Memorial Blood Bank*,[94] involved HIV transmission to a Mrs. Borchelt, who sub-

sequently died of AIDS. The case was settled during trial, with the stipulation that there was no test available in 1983 to detect either HIV or HIV antibody (HIV-ab), and that the blood bank failed to inquire whether the donor of the infected unit (who later was identified as being HIV-ab–positive) had a history of hepatitis. This question, one of a number mandated by the AABB Standards[95] for screening donors in 1983, presumably would have been answered in the affirmative because those who contract HIV infections through high-risk activity generally also have had hepatitis. Thus, the donor in question probably would have been precluded from making the donation.

Another possible argument is that the use of paid professional donors is evidence of negligence in and of itself, because of the increased risk of hepatitis associated with such donors. The courts have differed in the resolution of this issue, with a New Mexico court ruling that the use of paid donors was not evidence of negligence in the absence of contrary state laws or regulations.[96] On the other hand, the Oklahoma Supreme Court held that the use of paid donors could be considered by a jury as evidence of negligence.[97]

Still another issue is whether a blood bank would be negligent for failing to use surrogate testing.[98] While no cases could be located, it is doubtful that the courts would find the test required as the applicable standard of care in the absence of state statute or regulation requiring the test or the existence of a general practice or custom among blood banks to utilize the test.[99]

Hospital. A hospital may operate its own blood bank or may secure blood from one or more independent blood banks. Where the hospital operates its own blood bank, it would have the duties discussed for blood banks in the previous section.

Where the hospital acquired blood from one or more independent blood banks, it would have a duty to exercise reasonable care in the selection of the blood banks.[100] The application of the reasonable care standard to specific factual circumstances is difficult. For example, does a hospital have a duty to acquire that blood which is most likely to be free from hepatitis and other impurities (e.g., by refusing to accept blood drawn in the coastal cities)? Does a hospital have a duty to acquire blood that optimizes some cost-risk formula? If so, then how should such factors as availability, dependability, and speed of delivery be taken into account?[101] These issues will probably need to be resolved on a case-by-case basis. The issue is properly posed, however, not as whether the hospital made the best possible selection, but whether the selection of suppliers was reasonable. It should be added that in order to ship blood across state lines, both the shipper and receiving blood bank or transfusion service must be licensed by the Food and Drug Administration.[102]

Physician. While a number of plaintiffs have alleged that physicians negligently caused transfusion-associated hepatitis,[103] no reported case could be located finding a physician liable in negligence for transfusion-associated hepatitis.[104] Inasmuch as failure to obtain informed consent is considered to be a negligent act (see Chapters 3 and 9), one should inquire whether the risks of blood component therapy to be disclosed include hepatitis. That query is unsettled, at least at the present time.

Acquired Immunodeficiency Syndrome

Medical Background

The increasing incidence of transfusion-associated AIDS has caused concern among physicians, hospitals, and blood banks for a number of reasons. AIDS is defined by the Centers for Disease Control (CDC) as:

> a disease, at least moderately predictive of a defect in cell-mediated immunity, occurring in a person with no known cause for diminished resistance to that disease.[105]

AIDS is caused by HIV. Exposure to and infection by this virus, as indicated by the presence of antibodies, is apparently common, with estimates that 1 to 2 million U.S. citizens and more than 10% of the population in eastern Africa have been exposed to HIV.[106] It is the current belief that, absent any permanently effective treatment, 100% of those exposed will eventually develop the full-blown form of AIDS.[107] As is well known, HIV is transmitted through whole blood and blood products* as well other modalities. As of February 1, 1990, the CDC reported a cumulative total of 121,645 AIDS cases, with 72,578 deaths.[108] Of the 119,590 adult and adolescent (13 and older) cases, homosexual and bisexual males accounted for 60%; IV drug abusers, 21%; and homosexuals who abused drugs, 7%. The large majority (82%) of the 2055 pediatric cases acquired the infection from their mothers. Figure 17-1 shows the cumulative total numbers of adult and adolescent cases in each transmission category for the past 3 years. Figure 17-2 shows the percentage of cases in each transmission category over the same period. Note that while the cumulative total of blood-product-transmission cases has been rising slowly, the percentage of these cases in reference to the total number of cases has remained about the same.

The CDC consider 4347 of the 121,645 cases to be blood-product–related, broken down as shown in Table 17-1. It is important to note that these are cumulative data, covering more than 7 years, from the first report of blood-product transmission[109] to the present. While these numbers may not seem large in the light of the millions of units of blood products transfused over that interval, they are deceptive. They do not take into consideration the number of persons infected with HIV who have not yet developed AIDS. All of these cases may very well translate into a substantial amount of litigation against physicians, hospitals, and blood banks for transfusion-transmitted HIV infection, far beyond that which has already surfaced.[2,74,75,94,110]

Bases of Liability

The four theories of recovery that have been previously discussed are potentially applicable to transfusion-transmitted AIDS. The issues of causation and damages will not be discussed here, but the usual principles apply.

---

*Blood products include components and derivatives; components—whole blood, packed red cells, plasma, and platelet concentrate—are obtained mainly by physical means, i.e., gravitational separation; derivatives are "manufactured" from pooled plasma by physiochemical separation and concentration; derivatives include gamma globulin and factor concentrates to treat hemophilia.

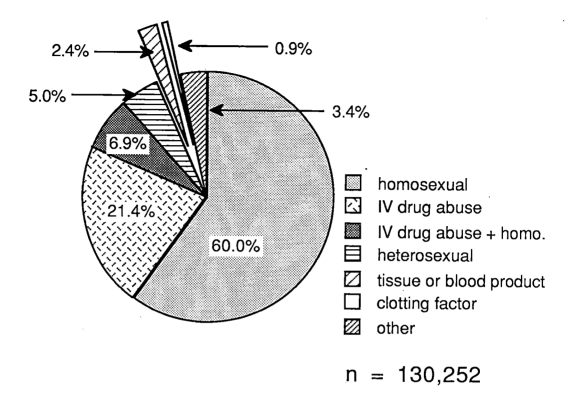

Figure 17–1 Sources of HIV infection among the 130,252 adults and adolescents who have developed AIDS since 1981. Third source includes both homosexual activity and IV drug abuse. (Data from Center for Infectious Diseases: HIV/AIDS Surveillance. Centers for Disease Control, Atlanta, April 30, 1990, p 8.

Lack of Informed Consent

If the transfusion resulting in AIDS occurred without a valid informed consent, the physician, and possibly the hospital, through the doctrine of *respondeat superior* discussed previously, would ordinarily be liable without regard to fault. The issue may be raised whether a failure to warn of the risk of transfusion-associated AIDS would lead to a defective consent. The resolution of this issue will probably vary from jurisdiction to jurisdiction, particularly because of the specific formulation of the standard for determining the adequacy of disclosure in each jurisdiction,[111] and the facts of each specific case. In cases involving hepatitis, the courts generally have not found a duty to warn of the risk of transmission, possibly because of the effectiveness of the B hepatitis antigen screening procedures currently employed.

Even though it is less likely that HIV will be transmitted by transfusion as compared

to hepatitis, it is not likely that courts would follow the hepatitis precedent and find that no duty exists to warn of the possibility of HIV transmission, for two reasons. First, the tests currently available screen only for the HIV-ab, and not the virus itself, as in the case of hepatitis screening. The "window" of infectivity without seroreactivity is both real and frightening. As discussed above, this window may extend for many months or even years.[112] Second, an HIV infection inevitably leads to AIDS, which in turn is fatal in all cases (at least at present). These two striking differences distinguish HIV from hepatitis viruses and, in my opinion, make disclosure of the risk of contracting the former mandatory.

Liability Without Fault

If strict liability in tort applied to blood and blood products in a jurisdiction, the blood bank and the hospital would be liable

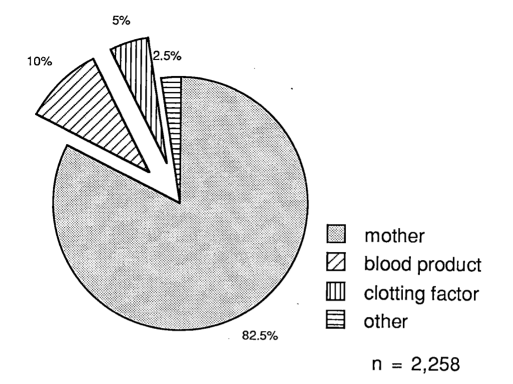

5%

10%

2.5%

mother

blood product

clotting factor

other

82.5%

n = 2,258

Figure 17–2 *Sources of HIV infection among the 2258 infants and children under 13 years of age who have developed AIDS since 1981. (Data from Center for Infectious Diseases: HIV/AIDS Surveillance. Centers for Disease Control, Atlanta, April 30, 1990, p 8.*

for any injury caused by the "defective" blood, absent a specific exception. One exception is an exclusion for unavoidably unsafe products of unquestioned utility that are accompanied by a warning. Because the risk of transfusion-associated AIDS cannot be completely eliminated, blood may be considered "unavoidably unsafe." Blood should be considered to be of "unquestioned utility," at least until a suitable substitute is developed. Thus blood banks and hospitals may institute a formal warning

TABLE 17–1. Cumulative Totals of AIDS Cases

Age Range (total number of AIDS cases)	HIV Acquired From Blood Component	HIV Acquired From Blood Derivative	Total Number of AIDS Cases (and Percent) Acquired From Blood Products in Age Range
Adults and adolescents 13 years and older (119,590 cases)	2923	1099	4022 (3.36)
Infants and children (2055 cases)	217	108	325 (15.82)
Totals	3140	1207	4347
Percent of all (121,645) cases	2.58	.99	3.57

Source: CDC data as of January 31, 1990.[108]

procedure to comply with this requirement of the exception, at least in those few states where strict liability may apply to blood transfusions.

Negligence Liability of Donor

A donor could face potential negligence liability for misrepresentations concerning questions posed in interviews and on questionnaires. He or she could also face potential negligence liability for deliberately donating blood with knowledge that he or she had AIDS or was an AIDS carrier.

Negligence Liability of Blood Bank

Four potential issues exist that might establish negligence[113] on the part of the blood banks—the thoroughness and effectiveness of procedures to screen out high-risk donors; the use, performance, and application of tests to detect units of blood harboring HIV; the failure to offer the availability of directed donations that *allegedly* may minimize risks; and the failure to popularize the availability of an autologous donation and transfusion service.

Adequacy of Donor Selection.   The first issue concerns procedures used to screen out high-risk donors, such as homosexuals and IV drug abusers. Long before it was possible to change the AABB standards and mandate verbal and written questionnaires pertaining to sexual preference, the Director of the Office of Biologics, National Center for Drugs and Biologics, Food and Drug Administration issued a letter to "All Establishments Collecting Human Blood for Transfusion." The purpose of this letter, dated March 14, 1983, was to have these establishments "institute additional measures designed to decrease blood collection from individual donors and donor groups known to be at increased risk for transmitting AIDS." The first recommended step was:

> 1 *Educational programs should be instituted to inform persons at increased risk of AIDS that until the AIDS problem is resolved or definitive tests become available, they should refrain from blood donation because of the potential risk to recipients of their blood. As presently defined, this group includes: persons with symptoms and signs suggestive of AIDS, sexually active homosexual or bisexual men with multiple*

> *partners, Haitian entrants to the United States, present or past abusers of drugs, and sexual partners of individuals at increased risk of AIDS. Educational programs should include the individual donor as part of the donor screening procedure.*[114]

These recommendations have been implemented from time to time since then, and in 1985 broadened to encompass all men who have had sex with more than one man since 1977.[115]

Unfortunately, screening donors verbally and via questionnaires is not always effective. A fairly recent article by Ward and associates[116] is disturbing. At the present time, screening is both verbal and via written questionnaire. More importantly, perhaps, is the manner in which each question should be phrased. Additionally, is any investigation required beyond taking the verbal history and having the questionnaire completed? These issues should be addressed carefully. One blood bank director and former AABB official stated his concerns (in the same journal issue as Ward's article) in the following manner:

> *The measures instituted to protect patients from acquiring HIV infection through blood transfusions have greatly improved the safety of the nation's blood supply. It is safer than it has ever been, but the slight risks that still remain can be reduced at this time only by intensified and appropriately focused education of blood donors [emphasis the editor's] and by more circumspect ordering of blood components by physicians.*[117]

Adequacy of Testing Donor Blood. The second issue concerns testing for infected units of blood. A direct test for the virus is not yet available. Two tests for antibodies to HIV are available, the enzyme-linked immunosorbent assay (acronym, ELISA) and Western Blot. The former is highly sensitive and is useful for the initial screen. The Western Blot is less sensitive but highly selective, and is used as a confirmative test. If the ELISA is positive, a second ELISA is performed. If the second is also positive, a specimen of the subject's serum is submitted for a Western Blot. If it, too, is positive, the subject is considered to be "triple-positive" or seroreactive. The FDA first licensed a manufacturer to market the ELISA in interstate commerce in

March 1985 (see Appendix 18-1). Soon after that, as ELISA testing was being implemented across this country, blood bank personnel expressed concern that informing donors of the test results might increase the incidence of transfusion-associated HIV infections. They rightly envisioned that those who engaged in high-risk behavior might deny their status and offer to donate blood to obtain the benefit of the test without charge.[118] The problem of those engaged in high-risk behavior offering to donate blood is still with us today, as discussed below.

Prior to the advent of the ELISA and Western Blot, it was suggested by some blood bankers that surrogate testing be employed in an effort to eliminate prospective donors infected with the AIDS virus.[90] Whether failure of a given blood bank to do so could constitute negligence would depend on whether the standard of care in the pre-1985 era required such surrogate testing.[119]

Even today, a number of legal and policy issues remain. Should blood that tests positive by ELISA but negative by Western Blot be used for donation? Reportedly, there are approximately 10,000 donors in this country who test in this manner. Donors who are triple-positive are notified. Should donors be notified if one or more ELISAs are positive, but not their Western Blot? What information should be provided to hospitals, physicians, and patients concerning these results? How can the blood bank ensure that the tests have been properly performed? Efforts currently are being made to resolve some of these issues, although not without controversy.

Opportunity for Directed Donations. A third blood bank liability issue might be the failure to allow directed donations. A directed donation is one made by a family member or friend of the recipient, with the recipient given first priority for that blood. In June 1983, the American Red Cross, the American Association of Blood Banks, and the Council of Community Blood Centers issued a joint statement recommending that directed donation programs not be conducted, primarily because of what was believed to be an onerous administrative burden.[120] In a situation wherein a particular recipient requested a directed donation, had been refused, and subsequently contracted HIV from another homologous

donor, the blood bank may have to litigate the issue of whether there was a duty to accept directed donations to safeguard against AIDS.* Recently, however, blood-banking interests in this country have reversed their stand; directed donations are accepted more or less universally.

Opportunity for Autologous Donations and Transfusion. Predeposit followed by autologous transfusion has been recommended for many years.[114] The AABB standards provide for predeposit, as well as intraoperative and postoperative and posttraumatic blood salvage.[121] The medical director of the blood bank should ensure that the bank has a protocol affording ready access of candidates for elective procedures to autologous donations and transfusions. He or she should also ensure that the medical staff of those institutions using the services of the bank are kept abreast with knowledge about pertinent advances in blood transfusion science.

Negligence Liability of Hospital

Primary negligence liability for the hospital for transfusion-associated AIDS might arise from the selection of the supplier of blood. If a particular supplier were known to have a high incidence of transfusion-associated AIDS or known to have deficient screening of donors or testing of blood, then the hospital may be liable for AIDS resulting from blood acquired from that supplier. Furthermore, it is the hospital's responsibility to help keep its medical staff apprised of the advantages and availability of a plant for predeposit of patients' blood for later use as an autologous transfusion. It is my opinion that the failure of a hospital to publicize and make readily available the autologous donation-transfusion option to candidates for elective operations in which a blood product will or might be needed would constitute a departure from the duty of care.

---

*Editor's Note: Blood bank directors should check with their legal counsel. It may be argued that there is no clear-cut legal duty to offer directed donations *provided that* the blood bank is able to justify its position through documented proof (e.g., employee time sheets) that it has insufficient resources to be able to do so. Collection of said documentation should be an ongoing process, which should have commenced at the time the decision is made not to offer these donations, not after the would-be donors are turned away and the recipient is inadvertently exposed to HIV.

Negligence Liability of Physician

Ordinarily—with two very important exceptions—the physician would have few responsibilities directly related to preventing the transmission of AIDS by transfusion. the first exception relates to the need to recommend an autologous transfusion to all those who might benefit from this procedure. Patients who are candidates for elective procedures during which there will or might be a need for the transfusion of a blood product are also candidates for predeposit and autologous transfusion. The standard of care of surgeons has changed to include the duty to apprise one's patients of the availability of this option. It is discussed more fully in the next chapter.

The *second exception* relates to therapy that is not medically indicated. If the physician orders an unnecessary transfusion that transmits an HIV infection, he or she very well could be found liable for the consequences of this infection.[122] This legal concept has been previously discussed as it pertains to transmission of hepatitis. The need for being certain that the blood product is really needed is obvious but cannot be overemphasized, especially in light of the conclusions of a consensus development conference on the perioperative use of red blood cells that was sponsored by the National Institutes of Health (NIH) as a part of the National Heart, Lung, and Blood Institute's National Blood Resource Education Program. These conclusions are discussed in the following section.

Guidelines for Transfusion

Consensus Development Conference Statement

The conference was held in Bethesda, Maryland, on June 27 to 29, 1988. The development panel was made up of 14 professionals representing primarily blood banking, clinical pathology, medicine, and surgery. Its 5-page statement ended with the following conclusions:

- *Available evidence does not support the use of a single criterion such as hemoglobin of less than ten grams per deciliter. No single measure can replace good clinical judgment as the basis for decision making regarding perioperative transfusion.*

- *There is no evidence that mild-to-moderate anemia contributes to perioperative morbidity.*
- *Perioperative transfusion of homologous red cells carries documented risks of infection and immune changes. Therefore, the number of homologous transfusions should be kept to a minimum.*
- *There are a variety of promising alternatives to homologous transfusion. These alternative will reduce the use of homologous transfusion to some extent and their development should be encouraged. However, in the foreseeable future, homologous blood will continue to be the therapeutic mainstay. Therefore, primary attention should be devoted to the promotion of safe and effective transfusions from carefully selected volunteer donors.*
- *Future research is necessary to define the best indications for red cell transfusion and the safest methods of blood conservation and delivery.*[123]

Transfusion Alert

In May 1989, the National Heart, Lung and Blood Institute of the NIH issued a *Transfusion Alert* titled *Indications for the Use of Red Blood Cells, Platelets, and Fresh Frozen Plasma.*[124] *Transfusion Alert* is a periodic publication of the Institute's National Blood Resource Program. Platelets and fresh frozen plasma are employed principally to treat bleeding and clotting problems. Excerpts from the *Alert* pertinent to the use of red cells follow:

Rationale for Component Use

Blood transfusion can be lifesaving therapy for patients with a variety of medical and surgical conditions. Advances in the use of blood components have made whole blood transfusions rarely necessary. Blood component therapy provides better treatment for the patient by giving only the specific component needed. Such therapy helps to conserve blood resources because components from one unit of blood can be used to treat several patients.

Red Blood Cell Transfusion

Red blood cell (RBC) transfusions increase oxygen-carrying capacity in anemic patients. Transfusing one unit of RBC will usually in-

crease the hemoglobin by 1 g/dL and the hematocrit by 2-3 percent in the average 70 kg adult.

Adequate oxygen-carrying capacity can be met by a hemoglobin of 7 g/dL (a hematocrit value of approximately 21 percent) or even less when the intravascular volume is adequate for perfusion. In deciding whether to transfuse a specific patient the physician should consider the person's age, etiology and degree of anemia, hemodynamic stability, and presence of coexisting cardiac, pulmonary or vascular conditions. To meet oxygen needs, some patients may require RBC transfusions at higher hemoglobin levels.

When a treatable cause of anemia can be identified, specific replacement therapy (e.g., vitamin B$_{12}$, iron, folate) should always be used before transfusion is considered. If volume expanders are indicated, fluids such as crystalloid or nonblood colloid solutions should be administered. RBC transfusions are often used inappropriately as volume expanders.

Do Not Transfuse Red Blood Cells:

- for volume expansion
- in place of a hematinic
- to enhance wound healing
- to improve general "well-being"

Risks Common to All Blood Components

Infection and alloimmunization are the major complications associated with transfusion of blood components. There is a relationship between these risks and the number of donor exposures. The risk of infection is geographically variable. The current estimated risks per unit transfused are:

- Human hepatitis viruses are the infectious agents most frequently transmitted by transfusions. Although non-A, non-B hepatitis [estimate: 1 case per 100 units transfused] may not be clinically evident in the months following transfusion, 30–50 percent of those infected develop chronic active hepatitis, and 10 percent of the latter group develop cirrhosis.
- Human immunodeficiency virus(es) presently poses a relatively small hazard. The wide range of estimated risk [1:40,000 to 1:1,000,000] reflects geographic variance.
- Other infectious diseases or agents may be transmitted via transfusion (e.g., hepatitis B, HTLV-I, cytomegalovirus, and those causing malaria).

- Fatal transfusion reactions are almost always caused by an ABO incompatibility due to errors in blood product labeling or patient identification [estimated risk— 1:100,000].
- Recipients of any blood product may produce antibodies against donor antigens, i.e., alloimmunization. This condition can result in an inadequate response to transfusion.
- Allergic reactions, febrile reactions, and circulatory overload may also occur.[124]

The just-cited estimated risks were obtained from the statement of the June 1988 Perioperative Red Cell Transfusion Consensus Development Conference[123] discussed above. Readers interested in a detailed review of the indications and contraindications for the use of platelets and fresh frozen plasma are referred to statements generated by the consensus conferences on those components.[125]

RECENT CASES

The failure of a hospital to offer directed donations, or predeposit and subsequent autologous transfusion, was not considered a departure from the duty of care in November 1981 in that it did not fly in the face of industry standards or acts of reasonably prudent practitioners. The hospital was not liable for the patient's infection with the AIDS virus, since it was not generally known that transfused blood was a vehicle for AIDS-transmission.[126]

United States liable for negligence of health care provider in performing tonsillectomy associated with excessive blood loss necessitating multiple transfusions in April 1983. Patient contracted HIV infection, and statistical evidence showed increased risk of HIV exposure from multiple units.[127]

A patient who allegedly contracted AIDS from blood given during an open heart operation in January 1984 may have a cause of action against the hospital for negligence, even though the ELISA had not yet been developed. The court held that the risk of AIDS was known, and it could have been a departure from the duty of care for the hospital to fail to use tests that were available (e.g., surrogate tests?).[128]

In a case involving HIV transmission in August 1984, the blood bank was found not liable even though it had not used available screening tests (presumably surrogate tests) because their failure rate was reported to be between 12% and 33%.[129]

A Jehovah's Witness who refused blood transfusion died of exsanguination following negligent delay in diagnosing postcolonic operation-associated hemorrhage. The court held that the patient's refusal to receive transfusion did not bar wrongful death claim by estate, but the award was to be proportionately reduced by the fact that death was proximately caused by patient's refusal to receive reasonable treatment (transfusion) that would have been lifesaving.[130]

CONCLUSION

For a good many years, blood products have been an essential element of medical practice. They will always remain so. Homologous whole blood, each of its components, and each of its derivatives carry a certain risk to every patient. Of course, the same is true of just about every other agent in the armamentarium of the physician. Intelligent application of any potentially hazardous therapeutic substance implies balancing the risks against the benefits. While needless transfusions are to be decried, so is the withholding of any blood product for which there is a real medical need. In the final analysis, the decision to transfuse should be a medical one, made by the physician and uncolored by any threat of legal action.

REFERENCES

1. Cumming, PD, Schorr, JB, and Wallace, EL: Annual Blood Facts, United States Totals—1986/87. American Red Cross, Washington, DC, June 1987.
2. *See, for example,* Kozup v. Georgetown University, 851 F.2d 437 (C.A.D.C. 1988) wherein the Court of Appeals for the D.C. Circuit held that the hospital was not liable for negligence, breach of warranty, strict liability, lack of informed consent, or violation of consumer protection statutes, but personnel at the hospital's newborn intensive care unit may have committed a battery by failing to obtain the Kozups' consent to transfuse their critically ill infant.
3. 51 Del. 554, 249 A.2d 749 (Sup. Ct. 1959).
4. 139 Ga. App. 457, 228 S.E.2d 596 (1976).
5. Two other courts have referred to this issue without providing an express holding; in Sloneker v. St. Joseph's Hospital, 223 F. Supp. 105, 108 (D.Colo. 1964) the court stated: "Whether there was such a duty [to warn that transfusions are a part of operative procedures and that serum hepatitis may result from the transfusion] ... and whether the plaintiff would have refused the surgery under these conditions is extremely doubtful." In Hoffman v. Misercordia Hospital of Philadelphia, 439 Pa. 501, 509, 267 A.2d, 871 (1970), the court stated: "Nor do we decide ... whether any duty existed on the part of the hospital or the physician to warn the patient of any risk that may exist in the performance of the blood transfusion due to hepatitis virus." [Footnote omitted.]
6. Ga. Code Ann. § 31—9—6(d) (1985). Discussed in Tanner, RG and Schroder, JS: Informed consent: New Georgia guidelines. Ga St BJ 12:197, 1976.
7. Hodge, RL: Comment: Consent to elective surgery valid even if doctor didn't warn of known risks. Mercer L Rev 28:377, 1976.
8. 522 F.2d 1102 (6th Cir. 1975) (applying Tennessee law).
9. Schloendorff v. Society of New York Hospital, 211 N.Y. 125, 105 N.E. 92 (1914).
10. Olmstead v. United States, 277 U.S. 438, 478 (1928) (Brandeis, J, dissenting).
11. Jehovah's Witnesses interpret the Bible quite literally. Their beliefs against the use of blood in any form (including autologous transfusions) are primarily based on the following Biblical passage: "Every moving animal that is alive may serve as food for you. As in the case of green vegetation, I do give it all to you. Only flesh with its soul—its blood—you must not eat." Genesis 9:3, 4. A comprehensive discussion on the interpretation of this passage by Jehovah's Witnesses is contained in : Jehovah's Witnesses and the Question of Blood. New York, Watchtower Bible and Tract Society 1977, pp. 5, 6.
12. One law-medicine specialist recommends the following:

   Should he decide to take the case, he does so at his peril. First, he should attempt to receive permission to transfuse blood. Failing this, he should secure "permission NOT to transfuse." In other words, he should fully notify the patient and the family of the dangers inherent in surgical procedures, and particularly when permission to administer a blood transfusion is refused. He should have the patient and all members of the immediate family sign such a release. Should the patient or his family now entertain the notion to enter suit against the physician, this release would be a powerful piece of evidence to deter them, and in court would weight heavily in the physician's favor.

Wasmuth, CE: Law for the Physician. Lea & Febiger, Philadelphia, 1966, p 366.

13. *See, generally*, Rozovsky, F: Consent to Treatment. Little, Brown, Boston 1984, pp. 414–442.
14. 331 F.2d 1000 (D.C. Cir. 1964), *reh'g denied*, 331 F.2d 1010 (D.C. Cir. 1964), *cert. denied sub nom.* Jones v. President and Directors of Georgetown College, 377 U.S. 978 (1964).
15. 331 F.2d at 1008–09. The issue of whether suicide was a crime in the District of Columbia at the time was not resolved, but the existence of a statute making suicide a crime may be a factor in subsequent cases.
16. 239 F. Supp. 752 (D. Conn. 1965).
17. Powell v. Columbian Presbyterian Medical Center, 49 Misc. 2d 215, 267 N.Y.S.2d 450 (Sup. Ct. 1965).
18. Kennedy Memorial Hospital v. Heston, 48 N.J. 576, 279 A.2d 670 (1971).
19. 294 A.2d 372 (D.C. 1972).
20. 32 Ill. 2d 361, 205 N.E.2d 435 (1965).
21. It is significant that the court quoted from Judge Burger's concurring opinion in *Application of President and Director of Georgetown College*, emphasizing the right of the patient to be left alone.
22. Erickson v. Dilgard, 44 Misc.2d 27, 252 N.Y.S.2d 705 (Sup. Ct 1962).
23. *See* Cantor, NL: A patient's decision to decline lifesaving medical treatment: Bodily integrity v. the preservation of life. Rutgers L Rev 26:228, 1973 (discussion of case law and policy considerations).
24. Rozovsky, *supra* note 13 at 237–239.
25. Colo. Rev. Stat. § 13-22-103 (1973).
26. People *ex. rel.* Wallace v. Labrenz, 411 Ill. 618, 104 N.E.2d 769, *cert. denied*, 344 U.S. 824 (1952); *In re* Ivey, 319 So.2d 53 (Fla. Dist. Ct. App. 1975) (*per curiam*); Brooklyn Hospital v. Torres, 45 Misc. 2d 914, 258 N.Y.S.2d 621 (Sup. Ct. 1965); State v. Perricone, 37 N.J. 463, 181 A.2d 751 (1962).
27. *In re* Sampson, 65 Misc.2d 658, 317 N.Y.S.2d 641 (Fam. Ct. 1970), *aff'd*, 37 A.D.2d 668, 323 N.Y.S.2d 253 (App. Div. 1971), *aff'd*, 29 N.Y.2d 900, 278 N.E.2d 918, 328 N.Y.S.2d 686 (1972) (*per curiam*); *In re* Green, 452 Pa. 373, 307 A.2d 279 (1973).
28. 42 N.J. 4521, 201 A.2d 537 (1964), *cert. denied*, 377 U.S. 985 (1964).
29. 410 U.S. 113 (1973).
30. Keeton, WP: Prosser and Keeton on Torts, ed 5. West, Minneapolis, 1984, p 39.
31. *Id.* at 164–165.
32. *Id.* at 263–269.
33. It should be noted that the doctrine of "proximate causation" exists for negligence liability but not for intentional torts such as battery. If the anesthesiologist failed to obtain consent for the transfusion that resulted in transmission of HIV, he or she would be liable for that transmission despite the unlikelihood or unforeseeability of transmitting the disease. Therapy that is not medically indicated is also considered a battery, and here, too, the doctrine of proximate causation would be inapplicable.
34. The procedural and substantive effect of the application of the doctrine of *res ipsa loquitur* has engendered considerable debate and confusion. The various jurisdictions differ in the substantive and procedural application of the doctrine. King, J: The Law of Medical Malpractice. West, Minneapolis, 1977, pp 132–135; Keeton, *supra* note 30 at pp 242–262.
35. Hubbell v. South Nassau Communities Hospital, 46 Misc. 2d 847, 260 N.Y.S.2d 539 (Sup. Ct. 1965).
36. In addition to negligence liability for misrepresentation, the donor may face possible prosecution for manslaughter or second-degree murder where deliberate lying leading to loss of life is established.
37. The term *blood bank* as used in this chapter includes nonprofit blood banks such as those operated by the American Red Cross, hospital-operated blood banks, and commercial blood banks.
38. *See, e.g.,* Klaus v. Alameda-Contra Costa Medical Assn. Blood Bank, Inc., 62 Cal. App. 3d 417, 133 Cal. Rep. 92 (1st Dist. 1976).
39. AABB Standards for Blood Banks and Transfusion Services, 11th ed. American Association of Blood Banks, Arlington, VA, 1984 (listed functions may overlap the hospital functions).
40. *See* AABB Technical Manual. American Association of Blood Banks, Arlington, VA, 1981.
41. Hutchins v. Blood Services of Montana, 161 Mont. 359, 364, 506 P.2d 449, 452 (1973).
42. Hines v. St. Joseph's Hospital, 86 N.M. 763, 766, 527 P.2d 1075, 1078 (Ct. App. 1974), *cert. denied*, 37 N.M. 111, 529 P.2d 1232 (1974).

43. *See, generally*, King, *supra* note 34 at pp 307–321.
44. *See, generally*, King, *supra* note 34 at pp 225–249; Keeton, *supra* note 30 at pp 499–516.
45. King, *supra* note 34 at pp 227–228.
46. Keeton, *supra* note 30 at p 375; while this statement represents the majority rule, some exceptions may exist in particular instances.
47. Franklin, MA: Tort liability for hepatitis; an analysis and a proposal. Stan L Rev 24:439, 1972.
48. Morton, JH: An evaluation of blood-transfusion practices on a surgical service. N Engl J Med 263:1285, 1960 (in retrospective study of 169 single-unit transfusions, transfusion was considered unnecessary in at least 34% of cases, and possibly as many as 72%). *But see* Allen, JG: Advantages of a single transfusion. Ann Surg 164:475, 1966.
49. *See, generally*, Boland, GL: Comment: Strict liability in tort for transfusion contaminated blood. Ark L Rev 23:236, 1969; Haut, IH and Alter, AA: Blood transfusions: Strict liability. St John's L Rev 43:557, 1969; Comment: Strict liability for disease contracted from blood transfusions. Nw UL Rev 66:80, 1971; O'Hara, DP: Strict liability: The medical service immunity and blood transfusions in California, UC Davis L Rev 7:196, 1974; Crump, D, and Maxwell, LA: Should health service providers be strictly liable for product-related injuries? A legal and economic analysis, Sw LJ 36:831, 1982.
50. Escola v. Coca Cola Bottling Co., 24 Cal.2d 453, 462, 150 P.2d 436, 440–41 (1944), stating: "Even if there is no negligence, however, public policy demands that responsibility be fixed wherever it will most effectively reduce the hazards to life and health inherent in defective products that reach the market. It is evident that the manufacturer can anticipate some hazards and guard against the recurrence of others, as the public cannot."
51. Franklin, *supra* note 47 at pp 463–465.
52. Restatement Second, the Law of Torts. American Law Institute, St. Paul, 1982, § 402A.
53. *Id.*, Comments j and k.
54. 308 N.Y. 100, 123 N.E.2d 792 (1954).
55. See Sloneker v. St. Joseph's Hosp., 223 F. Supp. 105 D.C.D. (Col. 1964); Baptista v. St. Barnabas Medical Center, 109 N.J. Super. 217, 262 A.2d 902 (Super. Ct., App. Div. 1970); Dibblee v. Dr. W. H. Groves Latter-Day Saints Hosp., 12 Utah 2d 241, 364 P.2d 1085 (1961); Gile v. Kennewick

Public Hosp. Dist., 48 Wash.2d 774, 296 P.2d 662 (Sup. Ct. Wash. 1956); Goelz v. J.K. and S.L. Waddley Research Institute and Blood Bank, 350 S.W.2d 573 (Ct. Civ. App., Texas 1961); Koenig v. Milwaukee Blood Center, 23 Wis. 2d 324, 127 N.W.2d 50 (Sup. Ct. 1964); Balkowitsch v. Minneapolis War Memorial Blood Bank, 270 Minn. 15t, 132 N.W.2d 805 (Sup. Ct., Minn. 196S); Whitehurst v. American National Red Cross, 1 Ariz. App. 326, 402 P.2d 584 (1965); Lovett v. Emory Univ., 116 Ga. App. 277, 156 S.E.2d 923 (Ct. App., Div. 3, 1967); Young v. Brooklyn Women's Hosp., 54 Misc. 2d 645, 283 N.Y.S.2d 212 (Sup. Ct., Spec. Term, Kings Co., Pt. 1, 1967).
56. Russell v. Community Blood Bank, 185 So.2d 749 (Ct. App., 2d Dist., Fla. 1966), *aff'd* as to blood bank, 196 So.2d 115 (Sup. Ct., Fla. 1967); Hoder v. Sayet, 196 So.2d 205 (Ct. App., 3d Dist., Fla. 1967).
57. Cunningham v. MacNeal Memorial Hosp., 113 Ill. App.2d 74, 251 N.E.2d 733 (Super. Ct. 1969); *aff'd with modification* 47 Ill.2d 443, 266 N.E.2d 897 (1970).
58. Jackson v. Muhlenberg Hosp., 96 N.J. Super. 314, 232 A.2d 879 (Sup. Ct., Law Div. 1967).
59. Carter v. Interfaith Hosp. of Queens, 60 Misc.2d 733, 304 N.Y.S.2d 97 (Sup. Ct., Spec. Term, Queens Co. Pt. 1, 1969).
60. *See* Gioia, DA: Comment: Blood transfusions and the transmission of serum hepatitis; the need for statutory reform. Am UL Rev 24:367, 1975.
61. For the complete text of each statute, see Dornette, WHL (ed): AIDS and the Law. Wiley, New York, 1987, Appendix M, pp 334–354.
62. *See, e.g.,* Utah Code Ann. § 26-31-1 (1984), which provides:

> *The procurement, processing, distribution, or use of whole human blood, plasma, blood products, and blood derivatives for the purpose of injecting or transfusing them into the human body together with the process of injecting or transfusing the same shall be construed to be the rendition of a service by the very person participating therein and shall not be construed to be a sale.*

63. *See, e.g.,* Ill. Ann. Stat. Ch. 111 1/2 § 5102 (Smith-Hurd Supp. 1985), which provides:

> *The procuring, furnishing, donating, processing, distributing or using human whole blood, plasma, blood prod-*

ucts, *blood derivatives and products, corneas, bones, or organs or other human tissue for the purpose of injecting, transfusing or transplanting any of them in the human body is declared for purposes of liability in tort or contract to be the rendition of a service by every person, firm or corporation participating therein, whether or not any remuneration is paid therefor, and is declared not to be a sale of any such items and no warranties of any kind or description nor strict tort liability shall be applicable thereto.*

64. Ariz. Rev. Stat. Ann. § 36-1151 (1974) provides:

    The procurement, processing, distribution, or use of whole human blood, plasma, blood products and blood derivatives for the purpose of injecting or transfusing them into the human body shall be construed as to the transmission of serum hepatitis to be the rendition of a service by every person participating therein and shall not be construed to be a sale.

    Added Laws 1964, Ch. 83, § 1.
65. Doe v. Miles Laboratories, Inc. 675 F.Supp. 1466 (D.Md. 1987).
66. Maryland Health-General Code § 18-402 (eff. 1986).
67. Baptista v. Saint Barnabas Medical Center, 109 N.J. Super. 217, 262 A.2d 902 (App. Div.); *aff'd* 57 N.J. 167, 270 A.2d 409 (1970) (strict liability not applicable to hospital for transfusion); Brody v. Overlook Hosp., 66 N.J. 448, 332 A.2d 596 (1975) (strict liability not applicable to blood bank or hospital for transfusion).
68. Fisher v. Sibley Memorial Hosp., 403 A.2d 1130 (D.C. Cir. 1979).
69. Partrillo v. Giroux, 426 A.2d 1313, 1317 (R.1. 1981) ("Strict liability and implied warranty are parallel theories of recovery, one in contract and the other in tort, with each having its separate analytical elements and procedural conditions precedent.").
70. U.C.C. § 2-314 (1978) provides that:

    (1) ... [A] warranty that the goods shall be merchantable is implied in a contract for their sale if the seller is a merchant with respect to goods of that kind.
    (2) Goods to be merchantable must be at least such as ... (c) are fit for the ordinary purposes for which such goods are used.

71. U.C.C. § 2-315 (1978) provides that:

    Where the seller at the time of contracting has reason to know any particular purpose for which the goods are required and that the buyer is relying on the seller's skill or judgment to select or furnish suitable goods, there is unless excluded or modified ... an implied warranty that the goods shall be fit for such purpose.

72. White, JJ and Summers, RS: Uniform Commercial Code. West, Minneapolis, 1980, p 51 and note 7.
73. McDaniel v. Baptist Hosp. 469 F.2d 230 (6th Cir. 1972).
74. Hyland Therapeutics v. Super. Ct. unty., 175 Cal. App. 3d 509J 7S Cal. Rptr. 509 (1986).
75. Coffee v. Cutter Biological, 809 F.2d 191 (C.A.2-Conn. 1987) (applying state statute); Zichichi v. Middlesex Memorial Hosp., 528 A.2d 805 (Conn. 1987); Jones v. Miles Laboratories, Inc., 705 F.Supp. 561 (N.D.Ga. 1987) (manufacturer of Factor VIII concentrate exercised sufficient control over plasmapheresis center to be liable for its negligence, but no negligence found); Poole v. Alpha Therapeutic Corp., 696 F.Supp. 351 (N.D.Ill. 1988) (Ill. Blood Liability Act barred strict liability claim, although supplier could be liable for negligent failure to warn of risk of HIV-transmission); McKee v. Cutter Laboratories, Inc., 866 F.2d 219 (C.A.6-Ky. 1989) (applying Kentucky's medical service statute); Doe v. Travenol Laboratories, Inc., 698 F.Supp. 780 (D.Minn. 1988) (applying state statute); Samson v. Greenville Hosp. System, 377 S.E.2d 311 (S.C. 1989) (S.C. statute did not violate equal protection clause); Doe v. Cutter Laboratories, 703 F.Supp. 573 (N.D.Tex.1988) (applying Texas's statute); Garvey v. St. Elizabeth Hosp., 697 P.2d 116 (Wash., 1985) (under medical service statute, hospital not strictly liable to patient who contracted non-A, non-B chronic active hepatitis).
76. Miles Laboratories v. Doe, 556 A.2d 1107 (Md. 1989) (medical service statute not retroactive); Doe v. Miles Laboratories, Inc., 675 F.Supp. 1466 (D.Md. 1987) (applying then existing state law, plaintiff could maintain strict liability claim for presence of HIV in factor concentrate, but not for failure to warn); Weber v. Charity Hosp. of Louisiana at New Orleans, 487 So.2d 148 (La.App. 1986) (blood bank but not hospital strictly liable for hepatitis transmission; no showing of negligence on

part of hospital); Shortess v. Touro Infirmary, 508 So.2d 938 (La.App. 1987) (blood bank but not hospital strictly liable for transmission of hepatitis); *aff'd* as to blood bank, *rev'd* as to hospital, which was also strictly liable, 520 So.2d 389 (La. 1988); *but see* Roberts v. Suburban Hosp., Ass'n., Inc., 532 A.2d 1081 (Md.App. 1987) (strict liability and breach of warranty claims of hemophiliac who contracted AIDS through contaminated blood product subject to dismissal for failure to pursue administrative remedy provided by state's Health Claims Arbitration Act).

77. *See, e.g.,* National Homeopathic Hospital v. Phillips, 181 F.2d 293 (D.C. Cir. 1940) (improper cross-matching); Mississippi Baptist Hospital v. Holmes, 214 Miss. 906, 55 So.2d 142 (1951) (mislabeling); Parker v. Port Huron Hospital, 361 Mich. 1, 105 N.W.2d 1 (1960) (mislabeling); Redding v. United States, 196 F. Supp. 871 (W.D. Ark. 1961), *appeal dismissed,* 298 F.2d 445 (8th Cir. 1962) (incompatible transfusion, unknown cause); Mazer v. Lipschutz, 327 F.2d 42 (3d.Cir. 1963), *cert. denied,* 385 U.S. 833 (1966) (mislabeling); Davis v. Wilson, 265 N.C. 139, 143 S.E.2d 107 (1965) (improper typing).

78. Mazer v. Lipschutz, *supra* note 77.

79. The "captain of the ship" doctrine holds the surgeon responsible for the negligence of those in the operating room under him or her despite the absence of a showing of fault on the part of the surgeon, because the surgeon is considered to be in command and responsible for the ultimate outcome. 327 F.2d at 51; for a further discussion of this doctrine, see Chapters 2 and 25.

80. Davis v. Wilson, 265 N.C. 139, 143 S.E.2d 107 (1965).

81. National Homeopathic Hospital v. Phillips, *supra* note 77 at pp 293–294; Davis v. Wilson, *supra* note 80 at pp 111–112.

82. 270 App. Div. 648. 61 N.Y.S.2d 832 (1946); *aff'd* 296 N.Y. 936, 73 N.E.2d 117 (1946).

83. 34 App. Div. 2d 632, 309 N.Y.S.2d 385 (1970).

84. 185 So.2d 324 (La. Ct. App. 1966).

85. 137 Cal. App.2d 589, 290 P.2d 894 (Dist. Ct. App. 1955).

86. 277 Or. 549, 561 P.2d 603 (1977).

87. Fields, B: Virology. Raven, New York, 1985, p 1436; subsequently analyzed studies suggest the incidence varies widely, depending on geographic area and time; Bove, JR: Sounding board. Transfusion-associated hepatitis and AIDS: What is the risk? N Engl J Med 317:242, 1987; *see also,* Office of Medical Applications of Research, National Institutes of Health: Perioperative red cell transfusion. JAMA 260(18):2700, 1988.

88. Bruce-Chwatt, L: Infection, immunity, and blood transfusion (editorial). Br Med J 288:1783, 1984.

89. Fields, *supra* note 87 at p 1447; antibody to the hepatitis B core antigen (anti-HBc) and reverse transcriptase activity have also been suggested as nonspecific markers for non-A, non-B hepatitis; Alter, H, and Holland, P: Indirect tests to detect the non-A, non-B hepatitis carrier state (editorial). Ann Int Med 101:859, 1984.

90. Silverstein, M, et al: Should donor blood be screened for elevated alanine aminotransferase levels? JAMA 252:2839, 1984; *see also* Aach, RD, et al: Serum alanine aminotransferase of donors in relation to the risk of non-A, non-B hepatitis in recipients, the Transfusion-Transmitted Viruses Study. N Engl J Med 304:989, 1981; Alter, HJ, et al: Donor transaminase and recipient hepatitis: Impact on blood transfusion services. JAMA 246:630, 1981; Koziol, DE, et al: Antibody to hepatitis B core antigen as a paradoxical marker for non-A, non-B hepatitis agents in donated blood. Ann Int Med 104:488, 1986; Stevens, CE, et al: Hepatitis B virus antibody in blood donors and the occurrence of non-A, non-B hepatitis in transfusion recipients: An analysis of the Transfusion-Transmitted Viruses Study. Ann Int Med 101:733, 1984.

91. *See, especially,* Kozup, note 2: this case is scheduled for trial on the merits, namely the extent to which parents, who in January 1983, when they acquiesced to the admission of their premature infant to a newborn intensive care unit, at the same time impliedly grant permission for procedures such as the transfusion of small volumes of blood.

92. Hubbell v. South Nassau Communities Hosp., 46 Misc. 2d 847, 260 N.Y.S.2d 539 (Sup. Ct. 1965).

93. Hoder v. Sayet, 196 So.2d 205, 206 (Fla. Dist. Ct. Appl. 1967).

94. Borchelt v. Irwin Memorial Blood Bank, No. 8193 (San Francisco Super. Ct. 1985) reported in 1 AIDS Policy and Law 1 (August 27, 1986).

95. Standard B1.261 Viral Hepatitis. Standards for Blood Banks and Transfusion Services, ed 11. American Association of Blood Banks, Arlington, VA, 1981, p 5.

96. Hines v. St. Joseph's Hosp., 86 N.M. 763, 766, 527 P.2d 1075, 1078 (Ct. App. 1974), *cert. denied,* 87 N.M. 111, 529 P.2d 1232

(1974) (the minority opinion, however, would have held that the use of paid donors did create a material issue of fact concerning negligence. *Id.*).

97. Gilmore v. St. Anthony Hosp., 598 P.2d 1200, 1205-06 (Okla. 1979).

98. Doe v. American Red Cross Blood Services, 377 S.E.2d 323 (S.C. 1989) (in action alleging negligent failure to employ surrogate testing prior to January 1985, plaintiff-recipient of HIV-infected blood must prove that defendant failed to conform to generally accepted practices of its profession; court held blood procurement and processing to be a skilled professional service).

99. *Cf.* Franklin, M: Tort liability for hepatitis: An analysis and proposal. Stan L Rev 24:439, (1972) (discussing HAA test); Hutchins v. Blood Services of Montana, 506 P.2d 449 (Montana 1973) (failure to use SGOT on accepted blood held not to be negligent); *but see* Belle Bonfils Memorial Blood Bank v. Hansen, 665 P.2d 118 (Colo. 1983), wherein the court held that adherence to the current standards of blood banking did not constitute an absolute defense in an action for strict liability for transmission of hepatitis.

100. Hoder v. Sayet, *supra* note 93 at p 210.

101. Franklin, *supra* note 99 at p 451.

102. *See, generally,* Schmidt, PJ: The blood banking system: Organization, economics, and regulatory framework; Zuck, TF: Food and Drug Administration perspectives: What to expect. Chapters 1 and 13 in Clark, GM (ed): Legal Issues in Transfusion Medicine. American Association of Blood Banks, Arlington, VA, 1986, pp 5–13 and 149–156.

103. Brody v. Overlook Hosp., 121 N.J. Super. 299. 296 A.2d 668 (1972), *rev'd on other grounds*, 127 N.J. Super. 331, 317 A.2d 392 (1974), *aff'd*, 66 N.J. 448, 332 A.2d S96 (1975); White v. Sarasota County Public Hospital Board, 206 So.2d 19 (Fla. Dist. Ct. of Appeal 1968); St. Martin v. Doty, 493 S.W.2d 95 (Tenn. App. 1972); Sawyer v. Methodist Hospital, 522 F.2d 1102 (6th Cir. 1975) (applying Tennessee law).

104. Brody v. Overlook Hospital, *supra* note 103, held that allegations of negligence were sufficient to allow presentation to a jury.

105. Update on acquired immune deficiency syndrome (AIDS)—United States. MMWR 31:507, 513, 1982. Miller, PJ, et al: Potential liability for transfusion-associated AIDS. JAMA 253:3419, 1985 (quoting and following CDC definition).

106. Quinn TC, et al: AIDS in Africa: An epi- demiologic paradigm. Science 234:955, 1986.

107. Johnstone, B: German survey's gloomy outlook. Nature 324:199, 1986.

108. HIV/AIDS Surveillance. Centers for Disease Control, Atlanta, 1990, pp 8, 13.

109. MMWR 31:365, 1982 (first cases of AIDS in hemophiliacs reported by CDC); MMWR 31:352, 1982 (first case of "possible" transfusion-associated AIDS reported, involving a 20-month-old California infant).

110. *See, e.g.,* Miles Laboratories v. Doe, Doe v. Miles Laboratories, Inc., Roberts v. Suburban Hosp., Ass'n., Inc., *supra* note 76; Matheson v. Irwin Memorial Blood Bank, No. 864196 (San Francisco Sup. Ct., filed September 18, 1986) reported in 2 AIDS Policy & Law 3 (January 14, 1987); Belle Bonfils Memorial Blood Center v. Denver District Court, slip op. 1988 WL 105300 (Colo., Oct. 17, 1988); Doe v. Cutter Biologicals, Civ. Action No. 870232 (D.C. Haw., filed January 8, 1988) (class action suit filed in Honolulu against several major manufacturers of factor concentrate on behalf of all hemophiliacs residing in the islands); Doe v. Children's Medical Center, No. 87-96 (Montgomery County, Ohio, Ct. Com. Pleas, filed January 14, 1987) reported in 2 AIDS Policy & Law 8 (January 28, 1987); Spiegel v. Fisher, No. C-88-7109 (Okla. Dist. Ct., Okla. County, filed July 7, 1988), reported in 3 AIDS Policy & Law 11 (July 27, 1988); Stenger v. Miller Memorial Blood Bank, No. 87-C-586, (Lehigh County Ct. 1987) reported in 2 AIDS Policy & Law 8 (June 3, 1987); Knight v. United States, Civ. Action No. SA-88-CA-0874 (W.D. Tex., filed July 29, 1988); Phipps v. United States, Civ. Action No. SA-87-CA-0396 (W.D. Tex., filed March 23, 1987); Valdiviez v. United States, Civ. Action No. SA-86-CA-1595 (W.D. Tex., filed December 2, 1986).

111. *See* prior discussion on informed consent; *see also* Appendix 9-1.

112. *See, especially,* Imagawa, DT, et al: Human immunodeficiency virus type 1 infection in homosexual men who remain seronegative for prolonged periods. N Engl J Med 320:1458, 1989.

113. DiMarco v. Hudson Valley Blood Service, 532 N.Y.S.2d 488 (N.Y. Sup. 1988) (action against blood supplier by patient who contracted HIV lies in negligence, not medical malpractice).

114. Petricciani, JC: Recommendations to decrease the risk of transmitting acquired immune deficiency syndrome (AIDS) from blood donors. Memorandum to Establish-

ments, Office of Biologics Research and Review, National Center for Drugs and Biologics, Food and Drug Administration. March 24, 1983; *see also* MMWR 32:101, 1983 [CDC issue guidelines for preventing spread of AIDS virus; these include having those at risk of AIDS to refrain from donating blood, minimizing the use of blood, and *encouraging the use of autologous transfusions* (emphasis the editor's)].

115. Revised definition of high-risk groups with respect to acquired immunodeficiency syndrome (AIDS) transmission from blood and plasma donors. Memorandum to Establishments, Office of Biologics Research and Review, National Center for Drugs and Biologics, Food and Drug Administration, September 3, 1985 (redefinition of high-risk behavior to include men who have had sex with more than one man since 1977); *see also* Bove, *supra* note 87.

116. Ward, JW, et al: Transmission of human immunodeficiency virus (HIV) by blood transfusions screened as negative for HIV antibody. N Engl J Med 318:473, 1988 [seven persons with negative HIV-antibody tests who donated blood later had detectable HIV antibodies; recipients of these seronegative donations acquired HIV infection; *six of the seven donors acknowledged risk factors* (emphasis the editor's)]; *see also* Jones v. Miles Laboratories, *supra* note 75 (plasmapheresis center not negligent in failing to inquire whether donor was homosexual inasmuch as donor had previously falsely stated that he was not).

117. Zuck, TF: Transfusion-transmitted AIDS reassessed (editorial). N Engl J Med 318:511, 1988.

118. Perkins, JT, Miceli, K, and Janda, WM: Does antibody screening increase the risk of transfusion-associated AIDS? (letter to the editor). N Engl J Med 313:115, 1985; *see also* Zuck, *supra* note 117.

119. *See, especially*, Doe v. American Red Cross Blood Services, *supra* note 98.

120. Bove, JR: Directed donations. In Clark, GM, *supra* note 102, pp 69–75.

121. AABB Standards, *supra* note 39, §§ L1.000 *et seq.*, pp 35–38.

122. A case alleging nonindicated blood product therapy is pending; *see* Doe v. Children's Medical Center, No. 87-96 (Montgomery County, Ohio, Ct. Com. Pleas, filed January 14, 1987) reported in 2 AIDS Policy & Law 8 (January 28, 1987) (parents of a Dayton, Ohio, boy filed a $10 million lawsuit against several physicians, a hospital, and four manufacturers of Factor IX concentrate, alleging that their son was negligently misdiagnosed as being a hemophiliac and thus received unnecessary factor concentrate that was contaminated with the HIV).

123. National Institutes of Health: Consensus Development Conference Statement 7 (no. 4) June 27–29, 1988; *see also* Office of Medical Applications of Research, *supra* note 87.

124. National Blood Resource Education Program: Transfusion Alert, NIH Publication No. 89-2974a, National Institutes of Health, Bethesda, MD, May 1989.

125. Office of Medical Applications of Research, National Institutes of Health: Fresh frozen plasma; indications and risks. JAMA 253(4): 551, 1985; Office of Medical Applications of Research, National Institutes of Health: Platelet transfusion therapy. JAMA 257(13):1777, 1987.

126. Hoemke v. New York Blood Center, 912 F.2d 550 (C.A.2-N.Y. 1990).

127. Doe v. U.S., 787 F.Supp. 155 (D.R.I. 1990).

128. Doe v. University Hosp. of New York University Medical Center, 561 N.Y.S.2d 326 (N.Y.Sup. 1990).

129. Snyder v. Mekhjian, 582 A.2d 307 (N.J. SuperA.D. 1990).

130. Corlett v. Caserta, 149 Ill.Dec. 793, 562 N.E.2d 257 (Ill. App. 1 Dist. 1990).

APPENDIX

17-1

STATUTES RELATIVE TO BLOOD TRANSFUSION

Statutory Citation	Year	Tissue Included	Other Provisions
Alabama Code § 7-2-314(4).		Yes	
Alaska Stat. § 45.02.316(e).		Yes	
Arizona Rev. Stat. Ann. § 36-11S1.	1964	No	
Arkansas Stat. Ann. § 85-2-316 (3)(d)(i).		Yes	
California Health and Safety Code § 1606.		No	
Colorado Rev. Stat. § 13-22-104	1973	Yes	
Connecticut Gen. Stat. § 19-139	1977	Yes	
Delaware Code Ann. § 2-316(5)		Yes	
District of Columbia—no statute, but see 403 A.2d 1130	1979		Blood is a medical service by common law decision
Florida Stat. § 672.316(5)		Yes	Warranties not applicable if defect cannot be detected or removed
Georgia Code Ann. § 51-1-28		Yes	
Hawaii Rev. Stat. § 325-91		No	Limited to hepatitis
Idaho Code § 39-3702	1977	No	Warranties not applble if defect cannot be detected or removed
Illinois Ann. Stat. § 5102		Yes	
Indiana Code § 16-8-7-2	1973	Yes	
Iowa Code § 142A-8	1969	Yes	
Kentucky Rev. Stat. Ann. § 139-125		Yes	
Louisiana Rev. Stat. Ann § 9.2797	1982	Yes	Limited to viral diseases not detectable by appropriate scientific tests
Maine Rev. Stat. Ann. title 11 § 2-108	1969	Yes	
Maryland Health-Gen. Code Ann. § 18 402	1986	No	Replacing 1971 statute limited to hepatitis
Massachusetts Gen. Laws, Ch. 106, § 2-316(5)		No	
Michigan Stat. Ann. § 333.9121	1978	Yes	
Minnesota Stat. § 525.928		Yes	
Mississippi Code Ann. § 41-41-1		No	
Missouri Ann. Stat. § 431.069		Yes	
Montana Code Ann. §§ 50-33-102, -103		No	As long as AABB recommended tests are used
Nebraska Rev. Stat. § 71-4001		Yes	
Nevada Rev. Stat. § 460.010		No	
New Hampshire Rev. Stat. Ann. § 507-8-b		No	
New Jersey—no statute			
New Mexico Stat. Ann. § 2410-5		No	Limited to hepatitis
New York Public Health Law § 580(4)		No	
North Carolina Gen. Stat. § 90-220.10		Yes	
North Dakota Century Code § 41-02-33(3)(d)		Yes	
Statutory		Tissue	Other

Statutory Citation	Year	Tissue Included	Other Provisions
Ohio Rev. Code Ann. § 2108.11	1969	Yes	
Oklahoma Stat. Ann. title 63, § 2151		Yes	
Oregon Rev. Stat. § 97.300	1973	Yes	
Pennsylvania Stat. Ann. title 35, § 10021	1977	Yes	
Rhode Island Gen. Laws § 23-17-30(a).	1986	Yes	
South Carolina Code Ann. § 44-43-10		Yes	
South Dakota Codified Laws § 557-4-33.1		Yes	
Tennessee Code Ann. § 47-2-316(5).		Yes	
Texas Civil Practice and Remedies Ann. § 4590-3		Yes	Forbids cash payment for blood
Utah Code Ann. § 26-31-1		No	
Vermont—no statute			
Virginia Code Ann. § 32.1-297		Yes	
Washington Rev. Code Ann. § 70.54.120	1971	No	Not retroactive
West Virginia Code § 16-23-1	1971	Yes	
Wisconsin Stat. Ann. § 146-31(2)	1965	Yes	
Wyoming Stat. § 35-5-110		Yes	

18

William H. L. Dornette, M.D., J.D.

HIV Infections
and Anesthesia Practice

BACKGROUND

Acquired immunodeficiency syndrome (AIDS) and its etiologic agent, the human immunodeficiency virus (HIV or HIV-1), have been given widespread publicity in the scientific literature and lay press during the past several years. Through a number of scientific publications, most notably the *Morbidity and Mortality Weekly Report* (MMWR) of the Centers for Disease Control (CDC) of the United States Public Health Service (USPHS), the American health care community has been kept abreast of the latest developments concerning the spread of the disease, as well as the precautions to take to minimize that spread.

Because of the HIV infectivity of most body fluids of carriers of the virus, anesthesia personnel face an occupational hazard of potentially devastating consequences. Additional problems are presented by the dual issues of confidentiality for, and concealment of the infection by, the HIV-infected person. Because of the possibility of transmission of HIV through blood products, those who administer these products face important therapeutic decisions that can literally pose a threat to life if the blood is given or if it is withheld. This chapter is concerned with the legal aspects of treating the infected patient, including maintaining confidentiality, and preventing the spread of HIV to persons who are not infected. A consideration of these legal issues is best begun with a review of the evolution of scientific knowledge about AIDS and HIV.

History of AIDS

The first cases in the United States of what is now known as AIDS were identified in homosexual males.[1] Cases were later identified among intravenous drug abusers.[2] From June 1981 to the present time, the CDC have been following the development of this disease and publishing their findings in the MMWR. Table 18-1 contains a list of the important scientific discoveries about AIDS and HIV in chronological order, together with the reference to the issue of the MMWR in which the discovery was reported. Also included are references to recommendations of the CDC for preventing the spread of HIV.

Of interest to anesthesia personnel are those reports concerned with transfusion-transmitted HIV infections and the protection of personnel. The first case of possible transfusion-associated HIV infection was reported on December 10, 1982. The CDC issued precautions for health care workers on September 2, 1983. On March 4, 1983, the CDC recommended that *the use of blood be minimized* and encouraged the use of autologous transfusions. On March 15, 1985, the Food and Drug Administration licensed the first company to market

an enzyme-linked immunosorbent assay developed to detect the presence of the HIV antibody. This test is known by its acronym, ELISA. Blood banks in the United States phased in the use of this screening test over the next several months.

Detailed recommendations for the prevention of transmission during invasive procedures were promulgated by the CDC on April 11, 1986. In June of that year the American Association of Blood Banks, the Council of Community Blood Centers, and the American Red Cross initiated the "look-back" program.*

On May 22, 1987, the CDC reported the first cases of HIV infections occurring in health care workers that *did not involve needle sticks.*[3] Because of the importance of this possible source of infection to anesthesia personnel (and all others who are exposed regularly to bodily secretions), a portion of this report is appended to this chapter (Appendix 18-1).

Incidence of AIDS and HIV Infections

Almost 125,000 known cases of AIDS had been reported to the CDC as of February 28, 1990.[4] In 1986, it was estimated by the USPHS[5] that between 1 and 1½ million Americans were infected with HIV but did not have symptoms of AIDS. In 1987, the CDC estimated the number to be between 945,000 and 1.4 million,[6] and in 1988 the reported estimate of the USPHS was "one million or more."[7] Assuming that the cor

---

*The look-back program is intended to identify recipients of blood products that were donated by a person later determined to be HIV antibody positive. When a blood product recipient is identified as having acquired an HIV infection from a blood product, the transfusion service records are reviewed and donors of all units of blood products received by that recipient are identified. These individuals are asked to return to the blood bank for an HIV antibody screen (an ELISA). If one of these donors is identified as being HIV antibody positive (called seroreactivity), his or her donor record is then reviewed, and all recipients of blood products obtained from that individual's donations are notified (generally through their health care provider) and asked to come to the blood bank for an HIV antibody screen. The look-back program has proved effective in identifying sources of transfusion-related HIV infections and, by notifying infected transfusion recipients, minimizing the danger of further spread of the virus by those individuals.

TABLE 18–1. Chronology of Events in the Development of Information About HIV Infections

June 5, 1981	First cases of *Pneumocystis carinii* pneumonia in homosexual men reported. MMWR* 30:250.
May 21, 1982	First cases of generalized lymphadenopathy (now known as *AIDS related complex* or ARC) in homosexual men reported. MMWR 31:249.
June 4	Term *acquired immune deficiency syndrome* (AIDS) first used by CDC in publication. MMWR 31:27.
June 16	First cases of AIDS in hemophiliacs reported by CDC. MMWR 31:365.
Nov. 5	CDC issue infection-prevention precautions for clinical and laboratory staffs. MMWR 31:577.
Dec. 10	First case of "possible" transfusion-associated AIDS reported. Case occurred in California and involved a 20-month-old infant. MMWR 31:352.
March 4, 1983	CDC issue guidelines for preventing spread of AIDS virus. These include having those at risk of AIDS to refrain from donating blood, minimizing the use of blood, and encouraging the use of autologous transfusions. MMWR 32:101.
April 13	USPHS issues strict guidelines as to screening donors. The American Red Cross publishes these guidelines, and they in effect become the standard of care for blood-drawing services in the United States.
Sept. 11	CDC issue precautions for health care workers and "allied professionals" including laboratory, dental, and anatomic pathological personnel. MMWR 32:450.
Jan. 11, 1985	CDC recommend use of ELISA for screening blood products, and apprising those likely to be infected to "refrain from donating blood, plasma, organs, other tissues, or sperm." MMWR 34:1.
March 15	The FDA licenses Abbott Laboratories to market an ELISA for detecting the presence of the HIV antibody in blood drawn for transfusion. Reportedly Irwin Memorial Blood Bank in San Francisco commences use of this test at 0001 hours.
May 24	CDC issue recommendations for preventing spread of HIV infection via donations of organs, other tissues, and semen. MMWR 34:294.
Aug. 30	CDC issue guidelines for education and foster care of children with HIV infections. MMWR 34:517.
	CDC issue guidelines for prevention of HIV infection through tears. MMWR 34:533.
Sept. 6	CDC redefine who should refrain from donating blood and plasma. MMWR 34:547.
Sept. 27	CDC publish an update on health care worker safety. MMWR 34:575.
Nov. 15	CDC issue recommendations for safety in the "workplace" (including personal-service and food-service workers). MMWR 34:691.
April 18, 1986	CDC publish recommendations for infection control in dental practice. MMWR 35:337.
June 14	American Association of Blood Banks, Council of Community Blood Centers and American Red Cross recommend initiation of "look-back" program.
May 22, 1987	CDC report first cases of HIV infections in health care workers *not involving needle-stick injuries*. MMWR 36:285.
Feb. 22, 1988	Ward and coworkers report 11 instances of HIV transmission from blood products screened negative for HIV-ab; the seven donors apparently failed to develop detectable HIV-ab for intervals as long as 16 months following putative infection. See Ward, JW, et al: Transmission of human immunodeficiency virus (HIV) by blood transfusions screened as negative for HIV antibody. N Engl J Med 318:473, 1988.
June 24	CDC issue update on what are termed *universal precautions* to be used in protecting workers from exposure to the HIV, hepatitis virus and "other bloodborne pathogens" in health-care settings. MMWR 37:377, 387.
Aug. 15	Office of Health Compliance Assistance of U.S. Department of Labor issues *OSHA Instruction CPL 2–2.44A* pertaining to guidelines for assuring health care worker safety when exposed to the HIV and hepatitis B virus.
Oct. 5, 1989	Cumming and coworkers evaluate risk of contracting HIV from HIV-ab–negative screened blood; in 1987 recipient of average transfusion (5.4 units) had odds of 1:28,000; "risk has been decreasing by more than 30 percent per year." Cumming, PD, et al: Exposure of patients to human immunodeficiency virus through the transfusion of blood components that test antibody-negative. N Engl J Med 321:941, 1989. Ward and coworkers evaluate factors influencing progression of HIV infection contracted from blood products. Ward, JW, et al: The natural history of transfusion-associated infection with human immunodeficiency virus. N Engl J Med 321:947, 1989.
July 27, 1990	CDC report possible instance of transmission of the HIV from a dentist with AIDS to one of his patients during extraction of two third-molar teeth. Patient reportedly had no risk factors. Patient developed malaise, moderately enlarged tonsils, and enlarged anterior cervical lymph nodes which were nontender. Two years after the extraction, she developed *pneumocystis carinii* pneumonia and was found to be seroreactive. MMWR 39:489.
Jan. 18, 1991	CDC issue update concerning transmission of HIV from a dentist to three of his patients during invasive procedures. MMWR 40:21.

*MMWR references are to *The Morbidity and Mortality Weekly Report* published by the Centers for Disease Control (CDC).

rect number lies somewhere in the middle, one then may calculate that there are about 10 infectious HIV carriers for each individual who has AIDS (i.e., 1.25 million divided by 125,000). This ratio should be a good point at which to commence a discussion of the overall risks to health care providers.

It is not known how many asymptomatic infected persons are unaware of their infectivity. One suspects that the number is quite large; the CDC is of the opinion that "most" are unaware.[8] Caring for such an individual will pose a threat to the health of any health care worker, a threat that is especially serious to those who handle the patient's bodily fluids. The risk of exposure is significant in the larger metropolitan areas wherein the greatest number of HIV-infected persons live. Figure 18-1, taken from the Center for Infectious Diseases' *Monthly Surveillance Report* of March 1, 1990,[4] shows the cumulative total number of AIDS cases per 10,000 population in some of these metropolitan areas. If one assumes that the number of HIV carriers is 10 times the number of active cases, as discussed

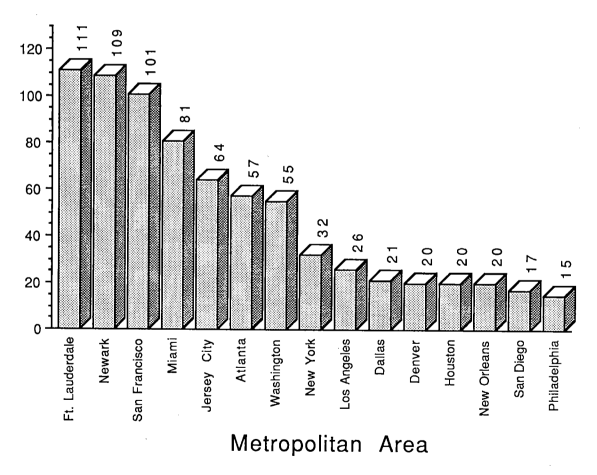

Figure 18–1 Depicting the cumulative total number of AIDS cases per 10,000 population in major metropolitan areas. Assuming that there are 10 HIV-infected persons for every AIDS case (see text), this figure also shows the number of infected persons per 1000 population. Calculated from population of metropolitan areas as of 1986 compiled by U.S. Department of Commerce and published in Statistical Abstract of the U.S.—1989, and from the cumulative total number of cases for these metropolitan areas compiled by Center for Infectious Diseases and published in HIV/AIDS Surveillance issued March 1990.

above, then this figure also shows the number of infected persons per 1000 population in each of these same metropolitan areas. Several studies[9-11] indicate that about 2% of admissions to hospitals in large cities are infected with HIV.

PATIENT CARE SITUATIONS

All those who treat HIV-infected patients, and especially anesthesia and surgical personnel, are at risk. In addition to the occupational exposure from coming into contact with bodily fluids of the infected person (notably blood), these personnel need to be concerned about protecting other patients from accidental cross-contamination, maintaining confidentiality, and, where they learn of the infected status of a patient during preoperative rounds,* warning their colleagues without allowing that potentially sensitive information to become general knowledge among hospital personnel. Another issue of concern to anesthesia personnel is the administration of blood products and possible consequent exposure of a patient to transfusion-transmitted infection. The problems relating to this route of transmission, and the associated informed consent questions, are discussed in Chapter 17. Health care personnel may encounter HIV-infected patients in at least four situations:

1 With a diagnosis of AIDS or "Rule out AIDS"
2 Known to be HIV-infected
3 HIV-infected but unaware of this status
4 Aware of infected status but unwilling to divulge that information to the health care provider

Patients who are hospitalized with AIDS may require a variety of operative procedures and associated anesthetic administrations. All who care for these patients

---

*One of the admonitions of the CDC to infected persons is, "When seeking medical or dental care for intercurrent illness, these persons should inform those responsible for their care of their positive antibody status so that appropriate evaluation can be undertaken and precautions taken to prevent transmission to other."[12]

will be on notice that precautions similar to those used for patients with hepatitis B must be taken (hereinafter referred to as *universal precautions*[13]). For anesthesia personnel, these precautions include masks, gowns, gloves, and at least eye (preferably full face) protection. Additionally, since these patients have a compromised immune system, extra care must be taken to prevent exposing them to any source of nosocomial infection. Inasmuch as the admitting diagnosis would be AIDS, which the patient's medical record would reflect, there should be no concerns related to breach of confidentiality by anesthesia personnel (other than the obvious ones of keeping the information within the health care setting). Universal precautions obviously must be employed for all HIV-infected patients. Because the HIV-carrier stage is not obvious, it is apparent that efforts be directed to avoiding dissemination of information about such patients' seroreactivity outside of the immediate health care setting. While this admonition is true of all diseases, it is especially important in the case of those infected with HIV because of the unpleasant connotations connected with such status (i.e., the implication of having been infected because of membership in a high-risk group).

Undoubtedly there are a significant number of persons who are aware that they are infected but who will not volunteer that information during history taking. Or, they may actively conceal their seroreactivity status from the health care provider, either through ignorance of the CDC's disclosure recommendations or otherwise. The possibility that persons who know they have been infected through "high-risk" activity will attempt to conceal their infectious status furnishes strong impetus for the argument that all candidates for invasive procedures should be screened routinely.

Routine Screening of Surgical Patients

As noted above, there may be as many as 10 HIV-infected persons for each patient with AIDS. These projected infection rates for certain metropolitan areas, noted in Figure 18-1, pose a definite threat to all health care providers, including anesthesia personnel, regularly exposed to bodily fluids who are working in those areas. One solution to this problem is the recommendation that all patients who are admitted to hospitals be screened for the HIV antibody, or at least all candidates for operative intervention. Some surgeons have recommended that all candidates for elective operative procedures be screened at the time of admission. Such a step would help prevent spread of HIV from patient to health care provider or patient to patient. Those who object to such a practice do so on several grounds:

1 It would be impossible to maintain confidentiality, and thus the identities of those who are seroreactive would be disseminated widely, thereby subjecting them to discrimination because they impliedly contracted HIV through "high-risk" activity.
2 Those patients who test negatively might have been in the "window" of infectivity without seroreactivity at the time the blood sample was drawn, thereby giving health care providers a dangerous false sense of security; thus, even if all admissions were screened, universal precautions still would have to be used on all patients.

Proponents of routine screening make very cogent arguments for their position:

1 Given the serious nature of this illness—with a probability that, given time, up to 100% of those who are infected with the virus will develop AIDS and that currently AIDS is ultimately lethal in all cases—it is imperative that every effort be taken within the health care setting to identify those who are infected and thus offer them early treatment[14] as well as help prevent the spread of HIV to other patients and staff; verifying who is infected is the necessary first step in that process.
2 Certain precautions, which extend beyond universal precautions and may have to be observed when caring for patients known to be infected, cannot, from a practical

standpoint, be undertaken for all patients; as one example, not allowing medical students or PGY-1 trainees to assist in the operating room during care of patients who are HIV antibody (HIV-ab) positive, inasmuch as such individuals might be more susceptible to making mistakes.
3 Persons who are infected but unaware of that status will not implement the CDC's recommendations for infected persons,[12] thereby needlessly exposing others.
4 There is ample and growing evidence that "early diagnosis can prolong the life of a person infected with the HIV."[13]
5 Health care providers have demonstrated the ability to maintain confidences for many, many years.

Universal Precautions

In the absence of routine screening of all patients (perhaps even in spite of it), all staff, and especially anesthesia and surgical personnel, must treat *all patients* as if they are infected. Those precautions—detailed in Appendix 18-2 and by the CDC (compare the MMWR updates cited in Table 18-1)—should be followed meticulously. Any health care or administrative personnel who do not want to take the time to, or incur the expense of, following these recommendations are referred to a publication of the Office of Health Compliance, Occupational Safety and Health Administration (OSHA) titled *OSHA Instruction CPL 2—2.44A* (1988).* This instruction details occupational safety standards for preventing exposure of health care workers to the hepatitis virus and HIV, guidelines for inspection of health care facilities to ensure compliance, and enforcement procedures should there be a failure in compliance. This standard thus imposes the force of law on institutions and personnel.

*Available gratis by mail or in person from the OSHA Publications Distribution Office, Room N3101, U.S. Department of Labor, 200 Constitution Avenue, N.W., Washington, D.C. 20210. This document should be required reading for risk managers, infection control personnel, and anesthesia department heads or their delegate.

CONFIDENTIALITY ISSUES

One of the duties of all health care providers to their patients (Chapter 2) is to keep confidences. Breach of confidence is the dissemination of confidential information about a person beyond that necessary for the protection of the individual, or society at large (see also Chapter 5). It is an intentional tort for which the person committing the breach may be held liable for potentially large damages. When the admission diagnosis is AIDS, the medical record should reflect that diagnosis. The hospital that regularly cares for AIDS patients will have developed guidelines for maintaining confidentiality while at the same time keeping pertinent members of the staff apprised of the infectious nature of those patients. Institutions that only care for the occasional AIDS patient should develop similar guidelines. A much more serious problem may arise from asymptomatic HIV-ab–positive patients admitted for a non–HIV-related illness. These patients create a much more serious threat to health care workers, because they do not pose an obvious risk. Yet, confidentiality issues will abound if such patients are manifestly identified as being seroreactive. Again, universal precautions must be employed.

Would an asymptomatic patient whose HIV infectivity becomes generally known have a cause of action against the health care provider who disseminated that information? Or against the hospital, either as employer of the health care provider or generically if no specific health care provider was involved? The patient could allege invasion of privacy (see also Chapter 5) or, more likely, breach of confidence. The patient would have to show that this information was disseminated beyond the extent necessary to afford protection of other members of the staff. The patient would also have to demonstrate some type of injury. What if a member of the staff posted a prominent sign outside the patient's door noting: "USE AIDS PRECAUTIONS"? Being infected with HIV does not mean that one has AIDS. While this distinction may seem to be one of semantics, in a lay sense (and cases are tried before jurors and judges who are laypersons as far as medical terminology is concerned) such a distinction very likely would become important. This problem could not occur if the phrase *universal precautions* were employed routinely.

PATIENT PROTECTION

Cross-Infection

Applying "universal precautions" to all patients and to their biological fluids would cover those known to be HIV-infected, as well as recently infected persons who were still in the "window" of infectivity without seroreactivity, and thus prevent spread of HIV to other patients.

Transmission Through a Blood Product

The study of case law generated by the spread of infectious diseases through blood transfusions[15] is fascinating. Chapter 17 brings the review of this blood transfusion case law up to date. Inasmuch as anesthesiologists and nurse anesthetists customarily monitor vital signs and frequently (because of early awareness of the signs of hypovolemia) participate in the decision to start blood in the operating room, the admonition of being certain that blood is medically indicated cannot be overemphasized. (See, especially, the discussion at the end of Chapter 17 of the May 1989 *Transfusion Alert* published by the National Heart, Lung, and Blood Institute titled *Indications for the Use of Red Blood Cells, Platelets, and Fresh Frozen Plasma*.[16]) The CDC stressed minimizing the use of blood as early as March 4, 1983.[17] Being certain that the blood is medically indicated is the first step (and a very critical one) in avoiding liability when participating in the decision to administer a blood product. The patient's consent and informed consent (see Chapter 9) are also essential. Testing blood for an HIV infection is far different than testing for hepatitis B. In the latter case, the diagnostic procedure actually detects the presence of the antigen. If the blood will transmit hepatitis B, the test will detect that fact. In the case of HIV infections, the tests that are currently in widespread use are only capable of detecting the presence of the HIV-ab. Inasmuch as an individual will become infected (and hence a carrier of the virus) at the time he or she first contracts HIV, but will not become seroreactive for 4 to 8 weeks (or, in rare instances, much longer [18,19]) after that, a window of infectivity without seroreactivity exists in every newly infected person. Blood given during this interval will pass all antibody screening tests. Estimates vary as to the number of units drawn each year from donors at a time when they are within this window. These estimates range from 1 in 64,000 to 1 in several hundred thousand.[19-22] Blood product recipients' exposure increases with the administration of each additional unit of that product.[19] In general, doubling the number of units will double the exposure. Although the risk is minimal, it is finite. Thus, it is imperative that the use of blood be minimized to the extent possible without otherwise compromising patient safety.

It is my opinion that anesthesia personnel should discuss the risks of blood product use with their patients if it is customary practice for those personnel to participate in the decision to initiate the use of that product. At the time the patient's informed consent for the anesthetic is being obtained, he or she should be apprised of this remote, yet finite, risk of HIV transmission should blood be needed.

The Seroreactive Health Care Worker

On November 15 and December 6, 1985, the CDC published detailed recommendations for preventing transmission of HIV from patients to health care workers and vice versa.[23] The CDC do not recommend routine testing of health care workers who perform or assist in invasive procedures inasmuch as it is the opinion of those at the Centers that the risk of transmission "in this setting is so low." The CDC do recommend that these precautions be applied in all situations. Presumably, if they were so applied, it would not make any difference whether a health care worker was seroreactive. Some health care workers have been identified as being members of a high-risk group.[24] It would seem logical that all such individuals would want to be

aware of their status, voluntarily subject a blood sample to an ELISA, and thus be alerted to the importance of using extra care in protecting their patients.

Although the risk of transmission is low, it cannot be considered to be absolutely zero. The infected surgeon, anesthetist, or anesthesiologist might not have a legal duty to *volunteer* to patients the fact that he or she is infected. In my opinion there is, however, a clear-cut legally recognized duty to inform the patient as part of the informed consent–risk disclosure discussion. In my opinion, failure to do so *would constitute both negligence and a breach of the fiduciary duty* (see Chapter 2) between health care provider and patient. Quite obviously, the precautions detailed by the CDC on April 11, 1986,[25] must be followed carefully in such a case.

Would a patient who acquired a nosocomial HIV infection during an invasive procedure performed by an infected health care worker have a cause of action against that worker? The patient first would have to prove that he or she was not infected prior to the procedure (an advantage to the patient of routine preoperative HIV-ab screening). Second, the patient would have to introduce evidence to the effect that the health care worker was infected at the time of the procedure. Third, proof of the patient's subsequent seroreactivity would have to be forthcoming. (The development of a "flulike" illness, as described in the case report of Health Care worker 1 detailed in Appendix 18-1, followed by the onset of seroreactivity would seem to wrap up such proof.) In that event, it would seem that the patient clearly would have a viable cause of action.

What if a patient, concerned about such exposure, inquired as to the seroreactivity status of the worker (i.e., "Are you infected with the AIDS virus?") and the worker, who was aware of his or her infectivity, said "No"? In that event, the patient could also allege fraudulent concealment, an intentional tort from which punitive damages (Chapter 3) may flow. A final cause of action might be failure to obtain informed consent; that is, "If I had known of the risk of catching the AIDS virus from my doctor, I never would have consented to the procedure." In all such actions, the patient would have to prove that he or she was not a member of a high-risk group and had no other source of exposure to HIV, as detailed above.

Would the hospital as employer of the infected worker (e.g., a resident or CRNA who worked for the hospital) be *vicariously* liable under the *respondeat superior* doctrine (See Chapter 6)? Assuming that the patient would be able to surmount the proof problems just alluded to and could prove that HIV was acquired by an act of the worker (i.e., negligently failing to take precautions to prevent infecting the patient), the answer also would be yes. Would the institution have *prime* liability, inasmuch as hospitals have a legally recognized duty to protect their patients from nosocomial infections? The answer to this query is not as clear-cut. If an infected health care worker had staff privileges as an independent contractor (e.g., a surgeon or anesthesiologist; see Chapter 6), rather than being a hospital employee, the patient could allege that the hospital had breached its duty to its patients by allowing unfit professionals to retain staff privileges.[26]

OTHER LIABILITY ISSUES

Protection of Employees

At the time of this writing, there are a number of queries pertaining to the protection of health care providers, some of which defy definitive answers. Would a health care worker who was exposed to and infected with HIV in the workplace have a cause of action? And, if so, against whom? All states have workers' compensation laws. These statutes provide an exclusive remedy for employees with work-related injuries (i.e., the employer has statutory immunity from a common law cause of action for negligence in maintaining an unsafe workplace, unless it is grossly unsafe). Such litigation might, however, be deemed to have merit if it could be proved that the hospital administration acted recklessly by intentionally concealing the identities of infected patients, thereby subjecting employees to needless exposure. The supreme courts in some states have carved out common law exceptions to the statutory immunity created by the workers' compensation laws if the employer acts wantonly or recklessly. Whether the institution was in compliance with *OSHA Instruction CPL 2—2.44A* (discussed above) would carry considerable evidential value in any such litigation.

The infected employee might sue the HIV-infected patient's personal physician if the latter was aware of the patient's status but failed to alert other health care providers. Such litigation would fail if the health care worker knew or suspected that a given patient was infected and failed to take appropriate precautions as set forth in the hospital's infection control manual.[27]

Protection of the Staff

Do physicians in private practice have the right to require that all prospective patients be screened for the HIV-ab as a prerequisite to accepting them as patients? Clearly they have such a right, based upon the common law interpretation[28] of the health care provider-patient contract (see Chapter 2). The contract is consensual, both parties must agree to its terms, and the physician may arbitrarily refuse to treat any patient. What if the members of the medical staff voted unanimously to recommend that all elective admissions be screened for HIV antibodies and the administration of the hospital refused because of concerns about possible breach of confidentiality? Hospital administrators are rightly concerned about possible exposure to such allegations. Any such direct confrontation between administration and medical staff would have to be resolved through use of existing hospital and staff by-laws. It has come to my attention[29] that all candidates for elective operations in certain Nevada hospitals are being screened for the HIV-ab, without any apparent adverse sequelae (this practice is further discussed below).

Testing Without Patients' Prior Knowledge and Consent

As just alluded to, one staff-protection issue that is foremost in the minds of many care professionals, perhaps most notably surgeons, is possessing knowledge of each patient's HIV-ab status.[30] May concerned members of the staff order an ELISA on their patients without those patients' knowledge and consent? Laws in some jurisdictions, notably California, Delaware, Florida, Georgia, Illinois, Iowa, Massachusetts, Missouri, Ohio, Oregon, Texas, Washington, and Wisconsin[31] (and possibly others), place some restrictions on nonconsensual testing and even may, as in California,[32] make it a criminal offense. In a state without such a law, the physician could make a strong case that knowledge of the test result was necessary to help deliver optimal care to that patient, for example, reasoning that, "If the result were positive, I would want to make certain that the patient would not be exposed unnecessarily to nosocomial infections." HIV-ab testing without consent might well generate a number of legal and possibly moral issues. First of all, the physician would have to inform patients who were identified as being seroreactive, based upon the legally recognized duty, discussed above, to protect third parties known to be at risk.[33] The infected patients thus could take appropriate personal precautions,[12] warn close relatives, and encourage any persons with whom there might have been sexual contact to obtain an ELISA.

Knowledge that one is infected should prove to be a powerful educational tool for limiting further spread of the virus. Unfortunately, being told that one has a probably lethal illness carries with it frightening implications, not the least of which is the risk of suicide.[34] A patient caught unawares by such startling news might sue the health care provider for battery (performing the test without consent), lack of informed consent (e.g., "If I had known you were going to do this to me, I would have gone to another hospital"), and possibly intentional infliction of emotional harm. It seems apparent that there should be a compelling medical reason before a health care provider orders an ELISA without the patient's consent.

Testing With the Patient's Consent

I believe that the solution to the testing issue is to adopt a policy of consensual testing of all candidates for elective procedures. One orthopedic surgeon uses the form

shown in Figure 18-2. He explains that knowledge of the test results will enable him to better protect other patients, his staff, and himself. He reports that for the most part, his patients think this testing is a good idea, because of its stated purpose.

Refusal to Care for an Infected Patient

There have been reports of pathologists refusing to perform autopsies on the bodies of AIDS victims[35] and of health care providers being reticent to treat HIV-infected patients.[36] The legal issues (if any) generated by such refusals differ, depending upon whether the individual making the refusal is an employee of a hospital or other entity, or is in private practice and, if the latter, whether there is any administrative regulation on the subject.

Private Practitioners

Since the earliest common law decisions,[28] private practitioners have had the right to refuse to accept anyone as a patient, especially in the elective case. This right has traditionally been recognized by the American Medical Association (AMA) in its Principles of Medical Ethics. For example, the 1957 version provides (in part):

> § 1 The principal objective of the medical profession is to render service to humanity.
> § 2 A physician may choose whom he will serve. In an emergency, however, he should render service to the best of his ability.[37]

The 1980 Principles of Medical Ethics provide (in part):

Principle VI

A physician shall in the provision of appropriate patient care, except in emergencies, be free to choose whom to serve, with whom to associate, and the environment in which to provide medical services.[38]

Since the advent of the AIDS crisis in this country, a number of physicians have expressed concern about caring for HIV-infected persons.[36] These concerns, and a variety of other reasons, undoubtedly caused

TO ALL OF MY PATIENTS

IN RE: AIDS ANTIBODY TESTING

In addition to the battery of laboratory studies that I normally require for all of my patients who are to undergo an elective operation, all of my patients will be tested for the presence of AIDS antibodies. This test is inexpensive and is carried out before the operation at the same time as the other routine blood tests— either in the hospital or at the pre-admitting center.

Because there is no cure for AIDS (acquired immune deficiency syndrome) at the present time, it is essential that every precaution be taken to protect my patients, operating room personnel, and me.

If your initial test is positive, your elective operation will be cancelled and additional testing carried out to confirm or rule out the presence of AIDS antibodies. It should be noted that all information about any positive test will, within the confines of public health rules and regulations, be kept confidential.

Your signature below will confirm your awareness of the importance of this test, and your permission to allow it to be performed.

_____   _____
DATE   PATIENT'S SIGNATURE

_____   _____
WITNESS   PATIENT'S NAME PRINTED

Figure 18–2 Form given each candidate for elective procedures by one orthopedic surgeon who practices in Las Vegas, alerting these patients to the forthcoming HIV-ab test and reasons for it.

the AMA Council to readdress its official position on ethics. In March 1988 the Council on Ethical and Judicial Affairs of the AMA issued a statement that contains the following paragraphs.

In summary, the Council on Ethical and Judicial Affairs believes that:

A physician may not ethically refuse to treat a patient whose condition is within the physician's current realm of competence solely because the patient is seropositive. Persons who are seropositive should not be subjected to discrimination based on fear or prejudice.

Physicians are dedicated to providing competent medical services with compassion and respect for human dignity.

Physicians who are unable to provide the services required by AIDS patients should make referrals to those physicians or facilities equipped to provide such services.[38]

The statement is clear-cut and unambiguous. It recognizes that not all practitioners are equipped by training or experience to treat HIV-infected patients. In addressing the issue of referral, the council clearly recognizes the importance of maintaining a continuum of care, which is also included in the administrative recommendations of several of the healing arts licensing boards noted below. Avoiding abandonment, as well as allegations of it, is obviously quite important.

Are private practitioners ever under a *legal* duty to treat? Some state licensing authorities by administrative regulation may require licensed practitioners to do so. Administrative regulations have the force of law on those governed by the administrative (in this case healing arts licensing) board that issues them. (For a listing of medical boards' positions by jurisdiction, see Appendix 18-3). Are there any other reasons compelling physicians to treat patients infected with HIV? One author[39] suggests that physicians have a strong *moral* obligation as members of a profession to treat AIDS patients:

> If physicians have an obligation to treat [AIDS] patients, it is derived from the concept of medicine as a profession and from the physician's particular professional role. The . . . objective of the medical profession is devotion to a moral ideal—healing the sick. . . . When a person joins the profession, he or she professes a commitment to these ideals and accepts the obligation to serve the sick.[39]

Employed Health Care Workers

Employee-employer relations are governed by the specific contract for employment, with labor relations law governing the interpretation of questionable contractual provisions. Decisions of the National Labor Relations Board and the courts[40] have upheld the right of employers to discipline employees who refuse to work in certain positions of risk, provided that the employer has conducted an education program for affected employees and has made reasonable protective measures (i.e., gowns, gloves, masks, and eye or full face protection) available to them. Any employee, including members of the house staff, will be governed by the provisions of their contracts, pertinent OSHA administrative regulations (discussed above), and any applicable contract or labor relations common law.

Addressing Concerns About Occupational Exposure

Administrative regulations, employment contracts, admonitions from ethicists, and statements about the risk being "low" notwithstanding, a significantly large number of health care professionals are genuinely concerned about the dangers of exposure to what at present is an inevitably fatal disease. Several authors addressed these concerns in a provocative commentary appearing in the *Journal of the American Medical Association* titled "Why Fear Persists: Health Care Professionals and AIDS."[41] The commentary begins with the following paragraph:

> *Acquired immunodeficiency syndrome (AIDS) is a frightening disease. Recent studies of dental professionals, physicians, and nurses have documented that fear is a basic and persistent reaction to the human immunodeficiency virus (HIV) epidemic. We have found, for example, that among a sample of dental providers in California, 81% of dentists and dental hygienists and 86% of dental assistants believed they would be at increased risk for infection if they treated people with AIDS [citations omitted]. Physicians who worry about AIDS have reported increased stress. In one study, 40% of medical house officers and 24% of pediatric house officers said their levels of stress had risen either moderately or extremely because they were concerned about getting AIDS. More than half of the nurses in one study (59%) believed that AIDS could be transmitted to hospital personnel despite infection control precautions. These studies and others show that getting AIDS from a patient is a frightening possibility for many health professionals.[41]*

These authors identify three reasons for this fear. First, they believe that public health authorities and others "have tended to downplay the real risk of occupational exposure." It is important to note that the authors do not make this statement in an accusatory manner. Second, they note the obvious fact that infection control procedures do not "guarantee against HIV transmission." Finally, they recognize that public health and infection control-oriented personnel do have different values and goals from health care professionals. In consequence, "communication" between these two groups is "hindered." The authors conclude their commentary with five recommendations. I am certain that I, too, if still engaged in the active practice of anesthesiology, would be worried about the risk of occupational exposure. Therefore, I quote these recommendations in toto, with the caveat that concerned health care professionals should read the entire commentary.[41]

First, discussions about the extent of risk for HIV transmission should include a clear recognition that risk does exist and that concern is warranted. Those who use the term "low" to describe risk should be sure to compare it with a specific referent, otherwise it conveys no useful information. They should also be aware that it can be perceived as problem-denying and as a paternalistic attempt at reassurance. It is best to acknowledge the risk and to enlist health care professionals in a joint effort to minimize it.

Second, the limitations as well as the benefits of infection control should be conveyed. Although conscientious use of infection control procedures can reduce the hazard posed by HIV in the health care environment, current technology cannot eliminate it. Because of this limitation, care must be taken not to present infection control as a panacea for health professionals' fear of AIDS.

Third, scientific and administrative authorities should cultivate their credibility as experts. As the facts about AIDS and HIV have changed and changed again, health care providers have lost confidence in the accuracy of the information they receive and in the motives of those conveying it. Authorities' status as experts can be strengthened if they clearly delineate what is known, what is unknown, and what is reasonable speculation. Interpretations of data should be conservative and inconsistencies should be acknowledged and explained. Preliminary findings should be reported with extreme caution and appropriate caveats. When a question cannot be answered, the status of research designed to answer the question should be described.

Fourth, a useful format for addressing health professionals' fears could be small discussion groups. Large meetings are the standard milieu for conveying information about AIDS and HIV and they are effective for that purpose. But they do not encourage health professionals to voice their concerns. Small groups, on the other hand, allow people to express their fears and share them with others. In these less intimidating surroundings, health professionals can feel free to ask questions. If peers have been trained to provide information and support, the small group format can be even more effective. Ideally, health professionals could meet in both large and small groups to receive information and voice their concerns.

Last, communication will improve when the groups involved recognize differences in their domains. With a cooperative effort, viewpoints that might have diverged can be channeled into a more effective educational strategy where all sides are heard and under-

stood. If differing interests are truly polarized and entrenched in their positions, intermediaries can be recruited from among groups of health professionals so that a commonality of language and concerns can be established. Whatever the arrangement, care should be taken to relate the message at hand to current information carried in the media.[41]

These authors have reviewed the problems generated by fears of occupational exposure in a humane, rational, and concise manner. Their concluding paragraph is also worth quoting:

Health professionals' fear of getting AIDS will persist as long as there is a risk that HIV can be transmitted in the workplace. The goal is not to eradicate that fear, but to prevent it from compromising the quality of patient care and from threatening the health professional's own well-being.[41]

Other Legal Issues

The statement of the AMA's Council on Ethical and Judicial Affairs[38] discussed earlier addresses three additional concerns that have legal ramifications—maintaining confidentiality, protecting endangered third parties at known risk of HIV infection, and protecting patients from exposure to HIV by an infected health care professional.

Physicians are ethically obligated to respect the rights of privacy and of confidentiality of AIDS patients and seropositive individuals.

Where there is no statute that mandates or prohibits the reporting of seropositive individuals to public health authorities and a physician knows that a seropositive individual is endangering a third party, the physician should: (1) attempt to persuade the infected patient to cease endangering the third party; (2) if persuasion fails, notify authorities; and (3) if the authorities take no action, notify the endangered third party.

A physician who knows that he or she is seropositive should not engage in any activity that creates a risk of transmission of the disease to others.

A physician who has AIDS or who is seropositive should consult colleagues as to which activities the physician can pursue without creating a risk to patients.[38]

Anesthesia personnel must acquire much confidential information about their pa-

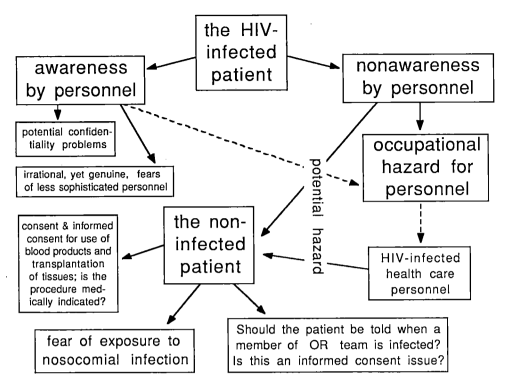

Figure 18–3 Diagram summarizing the various issues—legal and otherwise—and their interaction presented by patients who are HIV-infected and those who are not.

tients. The obvious importance of maintaining confidentiality is also discussed above, and in Chapters 2 and 6. Fortunately, anesthesiologists do not engage in primary care of the patient with AIDS, and thus are not placed in the dilemma between the common law duty to notify,[33] and a possible state statute (e.g., as in California) forbidding the notification of, a third party known to be at risk of HIV infection from one of his or her patients.

The issue of the HIV-infected health care provider is a very thorny one, and one that can involve anesthesia personnel. It is my opinion that patients have a common law–based (on the fiduciary nature of the relationship, see Chapter 2) right to know the seroreactivity of the health care provider who will be involved in an invasive procedure to be performed on them. By the same token, *that same provider has a right to know the seroreactivity of patients under similar circumstances.* This issue, too, is discussed above.

HIV infections and HIV-infected persons reach into just about every aspect of health care delivery. Some of the related issues

covered elsewhere in this book include informed consent, Chapter 9; anesthesia in obstetrics, Chapter 16; use of blood products, Chapter 17; and the training program, Chapter 19.

CONCLUSION

The widespread dissemination of HIV through members of high-risk groups, and the possibility of spread to some of those who are not necessarily members of such groups, do create both occupational and legal hazards for anesthesia personnel and others involved in health care delivery, especially those concerned with invasive procedures (see Figure 18-3). These personnel should understand the importance of taking appropriate precautions to protect themselves, their legal rights to appropriate protective measures, and the duty of their employer to supply those measures. They should also understand their duties under employment contracts, hospital regulations, licensing board regulations, and the common law. They should inform their fellow workers when they learn of the infectivity of one of their patients (commensurate with any statutory admonitions against such disclosure). And they must at the same time help assure that the patient's confidentiality will be protected to the extent possible.

Health care workers who are HIV carriers should be aware of their status, take steps to protect their patients, and inform those patients of their own potential for transmitting HIV, as appropriate.

The many medical, legal, moral, ethical and practical problems generated by AIDS and seroreactive persons will not soon pass away from the health care delivery scene. It seems almost inevitable that they will become more complex and troublesome before they ameliorate. Personnel who anticipate the problems that may arise in the future and, having recognized what those problems may develop into, create solutions before the problems are actually encountered, will have taken a major step toward protecting themselves, and preventing the legal and related entanglements that tend to flourish in the health care environment of today.

ADDENDUM

On January 18, 1991, the Centers for Disease Control reported three patients infected with a strain of the HIV closely resembling the strain taken from their dentist who subsequently died of AIDS.[42] The dentist had performed invasive procedures on each of these patients. The first of these cases generated widespread publicity in the lay press.[43] The CDC called a special meeting in Atlanta on February 21 and 22, 1991, "to review current information on risks of transmission of HIV and HBV to patients during invasive procedures and to assess the implications of these risks."[44]

REFERENCES

1. *Pneumocystis* pneumonia—Los Angeles. MMWR 30:250, 1981.
2. Update on acquired immune deficiency syndrome (AIDS)—United States. MMWR 31:507, 1982.
3. Update: Human immunodeficiency virus infections in health-care workers exposed to blood of infected patients. MMWR 36:285, 1987.
4. Center for Infectious Diseases: HIV/AIDS Surveillance, Centers for Disease Control, Atlanta, March 1990.
5. Institute of Medicine—National Academy of Sciences: Confronting AIDS. National Academy Press, Washington, DC, 1986, p 5.
6. Centers for Disease Control: Human immunodeficiency virus infection in the United States; a review of current knowledge. MMWR 36 (Suppl. 6):1, 1987.
7. Nichols, EK: Mobilizing Against AIDS. Harvard University Press, Cambridge, 1989, p 2.
8. Centers for Disease Control: Public Health Service guidelines for counseling and antibody testing to prevent HIV infection and AIDS. MMWR 36:509, 1987.
9. Baker, GD, et al: Unsuspected human immunodeficiency virus in critically ill emergency patients. JAMA 257:2609, 1987.
10. Lennox, JL, Redfield, RR, and Burke, DS: HIV antibody screening in a general hospital population. JAMA 257:2914, 1987.
11. Kelen, GD, et al: Unrecognized human immunodeficiency virus infection in emergency department patients. N Engl J Med 318:1645, 1988.
12. Centers for Disease Control: Additional recommendations to reduce sexual and drug abuse–related transmission of human T-lymphotropic virus type-III/lymphadenopathy-associated virus. MMWR 35:152, 1986.
13. *See, generally,* Centers for Disease Control: Update: Universal precautions for prevention of transmission of human immunodeficiency virus, hepatitis B virus, and other bloodborne pathogens in health-care settings. MMWR 37:377–382, 387–388, 1988.
14. Cf. Nichols, ref. 7 at pp 7, 109 *et seq.*; Friedland, GH: Early treatment for HIV; the time has come (editorial). N Engl J Med 322:1000, 1990.
15. *See, e.g.,* Dornette, WHL: The use of blood and blood products. In Dornette, WHL (ed): Legal Aspects of Anesthesia. FA Davis, Philadelphia, 1972, pp 249–284; Dornette, WHL: Legal problems in blood product use. J Leg Med 4:17, 1976.
16. National Blood Resource Education Program: Transfusion Alert, NIH Publication No. 89-2974a, May 1989.
17. Centers for Disease Control: Prevention of acquired immune deficiency syndrome (AIDS). MMWR 32:101, 1983.
18. Ward, JW, et al: Transmission of human immunodeficiency virus (HIV) by blood transfusions screened as negative for HIV antibody. N Engl J Med 318:473, 1988.

19. Cumming, PD, et al: Exposure of patients to human immunodeficiency virus through transfusion of blood components that test antibody-negative. N Engl J Med 321:941, 1989.

20. Zuck, TF: Transfusion-transmitted AIDS reassessed (editorial). N Engl J Med 318:511, 1988.

21. Institute of Medicine—National Academy of Sciences: Confronting AIDS, Appendix C. National Academy Press, Washington, DC 1986, p 309.

22. Koop, CE: Remarks as part of the 1988 Annual Ash Memorial Lecture, Armed Forces Medical Museum, June 1, 1988.

23. Centers for Disease Control: Recommendations for preventing transmission of infection with human T-lymphotropic virus typeIII/lymphadenopathy-associated virus in the workplace. MMWR 34:681, 1985.

24. Centers for Disease Control: Update: Prospective evaluation of health-care workers exposed via the parenteral or mucous-membrane route to blood or body fluids from patients with acquired immunodeficiency syndrome—United States: MMWR 34:101, 1985.

25. Recommendations for preventing transmission of infection with human T-lymphotropic virus type-III/lymphadenopathy-associated virus during invasive procedures. MMWR 35:221, 1986.

26. Corletto v. Shore Memorial Hospital, 138 N.J. Super. 302, 350 A.2d 534 (1975).

27. Livingston v. Gribetz, 549 Fed. Supp. 238 (S.D.N.Y. 1982).

28. Hurley, v Eddingfield, 156 Ind. 416, 59 N.E. 1058 (1901); ("In obtaining the state's license to practice medicine, the state does not require, and the licensee does not engage that he will practice at all or on other terms than he may choose to accept."); Limbaugh v. Watson, 12 O.L.Abs. 150 (Ohio 1932).

29. Marrone, GM: Personal communication, May 15, 1989.

30. Breo, D: Dr. Koop calls for AIDS tests before surgery. Am Med News, June 26, 1987, pp 1, 17-21; see also Hagen, MD, Meyer, KB, and Pauker, SG: Routine preoperative screening for HIV. JAMA 259:1357, 1988.

31. See, generally, Dornette, WHL: AIDS and the Law, 1989 Supplement, Appendix T. John Wiley & Sons, New York 1988, pp 72–74.

32. Cal. Health and Safety Code § 199.22(a), effective April 4, 1985, amended 1987.

33. Tarasoff v. Regents of the Univ. of Calif., SS1 P.2d 334 (1976).

34. Marzuk, PM, et al: Increased risk of suicide in persons with AIDS. JAMA 259:1333, 1988.

35. Ratzan, RM and Schneiderman, H: AIDS, autopsies, and abandonment. JAMA 260:3466, 1988.

36. Link, RN, et al: Concerns of medical and pediatric house officers about acquiring AIDS from their patients: Health care workers uncomfortable with AIDS. AORN J 50(4):742, 1989; Cooke, M and Koenig, B: Housestaff attitudes towards acquired immunodeficiency syndrome. Presented at the Third International Conference on AIDS, Washington, DC, June 4, 1967; Cooke, M, et al: The HIV epidemic and training in internal medicine; challenges and recommendations. N Engl J Med 321:1334, 1989; Loewy, EH: Duties, fears and physicians. Soc Sci Med 223:58, 1986.

37. Quoted in Wasmuth, CE and Wasmuth, CE, Jr: Law and the Surgical Team. Williams & Wilkins, Baltimore, 1969, p 402.

38. Council on Ethical and Judicial Affairs: Ethical issues involved in the growing AIDS crisis. JAMA 259:1360, 1988; see, also, Goldsmith, MF: (Medical News and Perspectives) AMA house of delegates adopts comprehensive measures on AIDS. JAMA 258:425, 1987; Board of Trustees: Prevention and control of acquired immunodeficiency syndrome. JAMA 258:2097, 1987.

39. Emmanuel, EJ: Do physicians have an obligation to treat patients with AIDS? N Engl J Med 318:1686, 1988.

40. See, generally, Leonard, AS: AIDS and employment law revisited. Hofstra L Rev 14:11, 1985.

41. Gerbert, B, et al: Commentary: Why fear persists. JAMA 269:3481, 1988.

42. Update: Transmission of HIV infection during an invasive dental procedure. MMWR 40:21, 1991.

43. Johnson, B and Grant, M: A life stolen early. People Weekly, 70 (October 22, 1990).

44. Ref. 42 at 27; for information on the conclusions of the meeting, any recommendations for preventing spread to patients, and other data on AIDS, contact the National AIDS Information Clearing House, P.O. Box 60003, Rockville, MD 20850.

APPENDIX

18-1

CASE REPORTS: HEALTH CARE WORKERS CONTRACTING HIV INFECTIONS OTHER THAN VIA NEEDLE STICKS

The following case reports involve three health care workers who contracted HIV infections other than via needle sticks. These reports are quoted from the *Morbidity and Mortality Weekly Report* of May 22, 1987, pp. 385–389, as reported by the Hospital Infections Program and AIDS Program, Centers for Infectious Diseases, CDC.

Health-Care Worker 1

A female health-care worker assisting with an unsuccessful attempt to insert an arterial catheter in a patient suffering a cardiac arrest in an emergency room applied pressure to the insertion site to stop the bleeding. During the procedure, she may have had a small amount of blood on her index finger for about 20 minutes before washing her hands. Afterwards, she may also have assisted in cleaning the room but did not recall any other exposures to the patient's blood or body fluids. She had no open wounds, but her hands were chapped. Although she often wore gloves when anticipating exposure to blood, she was not wearing gloves during this incident.
The patient with the cardiac arrest died. A postmortem examination identified Pneumocystis carinii pneumonia, and a blood sample was positive for HIV antibody by enzyme immunoassay (EIA) and Western blot methods. Twenty days after the incident, the health-care worker became ill with fever, myalgia, extreme fatigue, sore throat, nausea, vomiting, diarrhea, a 14-pound weight loss, and generalized lymphadenopathy (emphasis supplied) which her physician diagnosed as a viral syndrome. That illness lasted 3 weeks. She felt much better 9 weeks after the incident, and, when she was examined 6 months after the incident, all signs and symptoms had resolved. She had donated blood 8 months before the incident and was negative for HIV antibody by EIA. She donated again 16 weeks after the incident and was positive for HIV by EIA and Western blot (bands p24 and gp41). Serum samples obtained 20 and 23 weeks after the incident were also positive for HIV antibody. She stated that for over 8 years her only sexual partner had been her husband, who denied risk factors for HIV and was seronegative for HIV antibody. She denied ever receiving a blood transfusion, ever using intravenous drugs, or having any needle sticks or other significant exposures to blood or body fluids in the past 8 years. Her serologic test for syphilis was negative. Fifteen other employees who assisted in the care of the patient were seronegative at least 4 months after the exposure.

Health-Care Worker 2

A female phlebotomist was filling a 10-ml vacuum blood collection tube with blood from an outpatient with a suspected HIV infection when the top of the tube flew off and blood splattered around the room, on her face, and in her mouth. She was wearing gloves to protect her hands and was wearing eyeglasses so she did not think she got any blood in her eyes. She had facial acne but no open wounds. She washed the blood off immediately after the exposure. The outpatient's blood sample was positive for HIV antibody by EIA and Western blot, and a hepatitis B surface antigen test was negative. The phlebotomist's EIA was negative the day after the incident and again 8 weeks later. When she donated blood 9 months after the exposure, she was positive for HIV antibody by EIA and Western blot (bands p24 and gp41). She has had no symptoms. She denied having any sexual contact during the previous 2 years, ever using drugs intravenously, or ever receiving a transfusion. Two months after the incident, she scratched the back of her hand with a needle used to draw blood from an intravenous drug abuser of unknown HIV-antibody status. She did not bleed as a result of the scratch and has not had any needle-stick injuries in over 2 years. Her serologic tests for syphilis and hepatitis B were negative. A coworker who was splattered with blood on the face and in the mouth during the same incident remains seronegative 1 year after the incident.

Health-Care Worker 3

A female medical technologist was manipulating an apheresis machine (a device to separate blood components) to correct a problem that developed during an outpatient procedure when blood spilled, covering most of her hands and forearms. She was not wearing gloves. She does not recall having any open wounds on her hands or any mucous membrane exposure. However, she had dermatitis on one ear and may have touched it. She washed the blood off herself and the machine several minutes after the spill. The patient undergoing the apheresis had denied risk factors for HIV infection. However, a blood sample from the patient was positive for HIV antibody by EIA and Western blot methods and negative for hepatitis B surface antigen the next day. The technologist's HIV-antibody tests were negative 5 days after the exposure and again 6 weeks later. Eight weeks after the exposure, she had an influenza-like illness with fever, myalgia, diarrhea, hives, and a pruritic red macular rash on her arms and legs. The illness resolved after a few weeks, and her physician thought the illness was probably a viral syndrome. Three months after the incident, she was positive for HIV antibody by EIA and Western blot methods (band p24 alone). Four months after the incident, a Western blot was positive (bands p24 and gp41). She indicated that for more than 8 years her only sexual partner had been her husband, who denied risk factors for HIV infection and was seronegative for HIV antibody. She denied every receiving a transfusion, ever using intravenous drugs, or having any needle-stick injuries in over 2 years. Her serologic tests for syphilis and hepatitis B were negative. She has an immunologic disorder which had been treated with corticosteroids in the past, but she had not taken any immunosuppressive medication for the past year. A coworker with a similar exposure during the same procedure remains seronegative after 3 months.

The CDC commented editorially that these were the first such cases not caused by needle sticks, and that skin or mucous membrane exposure apparently will allow transmission of the virus, although only rarely. They concluded that the "cases again emphasize the need to implement and strictly enforce previously published recommendations for minimizing risk of exposure to blood and bodily fluids of all patients."

APPENDIX

18-2

CDC RECOMMENDATIONS FOR PREVENTION OF HIV TRANSMISSION IN CERTAIN HEALTH CARE SETTINGS*

1 All health-care workers should routinely use appropriate barrier precautions to prevent skin and mucous-membrane exposure when contact with blood or other body fluids of any patient is anticipated. Gloves should be worn for touching blood and body fluids, mucous membranes, or non-intact skin of all patients, for handling

*Extracted from *The Morbidity and Mortality Weekly Report* of August 21, 1987, Vol. 36, No. 2S (Second Supplement), a copy of which is available gratis from the National AIDS Clearinghouse, P.O. Box 6003, Rockville, MD 20850, or by calling 1-800-458-5321 (literature references omitted).

items or surfaces soiled with blood or body fluids, and for performing venipuncture and other vascular access procedures. Gloves should be changed after contact with each patient. Masks and protective eyewear or face shields should be worn during procedures that are likely to generate droplets of blood or other body fluids to prevent exposure of mucous membranes of the mouth, nose, and eyes. Gowns or aprons should be worn during procedures that are likely to generate splashes of blood or other body fluids.

2 Hands and other skin surfaces should be washed immediately and thoroughly if contaminated with blood or other body fluids. Hands should be washed immediately after gloves are removed.

3 All health-care workers should take precautions to prevent injuries caused by needles, scalpels, and other sharp instruments or devices during procedures; when cleaning used instruments; during disposal of used needles; and when handling sharp instruments after procedures. To prevent needlestick injuries, needles should not be recapped, purposely bent or broken by hand, removed from disposable syringes, or otherwise manipulated by hand. After they are used, disposable syringes and needles, scalpel blades, and other sharp items should be placed in puncture-resistant containers for disposal; the puncture-resistant containers should be located as close as practical to the use area. Large-bore reusable needles should be placed in a puncture-resistant container for transport to the reprocessing area.

4 Although saliva has not been implicated in HIV transmission, to minimize the need for emergency mouth-to-mouth resuscitation, mouthpieces, resuscitation bags, or other ventilation devices should be available for use in areas in which the need for resuscitation is predictable.

5 Health-care workers who have exudative lesions or weeping dermatitis should refrain from all direct patient care and from handling patient-care equipment until the condition resolves.

6 Pregnant health-care workers are not known to be at greater risk of contracting HIV infection than health-care workers who are not pregnant; however, if a health-care worker develops HIV infection during pregnancy, the infant is at risk of infection resulting from perinatal transmission. Because of this risk, pregnant health-care workers should be especially familiar with and strictly adhere to precautions to minimize the risk of HIV transmission.

Implementation of universal blood and body-fluid precautions for *all* patients eliminates the need for use of the isolation category of "Blood and Body Fluid Precautions" previously recommended by CDC for patients known or suspected to be infected with blood-borne pathogens. Isolation precautions (e.g., enteric, "AFB") should be used as necessary if associated conditions, such as infectious diarrhea or tuberculosis, are diagnosed or suspected.

Precautions for Invasive Procedures

In this document, an invasive procedure is defined as surgical entry into tissues, cavities, or organs or repair of major traumatic injuries (1) in an operating or delivery room, emergency department, or outpatient setting, including both physicians' and dentists' offices; (2) cardiac catheterization and angiographic procedures; (3) a vaginal or cesarean delivery or other invasive obstetric procedure during which bleeding may occur; or (4) the manipulation, cutting, or removal of any oral or perioral tissues, including tooth structure, during which bleeding occurs or the potential for bleeding exists. The universal blood and body-fluid precautions listed above, combined with the precautions listed below, should be the minimum precautions for *all* such invasive procedures.

1 All health-care workers who participate in invasive procedures must routinely use appropriate barrier precautions to prevent skin and mucous-membrane contact with blood and other body fluids of all patients. Gloves and surgical masks must be worn for all invasive procedures. Protective eyewear or face shields should be worn for procedures that commonly result in the generation of droplets, splashing of

blood or other body fluids, or the generation of bone chips. Gowns or aprons made of materials that provide an effective barrier should be worn during invasive procedures that are likely to result in the splashing of blood or other body fluids. All health-care workers who perform or assist in vaginal or cesarean deliveries should wear gloves and gowns when handling the placenta or the infant until blood and amniotic fluid have been removed from the infant's skin and should wear gloves during post-delivery care of the umbilical cord.

2 If a glove is torn or a needlestick or other injury occurs, the glove should be removed and a new glove used as promptly as patient safety permits; the needle or instrument involved in the incident should also be removed from the sterile field.

APPENDIX

18-3

POSITIONS OF LICENSING BOARDS ON TREATING HIV-INFECTED PERSONS

Arizona. Licensees are not required to care for patients with problems beyond their expertise. They may not, however, abandon one of their patients who tests positively, but must refer that individual to another practitioner who in turn agrees to care for the patient.

Delaware. The Board of Medical Practice feels it is unethical for a physician, utilizing appropriate safeguards, to withhold emergency care from any individual because of coexisting conditions or diseases or the suspicion of same. In order to provide optimal care and safeguards, the board feels it is essential that all patients make available to the treating physician any pertinent history or laboratory results and submit to any appropriate diagnostic procedures that are felt by the physician to be indicated to diagnose a coexisting condition or disease.

Florida. The board has no position. All licensees are required to complete 3 hours of continuing medical education relating to HIV and AIDS by December 31, 1989, as per Fla. Stat. § 55.2226, effective July 6, 1988.

Iowa. "A physician may choose whom they [sic] will serve. In an emergency, however, the physician should render service to the best of their ability. Having undertaken the case of a patient, the physician may not neglect the patient; and unless the patient has been discharged they may discontinue their services only after giving adequate notice."

Kansas. The board has no position; Kansas has a public accommodations statute that forbids discrimination against handicapped persons; AIDS is considered to be a handicapping condition in Kansas; no incidents involving health care providers who denied care to HIV-infected persons have come before the board, but it is the board's opinion that the public accommodations statute would be applicable in such a situation.

Maryland. The Medical Board has not taken a position; the Maryland Human Relations Commission interprets Article 49B of the Annotated Code of Maryland to mean that it embraces medical and dental services, that the "Commission has jurisdiction over the practices of virtually every health care provider in the State of Maryland," and that it is unlawful for a health care provider "to refuse, withhold from, or deny ... services because of the ... physical or mental handicap of any person."

Massachusetts. "[A]s a general rule, all licensed professionals [have an] affirmative duty to treat, care for or deliver services to persons with AIDS, ARC or HIV infection.... A professional's license carries with it a duty to provide needed services to the public.

Montana. The board has adopted the recent position of the AMA's Council on Ethical and Judicial Affairs.[38]

New Jersey. A physician possessing needed skills must treat HIV-infected persons unless that physician is overly susceptible to infections; in that event, the physician must arrange for referral of that patient to a colleague who will offer care.

Ohio.

> *Despite the extensive publicity devoted to acquired immune deficiency syndrome, the infection continues to spread....*
>
> *The probable universal fatality of AIDS is undisputed. Education remains the best method available to combat the spread of AIDS, and medical professionals are in a unique position to educate the public at large. The State Medical Board urges its licensees to continue taking a leadership role in educating health care consumers that, (1) AIDS is an infectious disease and a public health problem and (2), the impact on human life of AIDS goes far beyond social stigma or personal prejudice.*
>
> *Physicians are urged to identify patients in high risk categories and to educate them about the seriousness of AIDS and how it is spread. In particular, patients who are HIV positive should be alerted to activities that may jeopardize others, and should be encouraged to tell sexual partners and family members of their positive status.*
>
> *In conclusion, the Board urges its licensees to (1) promote AIDS control measures according to public health principles; (2) encourage contact tracing and alerting of potential victims; and (3) support all efforts to control AIDS as an infectious disease.*
>
> *Adopted 7/14/88*

Rhode Island. The board has had no complaints and has taken no formal position; if a case should come before it, the board most likely would adopt the position of the Rhode Island Medical Society: "All AIDS patients require competent, compassionate treatment. It is unethical for a physician to refuse to treat an AIDS patient within his/her realm of competence. Moreover, physicians should respond to the best of their abilities in cases of emergency, and should not abandon patients whose care they have undertaken." Physicians who are unable to provide appropriate care to AIDS patients should "make the appropriate referral to those physicians or facilities that are equipped to provide such services" [quotations adopted from the position of AMA Council on Ethical and Judicial Affairs[38]].

South Dakota. No formal policy adopted, but it would not be inconsistent with that of the Ethical and Judicial Council[38] of the American Medical Association.

Texas. The board has not taken a position; the Board of Councilors of the Texas Medical Association, however, has adopted the following position: "A physician shall either accept the responsibility for the care and treatment of a patient with AIDS, HIV, antibodies to HIV, or infection with any other probable causative agent of AIDS, or refer the patient to an appropriate physician who will accept the responsibility for the care and treatment of the patient."

None of the other boards has adopted a position.

4

Ancillary Activities

EDITOR'S NOTE

There are a number of activities in which not all anesthesia practitioners engage. These include teaching, practicing in a federal hospital, administering anesthesia in a dental office, and utilizing experimental drugs and equipment. The legal ramifications of these activities are covered in this part.

Just about every professional engaged in anesthesia practice today has undergone some amount of formal training. During that learning period, the trainee—knowingly or unknowingly—has been involved in a number of legal relationships and has had the potential for exposing himself or herself, as well as instructors, to liability. Once that individual matriculated and commenced professional practice, the legal implications of those pedagogical activities are of no further concern. Not so in the case of those who remain in the teaching environment—as instructors or departmental heads. Chapter 19 reviews the jurisprudence (effect of laws and legal processes on professional practice) of operating a training program and teaching residents and student nurse anesthetists. It is recommended reading for those whose livelihood revolves about such pedagogical pursuits.

The *scientific* aspects of anesthesia practice are similar in both private and federal sector health care institutions. The *jurisprudential* aspects differ markedly, however. This is so because of a number of federal statutes and common law decisions directed toward channeling liability toward the federal government and away from individual practitioners. These are covered in Chapter 20, which pertains to all branches of federal health care delivery—Veterans Administration, Public Health Service, and the uniformed services. This chapter is directed toward, and recommended reading for, professionals who are assigned to or considering a career in one of these federal health care systems.

A large number of analgesics and anesthetics are administered in dental offices across this country. The degree of sedation employed runs the gamut from analgesia to general anesthesia. These techniques are especially refined in the practice of the oral and maxillofacial surgeon. They are also regulated to a large degree by state dental licensing boards. Through the power of statutes and administrative regulations, these boards help protect the public by assuring that those who would employ consciousness-altering agents are equipped by training and experience to employ them safely. Chapter 21 reviews the jurisprudence of this type of anesthesia practice.

Donald E. Demkee, author of Chapter 21, is an oral and maxillofacial surgeon practicing in northeastern Ohio. He obtained his D.D.S. from Ohio State University and his oral surgery residency at the University of Cincinnati, where he received his anesthesiology training from the Editor. Dr. Demkee serves as a District Team leader for Office Evaluations of general anesthesia on behalf of the Ohio State Dental Board. In his chapter, he reviews the jurisprudence of anesthesia practice in the dental office.

Professionals who employ experimental drugs or highly complex equipment may be faced with the legal ramifications of the statutory and common law of products liability. Chapter 22 traces that common law from its early beginnings in England, and brings it up to date with recent landmark decisions during the latter part of this century. Appended to this chapter are examples of recent common law decisions relating to health care–related product liability cases.

W. H. L. D.

246

19

William H. L. Dornette, M.D., J.D.
Clement J. Markarian, C.R.N.A., M.A.

The Training Program

In this analysis of training programs, we shall review the legal relationships between the various entities and individuals involved—the institution, the training director, the supervisors, the accrediting board or association, and, finally, the trainee himself or herself. Each of these relationships revolves about either contract or agency law, branches of the law that are touched upon in Chapters 2 and 6, respectively. Our review begins with a consideration of the training process itself, and how the various entities and individuals relate to that process, from both a pedagogical and legal posture.

THE TRAINING PROCESS

Establishing and operating a training program is a rather complex multistep process. The associated legal relationships are even more complex. First, the program—topics for didactic instruction and clinical case load—must be structured according to the requirements of the agency that ultimately will be involved in the accreditation. The next steps involve applying for and obtaining accreditation, either from the Residency Review Committee of the American Board of Anesthesiology (ABA) or (in the case of student nurse anesthetists) the Council on Accreditation, a body that is autonomous from the American Association of Nurse Anesthetists (AANA). Once accreditation or provisional approval has been granted, the selection of trainees may begin. The training process itself involves:

- Offering didactic instruction
- Assigning cases
- Providing supervision in clinical activities
- Documenting work and progress of each trainee matriculating in the program
- Affiliating with other institutions, if any, to provide clinical experience not available at the home or base institution
- Helping the trainee prepare for the examinations intended to lead toward diplomate status or certification
- Terminating the trainee if that step becomes necessary

Structuring the Program

Once the decision is made to offer accredited training in anesthesia and the pro-

gram director is selected, steps must be taken to structure a program that will meet the educational standards of the Council on Accreditation or the ABA, as appropriate. The training director or a designee must determine the goals that all trainees must meet during their progression through the program. The material to be covered in the didactic instruction, the types of cases to be utilized for clinical experience, and all other goals must be carefully established and clearly documented. This documentation not only is a prerequisite to obtaining accreditation for the program but also is essential for the indoctrination of each incoming trainee. The latter must be made fully aware (for reasons that will become apparent later) of the expected goals to be achieved as that individual advances through the program.

Obtaining Accreditation

Once the program has been structured according to the standard of the respective accreditation organization, an application for accreditation is made. A program that has not yet been accredited stands somewhat in the same footing as an applicant for medical licensing or staff privileges. The courts have held that the license to practice medicine is not a *right*, but only a *privilege*.* Similarly, a program meeting all of the requirements of the accreditation agency still does not have a right to accreditation. Courts have held that a physician with a full staff appointment has a "valuable property right" of which he or she cannot be deprived without a complicated and time-consuming procedure described below. Newly accredited anesthesiology programs are granted accreditation for a predetermined period of time, not to exceed the length of a full accreditation period. These limitations on new programs place the new program in what amounts to a probationary

---

*The law distinguishes between a *right* and a *privilege* in the following manner. A right is something to which you are entitled, as for example, by reason of your being a citizen of these United States. A privilege, on the other hand, must be earned, for example, to gain the opportunity to practice medicine, one must matriculate from an approved medical school and pass the medical licensing board's examination.

status, which does not carry with it the "property right" of full accreditation. Thus, it is easier for the accrediting agency to take adverse action against the new and not yet fully accredited program that does not live up to expectations than it is to deaccredit a fully accredited program.

Selection of Trainees

Training directors should develop *objective standards* and methodology for selection of trainees. Such standards are much easier for admissions' committees to implement than are vague subjective ones. A good starting point for this objectivity is grade point average (GPA) in medical or nursing courses, including the GPA of student nurse anesthetists in their basic science courses. Next, efforts should be made to assess the aptitude of the prospective trainee. Will he or she be able to remain alert in boring situations? Will he or she be able to react quickly and correctly in those instances in which proper care of the patient abruptly demands almost instantaneous response? Will the individual be able to progress to increasing independence, a trait so necessary in anesthesia practice? Has the prospective trainee ever had problems with alcohol or drug abuse? This last question clearly deserves thorough exploration,* in the light of the ready availability of mind-altering drugs to those who administer anesthesia. If the training director is able to achieve as much objectivity as possible, any later allegations of discrimination in the selection process will be avoided.

Didactic Instruction

Standards of the ABA and Council on Accreditation require that each trainee be offered formal didactic instruction in a wide variety of basic science and clinical sub-

---

*An expert on substance abuse and rehabilitation of abusers *must* be consulted. Anyone who has become habituated to so-called hard drugs can never be cured; this "disease" can only be arrested, and that individual will forever after at some time or another feel the need for a "fix," a need which very likely will be impossible to overcome in an anesthesia service environment wherein drugs of abuse are readily available.

jects, informal conferences, morbidity and mortality meetings, journal clubs with review of current and historic literature, opportunities to listen to audio or audiovisual tapes, and, finally, periodic examinations to check the progress of trainees. *It is imperative that all trainees be relieved of clinical responsibilities during the times that these sessions are conducted.* The conferences should be held at regularly scheduled times, and attendance should be mandatory. An attendance record must be kept. This record is beneficial when applying for reaccreditation and when contemplating termination of a trainee.

Clinical Experience

Only so much learning comes from reading, attending lectures, and observing the work of others. To become skilled in any branch of the healing arts, trainees ultimately must perform the task themselves. Further, this practical experience must be gained while having greater and greater independence from immediate supervision. Initially, the trainee must be supervised continually, almost on a one-to-one basis. As one's experience grows, the need for independence in making judgments and carrying out various procedures becomes apparent. Eventually, trainees need to be treated with what we call *conscientious neglect*. That is, the trainee who comes to know his or her limitations (albeit fewer and fewer ones) must be left to administer anesthetics alone, but with readily available help close at hand. The training director, acting through those immediately supervising trainees' work, has the responsibility of assuring that each trainee moves progressively and satisfactorily from the point of one-on-one supervision to that of almost total independence. This procedure involves care in the assignment of cases, ready availability of supervisory personnel at all times, and adherence to the concept that the training process *should in no way compromise the care rendered each patient.*

Assignment of Cases

Personnel responsible for assigning cases to trainees must be aware of the capabilities of each trainee so that case assignments do not exceed the ability of each to deliver a safe anesthetic. Due consideration also must be given to the availability of supervisory personnel. The senior author of this chapter, in reviewing cases of alleged professional negligence over the years, has encountered instances in which residents in their first months of PGY-1 (first postgraduate year, formerly termed the internship) training were given complex cases without being afforded adequate supervision. If a patient is injured in such circumstances, it is literally impossible to defend such an activity.

Initially, the trainee follows the advice or dictates of the instructor in all phases of case management. As the trainee's knowledge and experience increases, he or she assumes increasing responsibility in selecting preliminary medication, anesthetic agents, anesthetic and monitoring techniques, and conduct of the case. The short, uncomplicated cases to which neophytes are first assigned are replaced by longer, more complicated ones. How quickly each trainee progresses becomes another factor in assessing the trainee's overall performance, and even predicting how well that individual might perform in posttraining practice.

Night Coverage

Conventionally, night coverage in the teaching institution is afforded by one or more residents who remain in-house, with a member of the attending staff being on call at home. Whoever prepares the on-call assignment roster must be aware of the potential need for an even greater (than during the weekdays) level of expertise during the evening, nighttime, and weekend periods, because only emergency operations are performed. By its very nature, the emergency case requires an extra level of skill, expertise, and training above that of the average elective operative procedure.

If the on-call staff supervisor comes to the hospital for every case, there should be no problem. On the other hand, it might be customary practice for the senior resident on call to cover the case with or without consultation with the on-call-at-home attending staff member. In such a situation, should the trainee on call notify the at-home staff before each case is started? Or,

should such notification be carried out only if it is anticipated that the case will be difficult? Can one always be certain that a pending case will not be difficult? Such decisions require a considerable amount of judgment on the part of the trainee who is on first call.

The need for this judgmental requirement for on-call trainees further emphasizes the importance of expertise in preparing the call roster. It is apparent that the individual who performs that function must be familiar with the capabilities of each trainee who will be assigned to that roster.

Night and weekend coverage by student nurse anesthetists is handled somewhat differently. A staff nurse anesthetist is always available for direct supervision, and the student and staff person collectively function as a team. This policy eliminates many of the problems noted in the previous paragraph. The student-to-staff ratio never is greater than 2 to 1.

It is also desirable to be aware of any personality conflicts between trainees and staff who afford night call, or feelings of superiority by a resident over a new staff member. Consider the following example of the latter that occurred many years ago while the senior author was a member of the anesthesiology staff of a university hospital.

The resident on first call failed to accurately apprise the staff person on call that evening of the patient's condition, possibly because he felt superior to her. He notified the staff person by telephone that the patient was physical status II, and that there was no need for her to come to the hospital. In actuality, the patient was much more severely ill, and was a physical status III. The trainee, however, felt that he could handle things and proceeded to administer the anesthetic. Complications and morbidity ensued. At the subsequent morbidity-mortality conference, the trainee reported that the patient was a physical status III, and the untoward result was a direct consequence of the patient's poor physical condition. No mention was made of his failure to report this condition to the staff member who was at home, ready and willing to come to assist.

It goes without saying that personal pride must never take precedence over obtaining consultation.

Instruction and Supervision of Other Trainees

As everyone is aware, it is common practice for senior trainees to instruct or supervise junior trainees. What is the standard of care in such a situation? What is the potential liability? In theory, an instructor will always be liable for incompetent instruction, inadequate supervision, or both. In practice, considering the impecunious condition of the average trainee, a competent lawyer representing a patient who suffered an adverse outcome while a trainee was supervising another trainee would direct the main thrust of his or her complaint against the institution, and possibly the training director. The lawyer would be utilizing what is semifacetiously called the "deepest pocket doctrine"* against the hospital, as well as the *respondeat superior* doctrine (see Chapter 6) against both the hospital and training director. The lawyer might also allege prime (as compared to vicarious) liability of the training director and immediate supervisor for failing to provide adequate supervision of the junior trainee.

Documentation of Progress of Trainees

There are a number of very cogent reasons why the progress of each trainee through the program should be accurately and continuously documented. Such a record forms a valuable yardstick when assessing the educational advancement of each trainee and comparing one trainee with another. It is useful for counseling purposes. It may be helpful in assigning cases, especially when that responsibility falls on the shoulders of a new staff member. This record furnishes vital evidence if a decision is made to place a trainee on probation or to terminate that individual. Quite

---

*Lawyers representing patients injured in the health care setting frequently name all providers who cared for the patient, ostensibly to avoid omitting an essential defendant whose care might have directly contributed to the adverse outcome. A more jaundiced view of this practice is that these lawyers are assuring the availability of as many "deep pockets" as possible to pay the large judgment they hope to win for their client.

obviously, every effort must be made to achieve total objectivity in assessing and documenting each trainee's progress.

Documenting didactic performance based on written examinations is a simple matter. Evaluating the trainee's clinical progress is more complex. Clinical performance may be documented with a clinical evaluation tool, completed on a daily basis by the supervising instructor. As the trainee progresses, this written evaluation form may be completed on selected procedures, weekly or biweekly, up to the completion of the program. The evaluation tool is supported by a document detailing the trainee's learning behavior. There must be guidance for each expected behavior relative to the degree of clinical instruction or supervision required for given achievement levels over specific intervals of time. Such a record not only aids in documenting deficiencies for the benefit of the training director but also provides expectations and goals in written form for the trainee. For example, assume in a school of nurse anesthesia that the sought-after behavior is to accurately and completely perform and document a preanesthetic physical examination. The achievement level should be assigned against the length of the training program and the degree of proficiency required at each point. The first-year student should require close supervision to complete the examination and documentation. At the beginning of the second year, supervision should be minimal, with total independence being given close to graduation toward the end of the second year.

Periodic audit of anesthesia and recovery room records can be a relatively easy and very accurate method for objective evaluation of each trainee's progress in anesthetic management. Duration of the interval between start of the anesthetic and when the patient is ready for the operation (not when the procedure actually starts—see discussion of the TOTS [turn over to surgeon] time in Chapter 10), whether protective reflexes are present at the termination of the case, and the PAR (postanesthesia recovery, see Chapter 13) scores are very useful yardsticks. These data can be tabulated from the records of all patients to whom the trainee has administered anesthesia during the period under study and compared with similar data from other trainees, or from the same trainee over time. Quite obviously, the patients' physical status and complexity of the operative interventions, as well as the immediacy of the supervision, must also be taken into consideration.

THE TRAINING DIRECTOR

The training director is much like the captain of a ship or pilot of an aircraft. He or she is ultimately responsible for all pedagogical activities, and all persons involved in implementing those activities. That this responsibility must rest on the shoulders of *only one individual* is reflected in the current practice of the ABA. Whenever the position of the director of a board-accredited program changes, that program must be reinspected and subjected to reaccreditation. The responsibilities, and legal relationships, of the director extend to the institution, to trainees, and to the patients under their care.

Relationship with the Institution

Training directors frequently are employees of the institution, although there are various exceptions to this rule. Whether an employee or an independent contractor, the training director functions as an agent for the institution in a number of ways. The training director is responsible for:

- Helping assure anesthesia coverage of the patients assigned to the training program
- Keeping the training program within the appropriate guidelines of the accrediting agency and thus assuring regular reaccreditation
- As a department head, serving on various committees of the organized medical staff of the institution as appropriate

As pertains to the accrediting authority, the training director acts as an agent for the institution in presenting the institutions's program for accreditation and reaccreditation, helping ensure that the program functions within the guidelines set forth by the

agency, and acting as a liaison between the institution and the accrediting agency. These responsibilities are, in fact, legally recognized duties.

The institution in turn owes the training director certain duties. These include furnishing or otherwise making available:

- Functional and up-to-date gas anesthesia apparatus and monitoring equipment
- Classroom and conference space
- An anesthesia library with current publications
- Quarters and meals (or equivalent) and stipend for the trainees
- Salaries for the required teaching staff (unless these individuals are engaged in private practice, and derive their income from that practice rather than teaching)
- Patients who as candidates for anesthesia will further the teaching program clinically as well as didactically

Would the training director ever have a cause of action for breach of contract against the institution? Conversely, would an institution that lost its accreditation have a cause of action against the training director? These questions are posed more for thought rather than for actual legal analysis. The answers would depend upon the facts. The courts have always recognized that a material breach of any binding contract creates a cause of action under American common law, one that ultimately may have to be litigated in a court of competent jurisdiction.

Responsibilities of the Director

The director is ultimately responsible for the organization and implementation of the instructional program. He or she oversees all didactic instruction and clinical experiences to assure their quality, and compliance with the requirements of the accreditation agency. Specifically, the director must ensure that:

1 The progress of each trainee is monitored closely.

2 All trainees are assigned to anesthetic administrations commensurate with their progress within the training program (or lack of it).

3 Each trainee is adequately supervised.

4 Each trainee is adequately and progressively instructed so that, at the termination of each year of the program, the trainee will have achieved those goals delineated as objectives of the formal training process.

5 Each trainee will have received sufficient didactic instructions to be able to qualify for, and have a reasonably good chance of passing, the written examination of the ABA or the Council on Certification, as well as become a well-rounded anesthesiologist or anesthetist.

6 Each trainee, at the time of reaching the end of the formal program, either as a board-eligible anesthesiologist or candidate for certification as a registered nurse anesthetist, will have had sufficient experience to be able to practice the art and science of anesthesia, independent from supervision.

Other duties ultimately falling on the shoulders of the director include developing and implementing the use of evaluation tools for evaluating the trainees *and* faculty; documenting the counseling of trainees; maintaining academic and associated records; preparing transcripts of trainees' grades; assigning instructors not only to clinical supervision but also to other departmental responsibilities to develop their own potential; consulting with the respective accreditation agency; overseeing the daily work schedule; preparing a budget; supervising and approving the program's functions, policies, and resources; and monitoring, auditing, and evaluating the curriculum to ensure conformance to program scope, purpose, and objectives.

With these broad duties in mind, one may then explore the potential areas of exposure of the training director to liability. These fall into three categories: to the patients who are cared for at the institution; to the trainee; and, possibly, to the future patients of the trainee.

Potential Liability to Current Patients

There is sufficient case law on point to justify the statement that a patient who is injured by a trainee can, and frequently will, sue the training director, as well as the immediate supervisor, the institution, and possibly the trainee as well. Consider the following case report:[1]

The Chief of Otology demanded that the operating room lights be extinguished while he was performing all of his otoplasties. The patient was a guitarist for a well-known band. The anesthesia was being administered by a resident who was a foreign medical graduate with a poor command of English. He had commenced his training at an institution wherein the medical gases were delivered to the anesthesia apparatus from central piping station outlets. The hospital at which the accident occurred did not have a central piping system. The supervising staff member was standing in the doorway observing the resident through the window. Sometime during the case the the cylinder of oxygen emptied. The resident failed to detect that he was delivering only nitrous oxide to his patient. The patient suffered massive central nervous system injury, and died subsequently. The case was ultimately settled in excess of one million dollars. Among those participating in the settlement was the insurance carrier for the training director, who was in Europe at the time of the accident. Consequent to the settlement, his carrier so increased his rates that he was forced to leave that private hospital and obtain employment at the local county hospital.

This is not the only instance of a training director being named as a defendant in such cases.[2] It is, therefore, important for all training directors to assure that they have adequate professional liability coverage, not only for those anesthetics they themselves administer, but for their role as director of the training program. It is customary practice in many teaching institutions to allow junior trainees to be supervised by senior trainees. The potential for exposure to liability in such situations is discussed below under "Rights, Duties, and Potential Liability of Trainees."

Potential Liability to Trainees

Thanks to the efforts of the ABA, requirements for academic and clinical instruction in anesthesiology are standardized throughout the United States. The Council on Accreditation performs a similar function for programs designed to prepare candidates for the examination of the Council on Certification, which allows them to become Certified Registered Nurse Anesthetists (CRNAs). What if an individual enters one of these programs as a trainee and does not receive the academic or clinical instruction either promised by the training director or set forth in the standards of the ABA or the Council on Certification? Would that individual have a cause of action against the institution,[3] the training director, or both? Although this interesting question does not have a straightforward answer, a review of the legal relationships among the trainee, the institution, and the training director may give some clues.

When a prospective trainee is accepted into a program, a contract is entered into. (For a brief discussion of contract law, especially as pertains to personal service contracts, see Chapter 2.) The duties of each party to this contract are outlined throughout this chapter. If the training program did not offer the clinical and didactic instruction substantially as covered in the discussions with the prospective trainee, the latter could very well have a cause of action for a breach of contract against either the hospital, the training director, or both. It is, therefore, very important that the precise scope and depth of the instruction be specifically delineated before the trainee enters the program and, further, that the training director make every effort to assure that these materials are in fact covered.

Potential Liability to Future Patients of the Trainee

Once the trainee finishes formal training and enters private practice, he or she should be able to practice independently, without any need for supervision. The question may well be asked, would a patient injured by an ex-trainee sue the lat-

ter's training director? Would he or she have a cause of action against the training director or the institution?[4] If the patient alleged that the training director was negligent in allowing the trainee to complete formal training and enter private practice, because he or she was not yet fully competent, could those allegations be proved? This question may seem farfetched to the reader of this book, yet there is one case in which a patient sued the college at which a chiropractic physician had his training.[5] This case underscores the ends to which the modern plaintiff's lawyer will go in an attempt to establish as broad a base of liability as possible, and hence garner as much in the way of funds as possible to compensate the client in the event of a plaintiff's verdict.

It seems clear that the training director is exposed, at least potentially, to liability from many sources.[6] Careful selection of candidates for the training program, careful adherence to educational standards, meticulous record keeping as far as the trainee's progress is concerned, and assuring that both the institution and the trainee live up to the provisions of the training contract—all will help assure that each newly graduated trainee will be someone of whom everyone can be proud and who will enter the anesthesia profession thoroughly capable of delivering the best possible anesthesia care.

THE IMMEDIATE SUPERVISOR

Supervisors are exposed to liability for inadequate supervision.[7] Would they be liable because of unavailability? This question relates directly to the staff-to-trainee ratio and to the intensity and quality of supervision available during evenings, nights, and weekends. Each of these elements deserves specific comment.

Staff-Trainee Ratio

No one would dispute that the ideal ratio would be one staff person for each trainee. Schools of nurse anesthesia generally endeavor to achieve this ratio. It is, however, probably neither practical nor achievable in anesthesiology residency programs. A ratio of 1 to 2 is more realistic. During the initial phase of the trainee's operating room experience, it is obvious that this ratio must be 1 to 1, or as close to that as possible. How long this intensive supervision lasts will depend upon the progress of the trainee and the complexities of the cases assigned. Unless the overall staff-to-trainee ratio is 1 to 1, it is apparent that whenever a new trainee is working in the operating suite, the staff member who might ordinarily be covering several rooms is restricted to the one room in which the trainee is working. Hence, while a ratio of 1 to 2 appears adequate "on paper," these ratios do suffer adversely when new trainees first begin their clinical exposure.

The question of liability of the individual supervisor will also depend upon a number of other factors. Incompetent supervision obviously will lead to potential liability.[7,8] On the other hand, what if a competent supervisor was in the process of covering another emergency when a trainee called for help?[9] Provision must always be made for the availability of a substitute supervisor under such circumstances. Lack of adequate supervision because of the presence of an excessive number of complicated cases requiring supervision on a one-to-one basis could expose the head of the department, or the institution itself,[10] to liability. In such a situation, the lawyer for the injured party, through interrogatories, depositions, and requests for production of records* such as assignment schedules, would endeavor to determine the adequacy of the staffing pattern at the time of the incident generating the lawsuit. The ready availability to the lawyer of this information, through appropriate discovery procedures, bespeaks the importance of maintaining current, accurate assignment rosters, and making certain that the staffing pattern reflected in those rosters is adequate.

Night Coverage

The incident cited earlier, involving failure to accurately apprise the staff on call of the condition of a candidate for an emer-

---

*For a discussion of the maneuvers used to obtain documents and other information from opponents during litigation, see Chapter 23.

gency operation, leads to an important question. What would be the potential liability of the supervising staff if he or she were *not notified at all* about a pending case? Members of the staff certainly are not expected to be clairvoyant, and come to the hospital without notification. Each teaching department should have a firm policy in reference to staff notification. If the problem is obviously one not requiring staff notification, that policy too should be set forth in the staff coverage guidelines of the department. A competent trial lawyer representing an injured plaintiff will name as an individual defendant the member of the staff who was on call, even though he or she was not notified about the pending case. Naming such an individual would relieve the lawyer of any allegations of legal malpractice on his or her part, that is, failure to make an essential person a party-defendant in the action. The fact that there might be sound legal grounds for naming the staff member as a defendant obviously would be of little solace to that individual, who frequently is not notified about impending cases that customarily would not require either notification or presence of a member of the staff. Unfortunately, that is one of the vicissitudes of being a supervisor in today's medical-legal climate.

RIGHTS, DUTIES, AND POTENTIAL LIABILITY OF TRAINEES

Contract law, as it pertains to the contract for health care, is covered in Chapter 2. Each party to every contract owes the other certain duties, duties that the courts consider to be legally enforceable. Each trainee has a contract, generally a written one, with the institution. This contract imposes certain duties upon both the institution and the trainee; the other party possesses correlative rights that these duties will be carried out.

Rights of Trainees

Trainees have certain rights. The *corollary* of a *right* is a *duty*. The duties of the institution to the trainee are threefold:

1 Furnish room and meals, or the equivalent stipend, as set forth in the agreement as the time the training process begins
2 Pay the agreed salary
3 Make available a patient load sufficient to expose the trainee to a broad-based clinical experience, as required by the accreditation agency

The training director has three duties to the trainee:

1 Provide the trainee with (preferably) written criteria used in the selection process (to help the trainee understand the importance of the admission requirements), and a written outline of the goals to be met before completion of or graduation from the program
2 Furnish academic instruction, including lectures, conferences, and accessibility to library materials
3 Furnish clinical experience of increasing complexity, with adequate supervision and, ultimately, increasing independence

The trainee must be made aware at the start of the program of the requirements for its successful completion. Such criteria usually include maintenance of a predetermined grade in each major subject area; demonstration of professional growth and acquisition of technical skills and academic knowledge meeting the program's and accreditation agency's requirements; presentation of case discussions; making other oral presentations; and, possibly, completion of a scholarly research project or paper for publication.

The purpose of being on notice of these pedagogical goals is obvious. The purpose of the training director's last two duties is also obvious; they are the primary reason why the trainee entered the program. Each trainee must attain sufficient intellectual expertise to have a reasonable chance at passing the written examination of the ABA or Council on Certification, and both intellectual and technical expertise to be able to administer safe anesthesia in a clinical practice setting. It is the responsibility of the institution to fulfill the first two duties and a portion of the last. The training director, acting as an agent of the institution, is re-

sponsible for assuring that both the didactic instruction and supervised clinical experience are adequate. If a trainee could prove that a program intended to lead toward board eligibility or council certification did not live up to the standards of the respective accreditation body, and could further prove that his or her failure to pass the qualifying examinations and become certified was not related to any failure on the trainee's part to apply himself or herself, that trainee might have a valid cause of action for breach of contract.

Considering the litigious climate that exists in this country today, such an action is within the realm of possibility. The most obvious defense—that the trainee did not apply himself or herself, or did not have the correct aptitude—will be bolstered by those records documenting the progress of the trainee, his or her (lack of regular) attendance at lectures and conferences, and the results of examinations of the trainee regularly conducted during his or her progression through the program.

Duties of Trainees

The trainee has duties both to the department and to the patients to whom he or she will be administering anesthetics. Duties to patients, discussed in Chapter 2 as they apply to all health care providers, include:

1 Practicing at the professed level of care, that is, as a resident in anesthesiology or student nurse anesthetist
2 Making full disclosure, that is, obtaining the patient's informed consent prior to the administration of an anesthetic*
3 Respecting confidences, that is, not divulging outside the health care setting private information obtained about a patient during history taking and evaluation of physical and laboratory findings
4 Offering continuing treatment
5 Seeking consultation when indicated

---

*Note: *Application of the informed consent doctrine in the teaching hospital differs somewhat from that in the nonteaching hospital; it deserves special consideration* and is discussed later in this chapter.

We cannot stress strongly enough the importance of trainees keeping foremost in mind the fifth just-cited duty, and adhering to it meticulously.

Duties of the trainee to the institution and training program are fivefold:

1 Arriving for work well-rested
2 Applying oneself fully and enthusiastically to the academic and clinical instruction
3 Attending and participating in departmental conferences, and all other formal and informal activities of the training program
4 Fulfilling the requirements for completion of the program
5 Maintaining a permanent record of clinical experiences as required by and in support of accreditation requirements

Normally, at the time a trainee applies for entrance into a residency or program for nurse anesthetists, he or she will be supplied with certain material covering some of these duties. It is the responsibility of the training director to be certain that the trainee is put on *actual, written* notice of these duties so that he or she may not later complain of unawareness of them. Although the prospective trainee may not enter into a formal written contract with the institution, it is desirable that the duties of the trainee, as well as those of the institution (which become the correlative rights of the trainee), be specifically delineated in the written documents supplied to the trainee at the start of the program. Making this information available will alleviate much future misunderstanding, especially if steps must be taken to terminate the trainee because of incompetence or for other reasons.

Potential Liability of Trainees

The trainee who is functioning independently must be aware of his or her own limitations and must keep the duty to seek consultation when indicated (see above) foremost in mind. *There is no place for the possession of excessive pride while undergoing training.* Knowing when to call for help and then doing so are not signs of ignorance, weakness, or inadequacy. They are

signs of an intelligent human being who recognizes that a problem exceeds his or her expertise and that help only can come from someone of greater expertise—a senior trainee or member of the staff. The trainee who calls for help when it is needed will be taking a major step toward gaining increasing independence as well as being assigned future cases of increasing complexity.

Each trainee can be held personally liable for his or her own negligence.[11] For this reason, trainees should either purchase their own professional liability insurance or be assured, via a written contract or other document, that coverage will be afforded them by the institution. These authors advise trainees to have such a statement in writing. This statement should be signed by either the chief of the anesthesia service or a responsible member of the hospital's administrative staff. In at least one case, a member of the house staff was sued by the institution to recover moneys paid as a result of litigation stemming from an act of alleged negligence of that individual.[11]

Clearly, the liability coverage afforded the trainee by the training institution would not cover activities outside the scope of his or her practice. It is mandatory that trainees who do engage in moonlighting purchase their own professional liability insurance with ample coverage.

Affiliation With Other Institutions

The significant degree of subspecialization within the specialty of anesthesia frequently mandates that trainees be sent to other institutions for those portions of their clinical exposure not available at the parent institution. The question of the liability of the parent versus the affiliated institution should the patient be injured by such a trainee frequently arises. Unfortunately, litigation may result when a resident commits an allegedly negligent act while on an affiliation.[7] The time to come to terms on the responsibility for indemnification is at the time the agreement for a formal affiliation is reached, *not* after the suit is filed. Both institutions involved should receive advice from their respective legal counsel, and a formal contract should be drawn up, specifying the responsibilities of each institution in such situations. Certain institutions may elect to assume the responsibility, and hence potential liability, of trainees from other institutions rotating through their service. Some institutions may require that the home institution of the trainee assume this responsibility. Certain advantages accrue to each arrangement. Whichever plan is utilized, the training directors at both institutions should be thoroughly familiar with the provisions of the agreement.

"Unofficial" Affiliation

This type of activity is commonly referred to as "moonlighting." It is our firm belief that residents should not be permitted to engage in any moonlighting without the express consent of the training director. Since this activity may broaden the trainee's experiences, as well as enhance his or her income, it may be beneficial in the long run to trainee, training director, and training program alike. It is important, however, that this activity not encroach upon the ability of the trainee to benefit from the clinical experiences and didactic material offered by the primary institution. Further, it is absolutely vital that such activity not produce trainees who come to work looking and feeling like "zombies." (A favorite question lawyers who represent patients in actions against institutions ask of house staff is, "How much sleep did you get the night before this accident occurred?") Those who moonlight must also understand that it is their responsibility to purchase their own professional liability insurance, unless of course the institution at which they are working agrees *in writing* to afford this coverage.

TERMINATION OF A TRAINEE

No matter how careful the process utilized in selecting candidates for anesthesia (or any other specialty for that matter) training, it should be obvious that some individuals simply do not have the aptitude for this type of work. They may be unable to remain alert in boring situations, ready to respond to an emergency on a moment's notice. They may lack sufficient self-confidence, so that they will not be able to function inde-

pendently. Or, there may be one or more of a host of other factors that preclude their becoming anesthesiologists or anesthetists capable of functioning competently and independently. For whatever reason, the termination process occasionally must be initiated. Over the years, a number of trainees have challenged their termination in court, and a significant body of pertinent case law has developed. The following discussion will summarize this case law and delineate the steps the training director must take to effectuate a legally effective termination.

Legal Underpinnings

The Fourteenth Amendment of the Constitution provides that *no person* shall be deprived of life, liberty, or property without *due process of law*. While it may be argued that a trainee has no inherent property right in his or her appointment within the program, once an individual has become a full-fledged member of the house staff or class of student nurse anesthetists, he or she has come into possession of some degree of property rights. In such situations, the courts have held that termination can only be achieved through due process. What is meant by due process? It is both substantive and procedural. Substantive due process means that each trainee must be required to meet the same criteria throughout the program and be graded on the same scale as all other trainees. That is, one cannot penalize one trainee for failing to progress faster or manage more difficult cases than other trainees. Procedural due process involves four elements—notice, hearing, representation, and the right of appeal, each of which deserves specific consideration.

Notice

As articulated by the courts in applying procedural due process, notice involves two elements. First, the trainee must be apprised of any deficiencies *before* the termination process is initiated, provided with information on how to correct them, and given an opportunity to do so. The notice should be specific, in writing, and given in a timely fashion. It should explain the action being taken and cite the reasons.

Generally, the reasons for probation or

dismissal can be grouped into one or several of three categories: academic, non-academic, and administrative. *Academic* reasons include failure to demonstrate minimum competency or personal attributes set forth in the evaluation plan of the program. *Nonacademic* reasons include failure to demonstrate dependability and conscientiousness in fulfilling pedagogical obligations; failure to maintain appropriate professional standards; lack of integrity; plagiarizing, or engaging in substance use or abuse. *Administrative* reasons include disability, prolonged absences, or requests for excessive personal or compassionate time off.

The trainee should acknowledge in writing receipt of the notice. At that point, the trainee may be placed upon probation. Generally, probationary status is a desirable prerequisite to formal termination. For this reason, many programs place each trainee on probation at the time he or she enters the program. If the trainee is apprised of the significance of this step, he or she should make extra efforts to complete the initial part of the program and pass from probationary to regular status in a timely fashion. Thus, initially placing trainees on probation is a sound idea. Furthermore, termination proceedings will be much more straightforward in the case of the trainee who from the beginning shows absolutely no aptitude, interest, scholarship, or other desirable traits.

Hearing

When the decision is made to formally terminate a trainee, he or she must be offered a hearing, which the trainee may decline. This offer, and any decision of the trainee to decline, must be in writing. At this time, formal allegations may be brought to the attention of the individual (in writing). That individual then should, according to relevant common law, have the opportunity to hear and question those who are advocating the termination, that is, testifying against him or her. The trainee must be given the right to present any mitigating factors or circumstances.

Representation

Courts have also held that those who do have a property right in an appointment also have the legal right to representation, either by a member of the legal profession or other person selected by them. This requirement only applies to situations in which the individual is in jeopardy of losing a legally accepted property right. It probably does not apply to the trainee during his or her initial probationary status. All trainees do have the right, however, to have others appear at the hearing and testify on their behalf.

Appeal

Finally, the courts have interpreted procedural due process to include the right of appeal. This right might not necessarily include appeal to a court of law, although if the aggrieved ex-trainee elected to sue the hospital, it would seem that some court would have to hear the case. The time allowed for the process of appeal should be limited to avoid protracted proceedings.

It is clear that the termination process involves the creation of an adversary relationship, in which the trainee is pitted against the institution. The ability of the institution to succeed in terminating the incompetent or otherwise undesirable trainee is greatly buttressed if the training director has kept accurate records of the progress of the trainee; mistakes of the trainee; and attendance of the trainee at the various seminars, meetings, and the like. Periodic testing of didactic knowledge, and of technical skills, can be of significant help in achieving successful termination of the trainee who has been determined not to be qualified to finish the program and, possibly, take the written examinations of the ABA or the Council on Certification. It should be obvious that all documentation involving termination proceedings must be kept on file for use in the event that the terminated trainee elects to litigate the issue.

INDEMNIFICATION OF PERSONNEL

It should be obvious that everyone in the health care delivery system must be protected against the catastrophic financial loss that might follow loss of litigation for professional negligence in that health care delivery. This protection, otherwise known as indemnification, conventionally has taken the form of professional liability insurance (see Chapter 29). Those professionals who are independent contractors (see Chapter 6) should purchase their own insurance, with an amount of coverage that is commensurate with their exposure. For example, if they are actively involved in the instruction of trainees, their exposure will probably be higher than their nonteaching colleagues, because of potential vicarious as well as additional prime liability.* If at all possible, their carrier should be the same as the one used by other members of the operating team, and the hospital as well.† Since the medical malpractice insurance crisis of the 1970s, a number of hospitals have become self-insured.[12] If the hospital plans to include members of its staff within the umbrella of its protection (either through self-insurance, the purchase of a deductible policy, or reinsurance), all hospital employees should be incorporated within the same plan or policy. Staff physicians and senior nursing personnel, including staff CRNAs, should be named *beneficiaries* under any such policy. If the hospital is self-insured, the employment contracts of these individuals should specifically reflect the hospital's intent to indemnify them for any professional negligence committed within the scope of their employment. It is also customary practice for hospitals to cover, through whatever modality selected, members of the house staff and other trainees. Medical schools should consider some form of indemnification of students who care for patients in the clinics or on the wards. (The subject of such protection for medical students is beyond the scope of both this chapter and Chapter 29.) It is our advice that the member of the

---

*If the trainee was considered to be a borrowed servant, the instructor would be vicariously liable for any negligence of the trainee; additionally, the plaintiff's lawyer might allege that the instructor was negligent in the process of supervision, and hence there was prime liability.

†If more than one carrier becomes engaged in complex litigation involving a number of members of the operating room team, disputes between carriers as to ultimate liability may ensue, in efforts to minimize the exposure of each individual carrier. The net result may be beneficial only to the plaintiff, inasmuch as lawyers for each carrier will endeavor to shift the blame to a defendant insured by one of the other carriers.

house staff who does not engage in moonlighting practices need not purchase insurance as long as the institution agrees *in writing* to afford coverage. A discussion of indemnification of house staff rotating through federal institutions is contained in Chapter 20. Physicians and nurses on active duty in one of the uniformed services or Public Health Service officially rotating through a private sector institution *may be covered* under the Federal Tort Claims Act, Gonzales Act, or similar legislation (see also Chapter 20). In one such case, however, the court held that a military physician partaking of residency training at a private hospital was a borrowed servant (see Chapter 6) and the United States was not liable for his acts.[13] Personal professional liability insurance protection obviously is necessary for those who moonlight (unless the institution at which this affiliation takes place agrees *in writing* to afford indemnification).

INFORMED CONSENT IN A PEDAGOGICAL SETTING

The doctrine of informed consent is covered in Chapter 9. The discussion here pertains solely to obtaining informed consent in the teaching situation. Several important issues may arise and must be addressed. For example, who should obtain informed consent? Should the patient be apprised of the role that trainees play in the care of that patient? And, should mention be made of agents or techniques that may be employed principally or solely for teaching purposes?

When a trainee will be responsible for the administration of the anesthetic, should he or she obtain this consent? There is no reason why a trainee should not obtain a patient's informed consent. The only *caveat* relates to the substantive nature of that disclosure. It is our opinion that trainees and their staff should adopt a more or less standardized disclosure, so that the trainee is disclosing the same risks as would the respective staff member *under similar circumstances*. That is, while the disclosure must be tailored to each patient's medical problems, contemplated operation, and proposed anesthetic and monitoring agents and techniques, the disclosure made to patients in similar circumstances must be the same, whether by staff or trainee.

The next issue relates to whether the patient should be told of the role that the trainee (or trainees) will play in the anesthetic administration. The preanesthetic visit *is not a time for evasion*. If patients ask, obviously they must be told. What if the patient does not ask? We have always felt, and taught, that individuals who are admitted to teaching hospitals should be considered to be on constructive notice (the law will *presume* that they were in possession of the information) of the role that trainees play in their care. Therefore, it is our opinion that the patient need not be specifically apprised of the activity of trainees, unless, of course, the patient inquires. Conversely, patients in community hospitals are not on such notice. Therefore, if trainees are assigned to a community hospital, the patients should be told of the role that trainees will play in their care. Times do change, however, and some departmental chairpersons in teaching hospitals may adopt a policy of full disclosure in all situations. There is, of course, no cogent reason for not doing so.

Are there any other concerns about the process of obtaining informed consent for anesthesia care during the educational process? We believe there are. For example, there might be situations in which certain procedures (e.g., invasive monitoring) are performed principally, or solely, for the education of a trainee. Inasmuch as such a procedure might pose a definite albeit limited risk, should the patient be apprised of that risk when informed consent is obtained? Frequently, photography is employed in the teaching hospital to illustrate an anesthesia or operative technique. What if the preparation of a videotape, motion picture, or series of still photographs will add 30 to 60 or more minutes onto the duration of the operative and anesthesia time? In spite of our best administrations, anesthesia is not without some risk, and the longer its duration, the greater that risk. Should the patient be counseled about this increased anesthesia and operative time, and his or her informed consent for this albeit slight increase in risk be obtained? We suggest that these factors be considered when germane to any teaching situation.

CONCLUSION

It is well known that we live in a litigious age and among a litigious society. Awareness by patients of other litigation, a breakdown in rapport, and other factors delineated in Chapter 7 suggest that those who participate in training programs, either at the level of the director, supervisor, or trainee, can expect increasing allegations of negligent conduct and potential exposure to liability in the coming years. This is an extremely unfortunate, but probably inevitable, consequence to engaging in anesthesia education today. Care in selecting trainees and assignment of cases to them, full implementation of pedagogical standards, up-to-date clinical and academic exposure of the trainees, and adequate supervision should contribute immeasurably toward promoting the delivery of quality anesthesia care and consequent minimization of incidents, accidents, untoward patient outcomes, and exposure to liability.

ADDENDUM

The problem of poor patient care afforded by the fatigued and unsupervised member of the house staff is the subject of a recent law review article.[14] The author cites examples of morbidity and mortality resulting from inadequate supervision coupled with judgment impaired by lack of sleep. One case that ended in a fatality resulted in a grand jury investigation. The American Council on Graduate Medical Education (ACGME) has promulgated guidelines for resident hours and supervision, to be defined by the residency review committees of the individual specialties. The author of this article believes these guidelines are inconsistent among the specialties and are not being uniformly implemented. The article reviews the theories of liability against the institution, and then comments on the potential personal liability of the house officers themselves. One lesson—*moonlight at your own risk!*[15] The final discussion concerns the program director who might ignore the ACGME guidelines.

The ACGME regulations will most likely charge the residency directors with enforcement of the Residency Review Committee's [for that particular specialty] recommendations. Heretofore, residency program directors generally have not been named as parties in lawsuits merely by virtue of their position as such. This may change, however, in light of the ACGME regulations, and the active role of program directors in the controversy surrounding these new rules.

Thus, residency program directors may find themselves named as defendants in all litigation involving allegations of resident negligence in this context. Moreover, residency program directors may be found liable for any discrepancy between the ACGME standards and any scheduling practices that lead to resident negligence.[16]

REFERENCES

1. Coleman v. Leffingwell, reported in *Time* (Nov. 2) 1970, p 36.
2. Barker v. Saltzman, 507 N.Y.S.2d 878 (N.Y.A.D. 1986).
3. The early cases alleging educational malpractice involved primary and secondary schooling; *but see* Huckaby v. Netterville, 263 So.2d 113 (La. App. 1972), wherein Mr. Huckaby, who had failed his bar examination three times, sued (unsuccessfully) his alma mater, Southern University Law School.
4. In two cases of alleged malpractice against chiropractors, the plantiffs also sued the Palmer College of Chiropractic, alleging that the College had improperly trained its graduates; the appellate court found for the College in both instances; *see* Salter v. Natchitoches Chiropractic Clinic, 274 s0.2d 490 (La. App. 1973); Moore v. Vanderloo, 386 N.W.2d 108 (Iowa 1986).
5. Salter v. Nachitoches Chiropractic Clinic, 274 So.2d 490 (La. App. 1973).
6. For a general review of case law containing allegations of professional negligence leveled against educators, see Morgan, D: Commentary: Liability for medical education. J Leg Med 8:305, 1987.
7. County of Riverside v. Loma Linda University, 118 Cal. App. 3d, 173 Cal. Rptr. 371 (1981); Morris v. Francisco, 238 Kan. 71, 708 P.2d 498 (1985).
8. Central Anesthesia Associates v. Worthy, 333 S.E.2d 829 (Sup. Ct. Ga. 1985) (patient injury associated with inadequate supervision of anesthesia assistant leading to liability of supervisor, anesthesiologist who should have been supervising, head of the anesthesia department, and institution; for a further discussion of this case, see Chapter 25).
9. *See* Battles v. Alderhold, 430 So.2d 307 (La. App. 3d 1983) (anesthesiologist supervising the transfusion of blood into a critically ill patient not liable for failure to respond to an emergency call for supervision in another operating room).
10. *See, generally,* Smith, JW: Vicarious liability. In Hospital Liability, §§ 3.02 *et seq.*, Law Journal-Seminars Press, New York, 1988.
11. Reported by Hall, CP: Professional liability insurance for the intern and resident. JAMA 193:55, 1965.
12. For a discussion of professional liability insurance and alternative coverage for hospitals, *see* Smith, JW: Hospital professional liability insurance. In Hospital Liability, §§ 5.01 *et seq.*, Law Journal-Seminars Press, New York, 1988.
13. Alfonso v. City of Boston, 587 F.Supp. 1342 (D.C. Mass. 1984).
14. *See, especially,* McNoble, DJ: Expanded liability of hospitals for the negligence of fatigued residents. J Leg Med 11:427, 1991.
15. Id. at 447.
16. Id. at 448.

20

William H. L. Dornette, M.D., J.D.

Practice in the Federal Sector

Anesthesia personnel working in the private sector may affiliate with or be assigned to a federal hospital. This practice is typified by the so-called Dean's Committee Veterans Administration (VA) Hospital that is affiliated with a private sector medical school. Additionally, many anesthesiologists and nurse anesthetists work full time in such hospitals. Some work for the Public Health Service. Finally, all branches of the uniformed services utilize anesthesiologists, nurse anesthetists, or both, as civilians and in uniform, in military hospitals in the continental United States and overseas. While the science and practice of medicine is essentially the same in both federal institutions and the private sector, there are vast differences as related to suing, and being defended against suits, for medical malpractice.

Before considering these differences, the reader should review the first three chapters of this book. Chapter 1 covers those aspects of health care law pertinent to all hospitals, both private sector and federal. This chapter serves as a supplement to Chapter 1, covering statutes and common law decisions that set federal practice apart from that in the private sector. These statutes include the Federal Tort Claims Act, the Gonzales Act and its VA and public health counterparts, and the Military Claims Act. Common law of import includes *Erie Railroad* and *Feres*. Chapter 2 covers the health care provider-patient relationship, which in essence is similar in both federal practice and the private sector. Chapter 3 reviews negligence law and the individual's exposure to liability. While negligence law is the same whether the act occurred in a federal or private setting, exposure of the individual to liability differs markedly. This difference, which is delineated in this chapter, should be understood by all who practice in federal health care facilities.

STATUTES AND COMMON LAW DECISIONS

The Erie Railroad Case

Trial courts customarily are bound by the common law set forth by the highest appellate court in the respective jurisdiction (generally the supreme court of that state). If the common law holding of a given state supreme court is favorable to a particular litigant, it would appear to be advantageous for that litigant to have his or her case tried within that jurisdiction, if at all possible. This process is called "forum shopping." An attempt at forum shopping became the focus of a famous 1938 decision of the Supreme Court of the United States, *Erie Railroad v. Tompkins.*[1]

Some time during the early 1930s Harry Tompkins was walking beside the Erie tracks in Hopkinsville, Pennsylvania, at 2:00 a.m. on a dark and moonless night. The footpath was on Erie Railroad property and located only 2 feet from the end of the cross-ties. An Erie freight train, traveling at 8 to 10 miles per hour, came by. A door on a refrigerator car happened to be unfastened. It swung open just as the car passed Harry. He was knocked down, and a car wheel severed his right arm. Harry hired a lawyer. The lawyer knew that in prior decisions the supreme court of Pennsylvania did not require companies to take extra precautions to prevent injuring trespassers. At law, Harry was a trespasser, since he was walking upon railroad property without permission. New York's highest court, on the other hand, required railroads to take precautions to avoid injuring trespassers. So Harry's lawyer filed suit in Federal District Court in New York State. He was able to obtain service of process there because the Erie had tracks in New York as well as in Pennsylva-

nia. The federal district judge, applying New York law, found for Harry and awarded him $30,000.

Lawyers for the railroad appealed, and the case ultimately reached the Supreme Court of the United States. That high court ruled against the concept of forum shopping, holding that the substantive law to be applied is that of the jurisdiction in which the allegedly tortuous incident occurred.

This decision has never been overturned. Thus, acts of alleged professional negligence of governmental employees, and hence the liability of the government, will be determined by the substantive law of the place where the allegedly tortuous act or omission occurred. It follows that a case involving a question of informed consent occurring in California would follow *Cobbs v. Grant,*[2] in Maryland, *Sard v. Hardy.*[3] When the Federal Tort Claims Act (see next section) was subsequently drafted, the Congress incorporated this legal principle as set forth in *Erie Railroad.*

The Federal Tort Claims Act

The origin and implication of sovereign immunity (freedom of a governmental entity from liability, derived from English Common Law) are discussed in Chapter 1. This concept has pervaded the American legal system. Governments, be they state, federal, or local, are simply immune from being sued, unless they waive this immunity by statute or ordinance. While there were limited waivers of immunity providing limited relief primarily for minor property claims, persons injured by the negligent act of an agent of the United States (e.g., a Postal Service driver delivering the mail) prior to World War II could not bring suit against the United States for their injuries. They could petition their senator or representative to file in the Congress a private bill of relief. This petition would be accompanied (in a case as just noted) by a police accident report (to establish liability) and automobile repair and medical invoices (to verify the damages). Needless to say, there was no paucity of these petitions. Members of Congress often were deluged with and inconvenienced by petitions, and much time at the end of each session of Congress was devoted to enacting these bills. Further, the legislators often had considerable difficulty in judging the merits of individual claims. These problems prompted the Congress in 1948 to enact the Federal Tort Claims Act (FTCA).[4]

This act waives the sovereign immunity of the United States government within a rather circumscribed area. This statute, as originally enacted, offered compensation only for acts of negligence committed by an agent (employee) of the United States acting within the scope of his employment,* and occurring within the United States, its territories and possessions. As an absolute condition precedent to filing suit, the injured party must first file an administrative claim, which should be initiated by the completion of a copy of *Standard Form 95*. The form is universal throughout the system and applies equally to cases of alleged medical malpractice, damage by Army tanks on maneuvers, sonic booms by military aircraft, or the like. The claim must be filed with the appropriate federal agency (or agencies if more than one is involved) within 2 years of the date of the accrual[†] of the claim. The Army, Navy, Air Force, Public Health Service, Veterans Administration, Postal Service, and other branches of the government each have their own claims services.

---

*The term "scope of employment" refers to the employee's specific duties and responsibilities. For example, an anesthesia trainee at a VA hospital might, officially and temporarily, be assigned to a children's hospital for exposure to pediatric cases. While performing training duties, the trainee would be "within the scope of employment," and the contract or agreement between the VA hospital and the children's hospital might specify that the U.S. government would assume responsibility for any act or acts of negligence of the trainee while on this affiliation. In a jurisdiction wherein the common law provides for the borrowed-servant doctrine (see Chapter 6), the trainee could be an employee of both the training hospital and the United States. On the other hand, the government would not cover "unofficial" affiliation (i.e., "moonlighting"), which would be "beyond the scope of employment."

†Accrual generally means the time the incident complained of took place, although in instances of alleged professional negligence, federal jurists have interpreted accrual to mean when the claimant became aware that the untoward result was caused by the health care.

The act specifies that the claimant has the right to bring suit after the expiration of 6 months from the date of receipt of the completed Standard Form 95. Regardless of the state of the claim, the claimant then may assume that the claim has been denied, and may file suit in a federal district court. (In cases involving alleged medical malpractice, most claimants will wait considerably longer before exercising their right to file a lawsuit, as it is well known that claims of this type may take longer to evaluate.) If the case does come to trial, it is decided by the judge, there being no right to trial by jury under the FTCA (although a judge may decide to use a jury to advise him or her). The Department of Justice, through the local assistant U.S. attorney, defends the government. Any judgment or settlement above $2500 is paid from the U.S. Treasury.

As noted above, as originally drafted and signed into law, the act provided that certain so-called intentional torts (see Chapter 5) would not be covered. This exception was subsequently modified relating to certain intentional torts committed within the health care setting. This modification, as it pertains to Veterans Administration and uniformed services health care providers, is discussed below.

The Feres Decision

When the FTCA was enacted, its provisions were made retroactive to the start of the Second World War. Three incidents involving death or injury to a service member resulted in the filing of claims, and subsequently lawsuits, following passage of this act.

Rudolph Feres, a lieutenant in the Army, was stationed at Pine Camp (now Ft. Drum), New York, during the early days of the war. The barracks in which he was housed caught fire, and he was unable to escape. After the passage of the FTCA, his widow sued the United States, alleging negligence in housing her husband.

The second case involved Arthur Jefferson, a noncommissioned officer who was ill during a major part of his military career. In the fall of 1944 he entered Ft. Belvoir Army Hospital where a cholecystectomy was performed by the chief of surgery. Some 8 months later, now discharged from the service, Jefferson was admitted to Johns Hopkins University Hospital because of continuing abdominal pain. A laparotomy revealed the presence of a towel measuring 18 x 30 inches and clearly identified as being the *Property of the Army Medical Department*. Jefferson retained legal counsel, and ultimately a lawsuit was filed on his behalf.

The third case stemmed from the death at Scott Field (now Scott Air Force Base) Hospital on November 17, 1947, of Lieutenant Colonel Dudley Griggs, U.S. Army, following an operative procedure. His widow also filed a claim and then a lawsuit.

The Supreme Court consolidated all three cases and in 1950 issued the famous *Feres* decision.[5] The substance of this opinion is that there is no right to file a claim, or a lawsuit, under the FTCA for injuries incident to active duty suffered by an active duty person.

The Military Claims Act

As noted above, the Federal Tort Claims Act does not cover torts arising in foreign countries. During the Second World War, Congress enacted the Military Claims Act.[6] This statute provides a somewhat more limited waiver of sovereign immunity than the FTCA, in that there is no ultimate right to trial. The remedy for those receiving an adverse ruling on a claim is an appeal to the secretary of the branch of the uniformed service having jurisdiction over the claim. This limitation gives broad powers to the respective claims service (Army, Navy, or Air Force) to effectuate settlements fair to both claimants and the United States. Customarily, a denial of an appeal by the secretary finally ended the matter. In recent years, however, plaintiffs' lawyers have found a method of "taking a second bite out of the apple," so to speak, as discussed below.

INDEMNIFICATION OF PERSONNEL

It is a common, and accepted, practice among trial lawyers to name as a party de-

fendant the institution, company, or other entity that has the greatest assets. This practice is only semifacetiously called the "deepest pocket doctrine." Thus, a lawyer would rather sue a physician than a nurse, a hospital than a physician, and a drug or equipment manufacturer rather than a hospital. Finally, the lawyer would prefer to sue the target with the greatest amount of assets of all, the U.S. government, rather than any private entity. When a Veterans Administration, Public Health Service, or uniformed services health care provider commits a proven act of negligence within the scope of his or her employment, the government would automatically be liable under the *respondeat superior* doctrine (discussed in Chapter 6). Lawyers are well aware of this application of agency law and very rarely (there are a few exceptions) name as an individual defendant a health care provider who was working for an agency of the United States. In spite of his dearth of cases, the Congress has felt it desirable, possibly to enhance recruitment, to adopt certain statutes specifically indemnifying (holding harmless, covering any losses) health care providers working in the federal sectors.

As noted earlier in this chapter, the FTCA initially provided in part that the sovereign immunity of the United States will be waived in cases of alleged negligence committed by an agent of the United States acting within the scope of his or her employment and committed within the United States, its territories and possessions. The terms *act of negligence* and *committed within the scope of his or her employment* must be stressed. For some years, federal health care personnel have been made statutorily immune (a freedom from liability created by statute). The provisions of these statutes, discussed below, differ slightly among each branch of the government's health care activities.

Veterans Administration Personnel

The provisions granting statutory immunity to personnel of the Department of Medicine and Surgery of the VA are contained in Title 38 of the U.S. Code. This statute provides in part:

The remedy . . . for damages for personal injury, including death allegedly arising from malpractice or negligence of a physician, dentist, podiatrist, optometrist, nurse, physician assistant, expanded-function dental auxiliaries, pharmacists, or paramedical (for example medical and dental technicians, nursing assistants and therapists) or other supporting personnel in furnishing medical care or treatment while in the exercise of such person's duties in or for the Department of Medicine and Surgery shall hereafter be exclusive of any other civil action or proceeding by reason of the same subject matter against . . . [such professionals or paraprofessionals].[7]

Additionally, the statute provides that the attorney general shall defend any such civil action, and, further, that if the civil action is brought in a state court against the individual health care provider, it will be removed by the assistant U.S. attorney to a federal court, and the United States will be substituted as the defendant. This statute was first adopted in 1965.[8] It has been amended several times since then, and its present wording, cited above, appears to offer coverage to all persons who directly care for patients in the VA's Department of Medicine and Surgery.

Public Health Service Personnel

Statutory immunity is granted Public Health Service personnel under Title 42.[9] This portion of the statute was enacted in 1970. It provides statutory immunity:

for damage for personal injury, including death, resulting from the performance of medical, surgical, dental or related functions, including the conduct of clinical studies or investigation, by any commissioned officer or employee of the Public Health Service while acting within the scope of his office or employment.[9]

The subsequent provisions of this statute are similar to those noted following the discussion of 38 U.S.C. § 4116, above.

Uniformed Services Health Care Personnel

Their indemnification statute, commonly known as the *Gonzales Act*, was enacted in 1976.[10] By virtue of 1982 amendments to FTCA, National Guard personnel are covered while on training duty or federal function.[11] This statute provides, in part:

The remedy against the United States for damages for personal injury, including death, caused by the negligent or wrongful act or omission of any physician, dentist, nurse, pharmacist, or paramedical or other supporting personnel (including medical and dental technicians, nursing assistants and therapists) of the Armed Forces, the National Guard while engaged in training or duty, the Department of Defense or the Central Intelligence Agency in the performance of the medical, dental, or related health care function (including clinical studies and investigations) while acting within the scope of his duties or employment therein or therefore, shall hereafter be exclusive of any other civil action or proceeding by reason of the same subject matter.[11]

The statute then provides a similar mandate to the attorney general to defend the proceeding and, if the action is brought against the individual health care provider in civil court, to remove the case to federal court and substitute the United States as the defendant.

From reading these statutes, it is apparent that anesthesia personnel are protected by statutory immunity afforded by the respective law, no matter which service branch they are serving in, as long as they remain within the confines of the United States, its territories and possessions. Whereas the wording of each of these immunity statutes is different, it is clear that health care personnel are treated essentially the same in all three government services. In the case of Public Health Service and the uniformed services, civilian employees as well as uniformed personnel are included in this protection. This means that health care personnel need not purchase professional liability insurance (unless, of course, they plan to moonlight in the private sector). In fact, it is the recommendation that they *do not* purchase such coverage. Were a member of the plaintiff's trial bar to learn of one of these policies, he or she might be tempted to sue the individual health care provider, necessitating a removal action (described above) and possibly complicating the defense problems.

The decision of whether to defend is to be

made by the United States. If the United States does defend, the government then is substituted as the defendant. If not, the physician remains the defendant, and his or her name could be placed in the National Data Bank created under the Health Care Quality Improvement Act[12] (see Figure 7-3 and Chapter 29).

In 1988 the Congress enacted the Federal Employees Liability Reform Act (FELRA),[13] which immunizes all federal employees from individual suit for "in-scope" acts. Inasmuch as this act did not repeal the above-referenced immunity statutes,[7–8] how they will be interpreted together ultimately will have to be decided by the courts. It is important to note that the FELRA contains no intentional tort exception, as do the other acts.

One must reiterate, however, that this protection is only afforded when the act is committed within the scope of employment.

In a recent case, an Army nurse was sued by a patient who alleged that the nurse had struck her. The Department of Justice certified that the nurse's actions were within the scope of her employment and moved to have the case transferred to the federal district court and the United States substituted as the defendant. The federal district judge overruled the Department of Justice's certificate, holding that the nurse's act was not within the scope of her employment and remanded the case to state court for trial on the merits.[14]

Thus, if an act is not compensable under the Federal Tort Claims Act, immunity would not be afforded by one of the just-cited statutes.

Recent Case Law Involving Personnel Serving Overseas

The past several years have seen lawsuits being filed in the United States against health care providers for care rendered in an area not covered by either the FTCA or Gonzales Act. A 1987 decision[15] of the Fifth Circuit Court of Appeals held that a civilian injured by an act of alleged medical malpractice could sue the health care provider in the country in which the injury took place. Two other appellate courts (ninth and eleventh circuits) in more recent decisions[16] have held that the allegedly errant health care provider may be sued in the United States upon his or her return there. The power to file such actions does not hinge on the outcome of any proceeding under the Military Claims Act. It should be noted that the assistant U.S. attorney will provide a defense, unless the employee desires to provide his or her own counsel or is insured. Any settlement or judgment may be paid by the government, in a manner similar to claims under the FTCA, if the requisite preconditions are met. These require that the United States be provided notice of the suit and afforded an opportunity to participate in any ensuing trial or settlement. These decisions should alert those practicing overseas to exercise extra care in treating their patients.

CONCLUSION

All anesthesia personnel who work for, or are temporarily assigned to work in, any U.S. government hospital should understand the various statutes and common law decisions cited in this chapter. They should be aware of the concept of sovereign immunity and how that immunity is waived by the Federal Tort Claims Act. They should fully understand the limitations imposed by that act. They should be aware of the concept of statutory immunity created by the sections of the U.S. Code cited in the preceding discussion. If persons working in each of the three health care delivery systems allow U.S. participation in any individual suits against them, they may be indemnified by the respective individual statute and do not need to purchase professional liability insurance. Should an act of alleged negligence occur within the scope of their employment and representation is requested, the U.S. attorney's office will take over defense of the case, and any judgment or settlement can be paid from the U.S. Treasury. The decision to defend, which must be made by the government, can have far-reaching implications for the health care provider, as noted above.

Statutory immunity obviously does not confer the right to practice just as one sees fit. The standard of care in these hospitals is the same as in the private sector, possibly even a little higher. Personnel who are working under the protection of this statutory immunity should be aware of their duties to their patients as well as their duties to their profession, to their country, and to themselves. Civilian personnel who commit acts of gross negligence can be subjected to disciplinary proceedings. Those on active duty can be court-martialed under the Uniform Code of Military Justice.

REFERENCES

1. Erie Railroad v. Tompkins, 304 U.S. 64 (1938).
2. Cobbs v. Grant, 104 Cal. Rptr. 505, 502 P.2d 1 (Sup. Ct. 1972).
3. Sard v. Hardy, 281 Md. 432, 379 A.2d 1014, 89 ALR3d 12 (C.A. 1977).
4. 28 U.S.C. § § 1346(b), 2671 *et seq.*
5. Feres et al. v. U.S., 340 U.S. 135 (1950).
6. 10 U.S.C. § 2733 (1948).
7. 38 U.S.C. § 4116.
8. 28 U.S.C. § 2680(e).
9. 42 U.S.C. § 233.
10. 10 U.S.C. § 1089.
11. 32 U.S.C. § 334.
12. 42 U.S.C. §§ 11101 *et seq.* (1986).
13. Signed into law on May 20, 1988, and codified in 38 U.S.C. § 4116(f).
14. Mitchell v. United States, 709 F.Supp. 767 (W.D.-Tex. 1989).
15. Powers v. Schultz, 821 F.2d 295 (C.A.5-Tex. 1987).
16. Newman v. Soballe, 871 F.2d 969 (C.A.-11 1989); Smith v. Marshall, 885 F.2d 650 (C.A.9-Cal. 1989).

21

Donald E. Demkee, D.D.S.

Anxiety and Pain Control in Dentistry

No other discipline within the healing arts profession is more dependent on anesthesia than dentistry. Furthermore, there is perhaps no other health care professional who, on a case-by-case, day-by-day basis is more knowledgeable in the use of local anesthesia of the maxillomandibular region than the dentist. Dentists do not, however, limit themselves to regional anesthesia as the only modality for pain control.

General anesthesia has become a major component in dentists' armamentarium, especially that of the oral surgeon. As everyone realizes, great strides have been made in the use of this technique since the founding father of general anesthesia, a dentist, demonstrated his ether inhaler in Boston's Massachusetts General Hospital surgical amphitheater in 1846. Dental anesthesia today must be thought of as a total spectrum of pain relief, from the "shot of Novocain" to the production of a totally unconscious state.

THE VICISSITUDES OF PAIN CONTROL

The safe administration of anesthetic agents in the dental office involves a number of carefully calculated steps, including assessing the patient's medical condition, selecting the appropriate agent and technique, obtaining the patient's informed consent to all procedures, administering that or those agents, monitoring the patient during and following use of the agent(s), and preparing a record that accurately reflects this administration. Each step deserves special emphasis.

The Patient's Medical History

One cannot stress strongly enough the importance of obtaining an accurate and complete history from a patient (see also Chapter 8). Failure to be aware of a patient's compromised cardiovascular status (e.g., because of hypertension), coupled with an apparent inadvertent intravenous injection of a local anesthetic containing epinephrine, could result in the patient suffering a cerebrovascular accident in the dental chair, with subsequent liability.[1,2] The following case,[3] while not involving any form of anesthesia, is illustrative of the strong admonition to obtain a complete history.

In some uniformed services dental clinics, military retirees are treated on a "space available" basis. One such retiree was awaiting a prophylactic cleaning. On the medical history form he checked "high blood pressure" and "heart disease" as problems in his past medical history. His blood pressure was taken and noted to be normal; no one asked him about the nature of the heart disease. A cancellation of an appointment by an active-duty person resulted in space becoming available. The cleaning was carried out. Three weeks later the retiree developed subacute bacterial endocarditis, for which he required hospitalization. He sued the United States, alleging negligence in performing the cleaning without

first initiating prophylactic penicillin therapy. The retiree had valvular heart disease, and later admitted he had been warned he should always receive prophylactic penicillin before having any procedures, including dental cleaning. When asked why he had not volunteered this important information, the retiree stated he assumed that the dentist had access to the information, inasmuch as it was on his dental records which were on file in the clinic. He also indicated that had he informed the dentist, he would have had to have taken penicillin and waited for it to become effective, thereby missing the "space-available" open appointment!

It obviously is imperative that each practitioner obtain a *complete* medical history before *any* therapy is initiated. The questioning must be probing. At times, keeping current all patients' health records may be overlooked. It may be thought unnecessary if the patient appears perfectly healthy. The astute practitioner, though, routinely inquires of each patient if there has been any change in his or her medical history subsequent to the prior visit. Even though patients may be under the care of a physician, the dentist still has a responsibility to verify the current status of their health.

Local Anesthesia

Almost 3 million local anesthetics are given in dental offices every year. Since the introduction of cocaine in 1884, many synthetic regional agents have been developed and marketed, starting with procaine in 1905. Many of these newer "caine" drugs reportedly possess more efficacy and less systemic or local toxicity than compounds of an earlier era. While regional agents tend to be inherently much safer than those that produce loss of consciousness and protective reflexes, serious complications can follow the use of regional anesthetics. A history of allergy to Novocain should alert one to the possibility of reactions to any kind of local anesthetic. Some of the newer regional agents are reported not to have the potentiality for producing a procainelike allergic reaction. It is important, nevertheless, to assess each patient's history accurately.

Skin testing should be conducted prior to the use of any of these new agents in any patient who gives a history of sensitivity. Even though the possibility of an allergic reaction would be in the realm of one in a million, the dentist still could be found liable for failing to question the patient and perform appropriate testing, or substitute another technique of anesthesia. Some practitioners recommend that patients with underlying cardiac, vascular, or respiratory disorders be examined by a physician shortly before undergoing any form of dental anesthesia. It is important to be certain that the examining physician fully understands the nature of the proposed dental procedure and associated pain or anxiety control in order to assess the total exposure of the patient fully. Frequently, only the dentist is completely aware of the problems posed by the contemplated therapy.

Beyond Local Anesthesia

When local anesthesia was the only modality employed for pain control, the techniques were readily understood and the legal issues far less complex than they are today. As the variety of techniques available for dental anesthesia has increased, so have associated complications, including morbidity and even mortality. Patient injuries in turn have forced the adoption of laws and administrative regulations (reviewed below) to regulate those who treat patients with something other than a "local."

To appreciate better these changes and the regulations evolving to address them, one should first review the altered states of consciousness employed in dentistry today. Every anesthesiologist, nurse anesthetist, and trainee in these areas understands the concept of general anesthesia. The Ohio State Dental Board in one of its administrative rules (adopted to regulate use of these techniques, as discussed below), defines *general anesthesia* as

> *A controlled state of unconsciousness, accompanied by partial or complete loss of protective reflexes, including inability to independently maintain an airway and respond purposefully to physical stimulation or verbal command, produced by a pharmacological or non-pharmacological, or a combination thereof.*[4]

In an effort to avoid the extremes of general (excessive depression with loss of protective reflexes) and local anesthesia (little anxiety control), dental practitioners during the 1970s developed two new techniques called *relative analgesia* and *conscious sedation*. Relative analgesia employs a variety of agents (including nitrous oxide in subanesthetic dosage) to produce pain relief without loss of consciousness or the use of a regional anesthetic. This technique thus allows the patient's protective reflexes to remain fully functional. Conscious sedation employs similar agents to sedate the patient, again without producing loss of consciousness. The Ohio State Dental Board defines *conscious sedation* as

> *A minimally depressed level of consciousness that retains the patient's ability to independently and continuously maintain an airway and respond appropriately to physical stimulation and verbal command, produced by a pharmacological or non-pharmacologic method, or a combination thereof.*[5]

Note the emphasis on "the ability to *independently and continuously maintain an airway.*" Clearly, the board is acutely aware of the potential risk of not doing so! The board also recognizes that it may be desirable to achieve a level of depression between conscious sedation and general anesthesia, and has included in its administrative regulations a definition of *deep sedation*, namely,

> *A controlled state of depressed consciousness, accompanied by partial loss of protective reflexes, including inability to respond purposefully to verbal command, produced by a pharmacologic or non-pharmacologic method, or combination thereof.*[6]

As states adopt administrative regulations for the use of general anesthesia, parenteral sedation, and nitrous oxide analgesia (see, e.g., Appendix 21-1), review of these regulations gives one a better appreciation of the widespread use of these techniques. One also obtains an inkling of the changing statutory and administrative laws that are being adopted to promote safety in the use of these techniques. As a dentist adds "a little something else" to his local anesthetic, or substitutes parenterally administered agents for the local, the patient approaches an altered state of sedation or even general anesthesia, with a concomitant *loss* of ability to *independently and continuously maintain an airway*. Consequently, a different set of laws or regulations controls that dentist's acts.

Informed Consent

The doctrine of informed consent is well accepted in this country (see Chapter 9). It applies to dental practice as well as medicine and other branches of the healing arts. The practitioner should inform each patient of the risks (if any) and benefits of the methodology of anxiety and pain control that will be employed. This disclosure should be made at the same time consent for the dental procedure is obtained. The fact that the patient's consent to both the anxiety or pain control and the dental procedure was obtained should be clearly documented in the office records.

Preparation and Administration

Traditionally, the alternative to regional anesthesia was a general anesthetic, frequently associated with the use of an endotracheal catheter. With the myriad of techniques now available for relative analgesia and conscious sedation, pure general anesthesia is an exception rather than the rule. Office anesthesia has, in truth, evolved into a new era, with many variables that must be addressed. I think patients have the feeling that to be "out" means simply going to sleep—something that is as complex as falling off a log. Such, of course, is not true. Giving the patient a mind-altering drug can be potentially hazardous under any circumstances, but especially in a nonhospital, ambulatory setting.

Perhaps foremost in the preparation of the candidate for relative analgesia or conscious sedation is the admonition "nothing by mouth" for *a minimum of at least 8 hours* before induction of anesthesia. The patient should be completely informed of the risks as well as benefits of the proposed course of action, and the risks and benefits of any alternative forms of pain or anxiety control. The patient must be made aware of these various possibilities, and the patient's informed consent obtained, not only

for the dental procedure but also for the anesthesia or sedation.

Furthermore, not only the individual administering the sedation but also the entire staff must be trained to recognize, evaluate, and treat—all in a timely fashion—any emergency that can arise during or following these procedures. Appropriate equipment and drugs, as well as oxygen, must be *readily* available. All office personnel must be aware of the location of these various therapeutic modalities, and the role of each in any emergency resuscitation. Patients who are having more than a local anesthetic must receive added attention, both during and following the procedure, as compared with those receiving only a local. Monitoring, too, must be more complete.

Monitoring

The subject of monitoring is covered in Chapter 12. It is my opinion that when general anesthesia is being administered, the monitoring practices in the dental office must be comparable to those carried out when general anesthesia is being employed in any ambulatory care facility (see also Chapter 15). I recommend the use of a blood pressure cuff and stethoscope, a digital oximeter–pulse-rate detector (MUI-5000), and electrocardiographic monitor with continuous display on an oscilloscopic screen.

Documentation

It should be obvious that the dentist's records must be thorough, accurate, and legible. Sketchy records, with a paucity of entries, do not create a positive image. The therapeutic agents administered, their dosage, the vital signs, and other events should be recorded accurately, along with the time of each event.

One cannot emphasize strongly enough the importance of not altering any record, or attempting to postdate any entries on it. Obliteration, alteration, or concealing the fact that entry was made after the fact, is called *spoliation.** When such an event oc-

---

*A legal term referring to alteration of documents or otherwise tampering with evidence; see Chapter 10. [Ed.]

curs and is discovered, the credibility of the person who committed the spoliation, and whatever defense he or she may have, will be lost forever. Everyone should realize that document analysis techniques now are available for determining the age of records, and whether entries were later inserted.

Introducing New Drugs

Each year a number of new agents are brought onto the market. Those who utilize these agents must keep abreast with the standard of care. Are the newer agents more efficacious, or safer, or both? The practitioner has a recognized duty to keep abreast of any change in the standard of care, and to be aware of how these new agents potentially fit into his or her armamentarium. Thus, the practitioner who understands the chemistry, pharmacology, applications, and contraindications of the new agent, and any potential interaction with the patient's medical problems, will be able to utilize the new agents as appropriate and deliver an even higher level of care.

THE CHANGING DENTAL PRACTICE ACTS

Traditionally, the granting of a license by a state dental board was all that was needed to practice dentistry in that jurisdiction. By virtue of the license the dentist could perform all acts relating to dentistry, including the administration of local and general anesthesia. Such is no longer the case, however. Augmentation of dental practice acts started in the late 1960s as a result of the number of unfortunate incidents involving one general dentist who was administering general anesthesia in Alaska. In 1970 a statute was passed amending Alaska's Dental Practice Act.[7] This amendment mandated that dental practitioners who would administer general anesthesia must have a special permit from the state Dental Board of Examiners.

The enactment of this amendment was only the beginning. Stricter control has spread across the entire United States. As of March 1989, licensing regulations in essentially all jurisdictions either regulate, or

have the power to regulate, general anesthesia practice in some way. Dental boards in all but seven states require permits for "intravenous or parenteral sedation," and permits for the use of nitrous oxide are required by 21 dental boards.[8] The state of Ohio offers a good example of this legislative activity and administrative rule making. The practice of dentistry is regulated by Chapter 4715 of the Ohio Revised Code. The dental board is mandated to regulate practitioners' use of sedatives:

> In accordance with Chapter 119 of the Revised Code, the board shall adopt, and may amend or rescind, rules establishing the eligibility criteria, the application and permit renewal procedures, and safety standards applicable to a dentist licensed under this chapter who applies for a permit to employ or use conscious intravenous sedation. These rules shall include all of the following:
>
> (1) The eligibility requirements and application procedures for an eligible dentist to obtain a conscious intravenous sedation permit;
> (2) The minimum educational and clinical training standards required of applicants, which shall include satisfactory completion of an advanced cardiac life support course [emphasis supplied];
> (3) The facility equipment and inspection requirements;
> (4) Safety standards;
> (5) Requirements for reporting adverse occurrences.[4]

Earlier versions of this section of the code date back to 1953. This latest version was enacted by the 1988 Ohio General Assembly, and became effective June 27, 1988.

At the time of this writing, Ohio has 6213 licensed dentists; 362 general anesthesia permits have been issued.[9] The requirements for obtaining such a permit are detailed in Appendix 21-1, and include completion of 1 year of advanced training in anesthesia and related academic subjects (or equivalent) beyond the undergraduate dental school (DDS) level.[10] These programs are described in Part 2 of the *Guidelines of Teaching the Comprehensive Control of Pain and Anxiety in Dentistry*, published by the American Dental Association (ADA).[11] These licenses are issued following both certification that the practitioner has had this training and an on-site evaluation of the practitioner, his or her staff, and operatory and other facilities by one or more representatives of the licensing board. Thus the dental profession, through its licensing board, as well as influence on state legislators, has responded to the need for safety (and occasionally public outcries). Clearly, a license to practice dentistry today no longer gives *carte blanche* to practice in any way that one sees fit.

MALPRACTICE IN DENTAL ANESTHESIA

Malpractice is negligence in a professional setting. Negligence is a breach of the duty or standard of care, followed by an injury proximally caused by that breach (see also Chapter 3). In 1971 the ADA approved the guidelines of the American Dental Society of Anesthesiology (ADSA). These guidelines are continuously upgraded and revised by the ADSA and ADA. They act as a national format for teaching pain and anxiety control. *They also set the standard of care.* The administration of anesthesia without the proper education outlined within these guidelines most probably would lead to allegations of a breach of the standard of care if an act caused an injury to a patient and litigation ensued.

Efforts are being made to assure that practitioners adhere to these standards. The various state organizations of oral and maxillofacial surgeons, sometimes in conjunction with state dental boards, have ongoing programs of office evaluations. An *Office Anesthesia Evaluation Manual*[12] is published by the American Association of Oral and Maxillofacial Surgeons (AAOMS). Most visitation teams use this schedule. Such visits afford an almost continuous process of education, evaluation, and review. The process has shown very positive results. In 1984 the AAOMS conducted a survey covering practice during the prior year. Approximately 2,427,177 general anesthetics were given in the dental office; these resulted in eight fatalities. Of the 1,568,720 intravenous sedation procedures, five fatalities were reported. There were no fatalities reported as the result of 2,974,945 local anesthetics administered.[13] No other medical discipline can boast such statistics of safety and accomplishment.

Professional Liability Insurance

It should be fairly obvious that oral and maxillofacial surgeons' professional liability insurance premiums are costly. Figure 21-1 shows premiums over the past 16 years covering practice, including use of general anesthesia, in northeastern Ohio. While attention still is focused on the office anesthesia setting as the basis for these high rates, actions for alleged malpractice against all subspecialties of dental practice are on the rise. The average dental malpractice settlement in 1978 was $6600. This amount rose to $20,000 in 1982. That rise resulted in an increase of 100% in professional liability insurance premiums over that same interval. (The fall in the cost of oral and maxillofacial surgeons' premiums during the last 2 years is discussed below.)

It is not certain, however, whether the more or less progressive increase up to 1988 is secondary to actions arising from anesthesia-related problems, from the new techniques being utilized in dentistry and particularly oral-maxillofacial surgery, or a combination thereof. These techniques— implants, full mouth rehabilitation, and orthognathic surgery—are at once innovative, complex, and productive of both excellent functional and cosmetic results. Unfortunately, they are not without side effects and create exposure to liability heretofore not present following a simple filling or extraction. One example stands out—numbness of the lower lip appears to be the leading cause of action in dental malpractice cases. Given the ongoing office evaluation programs, the changes in state dental laws, and the constant awareness of maintaining a high level of anesthesia practice, it is the opinion of knowledgeable dental professionals that the increase in professional liability insurance premiums should not be tied solely to the current widespread use of general anesthesia in dental practice. Whatever the cause of this rise in costs, rightly or wrongly dentistry has "arrived"—to take its place among other litigation-targeted health care fields.

Mistakes have been and will always be made. But now, the large judgments and settlements that were once limited to the province of the medical profession have crept into dental practice (and of course

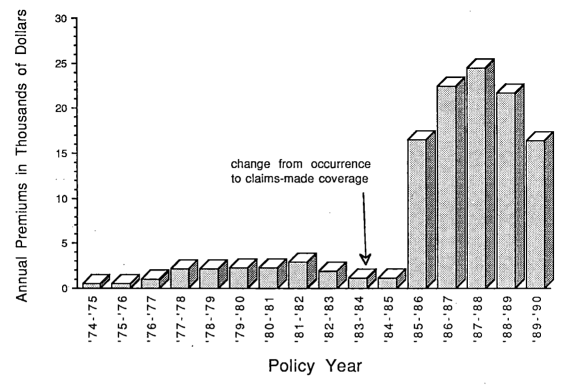

Figure 21-1 Professional liability insurance premiums for an oral and maxillofacial surgeon practicing in northeastern Ohio whose practice includes the administration of general anesthesia to ambulatory patients in his office. The fall in premiums during the last two years is discussed in the text.

into other professions as well, including law!). The attention of the public once again has been drawn to a newly recognized specialty of potential defendants, and an aggressive pursuit of dental practitioners by members of the bar appears to have commenced. The dental profession is not immune to society's current attitudes toward litigation. Social and economic trends have caused this increase, as they have in all the other health care professions (see the Preface and Chapters 7 and 29). Redress tomorrow for today's mistakes does generate large settlements or awards.

A carefully controlled profession will nonetheless promote a positive image. Thanks to the aforestated guidelines and the *AAOMS Manual,* the standard of care of all dentists who practice advanced anxiety and pain control has improved and is now of high quality. And it no longer is a so-called geographic or community standard, but rather a national one. In the advent of litigation stemming from dental

anesthesia, analgesia, or sedation, the same standard of care will be applied to those practicing in the "boondocks" as to a dentist utilizing a modern ambulatory care facility in a large city.

Attenuating the Risk

Taking into account the litigious attitude of society and the necessity of avoiding mistakes, what should practitioners do to avoid their turn in court? The importance of obtaining an adequate and complete medical history cannot be overstressed. One must never treat a stranger. One cannot reasonably and prudently treat patients when all is not known about them, their medications, and how the anticipated treatment will react with all. If one gets to know the patient's complete medical problems before any therapy is commenced, that patient is no longer a stranger. Failing to do so can result in an injury that is not readily defensible. Such efforts appear to be "paying off," so to speak, in the reduction of premiums during the past two policy years, as noted in Figure 21-1. It is, of course, uncertain whether this trend will continue. The reduction may have been influenced by competition, that is, the entry of another carrier into the northeastern Ohio insurance market.

Of course, not all untoward outcomes are attributable to negligence on the part of the practitioner. A classic case resulted from the break of a hypodermic needle. The practitioner was held to be a user and not a manufacturer or supplier thereof. The latent defect was held to be the responsibility of the manufacturer, who was subject to the doctrine of strict liability[14] (see also Chapter 22). Proper maintenance of all equipment, nevertheless, is as imperative as is using the equipment only for the purpose for which it is intended.

No matter the depth or type of anesthesia or sedation used, it is of paramount importance to be constantly aware of the status of each patient during the recovery stage. This responsibility must not be delegated to someone else when practicing within the office setting. Close observation during recovery is essential. A case is reported wherein the dentist left a patient who was still under the influence of relative analgesia. The unattended patient got up, fell through a window, and sustained injuries. The dentist was held liable.[15] Recovery areas that are easily observable and accessible provide an opportunity for this vigil by the operating room team.[16] Such a setting can lend itself to a continuum of contact, even though the operative procedure has been completed. In one case a patient suffered cardiorespiratory arrest in the recovery area and died a week later. A defense verdict for the oral surgeon resulted; the jury had found there had been adequate observation during the recovery process.[17] Adherence to accepted procedures offers a sound defense in any case of alleged professional negligence.

CONCLUSION

As I view the position of our profession, especially as pertains to anxiety and pain control, superior training will prevail.

Statutes and administrative regulations that will grant anesthesia privileges (via permits) only to those who have obtained such training are being promulgated across these United States. These laws also will attempt to define the techniques, and identify where each practitioner fits into the scope of practice. National standards of care have already ascended over local standards.

Patients have the right to know about expected complications that are significant. We professionals have a duty to so inform them. The operator must know the patient medically—*no strangers*. A complete awareness of our patients' problems, and skillful use of the correct technique, will all present a positive image should a defense in a court of law ever be needed. The implementation of sound risk management practices in the office, coupled with the delivery of anesthesia care at a high level, should help promote a leveling or lowering of insurance premiums, as noted above.

Caveat! One cloud lurks over the horizon. If the progressive and almost gargantuan increases in professional liability insurance premiums noted during the past decade resume, they may render any future office anesthesia prohibitively expensive. This issue still may have to be addressed; anesthesia surely will be no less expensive in the hospital and—statistics have proved—no safer!

REFERENCES

1. Sanzari v. Rosenfeld, 34 N.J. 128, 167 A.2d 625 (1961).
2. Le Beuf v. Atkins, 22 Wash. App. 877, 594 P.2d 923 (1979).
3. Dornette, WHL: Personal communication, December, 1988.
4. Ohio Administrative Code § 4715-3-01 (G) (1988).
5. *Id.* § 4715-3-01 (I) (1988).
6. *Id.* § 4715-3-01 (H) (1988).
7. Alaska Statutes, Title 8, Chap. 36, ¶¶ .08.36.110–.08.36.360; for an explanation of the events that led to this statutory enactment and complete text of the statute, *see* Dornette, WHL: Some problems in anesthesia. In Dornette, WHL (ed): Legal Aspects of Anesthesia. Davis, Philadelphia, 1972, p 329.
8. Office of Governmental Affairs, American Dental Association: Personal communication, May, 1989.

9. Yaple, NH, Secy., Ohio State Dental Board: Personal communication, June, 1989.
10. Ohio Administrative Code § 4715-5-05 (a)–(g).
11. American Dental Association: ADA Guidelines on the Comprehensive Teaching of the Control of Pain and Anxiety in Dentistry. Chicago. Part I was approved by the ADA Council on Dental Education on May 14, 1971; Part II on May 8, 1974; Part III by the House of Delegates on October 14, 1971; there have been several subsequent revisions.
12. American Association of Oral and Maxillofacial Surgeons: *Office Anesthesia Evaluation Manual.* Chicago, 1975. Approved by the American Association of Oral and Maxillofacial Surgeons' House of Delegates, 1975; available from the AAOMS, 211 East Chicago Avenue, Chicago, IL 60611.
13. These results are based on a survey conducted by the Committee on Anesthesia of the AAOMS in 1984. They are an extrapolation from a 40% response of the membership.
14. Magrine v. Spector, Krasua v. Spector, 100 N.J. Super. 223, 241 A.2d 637 (1968).
15. Langis v. Danforth, 308 Mass. 508, 33 N.E.2d 287 (1941).
16. The classic design for a close-proximity operatory and recovery room is described in Demkee, DE and Dornette, WHL: Toward safe outpatient anesthesia, Part 1. Anesthesia Progress, September/October 1970, p 105.
17. Johnson v. Bernard, 388 A.2d 490 (D.C. App. 1958).

RULES OF THE OHIO ADMINISTRATIVE CODE PERTAINING TO THE ADMINISTRATION OF GENERAL ANESTHESIA, DEEP SEDATION, AND CONSCIOUS SEDATION BY DENTAL PRACTITIONERS

Rule 4715-5-05   Use of general anesthesia and deep sedation

(A) No dentist shall employ or use general anesthesia or deep sedation on an outpatient basis for dental patients, unless such dentist possesses a permit of authorization issued by the Ohio state dental board. The dentist holding such permit shall be subject to review and such permit must be renewed annually. This rule is subject to the exception noted in paragraph (D) of this rule.

(B) In order to receive such permit, the dentist must apply on a prescribed application form to the Ohio state dental board, submit a fifty-dollar application fee and produce evidence showing that he or she:
   (1) Has completed a minimum of one year of advanced training in anesthesiology and related academic subjects (or its equivalent) beyond the undergraduate dental school level in a training program as described in part 2 of the "Guidelines for Teaching the Comprehensive Control of Pain and Anxiety in Dentistry"; or
   (2) Is a diplomate of the "American Board of Oral Surgery," or is a member of the "American Society of Oral Surgeons"; or
   (3) Is a fellow of the "American Dental Society of Anesthesiology"; or
   (4) Employs or works in conjunction with a trained M.D. or D.O. who is a member of the anesthesiology staff of an accredited hospital, provided that such anesthesiologist must remain on the premises of the dental facility until any patient given a general anesthetic or deep sedation regains consciousness; and
   (5) Has a properly equipped facility for the administration of general anesthesia or deep sedation staffed with a supervised team of auxiliary personnel capable of reasonably handling procedures, problems, and emergencies incident thereto. Adequacy of the facility and competence of the anesthesia or deep sedation team may be determined by the consultants appointed by the board as outlined in paragraph (C) of this rule.

(C) Prior to the issuance of such permit, the Ohio state dental board may, at its discretion, require an on-site inspection of the facility, equipment and personnel to determine if, in fact, the aforementioned requirements have been met. This evaluation shall be carried out in a manner following the principles, but not necessarily the specifics, described in the "American Society of Oral Surgeons Office Anesthesia" manual. The evaluation shall be carried out by a team of consultants appointed by the Ohio state dental board.

(D) Within one year of the effective date of these rules, each dentist who has been using or employing general anesthesia or deep sedation prior to adoption of this rule shall make application on the prescribed form to the Ohio state dental board if such dentist desires to continue to use or employ general anesthesia or deep sedation. If he meets the requirements of this rule he shall be issued such permit. An on-site evaluation of the facilities, equipment, and personnel may be, but is not necessarily, required, prior to issuance of such permit.

(E) For new applicants who are otherwise properly qualified, a temporary provisional permit of one year in duration may be granted by the board, based solely upon the credentials contained in the application, pending complete processing of the application and thorough investigation via an on-site evaluation as described in paragraph (C) of this rule.

(F) The board shall without charge renew the permit annually unless the holder is informed in writing that a reevaluation of his credentials and facility is to be required. In determining whether such reevaluation is necessary, the board shall consider such factors as it deems pertinent including, but not limited to, patient complaints and reports of adverse occurrences. Such reevaluation shall be carried out in the manner described in paragraph (C) of this rule.

(G) The Ohio state dental board, based on formal application stating all particulars which would justify the granting of such permit, may grant the permit authorizing the use or employment of general anesthesia and deep sedation to those licensed dentists who have been utilizing general anesthesia or deep sedation in a competent and effective manner in the past, but who have not had the benefit of formal training as outlined in this rule.

HISTORY: EFF. 10-1-88; 8-1-74; PRIOR DE-5-05

Rule 4715-5-06   Reports of adverse occurrences

(A) All licensees engaged in the practice of dentistry in the state of Ohio must submit a complete report within a period of thirty days to the Ohio state dental board of any mortality or other incident occurring in the outpatient facilities of such dentist which results in temporary or permanent physical or mental injury requiring hospitalization of said patient during, or as a direct result of, dental procedures or anesthesia related thereto.

(B) Failure to comply with this rule when said occurrence is related to the use of general anesthesia, deep sedation, or conscious IV sedation may result in the loss of such permits described in rules 4715-5-05 and 4715-5-07 of the Administrative Code.

HISTORY: Eff. 10-1-88; 8-1-74; prior DE-5-06

Rule 4715-5-07   Use of conscious intravenous sedation

(A) No dentist shall employ or use conscious intravenous sedation, in accordance with the definition of "conscious sedation," as defined in rule 4715-3-01 of the Administrative Code, unless such dentist possesses a permit of authorization issued by the Ohio state dental board. The dentist holding such permit shall be subject to review and such permit must be renewed annually. This rule is subject to the exception noted in paragraph (D) of this rule.

(B) In order to receive such permit, the dentist must apply on a prescribed application form to the Ohio state dental board, submit a fifty-dollar application fee and produce evidence showing that he or she:

(1) Has satisfactorily completed training in conscious intravenous sedation, which included a minimum of forty hours of didactic instruction and twenty hours of clinical experience, in accredited educational institutions or programs; or

(2) Has satisfactorily completed an accredited graduate program which included conscious intravenous sedation training equivalent to paragraph (B)(1) of this rule; or

(3) Has satisfactorily completed an internship or residency, which included conscious intravenous sedation training equivalent to paragraph (B)(1) of this rule, in an accredited educational institution or program; or

(4) Has satisfactorily completed qualifications governing the use of general anesthesia in rule 4715-5-05 of the Administrative Code; and

(5) Has a properly equipped facility, including the capability of delivering positive pressure oxygen ventilation, for the administration of conscious intravenous sedation staffed with supervised auxiliary personnel capable of reasonably handling procedures, problems and emergencies incident thereto. Adequacy of the facility may be determined by the consultants appointed by the board, as outlined in paragraph (C) of this rule; and

(6) Presents evidence acceptable to the board of satisfactory completion of an advanced cardiac life support course.

(C) Prior to the issuance of such permit, the Ohio state dental board may, at its discretion, require an on-site inspection of the facility, equipment and personnel to determine if, in fact, the aforementioned requirements have been met. The evaluation shall be carried out by a team of consultants appointed by the Ohio state dental board.

(D) Within one year of the effective date of this rule, each dentist who has been using or employing conscious intravenous sedation prior to adoption of this rule shall make application on the prescribed form to the Ohio state dental board, if such dentist desires to continue to use or employ conscious intravenous sedation. If he meets the requirements of this rule, he shall be issued such permit. An on-site evaluation of the facilities, equipment, and personnel may be, but is not necessarily required, prior to issuance of such permit.

(E) For new applicants who are otherwise properly qualified, a temporary provisional permit of one year in duration may be granted by the board, based solely upon the credentials contained in the application, pending complete processing of the application and thorough investigation as described in paragraph (C) of this rule.

(F) The board shall, without charge, renew the permit annually, unless the holder is informed in writing that a reevaluation of his credentials and facility is to be required. In determining whether such reevaluation is necessary, the board shall consider such factors as it deems pertinent, including, but not limited to, patient complaints and reports of adverse occurrences. Such reevaluation shall be carried out in the manner described in paragraph (C) of this rule.

(G) The Ohio state dental board, based on formal application stating all particulars which would justify the granting of such permit, may grant the permit authorizing the use or employment of conscious intravenous sedation to those licensed dentists who have been utilizing conscious intravenous sedation in a competent and effective manner in the past, but who have not had the benefit of formal training as outlined in this rule, provided said dentists meet the requirements of paragraphs (B)(5) and (B)(6) of this rule.

(H) A dentist holding a general anesthesia permit under rule 4715-5-05 of the Administrative Code may employ or use conscious intravenous sedation without a conscious intravenous sedation permit.

(I) No dentist shall use or employ ultra-short-acting barbiturates including, but not limited to, thiopental or methohexital for conscious intravenous sedation, unless he has a general anesthesia permit.
HISTORY: Eff. 10-1-88

Source: Ohio Administrative Code

22

William H. L. Dornette, M.D., J.D.

Products Liability

At the close of World War II, anesthesia personnel had available for their use seven inhalation anesthetic agents—chloroform, cyclopropane, diethyl ether, divinyl ether, ethylene, nitrous oxide, and trichloroethylene. Monitoring practices were limited to applying a stethoscope to the chest, taking the blood pressure indirectly utilizing a cuff and antecubital stethoscope, and counting the pulse rate with a finger placed upon one of the arteries in the head or neck.

Times have changed. With the advent of halothane in 1954, a variety of monohalogenated and polyhalogenated nonflammable agents have been introduced. The widespread application of these agents has led to the gradual demise in the use of flammable agents. Chloroform and trichloroethylene—the only nonflammable, total inhalation anesthetic agents available in those earlier times—have also fallen into disuse, either because of excessive toxicity, lack of desirable anesthetic properties, or both. The only inhalation agent to survive that earlier era is nitrous oxide. It, too, has come under attack[1] because of some undesirable properties. Over the ensuing years, those agents have been replaced with nonflammable ones—halothane, methoxyflurane, enflurane and, finally, isoflurane. Additionally, a large number of parenterally administered agents for balanced anesthesia have come onto the market.

Equipment available for the delivery of

inhalation anesthesia and the monitoring of the patient also has undergone dramatic change. Oscilloscopic electrocardiographic monitoring became a reality during the latter part of the 1950s. Since that time, a number of very innovative devices for both invasive and noninvasive monitoring have been designed, manufactured, and put to use (see Chapter 12). In the inhalation anesthesia field, universal vaporizers capable of dispensing any volatile liquid have given way to those calibrated for specific agents. Also added to the armamentaria of anesthesia personnel are newer muscle relaxants, analgesics, and regional, intravenous, and psychotropic agents intended to produce more complete forms of balanced anesthesia with (it is to be hoped!) fewer side effects.

This heavy influx of new agents, techniques, and equipment has changed the standard of anesthesia care. Unfortunately, many of these items have not proved to be unmixed blessings. The more potent the agent or complex the device, the greater the potential for side effects or malfunction. Whenever a product is responsible, even in part, for an injury to a patient and litigation ensues, it is very likely that the lawyer representing that individual will sue the manufacturer of the drug or device as well as the health care provider. The latter then may become enmeshed in a lawsuit in which the manufacturer endeavors to mitigate its own exposure to liability by alleging misuse by the health care provider. This maneuver immeasurably compounds the defense of the health care provider.

LEGAL BACKGROUND

Products liability is based primarily on the common law. In its beginnings, products liability litigation was similar to that involving professional negligence. The injured party had to establish a direct connection with the manufacturer of the product. That is, he or she had to have purchased the product directly from the person or firm that produced it. (Similarly, in the health care field, there must be an agreement with the physician to treat the patient if the latter is to have a viable cause of action against that provider.) Having established this connection (it is called *privi-*

ty of contract in products liability and is discussed further below), the injured person then had to demonstrate the defective steps in the manufacture of the product and prove how the injury resulted from use of that product. The comparable elements of proof in a malpractice action are breach of the standard of care and proximate causation (see Chapter 3). Over the years, this common law has undergone considerable metamorphosis, however, and proof in a modern products liability case is far more straightforward. This chapter first traces products liability law from its rudimentary common law beginnings to its present-day status of strict liability in tort. It will then orient the reader on how the current status of this law would be applied in a product-related injury to a patient. Finally, examples from current health care products liability case law will be cited.

When a physician agrees to treat a patient, a contract for *personal services* is entered into. Each party to that contract owes the other certain duties. These duties are discussed in Chapter 2. If the health care provider breaches one of these duties, the breach of duty injures the patient, and the latter sues the health care provider, the patient's lawyer customarily files an action for negligence rather than breach of contract (see Chapter 3). Perhaps the only instance in which a physician can be held liable for breach of contract would be guaranteeing a specific result (e.g., the plastic surgeon who promises his patient will have a perfect face) and then failing to achieve that goal. Physicians are sued for breach of contract only rarely, for a number of reasons discussed in Chapter 5.

A sales contract is somewhat different from a personal services one. Anesthetic-related pharmaceuticals and equipment are purchased principally by the hospital, using a sales contract that is customarily embodied in a written document (in contrast to contracts involving health care delivery, most of which are oral). The vendor may be the manufacturer, a wholesaler, or a local retailer who obtains the equipment or drugs either directly from the manufacturer or through a wholesaler. In many instances, the product passes through a number of hands in the chain of commerce from manufacturer to final user. Inasmuch as this passage involves drafting and executing at least one contract, and possibly a number of them, a failure of one party or another during execution of these transactions will result in allegations of breach of contract. Contract law thus formed the basis for products liability actions, at least initially.

EVOLUTION OF PRODUCTS LIABILITY LAW

As noted in Chapter 1, the common law is one source of the laws that govern us. Products liability originated from this common law in England during the 1840s. The first case involved a horse-drawn passenger coach with an apparently defective wheel. The wheel collapsed, and a passenger who was injured subsequently sued the manufacturer of the coach. In 1842 an English court in *Winterbottom v. Wright*[2] held that there could be no liability unless there was privity of contract between the passenger and the manufacturer of the coach. Privity simply means a direct connection or relationship existing between two or more contracting parties. The court reasoned that to allow litigation without such a direct connection between plaintiff and defendant would clog the courtrooms and impede commerce. Resale through an intermediary thus insulated the manufacturer from any liability for its own negligence. Thus, the early American colonists (except for those in Louisiana) adopted the privity requirement as part of the common law of England.

Abolition of the Privity Rule

Products liability law remained essentially the same in this country until the second decade of the 20th century. It was changed dramatically by an accident involving a vehicle then new to the common law, the automobile. A resident of New York State purchased a Buick automobile from a dealer. A defect in one of the wheels resulted in an accident and injury to its owner. The latter sued the manufacturer rather than the dealer. In a landmark decision[3] in 1916, Justice Benjamin Cardozo of the New York Court of Appeals held that

the offering of goods for sale carries the notion of a representation of safety, and that the Buick Motor Car Company was liable for negligence in the manufacture of the automobile. Cardozo reasoned that a vehicle such as an automobile could be expected to be capable of inflicting substantial harm if it was defective. Inasmuch as it was defective, the Buick Motor Car Company would be liable. Manufacturers henceforth were expected to use reasonable care, both in the design and construction of the item and in wording and publishing a warning when the use of the product created specific dangers. Inasmuch as the owner of the Buick had no direct dealings with the manufacturer, Cardozo's opinion effectively abolished privity of contract as an essential element in a products liability law suit in New York State.

In the ensuing years, the privity of contract requirement was gradually eliminated by common law decisions in other jurisdictions across the United States.[4] These courts also expanded the warning requirement, holding that to be sufficient, such warnings should not only protect the immediate user of the item, but also third persons who might come into contact with the product. The courts did state that the seller may assume that the user of the product would be a normal human being and that there was no duty to warn of obvious dangers.[5]

Truth in Advertising

In 1932 the Supreme Court of Washington handed down the decision of *Baxter v. Ford Motor Company*. The court held Ford liable for express representation of safety of its product when, in fact, the product was unsafe. Ford appealed, the case was retried, and the court articulated a new reason for holding for Baxter, namely strict liability for innocent misrepresentation.[6]

Genesis of Implied Warranties

The next radical changes in products liability related to foods and drugs. In the 1930s, consumers became aware of the presence of toxins and other deleterious substances in some foods on the American market. Their concern led to the imposition of strict liability in the case of sale of adulterated, poisonous, or otherwise defective food or drink.[7] In such an instance, the manufacturer will be liable to those injured by the product if it is defective, without the injured consumer having to prove negligence during its manufacture. In effect, these appellate courts were holding that the manufacturers *impliedly warranted* that their foods and drugs were safe and wholesome. (Presently, these implied warranties accompany the sale of all products in this country, thanks to the Uniform Commercial Code, which has been adopted by each United States jurisdiction; see Chapter 18.) The implied warranties relating to food and drink were extended to equipment in 1960 by a New Jersey court in *Henningson v. Bloomfield Motors,* which held that the seller impliedly warranted that the automobile would be safe.[8]

Creation of Strict Liability in Tort

The next development in products liability laws related to the adoption of 402A of the Restatement of Torts, 2d.* This section covers liability of the seller of a product for physical harm to the user or consumer. Paragraph 1 states:

1 One who sells any product in a defective condition unreasonably dangerous to the user or consumer or to his property is subject to liability for physical harm thereby caused to the ultimate user or consumer or to his property, if:
   a The seller is engaged in the business of selling such a product,
   b It is expected to and does reach the consumer without substantial change in the condition in which it is sold.
2 The rule stated in subsection 1 applies although:
   a The seller has exercised all possible care in the preparation and sale of his prod-

---

*Periodically, a number of legal scholars meet, review changes in the common law, and revise a group of publications known as the *Restatement of the Law, Second.* These publications in effect define the current status of that common law and cover various branches of the law, including torts.

uct, and the user or consumer has not bought the product from or entered into any contractual relationship with the seller.[9]

This new section in the *Restatement of the Law of Torts* abolished completely the last vestiges of privity of contract. It makes no mention of warranty and allows the "ultimate" user or consumer to sue the original seller (i.e., the manufacturer). The first case to apply this new section was *Greenman v. Yuba Power Products Inc.*[10] The user of a combination power tool was injured when a piece of wood flew from the tool and struck him in the head. He sued Yuba Power Products. The Supreme Court of California held that it was not a matter of warranty but simply one of strict liability in tort (i.e., negligence). This 1963 decision led to a variety of similar decisions across the United States substituting strict liability for contractual liability.

PRODUCTS LIABILITY AND HEALTH CARE

That is where products liability law stands today as it pertains to products that can be made safe or reasonably so. Of special importance to health care providers is the fact that the Restatement uses the term "unreasonably dangerous." Such products are to be distinguished from those that are or may be inherently dangerous, for example, pharmaceuticals with known serious side effects. The concept of the inherently dangerous product has also become a part of modern products liability case law, as discussed in the following section.

Potentially Dangerous Equipment and Pharmaceuticals

Although many modern pharmaceuticals and medical devices pose a risk to patients, the risk created by some is greater than others. Those agents and devices falling into the more risky category in turn create special duties on the part of both manufacturer and consumer or user (i.e., the health care provider). In the case of anesthesia personnel, some monitoring devices clearly fall into the risky category (see Chapter 12).

The manufacturer is under a duty to produce a product that is not unreasonably dangerous. There is a further duty to properly label the pharmaceutical or item of equipment, or supply it with package literature (or operation manual) specifying the indications, contraindications, applications, potential risks, and how to mitigate the latter. Once the manufacturer has done so, the article may no longer be unreasonably unsafe. As Prosser in his *Law of Torts* so aptly put it, "It seems clear that the product cannot be regarded as unreasonably unsafe merely because it is capable of doing harm."[11] Once the manufacturer produces such a product, and with proper labeling identifies whatever its capability is of causing harm, the burden then shifts to the user to be certain that it is employed properly. Properly employed means that it is used for the purpose intended within whatever limitations are set forth either by the package literature or operation manual, respectively.

Utilitarian Products That Are Unavoidably Dangerous

There are some products and equipment that, in the present state of knowledge, cannot be made inherently safe, and yet they have great utility; their advantages for the most part outweigh their risks. *Comment k* of § 402A of the *Restatement of Torts 2d* covers such items, limiting strict liability if the item is both of great utility and unavoidably safe, as long as the manufacturer provides adequate warnings.[12] Prescribing drugs of this nature may result in an adverse outcome, yet with proper warnings neither the physician nor the manufacturer may be liable.[13] When developing and marketing these items, however, the manufacturer has three duties:

1 To take every reasonable step in the design, development, and manufacture of the item to minimize the risk
2 To delineate carefully in the accompanying documentation (package literature or operation manual) the risks that remain
3 To suggest antidotes or remedial measures should sequelae develop

Significant duties also fall on the shoulders of the health care provider when using or prescribing one of these items. He or she must read carefully the package literature or operation manual, and become thoroughly familiar with all of the admonitions and safety precautions set forth therein. Based upon that knowledge, a determination then must be made whether the benefits outweigh the risks. In making this determination, the health care provider is acting, in the words of one appellate court, as a "learned intermediary" between the manufacturer and ultimate consumer, the patient.[14] If a decision is made to utilize the pharmaceutical or device, the following steps are mandatory:

1 The patient's informed consent must be obtained as appropriate (see Chapters 9 and 12).
2 The item must be employed only when it is indicated; there must not be any safer alternative of equal or greater utility.
3 The patient must be monitored carefully for side effects.
4 The therapy or use of the equipment must be terminated as soon as any side effects appear; the side effects then must be treated as appropriate.
5 The patient's medical record should clearly reflect the fact that consent was obtained, the indication(s) for the application of the drug or device, the techniques used to monitor for side effects, and remedial measures utilized (if any) to treat those side effects.

Fortunately for anesthesia personnel, there are few, if any, pharmaceuticals utilized in anesthetic practice that fall into the category of unreasonably dangerous but of great utility.

Reusable Items of Equipment

Perhaps an even greater risk is created when medical devices are used over extended periods of time. The cost of many of these items is significant, and their useful life may be expected to span a number of years. Both the manufacturer and the user have certain specific duties pertaining to this type of equipment.

Duties of Manufacturer

The manufacturer's duties are fourfold:

1 Take every reasonable step to design, develop, and manufacture the item of equipment to minimize any dangers and maximize its utility.
2 Furnish operation manuals and apply appropriate labeling to delineate the indications, contraindications, potential risks, and correct operation of the equipment.
3 Offer preventive maintenance service in the case of complex equipment, either directly from the manufacturer or through the local supplier; or, as an alternative, offer training for any in-house maintenance personnel.
4 Offer consultative service as appropriate to help resolve any future problems.

Duties of User

Major equipment purchases generally are made by the institution. Such items often are referred to as "capital equipment," to identify the source of funding. Within the context of hospital-owned equipment, the term "user" relates to both the institution itself and the health care provider who prescribes or applies the device to his or her patients. Duties of these persons or entities are eightfold:

1 Keep up with the standard of care; at some point in time the standard may mandate use of the new equipment, even though it is costly and has never been utilized before in that particular institution.
2 When the equipment is employed, make certain that its application is medically indicated.
3 Obtain the patient's informed consent as appropriate.
4 Utilize the equipment only for the purpose intended, and as recom-

mended by the operations manual.
5 Initiate and implement a *routine* check* for defects of those items of equipment that require such a check.
6 Keep the equipment in good repair; obtaining preventive maintenance contracts with the manufacturer or the manufacturer's representative may be highly desirable in the case of complex anesthesia and monitoring equipment.
7 Do not misuse any equipment; it is an invitation to liability; some equipment should be replaced regularly after a reasonable period of use.
8 Document carefully all dealings with manufacturers, distributors, and equipment service organizations; document carefully "in-house" service and maintenance activities.

Single-Use Items of Equipment

Anesthesia workrooms in the modern hospital contain a plethora of single-use items. It seems that just about every piece of equipment except the gas anesthesia apparatus and monitoring devices now are available in disposable form. Utilization of these items unquestionably reduces labor costs for reprocessing and totally eliminates the problems generated by reusable devices that are discussed in the preceding section. Single-use items are not an unmixed blessing, however. Storage problems may be created by the often large bulk of these devices, which, together with their packaging, may occupy considerable shelf or closet space. The same statement applies to the trash generated by their use, unless frequent trash pick-up policies are in effect.

Of much greater concern from a liability posture, however, is the *fire hazard issue*.[15] The uncontrolled combustion (as during a fire) of synthetic polymers results in the generation of large quantities of dense smoke. Over half of the products of combustion of these synthetics consist of complex hydrocarbons. (In contrast, when a natural polymer like wood burns, the large component of the smoke is made up of car-

---

*It may be desirable, for example, to check the equipment each time before it is put to use, or at least before the start of each day's cases; while patent defects may create liability for the manufacturer, the user's duty to check for them places a share of that liability on the user.

bon dioxide and water vapor.) Burning of polyvinylchloride and other chlorine-containing substances produces hydrochloric acid vapor; it is extremely irritating to the eyes and mucosa of the respiratory tract. When polyurethane burns, the higher oxides of nitrogen are released. These substances attack the alveolae, produce fulminating pulmonary edema, and may be rapidly fatal if inhaled for even a short period of time. Fires in hospitals pose a threat to patients not from flame but from the spread of products of combustion into patient care areas.

Reuse of One-Use Items

Should disposable items ever be reused? Some, of course, cannot, but a number can, especially those not intended for parenteral use or insertion into a body cavity. Many of these might seem to be ideal for reprocessing by hospital personnel. Manufacturers are naturally reticent to recommend methodology for reprocessing. A breakdown of one of these polymers during cleansing or resterilizing could well generate litigation against the manufacturer— for allegedly giving faulty reprocessing instructions, or not fabricating the item in such a manner that breakdown could not occur. Of course, the manufacturer has a purely economic incentive to discourage reprocessing—it reduces the market for the item! Personnel who would consider reuse of devices intended for single use must know the composition of the item (i.e., which polymer is involved) and the extent to which any of the substances used in the reprocessing might interact with that polymer. Although they do not undergo biodegradation, synthetic polymers are not inert (as, for example, corrosion-resistant steel). The legal implications of the improper reuse of one-use items should be obvious.

ENTERPRISE OR MARKET SHARE LIABILITY

The most recent development in products liability law has been the introduction of the concept of enterprise liability to the products field. This type of liability has no present implications for anesthesia personnel; it is mentioned here only for completeness. If two persons act negligently and in consort, either can be liable for any ensuing injury. For example, if two marksmen negligently engage in target practice and injure someone, the latter need not prove which one fired the injury-causing bullet.

This principle found firm common law roots in the recent spate of diethylstilbestrol (DES) litigation. Women who developed cervical carcinoma because their mothers took DES to avert a spontaneous abortion (so-called DES daughters) frequently have been unable to learn from their mothers the name of the manufacturer of the brand of DES that was prescribed. Many have been successful in learning which manufacturers were engaged in the sale of the DES in the community in which their mothers lived and the market share of each company. Litigation against all manufacturers (or just the major one or two) then would be initiated. The successful litigant would demand damages from each proportional to the market share, hence the term *market share liability*. Several of these cases are noted in Appendix 22-1.

CONCLUSION

The current standard of anesthesia care mandates the use of numerous pharmaceuticals and devices that may pose a risk to patients. Purchasing the equipment from a reputable pharmaceutical or equipment manufacturer, keeping equipment in good operating condition, utilizing drugs and devices appropriately and only when indicated, obtaining the patient's informed consent as necessary, monitoring the patient for side effects, and correcting problems whenever they occur should contribute to minimizing complications, promoting the delivery of anesthesia care of high quality, and avoiding troublesome products liability problems, including possible litigation.

REFERENCES

1. Eiger, EI and Saidman, LJ: Hazards of nitrous oxide anesthesia in bowel obstruction and pneumothorax. Anesthesiology 26:61, 1965.

2. Winterbottom v. Wright, 152 Eng. Rep. 402 (1842).
3. MacPherson v. Buick Motor Car Co., 217 N.Y. 382, 111 N.E. 1050 (1916).
4. *See, generally,* Noel, DW and Phillips, JJ: Products Liability, ed 2. West, St Paul, 1981, pp 17, 18.
5. *Id.* at 190, 191.
6. Baxter v. Ford Motor Co., 12 P.2d 409 (Wash. 1932).
7. Keeton, WP (ed): Prosser and Keeton on Torts, ed 5. West, St Paul, 1984, p 690.
8. Henningson v. Bloomfield Motors, 32 N.J. 358, 161 A.2d 69 (Sup. Cit. 1960).
9. Restatement Second, the Law of Torts. American Law Institute, St. Paul, 1965, § 402A.
10. Greenman v. Yuba Power Products, Inc., 377 P.2d 897 (Cal. 1963).
11. Prosser, WL: Law of Torts, ed 4. West, St Paul, 1971, p 660.
12. *Comment k* provides:

> There are some products which, in the present state of human knowledge, are quite incapable of being made safe for their intended and ordinary use. These are especially common in the field of drugs. An outstanding example is the vaccine for the Pasteur treatment of rabies, which not uncommonly leads to very serious and damaging consequences when it is injected. Since the disease itself invariably leads to a dreadful death, both the marketing and the use of the vaccine are fully justified, notwithstanding the unavoidable high degree of risk which they involve. Such a product, properly prepared, and accompanied by proper directions and warning, is not defective, nor is it unreasonably dangerous. The same is true of many other drugs, vaccines, and the like, many of which for this very reason cannot legally be sold except to physicians, or under the prescription of a physician. It is also true in particular of many new or experimental drugs as to which, because of lack of time and opportunity for sufficient medical experience, there can be no assurance of safety, or perhaps even of purity of ingredients, but such experience as there is justifies the marketing and use of the drug notwithstanding a medically recognizable risk. The seller of such products, again with the qualification that they are properly prepared and marketed, and proper warning is given, where the situation calls for it, is not to be held to strict liability for unfortunate consequences attending their use, merely because he has undertaken to supply the public with an apparently useful and desirable product, attended with a known but apparently reasonable risk.

13. Gaston v. Hunter, 588 P.2d 326 (Ariz. App. 1978).
14. Hill v. Searle Laboratories, 686 F.Supp. 720 (E.D. Ark. 1988).
15. Dornette, WHL and Yuellig DP: Disposables and the combustible load in hospitals. Fire J 66: 27, 1972.

22-1

RECENTLY REPORTED PRODUCTS LIABILITY CASES

The West Publishing Company (P.O. Box 64526, St. Paul, Minnesota 55164-0526), publishers of the National Reporter System and a plethora of excellent legal treatises, also produces *West's Personal Injury News*. This biweekly publication contains capsule reports of appellate decisions from current personal injury litigation in this country. At the end of each 26 issues, an annual compendium is prepared. The following case reports were selected from Volume 6, Numbers 1 to 26, covering the period of March 1, 1988, through February 14, 1989. These reports are included to show the broad scope of products liability litigation today, some of the principles by which liability is determined, representative examples of health care product liability, and (in a few cases) the ends to which some consumers will go to attempt to place blame on manufacturers for their (the consumers') own negligence.

The nonlawyer reader interested in review of any cases appearing in one of the National Reporter's state or federal publications will find them in all law school libraries and in the law libraries of many county court houses, some bar associations, and most large law firms. Law school libraries usually will admit health care providers to their open stacks, except during examination time. To find, for example, 747 S.W.2d 487, consult the law librarian for the location of the South Western Reporter. Look for Volume 747 of the second series. The report of *Prieto v. Val Verde Memorial Hospital* begins on page 487.

Alarm Systems

Hospital visitor sued manufacturer of hospital fire alarm system after alarm allegedly sounded and automatically closed interior fire door, injuring visitor. The appellate court held that manufacturer of the alarm system was not liable. The court found no evidence: of the presence at the hospital of any employee of the manufacturer; that a fire alarm was heard; or that its activation caused the door to close.
Prieto v. Val Verde Memorial Hosp., 747 S.W.2d 487 (Tex. Add. 1988)

Allopurinol

Patient sued manufacturer of Zyloprim for failing to warn that the simultaneous ingestion of penicillin and Zyloprim could be associated with genesis or exacerbation of Stevens Johnson syndrome. The appellate court held for the defendant.
Crisostomo v. Stanley, 857 F.2d 1146 (C.A.7-Ill. 1988)

Aminophylline

Wyeth Laboratories was found liable for central nervous system injuries in a 2 year old who was given aminophylline suppositories and Marax. The appellate court held that Wyeth breached its duty to physicians to warn of the danger of a synergistic reaction between the aminophylline and the ephedrine-containing Marax.
Batteast v. Wyeth Laboratories, Inc., 122 Ill. Dec. 169, 526 N.E.2d 428 (Ill. App. 1988)

Antabuse

Physician prescribed Antabuse for an alcoholic who alleged injuries and sued manufacturer

for failure to warn of severity of side effects. The appellate court held that although warnings may have been inadequate, the inadequacy could not have caused the alcoholic's injuries because the physician who prescribed the Antabuse did not rely on the warnings.
Mampe v. Ayerst Laboratories, 548 A.2d 798 (D.C. App. 1988)

Bendectin

Richardson-Merrell was not liable for congenital limb defects of a child whose mother had taken Bendectin during her pregnancy. The appellate court found that the expert who testified that the drug caused birth defects did not adequately substantiate his opinion. Chemical studies, in vitro studies, and in vivo animal studies did not prove causation in human beings, and no published work on Bendectin had concluded that there was statistically significant association between drug and limb reduction defects.
Richardson by Richardson v. Richardson-Merrell, Inc., 857 F.2d 823 (C.A.D.C. 1988)

Birth Control

Manufacturer of Cu-7 intrauterine device was not liable for perforated uterus suffered by user. Manufacturer's warnings of dangers of perforation were adequate. Federal district court predicted that Arkansas Supreme Court would adopt* the "learned intermediary rule," and that court would also adopt Comment k under § 402A of Restatement (Second) of Torts, which provides for utilitarian compounds an "unavoidably unsafe product" exception to strict liability rule. The district court further predicted that Arkansas Supreme Court would apply Comment k to prescription drugs, including intrauterine contraceptive devices. (For the text of Comment k, see ref. 12, Chapter 22. [Ed.])
Hill v. Searle Laboratories, 686 F.Supp. 720 (E.D. Ark. 1988)

Blood and Blood Products

Blood bank was not liable for death of infant from AIDS, resulting from receipt of transfusions of HIV-infected blood in January 1983. Suit was brought on theories of negligence, breach of implied warranty strict liability, and violation of consumer protection statutes.
Kozup v. Georgetown University, 85 F.2d 437 (C.A.D.C. 1988)

Blood supplier was not liable for death of patient who contracted AIDS after receiving transfusion during surgery in March 1985. Supplier was not negligent in failing to test blood for presence of HTLV-III (HIV) antibodies.
Kirkendall v. Harbor Ins. Co., 698 F.Supp. 768 (W.D. Ark. 1988)

Manufacturer of Factor VIII blood clotting product called "Koate" exercised sufficient control over plasma collection center to be held liable for any negligence by center in suit by hemophiliac alleging that he contracted AIDS after purchasing product in fall of 1983; however, center was not negligent in failing to inquire of plasma donor as to whether he was homosexual. Donor had previously falsely stated to center that he was not homosexual. In any event, evidence did not establish causation.
Jones v. Miles Laboratories, Inc. 70 F.Supp. 1127 (N.D. Ga. 1988)

Manufacturer of antihemophiliac factor was not strictly liable to hemophiliac who contracted AIDS after using factor. Illinois Blood Liability Act barred strict liability claims involving processing or distributing of blood derivatives and products. However, manufacturer could be held liable for negligent failure to warn of risk of contracting AIDS from using its product.

---

*Under the decision of *Erie Railroad v. Tompkins*, discussed in Chapter 20, federal judges must apply the substantive law of the jurisdiction in which the allegedly tortuous act occurred; if, as in this case, there is no state common law on the topic, the judge must predict how the supreme court of that state would hold, given a case with similar facts.

Poole v. Alpha Therapeutic Corp., 696 F.Supp. 351 (N.D. Ill. 1988); 698 F.Supp. 1367 (N.D. Ill. 1988)

Supplier of Factor VIII used to treat hemophiliacs was not liable for death of hemophiliac from AIDS following blood transfusion. Kentucky's medical service precluded holding supplier liable on strict products liability theory. Supplier was not liable on negligence theory, in light of standard of care for pharmaceutical companies in 1982 to 1983.
McKee v. Miles Laboratories, Inc., 675 F.Supp. 1060 (E.D. Ky. 1987)

Patient diagnosed as having AIDS-related complex after receiving units of blood-coagulation-factor concentrate "Konyne" in 1983 had strict products liability claim against product's manufacturer under Maryland law. Court had previously ruled that 1986 statute shielding blood providers from strict liability in tort did not apply to case retroactively. In instant opinion, court ruled that strict liability action was not barred by other Maryland statutes or by common law. Patient could maintain strict liability claim based on alleged defects in product, but could not maintain claim for strict liability based on duty to warn.
Doe v. Miles Laboratories, Inc., 675 F.Supp. 1466 (D. Md. 1987)

Hospital was strictly liable to patient for 1980 "sale" of defective blood, even though hepatitis virus present in blood could not have been detected by testing. Blood center that "sold" blood to hospital was also strictly liable.
Shortess v. Touro Infirmary, 520 So.2d 389 (La. 1988)

Two Louisiana statutes eliminating strict liability for hospitals and blood banks in connection with transmission of viral or infectious diseases through blood transfusions were unconstitutional. Final adopted versions of statutes were not read three times in legislature as required by Louisiana Constitution. The unconstitutionality extended only until July 15, 1982, however, the effective date of reenactment of one statute, which was nearly identical to the other statute. Constitutionality of reenacted statute was not challenged.
Casey v. Southern Baptist Hosp., 526 So.2d 1332 (La. App. 1988)

Patient's action against blood supplier arising from patient's contraction of AIDS following transfusion properly lay in negligence, and not in medical malpractice.
Di Marco v. Hudson Valley Blood Services, 532 N.Y.S.2d 488 (N.Y. Sup. 1988)

South Carolina's medical service statute, exempting providers of blood and blood products from liability based on breach of implied warranty, did not violate equal protection clause of constitution.
Samson v. Greenville Hosp. System, 368 S.E.2d 665 (S.C. 1988)

Bone Plate

Manufacturer of compression plates used for open reduction of fractures was not liable for alleged injuries resulting when a plate broke. Patient's fracture had not completely healed at time that plate broke, and there was no evidence that breakage of plate resulted in any injury to patient. Plate was found to be adequately designed for its intended purpose.
Padgett v. Synthes, Ltd. (U.S.A.), 677 F.Supp. 1329 (W.D.N.C. 1988)

Books

Publisher of nursing textbook was not liable for injuries sustained by nursing student when she treated herself for constipation by taking hydrogen peroxide enema after consulting textbook. Publisher did not make suggestions relating to section on treatment of consti-

pation, did not research or write any portion of book, and did not review contents of book for substantive accuracy. Strict liability did not extend to dissemination of idea or knowledge in books or other published material.
Jones v. J.B. Lippincott Co., 694 F.Supp.1216 (D. Md. 1988)

Cough Drops

Consumer did not establish submissible case against cough drop manufacturer based on allegations of failure to warn and product mislabeling. Consumer had suffered severe allergic reaction after taking three menthol cough drops. There was no evidence that manufacturer knew or had reason to know that some consumers might be allergic to those drops. Furthermore, no warning on package could have prevented consumer's reaction, as she did not know that she was allergic to menthol.
Burlison v. Warner-Lambert Co., 842 F.2d 991 (C.A.8-Iowa 1988)

Diethylstilbestrol

Persons born to mothers given DES could not recover against DES manufacturer without proof that manufacturer proximately caused their injuries. Neither Maryland nor District of Columbia had recognized any of the "nonidentification" theories of liability advanced by plaintiffs.
Tidler v. Eli Lilly and Co., 851 F.2d 418 (C.A.D.C. 1988)

Franchisor of pharmacy that filled DES prescription for pregnant woman was not liable for gynecological injuries suffered by woman's daughter. Suit alleged that franchisor had duty to warn physicians and franchisees of dangers of drug, even if manufacturer of DES was not liable to woman suffering from clear cell adenocarcinoma of vagina allegedly caused by in utero exposure to drug. Although there was evidence that condition in question is generally caused by synthetic estrogen drugs such as DES, there was insufficient nonspeculative, admissible evidence that woman's mother had in fact taken DES.
Shields v. Eli Lilly and Co., 697 F.Supp.12 (D.D.C. 1988)

Gas Anesthesia Apparatus

Manufacturer of gas anesthesia machine was not liable to patient for brain damage caused by lack of oxygen while anesthetized. Anesthesiologist and anesthetic nurse were determined to be solely at fault for inserting pressure control device into inhalation rather than exhalation hoses of the breathing circuit.
Meschino v. North American Drager, Inc., 841 F.2d 429 (C.A.1-Mass. 1988)

Manufacturers, sellers, and servicers of anesthesia vaporizer were liable for permanent brain damage suffered by patient as a result of overdose of anesthesia during minor surgical procedure; vaporizer apparently delivered gross overdose of volatile liquid anesthetic agent.
Ohio Medical Products, Inc. v. Suber, 758 S.W.2d 870 (Text. App. 1988)

High-Frequency Electrosurgical Unit

Manufacturer of HF electrosurgical unit used during circumcision of 2-year-old child was not liable for loss of child's penis, which was burned off as result of procedure. Although manufacturer failed to adequately warn of danger of using unit on small appendages, absence of adequate warning was not cause-in-fact of injury. Physician who supervised surgery admitted that she had never read instruction manual or warning label on device herself.
Felice v. Valleylab, Inc., 520 So.2d 920 (La. App. 1987)

Hospital was not strictly liable for patient's burns that were allegedly caused by defective

indifferent (ground) electrode on HF electrosurgical unit. Although patient may have been entitled to recover from manufacturer because of defect in electrode, hospital was itself a "consumer" of electrode and did not "transfer" it to patient.
North Miami General Hosp., Inc. v. Goldberg, 520 So.2d 650 (Fla. App. 1988)

Phenobarbital

Manufacturer of prescription of drug Bellergal-S, containing phenobarbital, was not liable to patient who allegedly had allergic reaction to drug. Manufacturer had warned physicians that drug contained phenobarbital and might produce allergic reaction.
Guevara v. Dorsey Laboratories Div. of Sandoz, Inc., 845 F.2d 364 (C.A.1-Puerto Rico 1988)

Pitocin

Fact issues existed as to whether manufacturer of Pitocin was liable for brain injuries allegedly suffered at birth by child of woman to whom drug had been administered.
Sacher v. Long Island Jewish-Hillside Medical Center, 530 N.Y.S.2d 232 (N.Y.A.D. 1988)

Plaster of Paris

Patient's malfunction theory strict liability claim should not have been submitted to jury in patient's suit against manufacturer of plaster of paris used to set patient's broken leg. Plaster of paris allegedly caused second- and third-degree burns on patient's leg. There was sufficient evidence of negligence on part of physicians as cause of malfunction to warrant submission of negligence theory to jury. Thus, patient failed to sustain burden of eliminating other reasonable secondary causes for malfunction.
Rogers v. Johnson & Johnson Products, Inc., 533 A.2d 739 (Pa. Super. 1987)

Prednisone

Physician's failure to warn prednisone user of risk of aseptic necrosis was intervening proximate cause, relieving manufacturer of liability for not warning user.
Glucksman v. Halsey Drug Co., Inc., 533 N.Y.S.2d 827 (N.Y. Sup. 1988)

Vaccines

Federal law did not preempt state law claims against manufacturer of DPT vaccine Tri-Immunol for defective design or failure to warn. Claims arose out of child's neurological injuries following her 1983 inoculation.
Abbot by Abbot v. American Cyanamid Co., 844 F.2d 1108 (C.A.4-Va. 1988)

Federal law did not preempt state law claims that vaccine manufacturer breached its duty to warn of product risks and its duty not to place unreasonably dangerous product into commerce. Issue arose in suit to recover for severe neurological damage sustained by infant, allegedly in reaction to pertussis component of DPT vaccine.
Hurley v. Lederle Laboratories Div. of American Cyanamid Co., 851 F.2d 1536 (C.A.5-Tex. 1988)

Parents of child who died after he was inoculated with diphtheria-tetanus-pertussis vaccine could maintain products liability action against one of three manufacturers of vaccine. Parents presented substantial circumstantial evidence from which reasonable jury could conclude that vaccine administered to their son was manufactured by that particular pharmaceutical company. However, Georgia law would not permit parents to maintain action against another manufacturer of vaccine under theory of alternative liability.
Chapman v. American Cyanamid Co., 861 F.2d 1515 (C.A.11-Ga. 1988)

5

Courts, Litigation, and Expert Testimony

EDITOR'S NOTE

When the editor first became interested in medical jurisprudence—the effects of laws and legal processes upon the practice of medicine—the incidence of medical malpractice cases was almost negligible. For example, in the early 1960s roughly one physician in 12 could expect to be named the defendant in a medical malpractice action *at some time during his or her professional career.* The incidence has increased almost exponentially. Today, reportedly one physician in three will be sued for medical malpractice during a professional career, about *one physician in 12 each year!* Nor have other health care providers—dentists, nurses, technicians, to name a few—been spared.

Given this wide potential exposure to allegations of negligence and litigation, the concern of health care providers is understandable. Inasmuch as few health care providers are knowledgeable in laws and legal processes, much concern arises from fear of the unknown. The purpose of the next two chapters is twofold—to explain the process of litigation to those unfamiliar with it, and to detail the role of the health care provider who agrees or is required to give testimony in any case involving personal injury.

The term *litigation* is derived from the Latin *litis.* It means a fight or quarrel. The litigation process, thus, as its name implies, involves a dispute between one party and another. To regulate these disputes, governmental entities have drafted procedural rules, called the rules of civil (or criminal) procedure. Medical malpractice cases are civil cases.

Chapter 23 explores the process of litigation, and some of the rules of civil procedure, from the standpoint of both the plaintiff and the defendant. Each step in the process is covered in some detail. Chapter 24 reviews what the witness should expect by way of preparation by a competent trial lawyer. If the lawyer does not address a particular subject, the health care provider who will be appearing as a witness should always *ask about it.* An understanding of these chapters will both add to the health care provider's knowledge and help to minimize fears based upon unawareness of pending events.

The author of Chapters 23 and 24, W. Stuart Dornette, graduated from Williams College with a dual major in physics and mathematics. He obtained his juris doctor degree from the University of Virginia College of Law in 1975, and currently is a partner in the litigation department of Taft, Stettinius & Hollister, Cincinnati, Ohio. Mr. Dornette is a member of the Ohio, Virginia, and District of Columbia bars.

W. H. L. D.

23

W. Stuart Dornette, J.D.

The Process of Litigation

A person who feels that he or she has been injured by a health care provider frequently seeks the services of legal counsel, and a lawsuit may be filed. These cases become civil cases. They are tried under the procedural law of that jurisdiction. The case is customarily filed in the community in which the defendant resides and practices. Thus, a patient coming to a Cincinnati hospital from another part of the country (e.g., northern Kentucky) and alleging an injury caused by improper care at that hospital would file the law suit in Hamilton County, Ohio. When both plaintiff and defendant reside in the same state, the suit will be filed in a state court; in Ohio, the Court of Commons Pleas. If, in the example just given, the plaintiff is a resident of Kentucky, the case could be filed in the Federal District Court under diversity jurisdiction. That is, when plaintiff and defendant are residents of different states, a federal court may be used, provided that the amount of damages claimed exceeds $50,000. It is probable that the average malpractice claimant would seek damages of at least that amount.

All litigation involves an adversary process. The positions of the plaintiff and defendant are diametrically opposite. The lawyer for each does his or her best to attack and destroy (within the context of the procedural rules) the opponent's case. The litigation process involves formal procedures, including filing the complaint, the answer, various motions (to produce or quash evidence, require the judge to rule on applicable law, and similar matters), and, if settlement discussions are nonproductive, the trial itself. Each of these steps deserves exploration.

PRETRIAL ACTIVITIES

Preparation

Not all lawyers try cases. Those who do specialize in this type of work are sometimes referred to as members of the trial bar. Among the trial bar there is a large group that specializes in handling cases for injured parties. They specialize in personal injury litigation. Many of these lawyers are members of the American Trial Lawyers Association. It is very likely that the plaintiff in the average malpractice case will be represented by a member of this association.

Before accepting a patient as a client, and long before any consideration is given to filing the lawsuit, the lawyer will amass as much information about that person and the allegedly negligent medical care as possible. Preliminary investigation is highly important; a competent personal injury lawyer will not take a frivolous case to court. Many patients have high expectations, and often equate imperfect results with negligent care. The lawyer cannot rely solely on the interview. After obtaining the prospective client's written release, the lawyer will purchase a copy of the medical records covering that particular hospitalization, as well as any previous care. Outpatient records may be helpful. The lawyer will want to find out as much else as he or she can about the potential client. Has this individual been involved in other litigation? Such a person may be lawsuit-prone, and interested in using the legal forum in an attempt to make more money from some insurance company. The potential client may pose other problems. Persons

who conceal vital parts of their medical history or who have been noncompliant during treatment may have contributed sufficiently to the untoward outcome by their own negligence to make their case totally frivolous. A good trial lawyer will identify these problems and may refuse to represent the client in such a case.

Assuming, however, that this research indicates that an act of professional negligence probably has occurred and that that act caused the patient to suffer some degree of injury, the lawyer will agree to represent the individual and will have the client sign a contingent fee contract.

The Contingent Fee Contract

The contract for professional services between patients and physicians rarely is written; generally, it is verbal. Physicians agree to offer patients their medical services. (The duties of the physician are covered in detail in Chapter 2.) Physicians expect that patients will support their end of the contract by making frank disclosure of pertinent medical, social, and other history; by complying with the therapeutic regimen; and by paying for services rendered. Physicians expect to be paid for their services whether patients recover completely, only partially, or not at all.

By contrast, the contingent fee contract involves a fee that the client owes the lawyer only if the lawyer wins the case. Winning the case is the contingency that triggers an obligation to pay the fee. Contingent fee contracts range anywhere from 15% to 50% of the amount of the recovery. The percentage may depend upon such factors as the difficulty of the case, the skill or reputation of the attorney, or the stage of the case at which recovery is had (before filing suit, before trial, or before or after appeal). Some states have adopted a sliding scale for such contracts—the greater the degree of recovery, the less the percentage of the lawyer's fee. In cases filed against the United States under the Federal Tort Claims Act (see Chapter 20), the lawyer's fee is limited to 20% for the administrative portion of the claim, 25% if a lawsuit is filed.

Many physicians and physicians' associations feel that the contingent fee is unethical and unfair in that it encourages unnecessary litigation. While it is true that some ill-grounded lawsuits may be filed simply because the lawyer has failed to take an adequate amount of time in investigating the facts before filing the case, in the long run the contingent fee is preferable to other alternatives. One of those alternatives would be making available at public expense a lawyer to represent all indigent patients. Many patients who are injured are out of work and unable to keep up with their own medical and other ongoing expenses, much less pay a legal fee. Thus, the contingent fee forms a valuable safeguard for the promotion of justice within the existing free enterprise legal system.

Expert Opinion

Having amassed the facts, the lawyer should (and if competent, will) obtain an expert opinion from a physician. Many physicians are reticent to talk to lawyers about care rendered by a colleague. For this reason, some lawyers must obtain such consultation from outside of the place where the defendant lives. While this process may be more time-consuming, it tends to promote objectivity. If the expert is of the opinion that the untoward result was caused by a departure from the duty of care, the lawyer will so advise the client, and will proceed with filing the lawsuit.

Complaint

The first formal step in the process of litigation involves drafting and filing a complaint in the appropriate court. That court, as noted above, generally is a civil court in the same county in which the defendant lives and practices. The complaint is a formal legal document setting forth the name and address of the defendant, the name and address of the plaintiff, the act or acts claimed to have caused the plaintiff's injury, the nature of the injury, and a demand for a specific amount of damages. Once the complaint is formally filed with the clerk of the court, a copy is sent by certified mail to the defendant.

Some lawyers have been accused of inflating the amount claimed to generate publicity for themselves or their firms. Because complaints, once filed, are available to the public and sometimes reports of them (notably a large lawsuit against a local hospital or physician) make their way into the news media, some states have enacted statutes precluding litigants from naming the amount of damages demanded.

Framing and Filing the Answer

Physicians who receive notice of the action pending against them, through receipt of the complaint, should notify their insurance carrier immediately. The carrier in turn will assign a lawyer of its selection to represent the physician. It will be the responsibility of that lawyer to follow through on all procedural steps that may ultimately lead to dismissal of the case, compromise (settlement), or if necessary the trial itself. The lawyer has a specific time to file an answer, and in doing so must respond to each of the allegations of the plaintiff. In order to be able to respond accurately and completely, the lawyer must obtain as much pertinent information from the defendant as possible within the relatively short time during which the answer must be framed and filed. The lawyer will schedule a meeting with the physician as soon as possible. This meeting, described below, will also serve as a beginning of the preparation of the defense.

If the amount of damages demanded exceeds the limits of the policy of that physician, it may be a wise idea to retain services of a personal lawyer in addition to the lawyer assigned to the case by the insurance carrier. The personal lawyer will represent the physician's interests and *only those interests*. The lawyer assigned by the insurance company to represent the physician has a direct responsibility to the physician, but *is being paid by the carrier*, and in many instances has an ongoing relationship with the carrier (that is, the carrier uses his or her services regularly). Were a conflict to develop between the interests of the carrier and those of the physician, the physician with no independent representation may well have doubts as to where the interests of the carrier's attorney lie.* For this reason, some medical-legal experts feel that *every* physician should be represented by a personal lawyer in addition to the one assigned by the carrier.

Preparation of the Case for the Defense

Generally, the initial conference between the lawyer assigned to the case and the defendant physician will be in the physician's office. A representative of the claims department of the carrier may attend this conference. If the physician has a personal lawyer, that lawyer should be present as well. The lawyer for the insurance carrier will review with the physician his or her personal recollection of the case, including any notes taken. The lawyer will want the physician to give an opinion on the quality of care rendered. It is highly important that the physician be totally honest with the lawyer at this time and throughout the proceedings. What the physician tells the attorney is confidential and remains that way. Any effort to conceal an act known by the defendant to be a departure from the duty of care can only result in later embarrassment and possibly an even larger judgment for the plaintiff. The lawyer also will want to know everything the physician knows about the patient, including past and present history, diagnosis, treatment, and the like. Having obtained this information, the lawyer will be in a reasonably good position to file the answer to the complaint. The answer may admit the allegation, deny it, or state that the defendant has insufficient evidence on which to base a reply. Once the answer is formally filed, the issues are joined and the preparation of the case may begin.

---

*For example, the conventional insurance policy covers professional negligence but not intentional torts. If an anesthesiologist failed to obtain *any* consent, the patient could allege that a *battery* had occurred, for which the carrier probably would deny coverage. Or, the carrier could agree to afford a defense in such a case, but with the reservation of rights to determine later whether to pay any damages. In this instance, the defendant would be well advised to retain independent legal representation. Issues concerning professional liability insurance and whether to retain such representation are covered more fully in Chapter 29.

The lawyer's next step is to obtain copies of all pertinent medical records, including records of any care rendered the patient prior to that given by the defendant. As noted in Chapter 2, much of what transpires between the patient and the physician is considered privileged in nature. That is, it is personal and in general not subject to being divulged by the physician without the consent of the patient. Once the patient places his or her health on the line, however, and alleges that it was impaired by some act of the defendant, the physician-patient privilege is usually abrogated, and the defendant physician has a right, not only of access to all other documents pertaining to the plaintiff's medical care, but also to disclose within the judicial proceedings information that he or she obtained from that relationship.

After the defense lawyer has assembled the medical records and all other necessary information, the next step is to discuss the facts with an independent medical expert and obtain an objective opinion about the patient's care. Defense lawyers generally do not have difficulty in obtaining such opinions. It is obviously essential that this opinion be totally objective. Efforts on the part of such an expert to conceal or play down acts of medical negligence will be counterproductive later on when the plaintiff's expert renders his or her opinion.

In the interests of justice and the speedy resolution of lawsuits, it is very important that all unfavorable as well as favorable aspects of each side be unearthed during the early evaluation of the case. Any weakness in the defense mandates that consideration be given to making a settlement offer. Conversely, weakness on the side of the plaintiff may mitigate the damages or even negate the entire case.

Discovery

The process of obtaining information from the opposing side is called *discovery*. It is a formal procedure that is encouraged by the courts to get all facts in possession of each side known to the other long before the case comes to trial. It may include requests for documents (medical records and the like) to be produced, written interrogatories, and examination of witnesses (including patient and health care provider) by oral deposition. By ferreting out this information, the issues (exactly what the defendant did to cause the plaintiff's injury) are narrowed. Early discovery promotes early resolution of cases, many before trial. Only a minute percentage of all of the civil cases filed ever go to trial.

Pretrial Conference

Depending upon the number of cases awaiting trial in a given jurisdiction, the suit may be set for trial 2 to as long as 6 years after it was initially filed. At some point, as the trial date approaches, the judge will call lawyers for the opposing sides into his or her office for a pretrial conference. The purpose of this conference is further to narrow the issues and explore all avenues of settlement or compromise. If the judge does not feel that the plaintiff has a case, there may be strong recommendations for dropping the case altogether. Few trial lawyers want to spend the time and energy trying a case knowing that they will lose before it even starts. Hence, there are strong reasons why lawyers will make every effort to resolve cases short of trial if at all possible. Few medical malpractice cases in which the patient's side has merit are tried. Generally, in those that are tried, the plaintiff has an exaggerated opinion of the amount of damages and makes an excessive settlement demand.

Medical malpractice cases are settled for three reasons:

1 The health care provider made a mistake and that mistake caused the patient to suffer a recognizable injury.
2 Even though the physician met the duty of care, it would be difficult to prove that fact in court because of poor documentation—records that are sketchy, illegible, or missing altogether—or because of unfortunate (from the physician's view) statements made by a health care provider.
3 Although the plaintiff's case has very little merit, it would be less costly to effectuate settlement for a minimal amount than to take the case to court.

Settling cases for the last reason generally causes considerable concern among members of the health care community. It must be remembered, however, that insurance carriers are in business to sell insurance and make a small return on their enterprise. Trying cases costs money. If a case has little merit, it may be far less expensive for the carrier to offer a nominal settlement than to defend it in court. Court costs and legal fees can be expensive and cost several times that of such a nominal settlement. This practice, while decried by health care professionals everywhere, does rest on a sound financial footing.

TRIAL OF THE CASE

Trials are conducted in an orderly fashion, similar to the conduct of the pretrial proceedings. The first step is selection of the jury if the case will be tried before one. There is in most states a constitutional right to trial by jury provided that the damages demanded exceed a certain amount. Generally, most injured plaintiffs feel that they would be better able to obtain a fair trial (read "high verdict") if a jury is used. Many physicians feel that jurors, being laypersons, do not understand medical terminology, tend not to be objective, and often equate injury with negligence. In practice, those feelings tend to be exaggerated, and jurors generally are quite objective and fair. They customarily listen carefully to the evidence and to the instructions given them, and generally bring in a fair verdict consonant with that evidence. Cases that are tried to the bench (by the judge) generally involve complex factual situations in which the lawyers on both sides feel that a judge would be in a better position to interpret the facts than would a group of laypersons. Cases tried under the Federal Tort Claims Act (see Chapter 20) must be tried by the judge.

Jurors are selected by a process called *voir dire*. They are questioned, either individually or as a group, in reference to knowledge of any of the parties in the case, employment and activities involved in the case ("Did you ever work for a hospital?"), and other potential sources of bias. If a specific bias is identified, the juror may be discharged for cause. Each side has an unlimited number of challenges for cause. In addition, each side has a certain number of additional preemptory challenges. The lawyer may use these challenges at will, without giving any specific reason.

Once the jurors are selected, they are sworn in. The judge makes a few opening remarks and turns the case over to the plaintiff's lawyer.

Opening Statements

Each side is given a certain amount of time to present an opening statement. The opening statement delineates what the lawyer intends to prove for his or her client. The lawyer will briefly review the evidence and also may touch upon the opponent's evidence as expected to materialize. These remarks are concluded with a statement such as

> *Ladies and gentlemen of the jury, my esteemed opponent and I expect you to listen carefully to the evidence as we present it. If you find that the client was injured but through no fault of defendant Dr. Blank, then you must bring in a verdict for Dr. Blank. On the other hand, if you feel that my client's injuries were directly caused by something that Dr. Blank did, then as the judge will instruct you, you must bring in a verdict for my client. I feel certain, having heard the evidence, that you will bring in a verdict for my client. Thank you very much.*

At this point, the defense presents its opening statement. It follows the same format as the plaintiff's opening statement, except that it stresses the position of the defense on each of the disputed issues. It, too, concludes with a stirring admonition to the jurors to bring in a fair verdict, stressing, of course, that if the jurors listen carefully to the evidence, they will inevitably conclude that the defendant did no wrong!

The Plaintiff's Case-in-Chief

Following the opening statements, the plaintiff introduces evidence to support the contention that the defendant breached the duty of care owed the patient-plaintiff, that the defendant's breach of duty caused the plaintiff to suffer the injury or injuries complained, and that those injuries should be compensated by a certain dollar amount. Evidence thus introduced is called the plaintiff's *case-in-chief.*

Evidence involves the testimony of witnesses and introduction of documents such as business records, memoranda, and other tangible things supporting the contention of the party introducing them. In a medical malpractice action, the medical record may become a key piece of evidence.

Much of the evidence may be highly technical. Generally, an expert in the specialty field of the defendant must testify as to what the standard of care is, how that standard was breached in the case, and how the damages sought resulted from that breach. (For a consideration of the health care provider as an expert witness, see Chapter 24; the elements of proof in an action for negligence are discussed at length in Chapter 3.) The plaintiff also will often retain the services of an economist to testify as to damages.

Damages take one of three forms. *Special damages* include medical expenses, past, present, and projected into the future; loss of income past, present, and projected into the future; and any cost of special training for a plaintiff suffering a permanent impairment. *General damages* compensate for pain and suffering. If the patient is married, the spouse customarily will file a derivative action to the plaintiff's action, alleging loss of care, comfort, and society of the injured spouse. Such loss of consortium, when awarded, is a part of general damages. If someone close to the injured patient observed the act of negligence, that individual may allege the negligent infliction of emotional harm. This cause of action, not universally recognized in all U.S. jurisdictions, is being alleged in increasing numbers of cases.

If the plaintiff feels that the negligence of the defendant was particularly egregious, an act that appeared to have *intended* to harm the plaintiff, the latter may ask for *punitive damages.* These damages are intended to punish the defendant, and the amount demanded is not equated to either the special or general damages, but to the nature of the act complained of. Punitive damages may be exceedingly large.

Each of the plaintiff's witnesses is subject to cross-examination by the lawyer for the defense (the role of the physician as a witness is covered in the next chapter). After all of the plaintiff's evidence is in, the plaintiff rests. Customarily, the lawyer for the defendant then moves for a directed verdict. The lawyer in effect says: "Your honor, you have heard the plaintiff's evidence. My opponent has not introduced sufficient evidence on all elements of the negligence action. [The lawyer then proceeds to delineate how the proof was lacking. For example, proof might be lacking that the negligent act of the defendant caused the injury.] Therefore, I move that your honor direct the verdict in favor of my client, the defendant." If the plaintiff has in truth failed to introduce enough evidence on each element, the judge must grant the defendant's motion. That, in effect, ends the case. In the usual case, the plaintiff generally is able to obtain a sufficient amount of evidence to overcome this motion. Furthermore, judges are naturally reluctant to grant this motion, inasmuch as almost half of the trial has already been conducted and would have to be repeated if the motion were granted only to have an appellate court determine it should not have been. If the motion is denied, it becomes the defendant's turn to present evidence.

The Defendant's Case-in-Chief

The defense then calls its witnesses and presents whatever documents and testimony it feels will support its side. The procedure is similar to that employed by the plaintiff. When all the defendant's evidence is in, the defense rests and a motion again is made for a directed verdict. Generally, the judge will deny this motion. The plaintiff then has the opportunity to introduce rebuttal evidence. The defense may then endeavor to rebut (by a process called *surrebuttal*) the plaintiff's rebuttal evidence. In a case involving alleged professional negligence, the defendant health care provider(s) is expected to sit at counsel table and actively assist his or her lawyers during the entire trial (see Chapter 24).

After all of the evidence, including any rebuttal evidence, has been introduced, both sides rest. Each side then has the opportunity to present closing arguments.

Closing Arguments

These "arguments" are really statements summarizing the evidence presented by each side, stressing the strong points and refuting the evidence presented by the opponent. The purpose of closing arguments is to refresh in the jurors' minds the material that has been presented to them. These statements are important, as some trials drag out over several weeks and the jurors, who are not usually permitted to take notes, would be hard-pressed to remember much of what was introduced. Customarily, the plaintiff, who comes first in both presentation of evidence-in-chief and closing arguments, reserves some time from the allotted interval to rebut the defendant's closing statement. Thus the sequence of closing statements is plaintiff-defendant-plaintiff. The theory is that the party who has the burden of proving his or her case to the jury has the opportunity to start *and* to end.

Instructions to the Jury

Following the completion of the closing statements, the judge instructs the jury on the applicable law. For example, the judge's instructions might state

Ladies and gentlemen of the jury, you have heard the evidence presented by the plaintiff and the defense in this case. You will recall that I instructed you at the beginning of this trial about what is called the "duty of care" of physicians, and the consequences of not meeting that duty. You have heard evidence about the duty of care of physicians such as the defendant, Doctor Blank. If you find that Doctor Blank has, as the plaintiff has alleged, departed from the duty of care and, further, that this departure caused the plaintiff's injury, then you must find for the plaintiff. You have also been given evidence as to the amount of damages that you may award if you determine that the plaintiff has established a case. The burden of proof lies with the plaintiff. Thus, upon consideration of all of the evidence, if you find that evidence of the plaintiff exceeds the evidence of the defendant on every one of the points in the negligence action that have been referred to, then you must render a verdict for the plaintiff. If, however, the evidence of the plaintiff does not exceed that of the defendant on any one of those points, then you must find for the defendant.

The members of the jury then are sequestered to discuss the case and render a verdict. Initially the jurors elect a foreman who controls their deliberations. The jurors may take anywhere from hours to weeks to sort over the evidence as they remember it, view the documents that are sent with them to the jury room, and reach a decision. When the jurors have reached a verdict, the judge is notified. The court is reconvened, the jurors are brought back into the jury box, and the judge requests that the foreman read the verdict, that is, "We find for the . . ."

Following the rendering of the verdict, both sides have the opportunity to make additional motions. The losing party may file a motion for judgment *non obstante verdicto*—not withstanding the verdict— or for a new trial. While the judge can grant a motion for a new trial, if he or she was convinced that the trial was conducted fairly and the verdict just, the motion would be denied. The losing party then has the opportunity to appeal to the next highest court.

APPELLATE PROCEDURE

The fact that one loses a case does not in and of itself furnish grounds for appeal. Appeals may be taken for a variety of specific reasons, all of which are set forth either in the procedural law of the jurisdiction or by common law decision. Common grounds for appeal include errors in instructing the jury, misinterpretations of the law, errors in admitting evidence, verdicts that fly in the face of the evidence, verdicts in which the measure of damages is grossly excessive or inadequate and, possibly, juror misconduct. Upon appeal, the complete transcript of the trial is made available to the appellate judges, and each side files an appellate brief supporting its position. At the time set in the future, the case is heard by the appellate judges, usually a panel of two or three. Each side presents its oral arguments specifically directed to the points on appeal. The appellate judges listen to the arguments, review the appellate briefs and the transcript of the trial, and make a decision. The losing party still may have the opportunity to appeal to the highest court (generally the Supreme Court) in that jurisdiction. Generally, unless a federal question is involved, the appellate process stops with the highest state court. In the federal court system, appeals may be taken all the way to the U.S. Supreme Court.

CONCLUSION

I was once involved in a matter in which our client's first question, upon being sued for several million dollars, was "If I do not immediately pay into court the full amount claimed in the complaint, will I go to jail?" The answer was "Absolutely not." The question, if posed by a first-year law student in class, would draw humor. But for a client, not trained in the process of litigation and as fearful of the unknown as of the possible verdict at the end of the road, there are no foolish questions.

It is likely that, at some time during his or her professional career, each anesthesiologist and anesthetist will be involved either as a witness or as a defendant in some type of lawsuit. Whatever the role, the practitioner is better able to perform if, in addition to a thorough knowledge of the facts of the case, he or she has an understanding of the process of litigation itself—how and why it is conducted. A review of the material contained in this chapter should go far toward accomplishing this last end.

24

W. Stuart Dornette, J.D.

The Health Care Provider as a Witness

With the number of lawsuits involving personal injuries currently active in the courts, health care providers often find themselves in court as factual witnesses, opinion witnesses, or some combination of the two. More frequently, given the fact that more than 90% of all lawsuits are settled before trial, the health care provider may be called upon before the trial commences to give a deposition—testimony taken under oath before a court reporter who transcribes the attorney's questions and the health care provider's answers.

Testifying in a legal proceeding of any sort involves far more than raising one's right hand, taking an oath "to tell the truth, the whole truth, and nothing but the truth," and answering the questions of the attorney. At whatever level or stage of a proceeding, testimony involves careful and thorough preparation to the end that nothing that occurs in the courtroom will come as any surprise to the witness or to the attorney who is preparing that witness. It is the purpose of this chapter to review the role of the health care provider as witness and to offer suggestions to help the medical witness fulfill that role.

FACTUAL TESTIMONY AND OPINION TESTIMONY

Health care providers are asked to appear to give either factual or expert opinion testimony in a lawsuit. The distinction is significant as to whether the medical witness is required to testify, the nature of the preparation required for the testimony, and the rules governing the giving of the testimony. Factual testimony involves describing the actual events that took place. The treating physician of a patient whose medical condition is the subject of litigation may give factual testimony describing the examination of the patient, the diagnosis made, the therapy prescribed, the results of that therapy, and the charges for the medical treatment—actual facts of which the treating physician is aware from participating in the patient's medical care. While a diagnosis, for example, may have constituted an opinion when it was made, once made, the diagnosis becomes another of the facts to which the factual witness testifies.

Opinion testimony is, as the name implies, the expression of the medical witness's opinion, based upon his or her expertise and the facts of what happened in the case, about some issue in the case. Examples of such testimony appear daily—in a homicide case, the coroner's opinion, based upon the results of the autopsy, that death was caused by the drug overdose that other testimony indicates was administered by the defendant; in a workers' compensation case, the orthopedic surgeon's opinion that the claimant will never regain full use of his or her injured arm; in the malpractice action, the nurse anesthetist's opinion that the defendant breached the standard of care owed by nurse anesthetists to the patient.

A physician or other health care provider can always be required to give factual testimony. The procedure involves the issuance of a subpoena—an order, usually from a court—requiring the medical witness to appear at a certain time and place to give testimony. It may also include a requirement that certain documents, including the patient's medical records, be produced at the time of the deposition.

One of the first questions a physician who receives a subpoena for the first time often has is: "Do I have to go on the date specified in the subpoena?" The answer is usually "No." If the subpoena is for a deposition, it will almost always be rescheduled for the convenience of the physician; if it is for testimony at a trial, judges are usually very accommodating when it comes to physicians' schedules.

The important things to remember are

1 Do not ignore the subpoena, but attend to it immediately, particularly if you have a scheduling problem.
2 Make certain your patient knows about the subpoena (usually his or her attorney will have received a copy of it, but make certain that is the case).
3 Do not discuss the case or the medical records with anyone without the consent of your patient.

These last two admonitions are necessary because you, as a treating physician, owe a duty to your patient to maintain confidences. The best thing to do upon receiving a subpoena of any sort is to call and send it to your own attorney to handle any issues of scheduling, notification of patient, and the like.

By contrast, the giving of opinion testimony by a medical provider is a matter of choice: you may choose to do it frequently; you may choose not to do it at all. Rare indeed is the circumstance in which a medical provider can be required to give opinion testimony. In a number of jurisdictions, however, one who is a party to the lawsuit may be compelled to give opinion testimony. For instance, in a case involving alleged medical malpractice, the defendant might be called to testify and required to give an opinion on whether the care given the patient met the standard of care and, if it did not, whether that departure from the duty of care caused the untoward result. This type of testimony is discussed below.

TYPES OF OPINION TESTIMONY FROM HEALTH CARE PROVIDERS

The role of the health care provider as an expert witness offering opinion testimony in a lawsuit will very much depend upon its nature. Many cases are personal injury actions in which the plaintiff was injured because of the acts or actions of the defendant. For example, in a case involving failure to recognize accidental esophageal intubation in a timely fashion, an anesthesiologist might be expected to testify about the appropriate steps that should be taken *routinely* after insertion of an endotracheal catheter, which, had they been carried out in the instant case, would have led to a speedy correction of the problem, rather than prolonged asphyxia. In any personal injury case, the plaintiff must establish that there was some physical injury incurred by him or her (e.g., central nervous system damage) as a result of the acts of the defendant, and it is for that physical injury that he or she is seeking to recover damages. The medical witness, usually a physician, will be called upon to help establish the nature and extent of the injury. In this setting, the expert testimony may be in any of the following areas:

- To explain the nature of the treatment which the plaintiff underwent (particularly if it was long, involved, or painful)
- To explain the nature of the injury
- To explain the prognosis for recovery or, if 100% recovery is not likely, any limitations on the patient's future ability to function
- To offer an opinion that the injury was caused by an act or acts of the defendant

As can be seen from this list, often there are not bright line distinctions between factual and opinion testimony. An explanation of the nature of the injury—for example, trauma to the larynx following allegedly inept intubation, including a description with illustrations of the cartilages, intrinsic muscles, and innervation—is not strictly speaking the offering of an expert's opinion. Nonetheless, the good expert witness is a teacher whose job it will be to instruct the judge and jury as to what happened. Usually their understanding is essential to the resolution of the issues in the case, and the expert who can provide it in a *simple, straightforward, and comprehensible* fashion goes a long way toward establishing his or her own credibility.

Because the treating physician already knows the patient's history and condition,

he or she frequently is asked to become the plaintiff's expert witness.* But that is not necessarily the case. Any party to a personal injury action is permitted to examine not only the medical records of the plaintiff but the plaintiff himself or herself in order to testify about the injury. A medical malpractice claim is a particular kind of personal injury action in which the claim is that a medical provider was negligent (see Chapter 3) and it was his or her negligence that caused the physical injury. In such a lawsuit, a medical witness's testimony may be in any of the areas listed above relating to the nature of the injury or the plaintiff's damages. It may also be directed to the threshold (key) question of whether the medical provider's conduct was negligent.

An expert testifying in this latter area rarely has treated, and frequently has neither seen nor examined, the patient. The medical witness bases his or her opinion on a review of the facts of the case, including the medical records, and expresses it through the answer to hypothetical questions derived from those facts. The lawyer conducting the examination will elicit the witness's expert opinion in the following manner. "Doctor, I want you to assume that the following facts are true...." The facts are summarized, and the witness then is asked to give an opinion about the diagnosis and appropriate course of therapy, and whether the care (diagnosis and treatment) met the standard of care (see Chapter 4). "Doctor, assuming all of those facts to be true, do you have an opinion, based upon reasonable medical certainty, whether...."

To be ready for a courtroom appearance and testimony as a witness, it is important to review the process of testifying, and how one prepares for it.

---

*Given the physician's obligation to maintain patient confidences, it is unlikely that the treating physician would be testifying as an expert for anyone other than the plaintiff. As noted above, a physician should always refrain from discussing a particular case with any outsider without the express consent of the patient. The only exception occurs in the areas of reporting requirements under certain (e.g., public health) statutes or when cooperating in a criminal investigation. Any of these exceptions should be explored carefully by the physician with his or her own personal lawyer.

PREPARATION OF THE WITNESS

The preparation of the witness is a multistep process that ideally should begin long before the witness is expected to testify. It involves affording the witness an understanding of

1 The facts in the case
2 The legal theories of the party for whom he or she is testifying, and those of the opposing party
3 Courtroom layout and procedure
4 How the witness is qualified
5 What areas are to be covered in direct examination
6 What to be watchful for during cross-examination
7 Courtroom demeanor

Knowledge of the Facts and Medical Background

It should be obvious that the witness, whether giving factual or opinion testimony, must be thoroughly familiar with the medical facts in the case. The treating physician should already possess this knowledge as a result of prior patient contacts, refreshed by a careful review of the medical record. The expert witness obtains this familiarity by reviewing the medical record and depositions given by other parties to the case, and consulting with the lawyer who called that professional to testify. In performing the chart review, the witness should be alerted to such items as missing laboratory data (e.g., was an arterial blood sample drawn for gas analysis? If not, why not?) Under certain circumstances, it may be desirable for the witness to examine the patient in preparation for giving testimony.

Medical records are the documents that are most essential for the preparation of the expert witness; the witness must become thoroughly familiar with them. If they are extensive, the witness should carefully digest them and might find it desirable to prepare a summary of them. The witness would be able to take such a summary to the stand when called to testify, to assist in referring to pertinent aspects of the record during the testimony. Medical records

should be among the first documents exchanged among lawyers early in the pretrial discovery (see Chapter 23), and they therefore should be readily available to the medical expert.

It is also critical that the expert witness be aware of pertinent scientific literature that will buttress or may be used to attack his or her opinion. The witness should furnish the lawyer for whom he or she is testifying references to or (better still) copies of this literature. The lawyer then can use them to prepare for his or her witness's direct examination and for the cross-examination of the opponent's expert. The witness also should be familiar with the opinions of eminent specialists, including published works, and may need to be able to distinguish the facts in the instant case from those in a case in which such a specialist gave an opinion opposite to that of the witness.

Legal Theories of the Case

After the witness has had the opportunity to become thoroughly familiar with the facts, he or she should be instructed by the lawyer on the legal theories of both the plaintiff and defendant, including the opinion of the opponent's expert witnesses. That is, what is the basis of the plaintiff's cause of action and of the defense's position that there is no cause of action? An example of a legal theory would be that even though the defendant had delayed making a diagnosis of carcinoma, it would have made no difference in the final outcome, at the earlier time when the defendant should have made the diagnosis. The witness should be prepared to support the theory of the client on whose behalf the testimony will be given and to refute the opponent's legal theories and experts' opinions.

Courtroom Layout and Procedure

Many health care providers have never before appeared as a witness in a court of law. The thought of being in the courtroom and undergoing cross-examination in an unknown environment generates real fear that may not be fully appreciated by the seasoned trial lawyer who regularly frequents the courtroom. It is the lawyer's responsibility to apprise the first-time witness of courtroom layout, possibly by making a diagram showing the locations of the bench, witness stand, court reporter's seat, counsel tables, and jury box. If the lawyer does not, the witness should ask. This simple step will help orient the witness and allay much apprehension.

With few exceptions, the right to trial by jury is a constitutional guarantee.* Either side may request a trial by jury. Many personal injury lawyers will automatically ask for a jury trial on behalf of their injured client. The number of jurors who will sit on a given case will depend on the jurisdiction and magnitude of the case. The jurors listen to the facts as they are presented through testimony and real evidence (see Chapter 23) and base their finding on those facts after applying pertinent law as instructed by the judge. The judge rules on legal questions and related issues. In a case tried by the judge (tried "to the bench"), the latter listens to the testimony and takes the place of the jurors as finder of fact as well as the arbiter of legal issues. When dealing with complex factual situations, many lawyers prefer a trial by the judge. Courtroom proceedings tend to be a little less formal when a case is so tried.

In all civil cases the plaintiff's evidence is introduced first, followed by that of the defendant (see Chapter 23). The medical witness will testify after the trial has already been in progress—the jury impaneled, the opening statements made, and possibly after other witnesses have already given their testimony. A courtroom appearance involves being sworn in, being qualified, giving direct testimony, and being subjected to cross-examination. These steps are discussed below.

Swearing In and Qualifying the Witness

The witness, after being called to the stand, will be "placed under oath"—asked to swear that the testimony about to be giv-

en will be "the truth, the whole truth, and nothing but the truth." The lawyer who calls the witness to testify on behalf of his or her client will then qualify the witness. The witness will be asked to state his or her name, address, occupation, and professional qualifications. Professional qualifications include undergraduate education and degrees, medical school attended and degree(s), postgraduate education including specialty training, and any subsequent seminars or other programs attended. Of special importance to older practitioners is their being able to attest that they have kept up with the continuing professional education requirements of their state licensing board, and also meet the requirements, if any, for reaccreditation by their specialty board. Putting the witness's "best foot forward" is especially important when qualifying the expert witness. The greater the apparent degree of the witness's expertise, the more weight the trier of fact will place on the testimony of that expert.

If a witness's qualifications are particularly impressive, opposing counsel may concede that the witness is qualified, and offer to waive this testimony. While such waiver may seem to speed up the process and get the health care provider out of the courtroom sooner, it may not be advisable. It is important for the jurors to be thoroughly exposed to all of these qualifications as a basis for their better appreciation of the witness's opinions.

Following qualification of the witness, the opposing counsel may want to cross-examine the witness about these qualifications, a process called *voir dire*. The purpose of the *voir dire* (French, meaning "to speak truthfully") is to allow the opposing counsel to challenge whether the background, education, and experience of the witness is appropriate to support the opinion testimony to be offered.

Direct Examination

Direct examination is the basic questioning of the witness by the attorney who has retained him or her. It starts with the identification and qualification set out above and then moves into the background, medical or otherwise, needed to understand the issues of the case, followed by

---

*Cases filed under the Federal Tort Claims Act (see Chapter 20) are exceptions to this guarantee; they are tried to the federal district judge without a jury.

what it was the expert witness was asked to do, followed by what the expert witness did, followed by what conclusions the expert reached. Those particular elements may be varied, but they are almost always to be found in the direct examination of an expert. That typically is the end of the direct examination and the cross-examination follows.

The one evidential rule of direct examination is that the examiner may not ask leading questions. "What is your opinion?" is an open-ended question and is proper. "Isn't it true that your opinion is . . ." is a leading question and is improper. Thus, direct examination is an opportunity for the witness to speak, through narrative answers, directly to the judge and jury.

Following are some basic principles for the medical witness to have in mind when preparing for *direct examination*. They may be discussed when being prepared by the attorney who will be calling the witness to the stand.

- Believe in the case of the client on whose behalf you will be testifying, or do not accept the engagement. Actors do not convince juries of the correctness of their position. Sincerity does. You are trying to establish your credibility and trustworthiness for the jury. You do that by presenting a position in which you believe.
- Use plain English wherever you can. Where you cannot, carefully explain to the jury or judge what it is you are talking about. Remember that *they are laypersons, with little or no medical background*. Work out with the attorney who is offering your testimony any analogies or examples that will be helpful to the judge and jury in understanding your testimony.
- If your research uncovers facts or opinions unfavorable to the side on which you will be testifying, inform the attorney of them. Surprises in the courtroom during trial can be devastating. The expert may need to offer a plausible explanation for changes in the medical record.
- Know exactly where the attorney is going on direct examination. You should review your testimony with

him or her so that you understand what points are to be brought out at what places in the examination. Do not review it to the point that it sounds rehearsed and stale.
- Do not give an expert opinion unless you are completely satisfied that you are qualified in the area of specialization involved and possess the appropriate expertise.
- Use visual aids where possible. Charts, illustrations, diagrams, blowups of key documents or even key pieces of testimony upon which you rely in your conclusions can be powerful learning tools for the jury and create a dramatic impact upon a case. Work with the attorney who is offering your testimony to develop a series of such visual aids to illustrate important aspects of your testimony, but do not rely solely upon his or her suggestions. You know your field, and you know what resources are available.
- Tell the truth. A lie, even on an extraneous point, can lose the case.
- Direct your answers to the jury or judge, not just to the attorney who is asking the questions. Do not be afraid to spend some time early in your testimony explaining a particular medical problem or procedure that is involved in the case, particularly if it is something the judge or members of the jury may have been hearing about in the press or elsewhere. Nothing sets up your testimony better in the mind of a decision maker than the thought "Oh I didn't know what these people were talking about when they kept saying 'CAT scan': I'm glad to find that out." The jurors now trust you when it comes to the opinion you are offering.
- Speak loudly enough to be heard. If you are looking at the jurors (or judge if there is no jury) when you answer lawyers' questions (see previous admonition), you will be able to tell from the listeners' reactions if you need to raise the level of your voice.
- Be brief. You need to maintain the jury's and judge's interest for the key points of your testimony. If some-

thing is not inherently of interest (few things are) or crucial to your testimony, leave it out.

- Unless you are a party (see below), when you are finished with your testimony, leave the courtroom. You are a disinterested person who has taken time out of a busy schedule to come and help the jurors understand this complicated matter; you are not someone with such a stake in the outcome of the case that you want to sit and watch the rest of it. Leave, or your credibility will decline with the judge or jury.
- Be courteous to everyone in the courtroom.

Cross-Examination

Cross-examination is far different from direct examination. It is usually an attempt to tear down the testimony the witness gave on direct examination or to otherwise discredit the witness. This examiner may (and should) ask leading questions. These questions attempt to lead the witness to answers that are favorable to the position of the cross-examiner but not to that of the client on whose behalf the witness is testifying.

A good cross-examination is an extensive narrative by the examiner punctuated by an occasional "Yes" or "No" from the witness. The witness should not be trapped into answering "Yes" or "No" when in fact the answer cannot be given exactly in that context. The witness should be watchful for "forked" questions. These have both a "Yes" and a "No" answer. The witness may forget about the first part of the question by the time the entire question is phrased. The answer to the second part is always opposite to that of the first. For example: "Doctor, isn't it true that when you made preoperative rounds you failed to ask my client about the drugs she was taking, and yet under 'Drug History' in the anesthesia record you wrote 'negative'? Just answer 'Yes' or 'No.'" The witness who follows the cross-examiner's lead and answers this question either "No" or "Yes," when it should have been answered "No and yes," will have fallen into a cleverly laid trap. There are many other such trick ques-

tions that the expert trial lawyer may use to attempt to confuse, frustrate, or anger, and then discredit the opponent's expert witness.

Some basic thoughts to have in mind when you are preparing for *cross-examination* are delineated below. As with the points for direct examination above, they should be discussed with the attorney who will be calling the witness to the stand.

- Tell the truth. If the question is "Did you meet with counsel before coming in to testify today," the answer is "Yes." If the question is "How much are you being paid for your testimony," the answer is you are receiving your normal rate for the time you are spending on this case—not for your testimony. (If the lawyer persists with this line of questioning, you should disclose your hourly fee.)
- Do not be intimidated by opposing counsel.
- Make certain you hear and understand the question before answering it. If you do not understand a question, ask the examiner to repeat or rephrase it.
- It is a good idea to pause briefly before answering the cross-examiner's questions. The lawyer on whose behalf you are testifying may want to enter an objection.
- If you do not know the answer to a question, say so. Furthermore, do not consider it an admission of ignorance to admit that your opinion is not conclusive. To attempt to gloss over such a point will detract from the impression you would like to leave with the jurors—one of frank openness.
- Answer only those questions that are asked. Nothing can be worse than trying to answer a question that the examiner has not asked but that you think the examiner should be asking.
- Listen to the attorney of the party who has retained you. His or her objection to a particular question may be overruled by the judge, but *may have some message for you*. If the attorney stands up and says "Objection, your honor, I do not understand

the question," ask the examiner to rephrase the question.
- Do not try to anticipate where the examiner is going with his or her questions. It will only serve to foul up your answers.
- Do not volunteer information. Answer only the question asked. This becomes particularly critical in the setting of a deposition. One piece of volunteered information can lead quite literally to another hour of questions.
- Never lose your temper.
- If there is a word used that is susceptible to more than one meaning, do not guess at which meaning is intended; ask the examiner.

The importance of this last principle may be illustrated by the following example. The action is one for malpractice against the treating physician.

The treating physician had referred the patient to a specialist (a Dr. Levy) to determine if a particular problem existed. The specialist rendered a 12-page report, most of which was window dressing. The treating physician, interested in the ultimate conclusion, scanned the report, and read the last two paragraphs carefully. The plaintiff's counsel is cross-examining the treating physician.

Q. Did you study the report Doctor Levy prepared for you?

[Thought processes of treating physician: Study? No, I didn't really study the report; I didn't have to. I knew most of that stuff he threw in there was window dressing, and I was interested in the conclusion. Does he mean did I look at it? The answer to that is "Yes." And if I say I did not look at it, the jury will think I was not doing my job.]

A. Yes.
Q. And that was because this was an important series of tests Doctor Levy was doing for you?
A. Yes.
Q. And Doctor Levy's expertise was in an area in which you did not have a lot of experience?
A. That is correct.
Q. In fact, you said your only prior experience with this problem was one afternoon class 17 years ago in medical school?

A. That is true.
Q. And his report was critical to the diagnosis you were making?
A. Yes.
Q. And you were relying upon his expertise in this area in doing his analysis and preparing his report?
A. Yes.
Q. And so you wanted to make sure you understood exactly what Dr. Levy had done and what he was saying in his report?
A. Yes, that's right.
Q. And you wanted to make sure what Doctor Levy reported to you was correct to the best of your knowledge?
A. Well, of course.

The examiner has now gotten the witness to adopt everything in the report as something he studied in diagnosing the plaintiff's ailment. The trap is about to be sprung shut as the examiner pulls out some statements on nonconsequential matters buried in the middle of the report and uses them to contradict the treating physician's prior testimony. The jurors are delighted they did not make the mistake of going to this boob for treatment. When the treating physician concedes that he really did study the last two paragraphs but did not go through the rest because the rest was unimportant, it sounds like a lame excuse for incompetence.

Compare that result with what might have happened on the first question of the series:

Q. Did you study the report Doctor Levy prepared for you?
A. What do you mean by "study"?
Q. Well, did you carefully review the entire report?
A. No. Most of the report was not important to the final conclusion. It was that final conclusion that I was interested in; that was the expertise of Dr. Levy upon which I was relying. So I studied carefully the final conclusion and really just skimmed through the remainder of the report.

Preparation and Demeanor

The lawyer who calls the witness should introduce the witness to some of the finer points of direct and cross-examination as part of the witness's preparation discussed above. This introduction helps the witness understand the nature of the questions that will be asked in the particular case and how best to respond. This preparation helps put the witness at ease and helps him or her avoid some of the traps that inevitably will be set by opposing counsel.

Perhaps the best method for achieving this end (especially in the case of an inexperienced witness) is for the witness to undergo simulated cross-examination some time before the trial. This simulated questioning may be effectively carried out by one of the partners of the lawyer who has called the provider to testify. If the law firm owns a video camera and recorder, the witness may then see himself or herself on tape while being subjected to simulated direct and cross-examination. By reviewing the tape, the witness may learn to avoid many problems inherent in being a first-time witness.

Finally, the witness should be aware of the proper dress (conservative) and demeanor while on the witness stand. As noted above, it is important that the witness be courteous to everyone in the courtroom. Yes, the witness is an important person who otherwise would not have been called into the case, but a pompous attitude will nullify the witness's effectiveness.

The witness should arrive at the courthouse well in advance of the time of the scheduled testimony and should be well rested. The witness should understand that there may be a delay before being called to the stand. Courts frequently do not run exactly on schedule.

When the testimony is finished, the judge will excuse the witness, who should leave the courtroom quietly and unobtrusively. Under certain circumstances, a witness may be subject to recall for rebuttal or other purposes. If that is the case, the witness will be instructed by the judge before leaving the stand.

THE EXPERT WITNESS'S FEE

Health care providers' time is valuable. It is customary for the provider who serves as an expert witness to submit an invoice covering the time spent in preparation and while giving testimony. The amount of that hourly fee should relate directly to the degree of expertise possessed by the provider. The hourly fee of many providers

is larger for giving testimony than it is for preparation. When testifying for a plaintiff in a personal injury action, it is unprofessional* to base the amount of the fee on amount of any plaintiff's award. The fee should be determined by mutual agreement when the prospective witness first meets the lawyer on whose behalf the provider will be testifying. At that time, the lawyer may ask the witness to approximate the number of hours that will be spent in preparation.

WHEN THE HEALTH CARE PROVIDER IS A DEFENDANT

At the current rate of litigation against health care providers, the odds are strong that the average reader of this book, if he or she practices long enough, will be named a defendant in a professional negligence action. The mechanics of the litigation process are discussed throughout this and the preceding chapter. Several additional queries come to mind, relating to the length of the trial and the presence of the defendant in the courtroom. Malpractice cases take from a number of days to several weeks to try. In general, the length of the trial is *directly proportional* to the complexity of the facts, the amount of disputed evidence, the number of witnesses that will be called, and the amount of the *ad damnum* (dollar value of damages demanded). The health care provider should be in the courtroom seated at the defense table *during the entire duration of the proceedings*. There are two very cogent reasons for his or her presence:

1 First, and perhaps foremost, professional liability insurance policies require the full cooperation of the insured. The defendant should listen carefully to the entire proceedings, and be prepared to inform his or her lawyer promptly of any untruths or distortion of facts by the opponent. Even with the best preparation, the defendant's lawyer may

*In addition, it would afford the witness an interest in the outcome of the litigation, thereby defeating his or her objectivity.

have missed some point that will be readily apparent to the defendant.

2 The second reason is psychological, but of almost equal importance. The defendant who sits in rapt attention for the duration of the trial, conferring with counsel and taking notes as appropriate, will create the impression among the jurors of strong interest in the defense. Absence(s), even of short duration, will have exactly the opposite effect. When the evidence on both sides is close, the defendant's presence or absence may make the difference in the verdict.

Self-employed health care providers, notably physicians, may express concern about the time away from a busy practice, and attendant loss of income. There is no way to compensate for this loss. Reimbursement is not provided by the usual professional liability insurance policy. The defendant who wins a totally frivolous case and files an action for malicious prosecution (see Chapter 5) might demand damages for loss of earnings as well as legal fees and other costs. This demand could very well be compensable if the physician-plaintiff obtains a verdict in the malicious prosecution litigation.

The defendant in a malpractice action undoubtedly will want or need to testify on his or her behalf. The preparation for and presentation of this testimony is the same as it would be for any expert witness.

Calling the Defendant "As on Cross"

Suppose that the defendant physician realizes he or she made a mistake and the mistake caused the untoward outcome. The physician so apprises his or her attorney, and the latter commences settlement discussions with the patient-plaintiff's lawyer. The patient's lawyer has already reviewed the case with a medical expert, has arrived at the same conclusion, and would like to depose the defendant to obtain an admission of his or her mistake. By doing so, the lawyer would hope to greatly increase his or her bargaining position at settlement.

As noted earlier in this chapter, in some jurisdictions a defendant may be compelled to give opinion testimony by and on behalf of the plaintiff's lawyer. In such a situation, the lawyer has the right to subject the witness to cross-examination, just as if the witness had previously given direct testimony. The rules for conducting this examination are the same as for "conventional" cross-examination, except that the questions need only relate to the facts of the case, because there was no prior direct examination.

CONCLUSION

Expert testimony is absolutely vital to the just adjudication of litigation involving many types of disputes, especially those arising from allegedly negligent health care. The likelihood of a physician being asked to testify, either as a factual or expert witness, is real. Physicians should understand their obligation to testify and the thorough preparation that must precede giving any sworn testimony in a court of law. This process is time-consuming but highly important. It should start months in advance, never just a few days before the trial commences. Keeping in mind the admonitions discussed in this chapter and following them carefully should help the physician make a satisfactory appearance for the client on whose behalf he or she is testifying and a valuable contribution to the client's cause and to that of justice.

6

Business and Other Relationships

Health care delivery has truly assumed the status of big business. Even individual practitioners may become enmeshed in the commercial ramifications of their professional activities. The final part of this book covers a variety of business-related issues—the legal status of the certified registered nurse anesthetist (CRNA), especially as an employee; the laws governing group practice and hospital privileges; the impact of antitrust laws on one's activities; and, finally, steps toward indemnifying one's self against liability for negligence via some form of professional liability coverage.

Nurses have been involved in the administration of anesthetics for many, many years. Inasmuch as giving anesthesia involves making diagnoses (determining the depth of anesthesia and the need for additional drugs) and prescribing therapy (administering anesthetics and other pharmaceuticals), it is clear that the nurse anesthetist's practice is akin to that of the physician. In every U.S. jurisdiction, by statute or administrative regulation, the practice of medicine is limited to those who have matriculated at an approved medical college and passed a qualifying examination administered by a state healing arts licensing board. Yet, as is well recognized, nurses everywhere are legally permitted to administer anesthetics. The status of their practice varies from state to state, inasmuch as it is defined by statute, healing arts board administrative regulation, the common law, or a combination thereof. How the "legalized" practice of the nurse anesthetist evolved, and his or her legal status today—with licensing board, hospital, and anesthesiologist—are the subjects of Chapter 25. An awareness of pertinent portions of this chapter would appear essential for nurse anesthetists, as well as those anesthesiologists who employ them in their practices.

Commencing the active practice of anesthesia is no longer a simple matter for many practitioners fresh out of their formal training. The start-up costs (e.g., the professional liability insurance premium, to name just one) may require that the newcomer to the specialty join an established group. Taking the latter step is no simple matter limited to call scheduling, paid vacations, and salary negotiations. Chapter 26, written by an expert in representing groups as well as individual practitioners, covers the many other detailed steps and contractual provisions involved in joining a group practice today. While this chapter is no substitute for competent legal counsel, understanding its contents will help both the new practitioner and his or her lawyer as well.

Except under unusual circumstances (e.g., work in a freestanding ambulatory care facility or pain clinic), anesthesia professionals must have hospital privileges in order to practice their specialty. While the application for and granting of such privileges may seem straightforward, numerous legal pitfalls await the novice. Professional advice, from a competent lawyer specializing in hospital law, may be indicated under many circumstances. Chapter 27, also written by a lawyer with considerable expertise in issues relating to such privileges, forms a good starting point for those who would become knowledgeable in the steps to take to optimize one's chances of being granted such privileges.

For a number of years, many professional associations have used membership criteria linked to quality performance standards ostensively to elevate the level of work of those professionals. Efforts to facilitate reimbursement by third-party payers led to the publication of so-called relative value guides. Any argument that such activities might be anticompetitive in nature was countered with the professional nature of the regulator and the practice regulated, the so-called professional exemption to the antitrust statutes. Beginning in 1975, courts began to overturn this exception. Recent decisions have involved individual employment contracts as well as concerted actions by groups of physicians. Chapter 28, written by a health care antitrust-law specialist, reviews these statutes and the common law they are based on, and suggests methodologies for avoiding entanglement in these laws.

For the large majority of health care professionals engaged in private practice in this country, some form of professional liability insurance—to indemnify that professional from liability for acts of negligence—is in order. Chapter 29 reviews the concepts of and mechanisms for casualty insurance underwriting. The chapter also covers some of the vicissitudes of such underwriting and considers methodologies for assuring continuing availability of such insurance in the private sector, including the value, disputed by some, of statutes intended to make it more difficult to obtain excessively large awards against health care providers (the so-called tort reform legislation). This chapter should be must reading for all practitioners concerned with the cost and availability of this type of indemnification.

Thomas C. Hill, the author of Chapter 27, is a partner in the litigation department of the Cincinnati law firm of Taft, Stettinius & Hollister. Since joining the firm, Mr. Hill has specialized in the representation of individual physicians and health care organizations. He was trial counsel for the defendants in *McElhinney v. The Medical Protective Company*, a staff-privileges antitrust case based on allegations that a surgeon's refusal to use anesthesiologists was a motivation for the formation of the conspiracy. He received his B.A. from Case Western Reserve University and his J.D. from the University of Chicago. He was admitted to practice in Ohio in 1973 and has since been admitted to practice before the Supreme Court of the United States as well as federal and state trial courts.

Susan Jenny is the international development attorney for the Marriott Corporation in Rockville, Maryland. At the time she coauthored Chapter 25, she was an associate at the Cincinnati law firm of Taft, Stettinius & Holister.

Ronald A. MacKenzie received his Doctor of Osteopathy from the Kansas City College of Osteopathic Medicine. He is a Diplomate of the American Board of Anesthesiology and Fellow in the American College of Anesthesiologists. Currently, he is Assistant Professor of Anesthesiology, Mayo Medical School, and Consultant and Vice Chairman, Department of Anesthesiology, Mayo Clinic, Rochester, Minnesota.

William B. Markovits, who wrote Chapter 28, is a partner in the Cincinnati law firm of Markovits & Greiwe. A 1971 *cum laude* graduate of Harvard Law School, Mr. Markovits spent his first few years of practice as a trial attorney with the Antitrust Division of the U.S. Department of Justice in Washington, D.C. Since moving to Cincinnati, he has continued to focus his practice on antitrust law and was an instructor of trade regulation at the University of Cincinnati College of Law. Mr. Markovits has been actively involved in health care law in recent years, and was plaintiffs' antitrust counsel in the *ChoiceCare* case, which resulted in a $100 million verdict in favor of a group of physicians suing a local health maintenance organization. Mr. Markovits provides counsel, consultation, and lectures to physician groups and other health care entities in problems relating to antitrust concerns.

Melvin S. Shotten, coauthor of Chapter 25 and author of Chapter 26, is a partner at Taft, Stettinius & Hollister, in Cincinnati, where he specializes in law relating to health care and finance. His health care practice concentrates on the rights and liabilities of, and fringe benefit possibilities for, individual physicians and their business organization. Mr. Shotten received his B.S. Aerospace Engineering in 1965 and his J.D. *(cum laude)* in 1968, both from the University of Michigan. He is licensed to practice law in the state of Ohio and before the Supreme Court of Ohio, the Federal District Court for the Southern District of Ohio and the Federal Sixth Circuit Court of Appeals.

W. H. L. D.

25

Susan A. Jenny, J.D.
Melvin S. Shotten, J.D.

The Legal Status
of the Nurse Anesthetist

Historical Background
Professional Providing Supervision
    Surgeon or Physician
    Anesthesiologist

Degree of Supervision
    State Statutes and Rules
    Case Law
    Federal Regulations

HISTORICAL
BACKGROUND

Nurses have provided anesthesia services since the discovery and first use of anesthetic drugs.[1] Today, nurse anesthetists are licensed, registered nurses with additional training who provide surgical anesthesia services, including preoperative evaluation, induction of anesthesia, endotracheal intubation, and intrasurgical and postsurgical monitoring of patients.[2] Most states specifically recognize the role of nurse anesthetists, by statute or administrative regulation, and authorize them to provide anesthesia services with varying amounts of supervision or input from licensed physicians. The particular role to be played by nurses in the provision of anesthesia service is a continuing subject of discussion and debate.

In the early part of the twentieth century, a paramount issue concerned whether the administration of anesthesia by a nurse anesthetist, under nonemergency circumstances, constituted the unlawful practice of medicine by a nonphysician.[3] A group of Ohio physicians filed charges before the Ohio Medical Board against the Lakeside Hospital School of Anesthesia for Nurses, alleging that the nurses were providing anesthesia illegally.[4] The medical board ruled in favor of Lakeside Hospital, and the Ohio Medical Practice Act was subsequently amended by the Ohio legislature to provide that

> Nothing in the act should be construed to apply to or prohibit in any way the administration of anesthetic by a registered nurse under the direction and in the immediate presence of a licensed physician, providing such nurse has taken a prescribed course in anesthesia at a hospital in good standing.[4]

By contrast, during the same era, the Kentucky Medical Society denied membership in good standing to physicians who employed nurse anesthetists or referred patients to hospitals employing nurse anesthetists. The society's position changed only after a Kentucky court of appeals defined the scope of practice for nurse anesthetists.[5] The court found that the practice of medicine, as defined broadly in a Kentucky statute, consisted of the diagnosis of an ailment, determination of the method of treatment of the ailment, and administration (or supervising the administration) of the treatment. The court noted that the nurse anesthetist was a licensed nurse who had made a special study of administering anesthetics to surgical patients, and who was employed by the defendant physician to "administer anesthesia under the physician's personal direction and supervision, in so far as it is possible for him to supervise and direct her work." The court concluded that administration of anesthesia by a nurse anesthetist, as one step in a plan of patient treatment determined by a licensed physician, does not constitute the practice of medicine.

In *Chalmers-Francis v. Nelson*, the California Supreme Court similarly concluded that the administration of anesthesia by a licensed nurse did not constitute the unlawful practice of medicine.[6] Because the then current statute did not specify the services and procedures a nurse could perform, the court relied upon case law from other jurisdictions, the California Medical Practice Act, and testimony regarding the uniform practice in operating rooms to illustrate the kinds of anesthesia and other nursing services that were recognized by the state. The court reasoned that adminis-

tration of anesthesia by nurses "under the immediate direction and supervision" of a surgeon is a uniform procedure that involves neither "diagnosing" nor "prescribing" within the meaning of the Medical Practice Act. The court therefore concluded that the nurse was merely carrying out the physician's order and ruled that anesthesia as practiced by the nurse anesthetist was within the scope of nursing practice. Today, there is little debate that administration of anesthesia by a nurse anesthetist does not constitute the unlawful practice of medicine.

This chapter will focus on the relationship between the nurse anesthetist and the surgeon or anesthesiologist in the administration of anesthesia in view of the basic tenet of the practice of anesthesia that a nurse anesthetist *shall* administer anesthesia under the supervision of or in collaboration with a physician.[7] Two different opinions about the amount of necessary supervision of a nurse anesthetist are promulgated by the American Society of Anesthesiologists (ASA) and the American Association of Nurse Anesthetists (AANA).

The ASA takes the position that anesthesia, particularly complicated anesthetic procedures such as regional anesthesia, should be administered by or under the medical direction and in the presence of a physician who is trained in the administration of anesthesia, preferably an anesthesiologist.[8] The ASA recognizes that "in areas where there is a shortage of physicians trained in anesthesiology, adequate anesthesia may be achieved through the use of certified registered nurse anesthetists (CRNA) to assist in the performance of the technical aspects of administering anesthesia . . . acting under the medical direction of an anesthesiologist or, if no anesthesiologist is available, another qualified physician." The ASA concludes, however, that approval of such delegation is not intended "to limit the eventual availability of optimal anesthesia for all, specifically the personal provision of anesthesia care by an anesthesiologist."[9] The ASA, therefore, "strongly encourages practice arrangements that provide access to the direct and exclusive attention of an anesthesiologist."

The AANA takes the position that nurse anesthetists are competent to provide anesthesia to patients undergoing care by a physician, dentist, podiatrist, or other health care professional with whom the nurse anesthetist works in varying degrees of collaboration or supervision.[10] A statement promulgated by the AANA defines the term *supervision* in reference to nurse anesthesia practice, and states that the term refers to

> a variety of different practice settings within a continuum. While all satisfy the legal requirements, practice settings take into account the education, experience, and capabilities of the nurse anesthetist, the rules and guidelines of the institution in which anesthesia is to be provided, and the needs and desires of the patient, nurse anesthetist, physician, dentist, podiatrist, or other health care professional. It is not unusual for nurse anesthetists to practice with the general agreement of the authorized health care provider. Supervision as required in licensing laws or nurse practice acts can be found in the consent of the authorized health care provider as manifested in an agreement to the proposed plan of anesthesia care, and may be either formal, informal or implied.[11]

A recent survey illustrates the practical application of the requirements of supervision, and the identity of the individual supplying that supervision (see Table 25–1). The survey indicates that more than half of the anesthesia services in the United States are provided by nurse anesthetists who practice in collaboration with, or under the direction of, surgeons, physicians, dentists, and other health professionals.[11] In rural areas where there are fewer anesthesiolo-

gists, nurse anesthetists provide more than 70% of the anesthesia care.[12]

The concept of supervision raises a number of specific issues:

1 The *identity* of the individual providing the supervision—(anesthesiologist, surgeon trained in anesthesia, or surgeon present in the operating room)
2 The *proximity of the supervisor*—actual presence in the operating room, presence somewhere in the operating suite, presence in the hospital, available by telephone, or unavailable but previously having coordinated with the anesthetist instructions on managing the anesthetic
3 *Supervision outside the operating room*—actual presence during induction, availability during induction, presence during maintenance, availability during maintenance, availability and supervision during emergence, and the nature of supervision during postemergence during the interval before all effects of the anesthesia have dissipated

PROFESSIONAL PROVIDING SUPERVISION

A number of state nurse practice acts require that a nurse anesthetist administer anesthesia only under the supervision or in the immediate presence of a physician.[13]

TABLE 25–1. Nature of Physical Supervision

Identity of Supervisor	Frequency (%)
Board-certified anesthesiologist	57.9
Non-board-certified anesthesiologist	12.1
Surgeon	21.3

Proximity of Supervisor	Frequency (%)
In operating room	22.5
In operating suite	65.1
By telephone	10.7
Not immediately available	1.6

Source: AANA Membership Survey Results. AANA J 53:35, 1985.

These statutes do not expressly require the physician to be an anesthesiologist. As a practical matter, however, a surgeon who "supervises" and operates at the same time has an increased risk of a vicarious liability for any negligence of a nurse anesthetist. Physicians working with nurse anesthetists have been held vicariously liable for a nurse's negligence under four related theories of liability:

1 The "captain of the ship" doctrine, wherein the surgeon is automatically deemed in charge of surgical procedures and is legally accountable for injuries caused by his or her assistants, including the operating room nurses and the anesthetist
2 The theory of *respondeat superior,* whereby the surgeon is liable for acts of nurses employed by him or her, or under his or her control
3 The "borrowed servant" doctrine, which holds a surgeon liable for the acts of nonemployees if he or she actually uses and controls the nonemployee or the nonemployee's services
4 Where the physician actually or potentially supervises or controls the nurse's actions (negligent supervision).

These theories all relate to the degree of control or supervision a physician (generally the surgeon) exercises over the nurse anesthetist.[14]

Surgeon or Physician

While the application of the "captain of the ship" doctrine, as such, has decreased, courts still usually consider the physician's ability to control or supervise, or the physician's actual control or supervision, over a nurse anesthetist to determine whether a nurse's negligence may be imputed to the physician.[15] In *Baird v. Sickler,*[16] an Ohio court rejected the "captain of the ship" doctrine, but applied a theory of *respondeat superior* to find a surgeon liable for an anesthesia-related injury. The case involved a CRNA, employed by an anesthesiology group, who administered anesthesia for a laminectomy. The patient had severe cervical arthritis, exposure of the vocal cords

for endotracheal intubation was difficult, and the surgeon assisted the CRNA during laryngoscopy and intubation. When the patient recovered from anesthesia, she was paraplegic. She subsequently brought an action alleging negligence in administration of the anesthetic. The Ohio Supreme Court considered whether the surgeon could be liable under the doctrine of *respondeat superior* if he had failed to properly supervise the nurse anesthetist. The court reasoned that the surgeon exercised and possessed the right to control the nurse anesthetist's actions as indicated by the surgeon's testimony that he instructed the nurse anesthetist regarding the intubation procedure and that he monitored the patient's position. The court concluded that where a surgeon controls, or realistically possesses the right to control, events and procedures, he or she must exercise a high degree of care.

A Texas court of appeals found a nurse anesthetist negligent in administering ether in a situation in which the nurse should have known that electrical instruments were being used for an operation.[17] The ether ignited, and the resulting fire killed the patient. The court, in considering whether the surgeon was liable for the nurse's negligence, framed the issue of terms of control. The court held that the surgeon was vicariously liable for the acts of the nurse anesthetist even though the surgeon was not in the operating room when the ether was administered. The court reasoned that the surgeon had the right to control the nurse anesthetist, even though he might not have chosen to exercise that right.

A number of courts have refused to impose liability on a surgeon when it can be shown that the surgeon neither controlled nor supervised the nurse anesthetist.[18] For example, in *Sesselman v. Muhlenburg Hospital,* a New Jersey court held that a surgeon was not vicariously liable for the negligence of his nurse anesthetist, and rejected the application of the "captain of the ship" doctrine. The court stated that a surgeon did not become liable for the acts of a nurse anesthetist merely because the surgeon was in charge of surgical procedures, and therefore would advise a nurse anesthetist of surgical procedures and the related anesthesia services to be performed.[19]

In *Parks v. Perry*, the court found that a patient sustained ulnar nerve damage when the nurse anesthetist failed to carefully monitor the patient's arm while administering general anesthesia.[20] The court stated that the surgeon had neither a duty to monitor the patient's arm nor a duty to supervise the nurse anesthetist's work, and therefore held that the surgeon was free from any liability.[21]

In summary, courts generally appear to be turning away from the automatic application of the "captain of the ship" doctrine when the surgeon neither supervises the nurse anesthetist nor has the power to control his or her acts. They seem to be recognizing the modern trend toward greater independence of nurse anesthetists for their own acts. On the other hand, under those factual situations wherein the power of supervision still resides with the surgeon, so does exposure to liability.

By contrast, when the anesthetic is administered by an anesthesiologist, most courts refuse to hold a surgeon liable for the former's negligence.[22] For example, in *McCullough v. Bethany Medical Center*, the Kansas Supreme Court reasoned that although a surgeon is "generally not liable for the negligence of an anesthesiologist"—under the doctrine of "captain of the ship"—the doctrine may be applied to hold a surgeon liable for the negligence of a nurse anesthetist if an anesthesiologist is not present.[23] Further, in *Marvulli v. Elshire*, a California court of appeals considered whether a surgeon could be held liable for the negligence of an anesthesiologist.[24] The court found that the anesthesiologist's negligence could not be imputed to the surgeon because there was no evidence of a standard of practice that gave the surgeon a right to exercise supervision or control over the anesthesiologist.[25]

In considering a surgeon's responsibility vis-à-vis a negligent anesthesiologist, a court will very likely frame the issue in terms of control. The reality of operating room procedure is that each individual represents a respective specialty that requires a unique set of skills and a high level of concentration; the surgeon performs an operation and the anesthesiologist controls the administration of the anesthetic.[26] However, there is at least one case with a contrary holding—a 1961 decision of the Pennsylvania Supreme Court. In *Rockwell v. Kent*,[27] surgeon Kent testified that he had the power to select the anesthetic agent and technique, although he had not exercised that power in Rockwell's case. The court held that as long as surgeon Kent possessed that power, he would be jointly liable along with the anesthesiologist for the loss of a portion of Rockwell's arm in consequence to the inadvertent intra-arterial administration of thiopental sodium.

Anesthesiologist

Anesthesiology is a medical specialty of recent advent (mainly since the Second World War). As anesthetic practices, agents, and equipment have become more complex, and the medical community has recognized this specialty, a strong argument may be made that a surgeon cannot be expected to control the administration of the anesthetic, particularly if an anesthesiologist is acting in a supervisory capacity. At least one expert in the field has asserted that the complexity of some anesthetics precludes the "cookbook recipe" approach to their administration by technicians who are not sufficiently experienced in anesthesia to make the judgmental decisions inherent in such complicated procedures.[28] An anesthesiologist assigned to a case may be held responsible for the control of complex anesthetic procedures.[29] An injured patient may therefore assert that the anesthesiologist is vicariously liable for the negligence of a nurse anesthetist over whom the anesthesiologist has control, even though the anesthesiologist might not choose to exercise control.[30]

When an anesthesiologist is supervising a nurse anesthetist, a court is more likely to find that the surgeon or physician in charge of the operation will not be deemed liable for the negligence of the nurse anesthetist. The ultimate liability for the nurse's negligence will probably fall on the shoulders of the anesthesiologist.

An analogy to the relationship between the surgeon and the operation may be relevant to the relationship between the anesthesiologist and the anesthetic. As the discussion in the previous section has shown, a surgeon may, to a large degree, be ultimately responsible for the procedures associated with the operation, even though the surgeon may not be in the operating room. If an operating room nurse negligently injures a patient during the surgical procedure, the surgeon may be considered vicariously liable.

Similarly, an anesthesiologist, to a large degree, may be considered ultimately responsible for the procedures involved in the administration of anesthesia, whether the anesthesiologist is actually present in the operating room or merely has talked with the patient preoperatively (particularly if the patient is given reason to believe an anesthesiologist is in charge) and recommended to the anesthetist the agent and technique to be administered. If the nurse anesthetist then negligently injures the patient, the anesthesiologist in charge may be considered liable for failure to provide adequate supervision.[29] The rationale for the court's imposition of liability is that proper supervision would enable the anesthesiologist to detect and correct the nurse anesthetist's negligence before any resulting harm befalls the patient. That is, the anesthesiologist is considered to be a *prime* tortfeasor by reason of inadequate supervision, rather than a *secondary* one because of vicarious liability for the nurse anesthetist's acts.

DEGREE OF SUPERVISION

Inasmuch as nurse anesthetists make both diagnoses (e.g., determine the depth of anesthesia) and therapeutic decisions (when to administer more agent, discontinue administration, and the like), it is understandable that nursing boards, and legislators via nursing practice acts, have adopted statutes and administrative regulations governing the nurse anesthetist's practice, notably by whom and to what degree supervision by a physician is required.

State Statutes and Rules

Nursing practice statutes differ from state to state regarding the degree of supervision a physician must maintain over the nurse who administers anesthesia.[31] References to the practice of the nurse anesthetist are found in 20 nursing practice acts and 29 board of nursing rules with a total of 38 states addressing the practice of the nurse anesthetist.[32] In some instances, the statute merely contains a definition of "nurse anesthetist" or a section addressing the administration of anesthesia in general. In the rules promulgated by boards of nursing, 13 states address the practice of the nurse anesthetist as a category under "advanced practice," or some other such broad term, while the remaining 16 states assign a separate section to this practice. Several states have statutory provisions stating that as long as a nurse anesthetist administers anesthesia under the supervision of a physician, the nurse will not be considered in violation of the medical practice act.[33] Two requirements that are referenced with some degree of frequency in the statutes or nursing board rules are "supervision" and "presence of a physician or surgeon." These are cited as requirements by 14 states.[34] A number of states refer to the working relationship between the physician or surgeon and the nurse anesthetist as "collaboration." Written protocols, guidelines, or agreements are required by 11 states.

The 14 states requiring supervision by a physician are Alabama, Arizona, California, Georgia, Indiana, Louisiana, New Hampshire, Ohio, Oklahoma, Pennsylvania, South Dakota, Utah, and West Virginia.[35] Of the 14 states requiring supervision, none specifically requires supervision by an anesthesiologist, although the Georgia statute requires that a supervising physician have some training in the administration of anesthetics.[36] The Arizona statute is typical in requiring that a nurse anesthetist administer anesthetics "under the direction of and in the presence of a licensed physician or surgeon." The statute defines *presence* as "within the same room or an adjoining room or within the same surgical or obstetrical suite."[37]

By contrast, some of the statutes requiring supervision do not explicitly require the presence of a physician. The South Dakota statute enumerates various "medical functions" that may be performed by a nurse anesthetist, including development of an anesthesia care plan, maintenance of life support functions and monitoring a patient during surgical procedures, managing a patient's emergence from anesthesia, and conducting postanesthesia follow-up.[38] The South Dakota statute also requires that such medical functions be performed only under the supervision of a licensed physician responsible for the medical care of the patient. Other states, such as Nevada, merely require that the nurse anesthetist administer anesthetics to persons under the care of professionals who are Nevada licensees in dentistry, surgery, or obstetrics.[39]

A number of states require both supervision and the development of protocols. Most of the states' statutes or administrative regulations mandating written guidelines merely require that a nurse anesthetist act pursuant to guidelines developed with collaborating physicians. At least one state (i.e., Massachusetts) by administrative rule enumerates several express functions of a nurse anesthetist and provides that a nurse anesthetist may perform additional functions pursuant to established guidelines. In other jurisdictions, statutes permit a nurse anesthetist, pursuant to a preset protocol, to determine the health status of a patient; determine, with the consent of a collaborating physician, the appropriate type of anesthesia; order preanesthesia medication; perform and administer anesthesia; monitor and support life functions of the patient during anesthesia; and participate in the patient's postanesthesia recovery.

Case Law

The statutes and administrative regulations present general guidelines for the administration of anesthesia by nurse anesthetists. Each of the cases that have been litigated, on the other hand, addresses a specific factual situation wherein the nature and scope of a physician's (anesthesiologist, obstetrician, surgeon) duty to supervise nurse anesthetists is explored in greater detail. The broad statutory variations in the amount of supervision required are reflected in these judicial decisions.

For example, in *Arkansas State Department of Health v. Drs. Thibault and Counsel*,[40] the Arkansas State Department of Health sought a declaratory judgment that registered nurses not specifically qualified in the field of anesthesia could administer epidural anesthesia to obstetrical patients. Typically, the obstetrician inserted the epidural catheter and administered the loading dose, waiting to note the effect of this first dose. The court found that thereafter the obstetrician instructed a nurse to reinject the local anesthetic as needed in specific amounts and at specific times. Although the physician then left the hospital, pursuant to hospital policy, he remained available within minutes if any problems arose. The court held that the Arkansas Nurse Practice Act, which provided that a nurse registered under the provisions of the act who had successfully completed an education program at an accredited school of anesthesia and held current certification, might "give or administer anesthesia in this State in the presence of a licensed physician or dentist," had to be strictly construed. The court held that because the act specifically required a licensed physician or dentist to be present when any nurse administered anesthesia, the hospital's practice of allowing nurses to administer subsequent doses of the local anesthetic should be discontinued.

A Louisiana court in *Brown v. Allen Sanitarium, Inc.*[41] broadly interpreted the state's nursing practice statutes in determining whether Allen Santarium was liable for failure to require a physician to supervise a CRNA in selection of either the method or administration of anesthesia to a patient. In that case, a patient died following a procedure performed under general anesthesia. The court determined that Allen Sanitarium was not liable, holding that the Louisiana legislature did not intend to require the degree of supervision over a person possessing the skill and qualification of a CRNA that would require a physician to supervise a CRNA in administration of anesthesia.

Another Louisiana court of appeals established the limits of the court's broad interpretation of the nurse practice statutes in *Keys v. Mercy Hospital of New Orleans*.[42] The court found that, in response to a patient's request for a general anesthetic, two staff anesthesiologists at Mercy Hospital assigned a nurse anesthetist to administer the anesthetic to the patient who was to undergo a cesarean section. While the nurse was attempting to perform endotracheal intubation, the patient regurgitated. Three minutes later the anesthesiologist arrived and took remedial action, but the patient later developed aspiration pneumonia and died. An action brought by the decedent patient's husband against the anesthesiologist was dismissed before trial. At trial, the plaintiff prevailed in a negligence action against both the nurse and her hospital employer.

On appeal, the court considered testimony on the standard of care in administering anesthetics. Dr. Levine, an anesthesiologist from Chicago, testified that the nurse was negligent in attempting intubation without an anesthesiologist assisting her. He also admitted, however, that different locations may have different standards in reference to the necessity of having an anesthesiologist present during intubation. Other anesthesiologists practicing in the New Orleans area testified that the nurse was not negligent in intubating the patient in the absence of an anesthesiologist. In light of these facts, the court found two grounds for imposing liability:

1 The nurse's failure to employ procedures during the intubation process that would minimize the risk of regurgitation
2 The hospital's failure to require both an anesthesiologist and an anesthetist to be present to jointly intubate such a patient

In *Central Anesthesia Associates P.C. v. Worthy*,[29] the Georgia Supreme Court reviewed a decision by a Georgia court of appeals[43] involving an attempt to define the degree of supervision that must be exercised over a nurse anesthetist according to Georgia statutes.[44]

The case involved a group of eight anesthesiologists who provided anesthetic coverage and operated a school of nurse anesthetists. The patient in question suffered brain damage during a tubal ligation because of alleged negligence of anesthesia personnel. A registered practical nurse, who was a student nurse anesthetist (SNA) at that time, had administered anesthesia under the supervision of a physician's assistant (PA) who had training in anesthesia. The facts showed that a Dr. Cortes was the first and only anesthesiologist to respond to the emergency, and he arrived by elevator from the second floor to the seventh floor operating room where the patient was being anesthetized. The facts also established that the PA had been present when the

SNA began administering the anesthetic, but he left the room for 10 to 15 minutes, during which time the patient's complications arose.

At the time in question, four of the central Anesthesia Associates' eight anesthesiologists were not in the hospital.[45] The fifth anesthesiologist was involved in an open heart operation and had no responsibility for the patient whose treatment was at issue in the case. Dr. Cortes was Central Anesthesia Associates' officer of the day and was in his office on the second floor of the hospital. He denied assigning either the SNA or the PA to the case and denied having any knowledge of the case until he entered the seventh floor operating room in response to the emergency.

The SNA placed a Dr. Chanta's name on the preoperative consultation, which prescribed the anesthesia plan and required approval by an anesthesiologist, but Dr. Chanta denied having signed or approved the plan. The SNA placed a Dr. Mani's name on the anesthesia record as the responsible anesthesiologist, but Dr. Mani denied having any involvement with the patient's treatment.

The court of appeals noted that the Georgia code defined and established the minimum qualifcations for CRNAs. The code also provided that a CRNA could lawfully administer anesthesia provided that such anesthesia is "administered under the direction and responsibility of a licensed physician with training or experience in anesthesia.[44] The court also noted that it was well-settled Goergia law that a statute created a standard of conduct, the violation of which became *negligence per se* [emphasis the Editor's]. The court analyzed the statute and stated that it set threshold qualifications that had to be met before a person would be permitted under the law to administer anesthesia.

The court added that statutory qualifications did not establish "how the anesthesia is to be administered, or what methods or instruments may be used, *but rather who may administer the anesthesia with whose supervision.*" [emphasis supplied][46] The court concluded that the statute prohibited unqualified individuals from administering anesthesia and further prohibited even a statutorily qualified person from administering anesthesia without prescribed supervision.

The court concluded that the physician members of the corporation providing the anesthesia services had the statutory duty to prohibit the administration of anesthesia by a nonqualified individual, and to ensure that a qualified person would be supervised by an anesthesia-qualified physician. The court then imposed liability upon the anesthesiologists, who were sued as individuals, since each had a position of responsibility with respect to patients being anesthetized under the auspices of the corporation. The court noted that all of the physicians denied involvement, showing that no anesthesiologist was in charge as required, and the breach was therefore a breach of omission rather than commission.

The court held the hospital liable even though the anesthesiology group, rather than the hospital, operated a school for anesthetists located on the premises of the hospital, and provided services to the hospital by contract. The court stated, however, that it was of "great import" that the hospital's surgical consent forms, to be signed by the patient, stated that anesthesia would be administered under the supervision of an anesthesiologist. The court concluded therefore that the hospital had a duty not to permit violations of the statute and therefore confirmed the trial court's granting of a motion for partial summary judgment on the basis of negligence per se for violation of the Georgia code.

The Georgia Supreme Court then granted *certiorari* (agreed to review the opinion of the court of appeals) to determine whether the trial court erred in finding the defendants negligent per se. The high court found a per se violation of the statute, and therefore adopted the reasoning of the court of appeals in holding that the trial court properly granted partial summary judgment against Central Anesthesia Associates, the three Central Anesthesia Associates' defendant anesthesiologists, the student nurse anesthetist, and the physician's assistant for having violated this section of the code.

Federal Regulations

The Medicare regulations recognize that an anesthesiologist may play a supervisory role in the provision of anesthesiology services and will reimburse the anesthesiologist on that basis. The Code of Federal Regulations (CFR) provides specifically that a physician may be reimbursed also on a reasonable-charge basis for the personal medical direction he or she furnishes to a qualified anesthetist such as a CRNA.[47]

These regulations, now embodied in the Medicare *Provider's Reimbursement Manual*,[48] specify that an anesthesiologist may be reimbursed for providing medical direction if the anesthesiologist is not supervising more than four anesthetic administrations concurrently with the assistance of CRNAs; performs a preanesthetic examination and evaluation and prescribes the anesthesia plan; personally participates in the most demanding procedures in the anesthesia plan, including induction and emergence; ensures that any procedures in the anesthesia plan that he or she does not perform are performed by a qualified individual; monitors the course of anesthesia administration at frequent intervals; remains physically present and available for immediate diagnosis and treatment of emergencies; and provides any postanesthesia care that is indicated. This provision in the manual adds that if anesthesiologists are in a group practice, one physician member may provide the preanesthesia examination and evaluation and another fulfill the other criteria.

The Medicare guidelines distinguish between those of the just-described services that are considered "medical directions" and those that constitute "supervision." These guidelines define supervision as "a general activity primarily concerned with monitoring performance of the anesthetist, with significantly diminished direct involvement of the anesthesiologist in delivery of services to the patients."[49] The guidelines add that if an anesthesiologist leaves the immediate area of the operating suite for more than short durations, devotes excessive time to aid another case, or is otherwise not available to respond to the immediate needs of the surgical patients, the physician's services to the surgical patients are considered supervisory in nature.[47]

CONCLUSION

The issues set forth in this chapter involve questions of potential professional liability, as well as potential violations of state statutes; licensing board regulations; and hospital protocols, guidelines, or agreements. Anesthesiologists, surgeons, and other physicians with a continuing business or professional relationship with nurse anesthetists should carefully review their practices in the light of their state's requirements for supervision and control, if any. Professional corporations and partnerships likewise should review their guidelines for supervision and control of any nurse anesthetists employed by the corporation or partnership. The same step should be taken in reference to any other nurse anesthetists with whom there is any relationship, including nurses employed by other organizations or hospitals. As part of this review, the existing requirements of any agreements with hospitals, HMOs, or other health-related entities, including payers, should be reassessed in reference to imposed contractual standards. Likewise, the hospital's medical staff guidelines, admission forms, and consent forms should be inspected to ascertain that actual practices confirm to the policies set forth in these documents.

It is far easier to carry out this review before any problem arises rather than to wait until one is endeavoring to straighten out an entanglement under the specter of pending litigation and possible substantial liability. Anesthesiologist-shareholders of professional corporations should take no particular satisfaction in the shield against personal liability provided by a corporate structure, at least for those physicians not actually involved in the supervision and immediate care of the injured patient. As long as there are cases such as *Worthy*,[29,43] there will be at least implied liability of all responsible anesthesiologists for failure to provide adequate supervision at the level of acceptable standards.

REFERENCES

1. *See* Brief of Amicus Curiae, the American Association of Nurse Anesthetists at 2, 3, Jefferson Parrish Hosp. Dist. No. 2 v. Hyde, 104 S. Ct. 1551 (1984); Mannino, MJ: The Nurse Anesthetist and the Law. Grune & Stratton, New York, 1982; Peters, JD, et al: Anesthesiology and the Law. Health Administration Press, Ann Arbor, 1983, p 86.
2. Lasky, PC (ed): Hospital Law Manual. Aspen Systems, Rockville, MD, 1984, § 3-1.
3. Fleming, P: Impact of the CRNA: The specialty and its future. AANA J 55:23, 1986.
4. *Id.; see also* Gunn, IP, Nicosia, J, and Tobin, M: Anesthesia: A practice of nursing. AANA J 55:99, 1987; Ohio Revised Code § 4731.34 (G.C. § 1286-2; 108 v PtI 131; adopted March 20, signed April 14, 1919).
5. Frank v. South, 175 Ky. 416, 194 S.W. 375 (1917).
6. Chalmers-Francis v. Nelson, 6 Cal. 2d 402, 57 P.2d 1312 (1936).
7. A Maryland court has stated that the terms *collaboration* and *supervision* are synonymous in the context of a physician's or anesthesiologist's duty to supervise or collaborate with nurse anesthetists. Kucera, WR: A defining of terms: Collaboration vs. supervision. AANA J 48:547, 1980; *also, see, generally,* Appendix 25-1.
8. American Society of Anesthesiologists: Statement on Regional Anesthesia (approved by House of Delegates on October 12, 1983); American Society of Anesthesiologists and the American Asosication of Nurse Anesthetists: Joint Statement Concerning Qualifications of Individuals Administering Anesthetics (issued January, 1972).
9. American Society of Anesthesiologists: Statement on the Anesthesia Care Team (amended by House of Delegates October 21, 1986).
10. American Association of Nurse Anesthetists: AANA Position Statement on Relationships Between Health Care Professionals (adopted by AANA Board of Directors, March 1, 1987).
11. Brief of AANA, *supra* note 1, p 8.
12. *Id. See also* Gunn, IP: Nurse anesthetists should control the teaching and practice of their profession. In Eckenhoff, JE (ed): Controversy in Anesthesiology. WB Saunders, Philadelphia, 1979, p 211; Mannino, MJ: Nurse anesthetists should administer regional anesthesia. In Eckenhoff, 225.
13. *See, e.g.,* Ark. Code Ann. § 17-86-302 (1987); 25 Indiana Stat. Ann. art 22-225-1-2(k) (Burns 1982); La. Rev. Stat. Ann. § 4731.3S (Balwin 1981); Ok. Stat. Ann. Ch. 59 §§ 67-51 (Supp. 1988); S. Dak. Codified Laws § 36-9-3.1 (1986); W. Va. Code 30-7-15 (1986); *see, generally,* Blumenreich, GA: CRNA's and their employment situations. AANA J 52:212, 1984.
14. Eskreis, T: The legal implications in utilizing the nurse anesthetist in place of the anesthesiologist. Whittier L Rev 7:855, 1985; Kucera, WR: Imputed negligence:

Captain of the ship is sinking. AANA J 48:282, 1980; Beal, J: Surgeons and the captain of the ship doctrine. In Eckenhoff, *supra* note 12.

15. *See* Blumenreich, GA: Legal requirements of physician supervision. AANA J 52:562, 1984; Anesthetic supervision and control. 8 Am. Jur. Proof of Facts 2d 598 (1984); Blumenreich, GA: A surgeon's liability for the anesthesia administration. AANA J 54:385, 1986.

16. Baird v. Sickler, 69 Ohio St. 2d 652, 23 Ohio Ops. 3d 532, 433 N.E.2d. 593 (1982).

17. McKinney v. Tromley, 386 S.W.2d 564 (Tex. 1964).

18. *See* Kiefer, MJ: The law and specialty health care practitioners. AANA J 51:562, 1983; Bernzweig, E: Liability of the nurse anesthetist. Today's OR Nurse 7:27, 1985.

19. Sesselman v. Muhlenburg Hosp., 124 N.J. Super. 285, 306 A.2d 474 (1973); *see also* Baird v. Sickler, *supra* note 16 (rejection of "captain of the ship" doctrine and imposition of *respondeat superior*).

20. Parks v. Perry, 68 N.C. App. 202, 314 S.E.2d 287; *rev. denied* 311 N.C. 761, 321 S.E.2d 142 (1984).

21. *Id.; see also* Kemalyan v. Henderson, 45 Wash. 2d 693, 277 P.2d 372 (1954) (surgeon free from liability for nurse anesthetist's negligence where surgeon testified that he left administration of anesthesia completely to nurse's discretion); Hughes v. St. Paul Fire and Marine Ins. Co., 401 So.2d 448 (La. 1981) (court found "captain of the ship" doctrine would not apply to imposed liability on surgeon for CRNA's negligence where surgeon neither controlled nor supervised the nurse anesthetist).

22. Peters, *supra* note 1, at p 71.

23. 683 P.2d 1258 (Kan. 1984).

24. 27 Cal. App. 3d 180, 103 Cal. Rptr. 461 (1972); *but see* Schneider v. Einstein Medical, 390 A.2d 1271 (Pa. 1978); Kitto v. Gilbert, 570 P.2d. 544 (Col. 1977) (surgeon liable for negligence of anesthesiologist because surgeon exercised control over management of anesthetic).

25. *Id.; see* Kennedy v. Gaskell, 78 Cal. Rptr. 753 (1964) (negligence of anesthesiologist could not be imputed to surgeon even though surgeon instructed anesthesiologist regarding type, nature, and purpose of the anesthetic).

26. *See, generally,* Peters, *supra* note 1, at p 73.

27. Rockwell v. Stone, 173 A.2d 48; Rockwell v. Kent, 173 A.2d 54 (Sup. Ct. Pa. 1961).

28. Jenkins, MT: Nurse anesthetists should not administer regional anesthesia. In Eckenhoff, *supra* note 12, pp 231–235.

29. *See* Central Anesthesia Associates P.C. v. Worthy, 333 S.E. 2d 829 (Sup. Ct. Ga. 1985)

30. *See* McKinney v. Tromley, *supra* note 17 (applying the principle in the context of nurse-surgeon).

31. *See, generally,* Gunn, IP: Professional territoriality and the anesthesia experience. In Nursing Issues and Nursing Strategies for the 80's. Springer, New York, 1983; Mannino, *supra* note 1.

32. *See, generally,* LeBar, *supra* note 2.

33. *See, e.g.,* Ohio Rev. Code Ann. § 4731.35 (Page's, 1985).

34. *See, generally,* LeBar, *supra* note 2, at p 67.

35. *See, e.g.,* 64 Ark. Stat. Ann. § 72-746 (1985) (any registered nurse anesthetist may give or administer anesthetics in the presence and under the supervision of a licensed physician or dentist); *see also* Utah Code Ann. 58-31a-4 (1986) (a nurse anesthetist may administer local anesthetics under "direct review"—a consulting physician is usually present on a daily basis, in the medical facility).

36. Geo. Code Ann. § 43-26-9 (1984) (a CRNA may administer anesthesia, "provided that such anesthesia is administered under the direction and responsibility of a duly licensed physician with training and experience in anesthesia").

37. Ariz. Rev. Stat. Ann. § 31-1661 (1986).

38. S. Dak. Codified Laws § 36-9-3.1 (1986).

39. Nev. Rev. Stat. § 632.010 (1986).

40. Ark. State Dept. of Health v. Doctors Thibault and Counsel, 664 S.W.2d 445 (Ark. 1984).

41. Brown v. Allen Sanitarium, Inc., 364 So.2d 661 (La. 1978), *cert. denied* 367 So. 2d 392 (La. 1979).

42. 485 So.2d 514 (La. App. 1986).

43. *See* Central anesthesia Assoc. P.C. v. Worthy, 325 S.E. 2d 829 (Ga. 1984).

44. *See* Geo. Code Ann. § 43-26-9 (d); *see also supra* note 43, at p 819.

45. Horty, J (ed): Defendants Without Defenses. Action Kit for Hospital Law, March, 1986.

46. *Supra* note 43, at p 823

47. Code of Federal Regulations §§ 405-552 (1986).

48. Department of Health and Human Services: Provider's Reimbursement Manual. [H.C.F.A. Publ. No. 15] Government Printing Office, Washington, DC, Part 1, § 2182.7 (1988).

49. *See* Medicare and Medicaid Guide § 8081 (1985).

26

Melvin S. Shotten, J.D.

Joining an Established Anesthesia Group Practice

When I was younger, and my elders would say, "Some things never change," I would laugh at such a statement. Yet, as I grew older, I noticed many things, personally and professionally, that seem to be proof of this theorem. For example, many of the points covered in this brief chapter on joining an anesthesia practice are identical to many if not most of those you would find in similar material written in 1968, the year when I began practicing in the specialty area of physicians' corporations. Some of the points might require a little clarification or updating, and there are, of course, a number of new developments—but most are the same or repetitions of cyclic events that seem to occur during a period of years (e.g., the "malpractice insurance crisis" described later in this chapter). Whether the points are new or old, however, a critical review by a young professional completing his or her anesthesia training (and ready to join the "real" world of practice) may still be the most important single activity of the posttraining professional career.

Although I call what follows an "analysis," it is in fact kept purposely brief, because it is intended to serve the young practitioner—and to a lesser extent an older practitioner switching to a new anesthesia practice—on strictly a practical "guideline" basis. I speak in terms of a "large" anesthesia practice only because most anesthesiologists who service a particular hospital or a number of area hospitals have chosen to band together into groups, usually containing more than two or three practitioners, in order to better handle the work load at such hospitals and the staff surgeons with whom they practice. At least, this has been the experience of our firm in the 22 years I have been involved in this area.

As an overview, Table 26-1 outlines the important topics to consider and evaluate when one reviews an opportunity for employment (and a later proprietary relationship) with a large anesthesia practice. Some of them (such as the relationship with the hospital) are of import regardless of the size of the practice.

The anesthesiologist seeking a new position should be careful to consider all of these various points, along with the general competence, stability, generosity, and overall standing of any anesthesia group he or she is considering joining. A failure to do so simply means that the anesthesiologist is not exercising the best judgment as to future prospects.

FEATURES OF A PRACTICE

Corporation Versus Partnership

The first consideration is the overall organization of the group under scrutiny. For a variety of reasons, not the least of which are benefits available under the law, most large anesthesia groups in the past have been, are, and continue to be incorporated. The reasons for this preference formerly were primarily centered on qualified retirement plan flexibility—that is, the ability of

a corporate plan to shelter more dollars from taxes for the physician-employees under better terms than the then available Keogh plans. The Tax Equity and Fiscal Responsibility Act of 1982 (TEFRA) has largely removed this advantage and (except for retirement plan loans), the old Keogh plan for self-employed individuals is now a practical equivalent of the benefits that can be obtained by employees under qualified corporate retirement plans.

Corporations are still the preferred practice mode in most states, however, for a number of reasons. These include

- Their clear and well-defined organizational concepts under state statutes
- The lack of any need for a complicated partnership agreement (which must be reconsidered in case of death or withdrawal of any of the partners)
- The ability to engage in tax planning because of possible use of different fiscal year ends
- The lower corporate tax rates on accumulations
- An array of additional tax shelter devices (that for the most part have not been altered by the new tax laws) through employee welfare benefit plans (i.e., group term life, medical-dental and disability insurance plans, plus reimbursement programs)
- And, most importantly, limited liability

In a partnership, the professional negligence of any of the physicians in the group endangers the personal assets of every other partner in the event that insurance coverage is insufficient. In the corporation, on the other hand, the physician employee-shareholder not involved in the malpractice usually faces only the loss of his or her investment in the corporation (which will always be liable as the "employer" of the physician who commits the negligent act). To a more limited extent, the same potential cutoff of liability extends to contractual matters. Therefore, for the physician reviewing possible practice affiliations, an anesthesia practice still operated as a general partnership *should be looked upon very carefully*.

TABLE 26–1. Topics to Review in Evaluating a Prospective Practice

Those aspects of an existing practice that should be investigated by a professional seeking to join an established group, be it a partnership, corporation, or other business entity, include:

1 Corporation versus partnership and related liability issues
2 Organization:
   a Number of shareholders or partner-physicians versus nonproprietary physicians
   b Rotation of directors and other officers
   c Receptivity to new ideas
3 Use of letter of intent relating to future relationship:
   a Specificity as to length of service required for proprietor status
   b Mechanism for valuing interest
   c Separation of practice as compared to investment assets
4 Use of employment agreement:
   a Moving expense reimbursement
   b Opportunity for additional compensation for productivity; "moonlighting" opportunities
   c Opportunity for retirement plan participation; protection of retirement plan participation if a debit from normal salary or additional compensation
   d Specification of illness, vacation, and educational time away from practice
   e Services for friends and relatives
   f Provision of malpractice insurance and amounts
   g Provision of other insurance benefits (health, disability, life); death or disability benefits
   h Guarantee of continued employment in event of disability
   i Termination provisions and required prior written notice or "cause" in connection with same
   j Access to records of patients
   k Residency limitations
   l Noncompete covenants
5 Participation arrangements as to compensation among shareholder-physicians (including allocation systems based on productivity or other indexes)
6 The stock valuation; ownership of properties and/or infusion of capitalized value of accounts receivable versus alternative payment-in and buy-out provisions (i.e., ease of entry and departure as a physician-shareholder)
7 Termination benefits owed deceased, disabled, or terminated physician-employee (and comparison with pro-rata share of accounts receivable)
8 Retirement plan opportunities and problems
9 Professional liability insurance
   a Coverage of individual physicians and nurse anesthetists, as well as corporation
   b Use of reputable carrier(s) (as compared to self-insurance or other insurance alternatives involving additional risks)
   c Length of insurance commitment—"occurrence" versus "claims made" coverage
   d Deductibles
   e Liability limitations on outside work
10 Invoicing system (who bills for patient services—the group, the hospital, or some third party?)
11 Relationship with hospital:
   a Exclusive arrangements for providing anesthesia coverage (i.e., "closed staff" as compared to "open staff")
   b Special requirements for staff membership? Peculiar provisions of staff regulations and bylaws?
   c Shareholder-physician the director of department of anesthesia?
   d Written contract involved? If so, length of contract and provisions for automatic renewal, termination, or both

TABLE 26–1.   (Continued)

12 Relationship with nurse anesthetists:
   a Employee of group versus hospital
   b Limitations on use by anesthesia practice imposed by hospital or staff bylaws or restrictive state laws?
   c Written employment agreement in effect?
   d Standardized procedures in effect on hours, overtime, and similar matters

Organization

The anesthesiologist seeking a long-term (in some cases you might say "lifetime") position with any established group is primarily interested in not only current compensation but in the chance of becoming a proprietor (i.e., shareholder or partner) under an organization that will allow him or her to have a voice in its affairs after a few years. A great deal can be gleaned about how an organization operates by looking into the number of physician-shareholders (or partners) versus the number of nonshareholders. A group with one or two shareholders and five or six nonshareholders—where there has been no sudden growth of the practice in the last few years that would justify this number of nonshareholders—is probably indicative of a situation wherein there is a great deal of exploitation of the younger anesthesiologists by established physicians. The latter, in turn, may control the relationship with the hospital in question or the referring staff. This is not to say such a situation should be rejected out of hand as a possible employment opportunity. Rather, the anesthesiologist who does go into the situation should keep his or her eyes open and look for a compensation package that may make up for any lack of potential future proprietary status.

Future Proprietor Relationship

It can be very meaningful for the anesthesiologist who is seeking a long-term relationship with an established group practice to require the group to spell out in writing his or her opportunity for future partner or shareholder status. This type of writing, sometimes called a letter of intent, should specify how many years of service are required before such status is available,

whether (after such service) full proprietor status equal with that of the other physicians will be available, the mechanism or formula for valuing any interest that the shareholder will be expected to purchase, and the interval over which he or she will be able to pay for that interest. Relevant to this point is the fact that it is advantageous to buy into practices that do not capitalize accounts receivable (see discussion *infra*). Also relevant to the matter of future buy-in is the question of whether the practice itself owns substantial investment assets (usually real estate, securities, or both), which can make purchase of an interest much more difficult and requires, in effect, that young physicians accept investment decisions in which they had no voice.

In a similar vein, one can judge somewhat the amenability of larger groups to new ideas by seeing whether the managing partners, directors, and officers rotate from time to time, or whether these positions are routinely held by a small number of senior physicians. In any situation such as this, it is obviously critical for the anesthesiologist being recruited to speak with one or two of the youngest anesthesiologists in the group (and, if possible, the nurse anesthetists used by the group).

Employment Agreement

It is critical that physicians joining a large practice require that their duties and obligations, and the benefits they are to receive, be delineated in a clear employment agreement with the group. Physicians should ask for samples of prior employment agreements used for anesthesiologists joining the group previously; there should be some concern when there have not been any such agreements in the past. Some of the points to consider in evaluating the terms of the agreement include moving expenses, productivity, exclusivity, retirement plans, time away, service for friends and relatives, professional liability insurance, other benefits, and the like.

Moving Expenses

These expenses to be incurred by the physician should be detailed. If possible, an actual figure should be used to avoid any future controversy as to the "reasonableness" of the requested reimbursement after the move is completed.

Exclusivity and Productivity

The contract should be clear as to whether the employment is exclusive—that is, whether there is an opportunity for the young anesthesiologist to moonlight in emergency rooms and in the many medicenters springing up across the country.

In addition, with respect to employment by the group itself, if there is an opportunity and enough information to define the amount of work expected from the young anesthesiologist, it is useful to place a specific "productivity" clause in the contract that will reward the physician for additional work. For example, such a clause might read that the compensation is to be based on 50% of all billings to patients cared for by him or her in excess of $100,000.

Retirement Plans

The terms of eligibility to participate in any qualified retirement plans should be detailed. This is obviously an additional fringe benefit that may be important. On the other hand, some groups have arrangements that provide for gross pretax compensation packages to the new physician, so that any retirement plan contributions reduce the contractual total compensation specified in the agreement. Whenever possible generally, and especially in the case of the latter type of agreement, the anesthesiologist should try to negotiate a clause providing that any vesting forfeiture (return of monies paid into retirement plan if termination occurs before vesting) of amounts under the retirement plans upon termination of employment will be paid to him as additional severance compensation. While

such additional compensation is not as useful as tax-sheltered benefits, it is obviously better than a total or partial forfeiture of these amounts.

Service for Friends and Relatives

There should be a provision allowing the physician to treat friends and relatives at his or her discretion, accounting to the employer only for any cash monies paid or reimbursement available through insurance.

Professional Liability Insurance

There should be a clear provision that the employer will cover the new anesthesiologist as a named beneficiary (not just the employer) under malpractice insurance, with specified primary and excess coverages (discussed further *infra*). Each professional, whether new or a seasoned member of the group, including CRNAs, should be a named beneficiary. The policy should also cover the business entity that comprises the partnership or corporation, to protect its assets as well as those of the individual professionals.

Additional Insurance Benefits

Any other insurance benefits funded by the corporation—including health, disability, life, or combinations thereof—should be specified, along with any uninsured death or disability coverage or reimbursement benefits.

Sickness

The contract should specify how much illness, either continuous or cumulative during the year, would be allowed before the employer may reduce or terminate compensation or employment.

Time Away

The agreement should be very specific on sick leave, vacation, leave for educational programs and seminars, and how such time accrues (i.e., available pro rata to services rendered or all available immediately) and whether the time will, if not taken, accumulate from year to year.

Termination

Termination provisions should be clear—for example, one would normally try to negotiate an agreement that provided for termination for any reason only on 60 days' prior written notice (although the young anesthesiologist may prefer less notice in order to maintain flexibility). In some unusual situations, it may even be possible for a physician to negotiate an agreement that provides for early termination by the employer (under an employment agreement having a 1- or 2-year term, for example) only "for cause," while maintaining his or her own right to terminate for any reason on short notice.

Records

As a minimum, the agreement should grant access and a right to copy records of the employer with respect to patients cared for by the anesthesiologist.

Location of Residence

Anesthesiologists should avoid, whenever possible, contracts with clauses requiring residency within a number of miles of a specific hospital. These requirements—usually inserted into agreements because of a similar agreement between the group and the hospital to afford "24-hour availability" of anesthesiologists—can be troublesome.

Noncompete Clauses

In a similar vein, whenever possible, the anesthesiologist should avoid agreements with restrictions on competition after termination. Even agreements with fairly limited restrictions—that is, for "1 year within 5 miles" of a certain hospital—can obviously narrow one's flexibility when terminating employment for a better position. If the opportunity is good, and such noncompete clauses or similar restrictive covenants must be accepted, often there is still the chance to negotiate downward applicable time periods or extent of geographic area. In some cases, the restrictions can be limited to situations where the employee terminates employment or the employee is terminated for "good cause."

Compensation Participation Arrangements

In any group in which an anesthesiologist hopes to make his or her future, there should be some clear arrangement among the existing proprietary physicians with respect to allocation of compensation. These arrangements deserve tactful investigation by the young anesthesiologist, even initially, since such arrangements are also indicative of the flexibility of the group and the likelihood of avoiding future controversies in this area. These participation arrangements range from strict equality (fully equal salaries) to "pure billing productivity," and everything in between (including seniority, supplements, special allocations for managing physicians, and the like). If productivity allocations are part of the calculation, one should inquire about the method of performing the calculations. For example, if productivity is based on gross billings, the fair share allocation of compensation within the group could be altered substantially by one or two physicians working with so-called service patients, that is, those of whom payment can be expected, if at all, only from third-party reimbursement agencies such as Medicare or Medicaid.

Valuation of Interest

As mentioned briefly above, the manner in which the proprietary interest (i.e., the partnership interest or the stock value) is calculated can mean a great deal to the ease of entry of a physician who expects to become a proprietor of the practice in the future. Many practices tend to maximize such value by including in the calculation the value of the accounts receivable, that is, "capitalizing" the receivables, which is usually the primary asset of most anesthesia groups. Others tend to increase the value of the practice by including in the valuation substantial amounts of real estate or securities.

From the point of view of easy of entry of a physician, the most desirable situations are those groups that do not engage in either of these practices. Such groups value the interest of the partner or shareholder on the basis of the depreciated book value or market value of tangible assets on hand. In these cases, accounts receivable are usually handled as part of a "purchase into" the existing accounts receivable of the practice. The mechanism employed is the employment agreement of the buying physician and his or her share of compensation involved. Such an arrangement allows, in essence, the buying physician to pay for his or her share of the primary asset of the practice (i.e., the accounts receivable) in "before-tax" dollars by allocating a portion of his or her compensation within the corporation to the other proprietary physicians.

As an example, take an anesthesia group of five established physician-shareholders, with $12,000 of book value of assets and $600,000 of accounts receivable, and with all shareholders equally sharing available compensation. If the group capitalizes these receivables, it would require the buying physician to purchase his or her one-sixth share of $102,000 in after-tax dollars. Not only is this a large debt to be shown on a personal financial statement, but it would have to be paid over a considerable number of years by a young physician who, in the process of moving into a new community, would be simultaneously incurring substantial new housing and other family expenses.

On the other hand, by not capitalizing accounts receivable, the purchase of the "pure" proprietary interest (in this example, the stock) is reduced to $2000 and the $100,000 obligation on accounts receivable could, for example, be handled by taking $20,000 less in salary during a period of 5 years. Each of the selling shareholders then would take $4000 additional compensation per year under the buy-in program. The existing shareholder-physicians do give up potential capital gain on the sale, and accept ordinary income, but they are usually in a financial position to do so easily. In addition, this treatment does not have the unusual effect of changing the tax characterization from ordinary income to capital gain for the value of the practice attributable to services provided by the physicians prior to the stock sale.

Termination Benefits

The other side of the buy-in issue is the type of termination arrangements found among the group of proprietary employees. In many cases, especially where accounts receivable have been capitalized (as noted *supra*), the only buy out is a purchase by the practice of the partnership interests or stock of a terminated employee, usually pursuant to provisions of the partnership agreement, the bylaws of the corporation, or a separate stock transfer agreement among the shareholders. In cases wherein accounts receivable have been handled as noted above to ease the entry of young anesthesiologists, however, such termination provisions are often also included in the employment agreements among the proprietary physicians.

A trade-off for easy entry is the willingness of the terminated physician-employee to accept a pay cut over a period of time. Such a cut is primarily based on the terminee's share of accounts receivable, and will be taxed as additional compensation. In such cases, there is also a question of the appropriate share of accounts receivable; this share often mirrors the decision on compensation allocations. That is, where compensation is equal, there is often an equal split of the estimated collectible accounts receivable to be paid as part of the termination. In productivity cases, a productivity share of accounts receivable is taken into account (usually based on pro-rata billings for a period prior to termination, such as 6 months).

In addition, the employee agreement among the proprietary physicians should clearly provide the periods in which he or she will not be terminated because of disability. It should also specify the disability benefits to be paid by the practice itself during a period of illness prior to such termination (see also earlier discussion of "Additional Insurance Benefits"). Many of the groups we represent provide such disability benefits to the full extent of the foresaid share of accounts receivable that would be available upon termination. A physician cannot adequately judge his or her personal need for disability insurance without knowing what benefits are available from the practice. Yet, to our great surprise, there are many practices that have no established provision whatsoever in this regard. Without specification of how these potential problems are to be handled, the practice is vulnerable to extreme problems that can arise in case of the long-term disability or death of one of the partners or shareholders (or even two at the same time). Often these claims will be pressed vigorously by the legal representative of a physician who is no longer capable of working, or who is deceased.

Retirement Plans

The practice, whether incorporated or a partnership, should have a clearly defined and easily understood retirement plan that allows for tax sheltering by any physician-employee. Obviously this is a complicated matter beyond the scope of this chapter. One can, however, judge somewhat the situation in any particular group by verifying that such plans exist and that they are not slanted in coverage or type to one or more of the proprietary physicians. For example, an existing corporation with mostly younger physician-employees normally should have a defined benefit pension plan extending beyond one that—because of age sensitivity—primarily benefits and maximizes the tax shelter of the older shareholder-physicians. In addition, these retirement plans should, whenever possible, have the type of provisions that would be of interest to a younger anesthesiologist in maintaining his or her own financial flexibility. These include provisions for "election out" of coverage for physicians who must have cash compensation, loans from the retirement plans (up to the maximum $50,000 allowed by TEFRA) and, where there are diverse investment philosophies among the group, provisions allowing each participant to direct the investment of his or her own accounts in any defined contribution retirement plans.

Professional Liability Insurance

The legal atmosphere that seems to encourage large claims and large judgments apparently is still with us today and may once again lead to the flight of insurance carriers from the professional liability market, just as it did in the mid-1970s. In consequence, there were at that time, and still may be in the current climate, those pro-

fessionals who choose to "go bare" by canceling all insurance coverage because of its cost. There are also those few groups that, because of their specialty (not usually anesthesiology), prior claims experience, or both, seem to be unable to procure any insurance. Obviously, becoming self-insured creates a dangerous situation, especially for the younger anesthesiologist who is considering joining a group. One of the benefits of malpractice insurance, apart from the liability coverage itself, is the legal defense provided by the insurance company. Without such a defense, even totally groundless claims can involve staggering legal fees that would become the obligation of the practice and the physicians involved.

In addition, insurance-free exposure to these types of claims requires a distortive modification of the physicians' personal financial and estate planning. Examples of such planning involve putting all assets in trusts, making premature gifts to wives and children, and other means of avoiding personal ownership of assets that may be subject to claims of creditors. (All of these moves must be completed prior to the filing of any such claims, or even an incident that leads to a filing, or be subject to voidance under various state "fraudulent conveyance" statutes.) Therefore, adequate coverage under a professional liability insurance plan, which covers each physician as a named insured as well as the practice, continues to be essential. The primary and excess liability limits obviously must be realistic for today's marketplace and legal climate. Eventually (it is to be hoped) state laws limiting malpractice judgments—such as those limiting "pain and suffering" damages to certain levels—will reduce premium levels and bring more carriers back into the market.

Another problem that probably will be faced in the future is the likelihood that those remaining carriers underwriting "occurrence" malpractice insurance policies will no longer do so because of the difficulty in adequately judging the reserves needed to cover possible future claims under such policies. Occurrence policies cover the insured whenever the claim is made, as long as the insurance was in effect at the time of the alleged malpractice. The replacement—"claims made" policies that provide for coverage only to the extent that the policy is actually in force when the claim is made—have been used by a number of malpractice insurance underwriters since the 1970s. This new underwriting policy makes it important that every anesthesiology group so insured be committed to "buy up the tail" when employment is terminated. This "tail" coverage offers continuing insurance for the departed physician and associated assets, just as if occurrence insurance coverage was still available.

In addition, all malpractice insurance packages, whether occurrence or claims made, should clearly specify whether there is any coverage for outside work that might be permitted under any employment arrangement with the practice. These policies also must clearly cover claims against any nurse anesthetists with whom the anesthesiologists work. (The many ramifications of liability insurance and complications of claims-made policies are beyond the scope of this chapter.) Nonetheless, a review of the insurance available in the practice remains a critical item in evaluating any practice that an anesthesiologist contemplates joining.

Billing System

In most anesthesia groups, the practice itself bills patients for its services. This procedure obviously maximizes the flexibility of the group in collecting for services rendered and in increasing fee levels. In some cases, however, either a hospital in which the group operates or some other third party bills on behalf of the anesthesiologists. There are obviously problems inherent in such practices. These in turn may be a factor in evaluating total practice economics, the amount of income that is currently available to the anesthesiologists, and that likely to be available in the future. Obviously, the worst case is the old system—which has gone out of use in most urban practice settings—that limits the anesthesia group to a mere percentage of anesthesia billings made by the hospital to its patients. Such a situation usually indicates very limited economic and political strength of the anesthesia group within the hospital system. It is often indicative of current and future problems with which a new anesthesiologist may not wish to become associated.

Relationship With the Hospital

Just as with the billing system noted immediately above, the particular relationship of the anesthesia group within the hospital or hospitals in which its members provide services is often indicative of the strength of the group and the regard in which it is held by the hospital management and staff physicians with whom the anesthesia group must deal on a day-to-day basis. The obvious sign of a strong relationship in this respect is an arrangement whereby the anesthesia group is, subject sometimes to limited exceptions, the exclusive provider of anesthesia services to the patients of the hospital. This is the so-called closed-staff (as opposed to open-staff) operation.

While such arrangements may be subject to certain antitrust problems (as indicated in Chapter 28), they are, without doubt, extremely advantageous for the anesthesia group involved. If there is such an arrangement, it is critical to its continuation that the arrangement be in writing. The existence of any service agreement between the hospital and the practice is something that should be explored (again, tactfully) by any anesthesiologist considering joining that group. If there is such a written contract, the secondary inquiry to be made relates to its term, and any provisions for automatic renewal, termination, or both. Obviously, a long-term exclusive contract or automatic renewal from year to year is most desirable in any case.

In most situations, it is also advantageous if one of the shareholders or partners of the established practice serves as the director of the anesthesia department at the hospital. This fact could be extremely important in situations in which there was an open staff—that is, where the practice does not have an exclusive right to provide anesthesia services at the hospital. Solutions to critical problems of patients and coverage allocations are obviously facilitated by having a member of the group serve in this capacity. Regardless of the closed-staff or open-staff status of the anesthesia department, it is also important for any anesthesiologist contemplating joining a group to review the hospital staff regulations and bylaws, seeking out any "peculiar" provisions that may impact future practice.

Relationship With Nurse Anesthetists

In today's economic climate, the efficient use of nurse anesthetists (CRNAs) may be critical to the financial stability of and coverage by the group. In that connection, it is important that any anesthesiologist joining a group inquire about the relationship of the physicians and the CRNAs and, if possible, actually speak to the CRNAs. In the more advantageous situations, the CRNAs are usually employees of the practice itself, as compared with allocated employees of the hospitals at which they render services. In any event, the inquiry also should include any limitations on use or coverage of CRNAs imposed by the hospital or its staff (or any statutory restrictions in effect—see Chapter 25). The inquiry should also be directed toward any standardized procedures in effect in the practice, hospital(s), or both in reference to hours, overtime, and most important, availability of scheduling CRNAs for anesthesia services to be rendered by the incoming anesthesiologist. Lastly, a written employment agreement with the CRNAs is often advantageous, guaranteeing the continuity of CRNA services to the group and clearly establishing their benefits so that future questions in these areas may be avoided.

CONCLUSION

This chapter covers the major points that should be considered by the anesthesiologist who should become adequately informed about a prospective position. These points are based upon my legal perspective and years of practice in the field of health care provider-physician relationships.

Anesthesiologists contemplating stepping into a large group practice would be well advised to refer to the outline of the needed information contained in Table 26–1 and check off each and every item during the recruiting process to which they are subject (or as part of their own search for an appropriate position). Obviously, it may be difficult to find a group practice that uses all of the "best" methods of operation that are discussed or implied in this chapter. On the other hand, merely making queries and listening to the openness of the answers can speak worlds about the nature of the practice and the physicians with whom the anesthesiologist will have to work very closely in future years.

Unlike days gone by, when many senior physicians were often "offended" by questions of this kind, most anesthesia groups today are, if not anxious, at least willing to discuss virtually all of the areas covered by this chapter—even though they may sometimes be reluctant to give out actual figures as to total compensation of some of their members. In most cases, the effort to be informed initially (rather than by hindsight) will prove worthwhile to those anesthesiologists who are willing to make the effort to appraise their future practice as suggested herein.

27

Thomas C. Hill, J.D.

Hospital Clinical Privileges and Staff Membership

The ability to treat patients in a hospital is of substantial importance to nearly every medical specialist; it is crucial to the practice of an anesthesiologist. Despite the ever-increasing proportion of operations and deliveries being performed outside the traditional hospital setting, it is still true that the bulk of anesthesia services are provided in acute care hospitals. For that reason, conducting a successful anesthesia practice requires obtaining clinical privileges at one or more hospitals. The conditions placed on such privileges are based in part on the practitioner's membership on the medical staff at that hospital. In order to enhance the likelihood of obtaining such privileges and such membership, it is helpful to have a knowledge of the workings of the hospital privilege system now prevalent in the United States.

PERTINENT HOSPITAL ACCREDITATION STANDARDS

The decisions as to the appropriate structure of hospital governance and the granting of privileges are, as a practical matter, determined by the standards included in the *Accreditation Manual for Hospitals* as promulgated by the Joint Commission on Accreditation of Healthcare Organizations (JCAHO). Compliance with the JCAHO standards is determined on the basis of an application and a "voluntary" survey of the particular facility by JCAHO inspectors. JCAHO accreditation, however, is accepted without further review as compliance with the standards for hospital licensing established under the Medicare program[1] and under the hospital licensing programs run by many states.[2] For many hospitals, the federal Medicare patients and the state Medicaid patients constitute a majority of admissions and revenues. Therefore, few hospitals are truly free to forego compliance with the JCAHO standards. Nominally, it is unnecessary for a hospital to meet every single standard in the *Accreditation Manual*:

> To be accredited, a hospital must demonstrate that it is in substantial compliance with the standards overall and not necessarily with each applicable standard.[3]

Thus, it is conceivable that a hospital might choose to ignore the medical staff standards in the *Accreditation Manual* and still receive an accreditation. As a practical matter, however, it is generally understood that a hospital that deliberately chose not to comply with the medical staff standards would have such deficiencies "written up" by its survey team. Rather than run the risk of loss of its accreditation, the typical hospital will adopt structures that comply with the JCAHO standards. Further, the theory behind the JCAHO standards has been widely accepted throughout the country and is the basis for comparison and evaluation of hospitals by patients, third-party payers, and physicians alike. The organizing theory is that the hospital and the practitioners with privileges at the hospital are engaged in a joint venture. The goal of the joint venture is to provide high-quality health care at a reasonable price.[4] All legal controversies involving clinical privileges or staff membership should ultimately be decided by reference to this almost universally accepted concept of the role of the hospital.

Distinguishing Clinical Privileges From Staff Membership

For many years, it has been common in the United States to use the expression *staff privileges* to describe the relationship between a hospital and the health care providers who practice there. To some extent, this nomenclature is a recognition of the reality that the medical care received in a hospital is critically dependent on the care given by physicians. Also, for many years it was true at most hospitals that only physicians and dentists were entitled to full staff membership, and only physicians were entitled to admit patients on their independent authority. The term *staff privileges* is, however, something of a misnomer, as it combines two distinct but closely interrelated benefits—staff membership and clinical privileges. For that and a large number of other reasons, including a recognition of the growing frequency of state laws granting admitting privileges to nonphysicians, the *Accreditation Manual* that became effective for surveys beginning in January 1985 substantially reduced the overlap between clinical privileges and staff membership.[5]

The *Accreditation Manual* now provides that "clinical privileges" are to be determined by the hospital on the basis of the scope of the state licensure of a practitioner and on the basis of that practitioner's training and experience.[6] "Clinical privileges" determine what care the practitioner can provide and under what conditions. For example, a nurse-midwife or a certified registered nurse anesthetist (CRNA) might by state law be granted privileges to perform certain procedures with physician supervision and certain others without. But the authority to treat patients independently, which is granted, documented, and circumscribed by the description of clinical privileges, does not constitute staff membership. Even admitting privileges do not constitute staff membership. The *Accreditation Manual* allows substantial flexibility in the structure of the clinical privileges other than admitting privileges, and no other level of clinical privileges must automatically include staff membership. Also, there is no prohibition against staff membership for practitioners without full admitting privileges.

In contrast to clinical privileges, "staff membership" connotes a role in governance of the "medical staff," concerning which the *Accreditation Manual* provides substantial detail in its Medical Staff (MS) Standards. It does not constitute authority to provide medical care to patients, though MS.4.3.1 suggests that no practitioner can authorize admission of inpatients unless he or she is a member of the medical staff.[7] The *Accreditation Manual* requires that there be written procedures for gaining admission to the staff and that the staff have a role in recommending bylaws and rules and regulations to the hospital's governing body. In recognition of the extreme diversity in structures and ownership of American hospitals, the standards adopted in the 1985 *Accreditation Manual* included few other definite substantive requirements for the staff membership. The 1985 revisions did add some definite requirements for giving authority to the medical executive committee, a group that has the power to act for the medical staff but need not be chosen by it. Membership on the medical staff is no longer limited only to physicians and dentists and others *required* by a particular state's laws, but the medical executive committee must still have a majority of members who are fully licensed physician members of the medical staff.

The new structure continues to involve a substantial overlap between admitting privileges and staff membership. The procedures for applying and the criteria for granting clinical privileges are to be set out in the medical staff bylaws.[8] The medical staff bylaws are ultimately adopted by the governing body, but they are based on recommendations directly from the medical staff. No individual is to have admitting privileges unless that person is also allowed to be a member of the medical staff. Both privileges and staff membership will be based on a showing of licensure in the particular state.[9] In summary, even though the anesthesia practitioner's inability to obtain admitting privileges does not by itself constitute a major impediment to the success of an anesthesia practice, an anesthesia practitioner will be closer to the source of the power in any hospital if he or she obtains staff membership.

ORGANIZATION OF THE MEDICAL STAFF

Under the new structure adopted with the 1985 *Accreditation Manual*, the medical staff consists of any allopathic and osteopathic physicians admitted to membership in accordance with established criteria, along with such nonphysician practitioners as are required by state law or allowed by the hospital governing body to be staff members. It will continue to be true that anesthesiologists, as physicians, will normally be members of the medical staff. Further, to the extent the associations of nurse anesthetists are successful in lobbying state legislatures or hospital governing bodies, staff membership could be granted to nurse anesthetists also. Thus, both physician and nonphysician anesthesia practitioners eventually may be on the medical staff.

Granting of Staff Membership

The procedures and criteria for granting membership in the staff are to be included in the staff bylaws.[10] Staff bylaws are to be recommended by the medical staff to the hospital governing body, which, however, retains the ultimate authority to establish the standards for staff membership and the levels of qualifications that will be required. The standards for admission must be disclosed in the staff bylaws, but the *Accreditation Manual* leaves substantial discretion to the governing body as to the substantive requirements. For example, it could be provided that staff membership would not be available to practitioners with certain specialties unless they were under contract to the hospital to provide that service. Such an arrangement has been more and more frequent in recent years for certain hospital-based specialties, such as pathology, radiology, emergency medicine, and anesthesia. The *Accreditation Manual* requires that contract physicians applying for staff membership meet the same quality standards as any other physician for admission or reappointment. It is explicitly provided, however, that the termination of a contract can, if clearly set out in the contract, entail automatic termination of staff privileges.[11] By this mechanism, an individual practitioner or group can be assured of the exclusivity of its right to perform a certain service in that particular hospital.

Once medical staff membership has been granted, the *Accreditation Manual* leaves greater flexibility (than before 1985) as to the extent of authority that must be given to the medical staff. Deleted from the manual were the substantial portions that discussed the consultation between the medical staff and the governing body on major aspects of the hospital's operation.[12] While the medical staff must still be involved in any amendment to its bylaws, the staff need not be involved in every hospital decision affecting the credentials or the quality of medical care. Rather, the post-1985 *Accreditation Manual* requires that the medical executive committee have responsibility in this area.

For reasons that are discussed in Chapter 29, the antitrust exposure of the hospital and its medical staff is reduced by delegating a number of competitively sensitive functions, including the granting of credentials and staff membership, to a small group of officials rather than to the vote of the staff as a whole. Currently, the granting of staff membership, then, will rise through some sort of membership committee to the executive committee and then will pass on with the executive committee's recommendation to the hospital's governing body. The *Accreditation Manual* requires this active involvement by the executive committee, a majority of whose members must be physicians, because of the importance of the staff membership and credentialing decisions to the provision of patient care. In recent years, the courts have been imposing on hospitals ever-greater responsibilities for ensuring the quality of the medical care given by those persons who have privileges at the hospital.[13] This exposure to damage judgments if certain practitioners do not deliver quality medical care has in turn led hospitals to seek a more rigorous screening of applicants. The practitioners on the medical executive committee are expected to ensure this quality-control function in its recommendation to the governing body. Within these broad outlines, the *Accreditation Manual* leaves it open for the governing bodies of hospitals with different ownership and different community situations to share more or less authority with the medical staff.

Granting of Clinical Privileges

The *Accreditation Manual* establishes a system for granting privileges that is parallel to the system for granting staff membership. The procedures for granting clinical privileges are to be set out in the medical staff bylaws and policies, subject to approval by the governing body.[14] The criteria must be uniformly applied to all applicants and in each case related to quality patient care. As with staff membership, clinical privileges for contract physicians are to be granted or renewed according to the same criteria used for economically independent practitioners, but the contract of employment can permissibly provide that clinical privileges will end upon termination of the contract.[15]

While the procedural framework for the decision on clinical privileges has been changed (vis-à-vis before and after 1985), the actual operation of the system is likely to be changed only slightly. Any credentialing decision would involve collecting information on the education and previous experience of the applicant. In light of recent revelations of the forgery, sale, or both, of false medical credentials, the hospital will have to make a serious attempt to confirm the past experience reported on the application form. The National Data Bank established by the Health Care Quality Improvement Act of 1986 and similar state data banks must be consulted.[16] If there are departments or services within the hospital, those bodies will recommend to the medical executive committee and then to the governing body the standards to be met by applicants for privileges in that department. After this process has been completed, the clinical privileges granted cannot have a duration of more than 2 years, so that there is a continuing opportunity for peer review of the quality of medical care provided by a particular practitioner and a renewed opportunity to check the National Data Bank or state banks.

The legal implications of this series of steps are varied. The responsibility for the initial confirmation of the applicant's experience and training rests on the hospital, which will have some risk of liability in any event if the physician is ultimately determined to be unqualified. For the most part, members of the staff committees reviewing qualifications of applicants are unlikely to be brought into lawsuits involving allegations of improper medical care.[17] There remains, however, the possibility that practitioners actively involved in reviewing applications for renewal of privileges, or in the suspension of privileges, may be charged with improper behavior by unsuccessful applicants. The major burden in many of the reviews will fall on the department for which the applicant seeks clinical privileges. Because the membership of that department will comprise the applicant's most direct competitors, *there are antitrust risks involved*. These risks are heightened if there is the appearance that economic considerations have control over quality-of-care considerations in making any of these decisions. (These risks are covered to some degree in Chapter 28.) The removal of the staff as a separate body from the appointment and reappointment processes, and its replacement with the medical executive committee, however, presumably will reduce the overall exposure of staff members.

THE IMPACT OF PRICE COMPETITION

Much of the medical community is busy in these times talking about price competition in medical services, either through prospective pricing systems or alternative delivery systems. Each of these developments is related to the granting of staff membership or clinical privileges.

Medicare and DRGs

Prospective pricing systems, the most prominent example of which are the diagnosis-related groupings (DRGs) adopted by Medicare,[18] have no direct relationship to the granting of clinical privileges or staff membership. The basic assumption of DRGs is that the same quality of care will be delivered under the DRG system as under the previous cost-based system. The adoption of DRGs, however, has skewed certain of the economic incentives in the medical system and therefore put certain pressures on the clinical privilege or staff membership questions.

Under the classic prospective pricing system, the health care provider agrees to perform a certain service for a flat charge determined in advance. Under the particular pricing system incorporated in Medicare's DRGs, the hospital receives a certain sum for each admission of a Medicare patient with a particular diagnosis, nominally without regard to the actual length of stay or services provided in order to treat that particular patient. This, of course, has the effect of encouraging the hospital to prefer to admit those patients whose treatment costs the hospital less than average over those patients whose treatment costs more than the average. Similarly, the hospital will prefer to deal with physicians whose patients tend to be in the preferred group. The open question is whether the hospital will be able to withdraw or reduce clinical privileges or staff membership of those physicians whose patterns of treatment appear to be costing the hospital money.

With certain prominent exceptions, the law has generally concluded that the granting of staff privileges is in the discretion of the hospital governing body and not subject to challenge except for some gross abuse of that discretion. For a publicly owned hospital, the analysis involves a determination of whether the hospital's procedures gave the applicant or terminated practitioner "due process of law," including a fair hearing before an impartial tribunal.[19] For the most part, practitioners seeking clinical privileges or staff membership at a private hospital are not owed due process, but courts often reach a quite similar result with regard to private hospitals by interpreting the staff bylaws as a contract between the individual practitioners and the hospital.[20] That the bylaws will provide for some hearing is made more likely by the *Accreditation Manual* standards suggesting that all staff bylaws provide a "fair hearing" to review adverse recommendations and by the civil damage immunity granted by the federal Health Care Quality Improvement Act of 1986 to professional review actions based on "adequate notice and hearing."[21]

Under whichever legal standard is applied, the essential question is whether the practitioner was given fair notice of the grounds for the refusal or termination of privileges or membership. Some years ago, the typical medical staff bylaws provided for termination of membership only for poor-quality medical care, and such provisions were sometimes interpreted not to allow termination for any reason not directly tied to patient care.[22] More recently, hospital staff bylaws have been written to include other possible grounds for refusal or termination, which can be generally summarized as "the good of the hospital." Under such provisions, the courts have upheld the termination of staff membership and clinical privileges for such behavior as denigrating the hospital in public speeches.[23] Under the more recent decisions, it would appear that a hospital giving its staff members and applicants adequate notice could, without undue legal risk, provide for the denial or termination of privileges or staff membership for physicians who consistently overuse hospital resources. The *Accreditation Manual* raises no obstacles to such a provision, as long as it is clearly spelled out for the applicants or the staff members in the hospital staff bylaws or policies.[24] This is perhaps a more obvious reliance on economic considerations than was previously the case, but practitioners should be prepared for this new environment.

HMOs and PPOs

In a parallel situation, the rise of alternative delivery systems, such as health maintenance organizations (HMOs), preferred provider organizations (PPOs), or competitive medical plans, has led to strong pressures for the control of utilization through active programs of utilization review. These various alternative delivery systems promise the purchaser a lower overall price based on reduction in utilization, often described as "more efficient" medical care. To deliver on these promises, the alternative delivery systems must ensure that the participating practitioners comply with the utilization review programs and reduce unnecessary utilization. Inevitably, some of the participating health care providers in

these alternative delivery systems will be determined not to be meeting the utilization standards and to be costing the sponsor money. Unlike the Medicare DRG system, the providers participating in alternative delivery systems will normally have participation contracts separate from any formal relationship to clinical privileges or staff membership at a particular hospital. In the typical case, a participating practitioner will be required to have privileges at some participating facility, but not every practitioner at the facility will be a member of the alternative delivery system. Certainly, if the practitioner loses privileges at the facility for any reason, the practitioner will also have his or her participation contract terminated, and that contract will explicitly so provide. Termination from the alternative delivery system, however, even on the grounds that the practitioner overuses services, will normally not directly affect the practitioner's clinical privileges. In short, participating in an alternative delivery system heightens the importance of maintaining clinical privileges and staff membership at a hospital, but in the typical case, participation will not increase the risks of loss of those privileges or membership.

CONCLUSION

In 1972, when F. A. Davis Company published a book on a subject similar to this one, *Legal Aspects of Anesthesia*, the greatest law-related concern of physicians was the risk of malpractice suits. Today, there are other legal problems of equal magnitude—namely, *the procuring of clinical privileges and staff membership*. These problems—the resolution of which is so important to a successful practice—seem to be based much more often on economics than on quality of care. Upon review, however, it becomes apparent that the changes in the clinical privileges and staff membership procedures in recent years have been heavily affected by the ever-broadening net of the malpractice-liability system. These changes in turn have led to greater pressure on practitioners by the hospital, by the state medical board, and by third-party payers. The courts and the legislatures have forced the hospitals to monitor the quality of care and the behavior of the practitioners within those hospitals ever more closely. In response, the hospitals have adopted more stringent procedures for the granting of clinical privileges and staff membership. Thus economic pressures have been brought to bear to achieve quality-of-care goals.

Understanding and working within this changing system should help the anesthesia professional to experience greater professional and economic success, as well as considerable peace of mind.

REFERENCES

1. 42 U.S.C. § 1395x(e).
2. *E.g.*, Ohio Admin. Code § 5122:3-3.
3. Joint Commission on Accreditation of Healthcare Organizations: Accreditation Manual for Hospitals, 1989. JCAHO, Chicago, 1988, p xxii, (hereinafter, AMH/89).
4. Pontius v. Children's Hospital, 1982–83 Trade Cases ¶ 65,176 (W.D. Pa. 1982); Kissam, PC, et al: Antitrust and hospital privileges: Testing the conventional wisdom. Cal L Rev 70:595, 656–657, 668–669, 1982.
5. Joint Commission on Accreditation of Healthcare Organizations: Accreditation Manual for Hospitals, 1985. JCAHO, Chicago, 1984, p iii. (hereinafter, "AMH/85"); AMH/89, p 122.
6. AMH/89, MS.4 (Medical Staff [standard] 4) 4, pp 110–115.
7. AMH/89, MS.1, MS.2, MS.3, pp 101–110.
8. AMH/89, pp 110–115.
9. AMH/89, pp 101, 110.
10. AMH/89, pp 101–104.
11. AMH/89, p 104.
12. *See, e.g.*, 1982 Accreditation Manual, at pp 55–56, 104.
13. *E.g.*, Elam v. College Park Hospital, 132 Cal. App. 3d 332, 183 Cal. Rptr. 156, *modified*, 133 Cal. App. 3d 94a (1982). *See, generally*, Chapters 7, 14, and 25.
14. AMH/89, MS.4, pp 110–115.
15. AMH/89, p 13.
16. AMH/89, MS.4.2.6, at p 111, now requires the hospital's inquiring into other denials or revocation of credentials. Health Care Quality Improvement Act of 1986, 42 U.S.C. § 11,101 *et seq.* National Data Bank established pursuant to 42 U.S.C. §§ 11,133 and 11,135; 45 C.F.R. § 60. For a similar but distinct state program, see Ohio Rev. Code § 4731.224.
17. *But see* Corletto v. Shore Mem. Hosp., 138 N.J. Super. 302, 350 A.2d 534 (1975), wherein a New Jersey intermediate appellate court held that a patient injured by the allegedly negligent act of a reportedly physically impaired (by old age) member of the staff may have a cause of action against the organized staff and administration of the hospital in which the negligent act took place for allowing that practitioner to continue to have clinical privileges.
18. 42 U.S.C. § 1395ww(d), 42 C.F.R. Part 412.
19. Sosa v. Board of Managers of Val Verde Mem. Hosp., 437 F.2d 173 (4th Cir. 1971). *Cf.* Greisman v. Newcomb Hosp., 192 A.2d 817 (N.J. 1963) (same standard for private hospitals).
20. Woodbury v. McKinnon, 447 F.2d 839, 842 (5th Cir. 1971); Shulman v. Washington Hosp. Center, 222 F. Supp. 59 (D.D.C. 1963) and 319 F. Supp. 252 (1970).
21. AMH/89, MS.1.2.3.1.9 (initial staff membership), MS.2.4.2 (mechanisms to be specified in medical staff bylaws), and MS.4.2.1 (clinical privileges); Health Care Quality Improvement Act of 1986, 42 U.S.C. §§ 11,101 *et seq.*, at § 11,112(b).
22. Miller v. Eisenhower Medical Center, 166 Cal. Rptr. 826, 614 P.2d 258 (1980); McElhinney v. William Booth Mem. Hosp., 544 S.W.2d 258 (Ky. 1976).
23. Siegel v. St. Vincent Charity Hosp. & Health Center, 35 Ohio App. 3d 143, 520 N.E.2d 249 (1987).
24. AMH/89, MS.1.2.2 and MS.4.2.1, pp 102, 110. It is unclear whether denial or termination of privileges for overutilization is based on "professional competence" and would therefore have to be reported to the National Data Bank under 42 U.S.C. § 11,133.

28

William B. Markovits, J.D.

Antitrust Problems in the Health Care Field

In the past decade or so, two emerging trends have converged to thrust the antitrust laws into a prominent position in the health care field. Judicial recognition of the application of the antitrust laws to professional services, coupled with a change in the nature of competition in the health care field, have caused the antitrust laws to be a subject the physician simply cannot ignore. What, then, is a physician to do to avoid undue antitrust exposure? Becoming aware of the basics of antitrust law—its theories and defenses—is the most important step. This chapter will explore antitrust basics, in the specific context of issues applicable to the health care practitioner.

COMPETITION IN THE HEALTH CARE FIELD

To say that the health care field has undergone a radical transformation in recent years would be an understatement. Not so long ago, the health care field could be characterized as consisting of localized hospitals and physicians, an absence of overt competition, and a total emphasis on public service. Today there is a shift to large medical care corporations, and the rising cost of health care has led to an open concern with price competition. In addition, there has been a dramatic increase in entrants onto the competitive playing field, challenging the business activities of hospitals and physicians.

In the past, hospitals competed only with other hospitals, and competition was limited to service (location, equipment, and personnel). Hospitals now compete with new entrants such as ambulatory surgical centers, freestanding emergency care centers, and even physicians' offices offering certain diagnostic services such as computed tomographic (CT) scanning or ultrasound. Rising costs and empty beds have led to an increase both in the visibility of competition (increased advertising by hospitals) and in the nature of competition (a greater emphasis on price).

The new marketplace has had an even greater effect on physicians. In the past, physicians competed only with other physicians, and again competition was limited to quality and service rather than price. Allied health professionals, for example, nurse anesthetists, podiatrists, and psychologists, are now encroaching upon the physicians' territory. New payment modes and alternative delivery systems, such as those found in health maintenance organizations (HMOs) and preferred provider organizations (PPOs), reduce the size of the fee-for-service market and provide competition for nonparticipant physicians.

Both hospitals and physicians have reacted to the increase in competition by diversification. Hospitals, for example, have expanded into the provision of durable medical equipment. Physicians have expanded into joint ventures for the provision of various diagnostic services, such as ultrasound. As a final example, hospitals and physicians have joined together in ventures

such as physician-hospital organizations (PHOs), to provide an alternative to being dictated to by third-party payors.

The potential for anticompetitive action caused by the changing health care marketplace is great. The emergence of price competition; the entrance of new competitors; and the shift to larger, more powerful health care entities are all antitrust warning signals. The recent spate of health care–related antitrust suits indicates that these signals have not gone unnoticed.

AN OVERVIEW OF THE ANTITRUST LAWS

The Statutes

The antitrust laws are intended to ensure that competition flourishes, free of unreasonable private restraints. There are four principal federal antitrust laws:

The Sherman Act of 1890. The Sherman Act[1] was the first antitrust law enacted by Congress and remains the most important. Section 1 of the act prohibits contracts, combinations, or conspiracies in restraint of interstate trade or commerce.[2] Section 2 prohibits monopolization or attempts to monopolize any part of interstate trade or commerce.

The Clayton Act of 1914.[3] This act's primary prohibitions involve exclusive dealing or tying arrangements, or certain mergers or acquisitions where the effect may be to substantially lessen competition or tend to create a monopoly.

The Robinson-Patman Act of 1936.[4] This act is an amendment to the Clayton Act; it prohibits price discrimination by sellers between purchasers in certain circumstances.

The Federal Trade Commission (FTCA) Act of 1914.[5] This act prohibits unfair methods of competition and deceptive practices.

In addition to the above statutes, most states have enacted antitrust laws that to some extent may mirror the federal laws but cover activities that are intrastate in nature.

The Danger Areas

Section 1 of the Sherman Act prohibits joint activity that "unreasonably" restrains trade, yet there are certain types of activity that are regarded as so inherently unreasonable they are held to be "per se" violations that may result in liability without further inquiry. These per se violations include

Price fixing. Agreements among competitors to raise, lower, or stabilize prices, discounts, or other terms and conditions of price

Group boycotts. Agreements among competitors that they will not deal with particular third parties

Market allocation. Agreements among competitors to divide up particular territories or customers

There are many other areas of antitrust concern that may not be per se offenses, yet still entail significant risk. These include

Exclusive dealing. Agreements with a customer that require the customer to purchase all, or substantially all, of its requirements for a particular product from a person or an entity are illegal if the effect is to deny a substantial portion of the market to a competitor.

Tying. Tying the purchase of a particular product to the purchase of another product. This practice may be per se illegal under certain conditions.

Monopolization. The improper acquisition or maintenance of monopoly power, that is, the power to control price or exclude competition.

Attempted monopolization. An entity without monopoly power may still be found liable for attempted monopolization in a situation wherein it takes actions with a specific intent to obtain a monopoly, and there is a dangerous probability that such actions would result in a monopoly.

Mergers. Mergers, acquisitions, or joint ventures may violate the antitrust laws where the effect is to substantially lessen competition, or tend to create a monopoly.

The Risks of Antitrust

By engaging in activity that might violate the antitrust laws, a physician risks criminal or civil liability. In addition, even if liability is not found, the physician involved as a target in an antitrust investigation or litigation will undoubtedly have spent much time and expense proving his or her innocence. It is therefore important to avoid, where possible, even the appearance of conduct that might lead to antitrust inquiry.

Sanctions for violations of the antitrust laws can be extremely severe. Certain violations of the Sherman Act are felonies, punishable by fines up to $250,000 and 3 years in prison. Physicians who say "It can't happen to me" are probably echoing the words of obstetricians in Georgia or allergists in Boston who, at the time of this writing, are undergoing criminal grand jury investigations for price-fixing violations. In a December 6, 1988, speech to the American Medical Association House of Delegates, the head of the U.S. Department of Justice Antitrust Division made it quite clear that physician activity was a subject of interest to the department, and that if physicians violate the antitrust laws, they could be subject to incarceration.[6]

Antitrust suits by private parties present an equally substantial risk to the physician. Anyone injured by an antitrust violation may bring suit and recover treble damages, as well as attorney's fees and costs. This makes the private antitrust suit a potent weapon, with frequent settlements at substantial cost in situations wherein liability may be present.

A case in which the author served as one of the plaintiffs' attorneys provides a good indication of the potential costs and benefits of an antitrust case.

In the ChoiceCare case,[7] a group of approximately 60 Cincinnati physicians brought a class action suit on behalf of more than 2000 physicians against a local health maintenance organization, alleging price-fixing and monopoly offenses, among other violations. The defendants counterclaimed, alleging antitrust and other violations by the plaintiffs, and sought $45 million in damages. More than 100 depositions were taken, and each of the physician-plaintiffs had to undergo a day or more of deposition testimony prior to trial. Each physician-plaintiff also had to answer two sets of extensive interrogatories (Chapter 23) and comply with document requests. The defendants incurred similar burdens: millions of ChoiceCare's records were produced, and more than 40 persons affiliated with Choice-Care were deposed.

The costs of the ChoiceCare case were tremendous. Plaintiffs' costs alone, for items such as deposition transcripts and expert witness fees, exceeded $400,000. Plaintiffs's attorney time expense was greater than $2 million. After a trial lasting 4 months, the jury returned a verdict in the plaintiffs' favor, with trebled antitrust damages totaling approximately $100 million. To forgo an appeal, the case was subsequently settled with the stipulation that certain management changes be made. The contingent liabilities to plaintiffs exceeded $60 million.

The ChoiceCare litigation illustrates the pitfalls of antitrust—the extensive time and expense of investigation and prosecution, and the great exposure to liability.

THE RISE OF HEALTH CARE–RELATED ANTITRUST ACTIONS

Until recently in the history of antitrust, the medical profession, like other learned professions, enjoyed a virtual exemption from antitrust scrutiny. This exemption was based on the notion that the medical profession was not engaged in "trade or commerce," and that the profession had special ethical and competency attributes that outweighed any antitrust concerns. The signal that this was to change came in 1975, when the U.S. Supreme Court rejected any antitrust exemption for the professions in holding that a minimum-fee schedule for lawyers set by a local bar association was a violation of the antitrust laws.[8] The one ray of hope for the professions was located in a footnote of the court's opinion, which stated,

The fact that a restraint operates upon a profession as distinguished from a business is, of course, relevant in determining whether that particular restraint violates the [antitrust laws]. It would be unrealistic to view the practice of professions as interchangeable with other human activities, and automati-

cally to apply to the professions other antitrust concepts which originated in other areas. The public service aspect, and other features of the professions, may require that a particular practice, which could properly be viewed as a violation of the [antitrust laws] in another context, be treated differently.[9]

Two subsequent attempts to use this "public service" defense have failed before the Supreme Court. In one case, a society of engineers adopted an ethical canon prohibiting competitive bidding by its members. The court rejected the defense that the regulation was necessary to promote the public interest by eliminating the potential for shoddy work resulting from cost cutting induced by competitive bids. Yet the potential "public service" defense lived on, with the court recognizing that with respect to the professions, the nature of competition may vary, and "[e]thical norms may serve to regulate and promote this competition."[10]

The medical profession's turn before the Supreme Court came in 1982, in a case that proved to be a poor vehicle for testing the "public service" defense.[11] The court struck down a maximum fee plan by doctors in two medical societies, rejecting the "public service" and "ethical norms" defenses. The court implicitly recognized the possibility of such defenses, yet stated that "the price-fixing agreements in this case . . . are not premised on public service or ethical norms."[12] In the ensuing years, antitrust cases involving physicians have increased dramatically, and the "public service" or "ethical norms" defenses have provided little solace.

ANTITRUST ISSUES FOR THE ANESTHESIOLOGIST

Every physician currently faces the risk of involvement in a health care antitrust investigation or suit. For the anesthesiologist, there are also certain specific areas of concern, such as exclusive contracts with hospitals (that may also be viewed as illegal tying arrangements or perhaps even monopolization or attempted monopolization) or dealings with nurse anesthetists (where restrictive actions may be viewed as boycotts or other restraints of trade). In addition, as with any physician, the anesthesiologist must be concerned with, in approximate order of importance: price fixing, boycotts or refusals to deal (troublesome in the context of peer review, staff privilege determinations, or in dealings with third-party payers), market allocation, joint ventures, such as the formation of an IPA, PPO, or HMO; and monopolization or attempted monopolization.

Exclusive Dealing Contracts and Tying

It is not unusual for a hospital to decide that, for a variety of valid reasons, it makes sense to enter into an exclusive contract for the provision of anesthesia care. These exclusive contractual arrangements have been attacked under a variety of antitrust grounds, with limited success. The primary bases for attack are characterization of these contracts as illegal exclusive dealing contracts or tying arrangements. An exclusive dealing contract, as the name implies, is a contract that restricts a given purchaser or seller from dealing with any of the parties' competitors. These contracts are unlawful under the antitrust laws if they foreclose so much of the market that they act as an unreasonable restraint on competition. Tying may be illegal per se under the antitrust laws, and is the use of market power in one product or service (the tying product) to gain a competitive advantage in a second product or service (the tied product), by forcing purchase of the tied product. In the context of an exclusive anesthesiology contract, the tying product would be use of the hospital's operating rooms, and the tied product would be anesthesia services.

A major Supreme Court case sheds light on the areas of legality and illegality. In *Jefferson Parish Hospital District No. 2 v. Hyde*,[13] an anesthesiologist brought an action based upon a hospital's exclusive contract with a competing firm of anesthesiologists. The Supreme Court found that the contractual arrangement in question was neither an illegal tying arrangement nor an illegal exclusive dealing arrangement. The justices began their analysis with the tying claim. They found that there were two separate products, rather than an integrated package as defendants claimed, because

anesthesiology services might be separately demanded by either the patient or the patient's physician, and anesthesiology services were billed separately from other hospital services. The plaintiff's tying claim failed, however, because the court found that the hospital did not have sufficient market power to "force" the purchase of the anesthesiology services. The hospital's 30% share of the operating room market in Jefferson Parish simply left too many alternatives to support the argument that patients were forced to go to that particular hospital and use that particular anesthesiology group. Note that a tying claim might be supported, however, if the hospital in question occupies a dominant position, which is likely to occur only in a relatively rural setting.

After finding that the contract was not an illegal tying arrangement, the court turned to the question of whether it was an illegal exclusive dealing arrangement. The court stated that the contract could be illegal if it foreclosed so much of the market for anesthesiological services that persons such as Dr. Hyde would be unreasonably restrained from competing. The record was insufficient before the court, so the court remanded the matter to the lower court for further inquiry. The Court of Appeals subsequently ruled that the exclusive contract in question was not unreasonably anticompetitive.[14]

The Federal Trade Commission (FTC) has also suggested that exclusive contracts for anesthesiology services may be "very different" from a classic tying arrangement.[15] The FTC suggests that the factors to consider in determining the legality of an arrangement under the antitrust laws include the proportion of the hospital and physician service markets involved in the contract, the purpose of the contract, the duration of the contract, the extent to which the contract deters entry into the market, the benefit to the public, and the extent of competition.

From the above, it seems clear that entering into an exclusive anesthesiology contract with an urban hospital should pose no problem under either an exclusive dealing or a tying analysis. Yet, this does not end the possible antitrust claims that might arise from such an arrangement. For example, if the evidence were to show that the arrangement was undertaken not for any valid reason, such as quality control, but rather with the intent and effect of excluding a competitor, a boycott or other agreement in restraint of trade might be found.

Relationship With Nurse Anesthetists

The relationship between anesthesiologists and nurse anesthetists is a subset of the relationship between physicians and allied health professionals (e.g., chiropractors, podiatrists, psychologists) generally. This is an area of concern, because the appearance, and sometimes actuality, may be that of an attempt to limit competition. Moreover, the courts have not proved receptive to the argument that physicians, because of their more extensive training, do not "compete" in the same market with allied health professionals. In *Bhan v. NME Hospitals, Inc,*[16] the Court of Appeals for the Ninth Circuit held that nurse anesthetists compete with anesthesiologists, despite a state statute requiring physician supervision of the nurse anesthetist. In *Bhan,* however, the plaintiff nurse anesthetist did not prevail in challenging a hospital's decision to allow only anesthesiologists to practice at its facility. A district court granted summary judgment for the hospital because it found that the decision could not have an anticompetitive effect because of the small (10%) market share of the hospital.[17] There was no unreasonable foreclosure for the nurse anesthetist in that there were as many as three other hospitals in the area that allowed nurse anesthetists to practice at their facilities.

The worse the facts of a given case, however, the less likely a court will be to strictly scrutinize market share. Where there is evidence that certain anesthesiologists are taking action to remove nurse anesthetists from the hospital staff or unreasonably restrict their activities, antitrust liability may be forthcoming. It was extremely significant that the allegations in *Bhan* of a conspiracy between the hospital and the anesthesiologists were weak. On the other hand, in *Oltz v. St. Peter's Community Hospital,*[18] a jury found a conspiracy existed between the hospital and the staff anes-

thesiologists to exclude nurse anesthetists from the hospital, and the court virtually ignored analysis of market share or anticompetitive effect.

Price Fixing

Fixing professional fees carries the greatest threat of criminal liability for an anesthesiologist or any other physician. While price fixing appears simple to understand, there are at least two common misconceptions regarding the nature of a price-fixing violation that must be clarified. The first misconception is that price fixing involves an agreement to raise specific fees to specific amounts. To the contrary, price fixing includes agreements among competitors to raise, lower, or stabilize prices or pricing terms, such as discount rates or terms of payment.[19] Relative value scales, or the publication of "average" fees for procedures, or an agreement on credit terms, all are examples of conduct that may be characterized as price fixing.[20]

The second misconception relating to price fixing is that a violation can only be shown if you have proof of an agreement, such as minutes of a meeting indicating that physicians in a smoke-filled room met and agreed to set fees. While this type of proof would obviously be welcomed by a plaintiff, it is unnecessary. Assent to a price-fixing agreement, and the agreement itself, may be inferred from circumstantial evidence. For example, if all the anesthesiologists in a given market attended a professional society meeting, and the following day they all adopted indentical fee structures, a price-fixing violation could be found.[21]

Although the penalty for a price-fixing violation may be harsh, the offense itself should be relatively easy to avoid. Physicians must not agree with other physicians on the fees to be charged patients or third-party payers, and they must not jointly determine the terms of payment. If a physician is involved in a meeting with other physicians and it appears the talk is turning to the price-fixing area, the physician should loudly and emphatically state that the discussion should cease, or that he or she will not be involved further. If the discussion persists, he or she should leave, and do so in an obvious manner. The reason these precautions are suggested is that a few years later, when there is an investigation, the physician wants everyone who testifies about that meeting to recall that he or she disagreed with the discussion and left. The possible benefit of the precautions outweighs any embarrassment suffered.

Boycotts or Refusals to Deal

If competing physicians join together to exclude a competitor from the market through a boycott or refusal to deal, an antitrust violation may have occurred. One example might involve anesthesiologists dealing with nurse anesthetists, as discussed above. Charges of boycotts or refusals to deal also often occur in the context of peer review or staff privilege determinations, and in dealings related to third-party payers.

Peer review and staff privilege determinations are fertile grounds for claims of boycott because of the clear risk for anticompetitive behavior. On the one hand, such activity may provide necessary and desirable quality and cost control and may in fact be explicitly required by statute. On the other hand, such activity often has physicians making decisions that may have a profound adverse effect on the business of the physician subject to the determination. Unfortunately, many physicians adversely affected by a peer review or staff privileges determination assume that the basis for the decision was anticompetitive in nature, and bring an antitrust claim, even though it might not be warranted.

Physicians serving on peer review bodies or involved in staff privilege determinations must take action to protect themselves from antitrust attack. Care must be taken to avoid even the appearance that a determination stemmed from an anticompetitive basis. To the extent possible, direct competitors of the subject of inquiry should minimize their involvement in the determination. Specific procedures should be established, set forth in written form in the bylaws or elsewhere, and *followed* to ensure that the subject of inquiry is given due process (i.e., that the process is fair). The term *followed* is emphasized, because many groups will write down detailed pro-

cedures, but will fail to adhere to them. This practice causes problems—it will be argued by a plaintiff physician that the failure to adhere to written procedure is evidence of an ulterior anticompetitive motive. The types of procedures that will satisfy due process concerns include a right to notice of a proposed adverse determination, a right to a hearing before impartial arbiters, a right to counsel, and a right to written explanations of the determination made. Compliance with due process may also qualify participants in a peer review group for antitrust immunity under the Health Care Quality Improvement Act of 1986 (HCQIA).[22] A physician involved in a peer review group should determine whether the group complies with the requirements of the HCQIA and, if it does not, action should be taken to bring about compliance.

Peer review participants also have another defense, applicable in the antitrust context generally, but of particular relevance to peer review—the so-called state action exemption from the antitrust laws.[23] In order to qualify for this exemption, the conduct in question must be "clearly articulated and affirmatively expressed as state policy," and must be "actively supervised by the state."[24] The Supreme Court in *Patrick v. Burget*[25] held that the second prong of this test—active state supervision—was not satisfied by Oregon's peer review statute, but clearly peer review activity can qualify under this doctrine.[26]

The facts of the *Patrick* case illustrate another important point.

Dr. Patrick declined partnership in the Astoria Clinic in Astoria, Oregon, and began a competing practice, at which point his former colleagues at the clinic took retaliatory action aimed at preventing Dr. Patrick from developing his practice. At the trial level, Dr. Patrick received a jury verdict of almost $2 million. This verdict was overturned on appeal, when the Ninth Circuit held that the state action doctrine immunized the conduct in question.

When the Supreme Court accepted the case for review, it was to some extent assumed that the appellate court decision would be reversed, as indeed occurred. The reason for the assumption, and the point illustrated by the facts of the Patrick case, is that no protection is likely to be afforded to blatantly anticompetitive conduct. The counterpoint is that where the plaintiff's antitrust claims in the peer review or staff privilege context appear baseless—for example, where no anticompetitive motive or conduct is found and proper procedures have been followed—a court may give the antitrust claims short shrift and dismiss them prior to trial.

Another area of physician activity that may result in a boycott or refusal to deal is physicians' responses to third-party payers. In these days of ever-increasing efforts at cost containment, physicians are often frustrated by restrictions placed upon them by insurance companies or alternative delivery systems (HMOs, PPOs, and the like). While there is clearly an imbalance of power when a physician negotiates with a large third-party payer, and while certain third-party payers may push cost containment too far, directly impacting on the ability of the physician to render quality care, the antitrust laws will not allow for "self-help" in the form of collective physician response.

Physicians have tried various methods of leveling the playing field with third-party payers, most of which have failed. It is crystal clear that agreements among physicians to refuse to deal with certain payers, or to deal only under certain conditions, are violations.[27] It is also a violation if physicians take other actions to accomplish the same goal, such as forcing hospitals to restrict privileges of physicians who belong to certain plans.[28] It will not aid the physicians if they call themselves a "union" or "federation" and attempt to fall under a labor law exemption to the antitrust laws.[29] Nor will it aid the physicians to claim that they did not know their actions were violations, as in the case of Tulsa, Oklahoma, physicians who banded together in attempting to deal with a new HMO entrant.[30] Even laypersons know that ignorance of the law is no excuse.

There are actions physicians can take to level the playing field that, if structured properly, will not violate the antitrust laws. For example, physicians who sufficiently integrate their practices, as in a corporation or independent practice association, may be able to deal collectively with third-party payers, depending upon the extent of integration; some physicians even go further and establish their own PPO or HMO, to serve as a competitive alternative.[31]

Physicians also may work together to remedy the problem if the actions taken involve litigation or lobbying activities, which are subject to a judicially created antitrust exemption known as the *Noerr-Pennington exemption.*[32] For example, it would be a violation if anesthesiologists jointly agreed to refuse to deal with a certain HMO unless the HMO changed certain outpatient procedure requirements. It would not be a violation, however, if the same physicians jointly agreed to lobby the legislature or regulatory authorities to require the HMO to make the same change. But physicians must be careful to undertake such activities in good faith, because there is a "sham" exception to Noerr-Pennington immunity.[33]

There are certain other actions that physicians can take to increase their ability to deal with third-party payers, while still maintaining their independent practice status. Professional societies can provide for evaluations of various third-party payer contracts in the area, allowing the physicians to make a more informed and intelligent choice. Similarly, certain data gathering and dissemination, if properly structured, could be undertaken to inform physicians of the different aspects of the plans prior to the physicians' contracting. This data gathering might include information regarding the plans' length-of-stay criteria, inpatient-outpatient restrictions, and even the physicians' general attitude about a plan's concern for quality of care.

Other Antitrust Violations

There are other antitrust violations of which a physician should be aware that have less prominence in health care antitrust case law than those violations discussed above, but may have equally severe consequences for the anesthesiologist. These include market allocation, joint ventures, and monopolization.

Market Allocation

This activity is a per se offense that should be simple to avoid. Competing physicians cannot agree with each other to allocate markets or customers by geographic area or by product (e.g., specialization).[34] For example, competing physicians cannot agree to relocate their offices to divide up a geographic market, or to service patients only from a certain geographic area, or to divide up patients requiring certain types of services.

Joint Ventures

This type of activity includes the formation of IPA, PPOs, or HMOs, discussed previously, and might also include physician entry into health care–related entities such as imaging centers. The legality of a joint venture among competitors will generally depend upon a number of factors, including

1 The nature of the market—is it competitive or noncompetitive?
2 The position of the venturers—are they market leaders?
3 The existence of other potential entrants into the market.
4 The foreclosure of the market by the joint venture.
5 Whether any of the joint venturers would have entered the market independently.[35]

Even if a joint venture is procompetitive, however, there may be certain actions, such as physician agreement on price, that must be carefully structured. For example, in physician-controlled PPOs or HMOs, it may be prudent to allow only nonphysicians to have fee-setting authority.

Monopoly

Monopoly and attempted monopoly may occur in relation to many of the offenses previously discussed. For example, a charge of monopolization or attempted monopolization may result from a hospital's exclusive contract with anesthesiologists, or from the action of anesthesiologists with respect to nurse anesthetists. The determination of each such claim will depend generally upon the market share of the defendant, the status of the plaintiff as a competitor in that market, and the actions taken by defendants. It is unlikely, in the examples above, that a charge of exclusive dealing or boycott would fail and a monopolization charge prevail.

HEALTH CARE ANTITRUST COMPLIANCE PROGRAMS

As previously stated, to avoid antitrust difficulties, the individual physician should have some knowledge of the antitrust laws. If that physician is an integral member of a hospital staff, the governing body of a PPO or HMO, a medical society, or similar organization, however, the best protection is an antitrust compliance program. While the exact form and content of antitrust compliance programs vary, there are four elements basic to all: (1) the antitrust audit, (2) antitrust education, (3) formal adoption of the program and its goals, and (4) ongoing review.

The first step in an antitrust compliance program is the *audit.* At this stage, antitrust counsel identifies the areas of antitrust risk through interviews with personnel and review of documents. As an example, for a hospital it would be critical to review the policies relating to staff privilege determinations, and then review documentation relating to the actual practice. Problems that are observed must then be remedied.

The next step is *education* of persons involved. The aim is to give the participants enough knowledge of the antitrust laws to recognize the problem areas. This education is usually accomplished through written handouts and presentations to different personnel, with the opportunity for questions and answers.

The entity involved in the compliance program should formally *adopt* the program and its goals. The details of this program should be conveyed to personnel or members by way of a written statement. This document should indicate that the entity supports the antitrust laws, and will not tolerate noncompliance.

The final step is to ensure there is *ongoing review,* and the ability to have problems addressed in a timely manner. Procedures should be implemented so that if personnel or members believe certain actions of the entity might pose an antitrust risk, these questions can be addressed and resolved by antitrust counsel as quickly as possible.

CONCLUSION

The antitrust laws may create a potentially costly minefield for the unwary health care provider. Because antitrust law in the health care field is rapidly changing, this chapter can do no more than afford an alert to the potential antitrust problems that may arise. It is hoped that the basic overview provided herein will aid the reader in recognizing potential antitrust problems, and thus promote timely and appropriate preventive or corrective action.

REFERENCES

1. 15 U.S.C. §§ 1 *et seq.* (1809).
2. The lack of interstate commerce is a potential defense in a federal antitrust case. There is currently a split among the federal courts as to the showing necessary to satisfy the interstate commerce requirement. The majority view would require a plaintiff to establish a connection between the defendant's challenged conduct and interstate commerce. *See, e.g.,* Furlong v. Long Island College Hospital, 710 F.2d 922 (2d Cir. 1983). The minority view is less stringent, requiring only that the defendant's business activities, not merely the challenged conduct, have an effect on interstate commerce. *See, e.g.,* Crane v. Intermountain Health Care, Inc., 637 F.2d 715, 720-24 (10th Cir. 1981).
3. 15 U.S.C. §§ 14, 18.
4. 15 U.S.C. § 13.
5. 15 U.S.C. § 45.
6. "Antitrust Enforcement and the Medical Profession: No Special Treatment," Remarks of Charles F. Rule, Assistant Attorney General, Antitrust Division, before the Interim Meeting of the American Medical Association House of Delegates (December 6, 1988).
7. Thompson v. Midwest Foundation Independent Physicians Association d/b/a Choice-Care, 124 F.R.D. 154 (S.D. Ohio 1988).
8. Goldfarb v. Virginia State Bar, 421 U.S. 773 (1975).
9. Goldfarb, 421 U.S., at 733, n. 17 (emphasis added).
10. National Society of Professional Engineers v. United States, 435 U.S. 679 (1978).
11. Arizona v. Maricopa County Medical Society, 457 U.S. 332 (1982).
12. Maricopa, 457 U.S., at 349.
13. 466 U.S. 2 (1984).
14. *See also* Ezpeleta v. Sisters of Mercy Health Corp., 800 F.2d 119 (7th Cir. 1986) (anesthesiologist's tying claims against hospital fail due to lack of hospital's market power); Dos Santos v. Columbus-Cuneo-Cabrini Medical Center, 684 F.2d 1346 (7th Cir. 1982) (vacating preliminary injunction, court held that plaintiff anesthesiologist could only prevail by showing that exclusive dealing arrangement resulted in substantial foreclosure of competition in the relevant market).
15. FTC Advisory Opinion to Burnham Hospital, 101 F.T.C. 991 (1983).
16. 772 F.2d 1467 (9th Cir. 1985).
17. Bhan v. NME Hospitals, Inc., 669 F. Supp. 998 (E.D. Ca. 1987).
18. 656 F. Supp. 760 (D. Mont. 1987), *aff'd* 861 F.2d 1440 (9th Cir. Nov. 28, 1988).
19. Catalan, Inc. v. Target Sales, 446 U.S. 643 (1980).
20. *See, e.g.,* FTC Advisory Opinion to American Society of Internal Medicine, 105 F.T.C. 505 (1985) (relative-value scale likely to be anticompetitive); The American College of Radiology, 89 F.T.C. 144 (FTC consent order regarding use of relative-value scale, accepted March 1, 1977). *But see* United States v. The American Society of Anesthesiologists, Inc., 473 F. Supp. 147 (S.D.N.Y. 1979) (relative-value guide at issue held not violative of antitrust laws).
21. *See* United States v. Foley, 598 F.2d 1323 (4th Cir. 1979) (after a dinner party attended by defendant real estate brokers, all defendants adopted substantially the same commission rate), *cert. denied,* 444 U.S. 1043 (1980).
22. 42 U.S.C.A. § 11101 (1986). To qualify for immunity under the HCQIA, actions taken by peer review bodies must meet the following criteria: (1) the action was undertaken in a reasonable belief that it furthered the quality of health care; (2) there was a reasonable effort to obtain the facts of the matter; (3) procedural due process protections were afforded to the physician involved; and (4) the participants reasonably believed that any action taken against the physician was warranted by the facts.
23. Parker v. Brown, 317 U.S. 341 (1943).
24. Southern Motor Carrier Rate Conference Inc. v. United States, 471 U.S. 48 (1985).
25. Patrick v. Burget, 108 S.Ct. 1658, 100 L.Ed.2d 83, 486 U.S. 94 (1988).
26. Subsequent to *Patrick*, the Eleventh Circuit held that under certain circumstances judicial review could satisfy the active state supervision requirement. Bolt v. Halifax Hospital Medical Center, 851 F.2d 1273 (11th Cir. 1988). The court held that judicial review would be sufficient if the courts review "the fairness of the procedures, the validity of the criteria used, and the suffi-

ciency of the evidence," 851 F.2d at 1284.

27. *See* Jose F. Calimlim, M.D. (FTC Consent Order issued March 8, 1988, 52 Fed. Reg. 10,367 [March 31, 1988]) (35 anesthesiologists agreed not to conspire to deal collectively with third-party payers or attempt to coerce third-party payers); *In re* Rochester Anesthesiologists (FTC Consent Order, 52 Fed. Reg. 44,408 [November 19, 1987]).

28. *See* Medical Staff of Doctors' Hospital of Prince George's County, No. C-3226 (FTC Consent Order issued April 14, 1988, 53 Fed. Reg. 18,273 [May 23, 1988]) (medical staff coercion of hospital to abandon plans to open HMO); United States v. Halifax Hospital Medical Center, 1981-1 Trade Cas. (CCH) ¶ 64, 151 (No. Fla. 1981) (Consent Decree).

29. "Health Care and Antitrust Enforcement: The Buyer's Eye View," Remarks of Charles F. Rule, Assistant Attorney General, Antitrust Division, before the Group Health Association of America (February 28, 1989); American Medical Association v. United States, 317 U.S. 519 (1943) (rejected labor exemption claim for physician groups attempting to prevent participation in prepaid group health plan).

30. McGinn, PR: Government Played Hardball on MD Antitrust Activity, American Medical News 10, January 6, 1989.

31. *See, e.g.,* FTC Enforcement Policy on Physician Agreements to Control Medical Prepayment Plans, 46 Fed. Reg. 48,982 (1982).

32. United Mine Workers v. Pennington, 381 U.S. 657 (1965); Eastern Railroad Presidents Conference v. Noerr Motor Freight, Inc., 365 U.S. 127 (1961).

33. California Motor Transport Co. v. Trucking Unlimited, 404 U.S. 508 (1972).

34. Timken Roller Bearing Co. v. United States, 341 U.S. 593 (1951).

35. Department of Justice Merger Guidelines, 2 Trade Reg. Rep. (CCH) ¶ 4490 (June 29, 1984); FTC Statement Concerning Horizontal Mergers, 2 Trade Reg. Rep. ¶ 4516 (June 14, 1982).

29

Ronald A. MacKenzie, D.O.

Professional Liability Insurance

The large majority of American health care providers are covered by some form of professional liability insurance. Currently, the charge for this coverage constitutes a major business expenditure—it makes up a significant portion of the cost of conducting a professional practice. The necessity for purchasing insurance—to afford protection against exposure to allegations of professional negligence in the conduct of one's practice—should be obvious to everyone. In this chapter, I shall review the reasons why professional liability insurance is so expensive; the complex nature of the overall problem; some of the sources of coverage by other than a conventional insurance carrier; the efforts by legislative bodies to ameliorate the liability problem and associated modalities for indemnification of health care providers; and, finally, the efforts by insurers and professional associations to identify risky practices and develop methods to correct those practices. While these last steps constitute the *injury prevention* component of *risk management* (which is discussed in detail in Chapter 7), they are reviewed in this chapter because the impetus to their development and implementation has in large measure emanated from efforts to assure *continuing availability* of professional liability insurance *at affordable cost*.

PROFESSIONAL LIABILITY LITIGATION

Professional liability suits were first observed in significant numbers in the 1930s. The science of medicine was expanding at the same time, both in sophistication and availability. During World War II there was a temporary reduction in the filing of suits, but in the postwar years, claims against physicians and hospitals steadily increased. As the government increasingly became involved with reimbursement for health care, the professional liability situation received increased attention. In 1971, President Richard Nixon ordered the Secretary of Health, Education and Welfare to study this growing insurance crisis, and the President's Commission on Medical Malpractice was appointed. One of the conclusions of the commission was that as more people could afford medical care, more people would visit physicians. The increased exposure to the medical profession led to more incidents that had the potential to develop into lawsuits.[1,2]

The ongoing crisis of availability and affordability of professional liability insurance is a result of the continuing increase in the *frequency* (ratio of number of claims

to the number of patient visits) of malpractice claims brought against physicians, as well as increases in the *magnitude* of claims (amounts of money spent for management, settlement, or judgment of each claim). This increase is similar to that experienced in the 1970s and is indicative of an unresolved problem.[3]

PROTECTING THE PROFESSIONAL

Most physicians, many nurse anesthetists, and other health care providers (hereinafter called "providers") carry professional liability insurance, and most cases become insurance claims before they become lawsuits. Many cases never reach the courtroom, and less than 10% reach a jury verdict. A sound understanding of professional liability insurance requires study of the mechanics of insurance underwriting, the insurance industry, tort reform, and beyond, and not just an anecdotal recitation of the occasional bizarre outcomes of individual malpractice cases.[4]

Mechanics of Underwriting

Casualty insurance, of which professional liability (malpractice insurance) is but one type, represents only a small portion of the total amount of insurance in effect in this country. Most individuals are familiar with life insurance, and the fact that the policyholder builds up equity in the assets of the company—in the form of a cash surrender value—as those portions of the premium not devoted to overhead or underwriting premature death of the insured are reinvested by the company. In the case of casualty insurance, however, the entire premium is absorbed by administrative costs and protection against loss.

Customarily, the provider purchases professional liability insurance from a casualty insurance broker who has entered into an agency agreement (see Chapter 5) with one or more carriers who underwrite this type of coverage. The broker agrees to act as an agent in soliciting business, in executing the insurance contracts with the provider, and in transmitting premium payments to the company, at a commission of about

20% of each premium. The company agrees to provide for the costs of defense, and pay judgments or settlements up to the limits of the policy, if the insured is accused of negligence in his or her professional practice. These obligations of the carrier are conditioned upon the insured complying with all terms of the policy.

The Insurance Contract

The contract for insurance is documented in the *policy*, which sets forth the rights and duties (see Chapter 2) of both the carrier and the insured. When a health care provider files an application for malpractice insurance, he or she must complete a statement of the prospective insured's type of practice, prior loss experience, and whether there are any partners or employees. This statement becomes a part of the contract, which is a conditional, unilateral one. The contract is unilateral because performance is unilateral unless and until the casualty occurs—that is, the performance of the insured in paying the premium results in only a promise of the insurer to pay on the policy if a casualty occurs. If no casualty occurs by the end of the policy period, the contract expires, bilateral performance never having occurred. If, on the other hand, a casualty occurs—the physician is threatened as having committed, or sued for, professional negligence—performance becomes bilateral. The insurer will investigate the allegations, settle or defend the insured, and pay any judgment, as long as the insured has met his or her duties to the carrier, as set forth in the provisions of the policy.

A lawsuit for professional negligence, or the threat of such a suit, is one of several events that must occur before the contract becomes bilateral. These events are commonly known as conditions—hence the term *conditional contract*. To effectuate protection under the customary professional liability insurance policy, the following conditions must be met:

1 The act of health care delivery that initiates the allegations of malpractice must have occurred within the scope of practice specifically underwritten by the policy (it should be obvious that the insurance cannot cover risks that were not taken into consideration when the policy was issued—for example, in general, the cost of premiums is directly related to the risk of exposure of each insured).

2 The applicant must not falsify any statements made in the application for coverage (again, the reasons for questions concerning employees and prior lawsuits reflect on future risks of the insured, and the importance of those queries, should be obvious).

3 The insured must be accused of allegedly negligent conduct, and the plaintiff's lawyer must so state in the complaint that initiates the litigation (Chapter 24). As a general rule, intentional torts such as abandonment, battery, breach of confidence, defamation, false imprisonment, fraud, and invasion of privacy are not covered by a malpractice insurance policy.

4 The provider must notify the carrier in a timely manner of any allegations of negligence leveled by a patient or former patient, irrespective of whether a lawsuit has been filed or is only threatened. Insurance carriers want to investigate promptly all problems, potential and real. Memories fade with time. In those instances in which the injured patient has a meritorious claim, it may be possible to take preventive measures to preclude the filing of a suit, or to effectuate early settlement (see, for example, the discussion in Chapter 7 of *claims prevention* as a component of *risk management*).

5 Each policy also notes other duties of the insured, including making available for defense purposes hospital and office records and other memoranda, including correspondence with the patient.

Importance of Prompt Reporting of Claims

If the insured commits a material (significant) breach of any of the conditions (which make up the duties of the insured) that are embodied in the insurance contract, the carrier may be able to avoid its duty to defend the physician and pay any judgment. Failure to notify the carrier promptly has been considered to be such a breach, as epitomized by an early Mississippi case.[5]

The insured physician received a telephone call from the injured patient's lawyer, notifying him of the possibility of a lawsuit. Eight months later, the suit was actually filed. One month after that, the physician, who claimed he had forgotten the name of his carrier, started contacting insurance companies. He finally learned which one had written his policy, and notified the carrier 11 months after his first notification, at which time the jury was being impaneled. The Supreme Court of Mississippi held that the physician's failure to notify the carrier in a timely fashion constituted sufficient negligence on his part that the carrier would be released from any duty to indemnify the physician for cost of legal defense or damages.

In another case,[6] the physician was well aware of his patient's pain following inguinal hernia repair. Additionally, at a subsequent operation a suture was discovered in the substance of the femoral nerve. The plaintiff's lawyer telephoned the physician at least twice and threatened litigation. In spite of these notices, the physician did not inform his insurance carrier of the injury until more than 7 months after the misplacement of the suture and only after he had received a letter from the patient's lawyer. One of the provisions of the policy required that the carrier be notified by the insured physician "as soon as practical (after) becoming aware of the alleged injury." The court interpreted this provision literally, indicating it did not mean that the physician could wait until he was sued before notifying the carrier.

A U.S. district court, in a similar case[7] involving delay in notification of the insurance carrier, stated: ". . . [a] provision in a liability insurance policy requiring that notice be given as soon as possible is a condition precedent to the imposition of liability [on the company] and failure to comply with the condition releases the insurer. . . ." In other words, the court held that the physician's delay constituted a material breach of the insurance contract.

The St. Paul Fire and Marine Insurance Company (hereafter referred to as the St. Paul Company) urges its insured physicians to promptly report claims, and *potential* claims as well. The company gives six reasons for prompt reporting.[8]

1 *Fresh facts.* Important details of an event can be more completely remembered and outlined soon after the occurrence. This allows for a more complete and accurate record for possible defense.
2 *Mitigation of damages.* Early reporting may result in a better resolution of the situation. Rehabilitation and prompt financial help to the patient, when appropriate, may make a difference in the ultimate resolution of the claim.
3 *Evidence.* Early protection and preservation of evidence is important to successful defense.
4 *Arbitration or mediation.* Early reporting may allow effective arbitration or mediation of a claim. This might result in fewer lawsuits.
5 *Support for insured.* The insured doctor early on receives the psychological support of the insurance company and its claim handlers. These people can answer questions and offer guidance about the claim process.
6 *Current standards.* A claim reported soon after the event would be evaluated by the standards of care current at that time. Delayed reporting of claims may result in the doctor being held accountable to a possibly higher standard present in the future.

Sources of Professional Liability Insurance

Anesthesiologists (and other health care professionals) can obtain malpractice insurance from various sources.[9]

Commercial Insurance

As claims and awards increased in the mid-1970s, many large and established insurance companies restricted their offerings of professional liability policies. It became difficult for physicians to purchase commercial malpractice insurance, even with annual premiums increasing more than 10-fold.[10] Because of strict regulations in many states, commercial insurance companies were not able to assign rates at a level believed by them to be appropriate. These regulations may have delayed serious interest by the commercial companies in writing additional physician malpractice policies.[9]

Captive Insurance

Institutions or professional associations frequently pool resources and form an insurance company for their staff or members. The company is owned (held *captive*) by the insured. A *captive*, then, is a closely held insurance company, the majority of whose business comes from the owners or a controlled group of policy holders.[11] Starting in 1975, many state medical societies formed such companies to handle the malpractice insurance needs of their members.[12]

The Physician Insurers Association of America (PIAA) is a national organization composed of 41 physician-owned medical professional liability insurance companies.[13] These companies currently write protection for more than half of the practicing physicians in the United States. The PIAA serves as a forum for member companies to share information, study issues of common concern, and seek long-range solutions to professional liability problems. At the end of 1988, member companies of the PIAA provided malpractice insurance for more than 179,000 physicians in at least 40 states and the District of Columbia. As an aggregate, assets exceeded $8.7 billion, capital or surplus was approximately $1 billion, and annual gross premiums were $2.0 billion.

Captive companies can provide primary coverage, excess (reinsurance) coverage, or both. When these companies provide primary coverage, they must be licensed in the state where the insurance is written. When they provide excess insurance, state licensure is not required. Frequently, captive insurance companies locate in foreign countries in order to enjoy favorable insurance laws and tax advantages.[9] *Advantages* of captive insurance include: (1) some protec-

tion from high prices or limited availability of commercial insurance, (2) some tax benefits for managers or owners of the business, (3) some protection from the erratic commercial insurance cycles, (4) ability to purchase excess liability coverage. Potential *disadvantages* of captive insurance include: (1) liability limits are aggregate, (2) state insolvency funds may not be available, (3) capitalization may be inadequate, (4) the long-term commitment may be questionable.[11]

Self-Insurance

An institution can entirely assume professional liability risks itself. No third party is involved in providing insurance. Self-insurance can be unfunded or funded. When no financial reserves are created to cover potential losses, the self-insurance is unfunded. It is funded when the institution develops reserves to cover potential losses. Instead of paying premiums to a third party, the institution places equivalent funds in reserve, thus in effect making premium payments to itself. Self-insurance is frequently combined with captive insurance or excess insurance. The self-insurance provides the deductible before any other insurance coverage is activated.[9]

Joint Underwriting Associations

As commercial professional liability insurance became increasingly more difficult for physicians to obtain, some states required insurance companies to join together and form *joint underwriting associations* (JUAs). These JUAs wrote policies for practitioners who would otherwise be uninsured. This type of professional liability insurance usually has little incentive for risk management and typically charges the highest premium rates.[9] In some cases, however, the rates permitted by the regulating agency have proven inadequate, and the JUA itself has become the major carrier.[12]

State Compensation Funds

Some states have developed compensation funds to provide professional liability insurance to health care providers. These funds are nonprofit and are supported through fees paid by participants. Florida established such a fund in 1975. Unfortunately, the fees charged were inadequate, the fund experienced financial instability, and in 1988 the legislature enacted extensive tort reform legislation.[9] In some states, payment to these funds is a requirement of licensure.[11] These funds were sometimes created to pay claims in excess of a predetermined maximum limit. Some funds were restricted in what they could charge and have accrued deficits. These shortfalls were frequently made up by additional assessments to participating health care providers.[12]

Channeling

Physicians can, in some instances, pool their liability risks with the hospital, a practice called *channeling*. The doctor is listed on the main hospital policy and may be assigned separate liability limits. This practice may enhance risk management activities and general cooperativeness within the hospital. If both the physician and hospital are named as defendants, however, there is a potential risk that the hospital's insurance carrier might "sacrifice" the individual physician in favor of the hospital.[11] A self-insured hospital can bring physicians into an insurance trust by having them contribute money into the hospital's reserve fund. Bringing for-profit physicians into a not-for-profit trust, however, might cause conversion of the trust into a taxable entity. This action could also possibly convert the trust into an insurance vehicle that becomes fully regulated under state insurance laws.[14]

Risk Retention Groups

The Liability Risk Retention Act[15] of 1986 allowed formation of special captive companies called *risk retention groups* (RRGs). These groups are chartered and regulated by the federal government and may operate nationwide after having met the state capitalization and licensing requirements for only one state.[16] They are designed to provide liability insurance for members of risk retention or purchasing groups at attractive rates. The group can design a policy to maximize protection and economy for its members.

In the first 2 years following the passage of the 1986 act, more than 50 employer groups and professional organizations established RRGs. Some states, however, have challenged the federal law and are establishing strong regulations for these organizations. RRGs can be established with much less capital than the amount required of commercial insurance companies.[17] RRGs usually do not have the backup of a state's guarantee fund (discussed *infra*). Potential customers should have questions about long-term financial solvency of RRGs. These groups should know their particular line of business and its accompanying risks very well and should be able to make positive contributions to effective risk management.[18] Some insurance industry experts have real concerns about RRGs in that they may undercharge and not be able to meet their claim obligations. Insolvency of an RRG would leave many physicians without professional liability insurance coverage.[19]

Legal Representation for the Defendant

The insurance company has a broad duty to defend the insured physician. When the carrier's attorney also represents the accused physician, the attorney may be pressured by a conflict of interest. Dual representation by the attorney can be beneficial since there is a common goal. In such a triangular arrangement, the insurance company's duty to defend usually includes the right to control the defense. The attorney's *ethical primary obligation*, however, is *to the insured physician*. If a conflict is probable, the insurance company should provide independent counsel for the insured physician. Most courts that have examined this issue of divided loyalty require the insurance company to provide independent counsel or an attorney of the insured's choice.[20] It is also advantageous to have a defense attorney who is familiar with the legal system in the local community. In selecting such an individual, it is wise to carefully examine track records of several local defense attorneys.[21]

Should You Retain Your Own Lawyer?

Melvin Belli[22] recommends that the

health care provider retain a personal attorney if: (1) the damages sought by the plaintiff exceed the policy limits; (2) a hospital is named codefendant and both the defendant health care provider and the hospital are covered by the same insurance carrier; or (3) the carrier expresses any reservations about certain aspects of coverage. The insurance company may elect to defend the physician under a "reservation of rights" if the damages exceed the policy limits, if some of the allegations are not covered by the policy, or if the physician may have breached certain policy provisions. Some courts have eliminated the potential for these conflicts by insisting that whenever an insurance company "reserves rights," it loses its right to control the defense. The company would then be required to provide independent counsel to the insured physician.

INSURANCE MECHANISMS

There are two basic types of professional liability insurance—*occurrence* and *claims-made*. The basic difference between these two types of coverage relates to *the interval of professional activity during which claims are covered* by a given policy.[23]

Occurrence Insurance

The traditional type of coverage, *occurrence insurance*, covers all claims that result from services rendered while the policy is in force, regardless of when the actual claim is reported. In the not-too-distant past, almost all physicians purchased occurrence-type coverage. The physician was covered literally forever from any claim for treatment delivered during the policy period. Five or more years might elapse before all claims arising from services performed in any given year are reported.[23,24] This delay in the claim reporting is called the "long tail" of medical professional liability insurance. On the average, in the first year only about 40% of the total claims are reported; in the second, an additional 30%; the third, 15%; the fourth, 10%; the fifth and subsequent years, the final 5%.[23] Any long-tail policies sold today can give rise to insurer liabilities years into the future. These policies would require cor-

respondingly large reserves, which would need to be continually adjusted to reflect the best current estimates of insurance commitments already made but not yet fulfilled.[25]

Claims-Made Insurance

The type of coverage now generally available throughout the United States is *claims-made* insurance. It covers claims reported ("made") while the policy is in force, regardless of when the service is rendered, so long as the service was rendered subsequent to the initial date the coverage was initiated. That is, these policies provide coverage for claims *made* while the policy is current for care *delivered* while the policy is (was) in effect. Claims-made coverage is not a new concept. It had been the basic mechanism for indemnifying other professionals for many years.[12] Coverage for claims for care rendered while the policy is in effect, but made after *discontinuation* of that policy, usually requires purchase of a separate policy called a *tail policy*.[21] The "tail" of a policy can be defined as the half-life of that policy. It is the average time between when the insurance was sold and when a claim against it is collected. A 1-year tail requires reserves about equal to 1 year's premiums or payments; longer tails require proportionally higher reserves. Reserves required for medical malpractice insurance tend to be four to five times annual premiums.[25] Since claims-made coverage terminates with the expiration of the policy year, the policyholder is not protected against a claim made after a claims-made policy expires.[24] Because most claims are not made in the year treatment is given, it is important for every health care provider to understand this aspect of claims-made insurance.

As noted above, the tail policy is purchased to cover acts that may have been committed while the claims-made policy was in effect, but which were not filed as a claim until after that policy *ceased* being in effect.[21] The costs of tail policies vary by specialty and state and have ranged from one-and-a-half to two times the current year's premium.

Inasmuch as tail policies now are customarily needed to protect against future claims, their cost becomes an issue for anyone retiring or having to change carriers because of a move to another jurisdiction. In group practices, particularly, each professional needs to have a clear understanding about who will pay for tail policies for departing group members. There are six options.

1 Purchase the tail from the carrier that wrote claims-made coverage.
2 Go "bare" and not purchase a tail; this practice carries an obviously significant risk, not only for the departing physician but also for the remaining partners, the hospital, or all three entities.
3 Purchase reduced-limits tail coverage; this reduces the cost, but carries some risk.
4 Purchase a tail with deductibles, thereby reducing cost yet still providing protection against large losses.
5 Continue coverage with same carrier in a new medical position; if the health care provider was covered for more than 5 years (a "mature" policy), the new policy will continue at the current, mature, rates and not at a year 1 level.
6 Purchase "prior acts" coverage from a different claims-made company.[26]

Neupauer, an underwriting manager with a captive insurance company, believes more education is needed regarding tail coverage.

> The fundamental problem is disclosing and communicating up front . . . what this is all about. You need to make clear that the first year premium is heavily discounted, that the premiums will increase over the next five years, and that if you leave for any reason other than death, disability, or retirement, you will have to pay this tail cost.[27]

The St. Paul Company, the largest single provider of professional liability insurance to physicians in the United States, states in a policyholder's brochure[23] that the reporting endorsement (tail) is free if "you die or become totally and continuously disabled for at least six months. There is also no charge if you retire at age 65 or older and have been insured . . . under claims-made

coverage for at least five years prior to retirement."

The St. Paul Company examines the 5-year development of reported claims by medical specialty and location (individual states and nationally). Special attention is paid to the most recent year. The company believes it can forecast what the claims experience should be 12 months into the future. With occurrence policies, as noted above, many incidents are not immediately reported as claims. The St. Paul Company believes occurrence claims must be forecast a minimum of 5 years into the future. The company also feels that incidents having occurred in the past, but not yet reported, must be forecast as well. Occurrence coverage has continued to be difficult for insurance companies to price accurately, with the error usually being an underestimate of ultimate cost.[12] The St. Paul Company reports that more than 50% of American hospitals and physicians currently have claims-made policies.[23] A reported benefit to doctors of claims-made insurance is that the insured is able to purchase higher limits of coverage, increasing them when indicated.[12]

A valid issue to consider when discussing claims-made policies and residual coverage is whether the carrier will be solvent a number of years hence when the claim is made and monies are needed for legal fees and possible settlement of judgment costs. One important protective insurance mechanism is a *state guarantee* [against insolvency] *fund*. Insurance companies approved by some states pay into such a fund a share proportional to the amount in force. If an approved carrier becomes insolvent, then a predetermined amount is available from this fund to meet the insured's liability. Some carriers may not be covered by a given state's guarantee fund. This is an important aspect to be considered when choosing a professional liability insurance company.[24]

THE BUSINESS OF UNDERWRITING INSURANCE

The profitability of the insurance industry has been the subject of close study. Whether there are annual profits on liability insurance depends upon the difference between the actual reserve and the estimated reserve to cover future liabilities. This estimated value is very difficult to predict. Insurance companies must also constantly deal with two opposing forces: (1) the Internal Revenue Service, which argues for lower reserves and therefore higher short-term profits and taxes; and (2) the state insurance regulators and commissions, which on the other hand demand higher reserves for conservative and safer management.[25] As one might gather, insurance underwriting is a very highly regulated business in the United States. Each state has its own insurance commission and statutes, both of which control the carriers underwriting within that jurisdiction. Insurers must operate under not only state regulations but also certain federal laws.

Pricing Insurance by Predicting Future Losses

Insurance premiums obviously must reflect expected payouts, that is, future losses. One key to successful insurance underwriting is the ability to predict the losses incurred by those insured by that carrier. During the professional liability crisis of the mid-1970s, the difficulties of pricing malpractice insurance were accentuated by an increase in the number and costs of claims and by the development of novel theories of liability and expensive types of claims. At the same time, the industry was undergoing a depletion of capital funds, caused by increased operating expenses and a drop in stock prices. Faced with limited resources and a troublesome line of business, several insurance carriers withdrew or curtailed their professional liability insurance offerings.[12,28,29] Inflation-adjusted average awards have been steadily arising ever since then. Insurance payouts have likewise increased, which in turn usually translates into higher premiums.

This cycle is once again being repeated. During the past few years, the unpredicted rises in frequency and severity of suits have made it difficult for insurance companies to project such losses accurately. Companies may have underwritten policies at premiums now determined to have been too low to adequately cover incurred losses. At the same time, declining interest rates ad-

versely impacted projected interest income, with the result that insurance companies have reported losses on medical malpractice business for several consecutive years.[24] The current situation is exacerbated by the lack of reinsurers—those carriers that take on additional risk for the primary insurers.[29]

Adverse Selection and Utilization of Premiums

In 1983, professional liability premiums totaled $2 billion, not counting the additional funding for self-insurance. This sum equals approximately 1% of the total U.S. health care spending for that year. Increasing insurance costs for doctors brings into play a process called *adverse selection*. Successful operation of an insurance pool depends critically on the companies' ability to attract low-risk customers into the pool. With rising rates, low-risk customers may change carriers. The loss of its best customers forces the insurer to raise premiums further, a step that in turn will stimulate still more customers to consider switching companies.[25] This selection process of the remaining customers is certainly an adverse one.

Virginia Insurance Reciprocal's analysis of claims paid revealed that its defense costs had increased 1327% during the period 1981 to 1985. The company estimated that each of its malpractice dollars is spent as follows:[30]

Payment to injured parties	31 cents
Defense costs, including legal fees	26 cents
Fees for plaintiffs' lawyers	20 cents
Insurer's operating costs	12 cents
Other (plaintiffs' court costs, expert witness fees, appeal expenses, and other medical costs)	11 cents

Calculating and Offsetting Losses

Insurance companies use combined ratios (CR) to reflect their underwriting results. A CR measures how each premium dollar is used to pay losses, loss expenses, and company operating expenses. For example, a CR of 90.0 indicates that 90 cents will be paid out for each $1.00 received in premiums—leaving a profit of 10 cents. A CR of more than 100.0 indicates that the company paid out more than it received in premiums. The St. Paul Company reported a CR of 106.1 for year-end 1988 (114.1 for 1987).[31,32]

A commercial insurance company usually has other lines of insurance (e.g., automotive liability, home owners) to offset any losses incurred insuring health care providers against medical malpractice. In 1987, the underwriting "profit" from medical professional liability insurance (nationwide) was *negative* 27.4%. The extremes were Rhode Island at minus 173.5% and Washington state at plus 41.0%. The "operating profit" (entire operations of a company) nationwide, however, on the average was a plus 11.6%. At the extremes were Connecticut at minus 74.3% and Washington state at plus 100.2%.[33]

Another measure of financial success or failure is *return on equity*, the return from all sources of income, including investment income, divided by the capital invested in the business.[32] Operating results from underwriting professional liability insurance for physicians nationwide averaged a 17% return on equity during the past 10 years, roughly 1.7% per year.

Underfunding and Other Problems

The difficulties of pricing malpractice insurance have led frequently to *underfunding*—the setting of premiums that turn out to be inadequate to cover the costs of claims. A carrier cannot allow underfunding to persist. In the interim, the needed funds can be obtained from the current policyholders, profits on other insurance lines, other capital funds, or guarantee (insolvency) funds.[12]

Beginning in 1985, the St. Paul Company observed a decrease in the number of claims against doctors. In 1985, the claims frequency was 17.3 (per 100 doctors). By 1987, the frequency was 14.4. At year-end 1988, the claim frequency had declined to 13.0. The cost of claims, however, continues to escalate[32] (Fig. 29-1). Future trends are discussed later in this chapter.

Purchasers of insurance tend to be rela-

tively fixed in their needs. Thus, demand remains quite steady in the face of a changing supply. Capital flows into insurance markets in bullish times, but the demand for insurance remains constant. The market for insurance becomes competitive (first half of the insurance "cycle"), and premiums must be reduced. In the second half of the cycle, these trends are reversed. In bearish times, funds become scarce; premiums rise and are further driven up by the prior competition-induced undervaluation of premiums. Captive companies owned by nonprofit medical associations may rush prematurely into the market during the first part of the cycle. They depress insurance premiums below true cost by underestimating future liabilities.[25] This practice in turn may stimulate another insurance cycle as the commercial companies reduce their premiums to remain competitive.

Unfortunately, the group of specialty carriers underwriting currently do not enjoy the same degree of financial backing from the commercial reinsurers and excess insurance carriers as did those carriers of the prior generation. A health care industry engaged in self-indemnification becomes a major player in a business for which it has little training or expertise—the insurance business.[34]

One industry observer believes the insurance "crisis" of the 1970s was self-made by the insurance companies. The problem

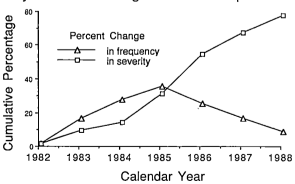

Physicians' and Surgeons' Claim Experience

Figure 29–1 *Physicians' and surgeons' claim experience from 1982 to 1988. While the frequency of claims declined, the severity or average cost of reported claims continues to increase. (Data from Medical Services Division, St. Paul Fire and Marine Insurance Company.)*

may have been the result of poor management practices by these carriers. The crisis came when interest rates dropped. The carriers' income on their invested reserves was then adversely affected. They responded by increasing premiums and dropping "high-risk" business.[35]

Comparative Medical Liability Insurance Rates

The St. Paul Company uses the rating classification depicted in Table 29–1 to price professional liability insurance. The premium rates for 1989 to cover each specialist in a given jurisdiction are calculated by multiplying the *conversion factor* shown in this table by the *basic rate* for that jurisdiction as depicted in Table 29–2.[32] The 1989 nationwide mean amount was $15,964; the median amount, $13,874. Thus, individual premiums are determined by the physician's specialty or rating class (anesthesiologists = 1.40), geographic location (state or in some cases city), limits of liability selected, and number of years insured under claims-made coverage.

Insurance Carrier Regulation

The insurance industry is regulated by the insurance commissioner (or commission) of each jurisdiction. Some consumer advocates and others[35] believe that many of the current insurance problems, including unavailability and escalation in premium costs, might be resolved by even closer regulation of the industry. To this end, in New York state the Governor's Advisory Commission on Liability Insurance has developed several recommendations[35] intended to strengthen the regulation of the insurance industry in that state:

1 *Price regulation.* Excessive and artificial swings in prices of professional liability insurance premiums could be minimized by setting upper and lower limits on permissible prices. The insurance companies could request rate changes periodically.
2 *Limiting cancellations.* Abrupt cancellations or nonrenewals are a major cause of the insurance "crisis" atmosphere. The commission proposed that the carriers be permitted to cancel physicians only in certain circumstances, such as fraud or nonpayment of premiums.
3 *Providing more resources.* State insurance regulatory agencies are generally understaffed. The state insurance commissions need more staff, more money, and more authority.
4 *Appointing a consumer advocate.* An individual should be appointed to work full time on behalf of the

TABLE 29–1. Rating Classification for Professional Liability Insurance

New Rating Class	Specialty	Conversion Factor
1A	Physicians—no surgery. Includes allergists, dermatologists, pathologists, and psychiatrists	0.32
1	Physicians—no surgery, no invasive procedures, no obstetrical procedures	0.40
2	Physicians—minor surgery, invasive procedures	0.60
3	Family or general practice—normal deliveries. Includes ophthalmologists and urologists	0.80
4	Family practice—major surgery Emergency medicine—no major surgery	1.00
5A	Anesthesiologists	1.40
5	Surgery—including general, emergency, and plastic, and otolaryngologists and gynecologists	1.60
6	Surgery—including cardiac and orthopedic	2.20
7	Obstetrics	2.76
8	Surgery—neurological	3.48

Source: Data supplied by the St. Paul Company.

TABLE 29–2. St. Paul Company Proposed Average Rates for Class 4 Doctors (Mature Claims-Made Rate; $1 Million/$3 Million Unless Otherwise Indicated)

State	Rate	State	Rate
AL	$15,801	NC	5,648
AR	6,809	ND	13,235
AZ	26,660	NE	5,055 †
CA	43,901	NH	— §
CO	14,762 §	NM	— §
FL	— §	NV	34,242 §
GA	15,049	NY	— §
IA	12,160	OH	18,873
ID	19,387	OK	17,450
IL	22,815	OR	20,197
IN	4,948‡	PA	10,034 †
KS	9,561†	SC	9,225
KY	11,046	SD	6,867
LA	8,816‡ §	TN	9,182
MA	— §	TX	32,747
ME	11,922 §	UT	15,359
MI	— §	VA	10,006
MN	14,199	VT	11,484
MO	29,455	WA	24,101
MS	13,874	WI	9,057 *
MT	18,526	WY	22,142

*$400,000 to 1,000,000
†$200,000 to $600,000
‡$100,000 to $300,000
§St. Paul Company does not offer medical liability.
Source: Data supplied by the St. Paul Company.

consumers, to represent the interests of consumers before the state insurance department.

5 *Allowing municipalities to pool risks.* Since one large claim could severely damage a small group of people, it is reasonable to allow many parties to share the risk of an event that will probably happen only to a few.[35]

ANESTHETIC LIABILITY AND THE STANDARD OF CARE

In its 1989 annual report,[32] the St. Paul Company noted 366 anesthesia claims, making up 3.7% of their total claims and 3.6% of total incurred costs (Table 29–3). There were 89 claims for *anesthesia and cardiac arrest.* These had an average cost (total value of claim including legal and oth-

TABLE 29–3. Major Allegation Groups by Frequency

Group	Number	Percent (%) of Total Claims	Percent (%) of Total Incurred Cost
Surgery	2,867	28.8	25.8
Failure to diagnose	2,771	27.8	34.4
Improper treatment	2,672	26.9	29.7
Anesthesia	366	3.7	3.6
Other issues	1,271	12.8	6.5
Total claims	9,947	100.0	100.0

Source: Data supplied by the St. Paul Company.

TABLE 29–4. Top 10 Allegations by Average Cost*

Allegation	Number of Claims	Average Cost†
1. Failure to diagnose, hemorrhage	73	$145,312
2. Failure to diagnose, bowel lesion	24	$129,742
3. Improper treatment, birth-related	661	$129,123
4. Failure to diagnose, diabetes	28	$121,902
5. Failure to diagnose, myocardial infarction	174	$106,961
6. Anesthesia, cardiac arrest	89	$101,370
7. Surgery, postoperative death	258	$ 97,609
8. Failure to diagnose, kidney disorder	35	$ 96,977
9. Failure to diagnose, cancer	607	$ 96,462
10. Failure to diagnose, circulatory problem, thrombosis	196	$ 96,107

*Based on the average cost of loss for allegations resulting in 24 claims or more.
†Includes total value of claim including legal and other expenses with no cap on individual claims.
Source: Data supplied by the St. Paul Company.

·er expenses) of $101,370 (Table 29–4). The company also reported an average paid medical liability claim, with losses capped at $200,000, in 1988 to be $102,380 (up 11% from 1987). When losses were capped at $1 million, the average 1988 paid claim was $132,800 (up 10% from 1987)[30] (Fig. 29–2).

The average medical liability *verdict* reached $924,416 in 1987, down from the all-time high of $1,478,028 reported in 1986. "This is the first time since 1980 that the number of million-dollar verdicts was less than the number reported for the previous year," reports *Jury Verdict Research (JVR).*[36] *JVR* states that 646 medical malpractice verdicts of $1 million or more have

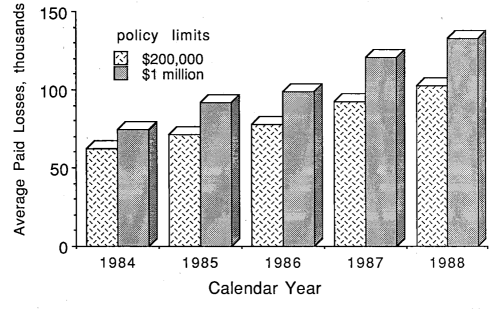

Figure 29–2 Physicians' and surgeons' average paid losses from 1984 to 1988. The average paid medical liability claim with losses capped at $200,000 and including defense costs was $102,380 in 1988. The average paid medical liability claim with losses capped at $1 million and including defense costs was $132,800 in 1988. (Data from Medical Services Division, St. Paul Fire and Marine Insurance Company.)

been reported since 1962. Of these verdicts, 75% (483) have been reported since 1980 (Table 29–5). *JVR* includes only initial jury verdicts in the data. Reductions in awards via appeals or subsequent negotiations are not calculated in this analysis of awards.[32,36]

In 1985, the Committee on Professional Liability of the American Society of Anesthesiologists (ASA) began a nationwide study of closed malpractice claims related to anesthetic care. Cases were selected from 17 insurance companies in the United States. Cheney et al.[37] reported on 1175 claims in their study data base. Death was the most common (372) complication that resulted in litigation. Nerve damage (157) and permanent brain damage (119) were the next most common adverse outcomes (Table 29–6). The most common critical incidences leading to patient morbidity and mortality were related to respiratory system management (Table 29–7). Cheney observed that payment was made to the patient in 42% of the cases in which anesthetic care was judged, by a peer group, to be appropriate, and that the incidence of payment increased to 83% of cases in which the anesthetic care was judged to be substandard.

An earlier study derived from this same data base[38] elucidated two anesthetic management patterns that may have contributed to unexpected circulatory arrest during spinal anesthesia. One pattern was sedation-related verbal nonresponsiveness and failure to detect cyanosis in a timely fashion as one of the initial clues of circulatory arrest. The second pattern was inadequate appreciation of the interaction between sympathetic blockade during high spinal anesthesia and the mechanisms of cardiopulmonary resuscitation (CPR). This important information was discovered during a review of closed malpractice claims related to anesthesia care. Improvements in patient care often result from critical assessment of previous litigation and similar medical-legal problems. The authors made three specific recommendations for future management.

1 Pulse oximetry should be used whenever intraoperative sedatives are given to patients under regional anesthesia.
2 Epinephrine should be used early in treatment of unexpected bradycardia in patients under spinal anesthesia.
3 A full resuscitation dose of epinephrine should be given immediately when cardiac arrest is diagnosed in these patients.

Keats, in a related editorial,[39] strongly endorsed such reviews of closed claims data as another approach to studying the etiology of anesthesia mortality. He emphasizes that the limitations of this methodology are outweighed by the important gains in improving patient safety.

The National Association of Insurance Commissioners (NAIC) studied approximately 75,000 closed claims covering a 3-year period. Anesthesia-related claims comprised about 3% of all the closed

TABLE 29–5. Annual Medical Liability Verdicts As Reported by Jury Verdict Research, Inc.[36]

Year	Awards, $	Verdicts	Number of Awards of $1 Million or More
1980	404,726	146	20
1981	850,396	186	45
1982	962,258	234	45
1983	887,938	322	69
1984	640,619	356	71
1985	1,179,095	233	79
1986	1,478,028	272	92
1987	924,416	279	62
1988*	732,445	121	31

*1988 data are incomplete

TABLE 29–6. Type and Severity of Common Anesthesia-Related Complications*

Complication	No. (%) of Lawsuits		No. (%)† of Deaths		Median SIS‡ of Survivors
Death	372	(37)	NA	(100)	NA
Nerve damage	157	(15)	1	(1)	5
Permanent brain damage	119	(12)	0	(NA)	8
Cardiovascular collapse	70	(7)	45	(64)	8
Prolonged ventilatory support	33	(3)	16	(48)	6
Eye injury	32	(3)	9	(0)	6
Hepatic dysfunction or failure	28	(3)	12	(43)	3–4
Burn	27	(3)	0	(0)	5
Pneumothorax	19	(2)	2	(11)	3
Aspiration	17	(2)	10	(59)	5
Pulmonary edema	17	(2)	10	(59)	6
Convulsion	17	(2)	7	(41)	3
Stroke	17	(2)	3	(18)	6–7

*Only complications with an occurrence rate of 2% or greater are included. Some lawsuits involved multiple complications. NA indicates not applicable.
†Percentages of deaths in lawsuits associated with this complication (percentage of column 1)
‡SIS indicates severity of injury score.
Source: Data from Cheney et al.[37]

claims, but represented 11% of indemnity payments. In the NAIC study, released in 1980, 94% of all claims paid resulted from pretrial settlement and only 4% from trial of the issues. The latter resulted in average payments 2.8 times higher than those following settlement. Court dispositions favored the physician defendant in 81% of cases in 1975; the percentage increased to 89 in 1978, the last year of the study.[40]

MITIGATING EXPOSURE TO LIABILITY

Because people seek medical care when they are sick, it is often difficult to ascertain whether an adverse outcome is caused by a failure of medical care, the underlying disease process, or a regrettable but unavoidable side effect of appropriate treatment.[4] Certain complications resulting

TABLE 29–7. Type and Severity of Common Anesthesia-Related Critical Incidents Leading to Patient Injury*

Incident	No. (%) of Lawsuits		No. (%)† of Deaths		Median SIS‡ of Survivors
Respiratory system critical incidents	333	(35)	217	(65)	7
Most common respiratory system critical incidents					
Inadequate ventilation	135	(14)	95	(70)	7–8
Esophageal intubation	68	(7)	54	(79)	7–8
Difficult intubation	56	(6)	26	(46)	5
Air embolism	18	(2)	9	(50)	7
Airway obstruction	16	(2)	7	(44)	7
Most common nonrespiratory system critical incidents					
Wrong drug or dose	25	(3)	13	(52)	7
Inadequate or inappropriate fluid therapy	21	(2)	15	(71)	8

*A critical incident was not identified in every lawsuit.
†Percentages of deaths in lawsuits associated with this complication (percentage of column 1).
‡SIS indicates severity of injury score.
Source: Data from Cheney et al.[37]

from the provision of anesthesia care, however, have been described as *correctable* health care problems.[41] As one thus might expect, there are a number of positive steps that each health care provider can take to reduce the exposure to risks inherent in practice, allegations of professional negligence, and financial liability.* Tillinghast, a firm providing actuarial consulting services,[34] recommends the following, which are related to both injury prevention and assuring the availability of a fiscally solvent carrier should litigation ensue.

1 Carefully review the commercial insurance policies to identify potential gaps in coverage. This review should include an analysis of tail provisions, retroactive dates, aggregate limits, and any exclusions.
2 Examine the financial viability of the insurance carrier (or the self-insurance plan). The long tail of malpractice liability can make an inadequately funded and inefficiently administered company initially appear financially sound.
3 Check for long-term commitment of all participants in insurance pool programs. The equitable distribution of profits and losses from these pools is essential to their long-range viability.
4 Institute comprehensive risk management programs (see Chapter 7). These programs should include incident reporting systems and quality assurance programs.
5 And, finally, sponsor meaningful public information programs.

The St. Paul Company[42] reminds its insured physicians that regardless of the level of care provided, an undesirable outcome can lead to a lost malpractice suit if the doctor has not fulfilled certain of what it describes as "legal" obligations. The company identifies five such obligations.

1 *Obtaining informed consent.* Additional procedures not consented to may constitute a battery and possibly even an assault (see Chapters 5 and 9).
2 *Achieving adequate medical documentation.* "More cases are lost because of inaccurate, incomplete, or illegible documentation than for any other reason" (see Chapter 10).
3 *Understanding and avoiding vicarious liability.* If the plaintiff's attorney believes the prime defendant(s) has insufficient liability protection to allow the client to achieve good economic recovery, he or she may involve a remotely connected health care provider in the lawsuit by alleging vicarious liability (see Chapters 6 and 27).
4 *Avoiding the guarantee of results.* Because of the often hidden nature of patients' illnesses and unpredictable nature of medical care, a physician should never guarantee a cure or other satisfactory outcome. (For a review of the legal implications of such a guarantee, see the discussion of *breach of contract* in Chapter 2.)
5 *Avoiding allegations of abandonment.* When a physician does not want to care for a patient, the patient must be made completely aware of the fact. A qualified substitute should be available to the patient before the doctor terminates the relationship (see Chapters 2 and 5).

In any risk-mitigation discussion, it is necessary to *stress* the importance of open communications between health care provider and patient. (See, especially, the discussion of the steps described in Chapter 7 that one should take following an adverse outcome.) *Lack of communication by physicians probably is the primary reason patients become plaintiffs.*[43]

As a substantial effort toward anesthetic risk management, the Mutual Insurance Company of Arizona (a captive company) in 1985 began providing professional liability insurance to anesthesiologists on a *preferred-risk* basis only. To qualify for this coverage, each physician had to agree to

---

*In any discussion of mitigating exposure to financial losses via adequate insurance coverage, it is important to remember that malpractice litigation is not a compensation system similar to workers' compensation. Rather, it is a tort system. As such, malpractice insurance does not provide financial protection for patients; it does provide liability, and hence financial, protection for physicians.[35]

practice in a very careful and attentive manner and use certain monitors. Failure to use a precordial or esophageal stethoscope, for example, would prompt an immediate $25,000 surcharge on further premiums. Conversely, if the physician maintained Advanced Cardiac Life Support certification, the premium would be reduced by 5%.[44]

TRENDS FOR THE FUTURE

The average annual rate of professional liability claims overall has declined by an average of 19.0% yearly since 1985. Anesthesiology claims experienced an annual *decline* of 21.7% for the years 1985 to 1987 (Table 29–8). The percent of anesthesiologists sued declined by an average of 25.2% for the years 1985 to 1987. The percent of anesthesiologists sued during their career was 31.5% as of 1987 (all physicians = 37.0%)[45] (Table 29–9).

Despite this pattern of moderation and decline in professional liability claim frequency, average insurance premiums continue to increase. Premiums for all physicians rose at a 20.9% annual rate from 1982 to 1987 (Table 29–10). The average annualized rate of inflation during this period was 3.3%; total medical practice revenues increased by 7.7% annually.[45] During the period 1985 to 1987, anesthesiologists' average premiums increased 13.1% annually. By way of comparison, in 1987, specialists in obstetrics and gynecology paid the highest average premium $35,300), while psychiatrists paid the lowest ($3800). In 1987, the average premium for anesthesiologists was $22,900[45] (Table 29–11).

Exposure to professional liability claims and litigation is not limited to the private sector. The Department of Defense reports[46] that the number of new malpractice claims filed consequent to uniformed services health care delivery increased from 689 in 1982 to 930 in 1985. The next 2 years demonstrated a reduction in number of claims. In 1986, there were 895; in 1987, 876. There has been, however, a steady increase in the amounts paid out. In 1982, $29 million was paid out. The amount paid increased to $67.6 million in 1987. The Department of Defense has developed a classification of allegations of negligence for use in analysis of military malpractice claims data (Table 29–12).

Alternatives to Tort Resolution

Understanding the malpractice crisis is difficult because of the coexistence of two fundamental, and independent, forces. According to Miccolls,[34] the first force is the persistent and substantial increase in the

TABLE 29–8. Annual Claims per 100 Physicians by Specialty, 1985–1987

	1985	1986	1987	Average Annual Rate of Change 1985–1987, %
All physicians	10.2	9.2	6.7[†]	−19.0
Specialty				
General and family practice	5.7	7.6	5.7	0.0
Internal medicine	6.2	5.5	4.5	−14.8
Surgery	16.8	15.8	12.7	−13.1
Pediatrics	7.2	6.8	4.5	−20.9
Obstetrics and gynecology	25.8	13.0*	8.0	−44.3[‡]
Radiology	12.8	11.5	8.0	−20.9
Psychiatry	2.9	4.5	1.6	−25.7
Anesthesiology	7.5	8.7	4.6	−21.7
Pathology	3.3	1.9	4.9	21.9
Other	10.4	9.1	5.9	−24.7

*1985–1986 change statistically significant at $p = .05$ level.
[†]1986–1987 change statistically significant at $p = .05$ level.
[‡]Total 1985–1987 change statistically significant at the $p = .05$ level.
Source: Data from the American Medical Association.[45]

TABLE 29–9. Percent of Physicians Sued Annually (1985–1987) and in Career by Specialty

	Percent Sued Annually			Average Annual Rate of Change 1985–1987	Percent Sued in Career as of 1987
	1985	1986	1987		
All physicians	8.5	7.6	6.0†	−16.0‡	37.0
Specialty					
General and family practice	5.5	6.3	5.1	−3.7	34.9
Internal medicine	5.4	4.8	4.3	−10.8	28.5
Surgery	13.6	12.3	11.0	−10.1	50.3
Pediatrics	6.6	5.7	3.9	−23.1	31.7
Obstetrics and gynecology	20.0	10.9*	6.7	−42.1‡	57.3
Radiology	11.2	10.5	6.5	−23.8	40.8
Psychiatry	2.9	4.1	1.6	−25.7	20.2
Anesthesiology	7.5	8.2	4.2	−25.2	31.5
Pathology	3.3	1.9	4.9	21.9	21.3
Other	7.5	7.4	5.7	−12.8	37.4

*1985–1986 change statistically significant at p = .05 level.
†1986–1987 change statistically significant at p = .05 level.
‡Total 1985–1987 change statistically significant at the p = .05 level.
Source: Data from the American Medical Association.[45]

underlying *cost* of malpractice claims. The root cause of this increase in cost is the "slow but steady and unmistakable erosion of the negligence concept in this country. The theory of negligence is giving way to the theory of 'entitlement.' Our society is simply becoming less and less willing to accept the risks of everyday life. When some unfortunate economic circumstance befalls us, we look to the nearest deep pocket, regardless of fault." The second force is the *pattern* of the underwriting cycle. "This second force has unfortunately focused attention on the periodic surges in prices, rather than on the unrelenting increase in cost."

One legal writer[47] describes four basic deficiencies in the present malpractice liability system: (1) fault of the doctor must be demonstrated, (2) the amount of the award is greatly influenced by subjective judgments, (3) most awards are granted in lump

TABLE 29–10. Professional Liability Insurance Premiums Paid and Total Practice Revenues of Self-Employed Physicians, 1982–1987

	Insurance Premiums Paid*	Total Practice Revenues*	Premiums as Percent of Revenues
1982	5.8	186.0	3.1
1983	6.9	199.3	3.5
1984	8.4	212.2	4.0
1985	10.5	226.8	4.6
1986	12.8	249.5	5.1
1987	15.0	269.5	5.6
1987 net of inflation (i.e., in 1982 dollars)	12.7	288.9	5.6
Annual percent increase			
1982–1987	20.9	7.7	—
1982–1987 net of inflation	17.0	4.2	—

*In thousands of dollars.
Source: Data from the American Medical Association.[45]

TABLE 29–11. Average Professional Liability Premiums Paid by Self-Employed Physicians, 1985–1987

	Average Premiums, in Thousands of Dollars			Average Annual Rate of Change 1985–1987, %
	1985	1986	1987	
All physicians	10.5	12.8*	15.0†	19.5‡
Specialty				
General and family practice	6.8	7.3	8.9	14.4‡
Internal medicine	5.8	7.1*	8.4†	20.3‡
Surgery	16.6	21.3*	24.5†	21.5‡
Pediatrics	4.7	6.3*	7.1	22.9‡
Obstetrics and gynecology	23.5	29.3*	35.3†	22.6‡
Radiology	8.9	10.4	9.5	3.3
Psychiatry	2.5	3.4*	3.8	23.3‡
Anesthesiology	17.9	20.5*	22.9	13.1‡
Pathology	3.1	4.4*	6.2†	41.4‡
Other	6.0	8.5*	8.4	18.3‡

*1985–1986 change statistically significant at p = .05 level.
†1986–1987 change statistically significant at p = .05 level.
‡Total 1985–1987 change statistically significant at the p = .05 level.
Source: Data from the American Medical Association.[45]

sums, and (4) the plaintiff is not required to deduct payment from collateral sources (e.g., other insurance, sick pay, etc.) and may collect more than once for the same injury. This author proffers two alternative approaches to the current tort system of recovery for medical malpractice injuries: (1) no-fault insurance and (2) contractual arrangement. No-fault insurance will be discussed later in this chapter. Contractual arrangements have successfully been used to bring down costs in some areas, notably high school sports–related injury insurance. The school district and the insurance carrier establish an arrangement wherein the injured student becomes a "third-party beneficiary." The company guarantees it will make a settlement offer covering medical and rehabilitation expenses and lost wages if the student forfeits his or her right to sue.

Trends Toward Anesthetic Injury Prevention

Anesthesiology was one of the specialties enmeshed in the severe insurance crisis of only a few years ago; premiums were increasing dramatically, and coverage became unavailable in certain areas of this country. Anesthesiologists began realizing

that they would need to participate in controlling their own loss experiences if the profession was to remain an insurable specialty.[48] The problem was attacked on a number of fronts. One involved the development and publication by the ASA of standards* of practice intended to elevate the quality of anesthesia care. The dissemination of the standards—which set forth what a prudent practitioner follows in identical or similar circumstances—was elevated countrywide in short order.[49]

A number of more or less formalized

*For a thorough discussion of the standard of care, plus the text of some of the standards of practice adopted by the ASA, see Chapter 4. [Editor]

TABLE 29–12. Classification of Allegations of Negligence

1. Diagnosis error
2. Anesthesia incident
3. Invasive procedure incident
4. Pharmacy and therapeutics incident
5. Obstetrical incident
6. Mental health related
7. Blood product use incident
8. Administrative error
9. Accidental trauma

Source: Data from the Department of Defense.[46]

steps are recognized for management of a loss exposure (see also Chapter 7). These include

1. *Identification* of the exposure through claims review. An attempt is made to identify the etiology of those claims.
2. *Evaluation* of the exposure and its causes. Various treatment methods to reduce the exposure are evaluated.
3. *Implementation* of the most appropriate treatment method.
4. *Close monitoring* of the exposure following implementation of treatment.[50]

Another advance came in the fall of 1985 with the establishment of the Anesthesia Patient Safety Foundation (APSF). The foundation resulted from a proposal presented at the 1984 International Symposium on Preventable Anesthesia Morbidity and Mortality.[51] The goals of the APSF are (1) to foster investigations that will provide a better understanding of preventable anesthetic injuries, (2) to encourage programs that will reduce the number of anesthetic injuries, and (3) to promote national and international communication of information and ideas about the causes and prevention of anesthetic injuries.[52] The APSF has a board of directors that includes representatives from anesthesiology, nurse anesthesia, device and pharmaceutical manufacturing, the insurance industry, hospitals, biomedical engineering, and the Food and Drug Administration. It was apparent from the beginnings of the APSF, and all parties agreed, that anesthesia needed to be safer and *could be made safer,* and that all participants had a major self-interest in achieving this goal.[53]

J. Holzer of the Risk Management Foundation believes the risk-reduction activities of the APSF have been very effective: "There is little doubt in my mind that the concerted efforts of ASPF have largely contributed to the creation of crucial risk management and quality assurance activities in hospitals throughout the country."[53] All of this, along with improved loss experience among anesthesiologists, is now translating into lower malpractice rates and discounted premiums in many parts of the country.[53] As an example, in 1976, the professional liability premium for anesthesiol-

ogists charged by The Doctor's Company in California was $15,389, while the average for all physicians was $9,743. In 1987, anesthesiologists' premium averaged $16,199, but the average for all physicians insured by the company had increased to $19,597. The insurance cost to anesthesiologists, which had decreased substantially below the overall average premium cost, may reflect a sharp turnaround in anesthesia loss experience.[48]

In 1985, MMI Companies, Inc., a professional liability insurance carrier, developed an anesthesia risk modification program that focused on clinical practice patterns that lend themselves to system failures, accidents, and potential liability exposure. The aim was to identify substandard practice patterns and change undesirable practices. Another goal was to develop an effective defense strategy against allegations of negligence. A major point was the importance of leadership in anesthesia departments in providing direction and encouragement for long-term positive change. The MMI risk modification program[54] has three components:

1. *Self-audit questionnaire.* The department chairman compares services actually provided with the MMI program guidelines.
2. *Statistical data.* An ongoing assessment of the department's statistics is developed by using data on volume and outcome criteria.
3. *Clinical care review.* Specific outcome indicators are identified for mandatory departmental review. Cases that result in actual or potentially liable situations are reviewed. The main issue is safety, not discipline.*

Tort Reform

Central to a discussion of professional liability insurance is the tort doctrine, which is based on the "fault concept." This concept determines who or what was responsi-

---

*Except in particularly egregious situations when a health care provider is repeatedly and grossly negligent, risk management activities within the institution should be separate and apart from recredentialling and decredentialling functions.

ble for an unfortunate event and who should pay for it. The premise underlying the fault concept is that the harmful event was preventable and with proper education and supervision should not occur.[55] Tort law, including that part related to professional liability, is governed by both state statutes and the courts (for decisions that make up the common law, see Chapter 1). Substantive rules and principles, as for example governing informed consent, are determined for the most part by the states. Procedural laws—rules of evidence, trial procedures, jury instructions, and the like—are federal or state statutory enactments intended to govern trials in the federal or state courts, respectively.

Starting in the mid-1970s, state legislatures began to wrestle with the malpractice problem and attendant insurance "crisis." The legislators in most jurisdictions enacted statutes directed toward what is loosely called *tort reform.*[56] The purpose of these statutes is to address professional liability issues and mitigate the exposure to liability of health care providers, especially those practicing in so-called high-risk but essential specialties (e.g., obstetrics). By doing so, these statutes were to assure the continuing availability of not only the professional liability coverage for these providers, but also the health care delivery that this insurance indemnifies.

The most common professional liability issues considered recently by state legislatures have been

1 *Disclosure of collateral sources*—Letting the jury know what compensation the plaintiff has already received from other sources for the same injury. Of claims paid after legal expenses, one-third to one-half duplicate payments already received from collateral sources.[4]

2 *Caps on noneconomic and punitive damages*—Limiting payment for pain and suffering. Caps generally do not affect compensation for medical expenses, wages lost, and other similar expenses.

3 *Structured settlement of large cases*—Provides that large awards may be paid over time, with consideration of immediate economic situations.

4 *Abolishment of joint and several liability*—Distributing the award between defendants according to the degree of fault of each.[56]

In 1986, Danzon[57] observed that the number and size of professional liability claims continued to increase steadily, but not as fast as they would have without the then-existing tort reforms. Danzon reported that cutting 1 year off the statute of limitation of actions for adults reduced claim frequency by 8%. Laws providing reduction in awards when plaintiff has collateral sources of compensation reduced claim costs by 11% to 18%. Caps ($250,000) on awards reduced the claim costs by 23%.[56,58]

Claims take a long time to be resolved. The U.S. General Accounting Office reported that of the malpractice claims closed in 1984, the average length of time from injury to claim filing was 16 months. Additionally, an average of 25 months elapsed until a claim was resolved. For claims closed with a payment of $1 million or more, about 5 years elapsed from claim filing until resolution.[19]

James Todd of the American Medical Association (AMA) states, "Tort reform has not been, in actuality, as successful as we would have liked to have seen it. It's been gutted by constitutional challenges and the further expansion of liability by the courts."[58] The greatest legal weakness of almost all tort reform measures that have been found to be unconstitutional is that they apply only to cases involving medical malpractice, and to no other kind of tort. Plaintiffs consequently claim violation of their constitutional rights of "equal protection of the laws." Tort reform that applies to all types of torts would be more likely to survive such constitutional challenges.[29] A damage cap of $750,000 established in Virginia was recently held to be constitutional by a federal appeals court. The fourth U.S. Circuit Court of Appeals ruled that the cap violated neither the right to trial by jury nor the guarantee to equal protection and due process. This decision may end speculation about whether damage caps violate a patient's federal constitutional right to a jury trial.[59]

The American College of Surgeons[55] recommends seven major reforms to the tort system:

1 *Limitation on noneconomic awards.*
The Rand Corporation believes regulation of noneconomic awards to be
one of the most important ways to
reduce the cost of professional liability. The great variation in professional liability jury awards depends
unpredictably on the emotional
"tone" existing in various areas of
the United States.
2 *Change of collateral source rules.*
Current rules prevent disclosure
during litigation of compensation
from other sources.
3 *Periodic payments.* Large awards
should be carefully structured over
the patient's life. The goal is to provide financial support for the patient during the course of his or her
lifetime, not a large lump sum all at
once.
4 *Regulation of contingent fees.* The
United States is the only country in
the world where unregulated contingent fees exist.
5 *Regulation of expert witness.* An expert should be fully qualified in the
specialty involved in the litigation,
both by training and by active practice. Currently, any licensed physician can testify as an expert on any
medical subject.
6 *Elimination of punitive damages.*
This activity should be left to state
medical boards and other disciplinary bodies.
7 *Modification of statutes of limitation of actions.* Most injuries are
obvious immediately or within a
short time after treatment. Without
shorter time limits (especially in
obstetrics), very large financial reserves must be maintained for
many years.[60]

These seven areas of reform are essentially
identical to those recommended by the
AMA.[28]

Beyond Tort Reform

The American Hospital Association recently published a report entitled *Non-traditional Approaches to the Medical Malpractice Crisis*.[61] This document discusses
the following five approaches:

1 *Contracts.* Contracts can be designed before care is delivered to define duties and modify rights of the
parties. These arrangements could reduce legal expenses and the amount
of defensive medicine practiced.
2 *Arbitration.* An impartial panel in-
vestigates all cases of alleged malpractice, renders its decisions, and
makes awards. All potentially liable
parties would submit to binding arbitration.
3 *Patient compensation funds.* This is
insurance administered by the state
and funded through premiums
charged to health care providers. The
fund pays claims over a predetermined maximum limit. Doctors are
protected against large premium increases because insurance companies
are protected against high awards.
These funds introduce some pre-
dictability into the insurance rate-
setting process. Indiana's patient
compensation fund has withstood
two constitutional challenges before
the Indiana Supreme Court,[62] and insurance premiums in that state have
remained moderate, despite an increase in the number of claims filed.
4 *Medical offer and recovery.* Physicians are given the option of paying a
claimant out-of-pocket expenses as a
result of unsatisfactory outcome. The
patient relinquishes the right to go to
court. Losses would be more predictable and payment would be
prompt and comprehensive. Legal
costs should be reduced. A greater
number of outcomes might be compensated.
5 *Scheduled benefits.* This would be
similar to workers' compensation,
but preserves fault as the basis for
compensation. Rewards are based
on a predetermined table or schedule. Awards would be more predictable. This system might be vulnerable to constitutional challenges
because of limiting awards and
eliminating right to trial by jury.[61]

No-Fault Insurance for Patients

Another proposal of professional liability
reform is to remove malpractice actions

from the tort system and adopt a *no-fault* compensation mechanism.[63] Determining fault under our present system can be very unpredictable and is protracted and costly as well. The jury and judge are asked to assign fault when even medical experts are unable to agree. Presently some patients receive windfall awards when no negligence has occurred; others who are truly injured through professional negligence incorrectly receive no award. Awards for noneconomic damages, such as loss of consortium and pain and suffering, are completely subjective and depend largely upon the jury's sympathy.[60] The system used in Sweden has proven effective and efficient. The total cost of that program averages about $1 per patient per year.[55] The U.S. Congress has considered the concept of a no-fault system for medical professional liability. It would resemble the workers' compensation programs now in place. The goal would be to create a more reasonable and fair system so that most funds paid go to the injured, rather than being used in the litigation process. Injured patients receive only an estimated 28 to 40 cents out of each dollar spent on malpractice insurance premiums.[56,60]

In contrast to malpractice insurance as it is used today, no-fault insurance would protect the patient, not the physician. In our society, the use of insurance for protection from unusual adverse events is widely accepted. Familiar examples include insurance protection from fire, automobile accident, or theft.[55] Critics of the no-fault concept believe identification of compensable events will be very difficult. They point out that it will be necessary to introduce a standard-of-care analysis in many cases involving diagnostic oversights. Rubsamen[64] argues: "Regardless of the standard finally decided upon by the administrative authorities, contention over the standard-of-care issue in a hearing would differ little, if at all, from the confrontation that now takes place in the courtroom between the doctor-defendant and the plaintiff's attorney." Some overseas insurers and reinsurers have withdrawn from the U.S. market because of the unpredictability of our present system and a fear of conversion of the fault system into an unlimited no-fault compensation system. They agree that a true no-fault system could greatly increase the amount of

each premium dollar actually received by the plaintiff, but fear that the total cost of all claims would rise to 4½ times the cost of our present fault system.[65]

A number of years ago, Mills[66] studied 23,800 hospital admissions to endeavor to learn whether some type of no-fault system would be economically feasible. He observed that in about 5% of admissions, there were unexpected events that he called PCEs (potentially compensable events). He grouped these PCEs into three categories.

1 *A misfortune*—A well-recognized complication of the disease being treated should not be compensated.
2 *A mishap*—An unusual event without gross negligence should be promptly reimbursed without litigation. This is the "designated compensable event" concept. It is similar to a workers' compensation program.
3 *An event caused by clear negligence*—These events belong in the tort system and should be litigated if simpler solutions are not satisfactory.

Determining which of these three types of adverse event a PCE represents can be difficult. Clear malpractice exists in only a minority of adverse events.[55]

Data Bank Identifying Incompetent Practitioners

A contract has been awarded to UNISYS, a Pennsylvania information systems company, by the Department of Health and Human Services, to establish and operate a National Practitioner Data Bank mandated by the 1986 Health Care Quality Improvement Act.[67] This act was passed by Congress with the intent to curb medical malpractice and improve the quality of medical care, and grants immunity from civil damage suits for people involved in peer review. The data bank will collect information relating to:

1 All payments made on behalf of any doctor as a result of a malpractice claim or settlement
2 Disciplinary actions taken by state medical boards

3 Professional review actions arising from peer review processes that adversely affect the clinical privileges of a physician

4 Adverse actions taken by professional societies against membership of a physician

One benefit of this data bank will be to restrict the ability of physicians to relocate their practices from one state to another in an attempt to elude discovery of previous substandard professional behavior. The national data bank will become a central repository of credentialing data on physicians. It will be directed by an executive committee composed of members from various professional organizations and federal agencies. Those authorized to have access to the bank's data include federal agencies, hospitals, state licensing boards, and individual physicians reviewing their own records.[68] Concerns have been expressed,[69] however, that these data will be subject to misuse.

Other Plans

Another alternative to the current professional liability system was announced in 1988 by the AMA and 32 national medical specialty associations. This proposal would include a fault-based administrative system under the jurisdiction of a strengthened state medical board (hereinafter referred to as the agency), which would totally replace the existing court and jury system.[70] This dispute resolution system is made up of three basic elements:

1 *Claims resolution function.* Complaints of malpractice would be first screened by experienced claims reviewers. Most claims would probably be settled, or dismissed, at this stage. Throughout this process, and ensuing stages, attorneys from the agency's office would be provided at no cost to any patient who wanted such assistance. If the claim was not satisfactorily resolved after the initial screening, it would be referred to an expert hearing examiner. This individual would conduct a full and prompt hearing on the merits of the claim. The hearing exam-

iner's decision would be reviewed by a medical board panel.

2 *Credentialing and disciplinary process.* Results of all settlements and awards would be submitted to the investigative branch of the agency. Here other malpractice or disciplinary findings would be reviewed to establish substandard conduct. Periodic physician credentialing reviews would occur.

3 *Codification of legal aspects of medical liability.* Including, for example, refinement of informed consent policies, definition of qualifications of expert witnesses, establishment of caps on noneconomic damages, and the like.[70]

Involving Health Care Providers and the Public

S. Loggans, a trial lawyer, issued the following admonishment to physicians: "You learn to avoid malpractice by learning about medicine. But you learn how to avoid malpractice claims by learning about the legal system. A lawyer has to teach you. Medical schools should institute more legal education courses."[43]

It is unlikely that effective resolution of the current professional liability crisis will occur until the public is involved in the cure. Education of the public about the degree to which the professional liability problem is harming medical care must be widespread.[43] The American College of Surgeons advises: "This effort must stress the extent to which the availability of orthopedic and obstetric services, among others, is being jeopardized; the mounting cost to the patient of defensive medicine; the increasing difficulty of obtaining services requiring high-risk procedures; and the rapid erosion of the traditional bond of trust between patient and physician."[55]

CONCLUSION

Insurance underwriting is basically a *predictive* business. Insurance pricing policies are established generally by estimates of future demand, not of the costs of policies already written. Insurance companies do not set rates to recover past losses. They determine their pricing structure in expectation of future claims and investment profits. As the legal system establishes broader liability definitions, and as the public demand for compensation increases, the professional liability insurance "crisis" will likely continue for some time.[25]

Despite these industrywide vicissitudes, professional liability insurance coverage remains an essential adjuvant to health care delivery. Fortunately, this coverage currently is almost universally available across this country, albeit at great cost for some specialists in some localities. Will it also remain so? Numerous efforts directed toward assuring continuing availability of this coverage are currently underway. Alternative dispute resolution, no-fault insurance coverage, statutory caps on recovery, modification of the collateral source rule, limitation of contingent fees, shortening the interval during which litigation may be filed, other tort reforms, or maintenance of the status quo—which one, or ones, will it be? Additionally, it is important to reiterate that although the common law for the most part defines malpractice, and judges and juries are the final arbiters in cases that are pursued to trial and judgment, the large majority of malpractice disputes are resolved through a private process of insurance claims settlement.[4]

Be that as it may, it is my opinion that the status quo cannot continue to survive for very long, that there are one or more alternatives to the status quo, that these must be explored, and that the sooner this exploration takes place, the better. As the malpractice problem inevitably deepens further and becomes a real crisis, as the cost of professional liability insurance becomes prohibitive, and as the public becomes aware of the destructive effects of maintaining the present system, society will demand a solution.[62] It would seem far better that this solution come from within the health care profession, rather than external to it—via statutory or common law!

REFERENCES

1. Minnesota Medical Association: Report of the Minnesota Commission on Professional Liability. The Minnesota Medical Association, Minneapolis, November, 1985.
2. American Medical Association Special Task Force on Professional Liability and Insurance: Professional Liability in the '80s: Report 1. Chicago, October, 1984.
3. American College of Emergency Physicians: Professional liability insurance, part I. Foresight March, 1987.
4. Bovbjerg, RR and Havighurst, CC: Medical malpractice: An update for noncombatants. Bus Health 2:38, 1985.
5. Aetna Life Ins. Co. v. Wally, 164 So. 16 (Miss. 1935).
6. Sohn v. United States Fidelity & Guaranty Co., 352 F.2d 65 6th. C.C.A. (1965).
7. United States Fidelity & Guaranty Co. v. Ditoro, 206 F. Supp. 528 (D.C., M.D. P2., 1962).
8. St Paul Fire and Marine Insurance Co.: Six Good Reasons Why You Should Report Claims and Potential Claims Early. St Paul, MN, 1987, pub. 7031.
9. MacDonald, MG, Meyer, KC, and Essig, B: Insurance issues. Health Care Law: A Practical Guide. Matthew Bender, New York, 1988, §§ 13.01–13.07.
10. Bickelhaupt, DL: General liability insurance. General Insurance. Richard D. Iwin, Homewood, IL, 1983, 528.
11. American College of Emergency Physicians: Professional liability insurance, part II. Foresight June, 1987.
12. MacGinnitie, WJ: Medical Malpractice: The Lingering Crises. Tillinghast Emphasis: May, 1985.
13. Physician Insurers Association of America: Membership Directory and Professional Services Section. Physician Insurers Association of America, Lawrenceville, NJ, 1989.
14. Anonymous: Liability reshapes hospital/physician relationships. *Hospitals* 61:56, 1987.
15. Liability Risk Retention Act, 15 U.S.C. §§ 3901 *et seq.* (1986).
16. Geisel, J: Risk Retention Act traces roots to 1979. Bus Ins, October 31: 88, 1988.
17. Burda, D: Risk retention law more trouble than its worth? Hospitals 61:46, 1987.
18. Foudree, B: The risk retention guaranty fund idea. Nat'l Underwriter August 24:15, 1987.
19. Kladiva, SD: Insuring for medical liability: The ongoing saga. Bus Health 4:31, 1987.
20. Brooks, RF: Can insurance defense counsel serve two masters? Va Bar News 8, June, 1987.
21. American College of Emergency Physicians: Evaluang medical malpractice insurance policies. Foresight July, 1988.
22. Belli, MM and Carlova, J: For Your Malpractice Defense. Medical Economics

Books, Oradell, NJ, 1986, p 135.

23. St Paul Fire and Marine Insurance Co: The Facts on Claims-Made Coverage for Medical Professional Liability Insurance. St Paul, MN, 1986, Pub. 4715.

24. American College of Emergency Physicians: Professional liability insurance, part I. Foresight March, 1987.

25. Huber, P: Injury litigation and liability insurance dynamics. Science 238:31, 1987.

26. Goldberg, D: Claims-made tails: A financial time bomb. Group Practice J 38:14, 1989.

27. Torry, K: Tail coverage need puts insurers at disadvantage, PIAA companies told. Am Med News 22, June 9, 1989.

28. American Medical Association Special Task Force on Professional Liability and Insurance: Professional Liability in the '80s, report 2. Chicago, November, 1984.

29. Anonymous: Malpractice insurance: The market gets tighter. Washington Report on Med and Health/Perspectives (Suppl) 40, February 3, 1986.

30. Anonymous: Malpractice from a carrier's point of view. Med Econ 63:17, 1986.

31. St Paul Fire and Marine Insurance Co: Physicians and surgeons update. The St Paul's 1987 Annual Report to Policy Holders. St Paul, MN, July, 1987.

32. St Paul Fire and Marine Insurance Co: Physicians and Surgeons Update. The St Paul's 1989 Annual Report to Policy Holders. St Paul, MN, May, 1989.

33. National Association of Independent Insurers: Estimated Underwriting and Operating Results by Line and by State. Des Plaines, IL, 1987.

34. Miccolis, JA: After the malpractice crises: What prognosis for the health care profession? Tillinghast Emphasis. April, 1987: 11–13.

35. Anonymous: The manufactured crises. *Consumer Reports* August:544, 1986.

36. From Jury Verdict Research, as cited in St Paul's 1989 Annual Report, *supra* note 32.

37. Cheney, FW, et al: Standard of care and anesthesia liability. JAMA 261:1599, 1989.

38. Kaplan, RA, et al: Unexpected cardiac arrest during spinal anesthesia: A closed claims analysis of predisposing factors. Anesthesiology 68:5, 1988.

39. Keats, AS: Anesthesia mortality: A new mechanism. Anesthesiology 68:2, 1988.

40. Brunner, EA: The National Association of Insurance Commissioners' Closed Claim Study. In Pierce, EC and Cooper, JB (eds): Analysis of Anesthetic Mishaps. Little, Brown & Co, Boston, 1984, pp 23–24.

41. Brunner, EA: Monitoring anesthetic care: New directions. JAMA 261:1633, 1989.

42. St Paul Fire and Marine Insurance Co: Tips to Prevent Medical Malpractice Claims. St Paul, MN, May, 1985, pub. 11326.

43. American Medical Association Special Task Force on Professional Liability and Insurance: Professional Liability in the '80s, report 3. Chicago, March, 1985.

44. American Society of Anesthesiologists: Examples of Approaches to Risk Management. American Society of Anesthesiologists, Park Ridge, IL, September, 1985, pub. 30506-2PS.

45. American Medical Association: Socioeconomic Characteristics of Medical Practice—1988. The American Medical Association, Chicago, December, 1988, pub. OP228/8.

46. Department of Defense: Information Paper: Management of Malpractice in the Department of Defense (undated).

47. O'Connell, J: A new approach to medical malpractice insurance. RI Med J 69:81, 1986.

48. Sabella, JD: California insurer notes fewer claims, lower premiums. Anesth Patient Safety Found Newsletter 2:22, 1987.

49. Ward, RJ and Lane, MJ: Anesthesiology and medicolegal outcome. In Brown, DL (ed): Risk and Outcome in Anesthesia. Lippincott, Philadelphia, 1988, p 398.

50. Wood, MD: Monitoring equipment and loss reduction: An insurer's view. In Gravenstein, JS and Holzer, JF (eds): Safety and Cost Containment in Anesthesia. Boston, Butterworth & Co, 1988.

51. St Paul Fire and Marine Insurance Co: Research helps prevent anesthesiology mishaps. Malpractice Dig 13:1, 1986.

52. Cooper, JB and Pierce, EC: Safety foundation organized. Anesth Patient Safety Found Newsletter 1:1, 1986.

53. Arcarese, JS and Carstensen, PB: FDA applauds APSF efforts. Anesth Patient Safety Found Newsletter 4:1, 1989.

54. DeBruine, P and Napier, JA: Insurer studies, cuts risks. Anesth Patient Safety Found Newsletter 3:1, 5, 1988.

55. Committee on Professional Liability, American College of Surgeons: Professional liability: A blueprint for reform. Am Coll Surg Bull 71:2, 1986.

56. Hollis, CD: Legislative remedies to the liability crises. J Med Assoc Ga 76:707, 1987.

57. Danzon, PM: New evidence on the frequency and severity of medical malpractice claims. Law Contemp Probs 49 (Spring): 57, 1986.

58. Quoted by Holthaus, D: After tort reform, what's next? *Hospitals* 62:48, 1988.

59. Boyd v. Bulala, 877 F.2d 1191 (4th Cir. 1989).

60. Roberts, DK: Resolving the crises: Where do

we go from here? In Roberts, DK, Shane, JA, and Roberts, ML: Confronting the Malpractice Crises. Eagle Press, Kansas City, 1985, pp 248–253.

61. Medical Malpractice Task Force, AHA, and American Academy of Hospital Attorneys: Non-traditional approaches to the medical malpractice crisis. American Hospital Association, Chicago, 1987.

62. Ind. Code § 19-9.5-2-2; Hines v. Elkhart Hosp., 465 F.Supp. 421 (N.D. Ind.), *aff'd* 603 F.2d 646 (1979); Johnson v. St. Vincent Hosp., 79 Ind. Dec. 131, 404 N.E.2d 585 (1980); *see also* Bowen, OR: The federal government's role in medical liability reform. Group Practice J 36:1987.

63. For a review of an early such proposal, see Dornette, WHL: Medical injury insurance: A possible remedy for the malpractice problem. J Leg Med 1:28, 1973; Dornette, WHL: Medical injury insurance: Proposed model legislation. J Leg Med 3:24, 1975; *see also* Freeman, R: Sounding board; professional liability: A no-fault solution. N Engl J Med 322:627, 1990; Manual, BM: Changing the malpractice liability system. N Engl J Med 322:628, 1990.

64. Rubsamen, DS: Why no-fault won't work. Am Coll Surg Bull 71:10, 1986.

65. Rinaman, JC: The tort liability system: Overview for the anesthesiologist. In Gravenstein, JS and Holzer, JF (eds): Safety and Cost Containment in Anesthesia. Boston, Butterworth & Co, 1988.

66. Mills, DH: Medical insurance feasibility study. West J Med 128:360, 1978.

67. Health Care Quality Improvement Act, 42 U.S.C. § § 11101 *et seq.* (1986).

68. Physician Insurers Association of America: The Physician Insurer 3:1, 1989.

69. Pinkney, DS: MDs predict rampant abuse of data bank. Am Med News July 7:22, 1989.

70. Gere, M: Alternative system proposed as a solution to the professional liabilities crisis. Am Coll Surg Bull 73:63, 1988.

Glossary of Legal Terminology

Abandonment.   In a health care context, the unilateral termination of needed care of a patient by the provider, without the latter first having made provisions for the continuation of that care by another provider.

Adversary system.   A system in which one party warns a second party of his or her intention to seek legal relief and the secondary party is given the opportunity to contest such action.

Affidavit.   A voluntary statement taken under oath before an officer of the court (e.g., a notary public) having authority to administer such an oath.

Agency.   Any relationship whereby one person authorizes another to act for or represent him or her.

Agency-by-estoppel.   When two parties engage in a relationship that on its face appears to be one of principal-agent, the principal will be estopped (prevented at law) from denying the existence of that relationship and hence any attendant liability for acts of the agent.

Answer.   A pleading by which the defendant in a lawsuit responds to a complaint and attempts to resist the action of the plaintiff either by denying the facts alleged by the plaintiff or by admitting them and alleging new matter that would negate the plaintiff's cause of action.

Assault.   The unlawful threat of actions by a person intended to inflict, by force, corporate injury; the fear of imminent danger created by would-be assailants must be substantiated by their capability to execute their threats; in the case of medical treatment, assault could be committed by a physician insisting on a method of treatment that the patient does not want and is fearful of having.

Assumption of the risk.   A party may be injured by the act of another, but if that party entered into a situation or relationship wherein he or she was voluntarily exposed to the risk of injury by the other, he or she is said to have *assumed the risk*; assumption of the risk is a defense against unintentional but not intentional torts.

Attorney.   One who acts on behalf of another.

Attorney, power of.   The document setting forth permission of one person to act on behalf of another.

Attorney, springing power of.   A power of attorney that becomes operative on the occurrence of a certain event, for example, when the person granting the power is no longer capable of making decisions for himself or herself.

Battery.   Any unlawful constraint or physical violence inflicted on a person without his or her consent. Any elective medical or surgical treatment performed without a patient's consent is a battery, under most circumstances.

Borrowed-servant doctrine.   Normally an employer is liable for injuries to others caused by an employee acting within the scope of his or her employment. If during the course of such employment, however, the employee comes under the direction and supervision of a third person who can direct the activities of the employee, the employee becomes a *borrowed servant*. His or her acts are imputed to his or her new master (the borrower).

Breach of confidence.   The dissemination of confidential information about a person beyond that required by statute or in the public interest.

Burden of proof.   The necessity of proving any fact disputed by opposing parties in a legal action.

Cause of action.   A matter for which a lawsuit may be initiated; an occurrence that gives rise to litigation; a redressable wrong.

Certiorari, writ of.   Permission, granted by a higher court (e.g., the U.S. Supreme Court), to appeal the decision of a lower court.

Common law.   A large and growing body of decisions handed down by appellate courts to finally resolve disputes between one party and another.

Comparative negligence.   A doctrine that reduces a plaintiff's damages if the plaintiff has also been at fault, in proportion to the extent of the plaintiff's own negligence, unless the negligence of the plaintiff equals or exceeds that of the defendant. (Compare **contributory negligence,** *infra,* in which the plaintiff's negligence forms an absolute defense.)

Complaint.   The initial pleading of a plaintiff in a civil action, which, when properly drafted, filed, and served upon the defendant, initiates the lawsuit.

Complaint, third-party.   Complaint filed by a defendant naming one who is not yet a party to the lawsuit; the third party then becomes a defendant; the action assures that any party who is or may be responsible for the act complained of in the original complaint is before the court and will be subject to any liability and damages.

Consent.   The voluntary acquiescence of one's will to the plans of another.

Contingent fee.   The fee for an attorney's services in some legal proceedings that is paid only if the client wins the case.

Contract.   An agreement between two or more parties, based upon sufficient consideration (e.g., money or performance of a service), to carry out a particular lawful act or refrain from doing so.

Contract, adhesion.   Contract that creates an undue or unfair advantage for the party who drafted it over the other party or parties to it; in general, courts will not enforce adhesion contracts.

Contract, breach of.   Failure of a party to adhere to the terms of a contract in the absence of a valid, legally acceptable reason for not doing so.

Contributory negligence.   Under the common law, if a plaintiff was negligent and that negligence in any way contributed to the plaintiff's injury, such contributory negligence constituted an absolute defense to a successful action against a defendant, even though the latter's actions may have been mainly responsible for the injury; a growing number of jurisdictions have rejected the harsh rule of contributory negligence and have adopted instead some form of **comparative negligence,** *supra.*

Corporation.   An artificial entity created under the laws of a jurisdiction for the purpose of carrying out some activity, usually a business activity.

Corporation, professional.   A corporation created for the delivery of professional services of some type (e.g., architecture, dentistry, engineering, law, medicine).

Counterclaim.   Pleading filed by a defendant in a lawsuit against the plaintiff asserting any claim the defendant has against the plaintiff (e.g., nonpayment for services); see **malicious prosecution,** *infra.*

Damages.   Monetary compensation for a person who has been injured in some manner by another.

Damages, actual.   In the case of personal injury, medical expenses, loss of wages, and cost of any rehabilitation, past, present, and projected into the future; dollar value of property damaged, destroyed, or lost; also called **special damages** or **specials.**

Damages, general.   Monies awarded for the successful plaintiff's pain and suffering, customarily calculated as a multiple of the total amount of actual damages.

Damages, punitive.   Damages far in excess of actual and special ones, intended to punish a defendant who has intentially and maliciously committed an egregious act.

Declaratory judgment.   A court's ruling as to the rights of the parties who have a dispute regarding a question of law (e.g., the proper meaning of a contract).

Deepest-pocket doctrine.   A semifacetious term applied to the tendency of some plaintiffs' counsel to name all possible parties as codefendants in order to reach the one or ones with the greatest assets.

Defendant.   The person opposing the party (plaintiff) trying to seek relief or compensation for damages in a suit.

Demurrer, or **motion to dismiss for failure to state a claim.**   A motion, filed by the defendant in response to the complaint, which says to the court, in effect, "Even if all the facts the plaintiff has alleged were true, the plaintiff still has not stated a cause of action, or there is some other legal defect in the claim; therefore, this case should be dismissed now."

Deposition.   The testimony of a witness who is asked questions under oath, not in a court of law but before a court reporter, with all parties in attendance; subsequently transcribed and able to be used in court.

Disability.   The lack of capacity to take full advantage of one's ordinary legal rights; a person who has no ability to change a legal relationship is under a disability.

Discovery. Formal process of obtaining information in possession of one's opponent during litigation.

Due process. Process owed a party based on rights granted under the constitution of the federal and local governments, plus pertinent laws of those governments.

Duty. The correlative of **right.** The physician is under a legal duty to treat the patient at the level of the standard of care, and the patient has a legal right to such treatment.

Emancipate. Literally, *to set free;* the act whereby one gains one's ability to act on one's own behalf.

Emancipated minor. A person who has not yet attained the age of emancipation (see, *infra*) but who, because of marriage, service in a branch of the armed forces, or self-support and living away from home, is considered at law to be capable of managing his or her own affairs, including consenting to health care.

Emancipation, age of. The age at which a person attains the ability to vote, make contracts, sue, and be sued; 21 years at common law, it has been lowered to 18 by legislatures in all U.S. jurisdictions.

Emancipation, statutory. All jurisdictions have statutes that allow unemancipated minors above a certain age (generally 12) to contract for health care in reference to certain problems such as substance abuse, and (possibly) unwanted pregnancy; the latter varies widely among the several states.

Estoppel. A bar recognized at law precluding a person from denying a certain set of facts, because of prior statements or acts, or a prior judgement.

Evidence. Any type of proof introduced at trial through testimony of witnesses, records, documents, models, or other concrete objects intended to convince the trier of fact of the contentions of the party introducing it.

Evidence beyond a reasonable doubt. Evidence that is fully convincing, clear, concise, and indubitable; the standard of proof required to convict in a criminal case.

Evidence, clear and convincing. The amount of evidence required, for example, in a sanity or commitment proceeding, or one to determine whether life support should be withdrawn; greater than a **preponderance** but less than evidence **beyond a reasonable doubt.**

Evidence, demonstrative. Evidence addressed directly to the senses, especially visual, as for example models, weapons, photographs, diagrams, and the like.

Evidence, preponderance of. The superiority of evidence produced by one side in a proceeding; evidence that carries more weight than that of the opponent, although to a lesser extent than **clear and convincing.**

Fellow servant doctrine. Under the common law, an employer could not be held liable for the injuries of an employee caused by a fellow employee; workers' compensation laws in all states have abolished this concept.

Fiduciary. A person in the position of a trustee in reference to guaranteeing confidentiality of information, or safeguarding assets, entrusted to him or her.

Forensic medicine. Medicine introduced into the *forum*, or public place of trial; the use of medical evidence to resolve disputes in civil cases, criminal cases, or workers' compensation proceedings.

Fraud. A false representation of a matter of fact intended to deceive another person and induce him or her to part with something of value or to lose a legal right.

Guardian. A person legally appointed to take care of the property and affairs of another person who is incapable of managing his or her own affairs because of some legal incapacity; see **incapacity,** *infra.*

Guardian *ad litem.* A guardian appointed by a court to represent a person who is legally incapacitated and to act on his or her behalf in a legal proceeding before that court.

Immunity. Freedom on the part of one person against having a legal relationship (a relationship with others recognized at and governed by law) altered by a given act or omission of another party; correlative of disability; the other party is under a disability in respect to altering the legal relationship.

Incapacity. Inability to act on behalf of oneself and manage one's own affairs, whether because of age, mental or physical illness, or the effects of mind-altering drugs.

Indemnify. To hold harmless, compensate for losses; for example, the professional liability insurance carrier agrees to pay damages caused by negligent acts of the insured professional covered by the terms, and within the monetary limits, of the policy.

Informed consent.   Within the health care context, consent to a diagnostic or therapeutic procedure based on the consenter's awareness of the risks (significant hazards) of that procedure, its likely outcome, and benefits, as compared with similar aspects of any other alternative procedure (if available) and with no procedure at all.

Informed refusal.   Within the health care context, refusal to consent to a recommended diagnostic or therapeutic procedure after being informed of its risks and benefits, and the risks of not having it performed.

Intentional tort.   A civil wrong stemming from an act by which the defendant intends to interfere with the interests of the plaintiff; giving any medical treatment without consent is the intentional tort of battery.

Interrogatory.   A series of questions formulated for the purpose of obtaining a written statement (under oath) from a witness in a suit.

Invasion of privacy.   A tort only recently recognized as such, and consisting in the unauthorized dissemination of private information about the plaintiff or the publication of his or her likeness without consent.

Liability.   A person subjected to having his or her legal relationship changed by one having a *power* is under a liability; any obligation that a person has a duty to perform because of the rules of law and justice; see also **immunity.**

Libel.   Defamation of a person's character by written statement or pictures.

Malicious prosecution.   A claim that can be raised by the defending party to a lawsuit against the plaintiff, the plaintiff's attorney, or both, after the original action is terminated in the defendant's favor, that the action was brought without proper foundation (not to be confused with **counterclaim**).

Malpractice.   Negligence committed by a professional during and as a part of his or her practice; see **negligence.**

Medical jurisprudence.   The effects of laws and the legal process on the practice of medicine. Laws and regulations that govern the physician's conduct in relation to fellow physicians, hospitals, and patients, including the privilege of practicing and holding staff positions.

Misrepresentation.   An untrue statement, an incorrect or false representation.

Negligence.   The failure to perform an action that a reasonably prudent person would do in similar circumstances, or the commission of an act that the same reasonably prudent person would not do.

Notice.   Information obtained by the use of one's senses, powers of observation, or deduction; knowledge of conditions that would make a reasonably prudent, similarly situated person aware of a fact.

Notice, actual.   Information actually and expressly given to or obtained by a party.

Notice, constructive.   Facts that ought to be known because of the circumstances, and that a court would so recognize; for example, anesthesia personnel would be expected to be on notice that a monitoring device that repeatedly tripped its electrical supply's circuit breaker and smelled of heated insulation had an electrical fault and should be repaired or replaced.

Notice, judicial.   The act whereby the presiding judge acknowledges certain facts generally known to be true within a community to be true without the necessity of proof by the introduction of evidence.

Partnership.   A voluntary association in which two or more persons agree to pool their assets, skills, talents, and labors, or one or more of those, for the conduct of some type of business enterprise, with proportionate sharing of profits and losses among those persons.

Partnership, general.   A partnership in which all partners share in the profits and liabilities, the latter not being limited to one's share in the partnership.

Partnership, limited.   A partnership consisting of both general and limited partners, the latter having liability limited to their interest in the partnership.

Plaintiff.   The person who brings an action in the courts in order to obtain relief from another party, who is the defendant.

Pleading, rules of.   The rules and principles by which the contentions of the parties to litigation are framed to produce uniformity and elucidate the specific issue or issues; originally embodied in the common law, pleadings in all jurisdictions now are codified in the (statutory) rules of civil and criminal procedure.

Power.   Correlative of liability. The ability of a person to produce a change in the legal status or a given legal relation—for example, the ability of persons to dispose of their own real or personal property as they see fit.

Power of attorney.   See **attorney, power of,** *supra.*

Prima facie.   Apparent, plain, on first appearance.

Prima facie **case.**   One that has evidence of such magnitude that will result in a verdict in the absence of contravening evidence by the opponent.

Privilege.   The legal freedom on the part of one person to do, or refrain from doing, a certain act.

Privileged communication.   A communication made within a certain relationship—for example, spouse to spouse, penitent to priest, client to lawyer, patient to physician—becomes privileged in the sense that the person making the communication has the power to prevent the other from divulging the nature of the communication; the physician-patient privilege is recognized by statute in all states except Alabama, Connecticut, Delaware, Florida, Georgia, Illinois, Louisiana, Maine, Maryland, Massachusetts, New Hampshire, New Jersey, Rhode Island, South Carolina, Tennessee, Texas, Vermont, and Virginia; it was not recognized at common law.

Proximate cause.   The factor or factors that, acting naturally and continuously and unbroken by any intervening cause, cause the injury, and without which the injury could not have occurred.

Reservation of rights.   In the context of professional liability insurance, the carrier agrees to defend a case but reserves the right to refuse payment for any damages if the cause of action is not covered by the policy (e.g., an action for abandonment or other intentional tort)..

Res ipsa loquitur.   Literally, "the thing speaks for itself." The negligence of the act can be proven by the fact that the plaintiff could not have suffered injury had there not been negligence on the part of the defendant. An inference is created that the defendant was negligent, and the order of proof is altered.

Res judicata.   A matter that is decided judicially so that such a decision is final.

Respondeat superior **doctrine.**   The master or employer is responsible for the actions of his or her servants or employees for breach of any duties that the master owes others if the breach of the duty occurs while the servant is engaged in work as an employee.

Right.   A legally enforceable claim of one person against another that the other shall or shall not do a certain act. For example, the physician has a right to payment of his or her invoice to the patient; the patient has a right to treatment at the level of current medical standards.

Slander.   Defamation of another person by verbal means.

Spoliation.   The destruction of evidence, for example, erasing, deleting, or discarding entries in a document that has evidential value in litigation.

Standard of care.   The level of care at which the average person is expected to conduct those business, professional, or daily activities that interact with other persons.

Statute.   A law enacted by a legislative body possessing the constitutional power to do so.

Summary judgment.   A judgment rendered after a short, concise proceeding based primarily upon deposition testimony, exhibits, and affidavits, by the court and without benefit of a jury.

Tort.   A civil wrong by which a person has violated a legally recognized duty to another; torts generally are of common law origin, may be created by statute.

A page number followed by a "t" indicates a table; a page number in italics indicates a figure.

constructive, 10
defective, 83–85
express, 10, 83
for HIV screening, 231–232
implied, 9–10, 83
informed. *See* Informed consent
language barriers and, 76
statutory, 10
to transfusion, 195–198, 208
types of, 9–11
verbal, 10
written, 10, 83–85
Consortium, loss of, 302, 379
Constitution, federal and state, 4, 6
Constructive consent, 10
Constructive contract, 10
Consultation
duty to seek, 13–14, *14*, 19
preanesthesia, 73–74, 78
Consumer advocate, 367–368
Contingent fee contract, 298–299, 378
Continuing treatment, duty to offer, 13, *14*
Contract
breach of. *See* Breach of contract
conditional, 359
constructive, 10
contingent fee, 298–299
definition of, *9*
exclusive, 350
express, 10
insurance, 359
personal service, 11
preventative maintenance, 131–132
privity of, 283–285
sales, 10, 283–284
service, 9–11, 15, 283
verbal, 10
written, 10
Contractual agreement, alternative to tort resolution
of claims, 375, 378
Contributory negligence, 14, 20–21
Convulsion, 371t
Copyright law, 4
Corporation, 48, 51, 330–332, 331t
Cough drops, 293
Counterclaim, 43–44
Courtroom, layout and procedure, 308–309
Cranial nerve injury, 118–119
Credentialing, 4, 380
CRNA. *See* Certified registered nurse anesthetist
Cross-examination, 311–312
Cross-infection, with HIV, 229
Cross-matching, of blood products, 204

Damages, 199–200
amount of, 299
general, 19, 302
mitigation of, 360
monetary, 18–19
punitive, 19, 43–44, 302, 377–378
special, 18–19, 302
Data base, risk management, 58–59, 59
Death, claims involving, 369t, 371t
Decredentialing, 4
Deep peroneal nerve injury, 122t
Deepest pocket doctrine, 251, 266
Defamation, 42, 359

Defective consent, 83–85
Defendant
calling "as on cross", 314
health care provider as, 313–314
legal representation for, 362–363
preparation of defense case, 300
Delivery. *See* Intrapartum care
Delivery room, fathers in, 191–192
Demeanor, of witness, 312–313
Dental anesthesia, 270–271
documentation of, 273–274
general, 270, 272–273, 279–281
HIV infection and, 234
informed consent for, 273
local, 271–272
monitoring of, 273
negligence in, 275–277
preanesthesia care, 271
standard of care, 275–276, 279–281
Dental injury, 164
Dental practice acts, 274–275
Deposition, 301, 305–306
DES. *See* Diethylstilbestrol
Diagnosis-related groupings (DRG), 343–344
Didactic instruction, 249
Diethylstilbestrol (DES), 288, 293
Dinemapp monitor, 126
Direct examination, 309–311
Directed donation, 211, 213
Directed verdict, 303
Disability benefits, 333, 335
Discharge
from ambulatory care facility, 177–178, 178t
from recovery room, 148, 149t
Disclosure, 82, 260–261
exceptions to requirement for, 87
extent of, 85–88
full, 12–13, *14*
by patient, 14
standards for, 85–86
professional, 86
reasonable-patient, 86
subjective, 86
Discovery, 67, 300–301
Disposable items, 287–288
Dispute resolution system, 380
Disseminated intravascular coagulation, 188
DPT vaccine, 294
DRG. *See* Diagnosis-related groupings
Droperidol, 165
Drugs, 285–286, 290–291, 293–294
new, introduction of, 26–27, 274
side effects of, 26
use of incorrect, 371t
Due process, 4–5
procedural, 4, 258–259
substantive, 4
Duty, 199
breach of, 17–18, 199, 302
of health care provider, 12–14, *14*, 283
of patient, 14, 78, 175–176
of trainee, 256–257
of training director, 256
Duty owing, 17, 19

Earning capacity, loss of, 18
Eclampsia, 188

A page number followed by a "t" indicates a table.